ᎠᏎᏉᏛ ᏣᏤᎩ-ᎭᏅᏍ ᏗᏍᏕᎶᏗ

Raven Rock Cherokee-English Dictionary

Michael Joyner
TommyLee Whitlock

Language and culture which are not shared and taught openly and freely will die.
If our language and culture die, as a people, so do we.

Raven Rock Cherokee-English Dictionary

Copyright 2015, Michael Joyner, TommyLee Whitlock

ISBN: 978-1-329-78831-2

Revision: 3.7

Last modified: 2016/01/07 20:38:50 EST

Contents

Preface   1

Introduction   3

    THE CHEROKEE LANGUAGE 3

    USING THE DICTIONARY 3

    PRONUNCIATION 8

    KEY TO PARTS OF SPEECH ABBREVIATIONS 10

    REMARKS ON SOME OF THE DIFFERENCES BETWEEN OKLAHOMA AND QUALLA BOUNDARY CHEROKEE 10

Dictionary   13

    D 13

    DⲎⲪⲆⳲ 16

    DEⰂⳫ 19

    DⲢⲪLBⲪⲆ 22

    Dⴼ OⳞVⲪⲆⲆⲆ 25

    DⰽZⳞ 26

    DⲎⳤⲪⳲ 27

    DⲪⳫⲆⳞⲆⲎⲦ 31

    DⲎⲪOⳲⳲ 34

    DLOⳞD 36

    DⲤⲪVⳲⳲ 40

    DⳜⳫⳲ 43

    DⳞⳲVⳲ 45

    DⲪD 47

    DBⲪⳲ 50

    R 51

    T 52

    Ⰺ 53

    OⳞ 53

    OⳞⲪLⳫT 55

    OⳞⲊⲪSⳞ 57

    OⳞZⳞⲪ 59

    OⳞⲪLⳫⲆⲦ 60

    OⳞSⳲⲪⳲ 62

    OⳞⳞGⳲ 64

    OⳞⰂSⳲ 66

    OⳞBG 68

i 68

Ꭶ 68

ᏚᎲᏤ ᏨᏫᏓ 71

ᏚᎾᎢᏓ 73

ᏚᏁᎵᏗᎦ 76

ᏚᏈᏯᏒ 78

ᏚᏫᎥᎦᏓ 81

ᏚᏉᎦᏦᏓ 83

Ꭷ 84

ᎧᏦᏬ ᎠᏤᏲ 86

Ᏸ 86

Ꭹ 87

A 87

AᏫᎵᏗhVᎧ 89

Ꭻ 89

E 90

Ꮛ 92

Ꮰ 93

᏶ 93

Γ 93

Ꮷ 93

Θ 93

Ꮈ 94

h 94

Z 94

Ꭾ 94

Ꭴ 95

Ꭲ 95

Ꮀ 95

Ꮄ 95

Ꮏ 96

Ꮁ 96

Ꮅ 96

Ꮛ 97

R 97

Ꮊ 97

ᏞhᏫᏬᏝᎶᎢ 99

W 102

Ꭶ 102

Ꮑ 104

Ꮧ 104

ᏧᏞᎢᏧᏨ 105

Ꮧ 105

V 105

S 106

Ꭷ 107

Ꮐ 107

Ᏼ 107

Ꮶ 108

Ꮰ 108

ᏫᏍᎪᎷ 109

Ꮯ 109

Ꮬ 109

Ꮼ 110

Ꮎ 110

Ꮼ 110

Ꮹ 110

Ꮾ 110

Ꭶ 110

Ᏼ 110

English to Cherokee Lookup   113

A 113

AMERICAN BLACK ELDERBERRY 113

ASHAMED 114

B 114

BED CLOTHES 115

BITING IT 115

BORROWING IT 116

BROTHER'S YOUNGER BROTHER 117

BY ONESELF 117

C 117

CATCHING FIRE 118

CHORDEILES MINOR 118

COME TO A POINT … 119

CRACKING 120

D 120

DOUGH 121

E 121

EVAPORATED 122

F 122

FEVER 123

FLYING 123

G 124

GOING DOWN HILL 124

GROUP 125

H 125

HEAD 126

HOLDING IT 126

I 127

J 128

K 128

L 128
Lindera benzoin 129
M 129
Meleagris gallopavo 130
Mounting it 131
N 131
Now 132
O 132
Overnight 132
P 132
Persuading him 133
Placing it 134
Post 134
Pushing it 135
Q 135
R 135
Red-tailed hawk 136
Rock shelter 137
S 137
Seine 138
Shirt 138
Slapping it 139
Solid 139
Spout 140
Striped wintergreen. Wintergreen 141
T 141
Thanking him 142
Tomorrow 142
Two hundred 143
U 143
V 143
W 144
Weaving 144
Winding it up 145
X 145
Y 146
Z 146

Grammar   **147**
Syllabary 149
Pronouns 150
Overview of Verbs 152
The Radical Conjugation 153
The Dative Conjugation 161

Bibliography   **165**

Preface

This dictionary was derived from the raw list of word roots and affixes collected by Dr. Duane King in his 1975 University of Georgia dissertation on the Cherokee language entitled A Grammar and Dictionary of the Cherokee Language of the Qualla Boundary in North Carolina. The word lists that were included at the end of Dr. King's dissertation provided word roots and basic affixes in a printout from his work using IBM computer punch cards that he created for a program he described in his seminal dissertation. This program was devised as a way to generate complete verb forms for the major tenses. The limitations of technology at the time forced Dr. King to break words down to very basic root phonemes and aspect forms that could fit onto the 88 column punch-card format of the day. Based on these entries and the phonetic rules that Dr. King meticulously derived and documented in his dissertation, in 1975 Bruce Delaney generated a punch card program which sadly no longer appears to exist. It was able to generate the correct form of any verb in the list for any pronominal prefix and tense.

Computer technology has, however, made dramatic advances since 1975. The major hurdle for this work was entering the data by hand from the barely legible photocopies of the 1975 printout that are available today. The raw data were painstakingly scrutinized, cross-checked, and manually entered into a database created for generating this dictionary which follows the format and layout of Dr. Durbin Feeling's well known work-horse, *The Cherokee-English Dictionary*. This format was chosen because of the widespread use and familiarity that most students of the Cherokee language already have with Dr. Feeling's dictionary. In addition, the very opaque academic phonetics of the time have been transcribed to a more readily accessible and more familiar format based on that of the *Cherokee-English Dictionary*. Syllabary version of the words have been generated, as well.

Dr. King's dissertation was a monumental work on the Cherokee language and his goal of computerizing the word list was extremely forward-thinking, ambitious, and praise worthy. Everyone working to promote, preserve, or learn the Cherokee language owes him a huge debt of gratitude for the tremendous amount of work and thought he put into his analysis of the Cherokee language and the word lists that he collected.

The hope that Dr. King expressed in his dissertation was to "someday facilitate the compilation of a nearly complete Cherokee dictionary." It is our hope that this dictionary furthers that worthy goal. In addition, it is our sincere hope that this dictionary will become an inspirational resource to help preserve and promote the Eastern Cherokee dialect as it is spoken on the Qualla Boundary by Dr. King's informants from Big Cove and their descendents. This dictionary is presented in the spirit of openness, gratitude to the ancestors, gratitude to the people who made the original work possible, and especially in the spirit of ᎦᏚᎩ (community cooperation). It is also our hope that this dictionary will not only expand and contribute to the preservation and growth of the Eastern dialects of the Cherokee language, but also be a resource that fills in gaps in other resources as it includes many words that are not in the *Cherokee-English Dictionary* or other sources.

-Michael Joyner
-TommyLee Whitlock

Introduction

Darrel Kipp, *Encouragement, Guidance, Insights, and Lessons Learned for Native Language Activists Developing Their Own Tribal Language Programs.*

- *Rule 1*: Never Ask Permission, Never Beg to Save the Language. *Never Beg.*
- *Rule 2*: Don't Debate the Issues. Don't let anyone debate you. Don't let them start in on you. Don't let them even start.
- *Rule 3*: Be Very Action-Oriented; Just Act.
- *Rule 4*: Show, Don't Tell. Don't talk about what you will do. Do it and show it.

—http://lakotalearners.com/Darrell%20Kipp.pdf

The Cherokee Language

Cherokee is grouped into three major dialects:

Elati (RWꝪ). This dialect was historically spoken by inhabitants of the Lower Towns in the vicinity of the South Carolina–Georgia border before the forced removal of 1838 and uses an "r" sound where the other two dialects use an "l" sound. This is also known as "The Lower" dialect. This dialect is believed to have become extinct around 1900.

Kituhwa (ᏛᏍᏭ). Commonly referred to as the "Eastern" dialect, it is spoken by the Eastern band on the Qualla Boundary in North Carolina, and is known as "The Middle" dialect.

Otali (ᎣᏔᏟ). This dialect is spoken in Oklahoma and by the Snowbird Community in North Carolina and is known as the "Western" or "Overhill" dialect.

Using the Dictionary

The main dictionary is composed of two main parts, a Cherokee to English section and an English to Cherokee section. The Cherokee to English section is what should be used to gain the best understanding of each Cherokee word. The English to Cherokee section's only purpose is to facilitate lookup of Cherokee entries in the Cherokee to English section. ☞ *Always refer to the Cherokee to English section to ensure correct usage of any word.*

In many instances a Cherokee to English entry can have multiple possible meanings in English. Such entries are separated with a semi-colon (;).

Many of the entries contain example sentences. These entries are provided in Syllabary and English.

Each Cherokee to English entry can be grouped into one of the following categories:

- Single entries.
- Dual entries, showing person.
- Dual entries, showing plurality.
- Multiple entries, showing person and plurality.
- Verb entries, showing the third, first, and second persons.
- Verb entries, only showing the third person.

The following provides a brief overview of each entry type.

Single entries.

Many of these entries are single words that are not inflected for person or quantity.

DSℓ [ạgada] (pt) "Much."

DSℱWↃ [ạgahyụladi] "Net."

Some of these entries, even though it is not shown, should be inflected. Familiarity with the language helps with determining which is which.

Dual entries, showing person.

These entries are identified by the second entry starting with ℱ-, Ⱶ-, DↃ-, or DↃ-.

Depending on the word, these changes are used to indicate "relationship", "ownership", "body part", "worn clothing", or "to whom it describes".

(For most of the following examples assume *he* could be substituted with *she* and vice-versa.)

Description

DⱵⱳ [ạgehya] (n) "Woman."

    ⱵⱵⱳ [tsịgehya]

- DⱵⱳ DAꞬↃⱷ: "She, a woman, sees it."
- ⱵⱵⱳ ⱵAꞬↃⱷ: "I, a woman, see it."
- DⱵⱳ ⱵAꞬↃⱷ: "I see her, a woman."

Ownership

OʼSⱳⱱVᴧ [uksdọhi] (n) "His pillow."

    DↃSⱳVᴧ [a¹gwạksdọhi]

- OʼSⱳVᴧ DAꞬↃⱷ: "He sees his pillow." or "He sees a pillow."
- OʼSⱳVᴧ ⱵAꞬↃⱷ: "I see his pillow." or "I see a pillow."
- DↃSⱳVᴧ DAꞬↃⱷ: "She sees my pillow."
- DↃSⱳVᴧ ⱵAꞬↃⱷ: "I see my pillow."

Description

OʼⱵWↃ [ugewodi] (n) "Bald."

    DↃⱵWↃ [a¹gịgewodi]

- OʼⱵWↃ DⱳSⱳ: "A bald man."
- ꞬⱵWↃ ⱥⱳSⱳ: "You are a bald man."

4

Relationship

ᎤᏁᏟ [unatsi] (n) "Parent-in-law."

    ᎠᏥᏁᏟ [a¹ginatsi]

- ᎤᏁᏟ ᏓᏳᏗᏍᎪᎢ: "He is seeing his parent-in-law."
- ᎤᏁᏟ ᏈᎠᏗᏍᎪᎢ: "I am seeing her parent-in-law."
- ᎠᏥᏁᏟ ᏓᏳᏗᏍᎪᎢ: "She is seeing my parent-in-law."
- ᎠᏥᏁᏟ ᏈᎠᏗᏍᎪᎢ: "I am seeing my parent-in-law."

Dual entries, showing plurality.

These entries are identified by the second entry starting with Ꮣ- or Ꮪ-.

Body Part

ᎠᎡᏍᎯ [aḳʏnogeni] (n) "His wing."

    ᏚᎡᏍᎯ [diḳʏnogeni]

- ᏈᎳᏗ ᎠᎡᏍᎯ ᏓᏳᏗᏍᎪᎢ: "She sees the bird's wing."
- ᏈᎳᏗ ᎠᎡᏍᎯ ᏈᎠᏗᏍᎪᎢ: "I see the bird's wing."
- ᏈᎳᏗ ᏚᎡᏍᎯ ᏞᎠᏗᏍᎪᎢ: "He sees the bird's wings."
- ᏈᎳᏗ ᏚᎡᏍᎯ ᏍᏈᎠᏗᏍᎪᎢ: "I see the bird's wings."

Description

ᎤᎣᏣᏗ [uhnvtsạti] (n) "Speckled trout."

    ᎤᏁᎣᏣᏗ [unahnvtsạti]

- ᎤᎣᏣᏗ ᏓᏳᏗᏍᎪᎢ: "He sees a speckled trout."
- ᎤᎣᏣᏗ ᏈᎠᏗᏍᎪᎢ: "I see a speckled trout."
- ᎤᏁᎣᏣᏗ ᏞᎠᏗᏍᎪᎢ: "She sees speckled trout."
- ᎤᏁᎣᏣᏗ ᏍᏈᎠᏗᏍᎪᎢ: "I see speckled trout."

Multiple entries, showing person and plurality.

These entries are identified by the third entry starting with Ꮪ-, Ꮔ-, ᎠᏥ-, or ᎠᎢ-.
These entries work the same as the dual entries showing person.
(For most of the following examples assume *he* could be substituted with *she*.)

Body Part

ᎠᏍᎦᎶ [ạktoli] (n) "His eye."

    ᏗᏍᎦᎶ [dịktoli]
    ᎥᏍᎦᎶ [tsịktoli]
    ᏗᏥᏍᎦᎶ [dịtsịktoli]

- ᎠᏍᎦᎶ ᎩᎦᎨ ᎮᏛ: "His eye was red."
- ᎥᏍᎦᎶ ᎩᎦᎨ ᎮᏛ: "My eye was red."
- ᏗᏍᎦᎶ ᏗᎩᎦᎨ ᎮᏛ: "His eyes were red."
- ᏗᏥᏍᎦᎶ ᏗᎩᎦᎨ ᎮᏛ: "My eyes were red."

Worn Clothing

Most clothing is treated as being as a part of a person.

ᎤᎤᎥᏗ [unỵsadi] (n) "Rattle wrapped around the leg."

    ᏊᎥᏗ [tsunỵsadi]
    ᎠᎢᎤᎥᏗ [a¹gwạnỵsadi]
    ᏗᎢᎤᎥᏗ [di¹gwạnỵsadi]

- ᎤᎤᎥᏗ ᏓᎠᎬᏗᎲ: "He sees her leg rattle. (Being worn by her.)"
- ᎠᎢᎤᎥᏗ ᎥᎠᎬᏗᎲ: "I see my leg rattle. (Being worn by myself.)"
- ᏊᎥᏗ ᏞᎠᎬᏗᎲ: "He sees her leg rattles. (Being worn by her.)"
- ᏗᎢᎤᎥᏗ ᏍᎥᎠᎬᏗᎲ: "I see my leg rattles. (Being worn by myself.)"

Verb entries, showing the third, first, and second persons.

Each Cherokee verb has five core forms or stems that are used to build new words. They are listed in the following order: 3rd person present, 1st person present, 3rd person remote past, 3rd person habitual, 2nd person immediate, and 3rd person infinitive.

ᎠᏍᏗᏗᎲ [agạsoh³dịha] (v) "He is going down hill."

    ᎦᎦᏍᏗᏗᎲ [gagạsoʔdịha]
    ᎤᏍᏗᏩᏅᎢ [ugạsoh³tạnv²³ʔi]
    ᎠᏍᏗᏗᏍᎪᎢ [agạsoh³dịsgo³ʔi]
    ᎲᏍᏗᏚ [hagạsoh³da]
    ᎤᏍᏗᎥᏗ [ugạsoh³dohdi]

The first entries of ᎠᏍᏗᏗᎲ refers directly to the English definition. The second entry of ᎦᎦᏍᏗᏗᎲ shows the 1st person inflection and in this case means "I am going down hill." The first form is referred to as the PRESENT TENSE stem. The second form is the 1st person of the present tense stem.

The next entry of ᎤᏍᏗᏩᏅᎢ is used when talking about what has happened as a completed event in the past. *This form is normally used for non-recent events.* In this case it means "He went down hill a while ago." This form is referred to as the REMOTE PAST stem.

The next entry of ᎠᏍᏗᏗᏍᎪᎢ indicates a state of having occurred repeatably in the past, with the expectation of the behavior or action continuing into the future. In this case it means "He often goes down hill." This form is referred to as the HABITUAL stem.

The next entry of ⊕ᏚᎱᏞ indicates that someone is being asked to do something or that something recently occurred. Because it is a form commonly used to ask someone to do something, it is listed in the 2nd person form. In this particular case, ⊕ᏚᎱᏞ could be translated as either "Let you go down hill" or "You recently went down hill" depending on how the final syllable is pronounced on the word. This form is referred to as the IMPERATIVE or IMMEDIATE MODE stem.

Finally there is the entry of ᎤᏚᎱᏙᏗ. This form is usually combined with another verb. It is used in a similar manner to the way "to do …" is used in English or can be used to indicate something someone needs to do. In this case it could be translated as either "for him to go downhill" or "he needs to go downhill." This form is referred to as the INFINITIVE or DEVERBAL stem.

In the following entry there are two 1st person present tense forms and two 3rd person immediate mode forms. This reflects a difference of pronunciation when referring to something animate (ᎯᏣᏌᎲᎥ, ᎠᏣᏎᎭ) vs something inanimate (ᏍᏌᎲᎥ, ⊕ᏌᎭ) caused by the use of different prefixes for each circumstance.

DᏌᏒᎥ [ąse³hįha] (vt) "He is counting.; He is pointing at him."

    ᎯᏣᏌᎲᎥ, ᏍᏌᎲᎥ [tsiyąse³hįha, gąse³hįha]

    ᎤᎬᏌᎯᎢ [uwąse³hlv²³ᵊi]

    DᏌᏅᎲᎢ [ąse³hįho³ᵊi]

    ᎠᏣᏌᎤ, ⊕ᏌᎤ [hiyąse³ka, hąse³ka]

    ᎤᎬᏌᎲᏗ [uwąse³sdi]

Some verb entries appear incomplete, such as DᎢ "He is walking". Many such verbs usually refer to an ongoing state of being or action, such as walking, and as such only refer to "is doing", "was doing", or "will be doing", etc, and do not have five stems.

DᎢ [aᵊi] (vi) "He is walking."

    ᏌᎢ [gaᵊi]

    ——

    DᎢᏒᎢ [aᵊiso³ᵊi]

    ——

    ——

Verb entries, only showing the third person.

These entries show five core stems in the same order as the other verb entries with the following exceptions. There is not listed a 1st person PRESENT TENSE stem. Instead of the 2nd person IMMEDIATE MODE stem, there is instead listed the 3rd person IMMEDIATE MODE stem. The entry has the Ꮻ- prefix added because it is normally used when saying "let him, it …". In this case the form listed is ᎳᏍᎵᎲ which could either mean "Let the sun shine" or "The sun was just shining (there)."

DᏒᎵᎲ [ągali³ha] (vi) "It (the sun) is shining."

    ——

    ᎤᏒᎵᎡᎢ [ugalih³sv²³ᵊi]

    DᏒᎵᏃᎠᎢ [ągalih³sgo³ᵊi]

    ᎳᏍᎵᎲ [wągali³hi] "Let it …"

    ᎤᏒᎵᎲᏗ [ugali³hįsdi]

Example Sentences

An example sentence is provided for many of the entries in the Cherokee-English section to help further show how the word is used. These sentences are given in Cherokee with an accompanying English translation.

These examples have been taken from works printed in Cherokee, including the Bible. Not all words in this edition have an example but it is our hope to provide example sentences for each entry in a following edition.

PRONUNCIATION

Vowel Sounds

Cherokee has six main vowels. They are "a", "e", "i", "o", "u", and "v".

They are generally pronounced as follows:

- a: as *a* in *father*, or short as *a* in *rival*,

- e: as *a* in *hate*, or short as *e* in *met*,

- i: as *i* in *pique*, or short as *i* in *pin*,

- o: as *o* in *note*, but approaching to *aw*, in *law*,

- u: as *oo* in *moon*, or short as *u* in *pull*,

- v: as *u* in *but*, nasalized (sounded through the nose).

Cadence   Each Cherokee vowel is pronounced "long" or "short". A long vowel is a vowel held for a normal length of time. A short vowel is a vowel spoken for a very brief length of time. Other than for the amount of time a vowel is spoken, the long and short vowels sound the same. Short vowels will be marked in the pronunciation guide with an "underdot".

☞ *Vowels that appear at the end of words in the pronunciation guide are always short and will not be displayed with an underdot. Vowels that are followed by a consonant then a tone mark are also always short and will not be displayed with an underdot.*

Examples (the number will be explained shortly):

nigada	short "i", long "a", short "a" *This means "all".*
agali³ha	short "a", long "a", short "i", short "a" *This means "the sun is shining".*
noya	long "o", short "a" *This means "sand".*

Consonant Sounds

All of the consonants in Cherokee sound the same as their English versions, with the following few exceptions:

- g: Sounds like either the "g" in "gaff" or the "k" in "kite". When in doubt, use the "g" sound. The pronunciation guide will be using both the "g" and "k".

- qu: Sounds like the "qu" in "question" or the "gw" in "Gwen". When in doubt, use the "gw" sound. The pronunciation guide will be using "kw" and "gw".

- s: Sounds like the "s" in "sight" for Otali Cherokee or the "sh" in "shell" for Kituhwa Cherokee.

- tl: This non-English sound is made by combining a "t" or "h" with the "l" sound while keeping the tongue's tip against the lower front teeth then dropping the tongue straight down. Those new to the language will many times think they are hearing the "cl" sound as found in "clack" or "clock". With a little practice, you will be able to tell the "tl", "hl", and "kl" sounds apart. When in doubt, use the "hl" sound. The pronunciation guide will be using "hl" and "tl".

- ts: Sounds like either the "j" in "John", the "ch" in "chair", the "ds" in "best buds", or the "tz" in "spritzer". In Otali Cherokee the "j" and "ch" soundings are more common. In Kituwah Cherokee, the "ds" and "tz" soundings are more common. The pronunciation guide will be using "ts".

- You will also see trailing and leading "h" sound indicators. These are not silent like they are in English, they are always sounded out.

Pronunciation Guide

Each entry is presented with its Cherokee Syllabary spelling, an English pronunciation guide in brackets ("[", "]"), and an English definition.

The following describes the different symbols used in the pronunciation guide.

Vowels

a, e, i, o, u, v - Usually these are long vowels.
> ☞ *Remember that when they are not immediately followed by a tone mark or when they appear at the end of a word they are short vowels.*

a̧, ȩ, i̧, o̧, u̧, v̧ - These are always short vowels.

Pausing

ʔ - A dotless question mark indicates a brief pause in speaking. This is called a *glottal stop*.
> Examples of this brief pause can be found in the middle of the English words: "uh-oh", "stoplight", and "workload".

Miscellaneous

, - This will be used to indicate pronunciation and spelling variations. Example:

ᏚᎶᏍᏗ, ᎪᎶᏍᏗ [ga̧hu̧sdi, go̧hu̧sdi] (pt) "Something.; Anything."

Tone   What is pitch or tone? Pitch or tone, when dealing with languages, refers to shifting the tone of the voice up or down. An example of this in English is the shifting of the tone upwards towards the end of a sentence when asking a question. In Cherokee shifts in tone are actually considered parts of words and can also be used to indicate things like "happened in the past" or "let it happen in the future". ☞ *The tones used in words or phrases can change their meaning, sometimes dramatically.*

In this material, the CED numbering system is being used, where:

- A "2" indicates a tone with a normal pitch. ☞ *This tone is commonly referred to as the "normal", "low", or "neutral" tone.*

- A "3" indicates a tone with a higher pitch. ☞ *This tone is commonly referred to as the "high" tone.*

Many words have parts with "contour" or "gliding" tones. These will be indicated by combining together the starting and ending pitches:

- A "23" indicates a tone that starts out at a normal pitch and then is glided higher in pitch. ☞ *This tone is commonly referred to as the "rising" tone.*

- A "32" indicates a tone that starts out at a higher pitch and then is glided down to a normal pitch. ☞ *This tone is commonly referred to as the "falling" tone.*

There are two more tones which will be only marked with single numbers and one special gliding tone that has no marking at all:

- A "1" indicates a tone that starts with a normal pitch and then is glided downwards. ☞ *This tone is commonly referred to as the "extra low fall" or "low fall" tone.*

- A "4" indicates a tone that starts out usually at either "normal" or "high", the closest matching the preceding syllable, and then is glided upwards in pitch to end higher than the "high" tone. ☞ *This tone is commonly referred to as the "extra high rise" or "high rise" tone.*

- At the end of every word, unless otherwise indicated, there is always a "43" gliding tone which starts out with an very high pitch and then is glided down very far. Because this is at the end of every word, it is not marked. ☞ *This tone is commonly referred to as the "extra high fall" or "high fall" tone.*

Only the most critical tones, as recorded by Dr. King, have been marked in the pronunciation entries.

Things of note

Stress   Unlike English, where you stress different syllables in words with loudness you should try and keep all the syllables in your Cherokee words held at an equal volume. As a general rule, one should only stress an ending vowel that has the high fall tone when speaking Cherokee. ☞ *Speaking with this different way of using stress takes a bit of practice. It is second nature for English speakers to stress certain parts of words without realizing they are doing so.*

Nasalization   When speaking Cherokee, the "v" and "ɣ" vowels are *always* nasalized. (Sending the sound through the nose). Additionally, the ending sound on each word is also nasalized. The English word "huh", contains an example of a nasalized "v".

Tongue Placement   Cherokee is spoken with the tip of the tongue against the lower front teeth most of the time. You should be using the middle of your tongue to make the "s", "d", and "t" sounds, not the tongue's tip. Keeping your tongue properly placed takes practice, but is critical for properly emulating native pronunciation. *Do not give up.*

The Intrusive "H"   Because of the way Cherokee is spoken, you will sometimes see an extra "h" added to the beginning of a syllable in the pronunciation guide, even though the matching syllabary character does not indicate any "h" sounds. This extra sound is called *The Intrusive "H"*. Except for the special Cherokee letters ₺, "hna", and G, "nah", this sound is not written. The amount of Intrusive "H" will vary from speaker to speaker, so you will hear the same words spoken with and without it to varying degrees.

KEY TO PARTS OF SPEECH ABBREVIATIONS

All entries in the Cherokee-English section of this dictionary are labeled with a traditional part of speech marker. We have taken the liberty to alter some of King's original word list parts of speech notations in this current edition for clarity and familiarity. King originally did not differentiate between transitive and intransitive verbs in his word lists and showed only VBST for all verbs . Since these parts of speech are familiar to students of language, we have opted to follow the example of the Feeling/Pulte *Cherokee-English Dictionary*, Montgomery-Anderson's *A Reference Grammar of Oklahoma Cherokee* and other works on the Cherokee language and added the distinction between the two verb types to this work. However, we have opted to simplify King's varying noun categories down to just one because they are less familiar to language learners.

The parts of speech noted in this work are:

(vi)   – *Intransitive Verb.* These are verbs that do not take a direct object. Verbs of motion and stative verbs are intransitive.

(vt)   – *Transitive Verb.* These are verbs that allow one or more direct objects.

(n)   – *Noun.*

(adj)   – *Adjective.*

(pt)   – *Particle.* Particles are words that do not change or do not easily fit into grammatical categories and include words that indicate passage of time, i.e. while, in a while, later. Note: King originally also included adverbs and adjectives as particles because the distinction between the two in Cherokee is often fluid.

REMARKS ON SOME OF THE DIFFERENCES BETWEEN OKLAHOMA AND QUALLA BOUNDARY CHEROKEE

One of the first noticeable differences between the two major dialects of Cherokee (West vs East or Oklahoma vs Qualla) is the pronunciation of /s/. In the west, this is generally pronounced like an English "s" sound. On the Qualla Boundary, however, before vowels it generally sounds like "sh" so we get forms that sound like "oshiyo", "shogwili", "shikwa". It is also generally pronounced as English "sh" in front of "g" or "k" so we get words that sound like "shgi" and "nashgi" or "hishgi" and "shgohi". However, before "d" and "t" it tends to remain as "s" so we hear "osda", "usdi", etc. in both dialects.

Another difference in pronunciation that has been documented is that often (not always) "tl" and "dl" in the West are "ts" in Qualla pronunciations. A few examples are:

10

West	East	English
tlesdi	tsesdi	don't!
didla	iditsa, itsa	towards
tla	tsa	no, not
galvladidla	galvladitsv	upwards
uyvdla	uyvts	cold
tlameha	tsamaha	bat

Sometimes the difference between Oklahoma Cherokee and Qualla Boundary Cherokee is that the /tl/ in the West is pronounced as an aspirated /hl/ on the Qualla Boundary. For example:

West	East	English
gitli	gihli	dog
adetlogwa'a	adehlogwa'a	he is learning
jundetlogwasdi	tsundehlogwasdi	school
uditlega	udihlegi	hot
odla	ohla	soap

Another difference often encountered between West and East is long /a/ (West) versus /o/ (East):

West	East	English
kawi	kowi	coffee
hawa	howa	Well!, Okay!
nagwu	nogwo	now
sagwu	shogwo	one
sadu	sho'adu	eleven

The /ts-/ syllables are represented and pronounced differently between the two, also. In Western pronunciation these syllables are usually pronounced /ch-/ or /j-/. On the Qualla Boundary, they tend to be pronounced /ts-/ or /dz-/. Examples:

West	East	English
jisdu	tsisdu	rabbit
jalagi	tsalagi	Cherokee
jisdvna	tsisvna	crayfish, crawdad

There are some specific words and usages also that are different. The following list by no means is exhaustive but these are some of the most used ones:

West	East	English
ale	nole	and
hatlv	gatsv (tl/ts!)	where?
hila	hvga	how?
hila iga	hvga iga	how many? (inanimate)
hila iyani	hvga iyani	how many? (animate)
hilayv	hvga iyv	when?
tla yi-	gesdi yi-	not (negating a sentence)
tla …. yigi	gesdi …. yigi	not (negating an adjective or noun)
tla yagwahnta	gesdi yitsigata	I don't know.
tlesdi	tsesdi or hesdi	Don't!
tla, vtla	hadi	No.
agilvgwodi(ha)	osd agiyeli, tsalvgwdiha	he likes it
tla gohusdi	(ges)di gohusdi	nothing
tamatli	uneguhisdi	tomato

☞ Tsalvgwdiha in NC (note the Type A prefix!) is more emphatic & means "I really like it" or "I love it!")
☞ Tamatli is a borrowing from Nahuatl.

Sometimes the differences are a little more subtle:

11

West	East	English
gado usdi	gado iyusdi, doyust	what?
dodagohvi	dedagohvyu	See you later!
donadagohvi	dendagohvyu	See you all later!

Plural nouns - In several cases, there is a difference between how plural nouns are treated between East and West, with Western dialect adding a plural marker prefix (di- or de-) whereas the Eastern dialect does not. Examples:

West		East		
Singular	Plural	Singular	Plural	English
yvgi	diyvgi	yvgi	yvgi	forks
telido	ditelido	telido	telido	plates

There are many more examples of differences but none of these are major enough to prevent communication between Eastern and Western fluent Cherokee speakers any more than the differences between an American and a British speaker, or for that matter, between Americans from different regions of the United States. For example, a "pan" in some parts of the United States means specifically a "frying pan" while in other places it refers to a "sauce pan" – which many speakers call a "pot". Folks in the Appalachian Mountains say "thar" and "whar" instead of "there" and "where" but communication still happens and it's still English. And, of course, there are many regional words in America that are well known. For instance, youse guys, you people, y'all, and – in Western NC – You'uns (which is "Youns" near Pittsburg)!

So don't get stuck over the differences in the Cherokee dialects. Just be aware of them and then relax and learn to appreciate and enjoy them!

Dictionary

D

DT [aʔi] (vi) "He is walking."

ᏩᎢ [gaʔi]

—

DTᏂᎢ [aʔiso³ʔi]

—

ᎢᎣᎢ DTᎡᎩ.
"He was walking in the fields."
[ᏚᎶᏗ ᏏᏲᎡᎡᎢ]

DiᚣᏩ [aʔvsga] (vt) "He is placing it (a solid) on the ground."

ᎢᎢᚣᏩ [tsiʔyʔsga]
Ꭳ'Ᏺ·Ꭲ [uʔnv²³ʔi]
DiᚣᎪᎢ [aʔvsgo³ʔi]
ᎤᎢᏚ [hiʔvga]
Ꭳ'iᚣᏅ [uʔvsdi]

DiᏏ [aʔvsi] (vt) "He is handing it (a solid) to him."

ᎢᎢᏏ [tsiʔyʔsi]
Ꭳ'ᎷᎦᎢ [uʔnelv²³ʔi]
DᎷᎢᎢ [aʔneho³ʔi]
ᎤᎢᏏ [hiʔyʔsi]
Ꭳ'ᎷᏅ [uʔnhdi]

ᎢᏴ Ꭳ'ᎷᏟ::Ᏺ; ᎤᚣᎩ ᎡᏚᏅ DᎬᏠᏈᏍ ᎢᎷᏈᏂ ᎤᚣᎩ
DᚣᎣ·Ꮔ ᎡᏚᏅ. Ꭳ'ᎠᎣ'Ꮓ DᎬᏠᏈᏍ Ꭳ'ᎷᏈᎩ ᏚᏞ
ᎢᚣᏚᎳᏗ ᏌᏟᏂ Ꭳ'ᏫᎢᎢ.
Jesus answereth, 'That one it is to whom I, having dipped the morsel, shall give it;' and having dipped the morsel, he giveth [it] to Judas of Simon, Iscariot.
[ᎶᏂ 13:26]

DᏚᏞᎣᎢ [agali³ha] (vi) "It (the sun) is shining."

—

Ꭳ'ᏚᏞᎡᎢ [ugalih³sv²³ʔi]
DᏚᏞᎣᎪᎢ [agalih³sgo³ʔi]
ᏓᏚᏞᎠ [wagali³hi]
Ꭳ'ᏚᏞᎠᚣᏅ [ugali³hisdi]

... ᏳᚣᏲ Ꭳ'ᏚᏞᎣᎬ DᎤᎥᏞᚣᎪᎢ DᏠ.
... and then when it is shined on by the sun the water is dried by the sun.
[ᏣᏫᏻ ᏔᏞᎷ ᏗᎥᏴᏚ ᏚᎥᎥᏙᏅ]

DᏚᏞᎣᚣᏚ [agaʔlisga] (vt) "He is cutting it (something flexible) off."

ᎢᏚᏞᎣᚣᏚ [tsigaʔliʔsga]
Ꭳ'ᏚᏞᎡᎢ [ugaʔlisv²³ʔi]
DᏚᏞᎣᎪᎢ [agaʔlisgo³ʔi]
ᎠᏚᏞᏚ [higaʔliga]
Ꭳ'ᏚᏞᎣᏅ [ugaʔlisdi]

DᏚᎤᎣᏬᎠᚣᏅ [aganawohisdi] (n) "Heater."

DᏚᎤᎷᚣᏅ [aganesdi] (n) "Button."

DᏚᎣᚣᎩ [agasgi] (n) "Rain."

DᏚᎣᚣᎬᎻᏗ [aksgynida] (n) "His left.; Left-handedness."

ᎢᏚᎣᚣᎬᎻᏗ [tsiksgynida]

DᏚᎢᏚᎣᎢ [agasoh³diha] (vi) "He is going down hill."

ᏩᏩᎢᏚᎣᎢ [gagasoʔdiha]
Ꭳ'ᏚᎢᏫᎣ·Ꭲ [ugasoh³tanv²³ʔi]
DᏚᎢᏚᎣᚣᎪᎢ [agasoh³disgo³ʔi]
ᎣᎢᏚᎢᏝ [hagasoh³da]
Ꭳ'ᏚᎢᏚᎠᏅ [ugasoh³dohdi]

DᏚᏝ [agada] (pt) "Much."

DᏚᏫ [akta] (n) "Eye ball."

DᎦWᎥᎵ [a̧ktaha] (vt) "He is knowing it."

ᏣᎦWᎥᎵ [tsi̧gataha]

—

DᏍWᏦT [a̧ktaho³ʔi]

—

—

OᎥVᎯGᎠᎥ, OᎢᎣ ᏪᏁGᎵ, iꞭ ᏍᏂᏣWᎥᎵ.
Truly, said *Christian*, I do not know.
[ᏪᏁGᎵ ᏏᎲᎩRRT]

DᎦWᎥᎠD [aktahyʔa] (vi) "He is turning."

ᏍᏍWᎥᎠD [ga̧gaʔtahyʔa]

OᎥᏍWᎥᎠRT [uktahysv²³ʔi]

DᎦWᎥᎠᎥAT [aktahysgo³ʔi]

ᎵᏍWᎥᎠꙨ [haktahyna]

OᎥᏍWᎥᎠᎥᎵ [uktahysdi]

ᎾᎥYZ ᎤᎥR OᎥᏍWᎥᎠRY; Dᵒ OᎢAᎥY ᏂᎠ ᏚVEY, Dᵒ
iꞭ GᎤᏞV ᏂᎠ ᏦRT.
and these things having said, she turned backward,
and seeth Jesus standing, and she had not known that
it is Jesus.
[Gh 20:14]

DᎦᏛꙨ [a̧gatena] (n) "Lace."

DᎦᏗᎥ [a̧ktiya] (vt) "He is watching for him, it.; He is waiting for him, it.; He is watching over him, it."

ᏂᏍᏗᎥ [tsi̧gatiya]

OᎥᏍᏗᎢT [u̧ktidʔv²³ʔi]

DᎦᏗᏂT [a̧ktiyo³ʔi]

ᎠᏍᏗᎵ [hi̧ktidi]

OᎥᏍᏗᎵᎥᎵ [u̧ktidi̧sdi]

ᏅᏂGᎬZ ᎠD ᎤᎥᎵᵒ ᏂᎭ, ᏦP RGOᏣ RᏜᏞ? ᎠDZ ᎤᎥᎵT,
Ꮣ ᏅᏂᏍWᎥᎵ: ᏂᎡ DB iYOᏣ ᏂᏍᏗᎥ?
And Jehovah saith unto Cain, 'Where [is] Abel thy
brother?' and he saith, 'I have not known; my
brother's keeper – I?'
[ᏃᏔ TEᏅᏅ 4:9]

DᎦVᏞ [a̧ktoli] (n) "His eye."

ᏗᏍVᏞ [di̧ktoli]

ᏂᏍVᏞ [tsi̧ktoli]

ᏗᏂᏍVᏞ [di̧tsi̧ktoli]

ᏗᏍVᏞ ᏍᎤᎥᎵ ᏪᏙᏬZ ᎾᎥYᎥ ᎲᏍꞬOᎥY.
"It had eyes lifted up to Heaven."
[ᏪᏁGᎵ ᏏᎲᎩRRT]

DᎦVᎥᎵᎵ [aktosdi̧ha] (vt) "He is looking at it."

ᏍᏍVᎥᎵᎵ [gakdosdi̧ha]

OᎥᏍVᎥᎵLOᎢT [uktosda̧nv²³ʔi]

DᎦVᎥᎵᎥAT [aktosdisgo³ʔi]

ᎵᏍVᎥᎵ [haktosda]

OᎥᏍVᎥᎵVᎵ [uktosdohdi]

DᎦᏐᎢᎠᎥᏍ [a̧kdv³hvsga] (vt) "He is investigating it."

DYᏍᎢʔiᎥᏍ [a¹gi̧kdv³ʔvsga]

OᎥᏍᎢᎢOᎢT [ukdv³hnv²³ʔi]

DᎦᏐᎢᎠᎥAT [akdv³hvsgo³ʔi]

ᎠᏍᎢᎠᏍ [hi̧kdv³hvga]

OᎥᏍᎢᎵ [ukdv³hdi]

DᎦᏐᎢᏨᎵ [akty³ʔleha] (vt) "He is going through.; He is
passing a grade."

ᏂᏍᎢᏨᎵ [tsi̧gaʔty³ʔleha]

OᎥᏍᎢᏨRT [ukty³ʔlesv²³ʔi]

DᎦᏐᎢᏨᎥAT [akty³ʔlesgo³ʔi]

ᎠᏍᎢᏨᎠ [hi̧kty³ʔlehi]

OᎥᏍᎢᏨᎥᎵ [ukty³ʔlesdi]

DᎦᏂOᎠᏍ [agatsi̧nvgoga] (vi) "It is rusting."

—

OᎥᏍᏂOᎠᏨT [ugatsi̧nvgotsv²³ʔi]

DᎦᏂOᎠAT [agatsi̧nvgogo³ʔi]

ᏣᏍᏂOᎠRᎥᎵ [wagatsi̧nvgoesdi]

OᎥᏍᏂOᎠTᎥᎵ [ugatsi̧nvgoʔisdi]

DᎦGWᎵ [a̧gahyuladi] (n) "Seine.; Net."

DᎦBᏞ [a̧gayvli] (adj) "One thousand."

ᎠDZ ᎾᎯY, DᎥAᎠ TᎥᏍBᏞ OᎥᏓᏳᎢ DᎥAᎠ
TᎥᏍBᏞ, Dᵒ DᎦBᏞ OᎥᏍBWᏂGᎢ.
— and the number of them was myriads of myriads,
and thousands of thousands —
[DᏂᎾᎤAᎤᎵᎢT 5:11]

DᎦBᏞᏦT [a̧gayvligȩʔi] (n) "Woman, elderly."

ᏂᏍBᏞᏦT [tsi̧gayvligȩʔi]

… Dᵒ TᏪW ᏛᎤᎥ DᎾᏍBᏞᏦ ᏦᎵT.
… and both were advanced in their days.
[MᏍ 1:7]

DᎥᎠᏅD [a̧ka̧hiyi̧ʔa] (vt) "He is leaving it (something
alive)."

ᏂᎤᏅTᏅD [tsi̧ka̧ʔiyi̧ʔa]

OᎥᎤᎠBT [uka̧hiyv²³ʔi]

DᎥᎠᏅᎥAT [a̧ka̧hiyi̧sgo³ʔi]

ᎠᎤᎠᎥ [hi̧ka̧hiya]

OᎥᎤᎠᏅᎥᎵ [uka̧hiyi̧sdi]

ᎠᎧᎲᎠ [ạkạhṿʔa] (vt) "He is moving it (a solid).; He is pushing it (something alive) aside.; He is clearing it (something alive) away."

ᏥᎧᎥᎠ [tsikạʔṿʔa]

ᎤᎧᎲᏒᎢ [ukạhṿsv²³ʔi]

ᎠᎧᎲᏍᎪᎢ [ạkạhṿsgo³ʔi]

ᎯᎧᎲᎾ [hikạhṿna]

ᎤᎧᎲᏍᏗ [ukạhṿsdi]

ᎠᎧᎲᎠ [akạhṿʔa] (vt) "He is moving it (something alive)."

ᏥᏯᎧᎥᎠ [tsiyakạʔṿʔa]

ᎤᎧᎲᏒᎢ [ukạhṿsv²³ʔi]

ᎠᎧᎲᏍᎪᎢ [akạhṿsgo³ʔi]

ᎯᏯᎧᎥᎾ [hiyakạʔṿna]

ᎤᎧᎲᏍᏗ [ukạhṿsdi]

ᎠᎧᎵᎢᎭ [ạkạliʔịha] (vt) "He is filling it."

ᏥᎧᎵᎢᎭ [tsịʔkạliʔịha]

ᎤᎧᎵᎸᎢ [ukạliʔlv²³ʔi]

ᎠᎧᎵᎢᎰᎢ [ạkạliʔịho³ʔi]

ᎯᎧᎵᏣ [hịkạlitsa]

ᎤᎧᎵᎢᏍᏗ [ukạliʔịsdi]

ᏂᎦᎥᏰᏃ ᏗᎧᎿᏩᏛᏍᏗ ᏚᎵᏁᏨ ᏌᏉᏉ ᎢᎧᏁᏨᎯ ᎠᎧᎵᎢᎭ, ᎯᎠᏉ ᎾᏍᎩ, ᎾᎥ ᎢᏗᏍᏓᏓᎳ ᎯᎨᏳᏎᏍᏗ ᎾᏍᎩᏯ ᏨᏒ ᏂᏣᏓᎨᏳᏒᎢ.
for all the law in one word is fulfilled — in this: 'Thou shalt love thy neighbour as thyself;'
[ᎨᎴᏏᏱ 5:14]

ᎠᎧᏁᎭ [ạkaneha] (vt) "He is giving it (something alive) to him."

ᏥᎧᏁᎠ [tsikanẹʔa]

ᎤᎧᏁᎸᎢ [ukanẹlv²³ʔi]

ᎠᎧᏁᎰᎢ [ạkaneho³ʔi]

ᎯᎧᎥᏍᏗ [hikạvsdi]

ᎤᎧᏁᏗ [ukanhdi]

ᎠᎧᏁᎵ [ạkaneli] (vt) "He is taking it (something alive) to him."

ᏥᎧᏁᎵ [tsikaneli]

ᎤᎧᏁᎸᎢ [ukaneʔlv²³ʔi]

ᎠᎧᏁᎵᏐᎢ [ạkaneliso³ʔi]

ᎯᎧᏁᎷᎦ [hikaneluga]

ᎤᎧᏁᎵᏗ [ukanehldi]

ᎠᎧᏂ [ạkạni] (vt) "He is returning an animal."

ᏥᎦᏂ [tsịgạʔni]

ᎤᎧᏁᏒᎢ [ukạnẹsv²³ʔi]

ᎠᎧᏂᏐᎢ [ạkạniso³ʔi]

ᎯᎧᏄᎦ [hịkạnuga]

ᎤᎧᏅᏍᏗ [ukạnṿsdi]

ᎠᎧᏅᎢ [ạkanvʔi] (n) "His eye."

ᏓᎧᏅᎢ [dạkanvʔi]

ᏥᎧᏅᎢ [tsịkanvʔi]

ᏕᏥᎧᏅᎢ [detsịkanvʔi]

ᎥᎵᏃ, ᏧᏓ ᎢᎬᏱ ᎡᎯ ᎤᏪᏥ ᎠᏍᎦᎾᎯᏳ ᎨᏎ ᏱᎰᏩ ᏓᎧᏅᎢ; ᏱᎰᏩᏃ ᎤᎴᎢ.
and Er, Judah's first-born, is evil in the eyes of Jehovah, and Jehovah doth put him to death.
[ᎼᏏ ᎢᎬᏱᏱ 38:7]

ᎠᎧᏍᎨᏂ [ạkasgeni] (n) "His hip."

ᏗᎧᏍᎨᏂ [dịkasgeni]

ᏥᎧᏍᎨᏂ [tsịkasgeni]

ᏗᏥᎧᏍᎨᏂ [dịtsịkasgeni]

ᎠᎧᏎᏍᏗᎭ [akạ³sẹsdịha] (vt) "He is watching it."

ᎦᎧᏎᏍᏗᎭ [gakạ³sẹsdịha]

ᎤᎧᏎᏍᏓᏅᎢ [ukạ³sẹsdạʔnv²³ʔi]

ᎠᎧᏎᏍᏗᏍᎪᎢ [akạ³sẹsdịsgo³ʔi]

ᎭᎧᏎᏍᏓ [hakạ³sẹsda]

ᎤᎧᏎᏍᏙᏗ [ukạ³sẹsdohdi]

ᎠᎧᏘᎭ [akạ³tịha] (vi) "He is peeking."

ᎦᎧᏗᎭ [gakạ³dịha]

ᎤᎧᏔᏅᎢ [ukạ³tanv²³ʔi]

ᎠᎧᏘᏍᎪᎢ [akạ³tịsgo³ʔi]

ᎭᎧᏔ [hakạ³ta]

ᎤᎧᏙᏗ [ukạ³tohdi]

ᎠᎧᏲᏍᎦ [ạkahyosga] (vi) "He is drying out."

ᏥᎧᏲᏍᎦ [tsịʔkahyosga]

ᎤᎧᏲᏒᎢ [ukahyosv²³ʔi]

ᎠᎧᏲᏍᎪᎢ [ạkahyosgo³ʔi]

ᎯᎧᏲᎯ [hịkahyohi]

ᎤᎧᏲᎯᏍᏗ [ukahyohịsdi]

ᎠᏅᎯᏗᏍ [akahyoh³diha] (vt) "He is drying it out.; He is preserving it."

    ᏥᏅᎯᏗᏍ [tsikahyoh³diha]

    ᎤᏅᎯᏩᏒᎢ [ukahyoh³tanv²³ʔi]

    ᎠᏅᎯᏗᏍᎪᎢ [akahyoh³disgo³ʔi]

    ᏍᏅᎯᏓ [hikahyoh³da]

    ᎤᏅᎯᏙᏗ [ukahyoh³dohdi]

    … ᏃᏍᎪ ᎤᏕᎶᏔᎬ ᎠᏅᎯᏗᏍᎪᎢ ᎠᎹ.
    … and then when it is shined on by the sun the water is dried by the sun.
    [ᏍᏫᎩ ᎳᏉᏗ ᏗᏂᏍᏓᏓᏗ ᏗᎦᏅᎯᏗ]

ᎠᎨᎯ [akęhi] (vt) "He is chasing him/it."

    ᏥᎨᎯ [tsiʔkęhi]

    ᎤᎨᎮᏒᎢ [ukęhęsv²³ʔi]

    ᎠᎨᎮᏐᎢ [akehʔso³ʔi]

    ᏍᎨᎽᎦ [hikęhuga]

    ᎤᎨᎯᏍᏗ [ukęhysdi]

    ᎠᏂᎨᎯ ᎠᏧᎦ ᎩᎶ.
    The dogs are chasing the boy.
    [King pg 110]

ᎠᎨᏯ [agęʔya] (vi) "He is flowing."

    ᏥᎨᏯ [tsigęʔya]

    ᎤᎨᏴᏒᎢ [ugęʔyvsv²³ʔi]

    ᎠᎨᏯᏐᎢ [agęʔyo³ʔi]

    ᏍᎨᏯ [higęʔya]

    ᎤᎨᏴᏍᏗ [ugęʔyvsdi]

ᎠᎨᏯ [agehya] (n) "Woman."

    ᏥᎨᏯ [tsigehya]

    ᏍᎩᏴᏃ ᎠᎨᏯ ᎠᏥᎮᏒᎢ.
    Actually, a woman was being killed.
    [King pg 121]

ᎠᎨᏯᏗᏍ

ᎠᎨᏯᏗᏍ [agehydiha] (vt) "He is refusing to give him."

    ᏥᎨᏯᏗᏍ [tsigęʔydiha]

    ᎤᎨᏯᏩᏒᎢ [ugehytanv²³ʔi]

    ᎠᎨᏯᏗᏍᎪᎢ [agehydisgo³ʔi]

    ᏍᎨᏯᏓ [higehyda]

    ᎤᎨᏯᏙᏗ [ugehydohdi]

ᎠᏱᎠ [agi³ʔa] (vt) "He is picking it (a solid) up.; He is getting it (a solid).; He is obtaining it (a solid)."

    ᏥᏱᎠ [tsigi³ʔa]

    ᎤᏱᏒᎢ [ugi³sv²³ʔi]

    ᎠᏱᏍᎪᎢ [agi³sgo³ʔi]

    ᏍᏱ [higi]

    ᎤᏱᏍᏗ [ugi³sdi]

    ᏥᏌ ᎤᎫᏨᏯ ᎤᏱᏒᎩ ᎦᏌ ᎠᎴ ᏌᏂᏯᎩ, ᎠᎴ ᎤᏂᎥ ᎠᎦᏗ ᏌᏂᏯᎩ.
    Jesus, therefore, doth come and take the bread and give to them, and the fish in like manner;
    [ᎧᏂ 21:13]

ᎠᏱᎠ [agiʔa] (vt) "He is eating it (a solid)."

    ᏥᏱᎠ [tsigiʔa]

    ᎤᎬᎢᎢ [ugʔv²³ʔi]

    ᎠᏱᏍᎪᎢ [agisgo³ʔi]

    ᏍᎦ [higa]

    ᎤᏱᏍᏗ [ugisdi]

    ᎣᏏᏴᏂ ᎤᎳᏩᏙᏗ ᏥᏞᏍ ᎠᏍᎥᎢᏍᏗ ᏬᏍᏛ ᎢᎧᏛ ᎠᎴ ᎤᎯ ᎢᎧᏛ, ᎢᎵ ᎬᏱᏍᏗ ᏬᎢᏆᏍᏗ, ᎣᎠᎬᏃ ᏔᎦ ᏍᎥᎦ ᎤᎥᎠᎬᎵ ᎬᎯᎠᏍᏗ ᎢᏆᏍᏗ.
    and of the tree of knowledge of good and evil, thou dost not eat of it, for in the day of thine eating of it – dying thou dost die.'
    [ᏍᏅ ᎢᏤᏒᏏ 2:17]

ᎠᏱᏒᎯ [agiʔeha] (vt) "He is taking it (a solid) from him."

    ᏥᏱᏒᎠ [tsigiʔęʔa]

    ᎤᏱᏒᎢ [ugiʔęʔlv²³ʔi]

    ᎠᏱᏒᎢᎢ [agiʔeho³ʔi]

    ᏍᏱᎢᎢ [higiʔi]

    ᎤᏱᏒᏗ [ugiʔehdi]

    ᏍᏱ ᎬᏁᏓᎠ ᎣᏍᏱ ᏥᏫᎬᎯᎢᎠ …
    receive, I pray thee, my blessing …
    [ᏍᏅ ᎢᏤᏒᏏ 33:11]

ᎠᏱᏟᏱᎠ [akiligiʔa] (vt) "He is removing an animal from pasture."

    ᏥᏱᏟᏱᎠ [tsikiligiʔa]

    ᎤᏱᏟᏱᏒᎢ [ukiligisv²³ʔi]

    ᎠᏱᏟᏱᏍᎪᎢ [akiligisgo³ʔi]

    ᏍᎢᏟᏱ [hikiligi]

    ᎤᏱᏟᏱᏍᏗ [ukiligisdi]

DYℏℏⵚ [agihlị³yoga] (vi) "He is suffering."

ℏYℏℏⵚ [tsigịʔlị³yoga]

O'Yℏℏⵎⵜ [ugihlị³yotsv²³ʔi]

DYℏℏAⵜ [agihlị³yogo³ʔi]

ⵚYℏℏⵍ [hịgihlị³yogi]

O'Yℏℏⵜⵌⵎ [ugihlị³yoʔịsdi]

ⵁⵌY ⵁⵌ⅄ⵜ O'ⵍⵚℙⵌⵎⵜ ⵘD ⵁⵌY ⅃ⵏⵌO'ⵜ
ℏYℏℏⵚ; D4Z iⵏ ⵌⵚⵚ⋔ⵌⵚ; …
for which cause also these things I suffer, but I am not
ashamed, …
[ⵏℙⵍ ⵍℙⵍ 1:12]

DYⵙⵌⵚ [akịʔlyʔvsga] (vt) "He is getting onto it.; He is
getting into it.; He is mounting it."

ⵚYⵙⵌⵚ [gakịʔlyʔvsga]

O'YⵙOⵜ [ukịʔlyʔnv²³ʔi]

DYⵙⵌAⵜ [akịʔlyʔvsgo³ʔi]

ⵜYⵙⵌⵚ [hakịʔlyʔvga]

O'Yⵙⵍ [ukịʔlvdi]

ℏⵡZ O'ⵠⵌⵌ DYⵁ ⵜℙℙ-ⵍⵚℙDO'ⵌⵜ', O'YⵙO'Y,
ⵁⵌYⵏ ⵘD ℏℏEO' ℏAⵌⵡ;
and Jesus having found a young ass did sit upon it,
according as it is written,
[ⵚℏ 12:14]

DYⵌⵚ [akịsga] (vt) "He is swallowing it."

ℏYⵌⵚ [tsikịsga]

O'YRⵜ [ukịsv²³ʔi]

DYⵌAⵜ [akịsgo³ʔi]

ⵚYⵙ [hịkịhi]

O'Yⵙⵌⵍ [ukịhịsdi]

ⵍℏⵜⵁ ⵍⵠⵍℏhVⵙ! ⵠR ⵜℏⵜⵜⵙⵌⵍⵌY ℏℏℙZ
ⵜℏYⵌY.
'Blind guides! who are straining out the gnat, and the
camel are swallowing.
[ℙⵚ 23:24]

DYⵌVD [agisdo³ʔa] (vt) "He is chewing it."

ℏYⵌVD [tsigịʔsdo³ʔa]

O'YⵌViⵜ [ugisdo³ʔv²³ʔi]

DYⵌVⵌAⵜ [agisdo³sgo³ʔi]

ⵚYⵌVⵚ [hịgisdo³tsa]

O'YⵌVⵌⵍ [ugisdo³sdi]

DYb [agisi] (vt) "He is fetching it (a solid)."

ℏYb [tsigisi]

O'YⵜRⵜ [ugisẹsv²³ʔi]

DYⵜAⵜ [agisẹgo³ʔi]

ⵚYⵢⵚ [hịgisụ³ga]

O'YRⵌⵍ [ugisvsdi]

DAⵙⵌⵚ [agohvsga] (vi) "It is burning."

———

O'AOⵜ [ugohnv²³ʔi]

DAⵙⵌAⵜ [agohvsgo³ʔi]

ⵠAⵙⵚ [wagohvga]

O'Aⵙⵌⵍ [ugohvsdi]

Dⵜ O'ⵍMO'Y TⵚZ O'hAⵙ ⵚⵚRⵌⵜ' ⵁⵌY
DAⵙⵌEⵜ …
and were crying, seeing the smoke of her burning …
[DℏⵁⵙAⵁⵜⵙⵜ 18:18]

DAⵙⵌⵚ [agohvh³sga] (vi) "It is burning up."

———

O'AOⵜ [ugoʔhnv²³ʔi]

DAⵙⵌAⵜ [agohvh³sgo³ʔi]

ⵠAⵁ [wagoʔhna]

O'Aⵙⵌⵍ [ugohvh³sdi]

… Dⵜ hⵚⵜ' Tⵠⵌ ⵌⵍⵌⵚ O'AO'Y.
… and all the green grass was burnt up.
[DℏⵁⵙAⵁⵜⵙⵜ 8:7]

DAⵙⵌⵍⵜ [agohysdịha] (vt) "He is burning it."

ⵚAⵙⵌⵍⵜ [gagoʔysdịha]

O'AⵙⵌⵍLOⵜ [ugohysdạʔnv²³ʔi]

DAⵙⵌⵍⵌAⵜ [agohysdịsgo³ʔi]

ⵜAⵙⵌⵍL [hagohysda]

O'Aⵙⵌⵚⵍ [ugohysduhdi]

DAℙⵝD [agoli³yẹʔa] (vt) "He is reading it.; He is studying.;
He is examining it."

ℏAℙⵝD [tsigoli³yẹʔa]

O'Aℙⵝiⵜ [ugoli³yẹʔv²³ʔi]

DAℙⵝⵌAⵜ [agoli³yẹsgo³ʔi]

ⵚAℙⵌ [hịgoli³ya]

O'Aℙⵝⵍ [ugoli³yedi]

… O'AℙⵝiZ ⵜⵜ' ⵚⵜⵌⵙ Dⵜ O'ⵌⵌOⵌY;
… and as he read, he wept and trembled;
[ⵍⵍⵚⵍ ⵚhYRRⵜ]

17

DAᎥD [ago꞉lv꞉a] (vi) "He is going then turning and coming back."

ᎦAᎥD [gago꞉lv꞉a]

ᏫAᎥRT [ugo꞉lvsv²³꞉i]

DAᎥᏬᎠT [ago꞉lvsgo³꞉i]

ᏬAᎥᎾ [hago꞉lvna]

ᏫAᎥᏬᎠᎫ [ugo꞉lvsdi]

ᎦᏀᏫᏰᏃ ᎢᏌᎤ ᏫᎾAᎥR ᏛᏞh ᏫᎾᏬᏞᎬᏚᎤ.
for already certain did turn aside after the Adversary.
[TEᏉᏦ ᎫᎩᎫ 5:14]

DAᎥD [ago³hlv꞉a] (vt) "He is turning it around."

ᏂAᎥD [tsigo꞉lv꞉a]

ᏫAᎥRT [ugo³hlvsv²³꞉i]

DAᎥᏬᎠT [ago³hlvsgo³꞉i]

ᏀAᎥᎾ [higo³hlvna]

ᏫAᎥᏬᎠᎫ [ugo³hlvsdi]

DAᎾ [agona] (n) "Starvation."

ᎾᏬᏃ ᎢᏀ ᎩᏳ DAᎾ ᏫᏟᏬᎤᏈᎠᎫ, ᏚᏬᏫᏴ DᏠᏬᏞᏈᏬᎤᏈᎠᎫ; ...
and if any one is hungry, at home let him eat, ...
[TEᏉᏦ ᏝAᏬᏪᏂᎡᏀ 11:34]

DAᏬᎩᏴᏬᎫꞈ [ako꞉sgisdị̈ha] (vt) "He is elbowing it."

ᏂᏬAᏬᎩᏴᏬᎫꞈ [tsiyako꞉sgisdị̈ha]

ᏫAᏬᎩᏴᏬᏞᎤᎢ [uko꞉sgisda꞉nv²³꞉i]

DAᏬᎩᏴᏬᎫᏬᎠT [ako꞉sgisdị̈sgo³꞉i]

ᏀᏬAᏬᎩᏴᏬᎫ [hiyako꞉sgisda]

ᏫAᏬᎩᏴᎫ [uko꞉skdi]

DAᏬᎡᏞᎩᏴᏬᎫᎫ [ago꞉sda̱ḳisdi] (n) "Lettuce.; biol. *Lactuca sativa.*"

DAᏬᏬᎫ [ago꞉sdi] (adj) "Raw.; Unripe."

DAᏬᏬᏚᎩᏴᏬᎫ [ago꞉sdu̱gisdi] (n) "Branch lettuce.; biol. *Saxifraga micranthidifolia.*"

DAᎬᏬ [ago̱dẹhi] (n) "Marsh hawk.; Hen Harrier.; biol. *Circus hudsonius.*"

DAᏩᎢᏬᎦ [ako̱dv꞉vsga] (vt) "He is sprinkling.; He is sifting flour."

ᏂᏞAᏩᎢᏬᎦ [tsiḳo̱dv꞉v꞉sga]

ᏫAᏩᎣᎣᎢ [uko̱dyunv꞉꞉i]

DAᏩᎢᏬᎠT [ako̱dv꞉vsgo³꞉i]

ᏀAᏩᎢᏚ [hị̈ḳo̱dv꞉vga]

ᏫAᏩᎫ [uko̱dv꞉di]

DAᎬᎫꞈ [ago³whtị̈ha] (vt) "He is seeing it."

ᏂAᎬᎫꞈ [tsigo̱whtị̈ha]

ᏫAᎬᎤᏬᏍᎢ [ugo³whtvhv²³꞉i]

DAᎬᎫᏬᎠT [ago³whtị̈sgo³꞉i]

ᏀAᎬᏪ [hị̈go³whta]

ᏫAᎬᎤᎫ [ugo³whtvhdi]

ii, ᏬᏴ ᏂAᎬᎫꞈ.
Yes, I see it well.
[ᏛᏁᎫ ᎦᏂᎩRRT]

DAᏓ [ago̱wv] (n) "Sand piper."

DᏚᎩD [a̱kugị꞉a] (vt) "He is dipping a liquid.; He is taking liquid from liquid.; He is removing liquid from a container."

ᏂᎫᎩD [tsiguị̈gị꞉a]

ᏫᎫᎩRT [ukugisv²³꞉i]

DᏚᎩᏬᎠT [a̱kugisgo³꞉i]

ᏀᎫᎩ [hị̈kugi]

ᏫᎫᎩᏬᎫ [ukugị̈sdi]

DᏚᏬᏞh [a̱ku̱sgeni] (n) "His elbow."

ᏛᏚᏬᏞh [dị̈ku̱sgeni]

ᏂᎫᏬᏞh [tsị̈ku̱sgeni]

ᏛᏂᎫᏬᏞh [dị̈tsị̈ku̱sgeni]

DᏚᏬᎩD [a̱ku̱sgị꞉a] (vt) "He is nudging it with his elbow."

ᏂᎫᏬᎩD [tsị̈ku̱sgị꞉a]

ᏫᎫᏬᎩᏪᎢᎢ [uku̱sgita̱nv²³꞉i]

DᎫᏬᎩᏬᎠT [a̱ku̱sgị̈sgo³꞉i]

ᏀᎫᏬᎩᏬᎫ [hị̈ku̱sgsda]

ᏫᎫᏬᎠᎫ [uku̱sgodi]

DᎬD [a̱kv³꞉a] (vt) "He is moving it (something alive).; He is moving it (a solid)."

ᏂᎬD [tsi꞉kv³꞉a]

ᏫᎬᎢT [ukv³꞉v²³꞉i]

DᎬᏬᎠT [a̱kv³sgo³꞉i]

ᏀᎬᎾ [hikv³na]

ᏫᎬᏬᎫ [ukv³sdi]

ᎠᎬᎦ [ạgvga] (vi) "He is drowning."

ᏥᎬᎦ [tsịgvga]

ᎤᎬᏨᎢ [ugvʔtsv^{23}ʔi]

ᎠᎬᎪᎢ [ạgvgo^{3}ʔi]

ᎯᎬᎩ [hịgvʔgi]

ᎤᎬᎢᏍᏗ [ugvʔisdi]

… ᎠᏥᎸᏱ ᎡᏛᎪᎢ ᎠᎴ ᎠᎹᏱ ᎠᎬᎪᎢ.
… for often he doth fall into the fire, and often into the water,
[ᎹᏚ 17:15]

ᎠᎬᎭᎴᏫᏓ [ạgṿhạlewịda] (n) "Quilt top."

ᎠᎬᎭᎵᎭ [ạgṿ^{3}hạlịha] (vt) "He is cutting it (a solid) off."

ᏥᎬᎠᎵᎭ [tsịgṿʔạlịha]

ᎤᎬᎭᎸᎲᎢ [ugṿ^{3}hạlṿhv^{23}ʔi]

ᎠᎬᎭᎵᏍᎪᎢ [ạgṿ^{3}hạlịsgo^{3}ʔi]

ᎯᎬᎭᎳ [hịgṿ^{3}hạla]

ᎤᎬᎭᎳᏗ [ugṿ^{3}hahldi]

ᎠᎬᎯᏓ [ạkṿhịda] (n) "Sheet.; Linen."

ᎠᎬᏃᎨᏂ [ạkṿnogeni] (n) "His wing."

ᏗᎬᏃᎨᏂ [dịkṿnogeni]

ᎠᎬᏍᏉᎠ [agvsgwoʔa] (vi) "He is washing his face."

ᎦᎬᏍᏉᎠ [gagṿʔsgwoʔa]

ᎤᎬᏍᏉᎥᎢ [ugvsgwoʔv^{23}ʔi]

ᎠᎬᏍᏉᏍᎪᎢ [agvsgwosgo^{3}ʔi]

ᎭᎬᏍᏉᏣ [hagvsgwotsa]

ᎤᎬᏍᏉᏍᏗ [ugvsgwosdi]

ᏂᎯᏍᎩᏂ ᎠᎹᏟ ᎲᏍᎨᏍᏗ, ᎭᏌᏁᏍᎨᏍᏗ, ᎠᎴ ᎭᎬᏍᏉᏍᎨᏍᏗ,
'But thou, fasting, anoint thy head, and wash thy face,
[ᎹᏚ 6:17]

ᎠᎬᏗᎨᏂ [ạgvdịgeni] (n) "His forehead."

ᏥᎬᏗᎨᏂ [tsịgvdịgeni]

ᎠᎬᏚᎶ [ạgvdụʔlo] (n) "Mask."

ᎠᎬᏩᎶᏗ [ạgvhwạldi] (vi) "It is worth."

ᎠᎩᎬᏩᎶᏗ [a^{1}gịgvwạʔldi]

ᎤᎬᏩᎶᏕᏍᏛᎢ [ugvhwạldesdv^{23}ʔi]

ᎠᎬᏩᎶᏙᎢ [ạgvhwạldo^{3}ʔi]

ᎯᎬᏩᎶᏓ [hịgvhwạlda]

ᎤᎬᏩᎶᏙᏗ [ugvhwạldohdi]

ᎠᎬᏯᏍᎦ [ạgṿʔyhsga] (vt) "He is drowning him."

ᏥᎬᏯᏍᎦ [tsigṿʔyʔsga]

ᎤᎬᏯᎲᎢ [ugṿʔyhv^{23}ʔi]

ᎠᎬᏯᏍᎪᎢ [ạgṿʔyhsgo^{3}ʔi]

ᎯᎬᏯ [higṿʔya]

ᎤᎬᏯᏍᏗ [ugṿʔyhsdi]

ᎠᎬᏱ [ạgvyi] (adj) "First.; Initially."

ᎠᎬᏱ ᎤᎦᏔ ᎤᏂᏫᏎ.
First they plant seed.
[ᏣᏔᎩ ᏔᎵᏁ ᏗᏂᏂᏙᎯ ᏗᎦᏲᏙᏗ]

ᎠᎬᏱᏗᏣ

ᎠᎬᏱᏗᏣ [ạgvyịditsa] (pt) "Before.; In the way."

ᎠᎬᏴᎵᎨᎢ [ạkṿyvlịgẹʔi] (adj) "Old (something alive)."

ᎠᎭᎨᏨᎯ [ạhạketsṿhi] (n) "A peeling."

ᎠᎭᏔᏍᎦ [ahạtasga] (vt) "He is hammering it in.; He is driving it in."

ᏥᎠᏔᏍᎦ [tsịʔạtasga]

ᎤᎭᏔᏅᎢ [uhạtạnv^{23}ʔi]

ᎠᎭᏔᏍᎪᎢ [ahạtasgo^{3}ʔi]

ᎯᎭᏔᎦ [hịhạtaga]

ᎤᎭᏘ [uhạti]

ᎠᎭᏫᏯ [ạhạwiya] (n) "Venison."

ᎠᎯᎭ [ahịha] (vt) "He is killing him."

ᏥᎢᎭ [tsiʔịha]

ᎤᎸᎢ [uhʔlv^{23}ʔi]

ᎠᎯᎰᎢ [ahịho^{3}ʔi]

ᎯᎷᎦ [hiluga]

ᎤᎯᏍᏗ [uhịsdi]

ᎠᏥᏁᏤᎴᏃ ᎯᎠ ᎤᏗᎠᏥᏭᏎᎴᎢ; ᏈᏓ, ᏔᎴᎲᎦ, ᎯᎷᎦ ᎠᎴ ᎭᎵᏍᏓᏴᎲᎦ, ᎠᎪᏎᎴᎢ.
and there came a voice unto him: 'Having risen, Peter, slay and eat.'
[ᎨᏥᏅᏏᏛ ᏄᎾᏛᏁᎵᏙᎸᎢ 10:13]

ᎠᎯᎵᏲᎦ [ahihlịyoga] (vi) "He is in agony, suffering."

ᏥᎢᎵᏲᎦ [tsịʔihlịyoga]

ᎤᎯᎵᏲᏨᎢ [uhihlịyotsv^{23}ʔi]

ᎠᎯᎵᏲᎪᎢ [ahihlịyogo^{3}ʔi]

ᎯᎯᎵᏲᎦ [hịhihlịyoʔga]

ᎤᎯᎵᏲᎢᏍᏗ [uhihlịyoʔịsdi]

ᎠᏒᎥᏍᎠ [ahiyiᵖa] (vt) "He is leaving it (a solid) or it (a liquid)."

ᏥᏔᎥᏍᎠ [tsiᵖiyiᵖa]

ᎤᎢᎥᏏᎢ [uhiyiv²³ᵖi]

ᎠᏒᎥᏍᎤᎠᎢ [ahiyisgo³ᵖi]

ᎭᎢᎭᏫ [hihiya]

ᎤᎢᎥᏍᎤᎠᏗ [uhiyisdi]

ᎠᏥᎵ [aholi] (n) "His mouth."

ᏥᏥᎵ [tsiholi]

iᏓᎾᎩh ᎾᎠᎩ Ꮎ ᎠᏥᎵ ᏃᏴᎦᎠ ᏍᏗᏛ ᎥᎦᏣᎱᏔ ᏴᎾ,
ᎠᏥᎵᎾᎩh ᎤᏝᏪᎦᏥᎠ ᎾᎠᎩ ᏍᏗᏛ ᎦᏣᎱᏔ ᏴᎾ.
not that which is coming into the mouth doth defile the man, but that which is coming forth from the mouth, this defileth the man.'
[ᎩᎠS 15:11]

ᎠᎢᏪᏥᏍ [ahulagega] (vi) "He is homesick."

ᏥᎤᏪᏥᏍ [tsiᵖulagega]

ᎤᎢᏪᏥᏓᎢᎢ [uhulagetsv²³ᵖi]

ᎠᎢᏪᏥᎠᎢ [ahulagego³ᵖi]

ᎭᎢᏪᏥᎢ [hihulageᵖi]

ᎤᎢᏪᏥᎥᎠᏗ [uhulagesdi]

ᎠᎢᎧᏉᎠᏍ [ahuleyvsga] (vi) "He is burning himself with hot food."

ᏥᎤᎧᏉᎠᏍ [tsiᵖuleyvsga]

ᎤᎢᎧᏴᎢᎢ [uhuleyvsv²³ᵖi]

ᎠᎢᎧᏉᎠᎢᎢ [ahuleyvsgo³ᵖi]

ᎭᎢᎢᎧᏉᎠ [hihuleyvhi]

ᎤᎢᎧᏉᎠᎠᎠᏗ [uhuleyvhisdi]

ᎠᎢᎵ [ahuᵖli] (n) "Drum."

… ᎾᎠᎩ ᏅᎠᏍ ᏔᏍᏞᎦ ᎬᎠᎻᏴᎥᎥᏫᏗᏍ, ᏗᎠᏃᏱᎦ ᎬᎥ,
ᎠᏉ ᎠᎢᎵ ᏔᎦᎯᎤ ᎬᎥ, ᎠᏉ ᎠᏆᏪᏍᎾᎦ ᏗᎠᏃᏱᎥᏘ ᎬᎥ?
… I send thee away with joy and with songs, with tabret and with harp,
[ᏅᏏ ᎢᎬᎥᎥ 31:27]

ᎠᎢᏗᎠ [ahudiᵖa] (vt) "He is putting it (something long) into a liquid."

ᏥᎤᎢᎠ [tsiᵖudiᵖa]

ᎤᎢᎢᎢᎢ [uhudᵖv²³ᵖi]

ᎠᎢᏗᎤᎠᎢ [ahudisgo³ᵖi]

ᎭᎢᏗ [hihuda]

ᎤᎢᏗᎤᎠᏗ [uhudisdi]

ᎠᎢᏣᏪᏫᎢᎢ [ahutsawoladvᵖi] (n) "Chimney."

ᎠᎢᎥᏓᏈ [ahuyi³siha] (vt) "He is taking it (something long) from a liquid."

ᏥᎤᎥᏓᏈ [tsiᵖuyi³siha]

ᎤᎢᎥᏓᎤᎢ [uhuyi³syhv²³ᵖi]

ᎠᎢᎥᏓᎤᎠᎢ [ahuyi³sisgo³ᵖi]

ᎭᎢᎥᏍᎤᎢ [hihuyiusa]

ᎤᎢᎥᏓᎤᎢ [uhuyi³svhdi]

ᎠᎤᎠᏍ [ahysga] (vt) "He is setting it (a solid) down."

ᏥᎢᎠᏍ [tsiᵖysga]

ᎤᎤᎢ [uhnv²³ᵖi]

ᎠᎤᎤᎠᎢ [ahysgo³ᵖi]

ᎭᎤᏍ [hihyga]

ᎤᎠᏗ [uhdi]

ᎠᎠᏓ ᏀᎤᏥᎢ, ᎤᎥᎠᏣᎠᏁ ᎢᏟᎦᏈᏓᏈ, ᎠᎠ ᎾᎠᎩ ᎤᎢ ᏔᎩᏟᎢᏓᏱ ᎤᏫᎥᏥᏣᎠ ᎤᎢᏟ ᎢᏍᎢ ᎠᎤᏍ ᎡᎤᏍᏅᏱ ᏏᏍᎦ ᎠᏥᎢᎢ.
and he said, 'Truly I say to you, that this poor widow did cast in more than all;
[ᎷᏍ 21:3]

ᎠᎤᎵᏴᎠ [ahvdagi³ᵖa] (vt) "He is taking it (something long) off a fire."

ᏥᎢᏗᎵᏴᎠ [tsiᵖvdagi³ᵖa]

ᎤᎤᎵᏴᎢᎢ [uhvdagi³sv²³ᵖi]

ᎠᎤᎵᏴᎤᎠᎢ [ahvdagi³sgo³ᵖi]

ᎭᎤᎵᏴ [hihvdagi]

ᎤᎢᎵᏴᎤᎠᏗ [uhvdagi³sdi]

ᎠᎤᏫᎤᏍ [ahvtah³sga] (vt) "He is putting it (something long) into a fire."

ᏥᎢᏫᎤᏍ [tsiᵖvtah³sga]

ᎤᎤᎢᎤᎢ [uhvtv³nv²³ᵖi]

ᎠᎤᏫᎤᎠᎢ [ahvtah³sgo³ᵖi]

ᎭᎤᏫᏍ [hihvta³ga]

ᎤᎤᏫᎵ [uhvtdi]

ᎠᏪᎤᎬᎠ [alasgvᵖa] (vi) "He is stepping."

ᏍᏪᎤᎬᎠ [galaᵖsgvᵖa]

ᎤᏪᎤᎠᎬᎢᎢ [ulasgvsv²³ᵖi]

ᎠᏪᎤᎬᎤᎠᎢ [alasgvsgo³ᵖi]

ᎤᏪᎤᎬᎾ [halasgvna]

ᎤᏪᎤᎬᎤᎠᏗ [ulasgvsdi]

DWⱻꙄꙅⱰD [ahlsdu³woʔa] (vi) "He is pulling corn slades off."

   ⱧWⱻꙄꙅⱰD [tsiʔlsdu³woʔa]

   OⵑWⱻꙄꙅⱰiT [uhlsdu³woʔv²³ʔi]

   DWⱻꙄꙅⱰꙭ₳T [ahlsdu³wosgo³ʔi]

   ꙅWⱻꙄꙅⱰG [hihlsdu³wotsa]

   OⵑWⱻꙄꙅⱰꙭ₳ [uhlsdu³wosdi]

DWⱻꙍ₵ⁱⱻꙄ [alasdyʔvsga] (vt) "He is stepping on it."

   ꙄWⱻꙍ₵ⁱⱻꙄ [galaʔsdyʔvsga]

   OⵑWⱻꙍ₵OⵑT [ulasdyʔnv²³ʔi]

   DWⱻꙍ₵ⁱⱻ₳T [alasdyʔvsgo³ʔi]

   ꙅWⱻꙍ₵ⁱꙄ [halasdyʔvga]

   OⵑWⱻꙍ₵Ꙇ [ulasdvdi]

DWꙨⱰⱵ [ahlawi³diha] (vi) "He is flying."

   ꙄWꙨⱰⱵ [gaʔlawi³diha]

   OⵑWꙍ₵₳T [uhlawi³dyhv²³ʔi]

   DWꙨⱰꙭ₳T [ahlawi³disgo³ʔi]

   ꙅWꙨⱰⱡ [hahlawi³da]

   OⵑWꙨⱰꙆ [uhlawi³tdi]

Dⷮ [ale] (pt) "And.; Or."

   ⱧA GⱡⵑT Dⷮ ⱰⅤⱧ DⱰⱵ?
   Hast thou a Wife and Children?
   [ⱰⱰGⱰ ꙄhⲨRRT]

DⷮhD [aleniʔa] (vt) "He is starting it.; He is beginning it."

   ꙅⷮꙍD [galewiʔa]

   Oⷮⷯ6iT [ulewyʔv²³ʔi]

   DⷮꙍꙭAT [alewisgo³ʔi]

   ⱵⷯⷷG [halewa]

   OⷮⷯⱵꙆ [ulewhdi]

DⷮOⵑⱰⱵ [alenhdiha] (vi) "He is beginning with."

   ꙅⷮOⵑⱰⱵ [galenyʔdiha]

   OⷮⷯOⵑWOⵑT [ulenhtanv²³ʔi]

   DⷮOⵑⱰꙭ₳T [alenhdisgo³ʔi]

   ⱵⷯOⵑⱡ [halenhda]

   OⷮⷯOⵑVꙆ [ulenhdohdi]

   ꙨꙭⱮ ꙠD OⷮⷯOⵑWOⵑⲨ ⱧⱵ OⵑꙭⱧhꙠꙆ ꙄꙅꙭꙭⱡⱰꙅⱮ Ⱨⱡⱡ Ⱨh ꙄꙄꙅⷷT, ...
   This beginning of the signs did Jesus in Cana of Galilee, ...
   [Gh 2:11]

DⱡRhD [aliʔenia] (vi) "He is crippled."

   ⱧⱡRhD [tsiliʔenia]

   OⵑⱡRhRⱻⷯꙮT [uliʔeniesdv²³ʔi]

   DⱡRhꙭT [aliʔenio³ʔi]

   ꙭⱡRhRⱻⱰ [hiliʔeniesdi]

   OⵑⱡRhRⱻⱰ [uliʔeniesdi]

DⱡT [aliʔi] (n) "Friendship."

DⱡꙠⱰⱵ [alikoneha] (vt) "He is wishing to accompany."

   ⱧⱸⱡⱠⱰⱵ [tsiyaligoʔneha]

   OⵑⱡⱠⱰ₵T [ulikoneʔlv²³ʔi]

   DⱡⱠⱰⱧT [alikoneho³ʔi]

   ꙭⱸⱡⱠⱠib [hiyaligoyʔsi]

   OⵑⱡⱠⱰꙆ [ulikonhdi]

   ... **TⱰꙭGZ ꙄGⱡⱠⱰⱧ ꙨꙭⲨ TⱧⱠⱰⱧⱸ.**
   ... and partly having become partners of those so living,
   [Dhⵟ̔M 10:33]

DⱡⱡEⲨD [aligvgiʔa] (vt) "He is ripping it."

   ⱧⱡⱡEⲨD [tsiligvgiʔa]

   OⵑⱡⱡEⲨRT [uligvgisv²³ʔi]

   DⱡⱡEⲨꙭ₳T [aligvgisgo³ʔi]

   ꙭⱡⱡEⲨ [hiligvgi]

   OⵑⱡⱡEⲨꙭꙆ [uligvgisdi]

DⱡⱡEⱥꙭꙄ [aligyyhsga] (vi) "He is diving."

   ꙅⱡⱡEⱥꙭꙄ [galigyyʔsga]

   OⵑⱡⱡEBT [uligyʔhyv²³ʔi]

   DⱡⱡEⱥꙭ₳T [aligyyhsgo³ʔi]

   ⱵⱡⱡEⱥ [haligyʔya]

   OⵑⱡⱡEⱥꙭꙆ [uligyʔhysdi]

DⱡⱵ [ahliha] (vi) "He is fighting."

   ꙅⱡⱵ [gaʔliha]

   OⵑⱡⱧT [uhlilv²³ʔi]

   DⱡⱧT [ahliho³ʔi]

   ⱵⱡⱡꙄ [hahlga]

   OⵑⱡꙭꙆ [uhlsdi]

   OⵑⲨⱢⱮⱢZ ꙄꙨⱰAVⷯ DOⱡꙨⷷT ...
   'On the succeeding day, also, he shewed himself to them as they are striving ...
   [ⱧⱧOⵑbⵑ ⱰOⵑⱰⱡⱡⱠVⱰⱧT 7:26]

ᎠᎵᎮᎵᎦ [alihe^{3}liga] (vi) “He is happy.; He is giving thanks.”

ᎦᎵᎡᎵᎦ [galịʔe^{3}liga]
ᎤᎵᎮᎵᏨᎢ [ulihe^{3}litsv^{23}ʔi]
ᎠᎵᎮᎵᎪᎢ [alihe^{3}ligo^{3}ʔi]
ᎭᎵᎮᎵᎩ [halihe^{3}ligi]
ᎤᎵᎮᎵᏍᏗ [ulihe^{3}lisdi]

ᎾᏍᎩᏃ ᎤᏭᏖᏒᎩ ᎠᎴ ᎤᎵᎮᎵᏨᎩ …
the which he took up and rejoiced therein …
[ᏧᏁᎶᏗ ᏚᏂᎩᏒᏒᎢ]

ᎠᎵᎮᎵᏤᎭ [alihelicheha] (vt) “He is thanking him.”

ᏥᏯᎵᎡᎵᏤᎭ [tsiyalịʔelicheha]
ᎤᎵᎮᎵᏤᎸᎢ [ulihelichẹʔlv^{23}ʔi]
ᎠᎵᎮᎵᏤᎰᎢ [alihelicheho^{3}ʔi]
ᎯᏯᎵᎡᎵᏥᏏ [hiyalịʔelichịsi]
ᎤᎵᎮᎵᏤᏗ [ulihelichehdi]

ᎢᎬᏱᏱ ᎨᏒᎢ, ᏥᏯᎵᎡᎵᏤᎭ ᎠᏆᏁᎳᏅᏯ ᎬᏗᎭ ᏚᏙᎥ ᏥᏌ ᎦᎶᏁᏛ …
first, indeed, I thank my God through Jesus Christ …
[ᎶᎻ 1:8]

ᎠᎵᏃᎮᏗᎭ [ahlịnọhẹ^{3}hdịha] (vt) “He is speaking to him.”

ᏥᏯᎵᏃᎮᏗᎭ [tsiyạʔlịnọhẹ^{3}hdịha]
ᎤᎵᏃᎮᏔᏅᎢ [uhlịnọhẹ^{3}tạnv^{23}ʔi]
ᎠᎵᏃᎮᏗᏍᎪᎢ [ahlịnọhẹ^{3}hdsgo^{3}ʔi]
ᎯᏯᎵᏃᎮᏓ [hiyạʔlịnọhẹ^{3}hda]
ᎤᎵᏃᎮᏙᏗ [uhlịnọhẹ^{3}hdohdi]

ᏧᏁᎶᏗ ᎠᎴ ᎤᏬᏯᏳᏯᏍᏛ ᎠᎾᎵᏃᎮᏔᏂᏏ ᎠᎾᎢᏒ ᎢᎾᎨᎢ, ᎯᎠ ᏄᏂᏪᏒ.
Christian and Pliable went talking over the Plain; and thus they began their discourse.
[ᏧᏁᎶᏗ ᏚᏂᎩᏒᏒᎢ]

ᎠᎵᏇᏅᏗ [algwehnvhdi] (n) “Bed cover.”

ᎠᎵᏌᎵᎭ [alsạliha] (vt) “He is teasing him.; He is picking on him.”

ᏥᏯᎵᏌᎵᎠ [tsiyalsạlịʔa]
ᎤᎵᏌᎳᏅᎢ [ulsahlanv^{23}ʔi]
ᎠᎵᏌᎵᏍᎪᎢ [alsạlisgo^{3}ʔi]
ᎯᏯᎵᏌᎳ [hiyalsạla]
ᎤᎵᏌᎵᏗ [ulsahldi]

ᎠᎵᏍᎦᏗ [alsgahdi] (n) “Ball.”

ᎠᎵᏍᎩᎠ [alsgị^{3}ʔa] (vi) “He is dancing.”

ᎦᎵᏍᎩᎠ [galsgị^{3}ʔa]
ᎤᎵᏍᎩᏒᎢ [ulsgị^{3}sv^{23}ʔi]
ᎠᎵᏍᎩᏍᎪᎢ [alsgị^{3}sgo^{3}ʔi]
ᎭᎵᏍᎩ [halsgị]
ᎤᎵᏍᎩᏍᏗ [ulsgị^{3}sdi]

ᎠᏂᎨᏯ ᎠᎾᎵᏍᎩᎠ.
The women are dancing.
[King pg 110]

ᎠᎵᏍᎫᏩᏍᎦ [ạhlsgụ^{3}whsga] (vi) “He is nodding his head.; He is shaking his head yes.”

ᎦᎵᏍᎫᏩᏍᎦ [gahlisgụ^{3}whsga]
ᎤᎵᎡᏍᎫᏩᎲᎢ [ụhlsgụ^{3}whv^{23}ʔi]
ᎠᎵᎡᏍᎫᏩᏍᎪᎢ [ạhlsgụ^{3}whsgo^{3}ʔi]
ᎭᎵᏍᎫᏩ [hạhlsgụ^{3}wa]
ᎤᎵᏍᎫᏩᏍᏗ [ụhlsgụ^{3}whsdi]

ᎠᎵᏍᏓᏴᎲᏍᎦ [alsda^{3}ʔyvhvsga] (vi) “He is eating a meal.”

ᎦᎵᏍᏓᏴᎥᏍᎦ [galsda^{3}ʔyỵʔvsga]
ᎤᎵᏍᏓᏴᏅᎢ [ulsda^{3}ʔyỵʔhnv^{23}ʔi]
ᎠᎵᏍᏓᏴᎲᏍᎪᎢ [alsda^{3}ʔyvhvsgo^{3}ʔi]
ᎭᎵᏍᏓᏴᎲᎦ [halsda^{3}ʔyvhvga]
ᎤᎵᏍᏓᏴᏗ [ulsda^{3}ʔyhdi]

ᏑᏠᏃ ᎠᏥᏝᏁᎴ ᎤᎵᏍᏓᏴᏗ; ᎠᏎᏃ ᎯᎠ ᏄᏪᏎᎢ, ᎥᏝ ᏴᎦᎦᎵᏍᏓᏴᎲᎦ ᎬᏂ ᏥᏃᏅᎭ ᏄᏍᏛ ᎠᎩᏃᎮᏗ ᎨᏒᎢ …
and setteth before him to eat; but he saith, ’I do not eat till I have spoken my word;’ …
[ᎼᏏ ᎢᎬᏱᏱ 24:33]

ᎠᎵᏍᏓᏴᏍᎦ

ᎠᎵᏍᏓᏴᏍᎦ [alsdahyyṿhsga] (vi) “He is going to eat.”

ᎦᎵᏍᏓᏴᏍᎦ [galsdayyṿʔsga]
ᎤᎵᏍᏓᏴᏒᎢ [ulsdahyyṿʔsv^{23}ʔi]
ᎠᎵᏍᏓᏴᏍᎪᎢ [alsdahyyṿsgo^{3}ʔi]
ᎭᎵᏍᏓᏴᎦ [halsdayyṿʔụga]
ᎤᎵᏍᏓᏴᏍᏗ [ulsdayyṿʔṿsdi]

ᎠᎵᏍᏙᏯᏙᏗ [alsdohydohdi] (n) “Razor.”

ᎠᎵᏍᏚᎩᎠ [ahlsdụgiʔa] (vt) “He is pulling leaves off of a tree.”

ᏥᎵᏍᏚᎩᎠ [tsịʔlsdụgiʔa]
ᎤᎵᏍᏚᎩᏒᎢ [uhlsdụgisv^{23}ʔi]
ᎠᎵᏍᏚᎩᏍᎪᎢ [ahlsdụgisgo^{3}ʔi]
ᎯᎵᏍᏚᎩ [hịhlsdụgi]
ᎤᎵᏍᏚᎩᏍᏗ [uhlsdụgi^{3}sdi]

DᏢᏬᏚᏈᏆ [alsduliha] (vi) "He is washing hair.; He is shampooing."

    ᏚᏈᏬᏚᏈD [galsduli?a]

    OᏈᏬᏚᏟᏇᎢ [ulsdulehv^{23}?i]

    DᏢᏬᏚᏈᏬAᎢ [alsdulisgo^3?i]

    ᏇᏈᏬᏚᏈ [halsduli]

    OᏈᏬᏚᏈᎫ [ulsduhldi]

DᏢᏬᏚᏪᎢ [alsdulohi] (n) "Bonnet.; Scarf."

DᏢᏬᎭᏔᏂᏆ [alsdy^{3}hniha] (vi) "He is shaking his head no."

    ᏚᏈᏬᎭᏔᏂᏆ [galsdy?niha]

    OᏈᏬᎭᏔᏂᎦᎢ [ulsdy^{3}hnilv^{23}?i]

    DᏢᏬᎭᏔᏂᏏᎢ [alsdy^{3}hniho^3?i]

    ᏇᏈᏬᎭᏔᏂᏏ [halsdy^{3}hnga]

    OᏈᏬᎭᏔᏂᏬᎫ [ulsdy^{3}hnsdi]

DᏈ4Ꮔ [aliseha] (vt) "He is carrying it on his back."

    ᏚᏈ4D [galise?a]

    OᏈ4ᎡᎢ [ulisesv^{23}?i]

    DᏈ4ᏏᎢ [aliseho^3?i]

    ᏇᏈᏤᏚ [halisuga]

    OᏈᎡᏬᎫ [ulisysdi]

    ᎢᏞ ᏏᏈ ᎬᎢᏞOᏇᏬᎫ ᏬᏴ, ᏂᏚᏈᏬᎧᎫ ᎭᎠ ᏚᏔᏋ ᏏᏚᏈ4Ꮔ.
    I cannot go so fast as I would, by reason of this Burden <u>that is upon my back</u>.
    [ᏧᏁᏋᎫ ᏏᏂᎡᎡᎢ]

DᏈᏏᏂᎫᏆ [alsi^{3}hndiha] (vi) "He is conserving."

    ᏚᏈᏏᏂᎫᏆ [galsi?ndiha]

    OᏈᏏᏂᏞOᎢ [ulsi^{3}hndanv^{23}?i]

    DᏈᏏᏂᎫᏬAᎢ [alsi^{3}hndisgo^3?i]

    ᏇᏈᏏᏂᏞ [halsi^{3}hnda]

    OᏈᏏᏂᎥᎫ [ulsi^{3}hndohdi]

DᏈᏇᏫꞋ [alitama] (n) "Carolina wren.; biol. *Thryothorus ludovicianus.*"

DᏈᏇᏚᏚ [ahltade^{3}ga] (vi) "He is jumping."

    ᏚᏈᏇᏚᏚ [gahltade^{3}ga]

    OᏈᏇᏚᎡᎢ [ultade^3?sv^{23}?i]

    DᏈᏇᏚᏏAᎢ [ahltade^{3}go^3?i]

    ᏇᏈᏇᏚᏚ [haltade^3?ga]

    OᏈᏇᏔᎢ [ultady^{3}hyi]

DᏈᏪᏂᏆ [altelv^{3}hniha] (vt) "He is swinging it."

    ᏚᏈᏏᏪᏂᏆ [gald?elv^{3}hniha]

    OᏈᏪᏂᏏᎢ [ultelv^{3}hnilv^{23}?i]

    DᏈᏪᏂᏏᎢ [altelv^{3}hniho^3?i]

    ᏇᏈᏪᏂᏏ [haltelv^{3}hnga]

    OᏈᏪᏂᏬᎫ [ultelv^{3}hnsdi]

DᏈᏗᎩD [ahlidgi?a] (vi) "He is taking off running."

    ᏚᏈᏗᎩD [ga?lidgi?a]

    OᏈᏗᎩᎡᎢ [uhlidgisv^{23}?i]

    DᏈᏗᎩᏬAᎢ [ahlidgisgo^3?i]

    ᏇᏟᎩ [hahlogi]

    OᏈᏗᎩᏬᎫ [uhlidgisdi]

DᏈᎥᎩᏙD [altogiyi?a] (vi) "He is racing."

    ᏚᏈᎥᎩᏙD [gald?ogiyi?a]

    OᏈᎥᎩᏙᎡᎢ [ultogiyisv^{23}?i]

    DᏈᎥᎩᏙᏬAᎢ [altogiyisgo^3?i]

    ᏇᏈᎥᎩᏫ [haltogiya]

    OᏈᎥᎩᏬᎫ [ultogiysdi]

DᏈᏟᏃᏬᏚ [alitsanosga] (n) "Indigo bunting.; biol. *Passerina cyanea.*"

DᏈᏥᏆ [altsiha] (vi) "It is boiling."

    —

    OᏈᏟᏍᎥᎢ [ultsy^{3}hiv^{23}?i]

    DᏈᏥᏬAᎢ [altsisgo^3?i]

    ᎬᏈᏟ [waltsa]

    OᏈᏟᎫ [ultshdi]

DᏈᏥᏬᏈᏬᏚ [altsiskwsga] (vt) "He is spitting."

    ᏚᏈᏥᏬᏈᏬᏚ [galtsisgw?sga]

    OᏈᏥᏬᎬᎢ [ultsiskwv^{23}?i]

    DᏈᏥᏬᏈᏬAᎢ [altsiskwsgo^3?i]

    ᏇᏈᏥᏬᏈ [haltsisgwi]

    OᏈᏥᏬᏈᏬᎫ [ultsiskwsdi]

    ᎾᎠᎩ ᏆᏫᎡ ᏍᎠᎠ OᏈᏥᏬᎬᎩ …
    These things saying, <u>he spat</u> on the ground …
    [Ꭻh 9:6]

DᏈᏥᎫᏆ [ahlidsdiha] (vt) "He is boiling it."

    ᏚᏈᏥᎫᏆ [ga?lidsdiha]

    OᏈᏥᏞOᎢ [uhlidsdanv^{23}?i]

    DᏈᏥᎫᏬAᎢ [ahlidsdisgo^3?i]

    ᏇᏈᏥᏞ [hahlidsda]

    OᏈᏥᎥᎫ [uhlidsdodi]

ᎠᎵᏥᏙᎲᏍᎦ [altsịdọ^{3}hvsga] (vi) "He is preaching."

ᎦᎵᏥᏙᎥᏍᎦ [galtsịdọʔvsga]

ᎤᎵᏥᏙᏅᎢ [ultsịdọ^{3}hnv^{23}ʔi]

ᎠᎵᏥᏙᎲᏍᎪᎢ [altsịdọ^{3}hvsgo^{3}ʔi]

ᎭᎵᏥᏙᎲᎦ [haltsịdọ^{3}hvga]

ᎤᎵᏥᏙᏗ [ultsịtdi]

… ᎠᎴ ᎠᎵᏥᏙᎲᏍᎬᎩ ᎣᏍᏛ ᎧᏃᎮᏛ …
… and proclaiming the good news …
[ᎹᏚ 9:35]

ᎠᎵᏥᏙᎲᏍᎩ [altsịdọhvsgi] (n) "Preacher."

… ᎠᎴ ᎦᏙ ᏱᎦᎵᏍᏙᏓ ᏯᎾᏛᎬᎦ ᎩᎶ ᎠᎵᏥᏙᎲᏍᎩ ᏄᏁᎲᎾ ᏱᎩ?
… and how shall they hear apart from one preaching?
[ᎶᎻ 10:14]

ᎠᎵᏰᎲᏍᎦ [aliyẹhvsga] (vi) "It (a plant) is growing.; It is sprouting."

—

ᎤᎵᏰᏅᎢ [ulịyehnv^{23}ʔi]

ᎠᎵᏰᎲᏍᎪᎢ [alịyẹhvsgo^{3}ʔi]

ᏩᎵᏰᎲᎦ [walịyẹhvga]

ᎤᎵᏰᏗ [ulịyehdi]

ᎿᏉᏃ ᎤᎵᏰᏅ ᎠᎴ ᎤᎦᏔᏔᏅ ᎾᏍᏉ ᎤᏂ ᎤᎾᏄᎪᏤᎢ.
and when the herb sprang up, and yielded fruit, then appeared also the darnel.
[ᎹᏚ 13:26]

ᎠᎵᏰᎵ [ahlịye^{3}li] (vi) "He is moving."

ᎦᎵᏰᎵ [gạʔlịye^{3}li]

ᎤᎵᏰᎴᏒᎢ [uhlịye^{3}lẹsv^{23}ʔi]

ᎠᎵᏰᎵᏐᎢ [ahlịye^{3}liso^{3}ʔi]

ᎭᎵᏰᎵᎦ [hahlịye^{3}lʔga]

ᎤᎵᏰᎸᏍᏗ [uhlịye^{3}lṿsdi]

ᎠᎵᏰᎶᏍᎦ [ahlịyẹ^{3}hlosga] (vi) "It is come to a point …."

—

ᎤᎵᏰᎶᎸᎢ [uhlịyẹ^{3}hlọʔlv^{23}ʔi]

ᎠᎵᏰᎶᏍᎪᎢ [ahlịyẹ^{3}hlosgo^{3}ʔi]

ᏩᎵᏰᎶᎦ [wahlịyẹ^{3}hloga]

ᎤᎵᏰᎶᎯᏍᏗ [uhlịyẹ^{3}hlohịsdi]

"ᎤᎾᏙᏓᏆᏍᎪᏃ ᎤᎵᏰᎶᎸ."
"And the sabbath having come."
[ᎹᎦ 6:2]
Literally - "And they often have holiday - it did come to that point."

ᎠᎵᏰᏑᎶ [ạlịyẹ^{3}sụlo] (n) "Gloves."

ᎠᎵᏰᏑᏍᏓᎩᎠ [aliyesusdạgị^{3}ʔa] (vt) "He is taking off a ring."

ᎦᎵᏰᏑᏍᏓᎩᎠ [galiyesusdạgị^{3}ʔa]

ᎤᎵᏰᏑᏍᏓᎩᏒᎢ [uliyesusdạgị^{3}sv^{23}ʔi]

ᎠᎵᏰᏑᏍᏓᎩᏍᎪᎢ [aliyesusdạgị^{3}sgo^{3}ʔi]

ᎭᎵᏰᏑᏍᏓᎩ [haliyesusdạgị]

ᎤᎵᏰᏑᏍᏓᎩᏍᏗ [uliyesusdạgị^{3}sdi]

ᎠᎵᏲᏪᏗᎭ [ahlịyowẹ^{3}hdịha] (vi) "He is pouting.; He is brooding."

ᎦᎵᏲᏪᏗᎭ [gạʔlịyowẹ^{3}hdịha]

ᎤᎵᏲᏪᏔᏅᎢ [uhlịyowẹ^{3}tanv^{23}ʔi]

ᎠᎵᏲᏪᏗᏍᎪᎢ [ahlịyowẹ^{3}hdịsgo^{3}ʔi]

ᎭᎵᏲᏪᏓ [hahlịyowẹ^{3}hda]

ᎤᎵᏲᏪᏙᏗ [uhlịyowẹ^{3}hdohdi]

ᎠᎶᏍᎦ [ạʔhlosga] (vt) "He is winning.; He is beating him in a game."

ᏥᎶᏍᎦ [tsi^{1}losga]

ᎤᎶᏒᎢ [uʔhlosv^{23}ʔi]

ᎠᎶᏍᎪᎢ [ạʔhlosgo^{3}ʔi]

ᎯᎶᎯ [hi^{1}lohi]

ᎤᎶᎯᏍᏗ [uʔhlohịsdi]

ᎠᎶᏕᎯᎭ [alo^{3}ʔdehịha] (vt) "He is kicking him."

ᏥᏯᎶᏕᎢᎭ [tsiyalo^{3}ʔdẹʔịha]

ᎤᎶᏕᎸᎢ [ulo^{3}ʔdehlv^{23}ʔi]

ᎠᎶᏕᎯᎰᎢ [alo^{3}ʔdehịho^{3}ʔi]

ᎯᏯᎶᏕᎦ [hiyalo^{3}ʔdẹga]

ᎤᎶᏕᏍᏗ [ulo^{3}ʔdesdi]

ᎩᎵ ᏧᎶᏕᎸᎩ.
He kicked the dog.
[King pg 72]

ᎠᎷᎸᎥᏍᎦ [alulv^{3}ʔṿʔhsga] (vt) "She is giving birth."

ᎦᎷᎸᎥᏍᎦ [galulv^{3}ʔṿ^{1}sga]

ᎤᎷᎸᎥᏅᎢ [ululv^{3}ʔṿnv^{23}ʔi]

ᎠᎷᎸᎥᏍᎪᎢ [alulv^{3}ʔṿʔhsgo^{3}ʔi]

ᎭᎷᎸᎥᎦ [halulv^{3}ʔvga]

ᎤᎷᎸᏗ [ululv^{3}di]

ᎠᎵᏯ [ahlv³įha] (vt) "He is tying up.; He is bandaging."

ᎦᎵᏯ [gaꭲlv³įha]

ᎤᏯᎵᎢ [uhlv³ꭲlv²³ꭲi]

ᎠᎵᎢᎰᎢ [ahlv³įho³ꭲi]

ᎭᎵᏣ [hahlv³tsa]

ᎤᏯᎥᏍᏗ [uhlv³sdi]

… Ꮩ ᎤᏟᏆᎥᏗᎣᎬᏯ ᎤᏯᎵᎢ.
… and because <u>he had bound him,</u>
[ᎠᎯᎣᏌᏂ ᏩᏔᎹᎵᏇᎥᎢ 22:29]

ᎠᎹ [ama] (n) "Salt."

ᎤᎯᏌᏃ ᎠᎯᎦ ᎬᎵ ⁻ᎠᎹ ᎭᏃᏞᏛᏗ ᎨᏄᎥᏗ, Ꮩ ᎾᏏ ᎠᎯᎦᎰᏫᎥᏗ ⁻ᎠᎹ ᎦᎣᏞᏛᏗ ᎨᏄᎥᏗ.
for every one with fire shall be <u>salted</u>, and every sacrifice with <u>salt</u> shall be salted.
[ᎹᎧ 9:49]

ᎠᎹ [ama] (n) "Water."

ᏩᏞᎾᏃ Ꮳ⸗ᎠᎠᎢᏴ ᎠᏉ ᎠᎹ ᏦᎦᏍᏇᏴ.
Again, as thou sawest the Damsel sprinkle the room with <u>Water.</u>
[ᏦᏁᏐᎯ ᏏᎯᏴᏣᏔ]

ᎠᎹ ᎤᏁᏍᏴᎥᏗ [ạm ạsdụgisdi] (n) "A water faucet."

ᎠᎹ ᎤᏍᏚᎢᎢᎢ [ạm ạsdvꭲi] (n) "A beach."

ᎠᎹ ᎤᏍᏚᎢꞏᎠᏚᎢ [ạm asdyhisdv] (n) "A pond."

ᎠᎹ ᎠᏍᎯᏲᎥᎢ [ạm ạdehyọhvꭲi] (n) "A whirlpool."

ᎠᎹ ᎠᏗᏉᏗ [ạm ạditodi] (n) "Queen of the meadow."

ᎠᎹ ᎠᎯᏍᏗ [ạm ạtsịsdi] (n) "A sink."

ᎠᎹ ᎠᏰᎵ [ạm ạyehli] (n) "An island."

ᎠᎹ Ꮾꮤꞏꭶ [ạm ẹgwohi] (n) "An ocean."

ᎠᎹ ᎤᏗᎮᎩ [ạm udihlẹki] (n) "Hot water."

ᎠᎹ ᎤᏣᏫᎶᏍᎥᏗ

ᎠᎹ ᎤᏣᏫᎶᏍᎥᏗ [ạm ụwadọꭲọhịsdi] (n) "Spicket.; Spout."

ᎠᎹ ᎤᏍᎳᎥᏗ [ạm ụwẹdạsdi] (n) "Water pipe.; Garden hose."

ᎠᎹ ᎤᏍᎯ [ạm uhyatsi] (n) "Cold water."

ᎠᎹ ᎦᏄᎪᎬᎢᎢ [ạm gạnugogvꭲi] (n) "A spring (of water)."

… Ꮩ ᎣᏣ ᎤᎾᏣᎶꭲᏛ ᎠᎹ ᎦᏄᎪᎬᎢᎢ.
…and find there <u>a well</u> of living water,
[ᏐᏈ ᏔᎬᏐᏐ 26:19]

ᎠᎹ ᎦᏙᎶᏍᎬᎢᎢ [ạm gạdoọsgvꭲi] (n) "A water fall."

ᎠᎹᎢᎢ [amagẹꭲi] (n) "Hominy soup.; Corn beer."

ᎠᎹᎢᏲᎢ [amageyvꭲi] (n) "Creek.; Branch."

ᎠᎹ ᏗᏍᏚᎵᎢ [ạm disdụhvꭲi] (n) "A lake."

ᎠᎹᏲ [ạmayi] (n) "River."

ᎠᏚ ᎤᎵᏏ [amọ ụlisi] (n) "Water cress.; biol. *Nasturtium officinale.*"

ᎠᎾᎦᎵᎯ [ạna³gạliha] (vi) "It is lightening."

ᎤᎾᏍᎦᎸᎢ [una³gạlvhv²³ꭲi]

ᎠᎾᎦᎵᏍᎠᎢ [ạna³gạlisgo³ꭲi]

ᏩᎾᎦᎳ [wạna³gạla]

ᎤᎾᎦᎵᏗ [una³gahldi]

… Ꮩ ᎤᏝᏚᎩᎢᏴ, Ꮩ ᎠᎾᎦᎵᏍᎥᏴ, Ꮩ ᏒᎦᎭ ᎤᏝᏓᎣᏴ.
… and thunders, and <u>lightnings</u>, and an earthquake.
[ᎠᎯᎾᎦᎠᎴᎯᎢ 8:5]

ᎠᎾᎦᎵᏍᎩ [ạnagạlisgi] (n) "Lightening.; Battery.; Electricity."

ᎠᎣᏃᏗᏍ ᎠᎾᎦᎵᏍᎩ ᎾᏯᏍ ᎨᎢ …
and his countenance was as <u>lightning</u> …
[ᎹᎧ 28:3]

ᎠᎾᎵᏍᎢᎳᎥᏴᏯ [ạnahlsgwạlysgi] (n) "Crowsfoot."

ᎠᎾᏣᎩᏴ [ạnakwanki] (n) "Delaware Indians."

ᎠᎾᏓᏌᎦᏫᎳꞏᎯ [ạnạdạsagwạle³hịha] (vi) "They are rolling."

ᎤᏓᏌᎦᏫꞏᎵᎢ [udạsagwạle³hlv²³ꭲi]

ᎠᎾᏓᏌᎦᏫꞏᎯᎢᎢ [ạnạdạsagwạle³hịho³ꭲi]

ᏩᎾᏓᏌᎦᏫᎳꞏᎦ [wạnạdạsagwạle³ga]

ᎤᏓᏌᎦᏫꞏᎥᏗ [udạsagwạle³sdi]

ᎠᎾᎳᏍᎳᏍᎩ [ạnạdạsdasgi] (n) "Violets."

ᎠᎾᏗᎯ [ạndatsi] (n) "Common evening-primrose.; Evening star.; Sun drop.; biol. *Oenothera biennis.*"

ᎠᎾᎯᏴᏯ [ạnạdạdsgiha] (vi) "They are assembling together.; They are gathering together.; They are congregating."

ᏆᏣᎳᏕᏴᎠ [otsạdạdsgiꭲa]

ᎤᎾᎳᏕᎠꞏᎢ [ụnạdạdskdv²³ꭲi]

ᎠᎾᎳᏕᏍᎠᎢ [ạnạdạdsgo³ꭲi]

ᏔᏣᎳᏕᎦ [itsạdạdsga]

ᎤᎾᎳᏕᎢᏗ [ụnạdạdskdi]

ᎠᎾᏗᏴᏫᏯᎩ [ạndayvtạsgi] (n) "Television."

ᎠᎾᏔᏍᎩᏍᎩ [ạntasgisgi] (n) "Popcorn."

ᎠᎾᏫᏴᎠ [ahnạwogiꭲa] (vt) "He is undressing.; He is taking off a shirt."

ᎦᎾᏫᏴᎠ [gạꭲnạwogiꭲa]

ᎤᎾᏫᏴᏒᎢᎢ [uhnạwọgisv²³ꭲi]

ᎠᎾᏫᏴᏍᎠᎢ [ahnạwogisgo³ꭲi]

ᎭᎾᏫᏴ [hahnạwọgi]

ᎤᎾᏫᏴᎥᏗ [uhnạwọgisdi]

DⱭⱰWⱯD [ahnelạdịꞌa] (vi) "He is traveling.; He is going on a trip."

ᏕⱰWⱯD [gạꞌnelạdịꞌa]

ᎤⱰWꝨᎢ [uhnelạdv²³ꞌi]

DⱭⱰWⱯᎨᎠᎢ [ahnelạdịsgo³ꞌi]

ᎮⱰWᏞ [hahnelạda]

ᎤⱰWⱯᎨᎠᏗ [uhnelạdịsdi]

DⱭⱱᎨᏲ [ahnesgeha] (vt) "He is building it."

ᏕⱰᎨᏲ [gạꞌnesgeha]

ᎤⱰᎨᏲꝨᎢ [uhnesgehv²³ꞌi]

DⱭᎨᏲᎨᎠᎢ [ahnesgesgo³ꞌi]

ᎮⱰᎨᎬᏞ [hahnesgvli]

ᎤⱰᎨᏲᏗ [uhneskdi]

ᎢᏳᏃ ᎩᎦ ᏚᎾᎨᎠᏞᎾᏒ ᎥⱰᎬᎦᎨᎠᎥꞌ ᎤᎡ ᎤⱰᎨᏲꝨᎢ, ᎾᎥᎩ DᏚᏳᎡᏒᏗ ᎥᎨᎠᏗ.

if of any one the work doth remain that <u>he built</u> on [it], a wage he shall receive;

[ᎠᎵᏂᏗᎥ ᎢᎬᏒᎥ 3:14]

DⱭᎨᎠᏗᏲ [ahnesdịha] (vt) "He is interpreting it.; He is translating it."

ᏕⱰᎨᎠᏗᏲ [gạꞌnesdịha]

ᎤⱰᎨᎠᏞᎤᎢ [uhnesdạꞌnv²³ꞌi]

DⱭᎨᎠᎨᎠᎢ [ahnesdịsgo³ꞌi]

ᎮⱰᎨᎠᏞ [hahnesda]

ᎤⱰᎨᎠᎣᏗ [uhnesdohdi]

DⱰᏓ [anetsa] (n) "Ball game (stickball)."

DⱭⱰᏗᎨᎠᏚ [ahnetsoꞌvsga] (vi) "He is playing ball."

ᏕⱰᏗᎨᎠᏚ [gạꞌnetsoꞌvsga]

ᎤⱰᏗᎧᎤᎢ [uhnetsoꞌnv²³ꞌi]

DⱭⱰᏗᎨᎠᎢ [ahnetsoꞌvsgo³ꞌi]

ᎮⱰᏗᎨᏚ [hahnetsoꞌvga]

ᎤⱰᏗᎧᏗ [uhnetsoꞌdi]

… ᏴᎡ ᎤꞌᎡᎣᎤꞌᎩ ᏪᎡᎨᎠᏞᏰᎯᎡᏒᎩ DᏘ ᏪᎡᎠWᎨᎡᏒᎩ, ᏕᎡᏗᎤꞌᎩ ᎤꞌᎡⱰᏗᎧᎤꞌᎩ.

… 'The people sat down to eat and to drink, and stood up to <u>play</u>;'

[ᎠᎵᏂᏗᎥ ᎢᎬᏒᎥ 10:7]

DⱭⱰᏗᎨᎠᎩ [anetsoꞌysgi] (n) "Ball player."

DⱭⱰᏗᏗ [anetsodi] (n) "Ball game (stickball)."

Dh [ani] (n) "Strawberry.; Virginia Strawberry.; biol. *Fragaria virginiana.*"

ᎤꞌᎦᎩⱯ ᏴᏞᏗ Dh ᏍᎢᎢ, ᏪᏀᏕ ᏕⱭᏰ. ᎮᏫᎢᏕ ᎢᏅ ᏂᏕᏞ Dh? Six <u>strawberries</u> were eaten, twelve remained. How many were all the <u>strawberries</u>?

[ᏪᏫᎩ ᎤꞌᎩⱭ ᏗᏂᎯᎠᏙ ᏗᏌᎮᎥᏗ]

DhᏕꞋᏗᏲ [anigạlvhtsi] (n) "Frenchmen."

DhᎨᎤ [anikạwi] (n) "Deer clan."

DhᎨᎤᎤW [anikạwita] (n) "Creek (lower)."

DhᎩᏞ [anigihli] (n) "Congaree (the dog people), see Mooney pg 508."

DhᎩᏞᏏ [anigịlịsi] (n) "Englishmen."

DhᎩᏪᎠ [anigịlọhi] (n) "Long hair clan (twister)."

DhᎩᎨᎠᎩ [aniksgi] (n) "People with no clan affiliation."

DhᎪᎨᏞᎠ [anigọsdahya] (n) "Chimney swift.; biol. *Chaetura pelagica.*"

DhⱯᏞᏲᎧ [anigodạgewi] (n) "Wild potato clan."

DhᏗᏏ [anikusi] (n) "Creek (upper)."

DhᎬᎧᏗᎢ [anigynạgeꞌi] (n) "Black people."

DhᏃᏲ

DhᏃᏲ [aninotsi] (n) "Natchez."

DhᎤᏞᏫᎩ [aninvdạwegi] (n) "Iroquois."

DhᏗᎤᎻ [anikwasasi] (n) "Osage."

DhᏫᎩ [anikwegi] (n) "Quakers."

DhᎤᏲh [anisạhoni] (n) "Blue clan."

DhᎤᎬᎦᎩ [anisawạnugi] (n) "Shawnee."

DhᎨᎠᏕᎬᏞ [anisgạloli] (n) "Tuscarora."

DhᎨᎠᏕᏲ [anisgatsi] (n) "Scotchmen."

DhᎨᎠᎩᎾ ᎤꞌᎡⱰᏲᏞ [anisginạ unạnẹsạda] (n) "Common greenbrier.; biol. *Smilax rotundifolia.*"

DhᎨᎠᎬᎿ [ahnsgvti] (n) "May."

DhᎨᎠᏘh [anisgwani] (n) "Spaniards."

DhᏮᎻᏃᏞ [aniseminoli] (n) "Seminole."

DhᏮhᎡ [anisenịka] (n) "Seneca."

DhᏴᏞ [anịsuli] (n) "Jury.; They are buzzards."

DhᏴᎬᏞ [anisụwali] (n) "Cheraw or sera."

DhᏒᎤᎦᏞ [anisynyhida] (n) "Horse corn."

DhᏞᏒ [anidatsi] (n) "Germans."

DhWᏫ [anitagwi] (n) "Catawba."

DhᏫᎡⱰᎠD [andvhnạdịꞌa] (vi) "It is grazing."

———

ᎤꞌhᏫᎡⱰᏗᎢᎢ [undvhnạdiv²³ꞌi]

DhᏫᎡⱰᏗᎨᎠᎢ [andvhnạdịsgo³ꞌi]

ᏪhᏫᎡⱰᏗᎢ [wandvhnạdịꞌi]

ᎤꞌhᏫᎡⱰᏗᎨᎠᏗ [undvhnạdisdi]

DhᏓᎡᎤW [anitsakta] (n) "Choctaw."

DhᏰᎡᎤ [anitsikạsa] (n) "Chickasaw."

DhᏰᎨᎠᏘ [anitsisgwa] (n) "Bird clan."

DhᏪᏗᏂh [aniwatsini] (n) "Virginians.; Federal government officials."

DhᏪᎦᎠ [anihwạya] (n) "Wolf clan."

DhᎤhᎨᎠᎩ [aniwọꞌnịsgi] (n) "Virginia water horehound.; Sweet bugleweed.; biol. *Lycopus virginicus.*"

ᎠᏂᏬᏗ [ąniwodi] (n) "Paint clan."

ᎠᏂᏳᏥ [ąniyutsi] (n) "Yuchi."

ᎠᏄᎩᏣᏍᎦ [ahnugįchasga] (vt) "He is hugging him."

> **ᏥᏯᏄᎩᏣᏍᎦ** [tsiyąʔnugįchasga]
> **ᎤᏄᎩᏨᏅᎢ** [uhnugįchvnv^{23}ʔi]
> **ᎠᏄᎩᏣᏍᎪᎢ** [ahnugįchasgo^{3}ʔi]
> **ᎯᏯᏄᎩᏣᎦ** [hiyąʔnugįchąga]
> **ᎤᏄᎩᏣᏗ** [uhnugįchahdi]

ᎠᏄᎳᏥᏴᎢ [ąnųlatsįyvʔi] (n) "Ribs."

> **ᏓᏄᎳᏥᏴᎢ** [dąnųlatsįyvʔi]
> **ᏥᏄᎳᏥᏴᎢ** [tsįnųlatsįyvʔi]
> **ᏕᏥᏄᎳᏥᏴᎢ** [detsįnųlatsįyvʔi]

ᎠᏅᎡᎭ [ąnvʔeha] (vt) "He is taking it (something flexible) or it (a solid) to him."

> **ᏥᏅᎡᎠ** [tsinvʔęʔa]
> **ᎤᏅᎡᎸᎢ** [unvʔęlv^{23}ʔi]
> **ᎠᏅᎡᎰᎢ** [ąnvʔeho^{3}ʔi]
> **ᎯᏅᎥᏍᏗ** [hinvvsdi]
> **ᎤᏅᎡᏗ** [unvʔehdi]

ᎠᏅᏬ [ahnvwo] (n) "Cloth.; A shirt."

ᎠᏅᏱ [ąnvhyi] (n) "March (month)."

ᎠᏆᎸᏂᎭ [akwąlvʔnįha] (vt) "He is slapping it."

> **ᏥᏆᎸᏂᎠ** [tsįkwąlvʔnįʔa]
> **ᎤᏆᎸᏂᎸᎢ** [ukwąlvʔnįʔlv^{23}ʔi]
> **ᎠᏆᎸᏂᎰᎢ** [akwąlvʔnįho^{3}ʔi]
> **ᎯᏆᎸᏣ** [hįkwąlvʔtsa]
> **ᎤᏆᎸᏂᏍᏗ** [ukwąlvʔnįsdi]

ᎠᏆᎸᏂᎭ [agwąlvʔnį^{3}ha] (vt) "He is spanking him.; He is paddling him."

> **ᏥᏯᏆᎸᏂᎠ** [jiyagwąlvʔnįʔa]
> **ᎤᏆᎸᏂᎸᎢ** [ugwąlvʔnį^{3}ʔlv^{23}ʔi]
> **ᎠᏆᎸᏂᎰᎢ** [agwąlvʔnį^{3}ho^{3}ʔi]
> **ᎯᏯᏆᎸᏂᎦ** [hiyagwąlvʔni^{3}ga]
> **ᎤᏆᎸᏂᏍᏗ** [ugwąlvʔnih^{3}sdi]

ᎠᏆᎾᏲᎯᎭ [ąkwąnąyǫ^{3}hįha] (vi) "He is playing cards."

> **ᏥᏆᎾᏲᎯᎭ** [tsįʔkwąnąyǫ^{3}hįha]
> **ᎤᏆᎾᏲᎸᎢ** [ukwąnąyǫ^{3}hlv^{23}ʔi]
> **ᎠᏆᎾᏲᎯᎰᎢ** [ąkwąnąyǫ^{3}hįho^{3}ʔi]
> **ᎯᏆᎾᏲᎭᎦ** [hįkwąnąyǫ^{3}haga]
> **ᎤᏆᎾᏲᏍᏗ** [ukwąnąyoh^{3}sdi]

ᎠᏆᏲᎯᎭ [agwąyohįha] (vt) "He is flipping it (something alive) with his finger."

> **ᏥᏯᏆᏲᎢᎭ** [tsiyagwąyǫʔįha]
> **ᎤᏆᏲᎸᎢ** [ugwąyohlv^{23}ʔi]
> **ᎠᏆᏲᎯᎰᎢ** [agwąyohįho^{3}ʔi]
> **ᎯᏯᏆᏲᎦ** [hįyagwąyǫʔga]
> **ᎤᏆᏲᏍᏗ** [ugwąyosdi]

ᎠᏇᎷᏍᎦ [agwelusga] (vt) "He is putting a ribbon in his hair."

> **ᎦᏇᎷᏍᎦ** [gagwelųʔsga]
> **ᎤᏇᎷᏅᎢ** [ugwelųʔnv^{23}ʔi]
> **ᎠᏇᎷᏍᎪᎢ** [agwelusgo^{3}ʔi]
> **ᎭᏇᎷᎦ** [hagweluga]
> **ᎤᏇᎷᏍᏗ** [ugwelusdi]

ᎠᏇᎷᏍᏗ [ągwehlusdi] (n) "Ribbon."

ᎠᏇᏄᎩᎠ [ągwęnugįʔa] (vt) "He is pinching."

> **ᏥᏇᏄᎩᎠ** [tsįgwęnugįʔa]
> **ᎤᏇᏄᎩᏒᎢ** [ugwęnugįsv^{23}ʔi]
> **ᎠᏇᏄᎩᏍᎪᎢ** [ągwęnugįsgo^{3}ʔi]
> **ᎯᏇᏄᎩ** [hįgwęnugi]
> **ᎤᏇᏄᎩᏍᏗ** [ugwęnugįsdi]

ᎠᏘᏍᏙᎯ ᎦᎸᏙᏗ [ąksdǫhį gąlvdohdi] (n) "Pillow case."

ᎠᏘᏱᎭ

ᎠᏘᏱᎭ [akwįyįha] (vt) "He is paying."

> **ᎦᏘᏱᎭ** [gagwįʔyįha]
> **ᎤᏘᏴᎲᎢ** [ukwįyyhv^{23}ʔi]
> **ᎠᏘᏱᏍᎪᎢ** [akwįyįsgo^{3}ʔi]
> **ᎭᏘᏯ** [hakwįya]
> **ᎤᏘᏱᏗ** [ukwįyhdi]
>
> ᏗᎦᏲᎲᏍᎩ ᎾᏢᏎᏥ ᎦᏩᏎᎢ ᏧᏂᏍᏗᎩᏍᏗ. $1.25 ᎦᏘᏴᏢᎢ. ᏅᎩ ᎦᏩᏎᎢ. ᎭᎳ ᎢᎦ ᎦᏘᏴᏢᎢ ᏂᎦᏓ?
> The teacher bought candy for eating. He paid $1.25. He bought four. How much did he pay for all of them?
> [ᏣᎳᎩ ᏅᎩᏁ ᏗᏂᏂᏙᎯ ᏗᎦᏲᏙᏗ]

ᎠᏘᏴᎡᎭ [akwįyvʔeha] (vt) "He is paying him."

> **ᏥᏯᏘᏴᎡᎭ** [tsiyagwįʔyvʔeha]
> **ᎤᏘᏴᎡᎸᎢ** [ukwįyvʔęlv^{23}ʔi]
> **ᎠᏘᏴᎡᎰᎢ** [akwįyvʔeho^{3}ʔi]
> **ᎯᏯᏘᏴᎥᎢ** [hiyagwįʔyvʔvʔi]
> **ᎤᏘᏴᎡᏗ** [ukwįyvʔehdi]

ᎠᏌᎧᎠ [asakaa] (vi) "He is lightweight."

ᏥᏌᎧᎠ [tsịʔsakaa]
ᎤᏌᎧᎮᏍᏛᎢ [usakahẹsdv^{23}ʔi]
ᎠᏌᎧᎰᎢ [asakaho^{3}ʔi]
ᎯᏌᎧᎮᏍᏗ [hịsakahẹsdi]
ᎤᏌᎪᏗ [usakohdi]

ᎠᏌᎩᎠ [asạkiʔa] (vi) "He is emitting body gas."

ᎦᏌᎩᎠ [gasạʔgiʔa]
ᎤᏌᎩᏒᎢ [usạkisv^{23}ʔi]
ᎠᏌᎩᏍᎪᎢ [asạkisgo^{3}ʔi]
ᎭᏌᎩ [hasạki]
ᎤᏌᎩᏍᏗ [usạkisdi]

ᎠᏌᎩᎠ [asạgiʔa] (vt) "He is removing it (a solid) from a shelf."

ᏥᏌᎩᎠ [tsịʔsạgiʔa]
ᎤᏌᎩᏒᎢ [usạgisv^{23}ʔi]
ᎠᏌᎩᏍᎪᎢ [asạgisgo^{3}ʔi]
ᎯᏌᎩ [hịsạgi]
ᎤᏌᎩᏍᏗ [usạgisdi]

ᎠᏌᎩᏏᏙᎠ [asạgisịdoa] (vt) "He is subtracting."

ᏥᏌᎩᏏᏙᎠ [tsịʔsạgisịdoa]
ᎤᏌᎩᏏᏙᎸᎢ [usạgisịdọʔlv^{23}ʔi]
ᎠᏌᎩᏏᏙᎰᎢ [asạgisịdoho^{3}ʔi]
ᎯᏌᎩᏏᏓ [hịsạgisịda]
ᎤᏌᎩᏏᏙᎠᏍᏗ [usạgisịdọasdi]

ᎠᏌᎲᎠ [asạhvʔa] (vt) "He is pushing it (a solid) aside."

ᏥᏌᎲᎠ [tsịʔsạhvʔa]
ᎤᏌᎲᏒᎢ [usạhvsv^{23}ʔi]
ᎠᏌᎲᎥᏍᎪᎢ [asạhvʔṿsgo^{3}ʔi]
ᎯᏌᎲᎾ [hịsạhvna]
ᎤᏌᎲᏍᏗ [usạhvsdi]

ᎠᏌᎲᏍᎦ [asạhvh^{3}sga] (vt) "He is putting it (a solid) up."

ᏥᏌᎲᏍᎦ [tsịʔsạhvh^{3}sga]
ᎤᏌᏅᎢ [usạʔhnv^{23}ʔi]
ᎠᏌᎲᏍᎪᎢ [asạhvh^{3}sgo^{3}ʔi]
ᎯᏌᎲᎦ [hịsạhv^{3}ga]
ᎤᏌᎣᏗ [usạohdi]

ᎠᏌᎳᏓ [asạladʔa] (vt) "He is raising it.; He is lifting it."

ᏥᏌᎳᏓ [tsịʔsạladʔa]
ᎤᏌᎳᏛᎢ [usạladv^{23}ʔi]
ᎠᏌᎳᏓᏍᎪᎢ [asạladʔsgo^{3}ʔi]
ᎯᏌᎳᏓᎦ [hịsạladạga]
ᎤᏌᎳᏙᏗ [usạladohdi]

… ᏇᎵᏲ ᎠᏴ, ᎠᎴ ᏂᎯ ᏂᎶᏁᏨᎾ ᎥᏝ ᎩᎶ <u>ᎤᏌᎳᏙᏗ</u> ᏱᎨᏎᏍᏗ ᎤᏬᏰᏂ ᎠᎴ ᎤᎳᏏᎦᏂ ᏂᎬᎾᏛ ᎢᏥᏈᏱ.
… 'I [am] Pharaoh, and without thee a man doth not <u>lift up</u> his hand and his foot in all the land of Egypt;'
[ᎼᏏ ᎢᎬᏱᏱ 41:44]

ᎠᏌᎳᏗᎠ [asạ^{3}ʔldịʔa] (vt) "He is lifting it."

ᏥᏌᎳᏗᎠ [tsịʔsạ^{3}ʔldịʔa]
ᎤᏌᎳᏓᏅᎢ [usạ^{3}ʔldạʔnv^{23}ʔi]
ᎠᏌᎳᏗᏍᎪᎢ [asạ^{3}ʔldịsgo^{3}ʔi]
ᎯᏌᎳᏗᎦ [hịsạ^{3}ʔldʔga]
ᎤᏌᎳᏙᏗ [usạ^{3}ʔldodi]

… ᎠᎴ ᎦᏙᎯ ᏧᎳᏏᏅᎯ, ᎦᎸᎳᏗ ᎢᏗᏢ <u>ᎤᏌᎳᏓᏅᎩ</u> ᎤᏬᏰᏂ,
… and upon the land, <u>did lift up</u> his hand to the heaven,
[ᎠᏥᎾᏄᎪᏫᏎᎸᎢ 10:5]

ᎠᏌᏂᏙᎭ [asạnidoha] (vt) "He is adding."

ᏥᏌᏂᏙᎭ [tsịʔsạnidoha]
ᎤᏌᏂᏙᎸᎢ [usạnidọʔlv^{23}ʔi]
ᎠᏌᏂᏙᎰᎢ [asạnidoho^{3}ʔi]
ᎯᏌᏂᏓ [hịsạnida]
ᎤᏌᏂᏙᎠᏍᏗ [usạnidọasdi]

ᎠᏌᏃ [ạsạno] (n) "A skirt.; A dress."

ᎠᏌᏆᎴᎭ [ạsạgwạ^{3}hleha] (vt) "He is rolling it."

ᏥᏌᏆᎴᎭ [tsịsʔạgwạ^{3}hleha]
ᎤᏌᏆᎴᎸᎢ [usạgwạ^{3}hlẹlv^{23}ʔi]
ᎠᏌᏆᎴᎰᎢ [ạsạgwạ^{3}hleho^{3}ʔi]
ᎯᏌᏆᎴᎦ [hịsạgwạ^{3}hlẹga]
ᎤᏌᏆᎴᏍᏗ [usạgwạ^{3}hlesdi]

ᎠᏌᏆᎴᎵ [ạsạgwạlehli] (vi) "He is rolling along."

ᏥᏌᏆᎴᎵ [tsịsʔạgwạlehli]
ᎤᏌᏆᎴᎴᏒᎢ [usạgwạlehlẹsv^{23}ʔi]
ᎠᏌᏆᎴᎵᏐᎢ [ạsạgwạlehliso^{3}ʔi]
ᎯᏌᏆᎴᎷᎦ [hịsạgwạlehluʔga]
ᎤᏌᏆᎴᎸᏍᏗ [usạgwạlehlṿsdi]

DᎻᏞᏉᏫᏍ [asagwąlesga] (vt) "He is rolling it around."

    ᏘᎻᏞᏉᏫᏍ [tsį?sagwąlesga]

    ᎤᎻᏞᏉᎠᎢ [usagwąlehlv²³?i]

    DᎻᏞᏉᏫᎠᎢ [asagwąlesgo³?i]

    ᎲᎻᏞᏉᏍ [hįsagwąlega]

    ᎤᎻᏞᏉᏗ [usagwahldi]

DᎻᏗᎠ [asa³dį?a] (vt) "He is putting it (something long) up."

    ᏘᎻᏗᎠ [tsį?sa³dį?a]

    ᎤᎻᏓᎠᎢ [usa³dᴐv²³?i]

    DᎻᏗᏫᎠᎢ [asa³dįsgo³?i]

    ᎲᎻᏗ [hįsa³da]

    ᎤᎻᏗᏫᏗ [usa³dįsdi]

DᎻᎠᎥᏗᎰ [asądo?ydįha] (vt) "He is knocking over a stack of objects."

    ᏘᎻᎠᎥᏗᎰ [tsį?sado?ydįha]

    ᎤᎻᎠᎥᎥᏙᎢ [usado?ytanv²³?i]

    DᎻᎠᎥᏗᏫᎠᎢ [asado?ydįsgo³?i]

    ᎲᎻᎠᎥᏗ [hįsado?yda]

    ᎤᎻᎠᎥᎤᏗ [usado?ydodi]

DᎻᎤᏫᏫᏍ [asądo³yhsga] (vt) "He is pushing it."

    ᏘᎻᎤᏫᏫᏍ [tsįs?ado³yhsga]

    ᎤᎻᎤᏫᎤᎤᎢ [usądo³yhv²³?i]

    DᎻᎤᏫᏫᎠᎢ [asądo³yhsgo³?i]

    ᎲᎻᎤᏫᏫᏗ [hįsado³yha]

    ᎤᎻᎤᏫᏫᏗ [usądo³yhsdi]

DᎻᎤᏈᎢᏫᏍ [asądv?vsga] (vt) "He is trapping.; He is setting a trap."

    ᏘᎻᎤᏈᎢᏫᏍ [tsį?sadv?vsga]

    ᎤᎻᎤᏈᎤᎢ [usądv?nv²³?i]

    DᎻᎤᏈᎢᏫᎠᎢ [asądv?vsgo³?i]

    ᎲᎻᎤᏈᎢᏍ [hįsadv?vga]

    ᎤᎻᎤᏈᏗ [usądv?di]

    ᎾᎥᎩ ᎠᏗ ᎯᎸᎾᎡᎩ DᎻᎤᏈᎢᏫᎡᎩ …
    and this they said, <u>trying him</u> …
    [Ꮧ8:6]

DᏫᏍᎢᎭ [asga?įha] (vt) "He is afraid of."

    ᏘᏫᏍᎢᎭ [tsį?sga?įha]

    ᎤᏫᏍᎠᎢ [usga?lv²³?i]

    DᏫᏍᎢᎯᎢ [asga?įho³?i]

    ᎲᏫᏍᏫ [hįsgaya]

    ᎤᏫᏍᎠᏗ [usgasdi]

    DᎣ DᏁ ᎬᏟᎣᎤᎠ ᏕᏙᎢᎢᎢ, DᎣ ᎤᏫᎶᎤᎣᎠ DᏫᏍᏘᎤᎢ.
    Here therefore he sweat and did quake <u>for fear</u>.
    [ᏚᎾᎦᏗ ᏏᎯᎩᎡᎡᎢ]

DᏫᏍᏈᏍ [asga³hlga] (vt) "He is biting it."

    ᏘᏫᏍᏈᏍ [tsį?sga³hlga]

    ᎤᏫᏍᏈᏟᎢ [usga³hltsv²³?i]

    DᏫᏍᏈᎠᎢ [asga³hlgo³?i]

    ᎲᏫᏍᏬ [hįsga³hla]

    ᎤᏫᏍᏈᏫᏗ [usga³hlsdi]

DᏫᏍᏃᏛ [asganola] (vi) "He is slow."

    ᏘᏫᏍᏃᏛ [tsį?sganola]

    ᎤᏫᏍᏃᏛᎤᎢ [usganoladv²³?i]

    DᏫᏍᏃᎬᎢ [asganolo³?i]

    ᎲᏫᏍᏃᏕᏫᏗ [hįsganolesdi]

    ᎤᏫᏍᏃᏛᏗᏫᏗ [usganoladįsdi]

DᏫᏍᏆᏍ [asganvga] (vi) "He is misbehaving."

    ᏘᏫᏍᏆᏍ [tsį?sganvga]

    ᎤᏫᏍᏆᏟᎢ [usganv?tsv²³?i]

    DᏫᏍᏆᎠᎢ [asganvgo³?i]

    ᎲᏫᏍᏆᎩ [hįsganv?gi]

    ᎤᏫᏍᏆᏙᏫᏗ [usganv?isdi]

    ᏥᏫᏫᎠᏃᎤ <u>DᎩᏫᏍᏆᏟ</u> ᏏᏴᎥᏈᏫᏗ?
    But may <u>my sin</u> be forgiven?
    [ᏚᎾᎦᏗ ᏏᎯᎩᎡᎡᎢ]

DᏫᏍᏫ [asgaya] (n) "Man."

    ᏘᏫᏍᏫ [tsįsgaya]

    ᎲᎠᎦ ᏆᏫᎡ DᏫᏍᏫ.
    The <u>Man</u> answered.
    [ᏚᎾᎦᏗ ᏏᎯᎩᎡᎡᎢ]

DᏫᏴᏇᎢᏫᏍ [asgilv?vsga] (vt) "He is sitting on it."

    ᏍᏫᏴᏇᎢᏫᏍ [gasgilv?vsga]

    ᎤᏫᏴᏇᎤᎢ [usgilv?nv²³?i]

    DᏫᏴᏇᎢᏫᎠᎢ [asgilv?vsgo³?i]

    ᎭᏫᏴᏇᏍ [hąsgilv?vga]

    ᎤᏫᏴᏈᏗ [usgilv?di]

DᏍᎩᎾ [ạsgina] (n) "Devil.; Spirit.; Soul."

... DᏍᎩᎾ ᎤᎪᎵᏰᏗᏱ ᎠᏰᎸᏉᎢ.
... to be tempted by the Devil,
[ᎹᎩ 4:1]

DᏍᎩᏦᏍᎦ [asgi³tsga] (vt) "He is dreaming about it."

ᎦᏍᎩᏦᏍᎦ [gasgi³tsga]
ᎤᏍᎩᏨᎢ [usgi³tsv²³ʔi]
DᏍᎩᏦᏍᎪᎢ [asgi³tsgo³ʔi]
ᎭᏍᎩᏦᏍᎩ [hasgi³tsgi]
ᎤᏍᎩᏦᏍᏗ [usgi³tsdi]

DᏍᎩᏨᎢᏍᎦ [ạsgichṿʔvsga] (vt) "He is dreaming of many things."

ᎦᏍᎩᏨᎢᏍᎦ [gạsgichṿʔvsga]
ᎤᏍᎩᏨᎢᎢᎢ [usgichṿʔvv²³ʔi]
DᏍᎩᏨᎢᏍᎪᎢ [ạsgichṿʔvsgo³ʔi]
ᎭᏍᎩᏨᎢᎦ [hạsgichṿʔvga]
ᎤᏍᎩᏨᏗ [usgichvdi]

DᏍᎪᎩD [asgogịʔa] (vt) "He is gnawing."

ᏥᏍᎪᎩD [tsịʔsgogịʔa]
ᎤᏍᎪᎨᎢ [usgogv²³ʔi]
DᏍᎪᎩᏍᎪᎢ [asgogʔsgo³ʔi]
ᎯᏍᎪᎦ [hịsgoga]
ᎤᏍᎪᎩᏍᏗ [usgogịsdi]

DᏍᎪᎵ [ạsgoli] (n) "His head."

ᏥᏍᎪᎵ [tsịsgoli]

... DᏧ DᎵᏍᏀ DᎦᏄ ᏝᏯᏂᎨᏍᏛᎲ DᏍᎪᎵ ᎦᏄᎳᏗᏢ ᏥᎦᎳ ...
... and that a Crown hangs over his head ...
[ᏧᏁᎶᏍᏗ ᏚᏂᎩᏒᏒᎢ - DᏁᏢᏗᏍᎩ]

DᏍᎪᏄᎦ [asgolṿga] (vi) "He is fading."

ᏥᏍᎪᏄᎦ [tsịʔsgolṿga]
ᎤᏍᎪᏄᏨᎢ [usgolvtsv²³ʔi]
DᏍᎪᏄᎪᎢ [asgolṿgo³ʔi]
ᎯᏍᎪᏄᎩ [hịsgolvgi]
ᎤᏍᎪᏄᎢᏍᏗ [usgolṿʔịsdi]

DᎦᏗᏲᏍᎩᏂ, DᏲᎩ, DᏧ DᎦᏓᎯᏲᎩ, DᏧ DᏍᎪᏄᎩ ᏂᎨᏒᎾ ...
I seek an *Inheritance incorruptible, undefiled, and that fadeth not away* ...
[ᏧᏁᎶᏗ ᏚᏂᎩᏒᏒᎢ]

DᏍᎪᏍᎦ [ạsgosga] (vt) "He is digging it."

ᎦᏍᎪᏍᎦ [gạsgosga]
ᎤᏍᎪᏒᎢ [usgosv²³ʔi]
DᏍᎪᏍᎪᎢ [ạsgosgo³ʔi]
ᎭᏍᎪᎳ [hạsgọla]
ᎤᏍᎪᏍᏗ [usgosdi]

... DᏧ ᎡᏩᏃᏁᏧ DᏤ DᏢᏗᏱ ᎤᎾᏍᎪᏒ ᎤᎨᏩᎵ, DᏧ ᎯD ᏂᎨᏩᏪᏎᏧᎢ, DᏤ ᏲᏥᏁᏩᏛ.
... the circumstances of the well which they have digged, and say to him, 'We have found water;'
[ᏔᏏ ᎢᎬᏱᏱ 26:32]

DᏍᏓᏓᎩD [asgudạgiʔa] (vi) "He is cutting off a head of cabbage."

ᏥᏍᏓᏓᎩD [tsịʔsgudạgiʔa]
ᎤᏍᏓᏓᎩᏒᎢ [usgudạgisv²³ʔi]
DᏍᏓᏓᎩᏍᎪᎢ [asgudạgisgo³ʔi]
ᎯᏍᏓᏓᎩ [hịsgudạgi]
ᎤᏍᏓᏓᎩᏍᏗ [usgudạgisdi]

DᏍᏓᏓᎳᏍᎦ [ạsgudạtasga] (vi) "It is budding."

—

ᎤᏍᏓᏓᎳᎠᏅᎢ [usgudạtạʔnv²³ʔi]
DᏍᏓᏓᎳᏍᎪᎢ [ạsgudạtasgo³ʔi]
ᏩᏍᏓᏓᎳᎦ [wạsgudạtaga]
ᎤᏍᏓᏓᏙᏍᏗ [usgudạtọsdi]

DᏍᎥᏓᎨᏂ [ạsgvdạgeni] (n) "His shin bone."

ᏥᏍᎥᏓᎨᏂ [tsịsgvdạgeni]

DᏍᏆᎨᏂ [ạsgwạgeni] (n) "The side of his body."

ᏥᏍᏆᎨᏂ [tsịsgwạgeni]

... DᏧ ᎶᏍᎦ ᎡᏅᎦ ᏦᏰᏂ ᏥᏍᏆᎨᏂ ᏩᎰᎾᏓ ...
... and bring thy hand, and put [it] to my side ...
[ᏣᏂ 20:27]

DᏍᏆᎵᏍᎦ [asgwạ³ʔlisga] (vt) "He is cutting it (something long) off."

ᏥᏍᏆᎵᏍᎦ [tsịʔsgwạ³ʔlisga]
ᎤᏍᏆᎵᏒᎢ [usgwạ³ʔlisv²³ʔi]
DᏍᏆᎵᏍᎪᎢ [asgwạ³ʔlisgo³ʔi]
ᎯᏍᏆᎳᎦ [hịsgwạ³ʔlaga]
ᎤᏍᏆᎵᏍᏗ [usgwạ³ʔlisdi]

ᎢᏳᏃ ᏦᏰᏂ ᎯᎦᏘᏏ ᎦᏦᎦᏍᏗᏍᎨᏍᏗ, ᎯᏍᏆᎵᏍᎨᏍᏗ, DᏧ ᏫᎦᎨᏍᏗ ...
'And, if thy right hand doth cause thee to stumble, cut it off, and cast from thee ...
[ᎹᎩ 5:30]

ᎠᏍᎢᏝᎣᏍ [asgwaʔlih³sga] (vt) "He is breaking it (something long)."

   ᎢᎤᏍᏝᎣᏍ [tsiʔsgwaʔlih³sga]

   ᎤᏍᏝᏒᎢ [usgwaʔlih³sv²³ʔi]

   ᎠᏍᏝᎣᎠᎢ [asgwaʔlih³sgo³ʔi]

   ᎲᏍᎢᏯᏍ [hisgwaʔlaga]

   ᎤᏍᏝᎣᏍᎵ [usgwaʔlih³sdi]

ᎠᏍᎢᎬᎠ [asgwaloʔa] (vt) "He is bumping someone's head."

   ᎢᎤᏍᎢᎬᎠ [tsiʔsgwaloʔa]

   ᎤᏍᏍᎢᎬᎢᎢ [usgwaloʔv²³ʔi]

   ᎠᏍᎢᎬᎣᎠᎢ [asgwalosgo³ʔi]

   ᎲᏍᎢᎬᏟ [hisgwalotsa]

   ᎤᏍᎢᎬᎣᎵ [usgwalosdi]

ᎠᏍᎢᎠᎢᎤ [asgwalv³ʔiha] (vt) "He is hitting someone in the head with it (something long)."

   ᎢᎤᏍᎢᎠᎠᎤ [tsiʔsgwalv³ʔiha]

   ᎤᏍᏍᎢᎠᎠᎢ [usgwalv³ʔlv²³ʔi]

   ᎠᏍᎢᎠᎢᎦᎢ [asgwalv³ʔiho³ʔi]

   ᎲᏍᎢᎠᏍ [hisgwalv³ʔga]

   ᎤᏍᎢᎠᎢᎣᎵ [usgwalv³ʔisdi]

ᎠᏍᎢᏁᏍᎢ

ᎠᏍᎢᏁᏍᎢ [asgwanegalvʔi] (n) "His abdomen."

   ᎢᎤᏍᏁᏍᎢ [tsisgwanegalvʔi]

ᎠᏍᎢᎯᎠᎣᏍ [asgwa³nigosga] (vt) "He is admiring it."

   ᎢᎤᏍᎯᎠᎣᏍ [tsiʔsgwa³nigosga]

   ᎤᏍᏍᎯᎠᏒᎢ [usgwa³nigosv²³ʔi]

   ᎠᏍᎢᎯᎠᎣᎠᎢ [asgwa³nigosgo³ʔi]

   ᎲᏍᎢᎯᎠᏟ [hisgwa³nigoʔli]

   ᎤᏍᏍᎯᎠᎣᎲᎵ [usgwa³nigohisdi]

ᎦᏯᎤᏃ ᎠᏗ ᎲᏍᎩᏅ ᎠᎢᎤᎣ ᏦᏣᏘ ᎤᎲᎤᏍᎢᎯᎠᏒᎩ …
At this his Relations were sore <u>amazed</u> …
[ᏦᏁᎬᎵ ᏍᎲᎩᏒᏒᎢ]

ᎠᏍᎢᎯᎠᏒᎢᎣᏍ [asgwanigosyʔvsga] (vi) "He is amusing himself."

   ᎢᎤᏍᎯᎠᏒᎢᎣᏍ [tsisgwanigosyʔyʔsga]

   ᎤᏍᏍᎯᎠᏒᎤᎢᎢ [usgwanigosyʔnv²³ʔi]

   ᎠᏍᎢᎯᎠᏒᎢᎣᎠᎢ [asgwanigosyʔvsgo³ʔi]

   ᎲᏍᎢᎯᎠᏒᎢᏍ [hisgwanigosyʔvga]

   ᎤᏍᏍᎯᎠᎣᎵ [usgwanigoshdi]

ᎠᏍᎢᎠᎲᏍ [asgwanu³tsga] (vt) "He is kissing (sucking)."

   ᎢᎤᏍᎠᎲᏍ [tsiʔsgwanu³tsga]

   ᎤᏍᏍᎢᎠᎬᏍᎢ [usgwanu³tsv²³ʔi]

   ᎠᏍᎢᎠᎲᎯᎠᎢ [asgwanu³tsgo³ʔi]

   ᎲᏍᎢᎠᎬ [hisgwanu³tsa]

   ᎤᏍᏍᎢᎠᎲᎵ [usgwanu³tsdi]

ᎠᏍᏩᏟᏲᎠ [asgweli³yeʔa] (vi) "He is spelling."

   ᎢᎤᏩᏟᏲᎠ [tsiʔsgweli³yeʔa]

   ᎤᏍᏩᏟᏲᎢᎢ [usgweli³yeʔv²³ʔi]

   ᎠᏍᏩᏟᏲᎠᎠᎢ [asgweli³yesgo³ʔi]

   ᎲᏍᏩᏟᏯ [hisgweli³ya]

   ᎤᏍᏩᏟᏲᎵ [usgweli³yedi]

ᎠᏍᏩᏎᎣᎵ [asgwetusdi] (n) "The cap over a stove pipe."

ᎠᏍᎤᎥᎣᏍ [asgwoh³sga] (vt) "He is craving it."

   ᎢᎤᎥᎣᏍ [tsiʔsgwoh³sga]

   ᎤᏍᎥᏒᎢ [usgwoh³sv²³ʔi]

   ᎠᎤᎥᎣᎠᎢ [asgwoh³sgo³ʔi]

   ᎲᎤᎥᏟ [hisgwoʔli]

   ᎤᏍᎥᎣᎲᎵ [usgwoʔhisdi]

ᎠᏍᎬᏁᏝ [asgwyneda] (n) "False hellebore.; Indian poke.; Indian hellebore.; biol. *Veratrum viride*."

ᎠᏍᏓᎬᎵ [asda³wadi] (vt) "He is following."

   ᎢᏍᏓᎬᎵ [tsiʔsda³wadi]

   ᎤᏍᏓᎬᏒᎢ [usda³wadeʔsv²³ʔi]

   ᎠᏍᏓᎬᎵᎢᎢ [asda³wadiso³ʔi]

   ᎲᏍᏓᎬᏚᏚ [hisda³waduga]

   ᎤᏍᏓᎬᎣᎵ [usda³wadysdi]

ᎦᎥᎤᏃ ᎬᎣᏄᏒᎩ, ᎠᏈᎩ ᎡᎣᏍ ᏟᏩᎬᏑ; ᏀᎤᎠᎬᎠᎯ
ᎤᎲᏍᏓᎬᏟᏑ, ᎠᏈᎩ Ꭾ ᏍᎬᎠᎵ ᏙᏟᎠᎠᏬᎣ.
so he went his way, and I came mine: <u>he after</u> Obstinate, and I to this Gate.
[ᏦᏁᎬᎵ ᏍᎲᎩᏒᏒᎢ]

ᎠᏍᏓᏯ [asdayi] (adj) "Hard.; Solid (object)."

ᏎᏈᎲᏍᎣᏍᎣᎲ ᎡᏲ <u>ᎠᏍᏓᏯᏞ</u> ᎠᏯᎮᎵ …
Fear followed me so <u>hard</u> …
[ᏦᏁᎬᎵ ᏍᎲᎩᏒᏒᎢ]

ᎠᏍᏓᏱᏗᎠ [asda^{3}ʔyidịʔa] (vi) "He is fastening.; He is making fast."

ᏥᏍᏓᏱᏗᎠ [tsịʔsda^{3}ʔyidịʔa]

ᎤᏍᏓᏱᏛᎢ [usda^{3}ʔyidv^{23}ʔi]

ᎠᏍᏓᏱᏗᏍᎪᎢ [asda^{3}ʔyidịsgo^{3}ʔi]

ᎯᏍᏓᏱᏓ [hịsda^{3}ʔyida]

ᎤᏍᏓᏱᏗᏍᏗ [usda^{3}ʔyidịsdi]

ᎠᏂᏧᏏᏃ ᎾᏍᏉ ᎤᏂᏍᏓᏱᏛᎩ, ᎤᏙᎯᏳᎯ ᎾᏍᎩ ᏄᏍᏗ, ᎤᎾᏛᏅᎩ.
and the Jews also agreed, professing these things to be so.
[ᎨᏥᏅᏏᏛ ᏄᎾᏛᏁᎵᏙᎸᎢ 24:9]

ᎠᏍᏓᏱᏗᎠ [asdąʔyi^{3}dịʔa] (vt) "He is strengthening it.; He is approving it.; He is signing it."

ᏥᏍᏓᏱᏗᎠ [tsịʔsdąʔyi^{3}dịʔa]

ᎤᏍᏓᏱᏛᎢ [usdąʔyi^{3}dv^{23}ʔi]

ᎠᏍᏓᏱᏗᏍᎪᎢ [asdąʔyi^{3}dịsgo^{3}ʔi]

ᎯᏍᏓᏱᏓ [hịsdąʔyi^{3}da]

ᎤᏍᏓᏱᏗᏍᏗ [usdąʔyi^{3}dịsdi]

… ᎠᎴ ᎩᎶ ᏥᏍᏓᏱᏓ ᎡᎳ ᎠᏍᏓᏱᏗᏍᎪᎢ.
… and to whom He willeth, He doth harden.
[ᎶᎻ 9:18]

ᎠᏍᏓᏲᎯᎭ [asdąyǫhịha] (vt) "He is firing a gun."

ᎦᏍᏓᏲᎯᎭ [gaʔsdąyǫhịha]

ᎤᏍᏓᏲᎸᎢ [usdąyohlv^{23}ʔi]

ᎠᏍᏓᏲᎯᎰᎢ [asdąyǫhịho^{3}ʔi]

ᎯᏍᏓᏲᎭᎦ [hịsdąyǫhaga]

ᎤᏍᏓᏲᏍᏗ [usdąyǫsdi]

ᎠᏍᏕᎵᎭ [asde^{3}lịha] (vt) "He is helping."

ᏥᏍᏕᎵᎭ [tsịʔsde^{3}lịha]

ᎤᏍᏕᎸᎲᎢ [usde^{3}lṿhv^{23}ʔi]

ᎠᏍᏕᎵᏍᎪᎢ [asde^{3}lịsgo^{3}ʔi]

ᎯᏍᏕᎳ [hịsde^{3}la]

ᎤᏍᏕᎵᏗ [usde^{3}hldi]

ᎠᏍᎦᏯ ᎤᎷᏤᎸᎩ, ᎠᏓᏍᏕᎵᏍᎩ ᏧᏙᎢᏛ …
that a man came to him, whose name was Help …
[ᏧᏁᎶᏗ ᏚᏂᎩᏒᏒᎢ]

ᎠᏍᏕᏲᏎᎭ [ąsdẹyoseha] (vt) "He is braiding hair."

ᏥᏍᏕᏲᏎᎭ [tsịsdẹyọʔseha]

ᎤᏍᏕᏲᏎᎸᎢ [usdẹyosẹlv^{23}ʔi]

ᎠᏍᏕᏲᏎᎰᎢ [ąsdẹyoseho^{3}ʔi]

ᎯᏍᏕᏲᏏ [hịsdẹyosi]

ᎤᏍᏕᏲᏎᏗ [usdẹyosehdi]

ᎠᏍᏗᎩᎠ [asdi^{3}gịʔa] (vt) "He is eating it (something long)."

ᏥᏍᏗᎩᎠ [tsịʔsdi^{3}gịʔa]

ᎤᏍᏗᎬᎢ [usdi^{3}gʔv^{23}ʔi]

ᎠᏍᏗᎩᏍᎪᎢ [asdi^{3}gịsgo^{3}ʔi]

ᎯᏍᏗᎦ [hịsdi^{3}ga]

ᎤᏍᏗᎩᏍᏗ [usdi^{3}gʔisdi]

ᏚᏯ ᏃᎴ ᏎᎷ ᏓᏍᏗᎩᎠ.
He is eating corn and beans.
[King pg 112]

ᎠᏍᏗᏰᏗᎭ [asdiyedịha] (vt) "He is begging him.; He is persuading him."

ᏥᏍᏗᏰᏗᎭ [tsiʔsdiyedịha]

ᎤᏍᏗᏰᏔᏅᎢ [usdiyetąnv^{23}ʔi]

ᎠᏍᏗᏰᏗᏍᎪᎢ [asdiyedịsgo^{3}ʔi]

ᎯᏍᏗᏰᏓ [hiʔsdiyeda]

ᎤᏍᏗᏰᏙᏗ [usdiyedohdi]

… ᎾᏍᎩ ᎠᎩᏍᏗᏰᏔᏅᎩ.
… who persuaded me.
[ᏧᏁᎶᏗ ᏚᏂᎩᏒᏒᎢ]

ᎠᏍᏙᎠ [asdoʔa] (vt) "He is pounding.; He is grinding.; He is churning."

ᏥᏍᏙᎠ [tsịʔsdoʔa]

ᎤᏍᏙᎥᎢ [usdoʔv^{23}ʔi]

ᎠᏍᏙᏍᎪᎢ [asdosgo^{3}ʔi]

ᎯᏍᏙᏣ [hịsdotsa]

ᎤᏍᏙᏍᏗ [usdosdi]

ᎠᏂᏔᎵ ᎠᏂᎨᏴ ᎠᏂᏍᏙᏍᎨᏍᏗ ᎠᏍᏙᏍᎩᏱ, ᎠᏏᏴᏫ ᎠᏥᏯᏅᏗ ᎨᏎᏍᏗ ᏐᎢᏃ ᎠᏥᎧᎯᏯᏍᏗ ᎨᏎᏍᏗ.
two women shall be grinding in the mill, one is received, and one is left.
[ᎹᏚ 24:41]

ᎠᏍᏙᏗ [ąsdohdi] (n) "Door."

ᎠᏍᏙᏰᎭ [asdo^{3}yeha] (vt) "He is shaving him.; He is cutting hair."

ᏥᏍᏙᏰᎭ [tsiʔsdo^{3}yeha]

ᎤᏍᏙᏰᎲᎢ [usdo^{3}yehv^{23}ʔi]

ᎠᏍᏙᏰᏍᎪᎢ [asdo^{3}yesgo^{3}ʔi]

ᎯᏍᏙᏰᎠ [hiʔsdo^{3}yẹa]

ᎤᏍᏙᏰᏗ [usdo^{3}yhdi]

DᎤᏍᎩᎠᎠ [asduᷠ³giʔa] (vt) "He is opening a door."

    ᏦᎤᏍᎩᎠᎠ [tsiʔsduᷠ³giʔa]

    ᎤᎤᏍᎩᎡᏘ [usduᷠ³gisv²³ʔi]

    DᎤᏍᎩᎤᎠᏘ [asduᷠ³gisgo³ʔi]

    ᎭᎤᏍᎩ [hisduᷠ³gi]

    ᎤᎤᏍᎩᏗ [usduᷠ³gidi]

DᎤᏍᏛᎤᏍ [asduhvh³sga] (vt) "He is shutting it.; He is closing it."

    ᏦᎤᏍᏛᎤᏍ [tsiʔsduhvh³sga]

    ᎤᎤᏍᎤᎢᏘ [usduhnv²³ʔi]

    DᎤᏍᏛᎤᎠᏘ [asduhvh³sgo³ʔi]

    ᎭᎤᏍᏛᏍ [hisduhv³ga]

    ᎤᎤᏍᏗ [usduhdi]

    … ᎳᎤᏗ ᎦᎤᏍᎣᎩ ᎥᏃᏱᎻ ᎠᏫᏓᎢᏞᎠ ᎠᏂ ᎠᎠ ᎠᏫᎱᎠ …
    … 'Thou mayest not <u>seal</u> the words of the prophecy of this scroll …
    [ᎠᏦᎾᎤᎠᎤᏝᏘ 22:10]

DᎤᏍᏦᎠᎥᎯ [asdutsidoha] (vt) "He is sprinkling."

    ᏦᎤᏍᏦᎠᎥᎯ [tsiʔsdutsidoha]

    ᎤᎤᏍᏦᎠᎥᎠᏘ [usdutsidoʔlv²³ʔi]

    DᎤᏍᏦᎠᎥᏦᏘ [asdutsidoho³ʔi]

    ᎭᎤᏍᏦᎠᏝ [hisdutsida]

    ᎤᎤᏍᏦᎠᎥᏗ [usdutsitdi]

DᎤᏛᎢᏘ [asdvʔi] (n) "At the edge of.; End."

    … ᏧᏞᎥ DᎤᏛᎢ ᏒᎷᏠᎤᎩ ᎧᏞᎢ DᎤᎠᎭᏗᏞ.
    … did come to <u>the borders</u> of Judea, beyond the Jordan,
    [ᎠᎵᏍ 19:1]

DᎤᏛᎢᎠ [asdv³ka] (vi) "It is deep."

    ⸺

    ᎤᎤᏛᎢᎡᏘ [usdv³hsv²³ʔi]

    DᎤᏛᎢᎠᏘ [asdv³ko³ʔi]

    ᎦᎤᏛᎢᏛᎯ [wasdv³hvhi]

    ᎤᎤᏛᎢᏛᎤᏗ [usdv³hvsdi]

    … ᎤᎤᏢᏃ ᎤᎤᎵᏞᏝ DᎤᏛᎢᎩ …
    … and darkness [is] on the face of <u>the deep</u> …
    [ᏉᏃ ᏔᎬᎥᎥ 1:2]

DᎤᏛᎢᎠᎤᏍ [asdvgoh³sga] (vt) "He is scraping (grit corn)."

    ᏦᎤᏛᎢᎠᎤᏍ [tsiʔsdvgoh³sga]

    ᎤᎤᏛᎢᎠᏒᏘ [usdvgoh³sv²³ʔi]

    DᎤᏛᎢᎠᎤᎠᏘ [asdvgoh³sgo³ʔi]

    ᎭᎤᏛᎢᎠᎵ [hisdvgo³ʔli]

    ᎤᎤᏛᎢᎠ᏿ᎤᏗ [usdvgo³osdi]

DᎤᏛᎢᎠᎠᎵᎥ [asdv³hisdiha] (vt) "He is making it deep."

    ᏦᎤᏛᎢᎠᎠᎵᎥ [tsiʔsdv³hisdiha]

    ᎤᎤᏛᎢᎠᎠᏫᎤᏘ [usdv³histanv²³ʔi]

    DᎤᏛᎢᎠᎠᎵᎤᏘ [asdv³hisdisgo³ʔi]

    ᎭᎤᏛᎢᎠᎠᎵ [hisdv³hisda]

    ᎤᎤᏛᎢᎠᎠᎥᏗ [usdv³hisdohdi]

DᎤᏛᎢᎵᏍᏁᎥ [asdvnegaliha] (vt) "He is scalping him."

    ᏦᎤᏛᎢᎵᏍᏁᎠ [tsisdvnegaliʔa]

    ᎤᎤᏛᎢᎵᏍᏘᏛᏘ [usdvnegalvhv²³ʔi]

    DᎤᏛᎢᎵᏍᏁᎤᎠᏘ [asdvnegalisgo³ʔi]

    ᎭᎤᏛᎢᎵᏍᏈ [hisdvnegala]

    ᎤᎤᏛᎢᎵᏍᏁᏗ [usdvnegahldi]

DᎤᏛᎢᎤᏍ [astvsga] (vi) "He is finishing.; He is coming to an end."

    ᏦᎤᏛᎢᎤᏍ [tsiʔstvsga]

    ᎤᎤᏛᎢᎢᏘ [ustvnv²³ʔi]

    DᎤᏛᎢᎤᎠᏘ [astvsgo³ʔi]

    ᎭᎤᏛᎢᏍ [histvga]

    ᎤᎤᏛᎢᎤᏗ [ustvsdi]

DᏀᏪᎥ [aseᷟ³heha] (vt) "He is showing him.; He is pointing for him."

    ᏦᏫᏀᏪᎥ [tsiyaseᷟ³heha]

    ᎤᏀᏇᏘ [useᷟ³helv²³ʔi]

    DᏀᏇᏓᏘ [aseᷟ³heho³ʔi]

    ᎭᏫᏀᏪᏘᏂ [hiyaseᷟ³heisi]

    ᎤᏀᏪᎤᏗ [useᷟ³hesdi]

    DᎵᎢᎬᎭᏂᎥᏗ ᏧᎥᏘᎢ DᎢᏀᏓᏋ …
    <u>I am directed</u> by a man, whose name is Evangelist …
    [ᏧᎾᎬᏗ ᏍᎲᏯᎡᏘᏘ]

DᏀᎠᎥ [aseᷟ³hiha] (vt) "He is counting.; He is pointing at him."

    ᏦᏫᏀᎠᎥ, ᏍᏘᎠᎥ [tsiyaseᷟ³hiha, gaseᷟ³hiha]

    ᎤᎦᏀᏓᏘ [uwaseᷟ³hlv²³ʔi]

    DᏀᎤᏓᏘ [aseᷟ³hiho³ʔi]

    ᎭᏫᏀᏓᎠ, ᏱᏀᎠ [hiyaseᷟ³ka, haseᷟ³ka]

    ᎤᎦᏀᎤᏗ [uwaseᷟ³sdi]

    … ᏪᎬᎩᎵᏁᎥ DᏀᏓᏛᏘ; ᎢᏞᏐᏃ ᎬᏀᎲᏛᎤᏗ ᏇᏀᏘ.
    … until that he hath ceased <u>to number</u>, for there is no number.
    [ᏉᏃ ᏔᎬᎥᎥ 41:49]

DᏀᎵᎵᎤᏴ [aseᷟlidanv] (n) "Affadavit."

D4Z [ạsehno] (pt) "Probably.; But yet."

D4Z AႶV⁹ FR hჰႶ⁹ O⁹SႶⁿⁿ.
but he will have all now.
[ᏠႶᏫᎫ ᏚhᎩRRT]

DᏏⁿ [ạsịha] (vt) "He is removing it from a shelf."

   ᏔᏏⁿ [tsị?sịha]

   O⁹RᏔT [usᴠhᴠ²³?i]

   DᏏᏬAT [asịsgo³?i]

   ᎧᏇ [hịsa]

   O⁹RᎫ [usᴠ?di]

DᏏWᏟ⁹iᏬᎦ [ạsịḷadv?vsga] (vi) "He is putting up a wire.; He is wiring."

   ᏔᏏWᏟ⁹iᏬᎦ [tsịsịḷadv?v?sga]

   O⁹ᏏWᏟ⁹O⁹T [usịḷadv?nv²³?i]

   DᏏWᏟ⁹iᏬAT [ạsịḷadv?vsgo³?i]

   ᎧᏏWᏟ⁹iᎦ [hịsịḷadv?vga]

   O⁹ᏏWᏟ⁹Ꭻ [usịḷadv?di]

DᏏƟⁿ [asi³nạha] (vi) "He is skilled."

   ᏔᏏƟⁿ [tsị?si³nạha]

   O⁹ᏏƟᏔRT [usi³nạhᴠsv²³?i]

   DᏏƟᏬAT [asi³nạsgo³?i]

   ᎧᏏƟᏔᎧ [hịsi³nạhᴠhi]

   O⁹ᏏƟRᏬᎫ [usi³nạsᴠsdi]

DᏏƟႾO⁹Ꭶ [asi³nạsạnvga] (vi) "He is becoming skilled."

   ᏔᏏƟႾO⁹Ꭶ [tsị?si³nạsạnvga]

   O⁹ᏏƟႾO⁹ᏟⁱT [usi³nạsạnvtsv²³?i]

   DᏏƟႾO⁹AT [asi³nạsạnvgo³?i]

   ᎧᏏƟႾO⁹Ꭷ [hịsi³nạsạnvhi]

   O⁹ᏏƟႾO⁹Ꭻ [usi³nạsạnvhdi]

D4Z O⁹VᏚ⁹Ꮀ DhᏏƟႾO⁹ET, DᏍ ᎪD hSᏫ4⁹T, ᏚVZ TᏬᎩႾⁿiᏬᎦ?
And he, having perceived their craftiness, said unto them, 'Why me do ye tempt?
[MᏚ 20:23]

DᏏh [ạsi³hni] (vi) "He is going there and lying down."

   ᏚᏏh [gạsi³hni]

   O⁹ᏏᎫRT [usi³hnᶒsv²³?i]

   DᏏhꞘT [ạsi³hnịso³?i]

   ⁿᏏᎦᎦ [hạsi³hnuga]

   O⁹ᏏOᏬᎫ [usi³hnᴠsdi]

DᏏO⁹ⁿᎫᏤⁿ [asi³nhᴠsdịha] (vi) "He is coaching."

   ᏔᏏO⁹ⁿᎫᏤⁿ [tsị?si³-nhᴠsdịha]

   O⁹ᏏO⁹ⁿᎫLO⁹T [usị³-nhᴠsdạnv²³?i]

   DᏏO⁹ⁿᎫᏤᏬAT [asị³-nhᴠsdịsgo³?i]

   ᎧᏏO⁹ⁿᎫL [hịsị³-nhᴠsda]

   O⁹ᏏO⁹ⁿᎫVᎫ [usị³-nhᴠsdọ³di]

DᏏBD [asi³yᴠ?a] (vt) "He is pushing it (something long) aside.; He is clearing it (something long) away."

   ᏔᏏBD [tsị?si³yᴠ?a]

   O⁹ᏏBiT [usi³yᴠ?v²³?i]

   DᏏBᏬAT [asi³yᴠsgo³?i]

   ᎧᏏBƟ [hịsi³yᴠna]

   O⁹ᏏBᏬᎫ [usi³yᴠsdi]

DꞘᏬO⁹Ꭻⁿ

DꞘᏬO⁹Ꭻⁿ [asọ?ohndịha] (vt) "He is dropping it (something long)."

   ᏔꞘᏬO⁹Ꭻⁿ [tsị?sọ?ohndịha]

   O⁹ꞘᏬO⁹WO⁹T [usọ?ohntạnv²³?i]

   DꞘᏬO⁹ᎫᏬAT [asọ?ohndịsgo³?i]

   ᎧꞘᏬO⁹L [hịsọ?ohnda]

   O⁹ꞘᏬO⁹VᎫ [usọ?ohndohdi]

DꞘᏬᏬᎦ [asọ?osga] (vi) "It (something long) is falling."

   ———

   O⁹ꞘᏬRT [usọ?osv²³?i]

   DꞘᏬᏬAT [asọ?osgo³?i]

   ᏣꞘᏬᎧ [wasọ?ohi]

   O⁹ꞘᏬᎧᏬᎫ [usọ?ohịsdi]

DꞘꓤWᏬᎦ [ạsolvtah³sga] (vt) "He is raising an arm."

   ᏚꞘꓤWᏬᎦ [gạsolvtah³sga]

   O⁹ꞘꓤWO⁹T [usolvtạ³nv²³?i]

   DꞘꓤWᏬAT [ạsolvtah³sgo³?i]

   ⁿꞘꓤWᎩ [hạsolvta³gi]

   O⁹ꞘꓤᎫᎫ [usolvtdi]

DꞘᏬᎫ [ạsosdi] (n) "A diaper."

34

ᎠᎾᏍᎦ [a̱su³geha] (vt) "He is mixing it.; He is stirring it."

ᏗᎾᏍᎦ [ga̱su³geha]

ᎤᎾᏍᎬᎢ [usu³gehv²³ʔi]

ᎠᎾᏍᎪᏍᏗᎢ [a̱su³gesgo³ʔi]

ᎲᎾᏍᎬᎵ [ha̱su³gvli]

ᎤᎾᏍᎩᏗ [usu³kdi]

… ᏍᎳ ᎲᏍᎣᏔᏫᏝ ᏪᏘ ᏘᏬᏨᎨᎵᎠ ᏣᎾᏍ ᏘᎡ; ᎲᎾᎬᎵᎵ,
ᏛᎧ ᏣᏁᏈᎤᎦᏍ.
… 'Hasten three measures of flour-meal, knead, and
make cakes;'
[ᏅᏛ ᎢᎬᏪᎥᎣ 18:6]

ᎠᎾᏍᎦᏟᎠ [a̱sugelvhi] (n) "Batter."

ᎠᎾᏍᎪᏍᏗ [a̱sugọsdi] (n) "Gritter."

ᎠᎾᏉᏯᏛ [a̱sula̱giʔa] (vt) "He is taking off a pair of pants."

ᏗᎾᏉᏯᏛ [ga̱sula̱giʔa]

ᎤᎾᏉᏯᎡᏘ [usula̱gisv²³ʔi]

ᎠᎾᏉᏯᏍᏗᎢᏘ [a̱sula̱gisgo³ʔi]

ᎲᎾᏉᏯ [ha̱sula̱gi]

ᎤᎾᏉᏯᏍᏗ [usula̱gisdi]

ᎠᎾᏍᏓ [a̱suleha] (vt) "He is wiping himself."

ᏗᎾᏍᏓ [ga̱suleha]

ᎤᎾᏍᏓᎬᎢᏘ [usulehv²³ʔi]

ᎠᎾᏍᏓᏍᏗᎢᏘ [a̱sulesgo³ʔi]

ᎲᎾᏍᏓᏛ [ha̱sulẹa]

ᎤᎾᏍᏗᏗ [usulhdi]

ᎠᎾᏍᏙᏗᏗ [a̱suhldohdi] (n) "Toilet paper."

ᎠᎾᏈᏛ [a̱suliʔa] (vt) "He is putting on a pair of pants."

ᏗᎾᏈᏛ [ga̱suliʔa]

ᎤᎾᏉᏬᏗ [usulaʔnv²³ʔi]

ᎠᎾᏈᏍᏗᎢᏘ [a̱sulisgo³ʔi]

ᎲᎾᏉᏬᎾ [ha̱sulaʔna]

ᎤᎾᏉᎦᏗ [usulodi]

ᎠᎾᏉ [asulo] (n) "A pair of pants."

ᎠᎾᏀ [a̱suʔʔyeha] (vt) "He is mixing stuff together."

ᏗᎾᏀ [ga̱su³ʔyeha]

ᎤᎾᏀᎬᎢᏘ [usu³ʔyehv²³ʔi]

ᎠᎾᏀᏍᏗᎢᏘ [a̱su³ʔyesgo³ʔi]

ᎲᎾᏀᏈ [ha̱su³ʔyvli]

ᎤᎾᏀᏗ [usu³ʔyhdi]

ᎠᎾᏟᏍᏗᏍ [a̱su³yọhohsga] (vi) "He is sliding."

ᏗᎾᏟᏍᏗᏍ [ga̱su³yọhohsga]

ᎤᎾᏟᎲᎡᏘ [usu³yọhọsv²³ʔi]

ᎠᎾᏟᏍᏗᏍᏗᎢᏘ [a̱su³yọhohsgo³ʔi]

ᎲᎾᏟᏟ [ha̱su³yọhọhi]

ᎤᎾᏟᏍᏗ [usu³yọhọsdi]

ᏗᎡᎢᏍᏍ [asv³vsga] (vt) "He is putting it (something flexible) up."

ᏟᎡᎢᏍ [tsiʔsv³vsga]

ᎤᎡᎣᏘ [usv³nv²³ʔi]

ᏗᎡᎢᏍᏗᎢᏘ [asv³vsgo³ʔi]

ᏍᎡᎢᏍ [hisv³vga]

ᎤᎡᏗ [usv³di]

ᏗᎡᏦᏫᏍᏍ [asvna̱tasga] (vt) "He is roasting it."

ᏟᎡᏦᏫᏍ [tsiʔsvna̱tasga]

ᎤᎡᏦᏫᎤᎢᏘ [usvna̱tanv²³ʔi]

ᏗᎡᏦᏫᏍᏗᎢᏘ [asvna̱tasgo³ʔi]

ᏍᎡᏦᏫᏍ [hisvna̱taga]

ᎤᎡᏦᏗ [usvna̱ti]

ᏗᎡᏆ [a̱sy³hnị̱ha] (vt) "He is feeling it.; He is touching
it."

ᏗᎡᏆ [ga̱sy³hnị̱ha]

ᎤᎡᏆᏗᏘ [usy³hnị̱lv²³ʔi]

ᏗᎡᏆᎢᏘ [a̱sy³hnị̱ho³ʔi]

ᏍᎡᏆᏍ [ha̱sy³hnga]

ᎤᎡᏆᏍᏗ [usy³hnsdi]

… ᏗᏍᏍᏫᏜ ᎤᎡᏃᏟᎣ ᎤᏓᏈᏍᏫᏫ ᎤᎡᏆᎢᏘ …
… for what cause she touched him declared to him
before …
[ᎷᏍ 8:47]

ᏗᎡᏝᏘᏉᏍᏗ [a̱svda̱gwa̱losdi] (n) "Log."

ᏗᎡᏟᏠᏛ [asvhtsa̱³dịʔa] (vt) "He is bridging it."

ᏟᎡᏟᏛ [tsiʔsvhtsa̱³dịʔa]

ᎤᎡᏟᏞᎢᏘ [usvhtsa̱³dv²³ʔi]

ᏗᎡᏟᏗᏍᏗᎢᏘ [asvhtsa̱³dịsgo³ʔi]

ᏍᎡᏟᏝ [hisvhtsa̱³da]

ᎤᎡᏟᏗᏍᏗ [usvhtsa̱³dịsdi]

ᏗᎡᏨ [a̱svtsv] (n) "Bridge."

Ꮪ [ahda] (n) "Wood.; Stick."

… ᏛᎧ Ꮪ ᏌᏪᎤᏫ ᏗᏢᏍᏘ, ᏛᎧ ᎤᏣᎣ ᎤᏗᏟ ᏰᏟᎩ, ᏛᎧ
ᏗᏆᏋ ᎡᏫᏜᏯᎣ ᎤᎢᏚᏘ, Ꮪ ᏗᏓᏈ ᏗᏍᏘ.
… and arrangeth the wood, and bindeth Isaac his son,
and placeth him upon the altar above the wood;
[ᏅᏛ ᎢᎬᏪᎥᎣ 22:9]

35

DLSᎯᏏᏴᎤ [ạdaktị?yeha] (vt) "He is baby sitting."

ᏱᏞᏚᎯᏴᎤ [gạdakdị?yeha]

ᎤᏞᏚᎯᏴᎯᎢ [udaktị?ye?lv²³?i]

DLSᎯᏏᎻᎢ [ạdaktị?yeho³?i]

ᎾᏞᏚᎯᏫ [hạdaktị?ya]

ᎤᏞᏚᎯᏫᏬᎠᏗ [udaktị?yạsdi]

DLᏈᏗ [ạdakehdi] (n) "Window pane.; Mirror."

Ꭰꭲ ᎠᎩᎪᏫ iᏞᎧ DLᏈᏗ ᎦᎬᎿᎤᏍ ᎾꭺᎩᎠᎢ ᎠᎮᎧ ᎤᏞᎥᎥ ᏆᎡᎩ …
and I saw as a sea of glass mingled with fire …
[ᎠᎮᎾᎧᎠᎾᎤᎧᎢ 15:2]

DLᏈᎥᎫ [ạdakẹdọdi] (n) "Mirror."

DLᎪᎾᎥᎫ [ạdagọnạdodi] (n) "Prize."

DL ᎡꭿᏏᏛ [adạ gyṇihidv] (n) "Cottonwood.; biol. *Populus spp.*"

DLᏗ [ạdahi] (n) "Young animal from a litter."

DLᏗ [ạda³hi] (n) "Killer."

DLᏯᎡᏗ [ạdahlsᎥhi] (n) "A bundle."

DLᎳᎡᏬᎤᏍ [ạda³hlsᎥhvsga] (vt) "He is wrapping it."

ᏱᏞᎳᎡᏬᎤᏍ [gạdạ?lsᎥhvsga]

ᎤᏞᎳᎡᎤᎢ [uda³hlsᎥ?hnv²³?i]

DLᎳᎡᏬᎤᎠᎢ [ada³hlsᎥhvsgo³?i]

ᎾᏞᎳᎡᏏ [hada³hlsᎥ?hni]

ᎤᏞᎳᎡᎫ [uda³hlsᎥ?hdi]

DLᎪᏬᎫ [ạdạ?losdi] (n) "Constitution."

DLᎾᎾᏴᎠ [adanạnagi³?a] (vi) "He is shopping."

ᏱᏞᎾᎾᏴᎠ [gạdanạnagi³?a]

ᎤᏞᎾᎾᏴᎡᎢ [udanạnagi³sv²³?i]

DLᎾᎾᏴᎠᎢ [adanạnagi³sgo³?i]

ᎾᏞᎾᎾᏴ [hadanạnagi]

ᎤᏞᎾᎾᏴᎠᏗ [udanạnagi³sdi]

DLᎾᎾᎢ [adạ?nạnv?i] (n) "Store."

DLᎾᎾᎯᎤ [adanạ³wịdiha] (vi) "He is jumping forward."

ᏱᏞᎾᎾᏗᎠ [gạdanạ³wịdi?a]

ᎤᏞᎾᎾᎪᎤᎢ [udanạ³wịdvhv²³?i]

DLᎾᎾᎯᎤᎠᎢ [adanạ³wịdisgo³?i]

ᎾᏞᎾᎾᏞ [hadanạ³wịda]

ᎤᏞᎾᎾᎯᎫ [udanạ³wịtdi]

ᎠꭺᏍᏫ, ᏱᎠᏍᏙᎾ ᏂᎪᎾᎾᏝᏐᎢ.
The fearless man jumped.
[King pg 117]

DLᏛᏣ ᎤᎵᏬᏯᎠᏗ [ạdanhᎥwạ ụnahlsgisdi] (n) "A war dance."

DLᏁᎤ [adahneha] (vt) "He is giving it (a solid)."

ᏱᏁᎤ [gạdạ?neha]

ᎤᏞᏁᎯᎢ [udahnẹlv²³?i]

DLᏁᎻᎢ [adahneho³?i]

———

ᎤᏞᏁᎫ [udahnehdi]

Ꭴꭰ ᎠᎮᎩᏫᎮᎠᏗᎥ ᎭᎭᏫᎰᎠᏗ ᏣᏁᎫ Ꭰꭲ ᎾᏞᎧᎰᎠᏗ …
leave there thy gift before the altar, and go …
[MᏚ 5:24]

DLᏁᎯᎢ [adanelv?i] (n) "A building."

ᏔᎡᏫᏫᏴᎢᏃ DLᏁᎯ ᎾᎻᎯᎩ ᎾᎥᎩ ᏚᏁᎩ.
and the first house you come at is his.
[ᏧᏁᎫ ᏍᏲᎡᎡᎢ]

DLᏁᎡᏴᎠ [adahnẹsagi?a] (vi) "He is conjuring.; He is witching."

ᏱᏞᏁᎡᏴᎠ [gạdạ?nẹsagi?a]

ᎤᏞᏁᎡᎢ [udahnẹsagv²³?i]

DLᏁᎡᏴᎠᎢ [adahnẹsagisgo³?i]

ᎾᏞᏁᎡᏍ [hadahnẹsaga]

ᎤᏞᏁᎡᏴᎠᏗ [udahnẹsạgisdi]

DLᏃᎾ [ạdahnọwi] (n) "War."

DLᏈᏈᎤ [adanu³lvha] (vi) "He is lazy."

ᏱᏞᏈᏈᎠ [gadanu³ly?a]

ᎤᏞᏈᏈᎤᎢ [udanu³lvhnv²³?i]

DLᏈᏈᎻᎢ [adanu³lvho³?i]

ᎾᏞᏈᏈᏍ [hadanu³lvga]

ᎤᏞᏈᏈᎢᎠᏗ [udanu³ly?isdi]

DLᎣᏛ

DLᎣᏛ [adạ³?nv?a] (vt) "He is moving his household from …."

ᏱᏞᎣᏛ [gadạ³?nv?a]

ᎤᏞᎣᎡᎢ [udạ³?nvsv²³?i]

DLᎣᏬᎠᎢ [adạ³?nvsgo³?i]

ᎾᏞᎣᎾ [hadạ³?nvna]

ᎤᏞᎣᏬᎫ [udạ³?nvsdi]

… ᏛᎠᎢ ᏣᎥᏋᏗ ᏆᎡᎢ, Ꭰꭲ ᏣᎸ ᏈᎡ ᏯᏬᎣᏬ, Ꭰꭲ ᏣᎳ ᏚᏁᎩ ᎾᏞᎣᎾ …
… 'Go for thyself, from thy land, and from thy kindred, and from the house of thy father …
[Ꮼᏸ ᏔᎡᏫᏫ 12:1]

DᏞOᏏᏏᏂVᎤ [adahnsi³nidoha] (vi) "He is crawling."

    ᏚᏞOᏏᏏᏂVᎤ [gadąᎥnsi³nidoha]

    OᎢᏞOᏏᏏᏂVᎥT [udahnsi³nidoᎥlv²³Ꭵi]

    DᏞOᏏᏏᏂVᏁT [adahnsi³nidoho³Ꭵi]

    ᎤᏞOᏏᏏᏂᏞ [hadahnsi³nida]

    OᎢᏞOᏏᏏᏂᏞᏍᎫ [udahnsi³nidąsdi]

DᏞOᏏᏏᎤ [adahnteha] (vi) "He is thinking.; He is planning to."

    ᏚᏞOᏏᏏᎤ [gadąᎥnteha]

    OᎢᏞOᏏᏏᎥT [udahntehlv²³Ꭵi]

    DᏞOᏏᏏᏍᎯT [adahntesgo³Ꭵi]

    ᎤᏞOᏏᏟᎮ [hadahntvli]

    OᎢᏞOᏏᎫ [udahntehdi]

    … DᏣ ᎾᏍᎩ ᎲᎠ ᎬᏞOᏏᎫ AᏚ TᏃᎤᎫ ᏨᏒT …
    … And for this thou must consider to whom he sent thee …
    [ᏣᏁᎬᎫ ᏍᏂᏴᏒᏒT]

DᏞOᏏᏏᎦᎤ [adante³siha] (vi) "He is considering."

    ᏚᏞOᏏᏚᎦᎤ [gadandᎥe³siha]

    ——

    DᏞOᏏᏏᎦᏍᎯT [adante³sisgo³Ꭵi]

    ——

DᏞᏓᎢᏟᏟᎮ [adąsagwąlę³hli] (vi) "He is rolling along."

    ᏚᏞᏓᎢᏟᏟᎮ [gadąsagwąlę³hli]

    OᎢᏞᏓᎢᏟᏟᏟᎯT [udąsagwąlę³hlᎥlv²³Ꭵi]

    DᏞᏓᎢᏟᏟᎮᏏT [adąsagwąlę³hliso³Ꭵi]

    ᎤᏞᏓᎢᏟᏟᏍ [hadąsagwąlęga]

    OᎢᏞᏓᎢᏟᏟᏍᎫ [udąsagwąlę³sdi]

DᏞᏍᎢᎢᏃᎯᏍᎤ [adasgwąlosdiha] (vt) "He is bumping his head."

    ᏚᏞᏍᎢᎢᏃᎯᏍᎫD [gadasgwąlosdiᎥa]

    OᎢᏞᏍᎢᎢᏃᎯᏞOᎢT [udasgwąlosdąnv²³Ꭵi]

    DᏞᏍᎢᎢᏃᎯᏞᏍᎯT [adasgwąlosdisgo³Ꭵi]

    ᎤᏞᏍᎢᎢᏃᎯᏞᏂ [hadasgwąlosdąni]

    OᎢᏞᏍᎢᎢᏃᎫ [udasgwąlhdi]

DᏞᏍᎯᏞᏟᎫ [adąsdahydi] (n) "Stove.; Kitchen."

    ᎯᏍᏳᏁ: ᎨᏔ ᏍᎯᏟᏁ DᏞᏍᎯᏞᏟᎫ.
    Fifth: The dough was collected into the stove.
    [ᏣᏫᏴ ᏫᎨᏁ ᏣᏂᏂᏏᎤ ᎫᏍᏫᎥᎫ]

DᏞᏍᏓᏚᏞᏨᏐᏒᎤ [adąsdedąliyyᎥeha] (vt) "He is trading."

    ᏚᏞᏍᏓᏚᏞᏨᏐᏒᎤ [gadasdedąliyyᎥeha]

    OᎢᏞᏍᏓᏚᏞᏨᏐᏒᎯT [udasdedąliyyᎥelv²³Ꭵi]

    DᏞᏍᏓᏚᏞᏨᏒᏂT [adąsdedąliyyᎥeho³Ꭵi]

    ᎤᏞᏍᏓᏚᏞᏨᏐᏴT [hadąsdedąliyyᎥi]

    OᎢᏞᏍᏓᏚᏞᏨᏐᏒᎫ [udasdedąliyyᎥehdi]

DᏞᏤᎮᏃᎫᎤ [adądolisdiha] (vi) "He is praying."

    ᏚᏞᏤᎮᏃᎫD [gadądolisdiᎥa]

    OᎢᏞᏤᎮᏃᏞOᎢT [udądolisdąnv²³Ꭵi]

    DᏞᏤᎮᏃᎫᏍᎯAT [adądolisdisgo³Ꭵi]

    ᎤᏞᏤᎮᏃᏞ [hadądolisda]

    OᎢᏞᏤᎮᏃᏴᎫ [udądolistdi]

    … DᏣ TᏴᏟᏃᎤ DᏞᏤᎮᏃᎫᏍᏁEᏴ.
    … sometimes praying.
    [ᏣᏁᎬᎫ ᏍᏂᏴᏒᏒT]

DᏞᏤᎮᏃᎫᎤ [adątolsdiha] (vt) "He is lending."

    ᏚᏞᏤᎮᏃᎫᎤ [gadądᎥolsdiha]

    OᎢᏞᏤᎮᏃᏞOᎢT [udątolsdąnv²³Ꭵi]

    DᏞᏤᎮᏃᎫᏍᎯAT [adątolsdisgo³Ꭵi]

    ᎤᏞᏤᎮᏃᏞ [hadątolsda]

    OᎢᏞᏤᎮᏃᎤᎫ [udątolsdohdi]

DᏞᏙᏎTᏃᎫᎤ [adądoduᎥisdiha] (vi) "He is making himself attractive."

    ᏚᏞᏙᏎTᏃᎫD [gadądoduᎥisdiᎥa]

    OᎢᏞᏙᏎTᏃᏞOᎢT [udądoduᎥisdąnv²³Ꭵi]

    DᏞᏙᏎTᏃᎫᏍᎯAT [adądoduᎥisdisgo³Ꭵi]

    ᎤᏞᏙᏎTᏃᏞ [hadądoduᎥisda]

    OᎢᏞᏙᏎTᏃᏴᎫ [udądoduᎥistdi]

DᏞᏟᏟᏏᏃᏍ [adątv³dvhvsga] (vt) "He is asking a question."

    ᏚᏞᏟᏟᏏᏃᏍ [gadatv³dvhvsga]

    OᎢᏞᏟᏟOᎢT [udątv³dvhnv²³Ꭵi]

    DᏞᏟᏟᏏᏃᏍᎯAT [adątv³dvhvsgo³Ꭵi]

    ᎤᏞᏟᏟᏏᏍ [hadątv³dvhvga]

    OᎢᏞᏟᏟᎫ [udątv³tdi]

    … ᏣᏁᎬᎫ OᎢᏟᏟOᎢᏴ ᎠD ᎤᏫRᏴ, ᏃᎠ ᏨᏓᏴᏰOᏍᏐᎫ ᏏᏴ ᎠD ᏍᏲ ᏨᏍᏞᏴᎤ OᎢᏟOᎢᏴ …
    … *Christian* asked him further If he could not help him off with his Burden that was upon his back …
    [ᏣᏁᎬᎫ ᏍᏂᏴᏒᏒT]

DᏞᏦᏍᎫ [adątsosdi] (n) "Belt."

DℒℴD [adạwo³ʔa] (vi) "He is swimming.; He is bathing."

SℒℴD [gadạwo³ʔa]

OꞋℒℴiT [udạwo³ʔv²³ʔi]

DℒℴℴAT [adạwo³sgo³ʔi]

ℴⱯLℴG [hadạwo³tsa]

OꞋℒℴℴⱭⱮ [udạwo³sdi]

ℴⱯⱲ DℒℴD iℒℙ.
An elephant is bathing in a lake.
[GWY WℙꞰ ⱮhhVℴ ⱮSⱧVⱮ]

DℒℴⱭℙⱮD [adạwohịldiʔa] (vi) "He is climbing over."

SℒℴTℙⱮD [gadạwọʔildiʔa]

OꞋℒℴⱭℙℴꞋT [udạwohịldv²³ʔi]

DℒℴⱭℙⱮℴⱭAT [adạwohịldịsgo³ʔi]

ⱯℴⱭℙⱮL [hadạwohịlda]

OꞋℒℴⱭℙⱮℴⱭⱮ [udạwohịldịsdi]

DℒⱮⱭⱭ [ạdạyahi] (n) "Oak.; biol. Quercus spp."

DℒⱭℬℴⱭY [ạdayesgi] (n) "Cancer."

Dℴ EhGꞋⱲ DℒⱭℬℴⱭY OꞋℙY OꞋMⱱ OꞋℒVℙℴⱭLⱮ́ꞋT …
and lo, a leper having come, was bowing to him …
[ⱯꞋS 8:2]

DℒⱧℴℴⱭS [ạdahyosga] (vi) "He is surrendering.; He is giving up."

Ɱ⊦DℒⱧℴℴⱭS [tsịdạʔyosga]

OꞋLⱧRT [udahyosv²³ʔi]

DℒⱧℴℴⱭAT [ạdahyosgo³ʔi]

ⱯℴLⱧⱭ [hạdahyohi]

OꞋLⱧⱭℴⱭⱮ [udahyohịsdi]

DℒℬKⱮℴⱭY [ạdạyvtsọdịsgi] (n) "The mumps."

DW [ata] (n) "Girl, teenage."

DWWSℴⱭS [ạtạlaksga] (vt) "He is penetrating it."

Ɱ⊦LWSℴⱭS [tsịdʔạlaksga]

OꞋWWSRT [utạlaksv²³ʔi]

DWWSℴⱭAT [ạtạlaksgo³ʔi]

ⱭWWS [hịtạlaga]

OꞋWWSℴⱭⱮ [utạlaksdi]

DWWSRT [ạtạlaksyʔi] (n) "A hole."

DWZℴⱭS [atạnoh³sga] (vi) "He is becoming big."

SLZℴⱭS [gadʔạnoh³sga]

OꞋWZRT [utạnoh³sv²³ʔi]

DWZℴⱭAT [atạnoh³sgo³ʔi]

ⱯℴWZⱭ [hatạnọ³hi]

OꞋWZℴⱭⱮ [utạnọ³hịsdi]

DWℴⱭS [atah³sga] (vt) "He is hanging it (a solid) up."

SLℴⱭS [gadʔah³sga]

OꞋWOꞋT [utạ³nv²³ʔi]

DWℴⱭAT [atah³sgo³ʔi]

ⱯⱲS [hata³ga]

OꞋⱮⱮ [utdi]

DWℴⱭYD [atasgiʔa] (vi) "It is popping."

———

OꞋWℴⱭYRT [utasgisv²³ʔi]

DWℴⱭYℴⱭAT [atasgisgo³ʔi]

ⱢWℴⱭY [watasgi]

OꞋWℴⱭYℴⱭⱮ [utasgisdi]

DWℴⱭYD [ạtasgi³ʔa] (vi) "He is bleeding."

SWℴⱭYD [gatasgi³ʔa]

OꞋWℴⱭYRT [utasgi³sv²³ʔi]

DWℴⱭYℴⱭAT [ạtasgi³sgo³ʔi]

ⱯWℴⱭY [hạtasgi]

OꞋWℴⱭYℴⱭⱮ [utasgi³sdi]

DWℴⱭYℴⱭET [ạtạsgisgyʔi] (n) "Sap.; Pus."

DWℴⱭYℴⱭⱮⱯ [atasgịsdịha] (vt) "He is popping it."

SLℴⱭYℴⱭⱮⱯ [gadʔasgịsdịha]

OꞋWℴⱭYℴⱭWOꞋT [utasgịstạnv²³ʔi]

DWℴⱭYℴⱭⱮℴⱭAT [atasgịsdịsgo³ʔi]

ⱯWℴⱭYℴⱭL [hatasgịsda]

OꞋWℴⱭYℴⱭVⱮ [utasgịsdohdi]

DWℒVℴⱭS [atạwe³dosga] (vt) "He is kissing her."

Ɱ⊦ℴⱢLℒVℴⱭS [tsiyadʔạwe³dosga]

OꞋWℒVOꞋT [utạwe³dọʔnv²³ʔi]

DWℒVℴⱭAT [atạwe³dosgo³ʔi]

ⱭℴⱢLℒVS [hiyadʔạwe³doga]

OꞋWℒVℴⱭⱮ [utạwe³dosdi]

DWℴⱭD [ahtạwo³ʔa] (vt) "He is combing it."

Ɱ⊦WℴⱭD [tsịʔtạwo³ʔa]

OꞋWℴⱭiT [uhtạwo³ʔv²³ʔi]

DWℴⱭAT [ahtạwo³sgo³ʔi]

ⱭWℴⱭG [hịhtạwo³tsa]

OꞋWℴⱭⱮ [uhtạwo³sdi]

38

ᎠᏔᏲᎯᎭ [ahtạyohịha] (vt) "He is asking.; He is asking for.; He is requesting."

ᏥᏔᏲᎯᎭ [tsịʔtạyohịha]

ᎤᏔᏲᎸᎢ [uhtạyohlv^{23}ʔi]

ᎠᏔᏲᎯᎰᎢ [ahtạyohịho^{3}ʔi]

ᎯᏔᏲᎭᎦ [hịhtạyohaga]

ᎤᏔᏲᏍᏗ [uhtạyosdi]

ᎥᏝ ᎡᎶᎯ ᏗᏨᏅᏍᏗᏱ ᏯᏥᏔᏲᎯᎭ ...
I do not ask that Thou mayest take them out of the world …
[ᏣᏂ 17:15]

ᎠᏔᏲᏎᎭ [ahtạyọ^{3}seha] (vt) "He is asking him for it."

ᏥᏔᏲᏎᎭ [tsiʔtạyọ^{3}seha]

ᎤᏔᏲᏎᎸᎢ [uhtạyọ^{3}sẹʔlv^{23}ʔi]

ᎠᏔᏲᏎᎰᎢ [ahtạyọ^{3}seho^{3}ʔi]

ᎯᏔᏲᏎᏏ [hiʔtạyọ^{3}sesi]

ᎤᏔᏲᏎᏗ [uhtạyọ^{3}sehdi]

ᎢᏳᏃ ᎩᎶ ᏂᎯ ᎢᏤᎲ ᎠᏕᏙᎥᎯᏍᏗ ᎨᏒ ᎤᏂᎬᎰᏍᏗ, ᎤᏁᎳᏅᎯ ᎠᏔᏲᏎᎮᏍᏗ, …
and if any of you do lack wisdom, let him ask from God, …
[ᏥᎻ 1:5]

ᎠᏕᎭ [ạdeha] (vt) "He is giving it (something long) to him."

ᏥᏕᎠ [tsidẹʔa]

ᎤᏕᎸᎢ [udelv^{23}ʔi]

ᎠᏕᎰᎢ [ạdeho^{3}ʔi]

ᎯᏗ Ꮟ [hidị si]

ᎤᏕᎯ [udehi]

ᎠᏕᎰᏍᎦ [adẹhoh^{3}sga] (vi) "He is ashamed."

ᎦᏕᎣᏍᎦ [gadẹʔoh^{3}sga]

ᎤᏕᎰᏒᎢ [udẹhoh^{3}sv^{23}ʔi]

ᎠᏕᎰᏍᎪᎢ [adẹhoh^{3}sgo^{3}ʔi]

ᎭᏕᎰᎯ [hadẹhọ^{3}hi]

ᎤᏕᎰᎯᏍᏗ [udẹhọ^{3}hịsdi]

ᎠᎴ ᎤᎪᎲᏊ ᎤᎴᏅᎲ ᎠᏕᎰᏍᎬᎢ.
at the sight also of whom he began to blush for shame.
[ᏧᏁᎶᏗ ᏚᏂᎩᏒᏒᎢ]

ᎠᏕᎲᏍᎦ [ạdẹhvh^{3}sga] (vi) "He is being born."

ᎦᏕᎥᏍᎦ [gạdẹʔvh^{3}sga]

ᎤᏕᏅᎢ [udehnv^{23}ʔi]

ᎠᏕᎲᏍᎪᎢ [ạdẹhvh^{3}sgo^{3}ʔi]

ᎭᏕᎲᎦ [hạdẹhv^{3}ga]

ᎤᏕᏗ [udehdi]

… ᎤᎲᎢ ᎠᏍᎦᏂ ᎨᏒ ᏣᏕᏅᎩ ...
… 'In sins thou wast born altogether …
[ᏣᏂ 9:34]

ᎠᏕᎳ [ạdela] (n) "Money."

ᎠᏕᎶᎣᏍᎦ [adelọʔosga] (vt) "He is noticing it."

ᎦᏕᎶᎣᏍᎦ [gadelọʔọʔsga]

ᎤᏕᎶᎣᏒᎢ [udelọʔosv^{23}ʔi]

ᎠᏕᎶᎣᏍᎪᎢ [adelọʔosgo^{3}ʔi]

ᎭᏕᎶᎣᎯ [hadelọʔohi]

ᎤᏕᎶᎣᎯᏍᏗ [udelọʔohịsdi]

… ᎯᎠᏃ ᏄᏪᏒᎩ, Ꮎ, ᎨᏩᏊ, ᎦᏕᎶᎣᏍᎦᏍᎩᏂ ᎠᏂ ᎪᏪᎵ ᏣᏆᎡᏕᎳ.
… He answered, Sir, I perceive by the Book in my hand, that I am condemned to die.
[ᏧᏁᎶᏗ ᏚᏂᎩᏒᏒᎢ]

ᎠᏕᎶᏆᎠ [adehlọ^{3}kwạʔa] (vt) "He is learning."

ᎦᏕᎶᏆᎠ [gadẹʔlọ^{3}kwạʔa]

ᎤᏕᎶᏈᎥᎢ [udehlọ^{3}kwiv^{23}ʔi]

ᎠᏕᎶᏆᏍᎪᎢ [adehlọ^{3}kwạsgo^{3}ʔi]

ᎭᏕᎶᏆ [hadehlọ^{3}kwa]

ᎤᏕᎶᏆᏍᏗ [udehlọ^{3}kwạsdi]

ᎾᏍᎩ ᏂᎪᎯᎸ ᎠᎾᏕᎶᏆᏍᎪᎢ, ᎠᏎᏃ ᎥᏝ ᎢᎸᎯᏳ ᏯᏩᏂᏰᎢᏳᎯᎭ ᏚᏳᎪᏛ ᎠᏕᏙᎥᎯᏍᏗ ᎨᏒᎢ.
always learning, and never to a knowledge of truth able to come,
[ᏔᎵᏁ ᏗᎹᏗ 3:7]

ᎠᏕᎸᎢ [ạdelỵʔhi] (n) "A dollar."

ᎠᏕᏗᏯᏍᏗ [ạdediỵyasdi] (n) "Indian beads."

DSꙅVᎫⱷ

DSꙅVᎫⱷ [adehytohdįha] (vt) "He is bothering someone.; He is being troublesome."

Ꮝ Ꮝ ꙅVᎫⱷ [gadęɂytohdįha]

ᎤꝯSꙅVWOᎢ [udehytotanv²³ɂi]

DSꙅVᎫꙫAᎢ [adehytohdįsgo³ɂi]

ⱷSꙅVᏝ [hadehytohda]

ᎤꝯSꙅVᎫ [udehytohdi]

… iᏞ Db ᏕV ᏇEᏩꙫᎫ ᎤꝯᏟ ᎤꝯꙨᏰꙫᎫ DᏊ ᎤꝯSꙅVᎫ ᏕᏀꙫᎫᏝ ᏇᏕᎩ ᏔꙫᎩ ᎠD Dh ᏢꙫᏒᏩ4ᏉᏋ …
… there is not a more dangerous and _troublesome_ way in the world than is that unto which he hath directed thee …
[ᏪᏁᏟᎫ ᏕhᎩᏒᏒᎢ]

DSꙧꝲⱷ [adehyįha] (vt) "He is denying it."

Ꮝ Ꮝ ꙧꝲⱷ [gadęɂyįha]

ᎤꝯSꙅꙨꝲᎢ [udehyalv²³ɂi]

DSꙧꝲᎥᎢ [adehyįho³ɂi]

ⱷSꙧꝲꝲᏍ [hadehyįga]

ᎤꝯSꙅꙫꙫᎫ [udehyasdi]

DSᏀ꙳ⱷ [adehyoha] (vi) "He is going in a circle."

Ꮝ Ꮝ Ꮥ꙳ⱷ [gadęɂyoha]

ᎤꝯSꙅꙨꝲᎢ [udehyalv²³ɂi]

DSᏀᎥᎢ [adehyoho³ɂi]

ⱷSᏀᎥᏍ [hadehyɂga]

ᎤꝯSꙅꙫꙫᎫ [udehyasdi]

DᏔWSⱷ [atę³ldeha] (vt) "He is joining."

ᏲꙫSWSⱷ [tsiyadɂę³ldeha]

ᎤᏔWSⱷOᎢ [utę³ldehanv²³ɂi]

DᏔWSᎥᎢ [atę³ldeho³ɂi]

ᏂꙫSWSD [hiyadɂę³ldęa]

ᎤᏔWSꙫᎫ [utę³ldęohdi]

DᏔ.ᏝᏢᏀ [ahtelidu] (n) "Plate."

DᏔꙫᏙᏂ [ahte³lyhvsga] (vt) "He is shaking it."

ᏲᏔᏙᏀꙫᏀᏚ [tsiɂte³lyhvsga]

ᎤᏔᏀOᎢ [uhte³lyɂhnv²³ɂi]

DᏔᏙᏀꙫAᎢ [ahte³lyhvsgo³ɂi]

ᎠᏔᏙꙫᏚ [hįhte³lyhvga]

ᎤᏔᏀᎫ [uhte³hldi]

DᏔꙫᎧᏂ [atęsgeni] (n) "Lower back."

ᏲᏔꙫᎧᏂ [tsitęsgeni]

DᏔꙫᎫⱷ [atesdiha] (vt) "He is startling him.; He is frightening him."

ᏂꙫSꙫᎫⱷ [tsiyądɂesdiha]

ᎤᏔꙫWOᎢ [utestanv²³ɂi]

DᏔꙫᎫꙫAᎢ [atesdisgo³ɂi]

ꙮꙫSꙫᎫᏝ [hiyądɂesda]

ᎤᏔꙫVᎫ [utesdohdi]

DᎫD [adįɂa] (vt) "He is saying it."

Ꮝ ᎫD [gadįɂa]

ᎤᏊꙩᎢ [udyɂnv²³ɂi]

DᎫꙫAᎢ [adisgo³ɂi]

ⱷᏝ [hada]

ᎤᎫᎫ [utdi]

ᎤꝯVꙫᏩꙫꙫ, ᎤᏊꙩ ᏪᏁᏟᎫ, iᏞ ꙧhᏒSWⱷ.
Truly, _said_ Christian, I do not know.
[ᏪᏁᏟᎫ ᏕhᎩᏒᏒᎢ]

DᎫD [adįɂa] (vt) "He is laying it (something long) down.; He is placing it (something long) on the ground."

ᏂᎫD [tsidįɂa]

ᎤᏊᎢ [uɂdɂv²³ɂi]

DᎫꙫAᎢ [adisgo³ɂi]

ᎠᏝ [hįda]

ᎤᎫꙫᎫ [udisdi]

DᎫSᏓꙫD [adigaleyaɂa] (vt) "He is scattering from a pile."

Ꮝ ᎫSᏓꙫD [gadigaleyaɂa]

ᎤᎫSᏓꙧ [udigaleyi]

DᎫSᏓꙫꙫAᎢ [adigaleyasgo³ɂi]

ⱷᎫSᏓꙫ [hadigaleya]

ᎤᎫSᏓꙫꙫᎫ [udigaleyasdi]

DᎫED [adi³kyɂa] (vi) "He is urinating."

Ꮝ ᎫED [gadi³kyɂa]

ᎤᎫꙨᎢ [udi³kalv²³ɂi]

DᎫEᎢ [adi³kvho³ɂi]

ⱷᎫᏚ [hadi³ga]

ᎤᎫEꙫᎫ [udi³kvsdi]

DᎫꙫSWꙫᏚ [adisgahlah³sga] (vi) "He is hiding."

Ꮝ ᎫꙫSWꙫᏚ [gadisgahlah³sga]

ᎤᎫꙫSᏀOᎢ [udisgahlv³nv²³ɂi]

DᎫꙫSWꙫAᎢ [adisgahlah³sgo³ɂi]

ⱷᎫꙫSWᏚ [hadisgahla³ga]

ᎤᎫꙫSWᎫ [udisgahldi]

ᎠᏗᏍᏚᏍᎦ [adị^{3}sdusga] (vi) "He is bowing."

ᎦᏗᏍᏚᏍᎦ [gadịsdusga]
ᎤᏗᏍᏚᏅᎢ [udị^{3}sdụnv^{23}ʔi]
ᎠᏗᏍᏚᏍᎪᎢ [adị^{3}sdusgo^{3}ʔi]
ᎭᏗᏍᏚᎦ [hadị^{3}sduga]
ᎤᏗᏍᏗ [udị^{3}sdi]

ᎠᏗᏏᏯ [ạdʔsiya] (vt) "He is leaving it (something long)."

ᏥᏗᏏᏯ [tsịdʔsiya]
ᎤᏗᏏᏴᎢ [udʔsiyv^{23}ʔi]
ᎠᏗᏏᏱᏍᎪᎢ [ạdʔsiyisgo^{3}ʔi]
ᎯᏗᏏᏱ [hịdʔsiyi]
ᎤᏗᏏᏱᏗ [udʔsiyhdi]

ᎠᏗᏔᏍᎦ [adị^{3}tasga] (vt) "He is drinking."

ᎦᏗᏔᏍᎦ [gaditasga]
ᎤᏗᏔᎲᎢ [udị^{3}tahv^{23}ʔi]
ᎠᏗᏔᏍᎪᎢ [adị^{3}tasgo^{3}ʔi]
ᎭᏗᏔ [hadị^{3}ta]
ᎤᏗᏔᏍᏗ [udị^{3}tasdi]

ᎯᎠᏃ ᏄᏪᏎᎢ, ᎭᏗᏔ ᏣᎬᏫᏳᎯ ᎠᏆᏤᎵᎦ; …
and she saith, 'Drink, my lord;' …
[ᎼᏏ ᎢᎬᏱᏱ 24:18]

ᎠᏗᏗᎠ [adidịʔa] (vi) "He is arising from lying."

ᎦᏗᏗᎠ [gadidịʔa]
ᎤᏗᏛᎥᎢ [udidvʔv^{23}ʔi]
ᎠᏗᏗᏍᎪᎢ [adidisgo^{3}ʔi]
ᎭᏗᏓ [hadida]
ᎤᏗᏘᏗ [uditdi]

ᎠᏗᏙᏗ [ạdịtohdi] (n) "Spoon."

ᎠᏗᏫᏍᎦ [adi-whsga] (vi) "It is healing up.; It is getting well."

—

ᎤᏗᏫᏒᎢ [udi-whsv^{23}ʔi]
ᎠᏗᏫᏍᎪᎢ [adi-whsgo^{3}ʔi]
ᏩᏗᏫ [wadi-whi]
ᎤᏗᏫᏍᏗ [udi-whsdi]

ᎠᏘᏂ [ahtihni] (vt) "He is taking someone along."

ᏥᏘᏂ [tsiʔtihni]
ᎤᏘᏁᏒᎢ [uhtihnẹsv^{23}ʔi]
ᎠᏘᏂᏐᎢ [ahtihniso^{3}ʔi]
ᎯᏘᏄᎦ [hihtihnuʔga]
ᎤᏘᏅᏍᏗ [uhtihnṿsdi]

ᎤᎩᏨᏛᏃ ᏧᎾᎩᎸᏗ ᎤᎾᏘᏅᏍᏗ ᏄᏅᏁᎸ, ᎠᏂᏯᏫᏍᎩ ᎤᎾᏨᏒᎩ, ᏗᏐᏴ ᏭᏂᏣᏒᎩ.
and on the morrow, having suffered the horsemen to go on with him, they returned to the castle;
[ᎨᏥᏅᏏᏛ ᏄᎾᏛᏁᎵᏙᎸᎢ 23:32]

ᎠᏘᏍᎩ [ạtisgi] (n) "His right.; Right-handedness."

ᏥᏘᏍᎩ [tsịtisgi]

ᎠᏘᏲᎯᎭ [atịyọ^{3}hịha] (vi) "He is arguing."

ᎦᏗᏲᎯᎭ [gadʔịyọ^{3}hịha]
ᎤᏘᏲᎸᎢ [utịyọ^{3}hlv^{23}ʔi]
ᎠᏘᏲᎯᎰᎢ [atịyọ^{3}hịho^{3}ʔi]
ᎭᏘᏲᎭᎦ [hatịyọ^{3}haga]
ᎤᏘᏲᏍᏗ [utịyoh^{3}sdi]

… ᏞᏍᏗᏉ ᎩᎾᏘᏲᎸᎩ ᎠᏴ, ᎠᎴ ᎦᎾᏝᎢ ᏗᎨᎩᏂᎦᏘᎦᎯ ᏞᏍᏗ ᎤᎾᏘᏲᎸᎩ; ᏗᎾᏓᏅᏟᏉᏰᏃ.
… 'Let there not, I pray thee, be strife between me and thee, and between my shepherds and thy shepherds, for we [are] men – brethren.
[ᎼᏏ ᎢᎬᏱᏱ 13:8]

ᎠᏙᎣᎸᏍᏙᏗ [ahdọʔolṿsdohdi] (n) "Saucer."

ᎠᏙᎥᏅᏗᎭ [adoʔvhndịha] (vt) "He is dropping it (something alive).; He is dropping it (something flexible)."

ᏥᏯᏙᎥᏅᏗᎭ, ᎦᏙᎥᏅᏗᎭ [tsiyadoʔvʔndịha, gadoʔvʔndịha]
ᎤᏙᎥᏅᏓᏅᎢ [udoʔvhndạnv^{23}ʔi]
ᎠᏙᎥᏅᏓᏍᎪᎢ [adoʔvhntsgo^{3}ʔi]
ᎯᏯᏙᎥᏅᏓ, ᎭᏙᎥᏅᏓ [hiyadoʔvhnda, hadoʔvhnda]
ᎤᏙᎥᏅᏙᏗ [udoʔvhndohdi]

ᎠᏙᎯᎠ [ạtohị^{3}ʔa] (vi) "He is yelling.; He is shouting.; He is hollering."

ᎦᏙᎯᎠ [gatohị^{3}ʔa]
ᎤᏙᎯᏒᎢ [utohị^{3}sv^{23}ʔi]
ᎠᏙᎯᏍᎪᎢ [ạtohị^{3}sgo^{3}ʔi]
ᎭᏙᎯ [hạtohị]
ᎤᏙᎯᏍᏗ [utohị^{3}sdi]

ᎠᏙᎳᏅᏍᏗ [ạdolạnṿsdi] (n) “Walking stick.; Walking cane.”

… ᎠᎴ ᎯᎠ ᏄᏪᏎᎢ, ᎭᏙᎴᎰᎯ, ᎦᎪ ᏧᏤᎵᎦ ᎯᎠ, ᎠᎵᏰᏨᏍᏚᏬ ᎠᎰᎥᏍᏙᏗ, ᎠᎴ ᎪᏄᏌᏛᏗ, ᎠᎴ ᎠᏙᎳᏅᏍᏗ.
… and she saith, ’Discern, I pray thee, whose [are] these – the seal, and the ribbons, and the staff.’
[ᎼᏏ ᎢᎬᏱᏱ 38:25]

ᎠᏙᎴᏘᎠ [adohlẹkwịʔa] (vt) “He is learning.”

ᎦᏙᎴᏘᎠ [gadọʔlẹkwịʔa]
ᎤᏙᎴᏋᎢ [udohlẹkwv²³ʔi]
ᎠᏙᎴᏆᏍᎪᎢ [adohlẹkwạsgo³ʔi]
ᎭᏙᎴᏆ [hadohlẹkwa]
ᎤᏙᎴᏆᏍᏗ [udohlẹkwạsdi]

“ᎢᏣᏙᎴᏆᏍᎨᏍᏗ ᏗᏓᏅᏬ ᏅᏬᏗ …
“You should be learning doctoring medicine …
[King pg 122]

ᎠᏙᎵᏍᎦ [ạtohlsga] (vt) “He is borrowing it.”

ᎦᏙᎵᏍᎦ [gatohlsga]
ᎤᏙᎵᏒᎢ [utohlsv²³ʔi]
ᎠᏙᎵᏍᎪᎢ [ạtohlsgo³ʔi]
ᎭᏙᎵ [hạtoli]
ᎤᏙᎵᏍᏗ [utohlsdi]

ᎠᏙᏌᏗᎠ [ạtosạ³dịʔa] (vt) “He is hanging it (something long) up.”

ᎦᏙᏌᏗᎠ [gatosạ³dịʔa]
ᎤᏙᏌᏛᎢ [utosạ³dʔv²³ʔi]
ᎠᏙᏌᏗᏍᎪᎢ [ạtosạ³disgo³ʔi]
ᎭᏙᏌᏓ [hạtosạ³da]
ᎤᏙᏌᏗᏍᏗ [utosạ³disdi]

ᎠᏙᏏᏏᎭ [ạtosisịha] (vt) “He is taking it (something long) down.”

ᎦᏙᏏᏏᎭ [gatosisịha]
ᎤᏙᏏᎥᎢ [utosiv²³ʔi]
ᎠᏙᏏᏏᏍᎪᎢ [ạtosisịsgo³ʔi]
ᎭᏙᏏᎠ [hạtosịa]
ᎤᏙᏏᏍᏗ [utosisdi]

ᎠᏙᏒᎥᏍᎦ [ado³svʔvsga] (vt) “He is covering it.”

ᎦᏙᏒᎥᏍᎦ [gado³svʔvʔsga]
ᎤᏙᏒᏅᎢ [udo³svʔnv²³ʔi]
ᎠᏙᏒᎥᏍᎪᎢ [ado³svʔvsgo³ʔi]
ᎭᏙᏒᎥᎦ [hado³svʔvga]
ᎤᏙᏒᏗ [udo³svʔdi]

ᎠᏙᏥᏗᎭ [ado³tsdịha] (vt) “He is ridiculing him.; He is making fun of him.”

ᏥᏯᏙᏥᏍᏗᎭ [tsiyado³dʔsdịha]
ᎤᏙᏥᏔᏅᎢ [udo³tstạnv²³ʔi]
ᎠᏙᏥᏗᏍᎪᎢ [ado³tsdịsgo³ʔi]
ᎯᏯᏙᏥᏍᏓ [hiyado³dʔsda]
ᎤᏙᏦᏗ [udo³tsohdi]

ᎠᏙᏪᎳᎩᎠ [ạdọwelagịʔa] (vi) “It is burning.”

—

ᎤᏙᏪᎳᎩᎥᎢ [udọwelagiv²³ʔi]
ᎠᏙᏪᎳᎩᏍᎪᎢ [ạdọwelagịsgo³ʔi]
ᏩᏙᏪᎳᎦ [wạdọwelaga]
ᎤᏙᏪᎳᎩᏍᏗ [udọwelagịsdi]

ᎠᏚᎯᏂᏙᎭ [adụhịnịdoha] (vi) “He is wading.”

ᎦᏚᎢᏂᏙᎭ [gadụʔịnịdoha]
ᎤᏚᎯᏂᏙᎸᎢ [udụhịnịdọʔlv²³ʔi]
ᎠᏚᎯᏂᏙᎰᎢ [adụhịnịdoho³ʔi]
ᎭᏚᎯᏂᏓ [hadụhịnịda]
ᎤᏚᎯᏂᏓᏍᏗ [udụhịnịdạsdi]

ᎠᏚᎯᏍᏗᎭ [ạdụhịsdịha] (vt) “He is blaming him.”

ᏥᏯᏚᎢᏍᏗᎭ [tsiyạdụʔịsdịha]
ᎤᏚᎯᏍᏔᏅᎢ [udụhịstạnv²³ʔi]
ᎠᏚᎯᏍᏗᏍᎪᎢ [ạdụhịsdịsgo³ʔi]
ᎯᏯᏚᎢᏍᏓ [hiyạdụʔịsda]
ᎤᏚᎯᏍᏙᏗ [udụhịsdohdi]

ᎠᏛᎩᎠ [ạtvgịʔa] (vt) “He is hearing it.”

ᎦᏛᎩᎠ [gatvgịʔa]
ᎤᏛᎦᏅᎢ [utvgạʔnv²³ʔi]
ᎠᏛᎩᏍᎪᎢ [ạtvgịsgo³ʔi]
ᎭᏛᎦᎦ [hạtvgaga]
ᎤᏛᎪᏗ [utvgodi]

ᎴᎹᏱ ᎧᏁᎬ ᎤᎾᏛᎦᏅᎩ …
‘A voice in Ramah was heard …
[ᎹᏚ 2:18]

ᎠᏛᎯᏍᏗᎭ [atvhị³sdịha] (vi) “He is rearing up.; He is raising.”

ᎦᏛᎯᏍᏗᎭ [gadʔvhị³sdịha]
ᎤᏛᎯᏍᏓᏅᎢ [utvhị³sdạnv²³ʔi]
ᎠᏛᎯᏍᏗᏍᎪᎢ [atvhị³sdịsgo³ʔi]
ᎭᏛᎯᏍᏓ [hatvhị³sda]
ᎤᏛᎯᏍᏙᏗ [utvhị³sdohdi]

DꞬꞋWꞋ [advlagʔa] (vi) "He is breaking his bone.; He is spraining his ankle."

ꞱꞬꞋWꞋ [gadvlagʔa]

OꞋꞬꞋWꞱRT [udvlaksv²³ʔi]

DꞬꞋWꞱꚙꞞAT [advlaksgo³ʔi]

ꝏꞱꞬꞋWꞋ [hadvlaga]

OꞋꞬꞋWꞱꚙꝆ [udvlaksdi]

DꞬꞋꝆꞋꞎ [advliha] (vi) "He is breathing."

ꞱꞬꞋꝆD [gadvliʔa]

OꞋꞬꞋꞆiT [udvlyʔv²³ʔi]

DꞬꞋꝆꚙAT [advlisgo³ʔi]

ꝏꞱꞬꞋꝆ [hadvli]

OꞋꞬꞋꝆꝆ [udvhldi]

DꞬꞋꞐꝆꞋꞎ [advnęliha] (vi) "He is acting up."

ꞱꞬꞋꞐꝆD [gadvnęliʔa]

OꞋꞬꞋꞐWRT [udvnęlasv²³ʔi]

DꞬꞋꞐꝆꚙAT [advnęlisgo³ʔi]

ꝏꞱꞬꞋꞐWꞋ [hadvnęlaga]

OꞋꞬꞋꞐWꝆ [udvnęladi]

DꞬꞋꞐꝆꞋꞎ

DꞬꞋꞐꝆꞋꞎ [advneliha] (vi) "He is acting."

ꞱꞬꞋꞐꝆD [gadvneliʔa]

OꞋꞬꞋꞐꞋOꞋT [udvnelyʔnv²³ʔi]

DꞬꞋꞐꝆꚙAT [advnelisgo³ʔi]

ꝏꞱꞬꞋꞐW [hadvnela]

OꞋꞬꞋꞐꝆꝆ [udvnehldi]

DꞬꞋꞐꝆꚙꝌ [advnelisgi] (n) "Actor."

DꞬꞋhꝆD [advhnidiʔa] (vi) "He is coming back to life."

ꞱꞬꞋhꝆD [gadvʔnidiʔa]

OꞋꞬꞋhꞬꞋT [udvhnidv²³ʔi]

DꞬꞋhꝆꚙAT [advhnidisgo³ʔi]

ꝏꞱꞬꞋhꞱ [hadvhnida]

OꞋꞬꞋhꝆꚙꝆ [udvhnidisdi]

… DꚙSh OꞋꞬꞋhꞬꞋꝌ, DBZ DꞋꝊꞐꞀꝆRꝌ.
… the sin revived, and I died;
[GH 7:9]

DꞬꞋOꞋTꚙꝆꞎ [advnvʔisdįha] (vi) "He is getting ready."

ꞱꞬꞋOꞋTꚙꝆꞎ [gadvnvʔįʔsdįha]

OꞋꞬꞋOꞋTꚙꞦOꞋT [udvnvʔisdąnv²³ʔi]

DꞬꞋOꞋTꚙꝆꚙAT [advnvʔisdįsgo³ʔi]

ꝏꞱꞬꞋOꞋTꚙꞦ [hadvnvʔisda]

OꞋꞬꞋOꞋTꚙꞦꝆ [udvnvʔisdohdi]

… ꝆꚙOꞋR WꞱꞟꞱ ꞞD DhꚙꞱꚙ, Dꝏ ꞫMꞱ Dꝏ
ꝏꞱꞬꞋOꞋTꚙꞦ …
… 'Bring the men into the house, and slaughter an
animal, and make ready …
[ꞀꞴ TEꚙꚙ]

DꞬꞋꚙꞞꞱ [atvsga] (vi) "He is growing."

ꞱꞬꞋꚙꞞꞱ [gadʔvsga]

OꞋꞬꞋRT [utvsv²³ʔi]

DꞬꞋꚙAT [atvsgo³ʔi]

ꝏꞱꞬꞋꞞ [hatvhi]

OꞋꞬꞋꞞꚙꝆ [utvhisdi]

DꞬꞋꚙꞦꞬꞞD [adysgwaloʔa] (vi) "It is cracking."

———

OꞋꞬꞋꚙꞦꞬꞞiT [udysgwaloʔv²³ʔi]

DꞬꞋꚙꞦꞬꞞꚙAT [adysgwalosgo³ʔi]

ꞬꞋꚙꞦꞱW [wadysgwala]

OꞋꞬꞋꚙꞦꞬꞞꚙꝆ [udysgwalosdi]

DꞬꞋꞀꞨ [advdaʔna] (n) "Brick."

DꞬꞋꞦꞱꝆꞎ [atvdasdįha] (vt) "He is listening."

ꞱꞬꞋꞦꞱꝆꞎ [gadʔvdasdįha]

OꞋꞬꞋꞦꞱꞦOꞋT [utvdasdąnv²³ʔi]

DꞬꞋꞦꞱꝆꚙAT [atvdasdįsgo³ʔi]

ꝏꞱꞬꞋꞦꞱꞦ [hatvdasda]

OꞋꞬꞋꞦꞱꞦꝆ [utvdasdohdi]

ꞞDZ hꞱꚙꝏꞬꞋT; Ꞟ, TꞬꞋꞦꞱꞦ ꞞD ꞨꚙꝌ DꞌꚙꝌꞱRT.
And he saith unto them, 'Hear ye, I pray you, this
dream which I have dreamed:
[ꞀꞴ TEꚙꚙ 37:6]

DꞬꞋVꞬ [advtǫwa] (n) "Moth.; biol. All Varieties."

DꞬ DꝌꚙVꚙꝆ [atsa ągisdosdi] (n) "Chewing gum."

DꞬꞱꚙꞱ [ahtsa³ksga] (vt) "He is clearing a path.; He is cutting weeds.; He is mowing."

ꞀrꞬꞱꚙꞱ [tsiʔtsa³ksga]

OꞋꞬꞱRT [uhtsa³ksv²³ʔi]

DꞬꞱꞱꚙAT [ahtsa³ksgo³ʔi]

ꞞꞬꞱ [hihtsa³ga]

OꞋꞬꞱꚙꝆ [uhtsa³ksdi]

DꞬꞬꞞ [atsahi] (n) "Rubber, pitch, gum."

ᎠᏣᏄᎵᏗᎠ [ạtsạnu³ldịʔa] (vt) "He is speeding it up."

ᏥᏣᏄᎵᏗᎠ [tsịtsạnu³ldịʔa]

ᎤᏣᏄᎵᏛᎢ [utsạnu³ldv²³ʔi]

ᎠᏣᏄᎵᏗᏍᎪᎢ [ạtsạnu³ldịsgo³ʔi]

ᎯᏣᏄᎵᏓ [hịtsạnu³lda]

ᎤᏣᏄᎵᏗᏍᏗ [utsạnu³ldịsdi]

ᎠᏣᏗ [ạtsạdi] (n) "Fish.; biol. *All Varieties.*"

… ᎾᏍᎩᏃ ᎤᏂᎬᏫᏳᎯ ᎰᏎᏍᏗ ᎠᏣᏗ ᎠᎺᏉᎯ ᎠᏁᎲᎢ …
… and let them rule over fish of the sea …
[ᎼᏏ ᎢᎬᏱᏱ 1:26]

ᎠᏣᏗ ᎠᏂᏆᏔ [ạtsadị ạnigwata] (n) "Yellow fringed orchid.; biol. *Platanthera ciliaris.*"

ᎠᏣ ᏗᏓᎾᎩᏍᎩ [atsạ didạnạgisgi] (n) "Elastic."

ᎠᏣᏯᎩᎠ [atsạʔyạkiʔa] (vi) "He is kicking up his leg."

ᎦᏣᏯᎩᎠ [gatsạʔyạkiʔa]

ᎤᏣᏯᎩᏒᎢ [utsạʔyạkisv²³ʔi]

ᎠᏣᏯᎩᏍᎪᎢ [atsạʔyạkisgo³ʔi]

ᎭᏣᏯᎩ [hatsạʔyạki]

ᎤᏣᏯᎩᏍᏗ [utsạʔyạkisdi]

ᎠᏣᏲᎵᎭ [ạtsạyọ³hlịha] (vt) "He is sticking it.; He is pricking it."

ᏥᏣᏲᎵᎭ [tsịtsạyọ³lʔịha]

ᎤᏣᏲᎸᎢ [utsạyọ³hlv²³ʔi]

ᎠᏣᏲᎵᎰᎢ [ạtsạyọ³hlịho³ʔi]

ᎯᏣᏲᎭᎦ [hịtsạyọ³haga]

ᎤᏣᏲᏍᏗ [utsạyọ³sdi]

ᎠᏤ ᎤᎾᏕᏘᏱᏍᎬᎢ [ạtse ụnạdetịyịsgvʔi] (n) "New year."

ᎠᏤᎯ [ạtsehi] (n) "New.; Green (of plants)."

ᎠᏤ ᏅᏙ [ạtse nvdo] (n) "New moon."

ᎠᏤᏌᏙ [ạtsesạdo] (n) "Apron."

ᎠᏤᏍᏙ [ạtsẹsdo] (n) "Mattress."

ᎬᏲᏎᎭ, ᏔᎴᎲᎦ, ᎠᎴ ᎯᎾᎩ ᏣᏤᏍᏙ, ᎠᎴ ᏗᏤᏅᏒ ᏫᏣᎯ.
I say to thee, Rise, and take up thy couch, and go away to thy house;'
[ᎹᎦ 2:4]

ᎠᏤᏓ [ahtsehd] (n) "Smooth alder.; Hazel alder.; biol. *Alnus serrulata.*"

ᎠᏤᏤᎭ [ạtse³cheha] (vt) "He is taking revenge on him."

ᏥᏯᏤᏤᎭ [tsiyạtse³dsʔeha]

ᎤᏤᏤᎸᎢ [utse³chẹʔlv²³ʔi]

ᎠᏤᏤᎰᎢ [ạtse³cheho³ʔi]

ᎯᏯᏤᏥᏏ [hiyạtse³dsʔịsi]

ᎤᏤᏤᏗ [utse³chehdi]

ᎠᏥᎠ [ạtsị³ʔa] (vt) "He is putting it (a liquid) into a container."

ᏥᏥᎠ [tsịtsị³ʔa]

ᎤᏥᏅᎢ [udsʔnv²³ʔi]

ᎠᏥᏍᎪᎢ [ạtsih³sgo³ʔi]

ᎯᏣ [hịtsa]

ᎤᏥᏍᏗ [utsisdi]

ᎠᏥᎠ [ạtsịʔa] (vt) "He is putting liquid into a liquid."

ᏥᏥᎠ [tsịtsịʔa]

ᎤᏨᎢ [utsv²³ʔi]

ᎠᏥᏍᎪᎢ [ạtsisgo³ʔi]

ᎯᏣ [hịtsa]

ᎤᏥᏍᏗ [utsisdi]

ᎠᏥᎪᎥᏍᎦ [atsgọʔvsga] (vi) "He is lying.; He is bearing false witness."

ᎦᏥᏍᎪᎥᏍᎦ [gadsiʔsgọʔvsga]

ᎤᏥᎪᏅᎢ [utsgọʔnv²³ʔi]

ᎠᏥᎪᎥᏍᎪᎢ [atsgọʔvsgo³ʔi]

ᎭᏥᎪᎥᎦ [hatsgọʔvga]

ᎤᏥᎪᏗ [utsgodi]

ᎠᏥᎳ [atsila] (n) "Mustard."

ᎠᏥᎳ [ạtsila] (n) "Fire."

ᎠᏥᎳᏃ ᎬᏗ ᏧᎳᏍᎩ ᎬᏂᏍᎦ ᎠᎵᏍᏓᏴᏗ.
The food is cooking in the pot in the fire.
[King pg 114]

ᎠᏥᎳᎯ [ạtsilahi] (n) "A fireplace."

ᎠᏥᎳ ᏓᏆᎴᎷ [ạtsilạ dạgwạlelu] (n) "A railroad train."

ᎠᏥᎳᏙᎣᏍᎦ [ạtsilạdọʔosga] (vi) "A corn tassel is falling off.; A flowers is falling off."

—

ᎤᏥᎳᏙᎣᏒᎢ [utsilạdọʔosv²³ʔi]

ᎠᏥᎳᏙᎣᏍᎪᎢ [ạtsilạdọʔosgo³ʔi]

ᏩᏥᎳᏙᎣᎯ [wạtsilạdọʔohi]

ᎤᏥᎳᏙᎣᎯᏍᏗ [utsilạdọʔohịsdi]

ᎠᏥᎳᏳᏗ [ạtsilayuhldi] (n) "Fireside."

ᎠᏥᎶᎠ [atsihlọ³a] (vt) "He is measuring it."

ᎦᏥᎶᎠ [gatsịʔlọ³a]

ᎤᏥᎶᎥᎢ [utsihlọʔv²³ʔi]

ᎠᏥᎶᏍᎪᎢ [atsihlọsgo³ʔi]

ᎭᏥᎶᏣ [hatsihlọtsa]

ᎤᏥᎶᏍᏗ [utsihlosdi]

ᎠᏥᎶᏍᏗ [ạtsịlosdi] (n) "Yardstick.; Ruler."

ᎠᏥᎸᏍᎩ [ạtsịlvsgi] (n) "A flower."

ᎠᏥᏂ [atsini] (n) "Cedar."

DⱠⱨⱺꝂⱢꞵ [a̱tsi³sdahlasga] (vt) "He is igniting it."

    ⱠⱨⱺꝂⱢꞵ [tsi̱tsi³sdạʔlasga]

    OꞋⱨⱺꝂⱢO·T [utsi³sdahlạnv²³ʔi]

    DⱠⱺꝂⱢⱺAT [a̱tsi³sdahlasgo³ʔi]

    ӘⱠⱺꝂꞵ [hi̱tsi³sdahlaga]

    OꞋⱨⱺꝀꝆꝆ [utsi³sdahldi]

DⱠⱺꝂꝆꞵ [atsi³sdahlga] (vi) "It is catching fire."

———

    OꞋⱨⱺꝂꝆꝀ̈·T [utsi³sdahltsv²³ʔi]

    DⱨⱺꝂꝆAT [atsi³sdahlgo³ʔi]

    ꞬⱨⱺꝂꝆY [watsi³sdahlgi]

    OꞋⱨⱺꝂꝆꝆ [utsi³sdahldi]

DⱠⱺꝆVꝆ

DⱠⱺVꝆ [a̱tsi̱³sdohdi] (n) "Container for it (a liquid)."

DⱨSiⱺꞵ [a̱tstuʔvsga] (vt) "He is flirting with her."

    ⱠⱳⱨSiⱺꞵ [tsiyạdsʔtuʔvsga]

    OꞋⱨSO·T [utstuʔnv²³ʔi]

    DⱨSiⱺAT [a̱tstuʔvsgo³ʔi]

    ӘⱳⱨSiꞵ [hiyạdsʔtuʔvga]

    OꞋⱨSꝆ [utstuʔdi]

DⱨꝲⱭꝳꝴ [adsyo³hyi̱ha] (vi) "He is weeping."

    ꞵⱠꝲⱭꝳꝴ [gadsyọʔyi̱ha]

    OꞋⱨꝲⱭꝲT [udsyo³hyi̱lv²³ʔi]

    DⱨꝲⱭꝳFT [adsyo³hyi̱ho³ʔi]

    ꝴⱨꝲⱭꞵ [hadsyo³hyga]

    OꞋⱨꝲⱭꝲⱺꝆ [udsyo³hysdi]

DKiⱺꝆⱴ [a̱tsoʔvsdi̱ha] (vt) "He is running over him."

    ⱠKiⱺꝆⱴ [tsitsoʔγʔsdi̱ha]

    OꞋKiⱺWO·T [utsoʔvstạnv²³ʔi]

    DKiⱺꝆⱺAT [a̱tsoʔvsdi̱sgo³ʔi]

    ӘKiⱺꝂ [hitsoʔvsda]

    OꞋKiⱺVꝆ [utsoʔvsdohdi]

DKꝋⱴ [atsoteha] (vt) "He is blowing on him."

    ⱠⱳKꞵⱴ [tsiyatsodʔeha]

    OꞋKꝋiT [utsotẹʔhv²³ʔi]

    DKꝋFT [atsoteho³ʔi]

    ӘⱳKꝂ [hiyatsodʔa]

    OꞋKꝋꝆ [utsotehdi]

DKꝋꝳⱴ [atsohyi̱ha] (vi) "He is crying.; He is weeping."

    ꞵKꝋꝳⱴ [gatsọʔyi̱ha]

    OꞋKꝋꝲT [utsohyi̱lv²³ʔi]

    DKꝋꝳFT [atsohyi̱ho³ʔi]

    ꝴKꝋꝲꞵ [hatsohyga]

    OꞋKꝋꝲⱺꝆ [utsohyi̱³sdi]

DKBT [atsohyvʔi] (n) "Fence."

DꝵⱭⱺꞵ [ahchu̱³hvsga] (vi) "He is fishing."

    ꞵꝵⱭⱺꞵ [gachu̱³hvsga]

    OꞋꝵO·T [uhchu̱³hnv²³ʔi]

    DꝵⱭⱺAT [ahchu̱³hvsgo³ʔi]

    ꝴꝵⱭꞵ [hahchu̱³hvga]

    OꞋꝵꝆ [uhchu̱³hdi]

DꝵꝆ [a̱tsu³di] (n) "Fish hook."

DꝵG [a̱chutsa] (n) "A boy."

    ⱠꝵG [tsi̱chutsa]

    ꝆⱠӘ DꝵG Yꝲ.
    The <u>boy</u> is chasing the dogs.
    [King pg 110]

DCⱴD [atsvʔa] (vi) "He is going to the bathroom."

    ꞵCⱴD [gatsvʔa]

    OꞋCⱴRT [utsvsv²³ʔi]

    DCⱴⱺAT [atsvsgo³ʔi]

    ꝴꝵꞵ [hatsuga]

    OꞋCⱴⱺꝆ [utsvsdi]

DCⱴiⱺꞵ [atsγʔvsga] (vt) "He is pouring it."

    ⱠCⱴiⱺꞵ [tsitsγʔγʔsga]

    OꞋCⱴiiT [uʔtsγʔγʔv²³ʔi]

    DCⱴiⱺAT [atsγʔvsgo³ʔi]

    ӘCⱴiD [hitsγʔva]

    OꞋCⱴiTⱺꝆ [uʔtsγʔγʔisdi]

DCⱴiⱺꞵ [a̱tsv³ʔvsga] (vt) "He is pouring it out.; He is spilling it (a liquid)."

    ⱠCⱴiⱺꞵ [tsitsv³ʔγʔsga]

    OꞋCⱴO·T [utsv³ʔnv²³ʔi]

    DCⱴiⱺAT [a̱tsv³ʔvsgo³ʔi]

    ӘCⱴiꞵ [hi̱tsv³ʔvga]

    OꞋCⱴꝆ [utsv³ʔdi]

DCⱴY TⱭFR.Ә [ahtsvgi̱ i̱nạgeḛhi] (n) "Spotted wintergreen.; Striped wintergreen. Wintergreen.; Rheumatism root.; biol. *Chimaphila maculata*."

DCⱴY OꞋꞵⱭⱺꝂ [atsvgi̱ u̱ganasd] (n) "Sweet birch."

ᎠᏣᏦᎧᎦᏍ [atsy³k-whsga] (vi) "He is boasting.; He is bragging."

ᎦᏦᎧᏍ [gatsvg-whsga]

ᎤᏣᏦᎡᎡᎢ [utsy³k-whsv²³ʔi]

ᎠᏣᏦᎧᎦᎥᎢ [atsy³k-whsgo³ʔi]

ᎰᏣᏦᎧ [hatsy³k-whi]

ᎤᏣᏦᎧᎦᎠ [utsy³k-whsdi]

ᎠᏣᏒᏪᎧᏍ [atsvstasga] (vt) "He is turning on a light."

ᏥᏣᏒᏍᏘᎧᏍ [tsitsvsdʔasga]

ᎤᏣᏒᏪᎤᎢ [utsvstanv²³ʔi]

ᎠᏣᏒᏪᎧᎦᎢ [atsvstasgo³ʔi]

ᎯᏣᏒᏪᎦ [hitsvstaga]

ᎤᏣᏒᎥᎠ [utsvstdi]

ᎠᏣᏒᎥᎠ [atsvstdi] (n) "Light.; Flashlight.; Matches.; Lamp."

ᎥᎵ ᎠᏜ Ꮓ ᏗᎯᏣᏒᏍ ᎠᏣᏒᎥᎠ ᎠᏣᎶᎥᎠ ᎦᏊᏣᎦᎢ
…
nor do they light a lamp, and put it under the measure
…
[ᎷᎩ 5:15]

ᎠᏣᏎᏏᏤᏓ [atsvsiyeʔa] (vi) "He is pacing back and forth."

ᎦᏣᏎᏏᏤᏓ [gatsvsiyeʔa]

ᎤᏣᏎᏏᏥᎢᎢ [utsvsiyeʔv²³ʔi]

ᎠᏣᏎᏏᏤᎦᎢ [atsvsiyesgo³ʔi]

ᎰᏣᏎᏏᎧ [hatsvsiya]

ᎤᏣᏎᏏᏤᎠ [utsvsiyeʔdi]

ᎠᏣᎥᎯᎧ [atsvdiya] (n) "Minnow."

ᎠᏣᏴᏪᎠᎥᎢ [atsywasdiha] (vt) "He is wringing it."

ᏥᏣᏴᏪᎠᎥᎢ [tsitsywaʔsdiha]

ᎤᏣᏴᏪᏪᎤᎢ [utsywastanv²³ʔi]

ᎠᏣᏴᏪᎠᎥᎧᎢ [atsywasdisgo³ʔi]

ᎰᏣᏴᏪᎥ [hitsywasda]

ᎤᏣᏴᏪᎥᎠ [utsywasdohdi]

ᎠᏣᏴᎢ [atsyvaʔi] (n) "Rooster."

ᎠᏣᏴ ᎤᏍᎪᎥᎠ [atsyya utsonydi] (n) "Timber rattlesnake, male.; biol. *Crotalus horridus.*"

ᎠᏩ ᎤᏍᏫᎾ [ahwa utana] (n) "Elk.; biol. *Cervus canadensis.*"

ᎠᏩᏂᎦᎳ [awanigala] (adj) "Weak."

… ᎤᏣᏒᎦᏃ ᏃᏪᏫ ᏏᎵᏎᎧᏫᏯ ᎠᏩᏂᎦᎳ ᎢᎡᎢ.
… since himself also is compassed with infirmity;
[ᎠᏏᎹᎻ 5:2]

ᎠᏩᏒᎤᎩᏍ [awhsyhasga] (vt) "He is whistling."

ᏥᏩᏒᎤᎩᏍ [tsiwʔsyhasga]

ᎤᏩᏩᏒᎤᎦᎢ [uwawsyhahv²³ʔi]

ᎠᏩᏒᎤᎧᎦᎢ [awhsyhasgo³ʔi]

ᎭᏩᏒᎤᎧ [hiwhsyhahi]

ᎤᏩᏩᏒᎤᎧᎠ [uwawsyhasdi]

ᎠᏩᏗᎧ [ahwa³tiha] (vt) "He is finding it (a solid)."

ᏥᏣᏗᎧ [tsiʔwa³tiha]

ᎤᏩᎢᏫᎢ [uhwa³tyhv²³ʔi]

ᎠᏩᏗᎧᎦᎢ [ahwa³tisgo³ʔi]

ᎭᏩᏪ [hihwa³ta]

ᎤᏩᎢᎠ [uhwa³tvhdi]

… ᏔᏴ ᎦᎢ ᎦᏎᏨ ᏥᎻᎬᏳ ᎠᏯᎯᏍᏳ ᎤᎵᏪᎤᎠ ᎠᎠ ᎾᎧᏯ ᎡᏏᏪᎢᎦᎠ ᏪᎡᎢ, ᎠᏪ ᎥᎵ ᎥᏥᏣᎠᏗ; ᎠᏅᎰᎵ; ᏍᎥᏃ ᎢᎤᏆᎠ ᏍᎥᎠ?
… three years I come seeking fruit in this fig-tree, and do not find, cut it off, why also the ground doth it render useless?
[ᎷᎩ 13:7]

ᎠᏩᎢᎠ [ahwatvhi] (vt) "He is going to go visit someone."

ᏥᏣᎢᎠ [tsiʔwatvhi]

ᎤᏩᎢᎡᎢ [uhwatvhesv²³ʔi]

ᎠᏩᎢᎠᎢᎢ [ahwatvhiso³ʔi]

ᎭᏩᎢᎡᏍ [hihwatvhuga]

ᎤᏩᎢᏫᎠᎠ [uhwatvhysdi]

ᎠᏩᎢᎠᎥᎤ [ahwatvhidoha] (vi) "He is visiting."

ᏥᏣᎢᎠᎥᎤ [tsiʔwatvhidoha]

ᎤᏩᎢᎠᎥᎤᎢ [uhwatvhidoʔlv²³ʔi]

ᎠᏩᎢᎠᎥᎢᎢ [ahwatvhidoho³ʔi]

ᎭᏩᎢᎠᎥᎠ [hihwatvhidoa]

ᎤᏩᎢᎠᎤᎣᎠ [uhwatvhida³sdi]

ᎠᎥ [ahwi] (n) "Deer.; White-tailed deer.; biol. *Odocoileus virginianus.*"

ᎡᏥ ᏂᎣ ᎤᏩᎣᎤ ᎠᎥ ᎥᎥᎤᎢ. "ᎠᎠᏩᏗᎧᎠ ᎠᏯᎧᎦ ᏂᎣ ᎠᎳ?"
Mother bear went to where the deer walk about. "Have you seen my baby bear?"
[ᏣᎳᎩ ᏪᎵᏃ ᏗᏂᏂᎥᎠ ᏗᏍᎯᎥᎠ]

ᎠᎥ ᎠᏍᏪ [ahwi akta] (n) "Deer-eye (black eyed susan)."

ᎠᎥ ᏍᏝᎢᎢ [ahwi gahngoʔi] (n) "Deer tongue.; biol. *Chelone spp.*"

ᎠᎥᎾ [awina] (n) "Boy, teenage."

DꙆꙨꙀ [ahwih³sga] (vt) "He is planting."

  ᏥꙆꙨꙀ [tsiʔwih³sga]
  ᎤᏬᎡᎢ [uhwih³sv²³ʔi]
  DꙆꙨꙨAT [ahwih³sgo³ʔi]
  ᎲᎲ [hįhwį]
  ᎤᏬꙨᏗ [uhwih³sdi]

  ƟꙨY DꙆꙨY ᎤᏃᎵ DꙆꙨAT.
  He who is sowing doth sow the word;
  [ᏗᏍ 4:14]

DꙆꙇᏗᎬ [ahwisvdiyu] (n) "A garden."

DꙆᎷᎲ [ąwidiha] (vt) "He is carrying it (a solid) off."

  ᏥᎦᎷᏗ [tsįwidiʔa]
  ᎤᏬᏊᎢ [uwidvhv²³ʔi]
  DꙆᎷꙨAT [ąwidisgo³ʔi]
  ᎲᎦᏗ [hįwida]
  ᎤᎦᎵᏗ [uwitdi]

DꙌᎭᎵ [ąwohįli] (n) "Bald eagle.; American eagle.; Eagle.; biol. *Haliaeetus leucocephalus.*"

Dꙍ [ąyʔa] (vt) "He is picking it (something long) up."

  Ᏺꙍ [tsiyʔa]
  ᎤᏴᎢ [uyvʔv²³ʔi]
  DꙍꙨAT [ąyisgo³ʔi]
  Ꮂꙍ [hiya]
  ᎤꙍᏗ [uyhdi]

DꙍD [ąyaʔa] (vi) "It (something alive) is in a liquid."

  —

  ᎤꙍᎡꙨᎢ [uyaʔesdv²³ʔi]
  DꙍᏦᎢ [ąyaʔo³ʔi]
  ᎬꙍᎡꙨᏗ [wayaʔesdi]
  ᎤꙍᎡꙨᏗ [uyaʔesdi]

DꙍD [ąyaʔa] (vi) "It (something alive) is in a container."

  —

  ᎤꙍᎡꙨᎢ [uyaʔesdv²³ʔi]
  DꙍᏦᎢ [ąyaʔo³ʔi]
  ᎬꙍᎡꙨᏗ [wayaʔesdi]
  ᎤꙍᎡꙨᏗ [uyaʔesdi]

DꙍD

DꙍD [ąyaʔa] (vi) "He is inside."

  ᏥꙍD [tsiyąʔa]
  ᎤꙍᎡꙨᎢ [uyaʔesdv²³ʔi]
  DꙍᏦᎢ [ąyaʔo³ʔi]
  ᎲꙍᎡꙨᏗ [hiyaʔesdi]
  ᎤᎬꙨᏗ [uwasdi]

  … ᎲꙍꙨᎩᎲ ᎡᏥᏍᏫᎤ, ᎢᏪᎠᏗᎥᎾᎬᏃᏃ, DᎧ ƟꙍY ᏔᎲꙨᎡꙨᏗ.
  … and ye know him, because he doth remain with you, and shall be in you.
  [Ꮼh 14:17]

DꙍYD [ąya³giʔa] (vt) "He is eating it (something flexible)."

  ᏥꙍYD [tsiya³giʔa]
  ᎤꙍYiᎢ [uya³giv²³ʔi]
  DꙍYꙨAT [ąya³gisgo³ʔi]
  ᎲꙍꙀ [hiya³ga]
  ᎤꙍYꙨᏗ [uya³gisdi]

DꙍꙶiꙨꙀ [ąyalvʔsga] (vt) "He is sticking it to something.; He is attaching it to something."

  ᏥꙍꙶiꙨꙀ [tsiyalvʔyʔsga]
  ᎤꙍꙶᎤᎢ [uyalvʔnv²³ʔi]
  DꙍꙶiꙨAT [ąyalvʔsgo³ʔi]
  ᎲꙍꙶiꙀ [hiyalvʔvga]
  ᎤꙍꙶᏗ [uyalvʔdi]

DꙍhᎲ [a¹ya³nįha] (vt) "He is calling out for him."

  ᏥꙍhᎲ [tsi¹ʔya³nįha]
  ᎤꙍᎤᏊᎢ [u¹ya³nvhv²³ʔi]
  DꙍhꙨAT [a¹ya³nįsgo³ʔi]
  ᎲꙍƟ [hi¹ʔya³na]
  ᎤꙍᎤᏗ [u¹ya³nhdi]

  DᎧ ᏞᎬᎤꙆᎩᏴ iᎠᏓᏰꙨᏗᏅᏮ
  and called after me to turn again.
  [ᏠᎾᎬᎵ ᏍᎲᎡᎡᎢ]

DꙍꙨᏢᎲ [ąyhsgeni] (n) "The crown of his head."

  ᏥꙍꙨᏢᎲ [tsiyhsgeni]

DꙍꙀᏰᏴꙨᎵᎲ [ąyadehysdįha] (vt) "He is surrounding it."

  ᏥꙍꙀᏰꙨᎵᎲ [tsiyadęʔysdįha]
  ᎤꙍꙀᏰꙨᏪᎢᎢ [uyadehystąnv²³ʔi]
  DꙍꙀᏰꙨᎵꙨAT [ąyadehysdįsgo³ʔi]
  ᎲꙍꙀᏰꙨᎵ [hiyadehysda]
  ᎤꙍꙀᏰꙨᎵᏙᏗ [uyadehysdohdi]

ᎠᏯᏖᎾ [ạyạte³na] (n) “Wide.; Flat.; A board.”

ᎠᏯᏙᎸᎢ [ạyadohlỵʔi] (n) “A portion.; A chapter.; A share.”

ᏓᏯᏙᎸᎢ [dạyadohlỵʔi]

ᎠᏯᏨᏗ [ahyạtsvhdi] (n) “Harness.; Collar.; Necklace.; Necktie.”

ᎠᏰᎦ [ạye³ga] (vi) “He is waking up.”

ᏥᏰᎦ [tsịye³ga]

ᎤᏰᏨᎢ [uye³ʔtsv²³ʔi]

ᎠᏰᎪᎢ [ạye³go³ʔi]

ᎯᏰᎩ [hịye³ʔgi]

ᎤᏰᎢᏍᏗ [uye³ʔisdi]

ᎠᏰᎧᎵ [ạyẹkahli] (n) “Quilt.”

ᎠᏰᎵ [ahyeli] (vt) “He is driving a car.”

ᏥᏰᎵ [tsịʔyeli]

ᎤᏰᎴᏒᎢ [uhyelẹ³sv²³ʔi]

ᎠᏰᎵᏐᎢ [ahyeliso³ʔi]

ᎯᏰᎵᎦ [hịhyelʔga]

ᎤᏰᎸᏍᏗ [uhyelỵsdi]

ᎠᏰᎵ [ạyehli] (pt) “Half.; In the middle.; Between.”

… ᎦᎸᎶᎢ ᏩᏙᏢᎾ ᎠᎹᏱ ᎠᏰᎵ …
… ’Let an expanse be in the midst of the waters …
[ᎼᏏ ᎢᎬᏱᏱ 1:6]

ᎠᏰᎵᎠ [a¹yelịʔa] (vt) “He is mocking him.”

ᏥᏰᎵᎠ [tsi¹ʔyelịʔa]

ᎤᏰᎸᎥᎢ [u¹yelỵʔv²³ʔi]

ᎠᏰᎵᏍᎪᎢ [a¹yelịsgo³ʔi]

ᎯᏰᎵ [hi¹ʔyeli]

ᎤᏰᎵᎢᏍᏗ [u¹yelịʔịsdi]

ᎠᏰᎶᎰ [a¹yehloha] (vt) “He is cutting it with a knife.”

ᏥᏰᎶᎰ [tsi¹ʔyehloha]

ᎤᏰᎶᎸᎢ [u¹yehlọʔlv²³ʔi]

ᎠᏰᎶᎲᎢ [a¹yehloho³ʔi]

ᎯᏰᏔᎦ [hi¹yehlạga]

ᎤᏰᎶᏍᏗ [u¹yehlsdi]

ᎠᏰᎸᎢ [ahyelv³ʔi] (n) “His body.”

ᏥᏰᎸᎢ [tsihyelv³ʔi]

… ᏂᎬ ᎯᏰᎸᎢ ᎤᎧᎵᏦᏅᎯ ᎨᏎᏍᏗ ᎢᎦᎦᏘ.
… all thy body shall be enlightened,
[ᎹᏚ 6:22]

ᎠᏰᏌᏛᎢ [ạ³hyẹsạdvʔi] (n) “Finger.”

ᏓᏰᏌᏛᎢ [dạ³hyẹsạdvʔi]

ᏥᏰᏌᏛᎢ [tsị³hyẹsạdvʔi]

ᏕᏥᏰᏌᏛᎢ [detsị³hyẹsạdvʔi]

ᎠᏎᏃ ᏕᏥᏰᏌᏛ ᏓᎩᏍᏕᏓᏅ ᏗᏥᎴᏂ.
but I put my fingers in my ears.
[ᏧᏁᎶᏗ ᏚᏂᎩᏒᏒᎢ]

ᎠᏱ [ạhyi] (vt) “He is carrying it (a solid).”

ᏥᏱ [tsịyʔi]

ᎤᏰᏒᎢ [uhyẹsv²³ʔi]

ᎠᏱᏐᎢ [ạhyiso³ʔi]

ᎯᏳᎦ [hịhyuʔga]

ᎤᏴᏍᏗ [uhyvsdi]

ᎠᏱᎠ [ạyị³ʔa] (vt) “He is fetching it (something long).; He is picking it (something long) up from the ground.”

ᏥᏱᎠ [tsịyị³ʔa]

ᎤᏱᎥᎢ [uyiv²³ʔi]

ᎠᏱᏍᎪᎢ [ạyi³sgo³ʔi]

ᎯᏯ [hịya]

ᎤᏱᏗ [uyhdi]

… ᎠᎴ ᏧᏓᏏᏩᏛ ᎠᏱᏍᎨᏍᏗ, ᎠᎴ ᎠᎩᏍᏓᏩᏕᎨᏍᏗ.
… and take up his cross, and follow me,
[ᎹᏚ 16:24]

ᎠᏲᎣᏍᎦ [ạyọʔosga] (vi) “He is lost (die).”

ᏥᏲᎣᏍᎦ [tsịyọʔọʔsga]

ᎤᏲᎣᏒᎢ [uyọʔosv²³ʔi]

ᎠᏲᎣᏍᎪᎢ [ạyọʔosgo³ʔi]

ᎯᏲᎣᎯ [hịyọʔohi]

ᎤᏲᎣᎯᏍᏗ [uyọʔohịsdi]

ᎠᏲᎦ [ạyo³ga] (vi) “It is becoming ruined.; It is becoming bad.; It is breaking.”

—

ᎤᏲᏨᎢ [uyo³ʔtsv²³ʔi]

ᎠᏲᎪᎢ [ạyo³go³ʔi]

ᏩᏲᎩ [wạyo³ʔgi]

ᎤᏲᎢᏍᏗ [uyo³ʔisdi]

… ᎠᎴ ᎪᏪᎵ ᎤᏲᎢᏍᏗ ᏂᎨᏒᎾ ᏱᎩ,
… and the Writing is not able to be broken,
[ᎶᏂ 7:23]

DfᎯᎤ [ayohįha] (vt) "He is shooting."

    ⱠhᎢᎤ [tsiyoꞏiha]

    OꞌfᎯᎢ [uyohlv²³ꞏi]

    DfᎯᏝ [ayohiho³ꞏi]

    ᎯfᎤᏒ [hiyohaga]

    OꞌfᏬᎫ [uyosdi]

DfᎯᎤ [ahyohįha] (vt) "He is bringing it (a solid)."

    ⱠfᎯᎤ [tsiꞏyohiha]

    OꞌfᎯᎢ [uhyohlv²³ꞏi]

    DfᎯᏝ [ahyohiho³ꞏi]

    ᎯfᏒ [hihyoga]

    OꞌfᎯᏬᎫ [uhyohisdi]

    … OꞌfᎯY ᏗᏬᎠᏬᎤ HW RWᎾZ, DᏬAᎯꞂ TBᎢᎭ TGᏝᎭ.
    … bearing a mixture of myrrh and aloes, as it were, a hundred pounds.
    [Ꮒh 19:39]

DfᎯᏬᎫᎤ [ayohisdįha] (vi) "He is quitting.; He is ceasing."

    ⱠhᎢᏬᎫᎤ [tsiyoꞏisdįha]

    OꞌfᎯᏬᎫᏞOꞋᎢ [uyohisdanv²³ꞏi]

    DfᎯᏬᎫᏬᎠᎢ [ayohisdisgo³ꞏi]

    ᎯfᎯᏬᎫᏞ [hiyohisda]

    OꞌfᎯᏬᎫᏙᎫ [uyohisdohdi]

DfᎯWOꞏiᏬᏒ [ayo³ꞏlanyꞏvsga] (vt) "He is carving it."

    ⱠhᎯWOꞏiᏬᏒ [tsiyo³ꞏlanyꞏvꞏsga]

    OꞌfᎯWOꞋOꞋᎢ [uyo³ꞏlanyꞏnv²³ꞏi]

    DfᎯWOꞏiᏬᎠᎢ [ayo³ꞏlanyꞏvsgo³ꞏi]

    ᎯfᎯWOꞏiᏒ [hiyo³ꞏlanyꞏvga]

    OꞌfᎯWOꞋᎫ [uyo³ꞏlanvdi]

DfᎯWOꞋOꞋ [ayohlanvnv] (n) "Carpenter."

DfᎯᏞ [ayohli] (n) "Child."

    ⱠfᎯᏞ [tsiyohli]

    ᏗhfᎯᏞ ᏞᏬᏞBᏬᏬᏒ RⱠh.
    Rachel is cooking for the children.
    [King pg 114]

DfᎯᏞᎤ [ayo³ꞏliha] (vt) "He is greeting him."

    ⱠfᎯᏞD [tsiyo³ꞏliꞏa]

    OꞌfᎯᏞᎢ [uyo³ꞏliįlv²³ꞏi]

    DfᎯᏞᏞᎢ [ayo³ꞏliho³ꞏi]

    ᎯfᎯᏞᏒ [hiyo³ꞏliįga]

    OꞌfᎯᏞᏬᎫ [uyo³ꞏlisdi]

    … Dꞡ OꞌᏞOꞋᏔꞡ ᏊᏬᎭ OꞋᏲᏝᎭ ᎠD ᎾᏬY OꞌfᎯᏞᎢ.
    … and was reasoning of what kind this <u>salutation</u> may be.
    [MᏚ 1:29]

DfᏬᎠY [aꞏyosgi] (n) "Soldier.; Mustard greens."

DfᏬᎫᎤ [ayo³sdiha] (vt) "He is ruining it."

    ⱠfᏬᎫᎠD [tsiyo³sdiꞏa]

    OꞌfᏬᎫWOꞋᎢ [uyo³stanv²³ꞏi]

    DfᏬᎫᏞᏬᎠᎢ [ayo³sdisgo³ꞏi]

    ᎯfᏬᎫᏞ [hiyo³sda]

    OꞌfᏬᎫᏙᎫ [uyo³stdi]

    … TⱠfᏬᎫᏞ ᎠD OꞋᎿOꞏᏞSWᎾᎢᏬᏞᏜ, KTᎮZ TᏚ ᏞⱠᏙᎮᎮ ᏠᎮ ᎧᏚᏗᏬⱠⱠh.
    … '<u>Destroy</u> this sanctuary, and in three days I will raise it up.'
    [Ꮒh 2:19]

DfᎭᏞᏴᏬᎢ [ayodasahvꞏi] (n) "Floor."

DfᎪ [ahyotsa] (n) "Girl, preteen."

    ⱠfᎪ [tsihyotsa]

DGᎢh [ahyuꞏini] (vi) "He is swimming along."

    ᏕGᎢh [gaꞏyuꞏini]

    OꞋGᎢᏗRᎢ [uhyuꞏinesv²³ꞏi]

    DGᎢhᏞᎢ [ahyuꞏiniso³ꞏi]

    ᎤGᎢᏍᏒ [hahyuꞏinuꞏga]

    OꞋGᎢOꞋᏬᎫ [uhyuꞏinysdi]

DGᎢh [ayukeni] (n) "Chin."

    ⱠGᎢh [tsiyukeni]

DGYᏞ [ahyugida] (n) "American hazelnut.; Hazelnut.; biol. *Corylus americana.*"

DGᎪᎢ [ahyugoꞏi] (n) "Jaw."

    ᏗGᎪᎢ [dihyugoꞏi]

    ⱠGᎪᎢ [tsihyugoꞏi]

    ᏗⱠGᎪᎢ [ditsihyugoꞏi]

ᎠᏳᏲᎰᏍᎦ [ayuyohosga] (vi) “He is driving recklessly fast on dangerous rural or mountain roads.; He is rolling or skidding logs downhill.; He is ball-hooting.”

ᎦᏳᏲᎣᏍᎦ [gayuyọʔosga]

ᎤᏳᏲᎰᏒᎢ [uyuyohosv²³ʔi]

ᎠᏳᏲᎰᏍᎪᎢ [ayuyohosgo³ʔi]

ᎭᏳᏲᎰᎯ [hayuyohohi]

ᎤᏳᏲᎰᎯᏍᏗ [uyuyohohịsdi]

ᎠᏴ [ạyv] (pt) “I.; We.”

ᎠᎴ ᎬᏂᏳᏉ ᎠᏴ ᏓᏥᏃᎤᎪᏔᏂ ᎡᎶᎯ …
’And I, lo, I am bringing in the deluge of waters on the earth …
[ᏑᏏ ᎢᎬᏱᏱ 6:17]

ᎠᏴᎡᎭ [ạyv³eha] (vt) “He is taking it (something long) from him.”

ᏥᏴᎡᎠ [tsiyv³ẹʔa]

ᎤᏴᎡᎸᎢ [uyv³ẹʔlv²³ʔi]

ᎠᏴᎡᎰᎢ [ạyv³eho³ʔi]

ᎯᏴᎢ [hiyv³i]

ᎤᏴᎡᏗ [uyv³ehdi]

ᎠᏴᎡᎭ [ạyvʔeha] (vt) “He is taking it (something long) or it (a liquid) to him.”

ᏥᏴᎡᎠ [tsiyvʔẹʔa]

ᎤᏴᎡᎸᎢ [uyvʔẹlv²³ʔi]

ᎠᏴᎡᎰᎢ [ạyvʔeho³ʔi]

ᎯᏴᎥᏏ [hiyṿvsi]

ᎤᏴᎡᏗ [uyvʔehdi]

ᎠᏴᎯᎭ

ᎠᏴᎯᎭ [ạyvhịha] (vt) “He is entering it.”

ᏥᏴᎢᎭ [tsịyṿʔịha]

ᎤᏴᎸᎢ [uyvhlv²³ʔi]

ᎠᏴᎯᎰᎢ [ạyvhịho³ʔi]

ᎯᏴᎭᎦ [hịyvhaga]

ᎤᏴᏍᏗ [uyvsdi]

… ᎥᏝ ᎾᎿ ᎤᏴᏍᏗ ᏱᎨᏎᏍᏗ.
… may not enter into it.’
[ᎷᎦ 18:17]

ᎠᏴᏈᏛᎥᏍᎦ [ạyṿgwịdv³ʔvsga] (vt) “He is bending.; He is hemming.”

ᏥᏴᏈᏛᎥᏍᎦ [tsịyṿgwịdv³ʔṿʔsga]

ᎤᏴᏈᏛᏅᎢ [uyṿgwịdv³ʔnv²³ʔi]

ᎠᏴᏈᏛᎥᏍᎪᎢ [ạyṿgwịdv³ʔvsgo³ʔi]

ᎯᏴᏈᏛᎥᎦ [hịyṿgwịdv³ʔṿga]

ᎤᏴᏈᏛᎠᏗ [uyṿgwịdṿ³ạdi]

ᎠᏴᏍᏉ [ạyhsgwo] (pt) “Me too.”

ᎠᏴᏍᏗᎭ [ạyvsdiha] (vt) “He is being carried by it (a solid).”

ᏥᏴᏍᏗᎠ [tsịyvsdịʔa]

ᎤᏴᏍᏔᏅᎢ [uyvstạnv²³ʔi]

ᎠᏴᏍᏗᏍᎪᎢ [ạyvsdisgo³ʔi]

ᎯᏴᏍᏓ [hịyvsda]

ᎤᏴᏍᏙᏗ [uyvstdi]

ᎠᏴᏐᎵ [ạyṿsoli] (n) “His nose.”

ᏥᏴᏐᎵ [tsịyṿsoli]

ᎠᏴᏓᏆᎶᎠ [a¹yvdạgwạlo³ʔa] (vi) “It is thundering.”

—

ᎤᏴᏓᏆᎶᎥᎢ [u¹yvdạgwạlo³ʔv²³ʔi]

ᎠᏴᏓᏆᎶᏍᎪᎢ [a¹yvdạgwạlo³sgo³ʔi]

ᏩᏴᏓᏆᎶᏣ [wa¹yvdạgwạlo³tsa]

ᎤᏴᏓᏆᎶᏍᏗ [u¹yvdạgwạlo³sdi]

… ᎠᎴ ᎡᎶᎯ ᏭᏗᏅᏒᎩ; ᏚᏃᏴᎳᏒᎩᏃ, ᎠᎴ ᎤᏴᏓᏆᎶᎥᎩ, ᎠᎴ ᎠᎾᎦᎵᏍᎬᎩ, ᎠᎴ ᎡᎶᎯ ᎤᎵᏖᎸᏅᎩ.
… and did cast [it] to the earth, and there came voices, and thunders, and lightnings, and an earthquake.
[ᎠᏥᎾᏄᎪᏫᏎᎸᎢ 8:5]

ᎠᏴᏓᏆᎶᏍᎩ [ahyvdạgwạlọsgi] (n) “Thunder.”

… ᎠᎴ ᎾᏍᎩ ᏉᎠᎾᏥ ᏚᏬᎡᎢ, ᎾᏍᎩ ᎠᏴᏓᏆᎶᏍᎩ ᏧᏪᏥ ᎦᏛᎦ;
… and he put on them names — Boanerges, that is, ‘Sons of thunder;’
[ᎹᎦ 3:17]

ᎠᏴᏣᏗᏍᏗᏍᎩ [ahyvtsạdịsdịsgi] (n) “Refrigerator.; Freezer.”

ᎠᏴᏤᏂ [ạyvhtseni] (n) “His neck, front of.”

ᏥᏴᏤᏂ [tsịyvhtseni]

… ᏧᏂᏁᎦᏄᏅᎯ ᏚᏪᏰᏋᏔᏁᎢ, ᎠᎴ ᎤᏪᏯᎵᏁ ᏓᎾᏍᎦᎨ ᎨᏒ ᎠᏴᏤᏂ;
… she hath put on his hands, and on the smooth of his neck,
[ᏑᏏ ᎢᎬᏱᏱ 27:16]

DBⲊꙆ⬧ [ạyɣ³hwtịha] (vt) "He is finding it (something long)."

ⲓrBⲊꙆ⬧ [tsiyɣɂwtịha]

OʼBⲊꙆⲊꙆ⬧T [uyɣ³hwtyhv²³ɂi]

DBⲊꙆⲟᎪꙆT [ạyɣ³hwtịsgo³ɂi]

ꙆBⲊꙆW [hiyɣ³hwta]

OʼBⲊꙆⲊꙆꙆ [uyɣ³hwtvhdi]

DBⲊⲟᎥ [ạyvwịya] (n) "Native American.; Cherokee."

ⲓrBⲊⲟᎥ [tsiyvwịya]

R

Rꙅ [ega] (vi) "He is going."

Ꝁꙅ [gega]

OʼꙍRT [uwesv²³ɂi]

RꙆT [ego³ɂi]

ꝀⲐ [heɂna]

OʼꙍⲐⲟᎪꙆ [uweny³sdi]

ꞓⲁ Zꭥ OꞮꝒ ꙆꞭⲐⲟ ꙍꙅⲐ!
You and Mary go to the store!
[King pg 112]

Rⲟ⬧ [ẹha] (vi) "He is alive.; He is living."

ꝀD [gẹɂa]

OʼꙍꝒⲟᎪꙆT [uwẹhesdv²³ɂi]

RꝒT [ẹho³ɂi]

ꝒꝒⲟꙆ [hẹhesdi]

———

Rⲁ [ẹhi] (vi) "He is dwelling.; He is living at."

ꝀT [gẹɂi]

OʼꙍꝒⲟᎪꙆT [uwẹhesdv²³ɂi]

RꝒT [ẹho³ɂi]

ꝒꝒⲟꙆ [hẹhesdi]

———

ꞒⲐ, DⲐ, Zꭥ EꝒ TⲊꞀ DꞭⲁ.
Bears, deer, and bobcats live in the wild.
[King pg 112]

RⲁⲟꙆ [ẹhịsdi] (n) "Pain.; Distress."

… LⲟꙆ OʼⲐVꭥꞝR DꞮꙆꝒT Dꭥ Ꙇⲱꞓr hꙅi RⲁⲟꙆ …
… that his Wife and Children should not perceive his distress, …
[ꝚꞭꞬꙆ ShᎽRRT]

RW [ehla] (vi) "He is in a group."

ꝀW [gẹɂla]

OʼꙍꞝⲟᏇꞀT [uwehlesdv²³ɂi]

RꞬT [ehlo³ɂi]

ꝒꞝⲟꙆ [hehlesdi]

OʼꙍꞭⲟꙆ [uwehlysdi]

RWꙆ [elạdi] (pt) "Lower.; Down below.; On the floor.; On the ground."

ꝓⲅⲱZ ꝒꞭꞬꙆ RWꙆ ꙅOʼWꙍE Ⲑi OʼꞞꞮRⲁ TꙆEVꝒⲟ
OʼOʼꞒꙅᎩ, OʼꙍMOʼᎩ …
Then Christian fell down at his foot as dead, crying
…
[ꝚꞭꞬꙆ ShᎽRRT]

RWꙆ TꙅꙆ [elạd igạdi] (adj) "Short height."

RWꙍꙆ [elạwohdi] (n) "The Yellow Hill Community."

RꝒD [elịɂa] (vt) "He is thinking that."

ꝀꝒD [gelịɂa]

OʼꙍꝒⲟᎽRT [uwelsgịsv²³ɂi]

RꝒꝒT [elihɂo³ɂi]

ꝒW [hela]

OʼꙍꝒⲟꙆ [uwelisdi]

iꞭꞴZ ⲟᎽVEꞬꞬꙆ ꝀꝒD …
for it doth seem to me irrational …
[ꝀrOʼꞵⲟ ꝗⲐꝒꞭꝒVꙅT 25:27]

RꞬⲁ [elọhi] (n) "Earth.; World."

ꙅVZ OʼⲟꙆ ꞬꞞꭥꙅ, ⲐⲟᎩ hꙅꝒⲟᎥꙆ hꙅꙆ RꞬⲁ
ꝀrꙅꞞⲟꙅ?
What are the things you seek, since you leave all the world to find them?
[ꝚꞭꞬꙆ ShᎽRRT]

RꞬꙆⲟᎩ [elọtịsgi] (n) "Bear huckleberry.; biol. Gaylus-sacia ursina."

RꞬꙍⲁ [elọwehi] (adj) "Quiet."

RꞝꙆ [ẹlvdi] (pt) "Down.; Below."

RꞒ [egwa] (adj) "Big.; Large."

ꞭhꞞꝒZ ꝀEꞝⲟꞮꞭ ꝸM Zꭥ ꙅⲱ RꞒ ꝵWⲟᎩ EꙆ Rꞓh.
Rachel is cooking the corn and beans in a large pot for the children.
[King pg 115]

RꞒ ⬧ꞴꞵWⲟꙆ [egwạ hạyelạsdi] (n) "Butcher knife."

RꝞh [egwoni] (n) "River."

… Dꭥ ꙅꞒꞭT, Dꭥ RꝞh ꙅꙍꝸVT, …
… and riseth, and passeth over the River, …
[ꝵꞲ TEꞵⲟꞵ 31:21]

RꙆⲟꙆ [edạsdi] (n) "Walkway.; Path."

RVⲱⱵ [edoha] (vi) "He is walking about."

　FVD [gedọꞋa]

　OꞋⱠVⱯT [uwedọꞋlv²³Ꞌi]

　RVFT [edoho³Ꞌi]

　P�L [heda]

　OꞋⱠⱢⱥⱭⱮ [uwedạsdi]

IⱶU ⱭD ⱰⱠⱿ4ⱯⱵ; WⱭⱠⱯ, ⱭⱺⱵ GVⱥV, Dꞌ P�L.
Jesus saith to him, 'Rise, take up thy couch, and be walking;'
[Gh 5:8]

RVPⱥⱭⱮVꞋD [edọꞋhesdigwoa] (vi) "He is staying."

　FVRⱥⱭⱮVꞋD [gedọ¹esdigwoa]

　——

　——

　——

　——

RVⱢVⱱⱵ [edọꞋli³doha] (vi) "He is loafing."

　FVⱢVD [gedọꞋli³dọꞋa]

　OꞋⱠVⱢVⱯT [uwedọꞋli³dọꞋlv²³Ꞌi]

　RVⱢVFT [edọꞋli³doho³Ꞌi]

　PVⱢL [hedọꞋli³da]

　OꞋⱠVⱢLⱥⱭⱮ [uwedọꞋli³dạsdi]

T

TRⱾ [ịꞋega] (vi) "He is going back."

　TFⱾ [igega]

　iOꞋⱠRT [vꞋuwesv²³Ꞌi]

　TRAT [ịꞋego³Ꞌi]

　IⱶꞋⱣⱧⱧ [tsịheꞋna]

　iOꞋⱠOⱥⱮ [vꞋuweny³sdi]

TⱾ [iga] (n) "Day.; Noon."

Dꞌ OꞋⱧⱧⱭOꞋTⱥWⱭⱮ OꞋhⱭⱰⱮ FR Db TⱾ hERⱧ KⱠ ⱧⱭG OꞋMⱥⱥⱮⱴ FRT; OꞋⱧꞋⱾⱠⱿZ Ⱨⱴ ⱮⱧPⱥⱠBhRT.
and they prepare the present until the coming of Joseph at noon, for they have heard that there they do eat bread.
[Ⴑb TEⱴⱴ 43:25]

TⱾ RVOꞋL [iga edonvda] (n) "Sun."

TⱾMⱧ [igaꞋlka] (vi) "He is returning.; He is arriving.; He is back."

　TIⱶMⱾ [itsịꞋluꞋga]

　iOꞋMⱧⱦT [vꞋuꞋlhtsv²³Ꞌi]

　TⱾMAT [igaꞋlko³Ꞌi]

　IⱶⱭMⱵ [tsịhịꞋlki]

　iOꞋMⱭⱥⱮ [vꞋuꞋluhịsdi]

ⱧⱥⱮꞋZ iOꞋMⱦⱵ hⱾⱮⱵꞋb, ⱧⱭⱵ TEⱴⱴ IⱶU RZⱴ OꞋMVⱰⱭ …
and Nicodemus also came — who came unto Jesus by night at the first …
[Gh 19:39]

TⱾⱧⱥⱮ [iganạsdi] (n) "Solomon's seal.; biol. Polygonatum biflorum."

TⱾⱮ [igạdi] (pt) "Height.; Tall."

TAⱭⱦꞋ [igọhidv] (pt) "As long as.; Until.; For the duration of."

RGⱭ TAⱭⱦꞋ FRT, iⱢ OꞋPⱥⱮⱮⱥⱮ ⱴⱵ …
during all days of the earth … do not cease.'
[Ⴑb TEⱴⱴ 8:22]

TAⱠⱥⱮ [igọwesdi] (n) "Pronunciation."

TEⱯTⱥⱮ [igyneꞋisdi] (n) "Word.; Speech."

TⱭⱥVꞋ [ịhisgwo] (pt) "You too."

TⱧ [ina] (pt) "Far."

TⱧI R.Ɑ WⱴⱭ [inạge ẹhi taya] (n) "Wild cherry."

TⱧIT [inạgeꞋi] (adj) "Wild."

TⱧL [inạda] (n) "Snake.; biol. All Varieties."

TⱧL ⱾⱯⱾ [inạda gahnga] (n) "American walking fern.; biol. Asplenium rhizophyllum."

TⱧL IⱭIT [inạda sọlvgeꞋi] (n) "Bullsnake.; biol. Pituophis catenifer sayi."

Th TⱾⱮ [in igạdi] (adj) "Tall height."

ThⱾⱮ [inigạdi] (adj) "Tall."

TZⱢ [ịnoli] (n) "Black Fox (Surname)."

TOⱭG [inᵥhiyu] (pt) "Far far away."

OꞋhⱰAⱦZ ⱾⱾⱠT, Dꞌ iⱢ Db TOⱭG ⱴGⱧT4T, …
they have gone out of the city — they have not gone far off …
[Ⴑb TEⱴⱴ 44:4]

TG [itsa] (pt) "Towards."

TⱵW [ịtsula] (pt) "Both."

ii ⱰⱺⱭGⱭRⱧ, Dꞌ OꞋⱺⱭGⱭⱥⱦꞋ TⱵW;
Yes, both Obstinate and Pliable;
[ⱮⱯGⱮ ShⱵRRT]

TⱴⱭ [ihya] (n) "River cane.; North American bamboo.; biol. Arundinaria spp."

TⱴⱭ [iya] (n) "Pumpkin."

TⱴⱭWbOⱭ [iyaꞋlạsihnᵥhi] (n) "One foot (12 inches)."

TⱴⱭOꞋL [iyạnvda] (n) "Several months ago."

TᏪᏏᏔᏪᏐᎠ [iyasitạdyhi] (n) "Inch."

TᏪᏔᏪᎤᏍᏫᎤ·Ꭺ [iyhtạwosdạnyhi] (n) "Minute(s)."

TᏳᏨᏉ [iyugwo] (pt) "Anytime.; Some other time."

... ᏫᏍᎢᏉ ᏍᎯᎷᏖᏫ TᏳᏨᏉ ᎤᏫᏳ ᏃᏉᏏ ᎤᏲᏓᏣᏜᏐᎢ.
... did inquire exactly from them the time of the appearing star,
[ᎹᏏ 2:7]

TᏳᏍᏂᎫ [iyụsdi] (pt) "Like."

ᎾᏃ ᎠᏂᏫᏍᎾᎬᎢ ᏍᏪᏍᏳᏩᎢᎢ ᏂᏍᏏᏯᏍᏫᎠ TᏳᏍᏂᎫ ᏂᎬᎮᎾᏞᏂᎢ.
Then, as it burned it popped and made a whistling-like sound.
[King pg 122]

TᏳᏍᏂᎫᏉ [iyụsdigwo] (pt) "Any."

... TᏳᏍᏂᎫᏉ ᏈᏫᎬ ᏍᏳᏪᏂᏏ, ᏔᏁᎵᏃ, ᎾᏳᏉ ᎠᏈᏎ ᏔᏏᏯ ᏲᏯ ᎾᎦ ᏓᏲᎬᎬᎠ ᎮᏍᎢ.
... 'Whatever thou mayest ask me, I will give to thee — unto the half of my kingdom.'
[ᎹᏏ 6:23]

TᏳᎳᎠ3Ꮝ [iyudạle3ga] (adj) "Several."

TᏳᎯᏒᎦᎷ [iyutsiloda] (n) "Mile.; Gallon.; Yard."

TᏳᏩᎯᏆᎠ [iyụwahnịlyhi] (n) "Time."

TᏳᏪᎤ·ᏍᎫ [iyụwenvsdi] (n) "Hour."

Ꭳ

ᏅᏍᎤ· [oganv] (n) "Groundhog.; Woodchuck.; biol. Marmota monax."

ᏅᏬ [ohla] (n) "Soap."

ᏅᎵᏍ [olịga] (n) "Red Horse."

ᏅᎵᏍᎯᏅᏍᏯ [ohneganiyịsgi] (n) "Catcher, hind (baseball)."

ᏅᎯ [ohni] (pt) "Last.; End."

ᏚᏁᎫᎵᏃ ᎢᏞ ᏔᏳᏉ ᏅᎯ ᏳᎠᏈᎢ.
and Christian saw him no more.
[ᏚᏁᎫᎵ ᏍᎯᏴᏲᏲᎢ]

ᏅᎯᏨᎢᏔᎬ [ohnịditsa] (pt) "Behind."

ᏅᏍᏫᎻᎾ [ọsgewi] (n) "Cabbage.; biol. Brassica oleracea."

ᏅᏍᏫᎦ [ọsda] (vi) "He is being good."

ᎠᏍᎫᎦ [gọsda]

ᎤᏬᎢᎢᎢ [uwoᏏv23Ꮟi]

———

ᎰᎠ [hohi]

ᎤᏬᏍᎦ [uwọsda]

ᏅᏍᎫ [osdi] (adj) "Good."

ᏅᏍᎦ ᎤᎥᏬᏬᏫᎢᎢ.
It was burning good.
[King pg 122]

ᏅᏏ [osi] (pt) "Good."

ii, ᏅᏏ ᏂᎦᎤᎫᎢᏲ.
Yes, I see it very well.
[ᏚᏁᎫᎵ ᏍᎯᏴᏲᏲᎢ]

ᏅᏏᏳ [osiyu] (pt) "Hello.; Very good."

... ᏅᏏᏳ ᏤᏙᎠ TᏳᏃ ᏎᏣᏍᏂᎫᏃ ᎤᎯᏔ ᏪᏪᎤ·Ꭺ ᏂᎲ."
... the ground is good when they are once got in at the Gate.
[ᏚᏁᎫᎵᎫ ᏍᎯᏴᏲᏲᎢ - ᎠᏈᏔᏒᏙᏲᏂᎠᏍᏃ]

ᏅᎳᏈ [odali] (n) "Mountain."

ᏔᏳᏉ ᎾᏳᏯ ᏨᎵᏃ ᎠᎾᎠ ᎠᏣᎵᎬᏲ ᏅᎳᏈ ᏣᎲᏣᎬᏲ; ...
then those in Judea, let them flee to the mountains;
...
[ᎹᏏ 21:21]

ᏅᎳᏈᏎᏈ [odạliga?li] (n) "Ginseng, American.; biol. Panax quinquefolius."

ᏅᎤᏫᎯᎢ [ọdvhla?tịᏏi] (n) "Garter snake.; Garden snake.; biol. Thamnophis spp."

ᏅᎤᏣᏍᎫ [ody-hlọohdi] (pt) "On the side of a mountain."

Ꭴ

ᎤᏍᎤᏏ [ugama] (n) "Gravy.; Soup."

ᎤᏍᎤᏅᏍᎦ [ụganạsda] (adj) "Sweet."

ᎤᎠᎫ ᎤᏍᎤᏅᏍᎦ ᏇᏯᎠ ᏅᎵᎳᎯᏍᏃᎵᎾ ᎤᏍᎤ·ᏪᎬ.
One cannot eat a lot of sweets without the possible result of rotten teeth.
[ᏣᏬᏴ ᏪᏈᏂ ᏒᎯᎲᏫᎠ ᎫᏍᎯᏉᎫ]

ᎤᏍᎤᏍᏍ [ugah3sga] (vi) "He is being rained on."

ᎠᏯᏍᎤᏍᏍ [a1gigaᏏᏍsga]

ᎤᏍᎤᏛᎤᎢ [ugạ3hnạnv23Ꮟi]

ᎤᏍᎤᏍᎠᎢᎢ [ugah3sgo3Ꮟi]

ᏣᏍᎤ [tsạga3na]

ᎤᏍᎤᏍᎫ [ugạ3hndi]

ᎤᏍᎤᏍᏙᎤᎠ [uksdọhi] (n) "His pillow."

ᎠᏍᎤᏍᏍᏙᎤᎠ [a1gwạksdọhi]

ᎤᏍᏥᏂ [ukseni] (n) "His anus."

ᎠᏍᎤᏍᏥᏂ [a1gwạkseni]

ᎤᏍᏩᎠ [ugsụhi] (n) "Blue racer (snake).; Eastern racer.; biol. Coluber constrictor."

ᎤᏍᏩᏍᎤᏍ [uksuhysga] (vi) "He is getting something in his eye."

ᎠᏯᏍᏩᎢᏍᏍ [a1gịksuᏏysga]

ᎤᏍᏩᎤᎢ [uksunv23Ꮟi]

ᎤᏍᏩᏍᎤᏍᎠᎢ [uksuhysgo3Ꮟi]

ᏣᏍᏩᏂ [tsạksuni]

ᎤᏍᏩᎫ [uksuhdi]

ᎣᏍᏚ [ukta] (n) "Seed."

    ... ᎡᎪᏫᎥ ᎠᏫᎥ ᎠᏫ ᎣᏍᏚ ᏔᎢᏯᏫᎵ, ᎠᏐ ᏞᎢᏠᏐ ᏒᎢᎠ.
    ... lo, __seed__ for you, and ye have sown the ground,
    [ᏅᏇ ᎤᎬᏯᏰᏮ 47:23]

ᎣᏍᏩᎤᏉᎸ [uktạnuloda] (n) "His eyelid."

    ᎠᏯᏍᏩᎤᏉᎸ [a¹giktạnuloda]

ᎣᏍᏓᎬᏉᎢ [uktiyuwạnvɂi] (n) "His eyebrow."

    ᎠᏯᏍᏓᎬᏉᎢ [a¹giktiyuwạnvɂi]

ᎣᏍᏛᎣᎠᏗᎥ [ugatsịnygotsidv] (adj) "Rusty."

ᎣᎥᎤᏆ [uɂkạha] (vi) "He has it (something alive)."

    ᎠᏯᎣᎠ [a¹gikạɂa]

    ᎣᎠᏇᎾᏫᎢᎢ [uɂkạhesdv²³ɂi]

    ᎣᎠᏏᎢ [uɂkạho³ɂi]

    ᏣᎣᏇᏫᎵ [tsakạhesdi]

    ᎣᎠᎵ [uɂkdi]

    ... ᎠᏐ ᎤᎾᏫ ᏣᎬᎾᏣᎠ ᏍᏆᎣᎤ ᏐᏞᎢ ᏛᎩᎾᏆᎣᎠ; ᎢᏞ
    ᏔᏬᏃᏃ ᎪᏫᎵ ᏏᏕᏝᏦᎤ ᎠᏍᏩᏫ ᏣᎬᎾᏣᎠ, ᎨᏛᏇᏋ ᎠᏐ ᏕᎤ
    ᎥᏲᏫ ᎣᎬᏪ.
    ... and __possession of__ the cattle [is] unto my lord, there
    hath not been left before my lord save our bodies, and
    our ground;
    [ᏅᏇ ᎤᎬᏯᏰᏮ 47:18]

ᎣᎥᎤᏆᎵ [ukạhadi] (n) "Fog."

ᎣᎥᎣᎠ [uka³hnạɂa] (vt) "He has livestock or animals."

    ᎠᏯᎣᎣᎠ [a¹gịɂka³hnạɂa]

    ᎣᎥᏂ [uka³hni]

    ᎣᎥᎣᎥᏔ [ukạ³hnạɂo³ɂi]

    ᏣᎥᎣᏍ [tskạ³hnvga]

    ᎣᎥᎣᎤᎵ [ukạ³hnvɂdi]

ᎣᎥᎤᎻᎾ [uktena] (n) "Snake, with deer horns (mythical)."

ᎣᎥᎤᏦᎢᎢ [ukạdvɂi] (n) "His eyelash."

    ᎠᏗᎠᎤᏦᎢᎢ [a¹gwạkạdvɂi]

ᎣᎥᎤᏦᎢᎢ [ukạdvɂi] (n) "His face."

    ᎠᏗᎠᎤᏦᎢᎢ [a¹gwạkạdvɂi]

    ᎠᎵ ᏣᎤᎠ ᏣᎤᏦᎢᎢ ᏎᏎ ᎠᏯᎥᎢᏫᎵ ᎡᏂ ᏒᎢᎠ ᎤᎠᎻᎢᎤᎣᎤᎤ,
    ᎿᎢᏰᏃ ᏮᎬᏬᎤᎢᎢᎠ; ᏑᎵᏋᏃ ᏂᎠ, ᎠᏐ ᏒᎢᎠ ᏿ᎧᎠᎻᎢᎤᏂ.
    by the sweat of __thy face__ thou dost eat bread till thy
    return unto the ground, for out of it hast thou been
    taken, for dust thou [art], and unto dust thou turnest
    back.'
    [ᏅᏇ ᎤᎬᏯᏰᏮ 3:19]

ᎣᎢᏫᎵ [ugewodi] (n) "Bald."

    ᎠᏯᎢᏫᎵ [a¹gigewodi]

ᎣᏯᏇᏫᎠᎬ [ukịhịsdiyu] (n) "His throat."

    ᎠᏯᏯᏇᏫᎠᎬ [a¹gikịhịsdiyu]

ᎣᎥᏯᏫ [ukịɂla] (vi) "He is on a horse."

    ᎠᏗᏲᏫ [a¹gwạɂkịɂla]

    ᎣᏯᎠᎣᎢ [ukịɂlvɂnv²³ɂi]

    ᎣᏯᏣᎢ [ukịɂlo³ɂi]

    ᏣᏯᎠᎢᏯ [tsakịɂlyɂvgi]

    ᎣᏯᎠᎵ [ukịɂlvɂdi]

    ᏘᏈᏃ ᎣᏣᎷᏫ ᎠᏳᎾ ᏔᏇᏗ-ᎫᏏᎮᏍᎣᎥᎾᏛ, ᎣᏯᎠᎣᎤᏯ,
    ᎨᏫᏯᏫ ᎠᎠ ᏘᏂᎡᎣ ᏘᏁᎠᏯᏫ;
    and Jesus having found a young ass __did sit upon__ it,
    according as it is written,
    [ᏣᏂ 12:14]

ᎣᎥᏯᏟᎵ [ugidahli] (n) "Feather."

ᎣᎥᎠᎦ [ugolv] (n) "Sun perch."

ᎣᎥᎠᏂᏟᏍ [ugoniyoga] (vi) "He is late."

    ᎠᏯᎠᏂᏟᏍ [a¹gigoniyoga]

    ᎣᎥᎠᏂᏟᏘᎾᏫᎢᎢ [ugoniyogesdv²³ɂi]

    ᎣᎥᎠᏂᏟᏗᎢᎢ [ugoniyogo³ɂi]

    ᏣᎠᏂᏟᏘᎾᏫᎵ [tsagoniyogesdi]

    ᎣᎥᎠᏂᏟᏘᎾᏫᎵ [ugoniyogesdi]

ᎣᎥᎠᏂᏟᏍ [ugo³hniyoga] (vi) "He is late."

    ᎠᏯᎠᏂᏟᏍ [a¹gigoɂniyoga]

    ᎣᎥᎠᏂᏟᏣᏘ [ugo³hniyotsv²³ɂi]

    ᎣᎥᎠᏂᏟᏗᎢᎢ [ugo³hniyogo³ɂi]

    ᏣᎠᏂᏟᏟᏯ [tsago³hniyogi]

    ᎣᎥᎠᏂᏟᏘᎾᏫᎵ [ugo³hniyoɂisdi]

ᎣᎥᎠᎣᎤ [ukohnv] (n) "His testicle."

    ᏧᎠᎣᎤ [tsukohnv]

    ᎠᏗᎠᎠᎣᎤ [a¹gwạkohnv]

    ᎵᏗᎠᎠᎣᎤ [di¹gwạkohnv]

ᎣᎥᏚᏚ [uguku] (n) "Hoot howl.; Barred owl.; biol. _Strix varia_."

    ᎠᎬᏅᏒᎡ, ᎣᎥᏚᏚ ᎣᏍᏍᎥᎵ.
    At first, __Owl__ asked a question.
    [ᏣᏫᏯ ᎧᏙᏫ ᏣᏂᏂᏮᎠ ᎵᏍᏨᏫᎵ]

ᎣᎥᏚᏚ ᎣᏫᎠᎵᏇ [uguku̠ uskoli] (n) "Yellow fringed orchid."

ᎣᎥᏚᏚᏫᎥ [ugukusdo] (n) "Wood betony.; Canadian lousewort.; biol. _Pedicularis canadensis_."

ᎣᎥᏦᏍ [ugulega] (vi) "He is belching."

    ᎠᏯᏦᏍ [a¹gigulega]

    ᎣᏦᏣᏘ [uguletsv²³ɂi]

    ᎣᏦᏗᏔ [ugulego³ɂi]

    ᏣᏦᏣᏯ [tsagulegi]

    ᎣᏦᏗᎵ [uguledi]

ᎤᎫᏇ ᎤᎳᏑᎳ [ụgkwẹ ụlạsụla] (n) "Lady's slipper orchids.; Slipper orchids.; Moccasin flower.; biol. *Cypripedium spp.*"

ᎤᎫᏇᎯ [ụgkwehi] (n) "Quail.; Northern bobwhite.; biol. *Colinus virginianus.*"

ᎤᎫᏍᏆᎶᎠ [ukụsgwạlo³ʔa] (vt) "He is bumping his elbow."

ᎠᎩᎫᏍᏆᎶᎠ [a¹giʔkụsgwạlo³ʔa]

ᎤᎫᏍᏆᎶᎥᎢ [ukụsgwạlo³ʔv²³ʔi]

ᎤᎫᏍᏆᎶᏍᎪᎢ [ukụsgwạlo³sgo³ʔi]

ᏣᎫᏍᏆᎶᏣ [tskụsgwạlo³tsa]

ᎤᎫᏍᏆᎶᏍᏗ [ukụsgwạlo³sdi]

ᎤᎬᎲᏬᎵᏗ [ụkỵhṿohldi] (n) "Tuberculosis."

ᎤᎬᏫᏳᎯ [ugvwịyụhi] (n) "King.; Chief.; Ruler."

ᎠᎩᎬᏫᏳᎯ [a¹gịgvwịyụhi]

ᎤᎬᏫᏳᎯ, ᎾᎿ ᎤᎬᏫᏳᏌᏕᎩ, ᎾᏍᎩ ᎤᏬᏪᎳ ᎯᎠ ᎪᏪᎵᎯ ...
The Lord, the Governor of the country, hath recorded that in this Book ...
[ᏧᏁᎶᏗ ᏚᏂᎩᏒᏒᎢ]

ᎤᎭ [uha] (vt) "He has it (a solid)."

ᎠᎩᎠ [a¹gịʔa]

ᎤᎮᏍᏛᎢ [uhesdv²³ʔi]

ᎤᎰᎢ [uho³ʔi]

ᏣᎮᏍᏗ [tsahesdi]

ᎤᎮᏍᏗ [uhesdi]

ᎯᎳᎢᎦ ᎠᏕᎳ ᏱᏗᏣᎭ?
How much money might you have?
[ᏣᎳᎩ ᏔᎵᏁ ᏗᏂᏂᏙᎯ ᏗᎦᏲᏙᏗ]

ᎤᎭᎨᏓ [ụhạgeda] (adj) "Thick."

ᎤᎭᎨᏗ ᎦᏌᎴᎾ [uhạgedị gasạlena] (n) "A heavy coat."

ᎤᎳᎾ [ulạna] (n) "Mother's brother's wife."

ᎠᎩᎳᎾ [a¹gilạna]

ᎤᎳᏏᏕᏂ [uhlạsihdeni] (n) "His foot."

ᎠᏆᎳᏏᏕᏂ [a¹gwahlạsihdeni]

ᎠᎴ ᎠᏓᎯᎯ ᏗᎪᏢᏒ ᎢᏗᏢ ᎨᎾᏗᏣᏕᎳᏁ ᏗᏣᎳᏏᏕᏂ.
And his setting thy feet in that way that leadeth unto the administration of Death.
[ᏧᏁᎶᏗ ᏚᏂᎩᏒᏒᎢ]

ᎤᎳᏑᎶ [uhlạsulo] (n) "Shoe."

ᎠᏆᎳᏑᎶ [a¹gwahlạsulo]

ᎤᎴᏍᏓᎸᎢ [ulesdahlvʔi] (n) "Her vagina."

ᎠᎩᎴᏍᏓᎸᎢ [a¹gịlesdahlvʔi]

ᎤᎴᏐᏓ [ulẹsoda] (n) "Poor.; Skinny."

ᎠᏆᎴᏐᏓ [a¹gwạlẹsoda]

ᎤᎵᎪᎭ [ulịgoha] (vi) "He is belonging to a group."

ᎠᏆᎵᎪᎠ [a¹gwạlịgọʔa]

ᎤᎵᎪᏅᎢ [ulịgọʔnv²³ʔi]

ᎤᎵᎪᎰᎢ [ulịgoho³ʔi]

ᏣᎵᎪᎲᎦ [tsalịgohvga]

ᎤᎵᎪᏗ [ulịkdi]

... ᏦᏩ ᎦᎵᏆᏚ ᎢᏳᏕᏘᏴᏛ ᎨᏎ ᏧᏂᎵ ᎤᎾᎵᎪᎭ ᏓᏅᎿᏗᏍᏗᏍᎨ ᎠᏫ; ...
... Joseph, a son of seventeen years, hath been enjoying himself with his brethren among the flock, ...
[ᎼᏏ ᎢᎬᏱᏱ 37:2]

ᎤᎵᏂᎩᏓ [uhlịnigida] (adj) "Strong."

ᎤᎵᏍᏆᏗᎠ [uli³sgwạdịʔa] (vi) "He has an earache."

ᎠᎩᎵᏍᏆᏗᎠ [a¹gịli³sgwạdịʔa]

ᎤᎵᏍᏆᏛᎢ [uli³sgwạdʔv²³ʔi]

ᎤᎵᏍᏆᏗᏍᎪᎢ [uli³sgwạdisgo³ʔi]

ᏣᎵᏍᏆᏓ [tsạli³sgwạda]

ᎤᎵᏍᏆᏗᏍᏗ [uli³sgwạdisdi]

ᎤᎵᏍᏆᏗᏍᎬᎢ [ulisgwạdịsgvʔi] (n) "Earache."

ᏚᎵᏍᏆᏗᏍᎬᎢ [dulisgwạdịsgvʔi]

ᎠᎩᎵᏍᏆᏗᏍᎬᎢ [a¹gịlisgwạdịsgvʔi]

ᏓᎩᎵᏍᏆᏗᏍᎬᎢ [da¹gịlisgwạdịsgvʔi]

ᎤᎵᏍᏇᏔᏬᎯ [ulsgwetạwọhi] (n) "Hat."

ᎠᏆᎵᏍᏇᏔᏬᎯ [a¹gwalsgwetạwọhi]

ᎤᎵᏍᏓ [uhlịsda] (pt) "Hurry.; Fast.; Quick."

ᎤᎵᏍᏓᎸᎢ [ulsdạlvʔi] (n) "Scab.; A sore."

ᎤᎵᏍᏓᏴᏗ [ulsdahydi] (n) "Food."

ᎠᏆᎵᏍᏓᏴᏗ [a¹gwalsdahydi]

ᎩᏟ ᎧᏴᏌᏛ ᎥᏍᏇ ᎤᏍᏕᎵᏍᎨ ᎤᎵᏍᏓᏴᏗ ᎤᏩᏛᏗ.
A dog's long (nose) also helps him to find food.
[ᏣᎳᎩ ᏔᎵᏁ ᏗᏂᏂᏙᎯ ᏗᎦᏲᏙᏗ]

ᎤᎵᏍᏗ [ulisdi] (adj) "Weak."

ᎤᎵᏏ [ulisi] (n) "Grandmother.; Granddaughter."

ᎠᏰᎵᏏ [a¹gilisi]

ᏑᏗᏩ ᏓᏞᏑᎠᏴᏓ ᏝᎤᎢ ᎤᎯ ᏚᏗᎵᎵ ᎤᎵᏏ ᎤᎬᏍᏛᏔ.
It was 8 o'clock when Sam Crock's grandmother found him.
[ᏣᏫᎩ ᏍᏔᎵᏗ ᏗᎯᎯᏙᎠ ᏗᏏᎵᏙᏗ]

ᎤᎵᏏᎯᏍᏇ [ulsihnidena] (n) "Evening."

ᎤᎵᏫᏗᎨ [uhlita³ʔneha] (vi) "He is eager."

ᎠᎢᎵᏫᏗᎨ [a¹gwaʔlita³ʔneha]

ᎤᎵᏫᏗᎾᏔ [uhlita³ʔnelv²³ʔi]

ᎤᎵᏫᏗᎮᏔ [uhlita³ʔneho³ʔi]

ᏣᎵᏫᏏ [tsahlita³si]

ᎤᎵᏫᏬᏗ [uhlita³ʔnhdi]

ᎤᎵᏗᏨ [ulditsv] (pt) "Beside.; Next to."

ᎤᎵᏬᎣᏨᎠ [uliwotsvhi] (n) "Dead."

ᏔᎤᎠᎱᎦᏃ ᎠᎢᏬᎵ ᎤᎵᏬᎣᏨᎠ ᎯᏍᏃᏔ, ᎤᎵ ᏧᎤᎦᎵᏈ ᏘᎤᏝᏣᏬᎠᏔ.
for wherever the carcase may be, there shall the eagles be gathered together.
[ᏓᏍ 24:28]

ᎤᎵᏰᎩᎤᏍᏛᎤ [uliyesusdawo] (n-nr) "His ring."

ᎠᎢᎵᏰᎩᎤᏍᏛᎤ [a¹gwaliyesusdawo]

ᎤᎵᏰᎯᎠ [uliyohi] (n) "His sock."

ᎠᎢᎵᏰᎯᎠ [a¹gwaliyohi]

ᎤᎬᎶᎩ [uhlogi] (n) "Father's sister."

ᎠᏰᎬᎶᎩ [a¹gihlogi]

ᎤᎶᎩᎵᏔ [ulogilv] (n) "Cloud."

ᏙᎤ ᎤᎶᎩᎵᏔ ᎤᎤᎠᏫᏛᏬᏗ; ᏙᎤ ᏍᏍᏍᎱᏬᏲᏗ ᏪᏬᏴ ᏗᎢᎤᏗᏬᏗᏙᏍ ᎤᎵᏫᏗᏬᏗ ᎯᏙᎡᏬ ᎤᏃᎠᏫ ᏏᏪᎤᏫᏬᏫ ᎤᏗᏪᎤᏗ ᏙᎤ ᎤᎯᏬᎵᏈ ᎯᎩᎩ, ᏪᏬᏴ ᎳᎬᏬ ᏣᏗᎨᏗ.
and the bow hath been in the cloud, and I have seen it – to remember the covenant age-during between God and every living creature among all flesh which [is] on the earth.'
[ᏏᏈ ᏔᎡᏫᏛ 9:16]

ᎤᎬᎠᏡᏬᏗ [ulogohosdi] (n) "Fall (season).; Autumn."

ᎤᎶᏫ [uloʔla] (vi) "He is lacking."

ᎠᏰᎬᏫ [a¹giloʔla]

ᎤᎬᏫᎤᏔ [uloʔlaʔnv²³ʔi]

ᎤᎬᎩᏔ [uloʔlo³ʔi]

ᏣᎬᏫᏍ [tsaloʔlaga]

ᎤᎬᎩᏗ [uloʔloʔdi]

ᎤᎶᏅᎥᏦᎭ [ulonv³tseha] (vi) "He is anxious."

ᎠᏰᎶᏅᎥᏦᎠ [a¹gilonv³tseʔa]

ᎤᎶᏅᎥᏙᎭᏔ [ulonv³tseʔlv²³ʔi]

ᎤᎶᏅᎥᎮᎭᏔ [ulonv³tseho³ʔi]

ᏣᎶᏅᎥᏦᏏ [tsalonv³tsesi]

ᎤᎶᏅᎥᏦᏬᏗ [ulonv³tsesdi]

ᎤᎶᏏᎤᎥ [ulosonv] (pt) "Afterwards."

ᏙᎤ ᎤᏴᏨᏍ, ᏗᎤᎤᏔᏫᎵᏗ ᏔᏏ ᎤᎶᏏᎤᎥᎠ, ᎤᎮᎡᎤᏟ ᏗᏥᎤᎵ-ᏗᏐᎦᎠ ᏙᎤ ᏗᎯᎢᎵᏏ ᏕᎬᏫᎤᎥ ᏔᏓᎵ,
And on the morrow that is after the preparation, were gathered together the chief priests, and the Pharisees, unto Pilate,
[ᏓᏍ 27:62]

ᎤᎶᏏᎤᎥ [ulosohnv] (pt) "Evaporated."

ᎤᎶᏗᏒᎬ [ulodskv] (n) "Fork in the branch of a tree.; An oarlock."

ᎤᎥᎷᎯᏍᏗ [uʔluhisdi] (n) "A place for receiving.; Receiving place."

ᎤᎥᏗ [ulvʔi] (n) "Sister's sister."

ᎠᏰᎥᏗ [a¹gilvʔi]

ᏣᎯᏃ ᎤᏫᏣᎴ ᎥᏍᏫ ᎯᏎᎹᏗᏬᏴ ᎢᏔᏔ, ᎤᎬᎬᎥᏣ ᎤᎥᏗ; ᎠᏙᏃ ᏡᏬᏐᏣ ᎥᏍᏫ, ᏗᎯᎲᏈ ᏗᏬᏯᏙᏏ, ᏔᎬᏃᏃ ᏛᎵ, ᏞᎯᎲᎤᏏ.
And Rachel seeth that she hath not borne to Jacob, and Rachel is envious of her sister, and saith unto Jacob, 'Give me sons, and if there is none – I die.'
[ᏏᏈ ᏔᎡᏫᏛ 30:1]

ᎤᎥᏂᏗᏍᎩ [ulvntisgi] (n) "Lunatic.; Degenerant."

ᎤᎥᏎᏘ [ulvsati] (n) "Transparent.; Quartz crystal."

ᎤᎥᏔᎭ [ulvteha] (vi) "He is fainting."

ᎠᏗᎠᏍᎭ [a¹gwalvdʔeha]

ᎤᎥᏔᎭᏔ [ulvtelv²³ʔi]

ᎤᎥᏔᎮᏔ [ulvteho³ʔi]

ᏣᎵᏔᏍ [tsalvtega]

ᎤᎥᏔᏬᏗ [ulvtesdi]

ᎤᎥᏗ [ulvdi] (n) "Poison ivy.; Poison oak.; biol. *Toxicodendron radicans*."

ᎤᎥᏗᎭ [ulvdiha] (vi) "He is crazy."

ᎠᏰᎥᏗᏓ [a¹gilvdiʔa]

ᎤᎥᏫᎤᏔ [ulvtanv²³ʔi]

ᎤᎥᏗᏬᏗᏔ [ulvdisgo³ʔi]

ᏣᎵᏓ [tsalvda]

ᎤᎥᏬᏗ [ulvdohdi]

ᎤᎾᎠ [uną?a] (vt) “He has it (something flexible).”

ᎠᎩᎾᎠ [a¹giną?a]

ᎤᎾᎡᏍᏛᎢ [uną?esdv²³?i]

ᎤᎾᎣᎢ [uną?o³?i]

ᏣᎾᎡᏍᏗ [tsąną?esdi]

ᎤᎾᎡᏍᏗ [uną?esdi]

ᎿᏉᏃ ᎯᎠ ᏂᏚᏪᏎᎴᎢ, ᎪᎯᏍᎩᏂ ᏥᎩ, ᎩᎶ ᎠᏕᎸ-ᏗᎦᎶᏗ ᎤᎾᎡᏍᏗ, ᎦᏁᎨᏍᏗ, ᎠᎴ ᎾᏍᏉ ᏕᎦᎶᏗ; ᎩᎶᏃ ᎠᏰᎳᏍᏗ ᎦᏅᎯᏛ ᏄᏩᏴᎾ ᎨᏎᏍᏗ, ᏫᏕᎾᏚᎦ ᎤᏄᏬ ᎠᎴ ᏭᏩᎯ.
Then said he to them, ‘But, now, he who is having a bag, let him take [it] up, and in like manner also a scrip; and he who is not having, let him sell his garment, and buy a sword,
[ᎷᎦ 22:36]

ᎤᎾᎦᎸᎦ [uhnągąlvga] (vi) “He is becoming angry.”

ᎠᎩᎾᎦᎸᎦ [a¹gị?nągąlvga]

ᎤᎾᎦᎸᏨᎢ [uhnągąlvtsv²³?i]

ᎤᎾᎦᎸᎪᎢ [uhnągąlvgo³?i]

ᏣᎾᎦᎸᎩ [chąnągąlvgi]

ᎤᎾᎦᎸᎢᏍᏗ [uhnągąlv?ịsdi]

ᎤᎾᎦᎸᎭ [uhnągąlvha] (vi) “He is angry.”

ᎠᎩᎾᎦᎸᎭ [a¹gị?nągąlvha]

ᎤᎾᎦᎸᏨᎢ [uhnągąlvtsv²³?i]

ᎤᎾᎦᎸᎰᎢ [uhnągąlvho³?i]

ᏣᎾᎦᎸᎩ [chąnągąlvgi]

ᎤᎾᎦᎸᎢᏍᏗ [uhnągąlv?ịsdi]

ᎤᎾᎵᎢ [unali⁴?i] (n) “His friend.; They are friends.”

ᏧᎾᎵᎢ [tsunali⁴?i]

ᎾᏉᏃ ᏧᏂᎶᏗ ᎤᎾᎵᎢᏃ ᏚᎾᏓᏲ.
Then Christian took his leave of his Friend.
[ᏧᏂᎶᏍᏗ ᏚᏂᎩᎡᏒᎢ - ᎣᏍᏛ ᏧᏰᎸᎯ ᏴᎾ]

ᎤᎾᎶᎢᏓ [ųnąlo?ịda] (adj) “Plaid.”

ᎤᎾᏄᏍᏗ [una?nųsdi] (n) “Frost on the ground (ice).; Hoar frost.”

ᎤᎾᏆᎸ [ųnągwahlv] (n) “Maryville, TN.”

ᎤᎾᏍᏕᏥ

ᎤᎾᏍᏕᏥ [ųnąsdetsi] (n) “Root.”

ᎤᎾᏕᎦ [unde³ga] (vt) “He is selling it.”

ᎠᎩᎾᏕᎦ [a¹ginde³ga]

ᎤᎾᏕᎡᏒᎢ [unde³ęsv²³?i]

ᎤᎾᏕᎪᎢ [unde³go³?i]

ᏣᎾᏕᎤᎦ [tsąnde³u?ga]

ᎤᎾᏕᎥᏍᏗ [unde³vsdi]

ᎢᏥᎾᏕᎨᏍᏗ ᎢᏥᎿᎥᎢ ᎠᎴ ᎢᏣᏓᏁᎸᎥᏍᎨᏍᏗ; …
sell your goods, and give alms, …
[ᎷᎦ 12:33]

ᎤᎾᏕᏘᏱᏍᎬᎢ [ųnądetịyịsgv?i] (n) “Christmas.”

ᎤᎾᏤᏥᏗ [ųntsetsdi] (n) “Candy roaster squash.; biol. *Cucurbita maxima.*”

ᎤᎾᏥ [unatsi] (n) “Parent-in-law.”

ᎠᎩᎾᏥ [a¹ginatsi]

ᎤᎾᏩ [uhnąwa] (n) “A dish.”

ᎤᎾᏫᎠ [unawį?a] (vi) “He is trembling.”

ᎠᎩᎾᏫᎠ [a¹ginawį?a]

ᎤᎾᏮᎢ [unahwv²³?i]

ᎤᎾᏫᎠᎪᎢ [unawį?ągo³?i]

ᏣᎾᏩ [tsąnahwa]

ᎤᎾᏫᎢᏍᏗ [unawįisdi]

ᎾᏉᏃ ᏧᏂᎶᏗ ᎦᎵᎡᎵᎦ, ᎠᎴ ᎠᎩᎾᏫᎠ ᎤᏛᏅᎩ.
Then said Christian, I rejoice and tremble.
[ᏧᏂᎶᏗ ᏚᏂᎩᎡᏒᎢ]

ᎤᏁᎦ [unega] (adj) “White.”

… ᏝᏰᏃ ᏰᎵ ᏌᏉ ᎩᏢ ᎤᏁᎬ ᎠᎴ ᎬᎿᎨ ᏱᏅᎦᏛᎦ.
… because thou art not able one hair to make white or black;
[ᎹᏚ 5:36]

ᎤᏁᎦᎸᎢ [unegą?lv?i] (n) “His skin.”

ᎠᎩᏁᎦᎸᎢ [a¹ginegą?lv?i]

ᎤᏁᎦᎸᏅ [unegąlv?nv] (n) “A peeling.”

ᎤᏁᎦᏓ [ųnegada] (n) “Yellow shafted flicker.; Yellowhammer.; biol. *Colaptes auratus auratus.*”

ᎤᏁᎫᎭ [uneguha] (vi) “He is mean.”

ᎠᎩᏁᎫᎠ [a¹ginegų?a]

ᎤᏁᎫᏨᎢ [unegu?tsv²³?i]

ᎤᏁᎫᎰᎢ [uneguho³?i]

ᏣᏁᎫᎩ [tsąnegu?gi]

ᎤᏁᎫᎢᏍᏗ [unegu?isdi]

ᎤᏁᎫᏣᏔ [unektsạta] (vi) "He is mischievious."

ᎠᎩᏁᎫᏣᏔ [a¹gịneguʔtsạta]

ᎤᏁᎫᏣᏖᏍᏛᎢ [unektsạtesdv²³ʔi]

ᎤᏁᎫᏣᏙᎢ [unektsạto³ʔi]

ᏣᏁᎫᏣᏖᏍᏗ [tsạnektsạtesdi]

ᎤᏁᎫᏣᏘ [unektsạti]

ᎤᏁᎭ [uneha] (vt) "He has it (a liquid)."

ᎠᎩᏁᎠ [a¹gịnẹʔa]

ᎤᏁᏅᎢ [unẹʔnv²³ʔi]

ᎤᏁᎰᎢ [uneho³ʔi]

ᏣᏁᎲᎦ [tsạnehvga]

ᎤᏁᏗ [unhdi]

ᎤᏁᎳᏅᎯ [ụnehlạnvhi] (n) "God."

… ᏂᎪᎯᎸ ᏗᎨᎦᏓᏂᎸᏨᎯᏉ ᎠᏂᏙᎾᎥ ᎤᏁᎳᏅᎯ ᎠᎦᏔᎲᎢ.
… every one walking in the sight of God,
[ᏧᏁᏣᏗ ᏕᏂᎩᎡᎡᎢ]

ᎤᏁᎸᏒ [ụnelvsv] (n) "Scar."

ᎤᏁᏍᎩᎸᎢ [uhnesgịlvʔi] (n) "Nest."

ᎤᏁᏍᏓᎳᏗᎠ [unesdaldịʔa] (vi) "He is freezing."

ᎠᎩᏁᏍᏓᎳᏗᎠ [a¹gịnẹʔsdaldịʔa]

ᎤᏁᏍᏓᎳᏛᎢ [unesdaldv²³ʔi]

ᎤᏁᏍᏓᎳᏗᏍᎪᎢ [unesdaldịsgo³ʔi]

ᏣᏁᏍᏓᎳᏓ [tsạnesdalda]

ᎤᏁᏍᏓᎳᏗᏍᏗ [unesdaldisdi]

ᎤᏁᏍᏓᎵ [unẹsdahli] (n) "Ice.; Glass."

ᎤᏁᏍᏓᎵ ᎪᏒᏍᎩ [ụnẹsdahl gọsvsgi] (n) "Ice plant.; Freezer."

ᎤᏁᏘ [ụneti] (n) "Freckles."

ᎤᏂᎬᎦ [uhnigvga] (vt) "He is needing.; He is running short of.; He is lacking."

ᎠᎩᏂᎬᎦ [a¹gịʔnigvga]

ᎤᏂᎪᏒᎢ [uhnigọsv²³ʔi]

ᎤᏂᎬᎪᎢ [uhnigvgo³ʔi]

ᏣᏂᎪᎯ [chạnigọhi]

—

ᎢᏳᏃ ᎩᎶ ᏂᎯ ᎢᏤᎲ ᎠᎦᏙᎥᎯᏍᏗ ᎨᏒ ᎤᏂᎬᎨᏍᏗ, …
and if any of you do lack wisdom, …
[ᏥᎻ 1:5]

ᎤᏂᎬᎦ [unigvga] (vt) "He is in need."

ᎠᎩᏂᎬᎦ [a¹gịnigvga]

ᎤᏂᎬᏨᎢ [unigvʔtsv²³ʔi]

ᎤᏂᎬᎪᎢ [unigvgo³ʔi]

ᏣᏂᎬᎦ [janigvʔga]

ᎤᏂᎬᎢᏍᏗ [unigvʔisdi]

ᎢᏳᏃ ᎩᎶ ᏂᎯ ᎢᏤᎲ ᎠᎦᏙᎥᎯᏍᏗ ᎨᏒ ᎤᏂᎬᎨᏍᏗ, ᎤᏁᎳᏅᎯ ᎠᏔᏲᏎᎮᏍᏗ …
and if any of you do lack wisdom, let him ask from God …
[ᏥᎻ 1:5]

ᎤᏂᎵ [unịli] (n) "Brother's older brother."

ᎠᎩᏂᎵ [a¹gịnịli]

ᎤᏂᎶᏇ [ụnịlogwe] (n) "Honey mushroom.; Slicky mushroom.; biol. *Armillaria mellea.*"

ᎤᏂᏁᎫᎯᏍᏗ [ụnineguḥịsdi] (n) "Tomato(es).; biol. *Solanum lycopersicum.*"

ᎤᏂᏆ [unịkwa] (n) "Black gum."

ᎤᏂᏍᏆᎵ [ụnisgwali] (n) "Heartleaf."

ᎤᏂᏍᏇᏚᎦ [ụnịsgweduga] (n) "Mayapple.; Wild mandrake.; Ground lemon.; biol. *Podophyllum peltatum.*"

ᎤᏂᏍᏕᎴᏍᏗ [ụnịsdẹlesdi] (n) "Wild comfrey.; Blue houndstongue.; biol. *Cynoglossum virginianum.*"

ᎤᏂᏏ [unisi] (n) "Father's father.; Grandson."

ᎠᎩᏂᏏ [a¹gịnisi]

ᎤᏂᏒᏙᏂ [unịsvdọni] (n) "Hollow mushrooms.; Morel.; Sponge morel.; They are hollow.; biol. *Morchella esculenta.*"

ᎤᏂᏖᎸᎳᏗ [ụnịtẹlvlahdi] (n) "Fox grapes.; Wild grapes.; biol. *Vitis labrusca.*"

ᎤᏂᏣᏘ [unitsạti] (n) "Mass of people."

… ᎠᎴ ᎤᏂᏣᏘ ᏫᎾᎾᎵᏍᏓ ᎾᎿ ᎠᏰᎵ ᎨᏒ ᎡᎶᎯ.
… and they increase into a multitude in the midst of the land.'
[ᎼᏏ ᎢᎬᏱᏱ 1:20]

ᎤᏂᏣᏛ [unitsạdv] (n) "Lots.; A group.; Many."

ᎠᎴ ᎾᎯᏳ ᎢᏳᏓᎴᏅᏛ ᎤᏂᏣᏛ ᎬᏩᏍᏓᏩᏗᏙᎯ ᎤᎾᏨᏒᎩ, ᎠᎴ ᎥᏝ ᎿᏉ ᎢᎸᎯᏳ ᏳᏁᏙᎴᎢ.
From this [time] many of his disciples went away backward, and were no more walking with him,
[ᏣᏂ 6:66]

ᎤᏂᏥᎸᎢ [ụnịtsilvʔi] (n) "A pepper on a vine."

ᎤᏂᏥᏯ [ụnịtsiya] (n) "Red earthworms.; Nightcrawlers.; biol. *Lumbricus terrestris.*"

ᎤᏂᏨᎾᏓᎵ [ụntsvndạli] (n) "Peas."

ᎤᎵᏴᏏ [uʔni³yha] (vt) "He is holding it (something alive) in hand."

ᎠᏯᎵᏴᏏ [a¹giʔni³yʔa]

ᎤᎵᏆᎶᎢ [uʔni³yvhv²³ʔi]

ᎤᎵᎯᎢ [uʔni³yho³ʔi]

ᏣᎵᏴᏏ [tsạʔni³ya]

ᎤᎵᏆᏗ [uʔni³yhdi]

ᎤᏃᎧ [uhnọka] (n) "Bigmouth bass.; Largemouth bass.; biol. *Micropterus salmoides.*"

ᎤᏃᎴᎯ

ᎤᏃᎴᎯ [ụnolẹhi] (n) "Wind."

ᎤᏃᏕᎾ [ụnọdena] (n) "Sheep.; biol. *Ovis aries.*"

ᎳᏍᎦ ᎤᎵᏃᏕᎾ ᏓᏂᎠᏫᏒ.
Count the sheep walking about.
[ᏣᎳᎩ ᎡᎶᏗ ᏗᎯᎯᏬᎯ ᏗᏍᎩᏃᏗᎢ]

ᎤᏃᏈ [unoyv] (n) "Cedar waxwing.; biol. *Bombycilla cedrorum.*"

ᎤᏃᏈᏃᏈᏆᏍ [uhnọyyʔnohyvhlga] (vi) "It is making a noise."

⸺

ᎤᏃᏈᏃᏈᏆᎡᏕ [uhnọyyʔnohyvhlsv²³ʔi]

ᎤᏃᏈᏃᏈᏆᎠᎢ [uhnọyyʔnohyvhlgo³ʔi]

ᎩᏃᏈᏃᏈᏆ [wuhnọyyʔnohyvhli]

ᎤᏃᏈᏃᏈᏆᏬᏗ [uhnọyyʔnohyvhlsdi]

ᎤᏇᎸᏬᏍ [unu³lvhvsga] (vi) "He is failing.; He is unable to do it."

ᎠᏯᏇᎸᏬᏍ [a¹ginu³lyʔvsga]

ᎤᏇᏃᎢᏔ [unu³lyʔhnv²³ʔi]

ᎤᏇᎸᏬᎠᎢᏔ [unu³lvhvsgo³ʔi]

ᏣᏇᎸᏍ [tsạnu³lvhvga]

ᎤᏇᏗ [unu³hldi]

ᏒᏏᏪᏈᏯᏃ ᏫᏬᏟᏣᎥᏪ ᎤᎵᏇᎠᏫᏲᏗᏁ; ᎠᏎᏃ ᎤᎵᏇᏃᎩ.
and I besought thy disciples that they might cast it out, and they were not able.'
[ᎷᏍ 17:16]

ᎤᏇᏂ [unutsi] (n) "Brother's younger brother.; Son-in-law."

ᎠᏯᏇᏂ [a¹ginutsi]

ᎤᏄᏍ [unvga] (vi) "He is hurrying."

ᎠᎦᏄᏍ [a¹gwanvga]

ᎤᏄᏟᏔ [unvʔtsv²³ʔi]

ᎤᏄᎠᏔ [unvgo³ʔi]

ᏣᏄᎩ [tsanvʔgi]

ᎤᏄᏔᏬᏗ [unvʔisdi]

ᎤᏄᏯᏅ [uhnyginv] (n) "American chinquapin.; Dwarf chestnut.; biol. *Castanea pumila.*"

ᎤᏄᎠᏫᏒ [uhnygọladv] (n) "Rainbow."

ᎠᏙ ᎠᏗ ᎤᎵᏏᏬᏪᎯ ᏜᏴ ᏂᏣᎩᏯᏪᏬᏗᏬᏓᏍᎤᏗ ᎡᏆᏗ, ᎤᏄᎠᏫᏒ ᏓᎦᏦᏗ ᎯᏍᏬᏗᏬᏓᏍᎤᏗ ᎤᎩᏯᏔ.
and it hath come to pass (in My sending a cloud over the earth) that the bow hath been seen in the cloud, [ᏅᏆ ᎿᎡᏳᏬ 9:14]

ᎤᏄᎭᏗ [unysadi] (n) "Rattle wrapped around the leg."

ᏤᏄᎭᏗ [tsunysadi]

ᎠᎦᏄᎭᏗ [a¹gwạnysadi]

ᏗᎦᏄᎭᏗ [di¹gwạnysadi]

ᎤᏄᏏᏴᏗ [ụnvsiyvʔi] (n) "Corner."

ᎤᏄᏓᎭ [uhndaha] (vt) "He is remembering it."

ᎠᎦᏄᏓᎭ [a¹gwạʔndaha]

ᎤᏄᏓᏉᏔ [uhndạdʔv²³ʔi]

ᎤᏄᎵᎢᏔ [uhndaho³ʔi]

ᏣᏄᏛᎸ [tsahndvda]

ᎤᏄᏓᏗᏬᏗ [uhndạdịsdi]

ᎡᏬᏓᏣᎵᏴᏫᏃ ᎤᏄᏓᏟᏯ ᎠᏗ ᎲᎡᏴ ᎠᏫᏔ; "ᎩᎥᏗ ᏓᏄᏝ ᏝᎻᎬ ᎠᏳᏬᏓ."
And his disciples remembered that it is written, 'The zeal of Thy house did eat me up;' [ᏣᎯ 2:17]

ᎤᏄᎵᎡᏔ [unvdạsvʔi] (n) "A mountain."

ᎤᏄᎳᏔᎴ [ụnytagwạli] (n) "Small pox."

ᎤᏄᏗ [ụnvdi] (n) "Milk."

ᏗᏴᏃ ᎤᏗᏬᏜ ᎤᏄᏗ, ᏗᏴᏬᏗ ᏗᏬᏗᏣᏍᏍ.
Color the ice cream a color according to the following.
[ᏣᎳᎩ ᎡᎶᏗ ᏗᎯᎯᏬᎯ ᏗᏍᎩᏃᏗᎢ]

ᎤᏄᏍᎭᏬᏓ [ụnvdụhisda] (n) "Groundcherry.; biol. *Physalis spp.*"

ᎤᏄᏟᏗ [uhnvtsạdi] (adj) "Speckled."

ᎤᏄᏟᏗ [uhnvtsati] (n) "Speckled trout."

ᎤᎾᏄᏟᏗ [unahnvtsati]

ᎤᏄᏂ [untsi] (n) "Snow on the ground."

ᎤᏄᏂᏓ [unvtsida] (n) "Brains."

ᎤᏅᏩᏍᏗᎭ [unvwasdịha] (vi) "He has chills."

ᎠᎩᏅᏩᏍᏗᎭ [a^{1}gịnvwạʔsdịha]

ᎤᏅᏩᏍᏔᏅᎢ [unvwastạnv^{23}ʔi]

ᎤᏅᏩᏍᏗᏍᎪᎢ [unvwasdịsgo^{3}ʔi]

ᏣᏅᏩᏍᏓ [tsạnvwasda]

ᎤᏅᏩᏍᏙᏗ [unvwasdohdi]

ᎤᏅᏪᏓ [ụnṿweda] (n) "Bowl."

ᎤᏆᎶᎦ [ugwạloga] (n) "Leaf."

ᎤᏆᏍᏓᎷᏱᏓ [ụgwạsdaluhyda] (n) "Ragweed.; Giant ragweed.; biol. *Ambrosia trifida.*"

ᎤᏇᏓᎸᎢ [ugwedahlvʔi] (n) "His flesh."

ᎠᎩᏇᏓᎸᎢ [a^{1}gịgwedahlvʔi]

ᎾᏍᎩᏃ ᎢᏳᏍᏗ ᎠᏍᎦᏯ ᎦᎬᎦᎨᏍᏗ ᎤᏙᏓ ᎠᎴ ᎤᏥ, ᎤᏓᎵᎢᏃ ᎠᏜᎾᏍᏗᏍᎨᏍᏗ, ᎾᏍᎩᏃ ᏌᏉᏉ ᎤᏂᏇᏓᎸᎢ ᎨᏎᏍᏗ.
therefore doth a man leave his father and his mother, and hath cleaved unto his wife, and they have become one flesh.
[ᎼᏏ ᎢᎬᏱᏱ 2:24]

ᎤᏌᎴᏂ [usạleni] (n) "A coat."

ᎠᏆᏌᎴᏂ [a^{1}gwasạleni]

ᎤᏍᎦᎡᏂ [ụsgạʔeni] (n) "Coward."

ᎤᏍᎦᎢ [ụsgạʔhi] (n) "Dwarf crested iris.; Crested iris.; biol. *Iris cristata.*"

ᎤᏍᎦᎩ [usgagi] (n) "His enemy."

ᎠᏆᏍᎦᎩ [a^{1}gwạsgagi]

ᎢᏣᏛᎦᏅᎯ ᎢᎩ ᎯᎠ ᎢᎦᏪᏛ ᎨᎡᎢ; ᎯᎨᏳᏎᏍᏗ ᎾᎥ ᎢᏗᏍᏓᏓᏔ, ᎯᏍᎦᎨᏍᏗᏃ ᏣᏍᎦᎩ.
'Ye heard that it was said: Thou shalt love thy neighbour, and shalt hate thine enemy;
[ᎹᏚ 5:43]

ᎤᏍᎦᏎᏗ ᎤᏗᎴᎩ [ụsgạsed ụdịlegị] (n) "Pneumonia."

ᎤᏍᎪᎸ [ụsgolv] (adj) "Pale."

ᎤᏍᎫᏩᏗᎠ [usgu^{3}wạdịʔa] (vi) "He has a headache."

ᎠᎩᏍᎫᏩᏗᎠ [a^{1}gịʔsgu^{3}wạdịʔa]

ᎤᏍᎫᏩᏛᎢ [usgu^{3}wạdʔv^{23}ʔi]

ᎤᏍᎫᏩᏗᏍᎪᎢ [usgu^{3}wạdịsgo^{3}ʔi]

ᏣᏍᎫᏩᏓ [tsasgu^{3}wạda]

ᎤᏍᎫᏩᏗᏍᏗ [usgu^{3}wạdịsdi]

ᎤᏍᏆᏅᏂ [ụsgwạnvhni] (n) "Mulligan blanket."

ᎤᏍᏆᏗ [usgwahdi] (n) "Safety pin.; Stick pin."

ᎤᏍᏆᏙ [ụsgwạdo] (n) "Red buckeye.; Firecracker plant.; biol. *Aesculus pavia.*"

ᎤᏍᏇᏅᎯ [usgwenṿhi] (n) "His fist."

ᎠᎩᏍᏇᏅᎯ [a^{1}gsgwenṿhi]

ᎤᏍᏉᎳᏗᎠ [usgwolạdịʔa] (vi) "He has diarrhea."

ᎠᎩᏍᏉᎳᏗᎠ [a^{1}gịʔsgwolạdịʔa]

ᎤᏍᏉᎳᏛᎢ [usgwolạdv^{23}ʔi]

ᎤᏍᏉᎳᏗᏍᎪᎢ [usgwolạdịsgo^{3}ʔi]

ᏣᏍᏉᎳᏓ [tsasgwolạda]

ᎤᏍᏉᎳᏗᏍᏗ [usgwolạdịsdi]

ᎤᏍᏓᎦᎸᎢ [ụsdagạlvʔi] (n) "Cave.; Rock shelter.; Cavern."

ᎤᏍᏓᎦᎸᎢ ᎠᏲᎭ. Ꮭ ᏯᏩᏗᎭ.
At the cave she is looking for him. She isn't finding him.
[ᏣᏔᎩ ᎧᎢᏁ ᏗᏂᏂᏙᎯ ᏗᎦᏲᏙᏗ]

ᎤᏍᏓᎸᎢ [usdahlvʔi] (n) "Clan."

ᎠᎩᏍᏓᎸᎢ [a^{1}gsdahlvʔi]

ᎤᏍᏓᎾᎵ [ụsdạnali] (n) "Shoals."

ᎤᏍᏓᏁᎦᎸᎢ

ᎤᏍᏓᏁᎦᎸᎢ [usdạnegạʔlvʔi] (n) "The sole of his foot."

ᎠᏆᏍᏓᏁᎦᎸᎢ [a^{1}gwạsdạnegạʔlvʔi]

ᎤᏍᏓᏍᏗ [ụsdạsdi] (n) "Mountain holly.; Catberry.; biol. *Ilex mucronata.*"

ᎤᏍᏗ [ụsdi] (adj) "Little."

ᏝᏍᎪᏃ ᏳᎾᎬᏯᏎᎵᎴ ᎤᏍᏗ ᎦᎶᎯᏍᏗ ᏗᎪᎵᎡᎢ ᎾᏣᎶᎯᏍᏗᏱ?
Did not I direct thee the way to the little Wicket-gate?
[ᏧᏁᎶᏗ ᏚᏂᎩᎡᎡᎢ]

ᎤᏍᏗᎢ [ụsdiʔi] (pt) "Baby."

ᎤᏍᏗᎢ ᎠᎩᏙ ᎡᎭ. ᏥᎦᏴᎵᏯ ᏏᏅ ᎠᎩᏙ ᎨᎡᎢ.
I have a baby brother. I am older than my brother.
[ᏣᏔᎩ ᏔᎵᏁ ᏗᏂᏂᏙᎯ ᏗᎦᏲᏙᏗ]

ᎤᏍᏗ ᎭᏰᎳᏍᏗ [ụsdị hạyelạsdi] (n) "Pocket knife."

ᎤᏍᏗᏳ [usdiyu] (n) "Place to look."

ᎠᎩᏍᏗᏳ [a^{1}gịsdiyu]

… "ᎢᏣᏙᎴᏆᏍᎨᏍᏗ ᏗᏓᏅᏬ ᏅᏬᏗ ᎢᏥᏍᏗᏳ ᏓᏨᏰᏲᏂ"
… "You should be learning doctoring medicine; I am going to teach you where to look".
[King pg 122]

ᎤᏍᏚᏥᎠ [usdutsịʔa] (vi) "He is dripping.; He is being spilled on."

ᎠᎩᏍᏚᏥᎠ [a^{1}gịʔsdutsịʔa]

ᎤᏍᏚᏨᎢ [usdudstsv^{23}ʔi]

ᎤᏍᏚᏥᏍᎪᎢ [usdutsịsgo^{3}ʔi]

ᏣᏍᏚᏥᏣ [tsasdudstsa]

ᎤᏍᏚᏥᏍᏗ [usdutsịsdi]

ᎤᏎᎳᏘ [usẹlati] (n) "Rattlesnake fern.; Held erect.; biol. *Botrypus virginianus.*"

ᎤᏌᏍᎩ [usẹsgi] (n) "Whooping cough."

ᎤᏇᏢᎦ [usihwah³sga] (vi) "He is coughing."

    ᎠᎩᏏᏢᎦ [a¹giʔsihwah³sga]

    ᎤᏇᏢᏫᏘ [usihwą³hv²³ʔi]

    ᎤᏇᏢᏍᎪᏘ [usihwah³sgo³ʔi]

    ᏣᏏᏢᎭ [tsasihwą³hi]

    ᎤᏇᏢᏍᏗ [usihwah³sdi]

ᎤᏐᏱ [usoyi] (adj) "Same."

ᎤᏇᎧᎵᎥᏘ [usụkahlvʔi] (n) "His toe nail."

    ᎠᏣᏇᎧᎵᎥᏘ [a¹gwasụkahlvʔi]

ᎤᏇᏩᏍ [usulągoga] (vi) "He is lonesome."

    ᎠᏯᏇᏩᏍ [a¹giʔsulągoga]

    ᎤᏇᏩᎩᏘ [usulągotsav²³ʔi]

    ᎤᏇᏩᎠᏘ [usulągogo³ʔi]

    ᏣᏇᏩᏯ [tsasulągogi]

    ᎤᏇᏩᏘᏍᏗ [usulągoʔisdi]

ᎤᏇᎵᎭ [usulịha] (vi) "He is full."

    ᎠᏯᏇᎵᎭ [a¹giʔsulịha]

    ᎤᏇᎸᏫᏘ [usulyhv²³ʔi]

    ᎤᏇᎵᏍᎪᏘ [usulịsgo³ʔi]

    ᏣᏇᎵ [tsasuli]

    ᎤᏇᎵᏗ [usuhldi]

ᎤᏒᎯ [usv³hi] (pt) "Yesterday.; Tonight.; At night."

    … ᎠᏎᏃ ᏠᎮᏫᎡ ᎤᏤᎵ ᎤᎤᏬᎯ ᎠᏯᎵᎥᎩᏴ ᎤᏒᎯ ᎡᏃᎲ, ᎠᏗ ᎬᎠᎡᏴ; …
    … but the God of your father yesternight hath spoken unto me, saying, …
    [ᏅᏛ ᎢᎬᏣᏓ 31:29]

ᎤᏒᏙᏂ [usỵdoni] (n) "Hollow."

ᎤᏓᎨᏳᎭ [udage³yuha] (vi) "He is loving."

    ᎠᏣᏓᎨᏳᎠ [a¹gwadage³yuʔa]

    ᎤᏓᎨᏳᏅᏘ [udage³yunv²³ʔi]

    ᎤᏓᎨᏳᎰᏘ [udage³yuho³ʔi]

    ᏣᏓᎨᏳᎦ [tsadage³yuga]

    ᎤᏓᎨᏳᏗ [udage³yhdi]

    ᎥᏣ ᎤᏬ ᏦᎬᎦᏍᏗ ᎡᎠᏍᏗ ᏘᏅᎵᎤᏄᎭ, ᏦᎤᏓᎨᏳᏮᏍᏴᎭ Ꮩ ᎦᎸᏍᎤᏆ.
    none of them are hurtful, but loving and holy.
    [ᏅᏛ ᎢᎬᏣᏓ]

ᎤᏓᎳᎭ [udạlehi] (adj) "Different."

ᎤᏓᎵ [ụdahli] (n) "Mistletoe.; biol. *Viscum album.*"

ᎤᏓᎵᎢᏘ [udạlịʔi] (n) "His wife."

    ᎠᏣᏓᎵᎢᏘ [a¹gwạdalịʔi]

    ᎿᏫ ᏂᏏ ᎡᏂᎭᎡᏫᏃ ᏂᏍᎦᎷᏣ ᎤᏓᎵᎢᏘ.
    Wherefore at length he brake his mind to his Wife and Children.
    [ᏅᏅᏣ ᏏᎮᏴᎡᎡᏘ]

    Note: ᎤᏓᎵ + ᎠᎵᎢᏘ.

ᎤᏓᎶᏒ [ụdalosv] (n) "Income."

ᎤᏓᏁᎦᎸᏓ [ụdąnegạlvda] (n) "Skinned place.; A sore."

ᎤᏓᏁᎳᏬᏓ [udạnelạwoda] (n) "A scald place.; Scalded."

ᎤᏓᏁᎶᎲ [udạnelohv] (n) "A bush."

ᎤᏓᏂᏖᏗᎭ [udanhte³hdịha] (vi) "He is worrying."

    ᎠᏣᏓᏁᏖᏗᎭ [a¹gwạdanʔte³hdịha]

    ᎤᏓᏂᏖᏓᏅᏘ [udanhte³hdạnv²³ʔi]

    ᎤᏓᏂᏖᏗᎠᏘ [udanhte³hdịsgo³ʔi]

    ᏣᏓᏁᏖᏓ [tsadanhte³hda]

    ᎤᏓᏂᏖᏍᏗ [udanhte³hduhdi]

ᎤᏓᏕᎥ [udando] (n) "His heart."

    ᎠᏣᏓᏕᎥ [a¹gwạdando]

    ᎠᎠᏑᏴ ᏍᎤᎬᎦ ᏴᎠ ᎤᏓᏕᎥ ᏏᏎᏲᏫ ᏴᏍᏫ ᎤᏬᏆᏕᎳᏅᏣᏑ ᏂᎮᎡᏅ.
    This parlour is the heart of a man that was never sanctified by the sweet Grace of the Gospel.
    [ᏅᏅᏣ ᏏᎮᏴᎡᎡᏘ]

ᎤᏓᏬᎭ [ụdatanyhi] (n) "Berry."

    ᎠᎡᏃᏃ ᎠᏗ ᏆᏔᏕᏙ ᎢᎥᎵ; ᏌᏫᏫ ᏏᎯᏴᏎᏗ ᎤᏓᏬᎭ ᏙᏬᏣᏍᎥ ᎢᏍᏫᏍ.
    And the woman saith unto the serpent, 'Of the fruit of the trees of the garden we do eat,
    [ᏅᏂ ᎢᎡᎥᎥ 3:2]

ᎤᏓᏨᏗ [ụdatsạkdi] (adj) "Rough."

ᎤᏓᏫᏯᏍᏗ [udạwelạgịsdi] (n) "Burner on a stove."

ᎤᏩᎦᏍ [utạloga] (vi) "He has his mouth open."

    ᎠᏣᏓᎦᏍ [a¹gwạdạʔaloga]

    ᎤᏩᎦᎥᏘ [utạloʔnv²³ʔi]

    ᎤᏩᎦᎢᎠᏘ [utạloʔysgo³ʔi]

    ᏣᏩᎦᎢᏍ [tsatạloʔyga]

    ᎤᏩᎦᏗ [utạlohdi]

ᎤᏩᎦᏴ [utạlogi] (n) "Kettle.; His open mouth."

ᎤᏩᎷᏯᎠ [uhtạlu³giʔa] (vi) "It is shining.; It is reflecting."

    ᎤᏩᎷᏏᏘ [uhtạlu³gaʔv²³ʔi]

    ᎤᏩᎷᏯᎠᏘ [uhtạlu³gịsgo³ʔi]

    ᏉᏩᎷᏍᏍ [wuhtạlu³gaga]

    ᎤᏩᎷᎠᏗ [uhtạlu³godi]

ᎤᏔᎷᎩᏍᎩ [ụtalugisgi] (n) "Satin."

ᎤᏔᎾ [utạna] (adj) "Grown-up.; Big."

ᎤᏔᏕᎩᎠ [uhtạdegịʔa] (vi) "He is thirsty."

> **ᎠᎩᏔᏕᎩᎠ** [a¹gịʔtạdegịʔa]
>
> **ᎤᏔᏕᎩᏒᎢ** [uhtạdegịsv²³ʔi]
>
> **ᎤᏔᏕᎩᏍᎪᎢ** [uhtạdegịsgo³ʔi]
>
> **ᏣᏔᏕᎩ** [tshtạdegi]
>
> **ᎤᏔᏕᎩᏍᏗ** [uhtạdegịsdi]
>
> … ᎢᏳᏃ ᎩᎶ ᎤᏔᏕᎩᏍᎨᏍᏗ, ᎠᏴ ᏩᎩᎷᏥ, ᎠᎴ ᏩᏗᏔ.
> … 'If any one doth thirst, let him come unto me and drink;
> [ᏣᏂ 7:37]

ᎤᏕᎦ [udega] (vt) "He is throwing it."

> **ᎠᏆᏕᎦ** [a¹gwạdega]
>
> **ᎤᏕᏒᎢ** [udesv²³ʔi]
>
> **ᎤᏕᎪᎢ** [udego³ʔi]
>
> **ᏣᏕᎦ** [tsadeʔga]
>
> —
>
> … ᎭᏓᏕᏖᏙᎢᏍᎨᏍᏗ, ᎠᎴ ᏣᏕᎨᏍᏗ; …
> … pluck it out and cast from thee, …
> [ᎹᏚ 5:29]

ᎤᏕᎰᏌᏘ [udẹhọsạti] (vi) "He is bashful."

> **ᎠᏆᏕᎣᏌᏘ** [a¹gwạdẹʔọsạti]
>
> **ᎤᏕᎰᏌᏛᎢ** [udẹhọsạtv²³ʔi]
>
> **ᎤᏕᎰᏌᏙᎢ** [udẹhọsạto³ʔi]
>
> **ᏣᏕᎰᏌᏖᏍᏗ** [tsadẹhọsạtẹsdi]
>
> **ᎤᏕᎰᏌᏖᏍᏗ** [udẹhọsạtẹsdi]

ᎤᏕᎵᎦ [udelịga] (vi) "He is going out of sight."

> **ᎠᏆᏕᎵᎦ** [a¹gwạdelịga]
>
> **ᎤᏕᎵᏨᎢ** [udelịtsv²³ʔi]
>
> **ᎤᏕᎵᎪᎢ** [udelịgo³ʔi]
>
> **ᏣᏕᎵ** [tsadeli]
>
> **ᎤᏕᎵᎢᏍᏗ** [udelịʔisdi]

ᎤᏕᏅ [ụdenv] (pt) "Birth.; Born.; Birthplace."

> ᏥᏌᏃ ᎤᏕᏅ ᏇᏚᏱ ᏇᏚᎲ ᏧᏗᏱ, …
> And Jesus having been born in Beth-Lehem of Judea, …
> [ᎹᏚ 2:1]

ᎤᏕᏗᏴᏌᏗᏒᎢ [udehdiyvsạdisvʔi] (n) "In the year.; During the year."

> ᏊᏕᏁ ᏏᏉᏯ ᎦᎵᏆᏚ ᏑᏓᎵᏍᎪ ᎦᎵᏉᎩ ᎤᏕᏗᏴᏌᏗᏒᎢ.
> Sequoyah was born in the year 1767.
> [ᏣᎳᎩ ᏔᎵᏁ ᏗᏂᏂᏙᎯ ᏗᏕᏲᏙᏗ]

ᎤᏕᏘᏱᎭ

ᎤᏕᏘᏱᎭ [udẹtịyịha] (vi) "He has a birthday."

> **ᎠᏆᏕᏘᏱᎭ** [a¹gwạdetịyịha]
>
> **ᎤᏕᏘᏴᎲᎢ** [udẹtịyỵhv²³ʔi]
>
> **ᎤᏕᏘᏱᎰᎢ** [udẹtịyịho³ʔi]
>
> **ᏣᏕᏘᏯ** [tsadẹtịya]
>
> **ᎤᏕᏘᏱᏗ** [udẹtịyihdi]

ᎤᏗ [udi] (n) "Corn cob."

ᎤᏗᎴᎩ [ụdịlegi] (n) "Fever."

ᎤᏗᎴᎬᎢ [ụdịlegṿʔi] (adj) "Heat.; Hot."

ᎤᏗᎴᎲᏍᎦ [udịlẹhvsga] (vi) "He has a fever."

> **ᎠᎩᏗᎴᎥᏍᎦ** [a¹gịdịlẹʔvsga]
>
> **ᎤᏗᎴᏅᎢ** [udịlehnv²³ʔi]
>
> **ᎤᏗᎴᎲᏍᎪᎢ** [udịlẹhvsgo³ʔi]
>
> **ᏣᏗᎴᎲᎦ** [tsạdịlẹhvga]
>
> **ᎤᏗᎴᎯ** [udịlẹhi]

ᎤᏗᎵᏍᏗ [ụdihlịsdi] (n) "Treacleberry.; False solomon's seal.; biol. *Maianthemum racemosum.*"

ᎤᏘᎾᎢ [utịnạʔi] (n) "Father's brother's wife."

> **ᎠᏆᏘᎾᎢ** [a¹gwatịnạʔi]

ᎤᏙ [udo] (n) "Sister's brother (female ego)."

> **ᎠᎩᏙ** [a¹gịdo]
>
> ᎤᏍᏗᎢ ᎠᎩᏙ ᎡᎭ. ᏥᏕᏴᎵᏯ ᏏᏅ ᎠᎩᏙ ᎨᏒᎢ.
> I have a baby brother. I am older than my brother.
> [ᏣᎳᎩ ᏔᎵᏁ ᏗᏂᏂᏙᎯ ᏗᏕᏲᏙᏗ]

ᎤᏙ [uto] (n) "Sister's daughter."

> **ᎠᏆᏙ** [a¹gwato]

ᎤᏙᎯ [udohi] (n) "Brother's sister (male ego)."

> **ᎠᎩᏙᎯ** [a¹gịdohi]

ᎤᏙᎳᏂ [ụdolạni] (n) "Smooth shadbush.; Allegheny serviceberry.; Serviceberry.; biol. *Amelanchier laevis.*"

ᎤᏙᏓ [udoda] (n) "Father.; Father's brother."

> **ᎠᎩᏙᏓ** [a¹gịdoda]
>
> ᎩᎳᏉᏃ ᎢᏴᏛ ᏚᏂᏲᏎ ᏥᏳ ᎠᎴ ᎤᏂᏙᏓ, ᎠᎴ ᎬᏩᏍᏓᏩᏛᏎᎢ.
> and they, immediately, having left the boat and their father, did follow him.
> [ᎹᏚ 4:22]

ᎤᏙᏓᏆᎠ [udo^{3}dągwąɂa] (vi) "He has a holiday."

ᎠᏆᏙᏓᏆᎠ [a^{1}gwądo^{3}dągwąɂa]

ᎤᏙᏓᏆᎥᎢ [udo^{3}dągwąɂv^{23}ɂi]

ᎤᏙᏓᏆᏍᎪᎢ [udo^{3}dągwąsgo^{3}ɂi]

ᏣᏙᏓᏆ [tsado^{3}dągwa]

ᎤᏙᏓᏆᏍᏗ [udo^{3}dągwąsdi]

ᎤᏙᏗᏍᎬ [ụdodisgv] (pt) "In the shade."

ᎤᏙᏛᏆᏛ [ụdodvgwądv] (n) "Day."

ᎤᏙᏪᎸᎢ [ụdowelvɂi] (n) "Birth mark."

ᎤᏙᏳ [ụdohyu] (pt) "Very."

ᎤᏚᎢᏍᎦ [ụduɂisga] (adj) "Dotted."

ᎤᏚᎦ [utuga] (vt) "He owes someone."

ᎠᎩᏚᎦ [a^{1}gịdɂuga]

ᎤᏚᏅᎢ [utuɂnv^{23}ɂi]

ᎤᏚᎪᎢ [utugo^{3}ɂi]

ᏣᏚᎥᎦ [tsạtuɂvga]

ᎤᏚᏗ [utuhdi]

... ᎢᎬᏱᏱᏃ ᎯᎠ ᏄᏪᏎᎢ, ᎢᎳᎪ ᎢᎦᎢ ᏣᏚᎦ ᎠᎩᏅᏏᏙᎯ.
... he said to the first, How much dost thou owe to my lord?
[ᎷᎦ 16:5]

ᎤᏚᎵᎭ [udu^{3}liha] (vt) "He is wanting it."

ᎠᏆᏚᎵᎠ [a^{1}gwądu^{3}lịɂa]

ᎤᏚᎸᎲᎢ [udu^{3}lvhv^{23}ɂi]

ᎤᏚᎵᏍᎪᎢ [udu^{3}lisgo^{3}ɂi]

ᏣᏚᎳ [tsadu^{3}la]

ᎤᏚᎵᏗ [udu^{3}hldi]

ᎠᏂᎨᏯ ᎤᎾᏓᏍᏓᏴᏗ ᎤᎾᏚᎵᎭ ᎠᏂᏍᎦᏯ.
The men want the women to cook.
[King pg 115]

ᎤᏚᎵᏗᎭ [uduhldịha] (vi) "He has an inclination to."

ᎠᏆᏚᎵᏗᎭ [a^{1}gwądụɂldịha]

ᎤᏚᎵᏔᏅᎢ [uduhltąɂnv^{23}ɂi]

ᎤᏚᎵᏗᏍᎪᎢ [uduhldịsgo^{3}ɂi]

ᏣᏚᎵᏓ [tsaduhlda]

ᎤᏚᎵᏙᏗ [uduhldohdi]

ᎤᏚᏓᎳ [udu^{3}dąɂla] (vi) "He is responsible for or to."

ᎠᏆᏚᏓᎳ [a^{1}gwądu^{3}dąɂla]

ᎤᏚᏓᎸᎥᎢ [udu^{3}dąɂlvɂv^{23}ɂi]

ᎤᏚᏓᎶᎢ [udu^{3}dąɂlo^{3}ɂi]

ᏣᏚᏓᎸᎥᎦ [tsadu^{3}dąɂlvɂvga]

ᎤᏚᏓᎸᏗ [udu^{3}dąɂlvdi]

ᎤᏚᏚ [ududu] (n) "Mother's father."

ᎠᎩᏚᏚ [a^{1}gịdudu]

ᎤᏚᏥ [udutsi] (n) "Mother's brother."

ᎠᎩᏚᏥ [a^{1}gịdutsi]

ᎤᏚᏥ [udutsi] (n) "Uncle."

ᎠᎩᏚᏥ [a^{1}gịdutsi]

ᎤᏛᎳᎦᏍᏛᏅ [udvlągsdvnv] (n) "Broken bone."

ᎠᏆᏛᎳᎦᏍᏛᏅ [a^{1}gwądvlągsdvnv]

ᎤᏛᏃ [udvno] (n) "A sheet sling used to carry a baby on one's back."

ᎤᏛᏐᏅ [utvsọnv] (n) "Man, elderly.; Patriarch."

ᎠᏆᏛᏐᏅ [a^{1}gwątvsọnv]

ᎤᏣᎳ [utsạla] (n) "Pot scrapings.; Lichen(s).; biol. *All Varieties.*"

ᎤᏣᎴᏍᏗ [utsạlesdi] (n) "Flour.; Wheat bread."

ᏔᎵᏁ ᎤᏂᎦᎵᏎ ᎤᏣᎴᏍᏗ.
Second they are cutting the wheat.
[ᏣᎳᎩ ᏔᎵᏁ ᏗᏂᏂᏙᎯ ᏗᎦᏥᏙᏗ]

ᎤᏣᏘ [ụtsati] (pt) "Much."

ᎠᎴ ᎤᏣᏘ ᎡᎯᏍᏗ ᎤᏓᏅᏛᎩ;
and greatly distressed in his mind;
[ᏧᏁᏣᏗ ᏚᏂᎩᎡᎡᎢ]

ᎤᏤᎦ [utse^{3}ga] (vi) "He is taking revenge."

ᎠᏆᏤᎦ [a^{1}gwątse^{3}ga]

ᎤᏤᏨᎢ [utse^{3}ɂtsv^{23}ɂi]

ᎤᏤᎪᎢ [utse^{3}go^{3}ɂi]

ᏣᏤᎩ [tsatse^{3}ɂgi]

ᎤᏤᎢᏍᏗ [utse^{3}ɂisdi]

ᎤᏤᎵ [utseli] (n) "His.; Hers.; Ownership.; Possession."

ᎠᏆᏤᎵ [a^{1}gwątseli]

"ᎫᏇ? ᎫᏇ! ᎭᏢ ᎠᏆᏤᎵ ᎠᏤᏈᎯᏍᏗ?"
"Quail? Quail! Where is my whistle?"
[ᏣᎳᎩ ᏔᎵᏁ ᏗᏂᏂᏙᎯ ᏗᎦᏥᏙᏗ]

ᎤᏤᏌᏗ [ụtsesadi] (n) "Overalls."

ᎤᏤᏥᏍᏗ [utsedsdi] (n) "Opossum.; biol. *Didelphis virginiana.*"

ᎤᏤᏫᎠ [utsewịɂa] (vt) "He is spilling a non-liquid."

ᎠᏆᏤᏫᎠ [a^{1}gwątsewịɂa]

ᎤᏤᏫᎥᎢ [utsewiv^{23}ɂi]

ᎤᏤᏫᏍᎪᎢ [utsewịsgo^{3}ɂi]

ᏣᏤᏩ [tsatsewa]

ᎤᏤᏩᏍᏗ [utsewąsdi]

ᎤᏥ [utsi] (n) "Mother.; Mother's sister."

ᎠᎩᏥ [a^{1}gịtsi]

ᎠᏓᏫᏃ ᎢᏫ ᏚᏬᎡ ᎤᏓᎵᎢ, ᏂᎦᏛᏰᏃ ᏴᏫ ᏗᏅᏃᏛ ᎾᏍᎩ ᎤᏂᏥ ᎨᏎᎢ.
And the man calleth his wife's name Eve: for she hath been mother of all living.
[ᎼᏏ ᎢᎬᏱᏱ 3:20]

ᎤᏥᎸ [utsịʔlv] (n) "Cotton.; Hot pepper."

ᎤᏥᎹ [utsịʔma] (n) "Gray catbird.; biol. *Dumetella carolinensis.*"

ᎤᏥᏓᎳᏗᎠ [utsdạlạdịʔa] (vi) "He has a sore."

ᎠᎩᏥᏓᎳᏗᎠ [a^{1}gịdʔsdạlạdịʔa]

ᎤᏥᏓᎳᏛᎢ [utsdạlạdv^{23}ʔi]

ᎤᏥᏓᎳᏗᏍᎪᎢ [utsdạlạdịsgo^{3}ʔi]

ᏣᏥᏓᎳᏓ [tsạtsdạlạda]

ᎤᏥᏓᎳᏗᏍᏗ [utsdạlạdịsdi]

ᎤᏥᏣᏗ

ᎤᏥᏣᏗ [ụtsitsạdi] (n) "Corn tassel."

ᎤᏦᎢ [utsoʔi] (n) "Daughter-in-law."

ᎠᎩᏦᎢ [a^{1}gịtsoʔi]

ᎤᏦᎦ [utsoga] (vt) "He is unable to find."

ᎠᏆᏦᎦ [a^{1}gwạtsoga]

ᎤᏦᎨᏍᏛᎢ [utsogesdv^{23}ʔi]

ᎤᏦᎪᎢ [utsogo^{3}ʔi]

ᏣᏦᎨᏍᏗ [tsatsogesdi]

ᎤᏦᎨᏍᏗ [utsogesdi]

ᎤᏦᎾᏗ [utsonạdi] (n) "Timber rattlesnake.; biol. *Crotalus horridus.*"

ᎤᏦᏁᏗ [ụtsonedi] (n) "Purple finch.; biol. *Haemorhous purpureus.*"

ᎤᏦᏅᎯᏓ [ụtsonṿhida] (n) "Soot."

ᎤᏧᎩ [ụtsugi] (n) "Tufted titmouse.; biol. *Baeolophus bicolor.*"

ᎤᏧᏬᏗ [ụtsuwọdi] (n) "Moccasin."

ᎤᏨᎦ [uhtsvga] (vi) "He is sick."

ᎠᎩᏨᎦ [a^{1}gịʔtsvga]

ᎤᏨᏨᎢ [uhtsvʔtsv^{23}ʔi]

ᎤᏨᎪᎢ [uhtsvgo^{3}ʔi]

ᏣᏨᎩ [tshtsvʔgi]

ᎤᏨᎢᏍᏗ [uhtsvʔịsdi]

ᎤᏨᎬ [utsvgv] (n) "Sickness."

ᎠᎩᏨᎬ [a^{1}gtsvgv]

ᎤᏩᎦ [uwạga] (n) "Passion flower.; Purple passionflower.; Maypop.; Wild passion vine.; biol. *Passiflora incarnata.*"

ᎤᏩᎨᏫᏍᎦ [uwkẹ^{3}whsga] (vt) "He is forgetting it."

ᎠᏋᎨᏫᏍᎦ [a^{1}gwṿʔkẹ^{3}whsga]

ᎤᏩᎨᏫᏒᎢ [uwkẹ^{3}whsv^{23}ʔi]

ᎤᏩᎨᏫᏍᎪᎢ [uwkẹ^{3}whsgo^{3}ʔi]

ᏨᎨᏩ [tsvkẹ^{3}wa]

ᎤᏩᎨᏫᏍᏗ [uwkẹ^{3}whsdi]

ᎤᏩᎫᏩᏍᏗ [ụwagụwạsdi] (n) "Hiccup."

ᎤᏩᏂ [uwạni] (n) "Wool."

ᎦᏙ ᏴᏫ ᎤᏩᏂ ᎦᏌᎴᎾ?
What person wears a wool jacket?
[ᏣᎳᎩ ᏦᎢᏁ ᏗᏂᏂᏙᎯ ᏗᎦᏲᏙᏗ]

ᎤᏩᏂᎦᎳᏅ [ụwanịgahlạnv] (n) "Limb.; Branch of a tree."

ᎤᏩᏅᎦ [uwanvga] (vi) "He is in a hurry.; He is hurrying."

ᎠᏋᏅᎦ [a^{1}gwvnvga]

ᎤᏩᏅᏨᎢ [uwanvʔtsv^{23}ʔi]

ᎤᏩᏅᎪᎢ [uwanvgo^{3}ʔi]

ᏨᏅᎩ [tsvnvʔgi]

ᎤᏩᏅᎢᏍᏗ [uwanvʔisdi]

ᎤᏩᏌ [uwạsa] (adj) "Alone.; By oneself.; Himself.; Herself."

ᎠᏋᏌ [a^{1}gwṿsa]

ᎦᏙᎦᏃ ᏧᎵᏍᏙᏓᏅ ᏨᏒ ᏥᎷᏥᎦ.
But how is it that you came alone?
[ᏧᏁᏣᏗ ᏚᏂᎩᏒᏒᎢ]

ᎤᏩᏍᎦ [uhwasga] (vt) "He is buying it."

ᎠᎩᏩᏍᎦ [a^{1}gịʔwasga]

ᎤᏩᏒᎢ [uhwasv^{23}ʔi]

ᎤᏩᏍᎪᎢ [uhwasgo^{3}ʔi]

ᏣᏩᎯ [chạwahi]

ᎤᏩᎯᏍᏗ [uhwahịsdi]

ᎡᎵᏉᏍ ᏱᏣᏩᎯ ᏓᏟᎶᏍᏛ? ᎥᎥ ᎠᎴ Ꮭ ᎯᎦᏬᏍᏓ.
Is it enough to buy the item? Choose between Yes and No.
[ᏣᎳᎩ ᏔᎵᏁ ᏗᏂᏂᏙᎯ ᏗᎦᏲᏙᏗ]

ᎤᏩᏍᏗ [ụwạsdi] (n) "Ramps (plant).; Spring onion.; biol. *Allium tricoccum.*"

ᎤᏩᏒᎥᏍᎦ [uhwạ^{3}sṿʔvsga] (vt) "He is buying things."

ᎠᎩᏩᏒᎥᏍᎦ [a^{1}gịʔwạ^{3}sṿʔvsga]

ᎤᏩᏒᏅᎢ [uhwạ^{3}sṿʔnv^{23}ʔi]

ᎤᏩᏒᎥᏍᎪᎢ [uhwạ^{3}sṿʔvsgo^{3}ʔi]

ᏣᏩᏒᎥᎦ [chạwạ^{3}sṿʔvga]

ᎤᏩᏒᏗ [uhwạ^{3}svdi]

ᎤᏩᏙᎵ [uwatoli] (n) "His penis."

ᎠᏆᏙᎵ [a^{1}gwạtoli]

ᎤᏩᏩᏒᎦ [uwąwsv³ga] (vt) “He is smelling it.”

ᎠᎩᏩᏒᎦ [a¹giwʔsv³ga]

ᎤᏩᏩᏒᏨᎢ [uwąwsv³tsv²³ʔi]

ᎤᏩᏩᏒᎪᎢ [uwąwsv³go³ʔi]

ᏣᏩᏒᎩ [tsąwhsv³gi]

ᎤᏩᏩᏒᎢᏍᏗ [uwąwsv̨³ʔįsdi]

ᎤᏩᏯ [uwaya] (vt) “He has it (something long).”

ᎠᏋᏯ [a¹gwvya]

ᎤᏩᏰᏍᏛᎢ [uwayesdv²³ʔi]

ᎤᏩᏲᎢ [uwayo³ʔi]

ᏨᏰᏍᏗ [tsvyesdi]

ᎤᏩᏰᏍᏗ [uwayesdi]

ᎤᏪᎯᏍᏓᏁᎭ [uwęhįsdaneha] (vi) “He is aching.”

ᎠᏇᎢᏍᏓᏁᎭ [a¹gwęʔįsdaneha]

ᎤᏪᎯᏍᏓᏁᎮᏍᏛᎢ [uwęhįsdanehęsdv²³ʔi]

ᎤᏪᎯᏍᏓᏁᎰᎢ [uwęhįsdaneho³ʔi]

ᏤᎯᏍᏓᏏ [tsehįsdąsi]

ᎤᏪᎯᏍᏓᏅᏗ [uwęhįsdanhdi]

ᎤᏪᎳ [ųwela] (n) “Liver.”

ᎤᏪᎳᎦᏏ [uwęlaksi] (n) “Sibling-in-law.”

ᎠᏇᎳᎦᏏ [a¹gwęlaksi]

ᎤᏪᎷᎧ [uhwęlųka] (vi) “He is hollering.; He is crying out.”

ᎠᏇᎷᎧ [a¹gwęʔlųka]

ᎤᏪᎷᏅᎢ [uhwęluhnv²³ʔi]

ᎤᏪᎷᎪᎢ [uhwęlųko³ʔi]

ᏤᎷᎲᎦ [tsehlųhvʔga]

ᎤᏪᎷᎱᏗ [uhwęlųhuhdi]

… ᎤᏪᎷᏅᏉ ᎠᏍᏓᏱᏳ ᎯᎠ ᏄᏪᏒᎩ, “ᎦᏙᏃ ᏓᎦᏛᏁᎵ ᏰᎵ ᎦᏴᎩᏍᎦᎸᏗ ᏅᏓᎦᎵᏍᏔᏂ?”
… he burst out, as he had done before, crying, “What shall I do to be saved?”
[ᏧᏁᎶᏗ ᏚᏂᎩᎡᏒᎢ]

ᎤᏪᏅᎦ [uwę³hnvga] (vi) “He is becoming rich.”

ᎠᏇᏅᎦ [a¹gwęʔnvga]

ᎤᏪᏅᏨᎢ [uwę³hnvʔtsv²³ʔi]

ᎤᏪᏅᎪᎢ [uwę³hnvgo³ʔi]

ᏤᏅᎩ [tse³hnvʔgi]

ᎤᏪᏅᎢᏍᏗ [uwę³hnvʔįsdi]

ᎤᏪᏅᏍᏛᎢ [uwenvsdvʔi] (n) “Stem.”

ᎤᏪᏅᏒᎢ [uwenvsvʔi] (n) “His home.”

ᏧᏪᏅᏒᎢ [tsuwenvsvʔi]

ᎠᏇᏅᏒᎢ [a¹gwenvsvʔi]

ᏗᏇᏅᏒᎢ [di¹gwenvsvʔi]

ᏗᏇᏅᏒᏃ ᏗᎩᎸᏫᏍᏓᏁᏗ ᏃᎴ ᎠᏆᏙᏪᏐᎸᏍᏙᏗ.
“I want to work and rest at home.”
[King pg 116]

ᎤᏪᏗ [ųwedi] (adj) “Old (inanimate only).”

ᎤᏁ ᏪᏙᎲᎢ, ᎤᏪᏗ ᎤᏍᏓᎦᎸ ᏊᏂᏴᏓᎢ.
There in his walking, was an old cold cave.
[ᏣᎳᎩ ᏦᎢᏁ ᏗᏂᏂᏙᎯ ᏗᎦᏲᏙᏗ]

ᎤᏪᏘ [ųweti] (n) “Mole (on the flesh).”

ᎤᏪᏛᎢ [ųwedvʔi] (n) “Meander.”

ᎤᏪᏥ [ųwetsi] (n) “His offspring.; His child.; An egg.”

ᏧᏪᏥ [tsųwetsi]

ᎠᏇᏥ [a¹gwetsi]

ᏗᏇᏥ [di¹gwetsi]

ᏅᏓ ᎢᎦ ᎡᎯ ᎤᏪᏥ ᎠᎨᏳᏣ
Daughter of the sun.
[ᏣᎳᎩ ᏅᎩᏁ ᏗᏂᏂᏙᎯ ᏗᎦᏲᏙᏗ]

ᎤᏫᎾ [uwina] (n) “Brother’s sister’s son.”

ᎠᎩᏫᎾ [a¹gįwina]

ᎤᏬᎩᎵ [ųwogįli] (n) “Beer.; Foam.”

ᎤᏬᎯᏳᎭ [uwohį³yuha] (vt) “He is believing in.”

ᎠᏉᎢᏳᎭ [a¹gwǫʔį³yuha]

ᎤᏬᎯᏳᏅᎢ [uwohį³yuhnv²³ʔi]

ᎤᏬᎯᏳᎰᎢ [uwohį³yuho³ʔi]

ᏦᎯᏳᏅᎦ [tsohį³yųnvga]

ᎤᏬᎯᏳᏗ [uwohį³yhdi]

… ᎠᎴ ᎾᏍᎩ ᎠᏍᎦᏯ ᎤᏬᎯᏳᏅᎩ ᏥᏌ ᏄᏪᏎᎢ, ᎠᎴ ᎤᏪᏅᏒᎩ.
… And the man believed the word that Jesus said to him, and was going on,
[ᏣᏂ 4:50]

ᎤᏬᎯᏳᏂ [ųwohįyųni] (adj) “Obedient.; Loyal.”

ᎤᏬᎰᏎᎭ [uwohǫ³seha] (vt) “He is dropping accidentally it (a solid).”

ᎠᏉᎣᏎᎭ [a¹gwǫʔǫ³seha]

ᎤᏬᎰᏎᎸᎢ [uwohǫ³sęlv²³ʔi]

ᎤᏬᎰᏎᎰᎢ [uwohǫ³seho³ʔi]

ᏦᎰᏏ [tsohǫ³si]

ᎤᏬᎰᏎᏗ [uwohǫ³sehdi]

ᎤᏬᎳ [uwohla] (vi) "He is sitting.; He is at home."

ᎠᏉᎳ [a^{1}gwọʔla]

ᎤᏬᎴᏍᏛᎢ [uhwọlesdv^{23}ʔi]

ᎤᏬᎶᎢ [uwohlo^{3}ʔi]

ᏦᎴᏍᏗ [tsohlesdi]

ᎤᏗ [uhdi]

ᎾᏍᎩ ᎤᏬᎳ ᎩᎶ ᎢᏳᏍᏗ ᎦᏁᎸ ᏌᏩᏂ ᏧᏙᎢᏛ, ᏗᏤᎾᏍᎩ, …
this one doth lodge with a certain Simon a tanner, …
[ᎨᏥᏅᏏᏛ ᏄᎾᏛᏁᎵᏙᎸᎢ 10:6]

ᎤᏬᏚᎭ

ᎤᏬᏚᎭ [uwodụha] (vi) "He is attractive.; He is pretty."

ᎠᏉᏚᎠ [a^{1}gwodụʔa]

ᎤᏬᏚᎮᏍᏛᎢ [uwodụhesdv^{23}ʔi]

ᎤᏬᏚᎰᎢ [uwodụho^{3}ʔi]

ᏦᏚᎮᏍᏗ [tsodụhesdi]

ᎤᏬᏚᎮᏍᏗ [uwodụhesdi]

ᎤᏬᏚᎯ [uwodụhi] (n) "Pretty."

ᎠᏉᏚᎯ [a^{1}gwodụhi]

ᏙᏳ ᎤᏬᏚᎯ ᎠᎨᏳᏣ, ᎨᏩᎦ?
"The little girl is very pretty, isn't she?"
[King pg 120]

ᎤᏬᏥᏗ [uwotsdi] (adj) "Silly.; Funny."

ᎠᏉᏥᏗ [agwotsdi]

ᎤᏬᏰᏂ [uwọʔyeni] (n) "His hand."

ᎠᏉᏰᏂ [a^{1}gwọʔyeni]

ᎾᏍᎩᏃ ᎤᎪᎲ ᎠᎵᏣᏙᏂᏙᎯ ᎠᎦᏗᏏ ᎤᏬᏰᏂ ᎤᏂᏴᎲᎩ, ᎯᎠ ᏄᏪᏎᎸᎩ, …
At the sight of which, *Evangelist* caught him by the right hand, saying, …
[ᏧᏁᎶᏗ ᏚᏂᎩᎡᎡᎢ]

ᎤᏯᎵ [uyhạli] (vt) "He is going after.; He is looking for."

ᎠᎩᏯᎵ [a^{1}giyʔạli]

ᎤᏯᎸᎢ [uyhạlv^{23}ʔi]

ᎤᏯᎵᏐᎢ [uyhạliso^{3}ʔi]

ᏣᏯᎵᎦ [tsạyhạlga]

ᎤᏯᏍᏗ [uysdi]

ᎤᏯᎶᏘᎭ [uyạlotịha] (vi) "He is overeating."

ᎠᎩᏯᎶᏗᎭ [a^{1}giyạlodʔịha]

ᎤᏯᎶᏔᏅᎢ [uyạlothạnv^{23}ʔi]

ᎤᏯᎶᏘᏍᎪᎢ [uyạlotịsgo^{3}ʔi]

ᏣᏯᎶᏔ [tsạyạlota]

ᎤᏯᎶᏙᏗ [uyạlotohdi]

ᎤᏯᎷᎦ [uhyạluga] (n) "Bark of a tree."

ᎤᏯᏍᎦ [uhyasga] (n) "Shell.; Mussel."

ᎤᏯᏛᎲ [uhyạtṿhv] (n) "Frost on ground (white)."

ᎤᏯᏪᎦ [uyạwe^{3}ga] (vi) "He is tired."

ᎠᎩᏯᏪᎦ [a^{1}giyạwe^{3}ga]

ᎤᏯᏪᎬᎢ [uyạwe^{3}ʔgv^{23}ʔi]

ᎤᏯᏪᎪᎢ [uyạwe^{3}go^{3}ʔi]

ᏣᏯᏪᎩ [tsạyạwe^{3}ʔgi]

ᎤᏯᏪᎢᏍᏗ [uyạwe^{3}ʔisdi]

ᎤᏯᏪᏐᎵᎭ [uyạwe^{3}sohlịha] (vi) "He is resting."

ᎠᎩᏯᏪᏐᎵᎭ [a^{1}giyạwe^{3}sọʔlịha]

ᎤᏯᏪᏐᎸᎢ [uyạwe^{3}sohlv^{23}ʔi]

ᎤᏯᏪᏐᎵᎰᎢ [uyạwe^{3}sohlịho^{3}ʔi]

ᏣᏯᏪᏐᎸᎦ [tsạyạwe^{3}sohlvga]

ᎤᏯᏪᏐᎸᏍᏗ [uyạwe^{3}sohlṿsdi]

… ᎿᏉ ᎢᏥᎵᏅᎩ ᎠᎴ ᎢᏥᏯᏪᏐᎸᎦ; …
… 'Sleep on henceforth, and rest! …
[ᎹᏚ 26:45]

ᎤᏰᎯ [uhyẹhi] (n) "Her husband."

ᎠᎩᏰᎯ [a^{1}gihyẹhi]

… ᎿᏉᏰᏃ ᎠᎩᏰᎯ ᎠᏎ ᎠᎩᎨᏳᏍᏗ.
… because now doth my husband love me.'
[ᎼᏏ ᎢᎬᏱᏱ 29:32]

ᎤᏰᎳᎭ [ụyelạha] (adj) "Naked.; Nude."

ᎤᏰᎶᎯᏎᎲᎢ [ụyelohịsehṿʔi] (n) "Infection."

ᎤᏰᎸᎭ [uyeh^{3}lvha] (vt) "He is intending.; He is meaning.; He is wishing to say."

ᎠᎩᏰᎸᎠ [a^{1}giyeh^{3}lṿʔa]

ᎤᏰᎸᏅᎢ [uyeh^{3}lvhnv^{23}ʔi]

ᎤᏰᎸᎰᎢ [uyeh^{3}lvho^{3}ʔi]

ᏣᏰᎸᎾ [tsạyeh^{3}lṿna]

ᎤᏰᎸᏗ [uyeh^{3}ldi]

ᎤᏰᏌᏛ [uhyesạdv] (n) "Dew on the ground."

ᎤᏰᏑᎧᎸᎢ [uhyesụkahlvʔi] (n) "His fingernail."

ᏚᏰᏑᎧᎸᎢ [duhyesụkahlvʔi]

ᎠᎩᏰᏑᎧᎸᎢ [a^{1}gihyesụkahlvʔi]

ᏓᎩᏰᏑᎧᎸᎢ [da^{1}gihyesụkahlvʔi]

ᎤᏰᏑᏨᏂ [uyesụtsvni] (n) "His wrist."

ᏚᏰᏑᏨᏂ [duyesụtsvni]

ᎠᎩᏰᏑᏨᏂ [a^{1}gịyesụtsvni]

ᏓᎩᏰᏑᏨᏂ [da^{1}gịyesụtsvni]

ᎤᏰᏥᎦ [uye^{3}tsga] (vi) "He is smiling."

ᎠᎩᏰᏥᏍᎦ [a^{1}gịye^{3}dsʔsga]

ᎤᏰᏨᎢ [uye^{3}tsv^{23}ʔi]

ᎤᏰᏥᎪᎢ [uye^{3}tsgo^{3}ʔi]

ᏣᏰᏣ [tsạye^{3}dstsa]

ᎤᏰᏥᏗ [uye^{3}tsdi]

ᎤᏲᎢ [uyoʔi] (n) "Bad."

ᎠᎩᏲᎢ [a^{1}gịyoʔi]

… ᎠᎴ ᎤᏁᎳᏅᎯ ᏄᏍᏛ ᎾᏍᎩᏯ ᏂᏍᏓᏍᎦᏍᏗ, ᎢᏍᏗᎦᏔᎮᏍᏗ ᎣᏍᏛ ᎠᎴ ᎤᏲ.
… ye have been as God, knowing good and evil.'
[ᎼᏏ ᎢᎬᏱᏱ 3:5]

ᎤᏲᎢᏯ [uyọ^{3}ʔiya] (vi) "He is being bad."

ᎠᎩᏲᎢᏯ [a^{1}gịyọ^{3}ʔiya]

ᎤᏲᎢᏲᏨᎢ [uyọ^{3}ʔiyotsv^{23}ʔi]

ᎤᏲᎢᏲᎪᎢ [uyọ^{3}ʔiyọgo^{3}ʔi]

ᏣᏲᎢᏲᎩ [tsạyọ^{3}ʔiyogi]

ᎤᏲᎢᏲᎢᏍᏗ [uyọ^{3}ʔiyọʔisdi]

ᎤᏲᎱᏎᎭ [uyohụ^{3}seha] (vt) "He is losing it."

ᎠᎩᏲᎤᏎᎭ [a^{1}gịyọʔụ^{3}seha]

ᎤᏲᎱᏎᎸᎢ [uyohụ^{3}sẹlv^{23}ʔi]

ᎤᏲᎱᏎᎰᎢ [uyohụ^{3}seho^{3}ʔi]

ᏣᏲᎱᏏ [tsạyohụ^{3}si]

ᎤᏲᎱᏎᏗ [uyohụ^{3}sehdi]

… ᎠᎴᏃ ᎾᏍᏉ, ᎦᎸᏉᏗᏳ ᎤᎬᏫᏳᎯ ᏣᏃᏁᎸ, ᎾᏍᎩ ᎩᎶ ᎬᏅ ᎢᎠᏩᏘᏍᎨᏍᏗ, ᎾᏍᎩ ᎤᏲᎱᏎᏗ ᎨᏎᏍᏗ; …
… Besides, the King of Glory hath told thee, that *he that will save his life* shall lose it: …
[ᏧᏁᎶᏗ ᏚᏂᎩᏒᏒᎢ]

ᎤᏲᎾ [uhyona] (n) "Horn of an animal."

ᎤᏲᏃᎪᏍᏓᎯ [uyonọgosdạhi] (n) "Bruise, to have a."

ᎠᎩᏲᏃᎪᏍᏓᎯ [a^{1}gịyonọgosdạhi]

ᎤᏲᏍᎦ [uyosga] (vt) "He is freeing.; He is turning loose."

ᎠᎩᏲᏍᎦ [a^{1}gịyọʔsga]

ᎤᏲᏒᎢ [uyosv^{23}ʔi]

ᎤᏲᏍᎪᎢ [uyosgo^{3}ʔi]

ᏣᏲᎯ [tsạyohi]

ᎤᏲᎯᏍᏗ [uyohịsdi]

ᎤᏲᏏᎭ [uyo^{3}siha] (vi) "He is hungry."

ᎠᎩᏲᏏᎠ [a^{1}gịyo^{3}sịʔa]

ᎤᏲᏎᏍᏛᎢ [uyo^{3}sesdv^{23}ʔi]

ᎤᏲᏏᏍᎪᎢ [uyo^{3}sisgo^{3}ʔi]

ᏣᏲᏎᏍᏗ [tsạyo^{3}sesdi]

ᎤᏲᏏᏍᏗ [uyo^{3}sisdi]

ᎾᏍᎩ ᎢᏳᏍᏗ, ᎢᏳᏃ ᏣᏍᎦᎩ ᎠᎪᏄ ᎤᏲᏏᏍᎨᏍᏗ, ᎯᏰᏣᎮᏍᏗ; …
I will recompense again, saith the Lord;' if, then, thine enemy doth hunger, feed him; …
[ᎶᎻ 12:20]

ᎤᏲᏒᎯ [ụyhosvhi] (n) "Dead."

ᎤᏲᏓᎩᎠ [uyo^{3}dạgịʔa] (vi) "He is itching."

ᎠᎩᏲᏓᎩᎠ [a^{1}gịyo^{3}dạgịʔa]

ᎤᏲᏓᎬᎢ [uyo^{3}dạgv^{23}ʔi]

ᎤᏲᏓᎩᏍᎪᎢ [uyo^{3}dạgisgo^{3}ʔi]

ᏣᏲᏓᎦ [tsạyo^{3}dạga]

ᎤᏲᏓᎩᏍᏗ [uyo^{3}dạgisdi]

ᎤᏲᏓᎵ [ụyodahli] (n) "Sweetflag.; biol. *Acorus calamus.*"

ᎤᏲᏓᎵᏳᏍᏗ [ụyọdahlịyụsdi] (n) "Fen orchid.; Yellow widelip orchid.; biol. *Liparis loeselii.*"

ᎤᏲ ᏗᎧᎾᏘ [ụyo dịkahndi] (n) "Ugly."

ᎤᏳᏆᏗᎠ [u^{1}yụ^{3}gwạdịʔa] (vi) "He has a toothache."

ᎠᎩᏳᏆᏗᎠ [a^{1}gi^{1}ʔyụ^{3}gwạdịʔa]

ᎤᏳᏆᏛᎢ [u^{1}yụ^{3}gwạdʔv^{23}ʔi]

ᎤᏳᏆᏗᏍᎪᎢ [u^{1}yụ^{3}gwạdịsgo^{3}ʔi]

ᏣᏳᏆᏓ [tsa^{1}yụ^{3}gwạda]

ᎤᏳᏆᏗᏍᏗ [u^{1}yụ^{3}gwạdịsdi]

ᎤᏳᏍᏆᏗᏍᎬᎢ [uyụsgwạdịsgvʔi] (n) "His toothache."

ᎠᎩᏳᏍᏆᏗᏍᎬᎢ [a^{1}gịyụsgwạdịsgvʔi]

ᎤᏳᏩᎾ [uyụwạʔna] (vi) "He is hairy."

ᎠᎩᏳᏩᎾ [a^{1}gịyụwạʔna]

ᎤᏳᏩᏁᏍᏛᎢ [uyụwạʔnesdv^{23}ʔi]

ᎤᏳᏩᏃᎢ [uyụwạʔno^{3}ʔi]

ᏣᏳᏩᏁᏍᏗ [tsạyụwạʔnesdi]

ᎤᏳᏩᏅᏗ [uyụwạʔnhdi]

ᎤᏴᎰᏒᎯ [uyvhosvhi] (n) "Corpse."

ᎠᎩᏴᎰᏒᎯ [a^{1}gịyvhosvhi]

ᎤᏴᎳᏛ [ụyvlạtv] (n) "A gap in the mountain."

ᎣᏍᏄᏱᎥᏘ [uʰyy³sgiludoga] (vt) "He is sniffling."

   ᎠᎩᏅᏱᎥᏘ [aʰgiʰʔyy³sgiludoga]

   ᎣᏍᏄᏱᎥᏘᎥᎢ [uʰyy³sgiludoʔlv²³ʔi]

   ᎣᏍᏄᏱᎥᎢ [uʰyy³sgiludogo³ʔi]

   ᏣᏍᏄᏱᎥᎩ [tsaʰyy³sgiludogi]

   ᎣᏍᏄᏱᎥᏗ [uʰyy³sgiludodi]

ᎣᏍᏄᎳᏴᎠ [uʰyysda³giʔa] (vi) "He is intoxicated."

   ᎠᎩᏅᎳᏴᎠ [aʰgiʰʔyysda³giʔa]

   ᎣᏍᏄᎳᎬᎢ [uʰyysda³gv²³ʔi]

   ᎣᏍᏄᎳᏴᏄᎢᎢ [uʰyysda³gisgo³ʔi]

   ᏣᏍᏄᎳᎦ [tsaʰyysda³ga]

   ᎣᏍᏄᎳᏴᏄᏗ [uʰyysda³gisdi]

ᎣᏍᏄᏗ [uhyysdi] (adj) "Bitter."

   ᎾᏍᎩ ᏗᎻᎵᏘ ᏗᎠᏳᏄᏍ ᏗᎳᏅᏲᏗᏄᏗ ᎡᏛ ᏙᎠ ᎣᏍᏄᏗ ᎡᏛᎢ.
   Whose mouth is full of cursing and <u>bitterness</u>.
   [GH 3:14]

ᎣᏍᏗᏄᏴ [uhyvtịnvta] (n) "Stem."

ᎣᏍᏣᏔ

ᎣᏍᏣᏔ [uhyvtsa] (adj) "Cold."

Ꭲ

ᎢᎢ [vv] (pt) "Yes."

   <u>ᎢᎢ</u> ᏙᎠ Ꮃ ᎮᏇᎠᏍ.
   Write <u>yes</u> or no.
   [ᏣᏫᏴ ᏫᎵᏄ ᏗᎻᎲᏙᎠ ᏗᏍᎲᏙᏗ]

ᎢᏨ [vle] (n) "Seven year locust.; Family: Acrididae."

   ... ᎣᎵᏄᎵᏴᏓᏃ ᎢᏨ ᎥᏄ ᏔᎾᎮᏃ ᏣᎠ ᏣᏍᏉᎬ.
   ... and his nourishment was <u>locusts</u> and honey of the field.
   [ᏝᏍ 3:4]

ᎢᎾᏗ [vnti] (n) "Pottery."

ᎢᏄᏴᎥ [vsgiyi] (n) "December."

ᎢᏄᏴᎥᏄ [vsgiyịha] (vt) "He is choking him."

   ᎮᏅᏄᏴᎥᏄ [tsiyyʔsgiyịha]

   ᎣᏣᏄᏴᏦᏘ [uwasgiyyhv²³ʔi]

   ᎢᏄᏴᎥᏄᏘ [vsgiyịsgo³ʔi]

   ᏄᏅᏄᏴᏄ [hiyyʔsgiya]

   ᎣᏣᏄᏴᏄᏗ [uwasgiyhdi]

Ꮥ

ᏍᏍᏣ [gagalo] (n) "Ham (whole)."

ᏍᏍᏣ ᎠᏍᏲᎭᎷ [gagalo ạgaḥạlvda] (n) "Ham, sliced.; Ham, portion of."

ᏍᏍᎷᎢ [gạgạluʔi] (n) "His thigh."

   ᎮᏍᎷᎢ [tsịgạluʔi]

ᏍᏍᏓᎢ [gạgạma] (n) "Cucumber.; biol. *Cucumis sativus*."

ᏍᏍᏔᏯᎯ [gakgwạleni] (n) "His cheek."

   ᏗᏍᏍᏔᏯᎯ [dịgakgwạleni]

   ᎮᏍᏔᏯᎯ [tsịkgwạleni]

   ᏗᎮᏍᏔᏯᎯ [dịtsịkgwạleni]

ᏍᏍᏐᎴ [gạktvda] (n) "Taboo.; Imposed restriction."

ᏍᎣᏆᏃᏍ [gạkaḥvh³sga] (vi) "He is setting up.; He is setting out.; She is giving birth."

   ᎮᏐᏆᏃᏍ [tsịʔkaḥvh³sga]

   ᎣᏆᎣᏘ [ukạʔhnv²³ʔi]

   ᏍᎣᏆᏃᏘ [gạkaḥvh³sgo³ʔi]

   ᏄᎣᏆᏍ [hịkaḥv³ga]

   ᎣᏐᎯᏗ [ukạohdi]

ᏍᏴᏢᎯᎯ [gạgihlgeni] (n) "His neck, the back of."

   ᎮᏴᏢᎯᎯ [tsịgihlgeni]

   ... ᏄᏆ ᏦᏰ ᎮᏣᏄᏴ ᏗᏂᏴᏢᎯᎯ ᏍᏄᏔᎦᏃᏗ, ᏣᎥᏓ ᏧᏇᎮ ᎡᏫᏗ ᏂᎮᏣᏫᏞᏃᏗ.
   ... Thy hand [is] on <u>the neck</u> of thine enemies, Sons of thy father bow themselves to thee.
   [ᎣᏈ ᎢᎡᏴᏈ 49:8]

ᏍᏴᏄᎥ [gạgisha] (vt) "He is gathering things."

   ᎮᏴᎲ [tsịgisʔa]

   ᎣᏴᏄᎣᏘ [ugisʔnv²³ʔi]

   ᏍᏴᏆᏃᏘ [gạgisisgo³ʔi]

   ᏄᏴᎲ [hịgisa]

   ᎣᏴᏔᏗ [ugisohdi]

ᏍᎠᏄᏗᎥ [gạgosdiha] (vt) "He is sifting."

   ᏍᎠᏄᏗᎠ [gạgosdịʔa]

   ᎣᎠᏄᏪᎣᏘ [ugostạnv²³ʔi]

   ᏍᎠᏄᏗᏄᏘ [gạgosdisgo³ʔi]

   ᏪᎠᏄᎵ [hạgosda]

   ᎣᎠᏄᎥᏗ [ugostdi]

ᏍᏲᏗ [gạhadi] (n) "Wedge."

   ᎾᏣᏅᏗ ᎡᏗ ᏊᎣᏞᏘ ᏍᏲᏗ ᏍᏙ ᏄᏔᏄᎭᏃᏗ.
   They made <u>a wedge</u> and maul from locust.
   [King pg 122]

ᏍᏏᎶᎭ [gahe³galiha] (vt) "He is skinning it."

 ᏥᏣᎶᎭ [tsi?e³galiha]

 ᎤᏢᏚᏓᎢ [uhe³galvhv²³?i]

 ᏍᏏᎶᏠᏓᎢ [gahe³galisgo³?i]

 ᎯᏢᏍᏫ [hihe³gala]

 ᎤᏢᏏᎵ [uhe³gahldi]

ᏍᏢᏠᎦ [gahehvsga] (vt) "He is laying down it (a liquid)."

 ᏥᏣᏠᎦ [tsi?ehvsga]

 ᎤᏢᎤᎢ [uhe?hnv²³?i]

 ᏍᏢᏠᏓᎢ [gahehvsgo³?i]

 ᎯᏢᏠᎦ [hihehvga]

 ᎤᏢᎵ [uhe?hdi]

ᏍᎢᏠᎵ, ᎠᎥᏠᎵ [gahusdi, gohusdi] (n) "Something.; Anything."

 Ᏸ ᏎᏍᎼᏍ DRPT! Ꮃ ᎠᎥᏠᎵ ᏂᏍᏢᏠᎵᏃᎢᏔ.
 Yet at the usual way on the bridge! Not <u>a thing</u> happened to us.
 [ᏣᏫᏯ ᏦᎦᏃ ᏗᎯᏥᏫᏯ ᏗᏍᎦᏫᎵ]

ᏍᏫ [gala] (vi) "It (something long) is in a container."

 ᎤᏣᏠᏅᎢᏔ [ulesdv²³?i]

 ᏍᏟᏔ [galo³?i]

 ᎤᏍᏣᏠᎵ [wigalesdi]

 ᎤᏣᏠᎵ [ulesdi]

ᏍᏫᏓ [gala?a] (vi) "It (something flexible) is in a container."

 ᎤᏫᏣᏠᏅᎢᏔ [ula?esdv²³?i]

 ᏍᏫᏣᏠᏔ [gala?o³?i]

 ᎤᏍᏫᏣᏠᎵ [wigala?esdi]

 ᎤᏫᏣᏠᎵ [ula?esdi]

ᏍᏫᏓ [gahlaa] (vi) "It (a solid) is in a container."

 ᎤᏫᏣᏠᏅᎢᏔ [uhla?esdv²³?i]

 ᏍᏫᏣᏠᏔ [gahlao³?i]

 ᎤᏍᎠᎦ [wigahlv?ga]

 ᎤᏫᏔᎵ [uhla?ihdi]

ᏍᏫᎰᏉᎢᏠᎦ [galage³hydv?vsga] (vt) "He is scattering.; He is broadcasting (seed or similar in concept)."

 ᏥᏫᎰᏉᎢᏠᎦ [tsilage?ydv?vsga]

 ᎤᏫᎰᏉᏅᏔ [ulage³hydv?nv²³?i]

 ᏍᏫᎰᏉᎢᏠᏓᎢ [galage³hydv?vsgo³?i]

 ᎠᏫᎰᏉᎢᎦ [hilage³hydv?vga]

 ᎤᏫᎰᏉᎢᎵ [ulage³hydv?di]

ᏍᏫᏴᏓ [galagi?a] (vt) "He is removing it (something long) or it (a liquid) or it (a solid) from a container."

 ᏥᏫᏴᏓ [tsilagi?a]

 ᎤᏫᏴᏒᏔ [ulagisv²³?i]

 ᏍᏫᏴᏠᏓᎢ [galagisgo³?i]

 ᎠᏫᏴ [hilagi]

 ᎤᏫᏴᏠᎵ [ulagisdi]

ᏍᏫᏴᎤ [galagina] (n) "Stag.; Buck.; Gobbler."

ᏍᏫᎠᎶᏠᎦ [galagohosga] (vi) "The leaves are turning."

 ᎤᏫᎠᎢᏒᏔ [ulagohosv²³?i]

 ᏍᏫᎠᎶᏠᏓᎢ [galagohosgo³?i]

 ᎤᏍᏫᎠᎶ [wigalagohohi]

 ᎤᏫᎠᎶᏠᎵ [ulagohosdi]

ᏍᏫᎠ [ga?lahi] (vi) "He is climbing (up)."

 ᏥᏫᏔ [tsi?la?i]

 ᎤᏫᏢᏒᏔ [u?lahesv²³?i]

 ᏍᏫᎠᎢᏔ [ga?lahiso³?i]

 ᎠᏫᎢᏍ [hi?lahuga]

 ᎤᏫᏠᏠᎵ [u?lahysdi]

ᏍᏫᏠᎦ [gahlasga] (vt) "He is putting it (a solid) into a container."

 ᏥᏫᏠᎦ [tsil?asga]

 ᎤᏫᏟᏔ [uhlanv²³?i]

 ᏍᏫᏠᏓᎢ [gahlasgo³?i]

 ᎠᏫᏍ [hihlaga]

 ᎤᏫᎵ [uhldi]

ᏍᏫᎵᏋᎭ [gahlso³?yeha] (vt) "He is shaking it off of a tree."

 ᏥᏫᎵᏋᎭ [tsilso³?yeha]

 ᎤᏫᎵᏋᏚᏔ [uhlso³?yehv²³?i]

 ᏍᏫᎵᏋᏠᏓᎢ [gahlso³?yesgo³?i]

 ᎠᏫᎵᏋᎭ [hihlso³?yeha]

 ᎤᏫᎵᏋᎵ [uhlso³?yhdi]

ᏍᏫᎵᏓ [galdi?a] (vt) "He is putting it (something long) into a container."

 ᏥᏫᎵᏓ [tsiladi?a]

 ᎤᏫᏟᏔ [uld?v²³?i]

 ᏍᏫᎵᏠᏓᎢ [galdisgo³?i]

 ᎠᏫᎵ [hilda]

 ᎤᏫᎵᏠᎵ [uldisdi]

ᏍᏫᎵᏠᏉᎵ [gahla?disdohdi] (n) "Container for something long."

ᏍᏐᏴ [ga?legi] (n) "Blacksnake.; Black rat snake.; biol. *Pantherophis obsoletus*."

ᎦᎴᏂ [gạleʔni] (n) "Ear."

ᏗᎦᎴᏂ [dịgạleʔni]

ᏥᎴᏂ [tsịleʔni]

ᏗᏥᎴᏂ [dịtsịleʔni]

… ᏕᎦᏰᏌᏛ ᏗᎦᎴᏂ ᏚᏭᎾᏕᎢ, ᎠᎴ ᏚᎵᏥᏍᏔᎢ, ᎠᎴ ᎦᏃᎪ ᎤᏒᏂᎴᎢ;
… he put his fingers to his ears, and having spit, he touched his tongue,
[ᎹᎦ 7:33]

ᎦᎴᏗᎭ [gạlhdịha] (vt) "He is burning it."

ᏥᎴᏗᎭ [tsịlẹʔdịha]

ᎤᎴᏔᏅᎢ [ulhtạnv²³ʔi]

ᎦᎴᏗᏍᎪᎢ [gạlhdịsgo³ʔi]

ᎯᎴᏓ [hịlhda]

ᎤᎴᏙᏗ [ulhdohdi]

ᎦᎴᏴᏍᎦ [gạle³yvsga] (vi) "He is hot."

ᏥᎴᏴᏍᎦ [tsịle³yṿʔsga]

ᎤᎴᏴᏒᎢ [ule³yvsv²³ʔi]

ᎦᎴᏴᏍᎪᎢ [gạle³yvsgo³ʔi]

ᎯᎴᏴᎥᎯ [hịle³yṿvhi]

ᎤᎴᏴᎯᏍᏗ [ule³yvhịsdi]

ᎦᎴᏴᏍᏗᎭ [gạlẹyvsdiha] (vt) "He is cutting a tree."

ᏥᎴᏴᏍᏗᎠ [tsịlẹyvsdịʔa]

ᎤᎴᏴᏍᏔᏅᎢ [ulẹyvstạnv²³ʔi]

ᎦᎴᏴᏍᏗᏍᎪᎢ [gạlẹyvsdisgo³ʔi]

ᎯᎴᏴᏍᏓ [hịlẹyvsda]

ᎤᎴᏴᏍᏙᏗ [ulẹyvstdi]

… ᎬᏂᏳᏉ, ᎿᏉ ᏦᎢ ᎾᏕᏘᏴ ᏥᎷᎬᎩ ᎠᎩᏲᎲᎩ ᎤᏓᏔᏅᎯ ᎯᎠ ᎾᏍᎩ ᎡᎦᏔ-ᎢᏳᏍᏗ ᏡᎬᎢ, ᎠᎴ ᎥᏝ ᏱᏥᏩᏛᎭ; ᎯᎴᏴᏍᏓ; …
… Lo, three years I come seeking fruit in this fig-tree, and do not find, cut it off, …
[ᎷᎦ 13:7]

ᎦᎵᎠᎦᎢᎭ [gạʔlịʔagaiha] (vi) "He is perspiring."

ᏥᎵᎠᎦᎢᎠ [tsịʔlịʔagạiʔa]

ᎤᎵᎠᎦᏒᎢ [uʔlịʔagạsv²³ʔi]

ᎦᎵᎠᎦᎢᏍᎪᎢ [gạʔlịʔagạisgo³ʔi]

ᎯᎵᎠᎦᎦ [hịʔlịʔagaga]

ᎤᎵᎠᎦᎢᏗ [uʔlịʔagạihdi]

ᎦᎵᎥᏂᎭ [gạliʔvniha] (vt) "He is assaulting him.; He is beating him up."

ᏥᎵᎥᏂᎠ [tsiliʔvnịʔa]

ᎤᎵᎥᏂᎸᎢ [uliʔvnịlv²³ʔi]

ᎦᎵᎥᏂᎰᎢ [gạliʔvniho³ʔi]

ᎯᎵᎥᎦ [hiliʔvʔga]

ᎤᎵᎥᏍᏗ [uliʔvsdi]

ᎿᏉᏃ ᏆᎴᏗ ᎤᏂᏴᎲᎩ ᏥᏌ ᎠᎴ ᎤᎵᎥᏂᎸᎩ.
Then, therefore, did Pilate take Jesus and scourge [him],
[ᏣᏂ 19:1]

ᎦᎵᎦᎵ [gahlgali] (n) "February."

ᎦᎵᎬ [gạligv] (n) "Fire, uncontrolled."

ᎢᏨᎨᏳᎢ, ᏞᏍᏗ ᎤᏍᏆᏂᎪᏗ ᏱᏥᏰᎸᏎᏍᏗ ᎦᎵᎬ ᏥᏥᏱᎵᎦᎭ ᎾᏍᎩ ᎢᏥᎪᎵᏰᏗ ᏥᎩ, …
Beloved, think it not strange at the fiery suffering among you that is coming to try you, …
[ᏈᏓ ᎢᎬᏱᏱ 4:12]

ᎦᎵᎭ [gahlịha] (vi) "He is asleep."

ᏥᎵᎭ [tsilʔịha]

ᎤᎸᏅᎢ [uhlvhnv²³ʔi]

ᎦᎵᎰᎢ [gahlịho³ʔi]

ᎯᎸᎾ [hịhlvna]

ᎤᎸᏗ [uhlvʔdi]

ᎦᎵᎲᎢ ᎠᏍᎦᏯ ᏳᏍᎩᏥᏒᎥᏍᎬᎩ.
The man that was sleeping, was dreaming.
[King]

ᎦᎵᏆᏍᎪᎯ [gahlkwasgohi] (adj) "Seventy."

… ᎴᎻᎩ [ᎤᎸᎯ] ᎦᎵᏆᏍᎪᎯ ᎦᎵᏉᎩ ᎢᏳᏩᎫᏗ ᎠᏎ ᎠᎦᏓᏤᏗ ᎨᏎᏍᏗ.
… And for Lamech seventy and sevenfold.'
[ᎼᏏ ᎢᎬᏱᏱ 4:24]

ᎦᎵᏆᏚ [gahlgwạdu] (adj) "Seventeen."

… ᏦᏩ ᎦᎵᏆᏚ ᎢᏳᏕᏘᏴᏛ ᎨᏎ ᏧᏂᎵ ᎤᎾᎵᎪᎭ ᏓᏅᎿᏗᏍᏗᏍᎨ ᎠᎾ; …
… Joseph, a son of seventeen years, hath been enjoying himself with his brethren among the flock, …
[ᎼᏏ ᎢᎬᏱᏱ 37:2]

ᎦᎵᏉᎩ [gahlgwogi] (adj) "Seven.; A frog."

… ᎡᏍᎦᏉ ᎦᎵᏉᎩ ᎢᏯᏂᏛ ᎠᏂᏍᎦᏯ ᎠᏂᎦᏔᎿᎢ ᎠᎴ ᏮᏍᏛ ᏗᎬᏩᏃᏏᎨᏗ ᏥᎨᎨᎢ.
… are wiser in their own eyes than seven men that can render a reason.
[ᏧᏁᎶᏗ ᏚᏂᎩᏒᏒᎢ]

ᎦᎵᏉᎩ ᎢᏳᏬᎵᏰᏓ [gahlkwogị ịyuwohlịyeda] (n) "Seven doctorings."

ᏍᎦᏬᎩ ᏧᏂᏁᎦ

ᏍᎦᏬᎩ ᏧᏂᏁᎦ [gahlkwogi tsuyasdu] (n) "Wild hydrangea.; Sevenbark.; biol. *Hydrangea arborescens.*"

ᏍᎵᏏᎭ [galisiha] (vt) "He is removing it (something long) from a container."

    ᏥᎵᏏᎭ [tsili?siha]

    ᎤᎵᏑᎾᏫ [ulisyhv²³?i]

    ᏍᎵᏏᏍᎪᎢ [galisisgo³?i]

    ᎲᎵᏌ [hilisa]

    ᎤᎵᏑᏗ [ulisvhdi]

ᏍᎵᏚᏅᏚᏂ ᏗᏗ [gahltanvtanv? ahdi] (n) "Can house."

ᏍᎵᏚᏅᏙᏗ [gahltanvdohdi] (n) "Container for solid items."

ᏍᎵᏣᏗ [gahltsadi] (n) "Bow."

ᏍᎵᏦᎭᏓ [gahltsohida] (n) "Fat."

    ᏥᎵᏦᎭᏓ [tsihltsohida]

ᏍᎵᏦᏕ [gahltsode] (n) "House.; Come in."

ᎠᏄᏃ ᏅᎾᏲ ᎠᎭᏅᏌᏫ ᎤᏌᏪᏅᏌᏍᎦᏍ, Ꮧ ᏍᎡᏣᎦᏛᏒ ᏣᏗ ᏍᎵᏦᏕ ᎬᏆᏫᏂ ᎠᎭᏫᎢᏘ, Ꮧ ᎤᎭᏅᏌᏁ ᏍᎦᏅᏗᏅ.
And the men put forth their hand, and bring in Lot unto them, into <u>the house</u>, and have shut the door; [ᎠᏅ TEᏌᏅ 19:10]

ᏍᎦᏗ [galo?a] (vt) "He is breaking it (a solid)."

    ᏥᎦᏗ [tsilo?a]

    ᎤᎦᎢᏘ [ulo?v²³?i]

    ᏍᎦᏍᎪᎢ [galosgo³?i]

    ᎲᎦᏟ [hilotsa]

    ᎤᎦᏍᏗ [ulosdi]

ᏍᎦᏐᎤᏗᎭ [galo?ohndiha] (vt) "He is making him fall."

    ᏥᎦᏐᎤᏗᎭ [tsilo?o?ndiha]

    ᎤᎦᏐᎤᏪᎢᏘ [ulo?ohntanv²³?i]

    ᏍᎦᏐᎤᏗᏍᎪᎢ [galo?ohndisgo³?i]

    ᎲᎦᏐᎤᏝ [hilo?o?nda]

    ᎤᎦᏐᎤᏅᏗ [ulo?ohndohdi]

ᏍᎦᏐᏍᎦ [galo?oh³sga] (vi) "He is falling."

    ᏥᎦᏐᏍᎦ [tsilo?o?sga]

    ᎤᎦᏐᎡᎢᏘ [ulo?oh³sv²³?i]

    ᏍᎦᏐᏍᎪᎢ [galo?oh³sgo³?i]

    ᎲᎦᏐᎯ [hilo?o³hi]

    ᎤᎦᏐᏍᏗ [ulo?o³hisdi]

ᏍᎦᎵᏗ [galogedi?a] (vt) "He is clearing a field."

    ᏥᎦᎵᏗ [tsilogedi?a]

    ᎤᎦᎵᏅᏘ [uloged?v²³?i]

    ᏍᎦᎵᏗᏍᎪᎢ [galogedisgo³?i]

    ᏗᎦᎵᏗ [hiLogeda]

    ᎤᎦᎵᏗᏍᏗ [ulogedisdi]

ᏍᎦᏲᏗ [galo³gi?a] (vt) "He is hoeing."

    ᏥᏲᏗ [tsilo³gi?a]

    ᎤᏣᏐᏘ [ulo³ga?nv²³?i]

    ᏍᏣᏲᏍᎪᎢ [galo³gisgo³?i]

    ᏗᏣᏣ [hilo³gaga]

    ᎤᏣᏗ [ulo³godi]

ᎢᎬᏃ ᏍᎥᏗ ᏍᎠᏣᏲᏍᏗᏍᏗ, ᎠᏗ ᎢᏣᏟᏦᏍᏈ ᎢᏢ ᏍᏑᏙᎰᏗᏅᏗ; ...
when <u>thou tillest</u> the ground, it doth not add to give its strength to thee ...
[ᏅᎾ TEᏌᏅ 4:12]

ᏍᎦᎵᏍᎦ [galogohosga] (vi) "The leaves are turning."

    ———

    ᎤᏣᎵᎡᏘ [ulogohosv²³?i]

    ᏍᏣᎵᏍᎪᎢ [galogohosgo³?i]

    ᏫᏍᏣᎵᏣ [wigalogohoga]

    ᎤᏣᎵᏍᏗ [ulogohosdi]

ᏍᏣᏗ [galogohdi] (n) "Hoe."

ᏍᏣᎯ [gahlohi] (n) "Cullowhee, NC."

ᏍᏣᎯᏍᏗ [galohisdi] (n) "Doorway."

ᏗᏗᏃ ᎤᎦᎡ ᎠᎵᏣᎲᏗᎯ. (ᎢᏚ Ꭰ ᎢᏧᎢᏘ) "ᏐᎠᏣᏗᏍᎠ Ꮠ ᎡᎤᎥᎵ ᏍᏣᎯᏗ ᏓᏚᎠᏈᏫ?" ᎠᏅᏌᏃ ᎠᏗ ᎦᏪᏛᏲ, "ᎢᏢ"
Then said Evangelist, pointing with his finger over a very wide field, "Do you see yonder Wicket-<u>gate</u>?" The Man said, "No."
[ᏧᏁᏣᏗ ᏍᏔᎾᏕᎢ]

ᏍᏣᎯᏗᎭ [galo³hisdiha] (vt) "He is passing a bill (legislation)."

    ᏥᏣᏘᏍᏗᎭ [tsilo?isdiha]

    ᎤᏣᏍᏫᏗᏘ [ulo³histanv²³?i]

    ᏍᏣᎯᏗᏍᎪᎢ [galo³hisdisgo³?i]

    ᏗᏣᎯᏗᏝ [hilo³hisda]

    ᎤᏣᎯᏍᏅᏗ [ulo³hisdohdi]

ᏍᏇᎠᏔᎾ [gạlọ³hịseha] (vi) "He is passing by."

ᏘᏓᎠᏔᎾ [tsịlọꭹịseha]

ᎤᏍᏇᎠᏔᎢᏔ [ulọ³hịsẹꭹlv²³ꭹi]

ᏍᏇᎠᏔᎨᏔ [gạlọ³hịseho³ꭹi]

ᎯᏍᏇᎠᏔᏏ [hịlọ³hịsesi]

ᎤᏍᏇᎠᏔᏗ [ulọ³hịsehdi]

ᎥhᏙᏆᏔ ᏍᏇᎠᏔᎾ ᏣᏎᏪ.
Crane is being passed by Hummingbird.
[ᏣᏩᎩ ᏭᎵᏗ ᏗhhᏙᎠ ᏗᏍ6ᏫᏗ]

ᏍᏇh [gạloni] (n) "August."

ᏍᏇᎣᎡᏔ [gạlonyꭹeha] (vt) "He is outwitting him."

ᏘᏋᎣᎡᎠ [tsịlonyꭹẹꭹa]

ᎤᏋᎣᎡᎯᏔ [ulonyꭹehlv²³ꭹi]

ᏍᏋᎣᎡᏫᎯᏔ [gạlonyꭹesgo³ꭹi]

ᎠᏋᎣᎥᎵ [hịlonyꭹꭹvli]

ᎤᏋᎣᎡᏗ [ulonyꭹehdi]

ᏍᏇᎣᏓᎾ [gạlonvheha] (vt) "He is cheating."

ᏘᏋᎣᎡᏔ [tsịlonyꭹeha]

ᎤᏋᎣᏓᎯᏔ [ulonvhehlv²³ꭹi]

ᏍᏋᎣᏓᏫᎯᏔ [gạlonvhesgo³ꭹi]

ᎠᏋᎣᎥᎵ [hịlonyꭹhvli]

ᎤᏋᎣᏓᏗ [ulonvhehdi]

ᏍᏇᏬᎣᎢᏫᎠᏎ [gạlhtạny³ꭹvsga] (vt) "He is canning it.; He is preserving it."

ᏘᏋᏬᎣᎢᏫᎠᏎ [tsịlọꭹtạny³ꭹvsga]

ᎤᏋᏬᎣᎣᏔ [ulhtạny³ꭹnv²³ꭹi]

ᏍᏋᏬᎣᎢᏫᎯᏔ [gạlhtạny³ꭹvsgo³ꭹi]

ᎠᏋᏬᎣᎢᏏ [hịlhtạny³ꭹvga]

ᎤᏋᏬᎣᏗ [ulhtạnv³di]

ᏍᏇᎥᏬᏗ [gạlọꭹyhsdi] (n) "Axe."

ᏍᎷᎥᏬᎠᏎ [gạlu³ꭹyhsga] (vt) "He is chopping it.; He is cutting it with an axe."

ᏘᎷᎥᏬᎠᏎ [tsịlu³ꭹyꭹsga]

ᎤᎷᎥᏬᏔ [ulu³ꭹyhv²³ꭹi]

ᏍᎷᎥᏬᎯᏔ [gạlu³ꭹyhsgo³ꭹi]

ᎠᎷᏬ [hịlu³ꭹya]

ᎤᎷᎥᏬᏗ [ulu³ꭹyisdi]

ᎠᏏᏪᏬᏗ ᎡᏗ ᏘᎷᎥᏬᎠᏎ.
"I am chopping it with a knife."
[King p40]

ᏍᎢᎢᏫᎠᏎ [gạlvꭹvsga] (vt) "He is putting it (something flexible) or it (something alive) into a container."

ᏘᏏᎢᏫᎠᏎ [tsịlvꭹvꭹsga]

ᎤᏍᎢᎣᏔ [ulvꭹnv²³ꭹi]

ᏍᎢᎢᏫᎠᏔ [gạlvꭹvsgo³ꭹi]

ᎠᏏᎢᏏ [hịlvꭹvga]

ᎤᏍᎵ [ulvꭹdi]

ᏠᏠ ᏖᎣᎣᏓᎸ ᎠᏏᎢᏏ ᎠᏫᏟ. ᏃᎢᏃ ᏓᏛ ᎡᏓ ᎠᎣᏟᏣ.
Put the paper into the jar. And then fill with water.
[ᏣᏩᎩ ᎤᎠᏑᏟ ᏗhhᏙᎠ ᏗᏍ6ᏫᏗ]

ᏍᎢᏪᏗ [gạlv³lạdi] (n) "Heaven.; Loft.; Upstairs."

… ᏗᎦᏃ, ᎡhᏣᏫᏆ, ᎢᏥᏃ ᏬᎷᎹᏣᏗ ꭹᎷhᏋᎾ ꭹᏣᏗᏫᏆ ᏍᎢᏪᏗ hᏎᏙ ᎤᏣᏫᏙᏔ …
… but behold, when he was got now hard by the Hill, it seemed so high …
[ᏗᏁᎦᏗ ᏏhᎩᏒᏒᏔ]

ᏍᎢᏪᎩᏣ [gạlvlạdịtsa] (n) "Upward.; Above."

ᏍᎢᎩᏔ [gạlvloꭹi] (n) "Sky."

ᏠᏟhꭹᏋᏔ ᎤᏁᏬᎣᏆ ᏏᏫᎯᏁ ᏍᎢᎩᏔ ᏛᏣ ᏃᎦᏒ.
In the beginning of God's preparing the heavens and the earth –
[ꭶᏏ ᎢᏎᏫᏅ 1:1]

ᏍᎢᏴ [gạlvꭹna] (n) "Gourd.; Bottle groud.; biol. *Lagenaria siceraria.*; Gourd dipper."

ᏍᎢᏫᎵᏔ [gạlvgwdiha] (vt) "He is loving it."

ᏘᏏᏫᎵᎠ [tsịlvgwdịꭹa]

ᎤᏍᎢᏫᎵᎣᏔ [ulvgwdạꭹnv²³ꭹi]

ᏍᎢᏫᎵᎯᏔ [gạlvgwdisgo³ꭹi]

ᎠᏏᏫᎵ [hịlvgwda]

ᎤᏍᎢᏫᎣᏗ [ulvgwdohdi]

ᏍᎢᏫᎵᏔ [gạlvkwohdịha] (vt) "He is glorifying it."

ᏘᏏᏫᎵᏔ [tsịlvkwodịha]

ᎤᏍᎢᏫᏬᎣᏔ [ulvkwọtạnv²³ꭹi]

ᏍᎢᏫᎵᎯᏔ [gạlvkwohdịsgo³ꭹi]

ᎠᏏᏫᎵ [hịlvkwohda]

ᎤᏍᎢᏫᏗᎵ [ulvkwohtdi]

… ᏘᏏᏫᎵᏔ ꭹᎥᎯ iᎢᏒᏍᎣᏔ;
… my ministration I do glorify;
[GH 11:13]

ᏉᎶᏍ [gahlvsga] (vi) "He is sleepy."

ᏥᎶᏍ [tsịlʔvsga]

ᎤᎵᏰᏍᏛᎢ [uhlỵesdv²³ʔi]

ᏉᎶᏍᎪᎢ [gahlvsgo³ʔi]

ᎮᎵᏰᏍᏗ [hịhlỵesdi]

ᎤᎶᏙᏗ [uhlỵohdi]

… Ꮩꭷ ᎤᎲᏟᎴꭲᏴ ᎥᏓ ᎥᏍᏉᎶᏍ.
… and their destruction <u>doth not slumber.</u>
[ᎠᎵ ᏉᎵᎵ 2:3]

ᏉᎵᏓᏍ [galvdasga] (vt) "He is cutting into strips."

ᏥᎵᏓᏍ [tsịlvdạʔsga]

ᎤᎵᏙᎢᎢ [ulvdạnv²³ʔi]

ᏉᎵᏓᏍᎪᎢ [galvdasgo³ʔi]

ᎮᎵᏓᏩᏍ [hịlvdạlaga]

ᎤᎵᏩᏩᏗ [ulvtạldi]

ᏉᎵᎥᎵ [galvdohli] (n) "Tall and skinny."

ᏥᎵᎥᎵ [tsịlvdohli]

ᏉᎵᎥᏗ [gahlvdohdi] (n) "Container for it (something flexi-ble)."

ᎤᎲᏥᎶᏴ ᏗᏍᏉᎥᏗ ᎤᏒᎾ.
The flower <u>vase</u> is empty.
[ᏣᏳ ᎺᏗᏂ ᏗᏂᎲᏙᎠ ᏗᏍᏟᎥᏗ]

ᏉᎵᏛᎲᎦ [galvdv³ʔniha] (vt) "He is flipping it.; He is call-ing (idiom).; He is telephoning (idiom)."

ᏥᎵᏛᎲᎠ [tsịlvdv³ʔnịʔa]

ᎤᎵᏛᎲᎠᎢ [ulvdv³ʔnịʔlv²³ʔi]

ᏉᎵᏛᎲᎢᎢ [galvdv³ʔniho³ʔi]

ᎮᎵᏛᎲᎦ [hịlvdv³ʔniga]

ᎤᎵᏛᎲꭷᏗ [ulvdv³ʔnisdi]

ᏉᎵᏨᎠ [galvweʔa] (vt) "He is winding thread or yarn."

ᏥᎵᏨᎠ [tsịlvweʔa]

ᎤᎵᏨꭲᎢ [ulvwev²³ʔi]

ᏉᎵᏨꭷᎢᎢ [galvwesgo³ʔi]

ᎮᎵᏨᎠ [hịlvwea]

ᎤᎵᏨᏙꭷᏗ [ulvweisdi]

ᏉᎵᏨꭱᎩᎠᎠ [galvweyagi³ʔa] (vt) "He is unwinding it."

ᏥᎵᏨꭱᎩᎠᎠ [tsịlvweyagi³ʔa]

ᎤᎵᏨꭱᎩᎡᎢᎢ [ulvweyagi³sv²³ʔi]

ᏉᎵᏨꭱᎩꭷᎢᎢ [galvweyagi³sgo³ʔi]

ᎮᎵᏨꭱᎩ [hịlvweyagi]

ᎤᎵᏨꭱᎩꭷᏗ [ulvweyagi³sdi]

ᏉᎵᏫꭱᏍᏗᎭᎤ [galvhwẹysdịha] (vt) "He is winding it up."

ᏥᎵᏫꭱᏍᏗᎭ [tsịlvwẹysdịha]

ᎤᎵᏫꭱᏍᏩᎣᎢᎢ [ulvhwẹystạnv²³ʔi]

ᏉᎵᏫꭱᏍᏗꭘꭷᎢ [galvhwẹysdịsgo³ʔi]

ᎮᎵᏫꭱᏍᏓ [hịlvhwẹysda]

ᎤᎵᏫꭱᏍᏙᎲᏗ [ulvhwẹysdohdi]

ᎦᎾᎠ [ganạʔa] (vi) "He is lying down."

ᏥᎾᎠ [tsịnạʔa]

ᎤᎾᎤᎤᎢ [unvʔnv²³ʔi]

ᎦᎾꭶᎢ [ganạʔo³ʔi]

ᎮᎾꭲᏍ [hịnạʔvga]

ᎤᎾᎤᏗ [unvʔdi]

ᎦᎾꭲᏍ

ᎦᎾꭲᏍ [ganạʔvsga] (vt) "He is placing it (something alive) on a raised surface."

ᏥᎾꭲᏍ [tsịnạʔɣʔsga]

ᎤᎾᎤᎢ [unạʔnv²³ʔi]

ᎦᎾꭲꭷᎢ [ganạʔvsgo³ʔi]

ᎮᎾꭲᏍ [hịnạʔvga]

ᎤᎾᏗ [undi]

ᎦᎾᏍᏗ [gạʔnakdi] (n) "Doctor."

<u>ᎦᎾᏍᏗ</u> ᏍᏉᎶᏫꭷᎠ ᏗᏍᎥᎵ.
<u>The doctor</u> investigates your eyes.
[ᏣᏳ ᏉᎵᎵ ᏗᏂᎲᏙᎠ ᏗᏍᏟᎥᏗ]

ᎦᎾᏍᏙ [gạʔnakdo] (n) "Hospital."

ᎦᎾᏍᏥ ᎤᏩᎾ [ganagatsị ụtana] (n) "Softstem bulrush.; Great bulrush.; biol. *Schoenoplectus tabernaemon-tani.*"

ᎦᎾᎩᎠ [ganagiʔa] (vt) "He is picking up it (something flex-ible) or it (something alive) from the ground."

ᏥᎾᎩᎠ [tsịnagiʔa]

ᎤᎾᎩᎡᎢ [unagisv²³ʔi]

ᎦᎾᎩꭷᎢ [ganagisgo³ʔi]

ᎮᎾᎩ [hịnagi]

ᎤᎾᎩꭷᏗ [unagisdi]

… ᏣᎥꭷᏙ ᎮᎾᎩ, Ꮩꭲ ᏗᏉᎤᏒ ᎨᎾ.
… take up <u>thy couch,</u> and go to thy house.'
[ᏗᎢᏎ 9:6]

73

ᎦᎾᎩᏤᎭ [ganagiʔeha] (vt) "He is taking it (something flexible) or it (something alive) from him."

    ᏥᎾᎩᏤᎠ [tsinagiʔeʔa]

    ᎤᎾᎩᏤᎸᎢ [unagiʔeʔlv²³ʔi]

    ᎦᎾᎩᏤᎰᎢ [ganagiʔeho³ʔi]

    ᎯᎾᎩᏤ [hinagiʔi]

    ᎤᎾᎩᏤᏗ [unagiʔehdi]

ᎦᎾᎩᎳ [ganagila] (vi) "He is residing."

    ᏥᎾᎩᎳ [tsinagila]

    ᎤᎾᎡᎵᏛᎢ [unaeldʔv²³ʔi]

    ᎦᎾᎩᎶᎢ [ganagilo³ʔi]

    ᎯᎾᎡᎳᏓ [hinaelada]

    ᎤᎾᎡᎳᏗᏍᏗ [unaeldisdi]

    ᎥᏓ **ᎦᎾᎩᎳ**.
    "He lives near me."
    [King p40]
    Qualla dialect.

ᎦᎾᎩᎸᎢ [ganagilvʔi] (n) "His house."

    ᏥᎾᎩᎸᎢ [tsinagilvʔi]

ᎦᎾᎩᏏ [ganagisi] (vt) "He is fetching it (something alive) or it (something flexible)."

    ᏥᎾᎩᏏ [tsinagisi]

    ᎤᎾᎩᏎᏒᎢ [unagisesv²³ʔi]

    ᎦᎾᎩᏎᎪᎢ [ganagisego³ʔi]

    ᎯᎾᎩᏚᎦ [hinagisuga]

    ᎤᎾᎩᏏᏍᏗ [unagisysdi]

ᎦᎾᎠᎩᏯ [gana³ʔgyʔa] (vt) "He is moving it (something flexible) off.; He is clearing it (something flexible) off."

    ᏥᎾᎠᎩᏯ [tsina³ʔgyʔa]

    ᎤᎾᎠᎡᏒᎢ [una³ʔgysv²³ʔi]

    ᎦᎾᎠᎡᏍᎪᎢ [gana³ʔgysgo³ʔi]

    ᎯᎾᎠᎡᏍᏗ [hina³ʔgysdi]

    ᎤᎾᎠᎡᏍᏗ [una³ʔgysdi]

ᎦᎾᏅᏍᎩ [gananesgi] (n) "Spider."

ᎦᎾᏅᏍᎩ [gaʔnanesgi] (n) "Clock."

ᎦᎾᏌ [gaʔnasa] (adj) "Tame."

ᎦᎾᏌᏛᎢ [ganasadvʔi] (n) "Toe."

    ᏕᎦᎾᏌᏛᎢ [deganasadvʔi]

    ᏥᎾᏌᏛᎢ [tsinasadvʔi]

    ᏕᏥᎾᏌᏛᎢ [detsinasadvʔi]

ᎦᎾᏍᏚᎩ [gansdugi] (n) "Washington, DC."

ᎦᎾᏏᏂ [gansi³ni] (vt) "He is dragging it."

    ᏥᎾᏏᏂ [tsinsi³ni]

    ᎤᎾᏏᏁᏒᎢ [unsi³nesv²³ʔi]

    ᎦᎾᏏᏂᏲᎢ [gansi³niso³ʔi]

    ᎯᎾᏏᏄᎦ [hinsi³nuʔga]

    ᎤᎾᏏᏅᏍᏗ [unsi³nysdi]

ᎦᎾᏑᎦᎸᎢ [gansugahlyʔi] (n) "A wall."

ᎦᎾᏑᏙᎶ [gansudylo] (n) "Witch-hazel.; American witch-hazel.; biol. *Hamamelis virginiana.*"

ᎦᎾᏚᏍᎩ [gandusgi] (n) "Auctioneer.; Seller.; Vendor."

ᎦᎾᏨᎭ [ga³nhtseha] (vt) "He is holding it (a liquid)."

    ᏥᎾᏨᎭ [tsi³nʔtseha]

    ᎤᎾᏨᏇᏍᏛᎢ [u³nhtsehesdv²³ʔi]

    ᎦᎾᏨᎰᎢ [ga³nhtseho³ʔi]

    ᎯᎾᏨᏇᏍᏗ [hi³nhtsehesdi]

    ᎤᎾᏨᏇᏍᏗ [u³nhtsehesdi]

ᎦᎾᏨᏗ [gantsehdi] (n) "A rattle."

ᎦᎾᏥ [ganhtsi] (vt) "He is carrying it (a liquid)."

    ᏥᎾᏥ [tsinʔtsi]

    ᎤᎾᏨᏒᎢ [unhtsesv²³ʔi]

    ᎦᎾᏥᏲᎢ [ganhtsi-so³ʔi]

    ᎯᎾᏨᎦ [hinhtsuʔga]

    ᎤᎾᏨᏍᏗ [unhtsysdi]

ᎦᎾᏨᏍᏗᎭ [gantsvsdiha] (vt) "He is being carried by it (a liquid)."

    ᏥᎾᏨᏍᏗᎠ [tsintsvsdiʔa]

    ᎤᎾᏨᏍᏩᏅᎢ [untsvstanv²³ʔi]

    ᎦᎾᏨᏍᏗᏍᎪᎢ [gantsvsdisgo³ʔi]

    ᎯᎾᏨᏍᏓ [hintsvsda]

    ᎤᎾᏨᏍᏛᏗ [untsvstdi]

ᎦᎾᎠᎯ [ganahwihi] (n) "Heart."

    ᏥᎾᎠᎯ [tsinahwihi]

ᎦᎾᎠᏗᎭ [ganawidiha] (vt) "He is carrying it (something alive) or it (something flexible) off."

    ᏥᎾᎠᏗᎠ [tsinawidiʔa]

    ᎤᎾᎠᏗᎥᏛᎢ [unawidvhv²³ʔi]

    ᎦᎾᎠᏗᏍᎪᎢ [ganawidisgo³ʔi]

    ᎯᎾᎠᏓ [hinawida]

    ᎤᎾᎠᏫᏗ [unawitdi]

ᏍᎣᎤᏗᏍ [gaṇa³whtịha] (vt) "He is finding it (something alive) or it (something flexible)."

    ᏥᎣᎤᏗᏍ [tsinạwhtịha]

    ᎤᎣᎣᎤᏫᎢ [uṇa³whtvhv²³ʔi]

    ᏍᎣᎤᏗᏬᎠᎢ [gaṇa³whtịsgo³ʔi]

    ᎮᎣᎣᏫ [hiṇa³whta]

    ᎤᎣᎣᎤᏱ [uṇa³whtvhdi]

ᏍᎵᏗ [gaṇeʔa] (vt) "He is picking it (something flexible) up."

    ᏥᎵᏗ [tsịneʔa]

    ᎤᎵᏒᎢ [unesv²³ʔi]

    ᏍᎵᏬᎠᎢ [gaṇesgo³ʔi]

    ᎮᎣᏱ [hịnagi]

    ᎤᎵᏬᎤ [unesdi]

ᏍᎵᎦ [gaṇeka] (vt) "He is carrying it (something flexible)."

    ᏥᎵᏍ [tsịnega]

    ᎤᎵᏒᎢ [unẹsv²³ʔi]

    ᏍᎵᎠᎢ [gaṇeko³ʔi]

    ᎮᎣᏍ [hịnuga]

    ᎤᎤᏬᎤ [unvsdi]

ᏍᎵᏴᏗ [gaṇegi³ʔa] (vt) "He is picking up it (a liquid)."

    ᏥᎵᏴᏗ [tsịnegi³ʔa]

    ᎤᎵᏴᏒᎢ [unegi³sv²³ʔi]

    ᏍᎵᏴᏬᎠᎢ [gaṇegi³sgo³ʔi]

    ᎮᎵᏴ [hịnegi]

    ᎤᎵᏴᏬᎤ [unegi³sdi]

    … ᎠᏗ ᎩᎦ ᎤᏍᏊᏬᏥᏬᎤ ᏍᎵᏴᏬᏥᏬᎤ ᎠᏲ ᎡᎯᏊ ᏕᎶᎵᏚ ᏤᏣᏓᎤ ᏥᏒᎦᎣ.
    … and he who is willing — let him <u>take</u> the water of life freely.
    [ᎠᏥᎣᏊᎠᎣᏎᏆᎢᎢ 22:17]

ᏍᎵᏴᏭᏍ [gaṇegi³ʔeha] (vt) "He is milking it.; He is taking it (a liquid) from him."

    ᏥᎵᏴᏭᏗ [tsịnegi³ʔẹʔa]

    ᎤᎵᏴᏭᎿᎢ [unegi³ʔẹlv²³ʔi]

    ᏍᎵᏴᏭᏝᎢ [gaṇegi³ʔeho³ʔi]

    ᎮᎵᏴᏝ [hịnegi³ʔi]

    ᎤᎵᏴᏭᎵ [unegi³ʔehdi]

ᏍᎵᏴᏏ [gaṇegisi] (vt) "He is fetching it (a liquid)."

    ᏥᎵᏴᏏ [tsịnegisi]

    ᎤᎵᏴᏴᏒᎢ [unegisẹsv²³ʔi]

    ᏍᎵᏴᏴᎠᎢ [gaṇegisego³ʔi]

    ᎲᎵᏴᎬᏍ [hịnegisuga]

    ᎤᎵᏴᏒᏬᎤ [unegisvsdi]

ᏍᎵᎪᎬᏍ [gaṇegoyụga] (vt) "He is wrinkling."

    ᏥᎵᎪᎬᏍ [tsịnegoyụga]

    ᎤᎵᎪᎬᏨᎢ [unegoyutsv²³ʔi]

    ᏍᎵᎪᎦᎢ [gaṇegoyụgo³ʔi]

    ᎮᎵᎪᎬᏴ [hịnegoyụgi]

    ᎤᎵᎪᎬᏔᏬᎤ [unegoyụʔisdi]

ᏍᎵᏍ [gaṇeha] (vt) "He is holding it (something long)."

    ᏥᎵᏗ [tsịnẹʔa]

    ᎤᎵᏢᏬᎤᎢᎢ [unehesdv²³ʔi]

    ᏍᎵᎩᎢ [gaṇeho³ʔi]

    ᎮᎵᏢᏬᎤ [hịnehesdi]

    ᎤᎵᏬᎤ [unẹsdi]

    … ᎠᏗ ᏪᏟ ᏦᎣᏬᎤ ᎠᏥᎤ <u>ᏍᏍᎵᏍ</u>; ᎠᏝᏃ ᎠᏝᏴᎣᎲ ᎨᏍᎩ, ᎠᎠᏃ ᏥᏉᎲᏪ?
    … who <u>hath</u> … two fishes, but these — what are they to so many?'
    [ᏣᎲ 6:9]

ᏍᎵᏍ [ga³hnẹha] (vt) "He is holding it (something flexible)."

    ᏥᎵᏍ [tsị³ʔnẹha]

    ᎤᎵᏢᏬᎤᎢᎢ [u³hnẹhesdv²³ʔi]

    ᏍᎵᎩᎢ [ga³hnẹho³ʔi]

    ᎮᎵᏢᏬᎤ [hị³hnẹhesdi]

    ᎤᎵᏢᏬᎤ [u³hnẹhesdi]

ᏍᎵᏍ [ganhẹha] (vt) "He is carrying it (something flexible)."

    ᏥᎵᏍ [tsịnʔeha]

    ᎤᎵᏒᎢ [unhẹsv²³ʔi]

    ᏍᎵᎩᎢ [ganhẹho³ʔi]

    ᎮᎵᏍ [hịnhega]

    ᎤᎤᏬᎤ [unhvsdi]

ᏍᎵᏫᎢ [gaṇehvʔi] (n) "A puddle."

ᏦᏗᎳ [gan̨ela] (vi) "He is residing."

ᏘᏗᎳ [tsin̨ela]
ᎤᏗᎳᏍᎢᎢ [un̨eld̨ʌv²³ʔi]
ᏦᎵᏣᎢ [gan̨elo³ʔi]
ᎯᏗᎳᏗ [hin̨el̨ada]
ᎤᏗᎳᏗᏍᏗ [un̨eldisdi]

Oklahoma Dialect.

ᏦᏗᎳᏗ [gan̨eladi] (adj) "Pregnant."

ᏘᏗᎳᏗ [tsin̨eladi]

ᏦᏗᎳᏬᏍ [gan̨elawo³ʔa] (vt) "He is scalding and scraping it."

ᏘᏗᎳᏬᏍ [tsin̨elawo³ʔa]
ᎤᏗᎳᏬᎢᎢ [un̨elawo³ʔv²³ʔi]
ᏦᏗᎳᏬᏍᏗᎢ [gan̨elawo³sgo³ʔi]
ᎯᏗᎳᏬᏨ [hin̨elawo³tsa]
ᎤᏗᎳᏬᏍᏗ [un̨elawo³sdi]

ᏦᏗᏟᎮ [gan̨e³liha] (vt) "He dislikes him."

ᏘᏗᏟᎠ [tsin̨e³liʔa]
ᎤᏗᎦᏩᎢ [un̨e³lvhv²³ʔi]
ᏦᏗᏟᏍᎢᎢ [gan̨e³lisgo³ʔi]
ᎯᏗᎳ [hin̨e³la]
ᎤᏗᏟᏗ [un̨e³hldi]

ᏦᏗᏟᏗᎮ

ᏦᏗᏟᏗᎮ [gan̨ehldiha] (n) "A try."

ᏦᏗᏗᎮ [gan̨eneha] (vt) "He is giving it (a liquid) to him."

ᏘᏗᏗᎠ [tsin̨en̨eʔa]
ᎤᏗᏗᏍᎢ [un̨en̨elv²³ʔi]
ᏦᏗᏗᎭᎢ [gan̨eneho³ʔi]
ᎯᏗᎵᏏ [hin̨evsi]
ᎤᏗᏗᏗ [un̨enhdi]

ᏦᏗᏃᏗᏍᎩ [gan̨enodisgi] (n) "Measles."

ᏦᏗᏉᏟᎠ [gan̨enų³liʔa] (vt) "He is challenging.; He is bullying."

ᏘᏗᏉᏟᎠ [tsin̨enų³liʔa]
ᎤᏗᏉᎳᏬᎢ [un̨enų³lanv²³ʔi]
ᏦᏗᏉᏟᏍᎢᎢ [gan̨enų³lisgo³ʔi]
ᎯᏗᏉᏬᏍ [hin̨enų³l̨aga]
ᎤᏗᏉᏟᏗ [un̨enų³hldi]

ᏦᏗᏬᏛᏙᎭᏓ [gan̨esdalgi³ʔa] (vt) "He is thawing it out."

ᏘᏗᏬᏛᏙᎭᏓ [tsin̨esdalgi³ʔa]
ᎤᏗᏬᏛᏙᎭᎢᎢ [un̨esdalgi³sv²³ʔi]
ᏦᏗᏬᏛᏙᎭᏍᎠᎢ [gan̨esdalgi³sgo³ʔi]
ᎯᏗᏬᏛᏙᎭᏓ [hin̨esdalgi]
ᎤᏗᏬᏛᏙᎭᏍᏗ [un̨esdalgi³sdi]

ᏦᏗᏏ [gan̨esi] (n) "Golden-club.; biol. *Orontium aquaticum.*"

ᏦᏗᏁᏙᏍᏇᏍ [gan̨esoʔosga] (vi) "It is hailing."

ᎤᏗᏁᏙᏍᏅᎢ [un̨esoʔohv²³ʔi]
ᏦᏗᏁᏙᏍᏍᎠᎢ [gan̨esoʔosgo³ʔi]
ᏇᏍᏗᏁᏙᏍᏗ [wigan̨esoʔohi]
ᎤᏗᏁᏙᏍᏗ [un̨esoʔosdi]

ᏦᏗᏁᏙᏍᏙᎥᏗ [gan̨esolysdoʔdi] (n) "Collander.; Strainer."

ᏦᏗᏗᏍᎩ [gan̨edi³sgi] (n) "Black birch.; River birch.; Water birch.; biol. *Betula nigra.*"

ᏦᏗᏫᎮ [gan̨htseha] (vt) "He is holding it (a liquid).; He is bringing it (a liquid)."

ᏘᏗᏫᎮ [tsin̨ʔtseha]
ᎤᏗᏫᏁᏍᎢᎢ [unhtsehesdv²³ʔi]
ᏦᏗᏫᏴᎢ [gan̨htseho³ʔi]
ᎯᏗᏫᏁᏍᏗ [hinhtsehesdi]
ᎤᏗᏫᏁᏍᏗ [unhtsehesdi]

ᏦᏗᏘᎢ [gan̨etsiʔi] (n) "Chest (of the body)."

ᏘᏗᏘᎢ [tsin̨etsiʔi]

ᏓᏲᏃ ᏘᏴ ᏦᏗᏘᎢ ᎤᏍᏍᏛᎵ ᎠᏗ ᏆᏫᏄᎯᏴ; ᏓᎡᏐᏗᎠ, ᏦᎠ? and that one having leant back on the breast of Jesus, respondeth to him, 'Sir, who is it?' [Ꮵh 13:25]

ᏦᏘᏗᏍᎩ [gahn̨etsdisgi] (n) "An interpreter."

ᏦᏗᏫᏗᎮ [gan̨ewidiha] (vt) "He is carrying it (a liquid) off."

ᏘᏗᏫᏗᎠ [tsin̨ewidiʔa]
ᎤᏗᏫᏍᎠᎢ [un̨ewidvhv²³ʔi]
ᏦᏗᏫᏗᏍᎠᎢ [gan̨ewidisgo³ʔi]
ᎯᏗᏫᏓ [hin̨ewida]
ᎤᏗᏫᏗᏗ [un̨ewitdi]

ᏚᏁᏬᏗᎠ [gane³hwdịha] (vt) "He is finding it (a liquid)."

    ᏥᏁᏬᏗᎠ [tsịne?wdịha]

    ᎤᏁᏬᎭᎥᎢ [une³hwdyhv²³?i]

    ᏚᏁᏬᏍᎪᎥᎢ [gane³hwdịsgo³?i]

    ᎯᏁᏬᏓ [hịne³hwda]

    ᎤᏁᏬᎥᏗ [une³hwdvhdi]

ᏵᏂ [ga?ni] (n) "Mountain cane.; Bullet.; Lead."

ᏽᏂᎨᏂ [ganigeni] (n) "Knee."

    ᏥᏂᎨᏂ [tsịnigeni]

ᏽᏂᎪᎢ [gango?i] (n) "His tongue."

    ᏥᏂᎪᎢ [tsịngo?i]

ᏽᏂᎵᏕᎭ [gani³lǝdeha] (vt) "He is urging him."

    ᏥᏂᎵᏕᎠ [tsini³lǝdẹ?a]

    ᎤᏂᎵᏕᎥᎢ [uni³lǝdẹlv²³?i]

    ᏽᏂᎵᏕᎰᎢ [gani³lǝdeho³?i]

    ᎯᏂᎵᏗᏏ [hini³lǝdịsi]

    ᎤᏂᎵᏗ [uni³lǝtdi]

ᏽᏂᎬᏔᎭ [ganigwa³tiha] (vt) "He is hating him."

    ᏥᏂᎬᏔᎭ [tsịnigwatiha]

    ᎤᏂᎬᏔᎥᎢ [unigwa³tihlv²³?i]

    ᏽᏂᎬᏔᎰᎢ [ganigwa³tiho³?i]

    ᎯᏂᎬᏔᎦ [hịnigwa³tiga]

    ᎤᏂᎬᏔᏬᏗ [unigwa³tị³sdi]

    ᎾᏬᏯᏃ ᎢᎪᏅᏗ ᎩᎦ <u>ᏗᏂᎲᏌᏗᎠ</u>, ᎥᏝ ᏴᏃ <u>ᎥᏚᏂᎬᏔᎭ</u>, …
    he, therefore, <u>who is despising</u> — doth not <u>despise</u> man, …
    [᏶ᏏᎦᎲᏍ ᎢᎬᏬᏬ 4:8]

ᏽᏂᏌᎥᎢ [ganisahv?i] (n) "Burial.; Grave."

    Ꮮ ᎩᎦ ᎬᎠᏫ ᎤᎵᎢ <u>ᏽᏂᏌᎥᎢ</u>
    No one knows the whereabouts of <u>his burial</u>.
    [ᎬᏯ ᏪᎵᏂ ᏗᎯᎲᏬ ᏗᏕᎲᏗ]

ᏽᏂᏌᎲᏍᎦ [ga?nisa³hvsga] (vt) "He is burying him.; He is disposing of a body."

    ᏥᏂᏌᎥᏍᎦ [tsi?nisạ?vsga]

    ᎤᏂᏌᎿᎥᎢ [u?nisạ³hnv²³?i]

    ᏽᏂᏌᎲᎪᎥᎢ [ga?nisạ³hvsgo³?i]

    ᎯᏂᏌᎦ [hi?nisạ?vga]

    ᎤᏂᏌᎣᏗ [u?nisạohdi]

ᏽᏂᏏ [ganịsi] (n) "Bed."

ᏽᏂᎡᎥ [gani³svyi] (pt) "Under the house."

ᏽᏂᏓᏓ [ganidạda] (vi) "He has a tail."

    ᏥᏂᏓᏓ [tsịnidạda]

    ᎤᏂᏓᏍᎣᎢᎢ [unidạdesdv²³?i]

    ᏽᏂᏓᏙᎢ [ganidạdo³?i]

    ᎯᏂᏓᏍᏗ [hịnidạdesdi]

    ᎤᏂᏓᎥᏗ [unidạdvhdi]

ᏽᏂᏯᎠ [ga?ni³yị?a] (vt) "He is leaving it (something flexible)."

    ᏥᏂᏯᎠ [tsị?ni³yị?a]

    ᎤᏂᏯᎢᎢ [u?ni³yiv²³?i]

    ᏽᏂᏯᎪᎥᎢ [ga?ni³yisgo³?i]

    ᎯᏂᏯ [hị?ni³ya]

    ᎤᏂᏯᏗ [u?ni³yhdi]

ᏽᏂᏯᎭ [ga?ni³yiha] (vt) "He is catching something thrown or chased."

    ᏥᏂᏯᎠ [tsị?ni³yị?a]

    ᎤᏂᏴᎥᎢ [u?ni³yvhv²³?i]

    ᏽᏂᏯᎪᎥᎢ [ga?ni³yisgo³?i]

    ᎯᏂᏯ [hị?ni³ya]

    ᎤᏂᏯᏗ [u?ni³yhdi]

    … ᎾᏬᏯᏃ ᎤᎠᏫ ᎠᎵᎬᎲᎠᏬ ᎠᏚᏗ ᎤᏪᏯᏂ <u>ᎤᏂᏴᏫᏱ</u>, ᎠᏗ ᏊᏬᏓᏱ, …
    … At the sight of which, *Evangelist* <u>caught</u> him by the right hand, saying, …
    [ᏗᏁᏗ ᏒᏯᎡᎢ]

ᏇᏃᎨᏂ [gahnogeni] (n) "His arm."

    ᏥᏃᎨᏂ [tsihnogeni]

    ᎠᎵ ᎤᏂᏌᏫ ᏞᏉ ᎩᎬᏯ? Ꭰ) <u>ᏗᏇᏃᎨᏂ</u>, Ᏼ) ᎠᎬᏥᏂ.
    Where does a chipmunk keep his seeds? a) In <u>his arms</u>, b) In his cheeks.
    [ᎬᏯ ᎧᎢᏂ ᏗᏂᎲᏬ ᏗᏎᎲᏗ]

ᏇᏃᎮᎾ [ganohena] (n) "Rice."

ᏇᏃᎮᏂ [ganoheni] (n) "Hominy grits."

ᏇᏃᎰᎭ [ganhohịha] (vt) "He is bringing it (something flexible)."

    ᏥᏃᎰᎭ [tsịn?ohịha]

    ᎤᏃᎡᎢ [unhohlv²³?i]

    ᏇᏃᎰᎢᎢ [ganhohịho³?i]

    ᎯᏃᎦ [hịnhoga]

    ᎤᏃᎰᏗ [unhohịsdi]

SZᎯᏢ [gạnohi³li] (vt) "He is flying."

  ᏍZTᏢ [tsịnọʔi³li]

  ᎣᎡZᎯᏣRT [unohi³lẹsv²³ʔi]

  SZᎯᏈᏗT [gạnohi³liso³ʔi]

  ᎯZᎯMᏚ [hịnohi³luʔga]

  ᎣᎡZᎯᎶᏗᎵ [unohi³lv³sdi]

SZᏢ [gạno³li] (vi) "He is slipping up on.; He is sneaking up on."

  ᏍZᏢ [tsịno³li]

  ᎣᎡZᏣRT [uno³lẹsv²³ʔi]

  SZᏢᏗT [gạno³liso³ʔi]

  ᎯZMᏚ [hịno³luʔga]

  ᎣᎡZᎯᏗᎵ [uno³lvsdi]

SZᏢVD [gạno³hlidọʔha] (vt) "He is hunting animals."

  ᏍZᏢVD [tsịnọʔlidọʔha]

  ᎣᎡZᏢVᎠT [unọ³hlidọʔlv²³ʔi]

  SZᏢVᎶᏓT [gạno³hlidọʔho³ʔi]

  ᎯZᏢD [hịnọ³hlia]

  ᎣᎡZᏢDᏗᎵ [unọ³hliạsdi]

SZᎯᎶᏚ [gạnolv³ʔvsga] (vi) "The wind blowing."

  ———

  ᎣᎡZᎯᎣᏔ [unolv³ʔnv²³ʔi]

  SZᎯᎶᏗT [gạnolv³ʔvsgo³ʔi]

  ᎾᏍZᎯᏚ [wịganolv³ʔga]

  ᎣᎡZᎯᎵ [unolv³ʔdi]

SZᎤᎠYD [gạnosgị³ʔa] (vt) "He is stealing."

  ᏍZᎤᎠYD [tsịnọʔsgị³ʔa]

  ᎣᎡZᎤᎠYRT [unosgị³sv²³ʔi]

  SZᎤᎠYTᏗAT [gạnosgị³isgo³ʔi]

  ᎯZᎤᎠY [hịnosgị]

  ᎣᎡZᎤᎠYᏗᎵ [unosgị³sdi]

  ... LᏗᎵ GZᎤᎠYRY, ...
  ... Thou mayest not steal, ...
  [ᎠᎢᏚ 10:19]

SZRᎥᎠᏚ [gạnosyʔvvsga] (vt) "He is putting on his shoulder."

  SZRᎥᎠᏚ [gạnosyʔvvsga]

  ᎣᎡZRᎣᏔ [unosyʔnv²³ʔi]

  SZRᎥᎠᏔT [gạnosyʔvvsgo³ʔi]

  ᏴZRᎥᏚ [hạnosyʔvga]

  ᎣᎡZRᎵ [unosvdi]

SZBᏚ [gạnoyv³ga] (vi) "He is drowning.; He is sinking."

  ᏍZBᏚ [tsịnoyv³ga]

  ᎣᎡZBᏣᎢT [unoyv³tsv²³ʔi]

  SZBAT [gạnoyv³go³ʔi]

  ᎯZBᎩ [hịnoyv³gi]

  ᎣᎡZBTᏗᎵ [unoyy³ʔisdi]

SZBᏢᎤᏗᎦ [gahnọyy³hẹsdịha] (vt) "He is ringing it (bell)."

  ᏍZBᏢᎤᏗᎦ [tsịnọʔyy³hẹsdịha]

  ᎣᎡZBᏢᎤᎯᏐᎢT [uhnọyy³hẹsdạʔnv²³ʔi]

  SZBᏢᎤᏗᎤᎠT [gahnọyy³hẹsdịsgo³ʔi]

  ᎯZBᏢᎤᏗᎢ [hịhnọyy³hẹsda]

  ᎣᎡZBᏢᎤᎠVᎵ [uhnọyy³hẹsdohdi]

ᏌᎤᎠᎶᎤᏚ [gạnugoʔọsga] (vi) "It is falling (multiple falls)."

  ———

  ᎣᎡᎤᎠᎶᎢRT [unugoʔọsv²³ʔi]

  ᏌᎤᎠᎶᎤᎠT [gạnugoʔọsgo³ʔi]

  ᎾᏍᏌᎤᎠᎶᎢT [wịganugoʔọʔhi]

  ᎣᎡᎤᎠᎾᏗᎵ [unugohịsdi]

ᏌᎤᎠᏚ [gạnugo³ga] (vt) "He is exiting.; He is going out of it."

  ᏍᎢᏌᎠᏚ [tsịnugo³ga]

  ᎣᎡᏌᎠᏣᎢT [unugo³ʔtsv²³ʔi]

  ᏌᎤᎠAAT [gạnugo³go³ʔi]

  ᎯᏌᎠAT [hịnugo³ʔi]

  ᎣᎡᏌᎠTᏗᎵ [unugo³ʔisdi]

  ... ᎪᎢᎤᏓᏚ DᏍ TᏍᏌAT Dh; ᏛᏲᏣᎦᎤZ ᏅᏔᏅᎤᎳh ᎠD SSᏗᎢT. ...
  ... 'Rise, go out from this place, for Jehovah is destroying the city;' ...
  [ᎤᎦ TEᏛᏗᏛ 19:14]

ᏌᎤᎯᎵᎵ

ᏌᎤᎯᎵᎵ [gạnụhihldi] (n) "Plate."

ᏌᎠᎢᎵᎵ [gạnụhuhldi] (n) "Cup."

ᏌᎠWᎤD [gạnulah³sạʔa] (vi) "He is covered with dirt."

  ᏍᎠWᎤD [tsịnulaʔʔsạʔa]

  ᎣᎡᏌWRᎣᏔ [unulah³svhnv²³ʔi]

  ᏌᎠWᎤᎶᏔT [gạnulah³sạʔo³ʔi]

  ᎯᏌWᎤᏓᏚ [hịnulah³sahvga]

  ᎣᎡᏌWRᎵ [unulah³svhdi]

78

ᎦᏄᎳᏒᎥᏍᎦ [gạnulah³sṿʔvsga] (vt) "He is covering it with dirt.; He is burying it."

ᏥᏄᎳᏒᎥᏍᎦ [tsịnulạʔsṿʔvsga]

ᎤᏄᎳᏒᏂᎥᎢ [unulah³sṿʔhniv²³ʔi]

ᎦᏄᎳᏒᎥᏍᎪᎢ [gạnulah³sṿʔvsgo³ʔi]

ᎯᏄᎳᏒᎥᎦ [hịnulah³sṿʔvga]

ᎤᏄᎳᏒᏱ [unulah³sṿʔyi]

ᎦᏄᎸᎯ [gạnulṿhi] (n) "Grass.; Weeds."

ᎤᏁᎳᏅᎯᏃ ᎯᎠ ᏄᏪᏎᎢ; ᎡᏂᏣᏊ ᏂᎦᎥ ᎦᏄᎸᎯ ᎠᎦᏔᏛᏍᎩ ᎾᏍᎩ ᏂᎬᎾᏛ ᎦᏙᎯ ᏣᏛᏍᎦ, …
And God saith, 'Lo, I have given to you every herb sowing seed, which [is] upon the face of all the earth, …
[ᎼᏏ ᎢᎬᏱᏱ 1:29]

ᎦᏄᏖᏲᎭ [gạnutẹʔyoha] (vt) "He is twisting it."

ᏥᏄᏕᏲᎭ [tsịnudʔẹʔyoha]

ᎤᏄᏖᏲᎸᎢ [unutẹʔyohlv²³ʔi]

ᎦᏄᏖᏲᏍᎪᎢ [gạnutẹʔyosgo³ʔi]

ᎯᏄᏖᏲᎧ [hịnutẹʔyka]

ᎤᏄᏖᏲᏍᏗ [unutẹʔyosdi]

ᎦᏅᎥᏍᎦ [gạnv³ʔvsga] (vt) "He is placing it (something flexible) on the ground.; He is placing it (something alive) on the ground."

ᏥᏅᎥᏍᎦ [tsịnv³ʔṿʔsga]

ᎤᏅᏅᎢ [unv³ʔnv²³ʔi]

ᎦᏅᎥᏍᎪᎢ [gạnv³ʔvsgo³ʔi]

ᎯᏅᎥᎦ [hịnv³ʔvga]

ᎤᏅᏗ [unv³ʔdi]

… ᎥᏝ ᎠᏂ ᏱᎦᏅ; ᏗᏣᎾᏅᎦ Ꭰ ᎤᏂᏅᏅᎢ.
… he is not here; lo, the place where they laid him!
[ᎹᎦ 15:47]

ᎦᏅᎦ [gạnv³ga] (vi) "He is falling to the ground."

ᏥᏅᎦ [tsịnv³ga]

ᎤᏅᏨᎢ [unv³ʔtsv²³ʔi]

ᎦᏅᎪᎢ [gạnv³go³ʔi]

ᎯᏅᎩ [hịnv³ʔgi]

ᎤᏅᎢᏍᏗ [unv³ʔisdi]

… ᎠᏎᏃ ᎥᏝ ᏌᏉ ᎡᎳᏗ ᎤᏅᎢᏍᏗ ᏱᎩ ᎢᏥᏙᏓ ᎤᏓᏅᏖᎸᎯ ᏂᎨᏒᎾ.
… and one of them shall not fall on the ground without your Father;
[ᎹᏚ 10:29]

ᎦᏅᎦ [gạhnṿ³ga] (vi) "He is in the process of lying down."

ᏥᏅᎦ [tsịʔnṿ³ga]

—

ᎦᏅᎪᎢ [gạhnṿ³go³ʔi]

—

—

ᎢᏏᎦ ᏗᎦᎵᎠᏅᎯᏛ ᎤᎵᏂᎩᏛ, ᏗᏴᏙᏗᏱ ᎠᏰᎵ ᎦᏅᎦ.
Issacher [is] a strong ass, Crouching between the two folds;
[ᎼᏏ ᎢᎬᏱᏱ 49:14]

ᎦᏅᎦᎵᎠ [gạnvgạ³lịʔa] (vt) "He is cleaning (1)."

ᏥᏅᎦᎵᎠ [tsịnvgạ³lịʔa]

ᎤᏅᎦᎸᎥᎢ [unvgạ³lṿʔv²³ʔi]

ᎦᏅᎦᎵᏍᎪᎢ [gạnvgạ³lisgo³ʔi]

ᎯᏅᎦᎳ [hịnvgạ³la]

ᎤᏅᎦᎵᏗ [unvgạ³hldi]

ᎦᏅᎦᎵᎭ [gạnvgạ³liha] (vt) "He is cleaning (2)."

ᏥᏅᎦᎵᎠ [tsịnvgạ³lịʔa]

ᎤᏅᎦᎸᎲᎢ [unvgạ³lvhv²³ʔi]

ᎦᏅᎦᎵᏍᎪᎢ [gạnvgạ³lisgo³ʔi]

ᎯᏅᎦᎳ [hịnvgạ³la]

ᎤᏅᎦᎵᏗ [unvgạ³hldi]

ᎦᏅᎩ [gạnvgi] (n) "Blackburnian warbler.; biol. *Setophaga fusca.*"

ᎦᏅᎯᏓ [gạnṿhida] (adj) "Long."

ᎦᏅᎱᎩᎠ [gạnvhugịʔa] (vi) "It is flooding."

—

ᎤᏅᎱᎦᏅᎢ [unvhugạnv²³ʔi]

ᎦᏅᎱᎩᏍᎪᎢ [gạnvhugịsgo³ʔi]

ᏫᎦᏅᎱᎦᎦ [wịgạnvhugaga]

ᎤᏅᎱᎪᏗ [unvhugohdi]

ᎦᏅᏁᎭ [gạnvneha] (vt) "He is giving it (something flexible) to him."

ᏥᏅᏁᎠ [tsinvnẹʔa]

ᎤᏅᏁᎸᎢ [unvnelv²³ʔi]

ᎦᏅᏁᎰᎢ [gạnvneho³ʔi]

ᎯᏅᎥᏏ [hinvvsi]

ᎤᏅᏁᏗ [unvnhdi]

ᎠᏍ ᎠᏣᏗ ᏯᏔᏲᎯᎭ, ᏥᎪ ᎢᎾᏛᏉ ᏴᎦᏅᎥᏏ?
and if a fish he may ask — a serpent will he present to him?
[ᎹᏚ 7:10]

ᎦᏅᏃᏩ [gạnvnọwa] (n) "A pipe use for smoking."

ᎦᏅᏅ [gạnvhnv] (n) "A road."

Ꮎ'ᏂᎩᏰᏃ ᎦᏅᏅ ᏭᎷᏨ ...
And as he is going forth into the way ...
[ᎹᎦ 10:17]

ᎦᏅᏆᎶᎠ [gạnvgwạlọ³ʔa] (vt) "He is beating it."

ᏥᏅᏆᎶᎠ [tsịnvgwạlọ³ʔa]
ᎤᏅᏆᎶᎢᎢ [unvgwạlọ³ʔv²³ʔi]
ᎦᏅᏆᎶᏍᎪᎢ [gạnvgwạlọ³sgo³ʔi]
ᎯᏅᏆᎶᏣ [hịnvgwạlọ³tsa]
ᎤᏅᏆᎶᏍᏗ [unvgwạlọ³sdi]

ᎦᏅᏆᎶᏍᏗ [gạnvgwạlosdi] (n) "A hammer."

ᎦᏅᏆᎶᏍᏗ [gạnvkwạlọsdi] (n) "A hammer."

ᎦᏅᏌᏩᏍᎦ [gạnhsạhvh³sga] (vt) "He is robbing him.; He is stealing from him."

ᏥᏅᏌᏩᏍᎦ [tsinʔsạhvh³sga]
ᎤᏅᏌᏅᎢ [unhsạʔhnv²³ʔi]
ᎦᏅᏌᏩᏍᎪᎢ [gạnhsạhvh³sgo³ʔi]
ᎯᏅᏌᏩᎦ [hinhsạhv³ga]
ᎤᏅᏌᏬᏗ [unhsạohdi]

ᎦᏅᏍᎦ [gạnvsga] (vt) "He is delegating him to do ....; He is asking him to do ...."

ᏥᏅᏍᎦ [tsinỵʔsga]
ᎤᏅᏒᎢ [unvsv²³ʔi]
ᎦᏅᏍᎪᎢ [gạnvsgo³ʔi]
ᎯᏅᎵ [hinvʔli]
ᎤᏅᏍᏗ [unvsdi]

ᎦᏅᏍᎨᏂ [gạnvsgeni] (n) "His leg."

ᏥᏅᏍᎨᏂ [tsịnvsgeni]

... ᎥᏝ ᏱᎦᏂᏍᏆᎵᏦ ᏗᎦᏅᏍᎨᏂ;
... they did not break his legs;
[ᏣᏂ 19:33]

ᎦᏅᏍᏗᎭ [gạnỵsdiha] (vt) "He is being carried by it (something alive) or it (something flexible)."

ᏥᏅᏍᏗᎠ [tsịnỵsdịʔa]
ᎤᏅᏍᏔᏅᎢ [unỵstạnv²³ʔi]
ᎦᏅᏍᏗᏍᎪᎢ [gạnỵsdisgo³ʔi]
ᎯᏅᏍᏓ [hịnỵsda]
ᎤᏅᏍᏙᏗ [unỵstdi]

ᎦᏅᏍᏗᎭ [gạnỵsdịha] (vt) "He is being carried by it (something long)."

ᏥᏅᏍᏗᎭ [tsịnỵsdịha]
ᎤᏅᏍᏔᏅᎢ [unỵstạnv²³ʔi]
ᎦᏅᏍᏗᏍᎪᎢ [gạnỵsdịsgo³ʔi]
ᎯᏅᏍᏓ [hịnỵsda]
ᎤᏅᏍᏙᏗ [unỵsdohdi]

ᎦᏅᏐᎮᎭ [gạnỵsoheha] (vt) "He is winding a clock."

ᏥᏅᏐᎡᎭ [tsịnỵsọʔeha]
ᎤᏅᏐᏝᎢ [unỵsọʔhlv²³ʔi]
ᎦᏅᏐᎮᎰᎢ [gạnỵsoheho³ʔi]
ᎯᏅᏐᎧ [hịnỵsoka]
ᎤᏅᏐᏍᏗ [unỵsọʔhsdi]

ᎦᏅᏐᎯᎭ [gạnvsọ³hịha] (vt) "He is tightening it.; He is applying brakes."

ᏥᏅᏐᎢᎭ [tsịnvsọʔịha]
ᎤᏅᏐᏝᎢ [unvsọ³hlv²³ʔi]
ᎦᏅᏐᎯᎰᎢ [gạnvsọ³hịho³ʔi]
ᎯᏅᏐᎦ [hịnvsọ³ga]
ᎤᏅᏐᏍᏗ [unvsoh³sdi]

ᎦᏅᏋᏨᎢ [gạnvsỵtsvʔi] (n) "His ankle."

ᏥᏅᏋᏨᎢ [tsịnvsỵtsvʔi]

ᎦᏅᏙᎧ [gạndọka] (n) "Tooth."

ᏕᎦᏅᏙᎧ [degạndọka]
ᏥᏅᏙᎧ [tsịndọka]
ᏕᏥᏅᏙᎧ [detsịndọka]

ᎦᏅᏙᎩ [gahndogi] (n) "Saw."

ᎦᏅᏅᏍᏗᎭ [gahnỵwsdịha] (vt) "He is urging him.; He is driving it."

ᏥᏅᏅᏍᏗᎭ [tsịnỵʔwsdịha]
ᎤᏅᏅᏍᏓᏅᎢ [uhnỵwsdạʔnv²³ʔi]
ᎦᏅᏅᏍᏗᏍᎪᎢ [gahnỵwsdịsgo³ʔi]
ᎯᏅᏅᏍᏓ [hịhnỵwsda]
ᎤᏅᏅᏍᏙᏗ [uhnỵwsdohdi]

ᎦᏅᏬᎦ [gạnvwoʔga] (vi) "It is getting shallow."

—

ᎤᏅᏬᏨᎢ [unvwoʔtsv²³ʔi]
ᎦᏅᏬᎪᎢ [gạnvwoʔgo³ʔi]
ᏫᎦᏅᏬᎩ [wigạnvwoʔgi]
ᎤᏅᏬᎢᏍᏗ [unvwoʔisdi]

ᏎᎣᏍᏪᏍ [gạnvwọsga] (vi) "It is receding."

⸺

ᎤᎣᎧᎤᎡᎢ [unvwọsv²³ʔi]
ᏎᎣᏪᏌᎯ [gạnvwosgo³ʔi]
ᏪᏎᎣᏍ [wịganvwoga]
ᎤᎣᎠᏪᏌᎠᎫ [unvwohịsdi]
ᏎᎣᏪᎶᏆ [gạnvwo³diha] (vt) "He is making it shallow."

ᏥᎣᏪᎫ [tsịnvwo³dịʔa]
ᎤᎣᎣᎤᎡᎢ [unvwo³dv²³ʔi]
ᏎᎣᏪᏆᏌᎯ [gạnvwo³disgo³ʔi]
ᎠᎣᎤᏞ [hịnvwo³da]
ᎤᎣᎤᏪᏆᏌᎫ [unvwo³disdi]
ᏎᏞᎡᏎ [gạgwsvga] (adj) "Smelly."
ᏎᎤᏣᎾ [gạsạlena] (n) "Coat.; Jacket.; Sweater."

ᏎᎤᏣᎾ ᎿᏌ ᏣᏥᎩᎲᏏᎩ ᏎᏣ ᏎᏆᏲ ᏛᎡ ᏊᏆᎳᏉ, …
the cloak that I left in Troas with Carpus, coming, …
[ᏔᎵᏐ ᎫᎱᏆ 4:13]

ᏎᎤᏞᎣᏨᎢᎴᏍ [gạsạne³ndyʔvsga] (vt) "He is threading a needle."

ᏥᎤᏞᎣᏨᎢᎴᏍ [tsịsane³ndyʔyʔsga]
ᎤᎤᏞᎣᏨᎣᎢ [usane³ndyʔnv²³ʔi]
ᏎᎤᏞᎣᏨᎢᎴᏌᎯ [gạsane³ndyʔvsgo³ʔi]
ᎠᎤᏞᎣᏨᎢᏎ [hịsane³ndyʔvga]
ᎤᎤᏞᎣᏨᎫ [usane³ndvdi]
ᏎᎴᎨᎭ [gạsgeni] (n) "His armpit."

ᏥᎴᎨᎭ [tsịsgeni]
ᏎᎴᏎᏣᎠ [gạsgịlọhi] (n) "Chair."
ᏎᎴᏎᏯᎢ [gạsgịlvʔi] (n) "Table."

… ᎴᎾ ᏍᎹᏣᎣᏒᏯ ᏎᏎᎴᏯᎢ.
… and the tables he overthrew,
[ᏅᎭ 2:15]

ᏎᎴᎥᎸᎶᏍ

ᏎᎴᎥᎸᎶᏍ [gạsgwolvsga] (vi) "It is dripping."

⸺

ᎤᎴᎥᎸᎡᎢ [usgwolvsv²³ʔi]
ᏎᎴᎥᎸᎶᏌᎯ [gạsgwolvsgo³ʔi]
ᏪᏎᎴᎥᎸᎠ [wịgasgwolvhi]
ᎤᎴᎥᎸᎶᏌᎫ [usgwolvsdi]
ᏎᎴᏡᎨᎭ [gạsdgeni] (n) "His calf of the leg."

ᏆᏎᎴᏡᎨᎭ [dịgạsdgeni]
ᏥᎴᏡᎨᎭ [tsịsdgeni]
ᏊᏥᎴᏡᎨᎭ [dịtsịsdgeni]

ᏎᎴᏆᎩᏠᎶᏍ [gạsdịwụʔosga] (vi) "The leaves are falling."

⸺

ᎤᎴᏆᎩᏠᎡᎢ [usdịwụʔosv²³ʔi]
ᏎᎴᏆᎩᏠᎥᏌᎯ [gạsdịwụʔosgo³ʔi]
ᏪᏎᎴᏆᎩᏠᎠ [wịgasdịwụʔohi]
ᎤᎴᏆᎩᏠᎠᏌᎫ [usdịwụʔohịsdi]
ᏎᎠᏠᎢ [gạsohiʔi] (n) "His upper back."

ᏥᎠᏠᎢ [tsịsohiʔi]
ᏎᏒᎾᏐ [gạsỵnali] (n) "Roof."
ᏎᏒᏪᎶᏍ [gạsvtasga] (vt) "He is stacking it."

ᏥᏒᏞᎶᏍ [tsịsvdʔasga]
ᎤᎡᏒᏫᎣᎢ [usvtạnv²³ʔi]
ᏎᏒᏪᎶᏌᎯ [gạsvtasgo³ʔi]
ᎠᏒᏫᏎ [hịsvtaga]
ᎤᎡᏒᏡᏆ [usvtdi]
ᏎᏛ [gahda] (n) "Dirt."

ᏔᏎᎤᏃ ᎤᏫᏌ ᏥᎡ ᎤᎥᏞᎶᎥᏫᎢ, ᏎᎯᏢ ᏎᏛ ᏎᏫᎤᎡᏔ, ᎩᏪᎷᏃ ᏔᏆᎤ ᎤᎡᏒᏞᏆᎢ, ᎤᏆᏎᎶᎥᏆᎶᎢ ᎤᎢᏔᎬ ᏥᎡ ᏎᏛ.
and others fell upon the rocky places, where they had not much earth, and immediately they sprang forth, through not having depth of earth,
[ᎹᎠ 13:5]

ᏎᏡᎠ [gạdaʔa] (vi) "He is being hanged."

ᏎᏡᎠ [gạdaʔa]
ᎤᎣᎣᎢ [udvʔnv²³ʔi]
ᏎᏡᏌᎢ [gạdaʔo³ʔi]
ᎿᏡᎢᎢᏎ [hạdayʔvga]
ᎤᎣᏡ [utdi]
ᏎᏡᎩᏓ [gạdạgiʔa] (vt) "He is taking it (something alive) or it (a solid) or it (something flexible) down."

ᏥᎦᏡᎩᏓ, ᏎᏡᎩᏓ [gạdạgiʔa, jịyạdạgiʔa]
ᎤᏡᎩᏒᎢ [udạgisv²³ʔi]
ᏎᏡᎩᏌᎯ [gạdạgisgo³ʔi]
ᎠᎦᏡᎩ, ᎿᏡᎩ [hạdạgi, hịyạdạgi]
ᎤᏡᎩᏌᎫ [udạgisdi]
ᏎᏡᏕ [gạdạguga] (n) "A churn."
ᏎᏡᏕ [gạdạguga] (n) "A jug."
ᏎᏡᏆ [gahdạha] (adj) "Dirty."

ᏛᎭᏪᏓᏆᏏᏃ ᏓᏒᎡ ᏓᏎᏌ ᏎᏡᏆ ᏆᏢᎥ ᎤᏌᎢ, ᏕᎣ ᎤᏪᎹᏆ,
And there was in their synagogue a man with an unclean spirit, and he cried out,
[ᎹᎠ 1:23]

ᏎᏡᏏᏢ [gạdahlịda] (n) "Arrow."

81

ᏍᎷᎹᎮᎠ [gạdạlu³gịʔa] (vt) "He is plowing."

Ꮵ�319ᎾᎠ [tsịdạlu³gịʔa]

ᎤᏝᎹᏍᎾᎢ [udạlu³gaʔnv²³ʔi]

ᏍᎷᎹᏯᏗᎯ [gạdạlu³gisgo³ʔi]

ᎠᎷᎹᏍᏍ [hịdạlu³gaga]

ᎤᏝᎹᎠᏗ [udạlu³godi]

ᏍᏚᎤᏈ [gạdạgwali] (n) "Clay."

ᏍᏝᏗ [gadạti] (n) "A flag."

ᎷᏁᏈᏗ ᏍᏝᏗ ᏯᏍᎮᏓ ᎠᏯᏇ.
Color the ninth flag red.
[ᏩᎶ ᏪᏈᏁ ᏗᎯᎲᎥᏓ ᎠᏍᎮᎥᏗ]

ᏍᏝᏫᎠᏕᎾ [gạda³yohịha] (vi) "He is playing marbles."

ᏥᏝᎮᏔᎾ [tsịda³yọʔịha]

ᎤᏝᎮᎣᎢ [uda³yohlv²³ʔi]

ᏍᏝᎮᎠᎮᏔ [gạda³yohịho³ʔi]

ᎠᏝᎮᎣᏍ [hịda³yohaga]

ᎤᏝᎮᎥᏗ [uda³yosdi]

ᏍᏝᎮᎥᏗ [gạdayọsdi] (n) "A marble."

ᏍᏚᎤᏗ [gạtesạdi] (n) "A skillet."

ᏍᏚᏯᎢᎭ [gạtesgeni] (n) "His back, the lower part."

ᏥᏚᏯᎢᎭ [tsịtesgeni]

ᏍᎵᎥᎭ [gạdigeni] (n) "His heel of the foot."

ᏍᏍᎵᎥᎭ [degạdigeni]

ᏥᎵᎥᎭ [tsịdigeni]

ᏍᏥᎵᎥᎭ [detsịdigeni]

... "ᎢᏛᏫᏱ ᏪᏡᎵᎣᏅ�B&ᎥᏯ ᎤᏴᏫᏠᎤ ᏍᎵᎥᎭ
ᎠᎢᎿᏯᎾᎨᎢᎢ."
... He who is eating the bread with me, did lift up
against me his heel.
[ᎬᎯ 13:18]

ᏍᎵᎢᎠᏍᎵᎠᏕᎯ [gạdigwạlvdehdịha] (vt) "He is twirling it."

ᏥᎵᎢᎠᏍᎵᎠᏕ [tsịdigwạlvdedịha]

ᎤᎵᎢᎠᏍᏬᎣᎢ [udigwạlvdẹtạnv²³ʔi]

ᏍᎵᎢᎠᏍᎵᎠᏕᎯᏗᎰ [gạdigwạlvdehdịsgo³ʔi]

ᎠᎵᎢᎠᏍᎡ [hịdigwạlvdehda]

ᎤᎵᎢᎠᏍᎤᏗ [udigwạlvdehdohdi]

ᏍᎥ [gạdo] (pt) "What."

(Ꮪ)�``ᏔᏟᏁᎦ?
"What are you doing?"
[King pg 120]

Oklahoma dialect.

ᏍᎥᏠᎤᏍ [gạdoʔosga] (vi) "It (something flexible) or it (a
liquid) is falling."

———

ᎤᎥᏠᏏᎢ [udoʔosv²³ʔi]

ᏍᎥᏠᎠᏗᎯ [gạdoʔosgo³ʔi]

ᎤᏍᎥᏠᎠ [wịgạdoʔohi]

ᎤᎥᏠᎠᏁᏗ [udoʔohịsdi]

ᏍᎥᎦ [gạdoga] (vi) "He is standing."

ᏥᎥᎦ [tsịdoga]

ᎤᎥᎥᏦᎢ [udogesdv²³ʔi]

ᏍᎥᎠᎢ [gạdogo³ʔi]

ᎠᎥᎥᏗ [hịdogesdi]

ᎤᎥᎥᏗ [udogesdi]

ᏚᏴᏃ ᎠᎠ ᏐᏯᏒ ᎠᎨᏝᎲᏄᎠ, ᎠᎥᎥᏗ ᏞᏍ, ᎤᏯᏃ
ᏞᎡᏃᏈ ᏥᏗ ᎤᎵᏫᎣᎠ ᎤᏁᏫᎠ. ᎤᏯᏃ ᏍᎥᎠ
ᎤᏫᎤᎥᏗ.
Then, said *Evangelist*, stand still a little, that I may
shew thee the words of God. So he stood trembling.
[ᏗᏁᏥ ᏍᎯᏯᏒᏗ]

ᏍᎥᎤᏝᏗᎥᏗ [gatosạdịsdohdi] (n) "A hinge, hinges."

ᏍᎥᎤᎵᎠᎭ [gạdọwidịha] (vt) "He is mashing it."

ᏥᎥᎤᎵᎠᎢᎠ [tsịdọwidịʔa]

ᎤᎥᎤᏫᎤᎢ [udọwitạnv²³ʔi]

ᏍᎥᎤᎵᎠᏗᎰ [gạdọwidịsgo³ʔi]

ᎠᎥᎤᎤ [hịdọwida]

ᎤᎥᎤᎥᏗ [udọwitdi]

ᏍᏚ [gadu] (n) "Bread."

ᎥᏍᎨᏃ ᏍᏚ ᎠᏓ ᏐᏗ ᏔᎦᎤᎥᏗ ᏗᏠᎠᎠ ᏍᏄᏕ ᏔᎮ,
ᎤᏈᏫᎷᏢᏁᏃ, ᎠᏓ ᎤᎵᏫᏈᏔ, ...
and Jacob hath given to Esau bread and pottage of
lentiles, and he eateth, and drinketh, ...
[ᏃᏚ ᏔᎡᏯᏒ 25:34]

ᏍᏚᏯ [gadugi] (n) "County.; Free labor company."

ᏍᏚᏪᎥᏗ [gạdụlasdi] (n) "Dough."

ᏍᏚᏚ [gadusi] (pt) "Up the mountain."

ᎠᏯᏪ ᎤᏍᎢᎬᏝ ᏍᏔᏫᏗ ᏍᏚᏚ ᎩᎹᎠᎥᏗᎢ.
Help the goat arrive high up the mountain.
[ᏩᎶ ᏪᏈᏁ ᏗᎯᎲᎥᏓ ᎠᏍᎮᎥᏗ]

ᏍᏦᎢᎥᏍ [gạdv³ʔvsga] (vt) "He is hanging it (something
flexible) up."

ᏍᏦᎢᎥᏍ [gạdv³ʔvʔsga]

ᎤᏦᎤᎢ [udv³ʔvnv²³ʔi]

ᏍᏦᎢᎥᏗ [gạdv³ʔvsgo³ʔi]

ᏔᏦᎢᏍ [hạdv³ʔvga]

ᎤᏦᎢ [udv³ʔdi]

ᏍᏦᎢ [gạdvdi] (n) "A fishing pole."

82

ᏍᏣᏲᎯᎭ [gatsayo³hiha] (vt) "He is stabbing him."

    ᏥᏯᏣᏲᎯᎭ [tsiyatsayo²iha]

    ᎤᏣᏲᎸ [utsayo³²lv²³²i]

    ᏍᏣᏲᎯᎰ [gatsayo³hiho³²i]

    ᎯᏯᏣᏲᎠᎦ [hiyatsayo³²aga]

    ᎤᏣᏲᎥᏗ [utsayo³sdi]

ᏍᎦᎺᎩᏍᏙᏗ [gatsehlukisdohdi] (n) "Horn.; Flute.; Clarinet.; Bugle."

ᏍᎥ [gatsv] (pt) "Where."

ᏍᎥᏄᎳ [gatsvnula] (pt) "Fast.; Quick.; In a hurry."

ᏍᎥᎲᏍᎦ [gatsvhyhsga] (vt) "He is stinging him."

    ᏥᏯᏨᎲᏍᎦ [tsiyatsv²ysga]

    ᎤᏨᎲᏳᎥ [utsvhyhv²³²i]

    ᏍᎥᎲᏍᎰᎢ [gatsvhyhsgo³²i]

    ᎯᏯᏨᎲ [hiyatsv²ya]

    ᎤᏨᎥᎯᏍᏗ [utsvhyisdi]

ᏍᎦᎥᏏᎩ [gawhsvgi] (n) "Cantaloupe.; biol. *Cucumis melo*."

ᏍᏫᏯᏟᎠᏍ [gawo³kilasga] (vi) "It is foaming."

———

    ᎤᏫᏯᏟᎠᎥ [uwo³kilanv²³²i]

    ᏍᏫᏯᏟᎠᏍᎰᎢ [gawo³kilasgo³²i]

    ᎤᏍᏫᏯᏟᎠᎦ [wigawo³kilaga]

    ᎤᏫᏯᏟᏗ [uwo³kildi]

ᏍᏫᎯᎶᏍᎦ

ᏍᏫᎯᎶᏍᎦ [gawohilosga] (vi) "He is going over a hill."

    ᏍᏫᏔᎶᏍᎦ [gawo²ilosga]

    ᎤᏫᎯᎶᏏᎥᎢ [uwohilosv²³²i]

    ᏍᏫᎯᎶᏍᎰᎢ [gawohilosgo³²i]

    ᎭᏫᎯᎶᎯ [hawohilohi]

    ᎤᏫᎯᎶᎯᏍᏗ [uwohilohisdi]

ᏍᏫᏂᎭ [gawoniha] (vi) "He is talking.; He is speaking."

    ᏥᏫᏂᎠᎠ [tsiwoni²a]

    ᎤᏫᏂᏏᎥᎢ [uwonsv²³²i]

    ᏍᏫᏂᎰᎢᎠᎢ [gawonisgo³²i]

    ᎭᏫᏂᎠ [hiwonhi]

    ᎤᏫᏂᎠᏍᏗ [uwonhisdi]

ᏰᏫ ᎡᏗ ᏛᏥᏫᏂᏏ.
"I will speak in Cherokee."
[King p40]

ᏍᏫᏂᏍ ᎠᏱᎠᏱ [gawonisv agisgi] (n) "A tape recorder."

ᏍᏫᎥᎬ [gawosgv] (n) "Ulcer."

ᏍᏯᎳᏁ [gayalena] (n) "North Carolina."

ᏍᏯᎸᎾᎦ [gayalvnga] (vi) "It is sticking to it.; It is attached to it."

———

    ᎤᏯᎸᎾᏨᎢ [uyalvntsv²³²i]

    ᏍᏯᎸᎾᎣᎢ [gayalvngo³²i]

    ᎤᏍᏯᎸᎢᎦ [wigayalvvga]

    ᎤᏯᎸᎾᎯᏗ [uyalvnhdi]

ᏍᏯᎸᏗ [gayalvdi] (n) "Postage stamp."

ᏣᏂ ᏚᏩᏍ ᏨᏍᏯᎸᏗ ᏍᎦᏘᎢ. ᎤᎠᎢᎢ ᏩᎵ ᏔᏍᏘ ᏨᏍᏯᎸᏗ ᎡᎶᏓ ᎤᏍᎠᏳᏍ ᏍᎢᎡᎢ. ᏟᏩ ᏔᏍ ᏨᏍᏯᎸᏗ ᏕᎵᏯᏓ ᏖᏝᏫᏓ ᏍᎢ4Ꭲ?
John bought twelve <u>postage stamps</u>. He saw that two <u>postage stamps</u> were grey. How many <u>postage stamps</u> were differently colored?
[ᏣᏫᎩ ᎪᏔᏗ ᏘᏂᏴᏓ ᏨᏍᎯᏙᏗ]

ᏍᏯᏍᎦᏝᎥ [gaysgwalenv] (n) "Rose-breasted grosbeak.; biol. *Pheucticus ludovicianus*."

ᏍᏯᏩᏗᎭ [gayawidiha] (vt) "He is carrying it (something long) off."

    ᏥᏯᏩᏗᎠᎠ [tsiyawidi²a]

    ᎤᏫᏯᏗᎥᏳᎢ [uyawidvhv²³²i]

    ᏍᏯᏩᏗᎰᎢᎠᎢ [gayawidisgo³²i]

    ᎭᏯᏩᏗ [hiyawida]

    ᎤᏯᏩᏗᏗ [uyawitdi]

ᏍᏰᎭ [ga¹yeha] (vt) "He is holding it (a solid)."

    ᏥᏰᎭ [tsi¹²yeha]

    ᎤᏰᏝᎥᏒᎢ [u¹yehesdv²³²i]

    ᏍᏰᎢᎢ [ga¹yeho³²i]

    ᎠᏰᏝᏗ [hi¹yehesdi]

    ᎤᏰᏝᏗ [u¹yehesdi]

ᎾᎯᏰᏃ ᎤᎤᏰ ᏍᎤᏢᎤᎡᏗᏍᎬ ᏗᏂᏰᏝᏗ.
for each one his own burden <u>shall bear</u>.
[ᎡᎩᏬ 6:5]

ᏍᏰᏟᎤᎡᎢ [gayekwsgy²i] (n) "A stitch."

ᏍᏰᏫᏍᎦ [gaye³wisga] (vt) "He is sewing."

    ᏥᏰᏫᏍᎦ [tsiye³wi²sga]

    ᎤᏰᏫᏒᎢ [uye³wisv²³²i]

    ᏍᏰᏫᏍᎰᎢ [gaye³wisgo³²i]

    ᎠᏰᏫ [hiye³wa]

    ᎤᏰᏫᏍᏗ [uye³whsdi]

ᏗᏴᎩ Ꮓ ᏗᎷᏃ ᏍᏍᏰᏫᏍᎦ.
<u>She is sewing</u> pants and dresses.
[King pg 112]

ᏍᏰᏫᎥᏏᎥᏱ [gayewhsv²ysgi] (n) "Sewing machine.; One who sews."

ᎦᏏᏉᎵ [gayohli] (pt) "Little.; Small amount."

    ᎦᏏᏉᎵ ᎠᎹ ᏓᎭᎵᎩ, ᎠᎴ ᏗᏣᏩᏍᎦ ᏗᎦᏪᎵ, ᎠᎴ ᎢᎦᎦᏫᏃᏓᎴ ᎧᎬ ᎦᎣᎭᎵᏇ;
let, I pray thee, a little water be accepted, and wash your feet, and recline under the tree;
[Ꮧꮞ ᎀᎥᏒᎥ 18:4]

ᎦᎤᎳ [gayula] (pt) "Already."

    ᎠᎴ ᏍᎥᏣᎪᏍ ᎦᎤᎳ ᎠᎢᎣᎵᎫ ᏣᏍᎧᎵᏫᎫᎥᎢ;...
Thou hast met with something (as I perceive) already; ...
[ᏗᏁᎩᎵ ᏍᎯᏴᎡᎡᎢ]

ᎦᏴᎭᎶ [gayyhulo] (n) "Saddle."

Ꭹ

ᎦᏥᎤᏍᏗ [kagiyusdi] (pt) "Who is it?"

ᎦᎪ [kago] (pt) "Who?"

    ᎦᎪ ᎢᎦᎢ?
"Who was that?"
[King pg 120]

ᎧᎵ ᎤᎾ [kali nvda] (n) "Full moon."

ᎧᎵᏎᏥ [kahlsetsi] (n) "Sugar.; Honey locust.; Thorny locust.; biol. *Gleditsia triacanthos*."

    ᏗᏍᎯᏫᎥᏴ ᎧᎵᏎᏥ ᏍᎦᏑᎢ ᏚᎰᏍᎵᏴᏍᏗ. $1.25 ᏍᏇᏈᏯᎢ. ᎤᏯ ᏍᎦᏑᎢ. ᏋᎳ ᎢᏒ ᏍᏇᏈᏯᎢ ᏂᏍᏚ?
The teacher bought candy for eating. He paid $1.25. He bought four. How much did he pay for all of them?
[ᏣᏩᏯ ᎤᎤᏯᏁ ᏗᎯᎲᏙ ᏗᏍᎯᏙᏁ]

ᎧᎵᏦᏓᏍᎦ [kaltsotah³sga] (vt) "He is roofing a house."

    ᏥᎵᏦᏓᏍᎦ [tsiʔltsotah³sga]

    ᎤᎵᏦᎣᎢ [uhltsota³nv²³ʔi]

    ᎧᎵᏦᏫᏍᎪᎢ [kaltsotah³sgo³ʔi]

    ᎮᎵᏦᎥᏍ [hihltsota³ga]

    ᎤᎵᏦᏗᏗ [uhltsotdi]

    ᎠᎴ ᎤᎪᏎ ᎢᏋᎵ ᎢᎩᏘ ᏋᎵᏇ, ᎥᏖ ᎤᎵᏦᎣᎢ, Ꮶ ᏧᏫᏥ ᏍᎦᏫᎷᎢ, ...
and he buyeth the portion of the field where he hath stretched out his tent, ...
[Ꮧꮞ ᎀᎥᏒᎥ 33:19]

ᎧᎶᎬᏗ [kalogwedi] (n) "A gun.; Black locust.; biol. *Robinia pseudoacacia*."

    ᎧᎶᎬᏗ ᎬᏗ ᏳᎤᎵᏒᎢ ᏍᏲᏗ ᏃᏛ ᏫᎢᏥᎲᏗ.
They made a wedge and maul from locust.
[King pg 122]

ᎧᎵᎩᎥᎢ [kalygvʔi] (n) "East."

ᎧᎸᏅᎯᎥ [kalvdvnịʔa] (vt) "He is telephoning."

    ᏥᎸᏅᎯᎥ [tsiʔlvdvnịʔa]

    ᎤᎸᏅᎣᎢ [uhlvdvnv²³ʔi]

    ᎧᎸᏅᎯᏍᏁᎢ [kalvdvnịsgo³ʔi]

    ᎮᎸᏅᎠ [hihlvdvna]

    ᎤᎸᏅᎣᏗ [uhlvdvnhdi]

ᎧᎻᎻ [kamama] (n) "Butterfly.; Elephant."

ᎧᎾᎫᏣᏗ [kahngutsati] (n) "Turk's cap lily.; Swamp lily.; American tiger lily.; biol. *Lilium superbum*."

ᎧᎾᎷᎯᏍᎦ [kanaluh³sga] (vi) "He is climbing a hill.; He is going up a hill."

    ᏥᎾᎷᎯᏍᎦ [tsiʔnaluh³sga]

    ᎤᎾᎷᏒᎢ [uhnaluh³sv²³ʔi]

    ᎧᎾᎷᏍᎪᎢ [kanaluh³sgo³ʔi]

    ᎮᎾᎷᎯ [hihnalụ³hi]

    ᎤᎾᎷᎯᏍᏗ [uhnalụ³hịsdi]

ᎧᎾᎻᏍᎩ [kanahnesgi] (n) "Spider."

    ᎧᎾᎻᏍᎩ 8 ᎲᏍᎣᎾ ᏗᎲᎣᏫᎰ.
A spider has 8 legs to stay up with.
[ᏣᏩᏯ ᎨᎢᎵ ᏗᎯᎲᏙ ᏗᏍᎯᏙᏁ]

ᎧᎾᏍᎦᎣ [kansgawi] (n) "Crane.; Whooping crane.; biol. *Grus americana*."

ᎧᎾᏍᏓᏥ [kansdatsi] (n) "Sassafras.; biol. *Sassafras albidum*."

ᎧᎾᏥᏍᏕᏥ [kantsịsdetsi] (n) "A wasp.; biol. *Order Hymenoptera*."

ᎧᎾᏬᎦ [kanawo³ga] (vi) "He is cold."

    ᏥᎾᏬᎦ [tsiʔnawo³ga]

    ᎤᎾᏬᏨᎢ [uhnawo³tsv²³ʔi]

    ᎧᎾᏬᎪᎢ [kanawo³go³ʔi]

    ᎮᎾᏬᎩ [hihnawo³gi]

    ᎤᎾᏬᎢᏍᏗ [uhnawo³ʔịsdi]

ᎧᏁᎦ [kane³ga] (vi) "He is speaking."

    ᏥᏁᎦ [tsiʔne³ga]

    ᎤᏁᏨᎢ [uhne³tsv²³ʔi]

    ᎧᏁᎪᎢ [kane³go³ʔi]

    ᎮᏁᎩ [hihne³ʔgi]

    ᎤᏁᎢᏍᏗ [uhne³ʔịsdi]

    ᏍᎢᎲᏃ ᎠᏗ ᏳᏫᏅᎢ, ᏆᎬᏴ, ᎾᏍᏯ ᏳᏅᏍᎥᏗ ᎾᏍᏯᏫ ᏣᏁᏨᎢ.
And Laban saith, 'Lo, O that it were according to thy word;'
[Ꮧꮞ ᎀᎥᏒᎥ 30:34]

ᎧᏁᎬᏙ [kanegwoda] (n) "Cottonmouth.; Water moccasin.; biol. *Agkistrodon piscivorus*."

ᎧᏁᏌ [ka̧nesa] (n) "A box."

ᎭᎳᎢᎦ ᎠᏕᎳ ᏕᎦᏘᎦ ᎧᏁᏌᎢᎢ?
How much money is piled up in each box?
[ᏣᎳᎩ ᎤᎩᏁ ᏗᏂᏂᏙᎯ ᏗᎦᏲᏙᏗ]

ᎧᏁᏍᎦ [ka̧nesga] (n) "Hay.; Panic grass.; biol. *Panicum spp.*; Slender rush.; Wiregrass.; biol. *Juncus tenuis.*"

ᎯᎠᏃ ᎾᏍᏉ ᏂᎤᏪᏎᎴᎢ, ᎢᏧᎳ ᎧᏁᏍᎦ ᎠᎴ ᎨᏣᏄᏗ ᏰᎵᏉ ᏬᎩᎭ, …
She saith also unto him, 'Both straw and provender [are] abundant with us, …
[ᎼᏏ ᎢᎬᏱᏱ 24:25]

ᎧᏁᏍᎦ ᏬᏗ [ka̧nesga̧ wodi] (n) "Broomsedge bluestem.; biol. *Andropogon virginicus.*"

ᎧᏂ [ka̧ni] (vt) "He is bringing it (something alive)."

ᏥᏂ [tsiʔni]
ᎤᏁᏒᎢ [uhnȩsv[23]ʔi]
ᎧᏂᏐᎢ [ka̧niso[3]ʔi]
ᎯᏄᎦ [hihnuʔga]
ᎤᏅᏍᏗ [uhnv̧sdi]

ᎧᏂᎩᏓ [ka̧nigi̧da] (pt) "None.; Not any."

ᎧᏂᎩᏓ [ka̧nigi̧da] (pt) "Nothing.; Not any.; None."

ᎧᏂᏍᎦᏩ [ka̧ni̧sga̧wa] (n) "Graty blue heron.; biol. *Ardea herodias.*"

ᎧᏃᎩᏍᏗ [ka̧nogisdi] (n) "A song.; A radio."

ᎧᏃᎩᏍᏗᎭ [ka̧nogisdi̧ha] (vt) "He is playing music."

ᏥᏃᎩᏍᏗᎭ [tsi̧ʔnogisdi̧ha]
ᎤᏃᎩᏍᏔᏅᎢ [uhnogistanv[23]ʔi]
ᎧᏃᎩᏍᏗᏍᎪᎢ [ka̧nogisdi̧sgo[3]ʔi]
ᎯᏃᎩᏍᏓ [hi̧hnogisda]
ᎤᏃᎩᏍᏙᏗ [uhnogisdohdi]

ᎧᏃᎩᏍᏙᏗ [ka̧nogisdohdi] (n) "A musical instrument (of any kind)."

… ᎠᏤᎷᎯᏍᏗ ᎠᎴ ᏗᎧᏃᎩᏍᏙᏗ ᏱᎩ, ᎢᏳᏃ ᏧᏓᎴᏅᎢ ᏂᏚᏃᏴᎬᎾ ᏱᎩ, ᎦᏙ ᏱᎦᎵᏍᏙᏓ ᏴᏙᎴᎰᎯ ᎾᏍᎩ ᎠᏤᎷᎯᏛ ᎨᏒ ᎠᎴ ᎾᏍᎩ ᏗᎧᏃᎩᏛ ᎨᏒᎢ?
… whether pipe or harp — if a difference in the sounds they may not give, how shall be known that which is piped or that which is harped?
[ᎪᎵᏂᏗᏱ ᎢᎬᏱᏱ 14:7]

ᎧᏃᎮᎭ [ka̧no̧heha] (vt) "He is telling it."

ᏥᏃᎮᎭ [tsi̧ʔno̧heha]
ᎤᏃᎮᎸᎢ [uhno̧hehlv[23]ʔi]
ᎧᏃᎮᏍᎪᎢ [ka̧no̧hesgo[3]ʔi]
ᎯᏃᎥᎵ [hi̧hno̧ʔhvli]
ᎤᏃᎮᏗ [uhno̧hehdi]

ᎠᎴ ᎾᏍᎩ ᎤᎪᎲᎢ ᎤᏛᎦᏅᎾᏍᎩ ᎧᏃᎮᎭ, ᎠᏎᏃ ᎥᏝ ᎩᎶ ᏱᏓᏓᏂᎸᎦ ᎾᏍᎩ ᎤᏃᎮᎸᎢ.
'And what he hath seen and heard this he doth testify, and his testimony none receiveth;
[ᏣᏂ 3:32]

ᎧᏃᏅ [ka̧nonv] (n) "Pounding block."

ᎧᏃᏍᎬ [ka̧nosgv] (n) "Coal.; Charcoal."

ᎧᏄᎦᎵ [ka̧nugali] (n) "Briar."

ᎧᏄᎯ [ka̧nu̧hi] (vi) "He is floating."

ᏥᏄᎯ [tsi̧ʔnu̧hi]
ᎤᏄᎮᏒᎢ [uhnu̧hȩsv[23]ʔi]
ᎧᏄᎯᏐᎢ [ka̧nu̧hiso[3]ʔi]
ᎯᏄᎰᎦ [hi̧hnu̧hoga]
ᎤᏄᎲᏍᏗ [uhnu̧hv̧sdi]

ᎧᏄᎲᏗᎭ [ka̧nu̧hv̧[3]hdi̧ha] (vt) "He is floating it."

ᏥᏄᎲᏗᎭ [tsi̧ʔnu̧hv̧[3]hdi̧ha]
ᎤᏄᎲᏔᏅᎢ [uhnu̧hv̧[3]ta̧nv[23]ʔi]
ᎧᏄᎲᏗᏍᎪᎢ [ka̧nu̧hv̧[3]hdi̧sgo[3]ʔi]
ᎯᏄᎲᏓ [hi̧hnu̧hv̧[3]hda]
ᎤᏄᎲᏙᏗ [uhnu̧hv̧[3]hdohdi]

ᎧᏄᏄ [ka̧nunu] (n) "Bullfrog.; biol. *Rana catesbeiana.*"

ᎧᏅᎠ [ka̧nvʔa] (vt) "He is pushing aside.; He is clearing stuff away."

ᏥᏅᎠ [tsi̧ʔnvʔa]
ᎤᏅᏒᎢ [uhnvsv[23]ʔi]
ᎧᏅᏍᎪᎢ [ka̧nvsgo[3]ʔi]
ᎯᏅᎾ [hi̧hnvna]
ᎤᏅᏍᏗ [uhnvsdi]

ᎧᏅᏥ [ka̧nvtsi] (n) "Hickory nut soup."

ᎧᏅᏧᏩ [ka̧nvtsuhwa] (n) "Fish hawk.; Osprey.; biol. *Pandion haliaetus.*"

ᎨᎣᎤᎠᏗ [kạnvwị?a] (vt) "He is doctoring him."

    ᏥᎣᎤᎠᏗ [tsị?nvwị?a]

    ᎤᎣᎬᎣᎢ [uhnvwạ?nv²³?i]

    ᎨᎣᎤᏋᎠᎢ [kạnvwịsgo³?i]

    ᏁᎣᎬᏏ [hị?nvwaga]

    ᎤᎣᎤᏋᎠ [uhnvwọ³di]

        … Ꮣꭶ ᎤᎣᎬᎣᎩ; ᎣᏋᎩᎩ ᎵᏄ Ꮣꭶ ᎤᎬᎷᏴ ᎤᏬᏂᎡᎩ
        Ꮣꭶ ᎤᎪᏫᎩ.
        … and <u>he healed him</u>, so that the blind and dumb
        both spake and saw.
        [ᎶᏍ 12:22]

ᎨᎬᏌ [kawạya] (n) "Black huckleberry.; Huckleberry.;
Blueberry.; biol. *Gaylussacia baccata.*"

ᎨᎬᏌ ᎠᏆᏍᏬ

ᎨᎬᏌ ᎠᏆᏍᏬ [kạwaya ạsụ?yi] (n) "Huckleberry bread."

ᎨᏬᎬ [kạwogv] (n) "Wood thrush.; biol. *Hylocichla
mustelina.*"

ᎨᏬᎾ [kạwonu] (n) "Duck.; biol. *Family Anatidae.*; April."

Ꮎ

ᏉᏪᎵ [kelạdi] (n) "Possum grapes.; biol. *Vitis baileyana.*"

ᏉᏪᎵᏗ [gẹ³hlạdị?a] (vt) "He is putting something into a
group."

    ᏉᏪᎵᏗ [gẹ?lạdị?a]

    ᎤᏋᎱᎢ [uwhdv²³?i]

    ᏉᏪᎵᏋᎠᎢ [gẹ³hlạdisgo³?i]

    ᏇᏙ [heh³da]

    ᎤᏋᎵᏋᎠ [uwhdịsdi]

ᏉᏪᎵᏙᎲ [kẹlạdi³dọha] (vi) "He is attending.; He is mingling."

    ᏉᏪᎵᏙᎲ [gẹ?lạdi³dọha]

    ᎤᏋᏬᎵᏙᏋᎠᎢ [uhwẹlạdi³do?lv²³?i]

    ᏉᏪᎵᏙᏍᎢ [kẹlạdi³dọho³?i]

    ᏇᏪᎵᏙ [hehlạdi³da]

    ᎤᏋᏬᎵᏙᏋᎠ [uhwẹlạdi³dạsdi]

        ᏁᎠᏓᏍᏂ ᎢᎯ ᎤᎲᎧᎣᏋᎥ, ᎣᏃᎩ ᏣᏀᏁᏄ ᏌᎬᏉᎵ
        ᏓᎯᏴᏄ ᎤᎲᎵᎳᏂᎬ ᎤᏋᏬᎵᏙᏋᎢ, ᏔᏄᏃ ᏍᎧᏇᏬᏄ
        ᎬᏍ ᏓᏴᎾ.
        but when thy son — this one who did devour thy liv-
        ing <u>with</u> harlots — came, thou didst kill to him the
        fatted calf.
        [ᎷᏍ 15:30]

ᏉᎸᏏᏂ [gelịsini] (vt) "He is leading him."

    ᏥᎦᎸᏏᏂ [tsiyelịsini]

    ᎤᏋᎸᏏᎷᏔᎢ [uwelịsinẹsv²³?i]

    ᏉᎸᏏᏂᏐᎢ [gelịsiniso³?i]

    ᏁᎦᎸᏏᏄᏍ [hiyelịsinu?ga]

    ᎤᏋᎸᏏᎥᏋᎠ [uwelịsinysdi]

ᏉᎸᏥᎩ [gelidsgi] (n) "A pie."

ᏉᎦᎵ [kẹloha] (vt) "He is feeding."

    ᏉᎦᎵ [gẹ?loha]

    ᎤᏋᏪᎢ [uhwẹlalv²³?i]

    ᏉᎦᎵᎢ [kẹloho³?i]

    ᎮᎬᏍ [hehlga]

    ᎤᏋᏬᏋᎠ [uhwẹlạ³sdi]

        … Ꮣꭶ ᎤᎵᏪᎣᏄ <u>ᏍᎦᎢᎢ</u>. ᎲᏏ ᎤᎢᏟ ᏞᏏᏊᏴᏋ ᎲᏁ
        ᎡᏋᏍᏴᏢ ᏥᏋᏓ.
        … and God <u>doth nourish them</u>; how much better are
        ye than the fowls?
        [ᎷᏍ 12:24]

ᏉᎷᏂ [gelụ³hni] (vt) "He is talking to him.; He is tracking
him."

    ᏥᎦᎷᏂ [tsiyelụ?ni]

    ———

    ᏉᎷᏂᏍᎢ [gelụ³hniso³?i]

    ᏁᎦᎷᏟᏎ [hiyelụ?nẹsi]

    ᎤᏋᎷᏄᏍ [uwelụ³hnu?ga]

ᏉᎻᎵ [kemịli] (n) "Camel."

    ᎵᏄᏃᏃ ᏍᎤᏪᎵᏂ ᏗᏍᏫᎵ, ᎡᏝᏃᏃ ᎤᎠᏊ, ᎤᏥᏓᏎ <u>ᏉᎻᎵᏋ</u>.
    And Rebekah lifteth up her eyes, and seeth Isaac, and
    alighteth from off <u>the camel</u>;
    [ᏅᏆ ᎢᎡᏬᏬ 24:64]
    English borrowing.

ᏉᏄᎩᏗ [gẹnugị?a] (vi) "He is pulling up weeds."

    ᏉᏄᎩᏗ [gẹnugị?a]

    ᎤᏋᏄᎩᏏᎢᎢ [uwẹnugisv²³?i]

    ᏉᏄᎩᏋᎠᎢ [gẹnugisgo³?i]

    ᏇᏄᎩ [hẹnugi]

    ᎤᏋᏄᎩᏋᎠ [uwẹnugisdi]

ᏉᎩᏬᎬ [gẹ?gwogv] (n) "Pileated woodpecker.; biol. *Dryocopus pileatus.*"

ᏉᏋᎠ [gẹsdi] (pt) "Not."

ᏉᏋᎠ ᎠᎢᏋᎠ [gẹsd gohụsdi] (n) "Nothing."

ᏉᏟ [kedạli] (pt) "Downhill."

ᎨᏯ [gẹʔya] (vi) "It is flowing."

—

ᎤᏪᏴᎢ [uwẹʔyv^{23}ʔi]

ᎨᏲᎢ [gẹʔyo^{3}ʔi]

ᏫᎨᏯ [wịgẹʔya]

ᎤᏪᏴᏗ [uwẹʔyhdi]

ᎨᏯᏔᎯ [gẹyaṭahi] (adj) "Wild (not tame)."

ᎨᏴᎯᏍᏗᎭ [geʔyvhisdịha] (vt) "He is causing it to flow."

ᎨᏴᎢᏍᏗᎭ [geʔyvʔisdịha]

ᎤᏪᏴᎯᏍᏓᏅᎢ [uweʔyvhisdạʔnv^{23}ʔi]

ᎨᏴᎯᏍᏗᏍᎪᎢ [geʔyvhisdịsgo^{3}ʔi]

ᎮᏴᎯᏍᏓ [heʔyvhisda]

ᎤᏪᏴᎯᏍᏙᏗ [uweʔyvhisdohdi]

Ꭹ

ᎩᎦ [giga] (n) "Blood."

... ᏩᎦ ᎠᏂᎩᎾ ᎤᏂᎩᎬ ᎠᎴ ᎠᏫ ᏗᏂᎭᎸᎸᎯ ᎤᏂᎩᎬ ᎤᏁᎩᏎᎢ, ᎠᎴ ᎠᏧ ᎠᎴ ᎤᏩᏅ ᎩᎦᎨᎢ, ᎠᎴ ᏗᏑᏈ, ᏕᏍᏕᏓᏃ ᎪᏪᎵ ᎠᎴ ᎾᏂᎥ ᏴᏫ.
... having taken the blood of the calves and goats, with water, and scarlet wool, and hyssop, he both the book itself and all the people did sprinkle,
[ᎠᏂᏈᎷ 9:19]

ᎩᎦᎨᎢ [gịgạgeʔi] (adj) "Red (color)."

... ᎠᎴ ᎬᏂᏳᏉ ᎤᏔᏅ ᎩᎦᎨ ᎢᎾᏛ [ᏫᏥᎪᎥᎩ,] ᎦᎸᏉᎩ ᏓᏍᎫᏓᏛᎩ, ...
... and, lo, a great red dragon, having seven heads ...
[ᎠᏥᎾᏄᎪᏫᏎᎸᎢ 12:3]

ᎩᎦᎨ ᎤᏍᎪᎸᎢ [gịgạge ụsgolvʔi] (adj) "Pink."

ᎩᎦᎨ ᎦᎳᏍᎩ [gịgạgẹ gahlasgi] (n) "Beet, red.; biol. *Beta vulgaris.*"

ᎩᎦᎨᏨᏩᎩ [gịgagetsvhwạgi] (n) "Red maple.; biol. *Acer rubrum.*"

ᎩᎩ [gigi] (n) "Sparrow hawk.; American kestrel.; biol. *Falco sparverius.*"

ᎩᎵ [gihli] (n) "Dog.; biol. *Canis lupus familiaris.*"

ᎩᎵ ᏛᏩᎦᎵ.
He will kick the dog.
[King pg 72]

ᎩᎶᎢ [kịloʔi] (pt) "Someone.; Somebody."

... ᎠᏎᏃ ᎥᏝ ᎩᎶ, ᎦᏙ ᏣᏲᎭ? ᎠᎴ ᎦᏙᏃ ᎢᎯᏢᏃᎮᏍᏗ? ᏳᏬᏎᎴᎢ.
... no one, however, said, 'What seekest thou?' or 'Why speakest thou with her?'
[ᏣᏂ 4:27]

ᎩᏳᎦ [kịyuga] (n) "Chipmunk, eastern.; biol. *Tamias striatus.*"

ᎩᏳᎬ [kịyugv] (n) "Worm-eating warbler.; biol. *Helmitheros vermivorum.*"

Ꭺ

ᎪᎢ [goʔi] (n) "Grease.; Lard.; Gasoline.; Ground snake."

... ᎠᎴ ᎤᏪᏘᏁᎢ, ᎠᎴ ᎪᎢ ᎤᏍᎪᎵ ᎤᏍᏕᏓᎢ.
... and maketh it a standing pillar, and poureth oil upon its top,
[ᎼᏏ ᎢᎬᏱᏱ 28:18]

ᎪᎦ [koga] (n) "Crow.; biol. *Corvus brachyrhynchos.*"

ᎪᎦᏍᏗ [goksdi] (n) "Cigarette.; Cigar."

ᎪᎩ [gogi] (n) "Summer (1st new moon in April to the 1st new moon in October)."

... ᎤᏩᏂᎦᎸ ᎿᏉ ᎤᏓᎨ ᏂᎦᎵᏍᏓ, ᎠᎴ ᏥᎦᎵᏍᏕᎲᏍᎪᎢ, ᎢᏥᎦᏔᎨ ᎪᎩ ᎾᎥᏂᏳ ᎨᏒᎢ;
... when the branch may already become tender, and may put forth the leaves, ye know that nigh is the summer;
[ᎹᎦ 13:28]

ᎪᎩᏍᎦ [gogh^{3}sga] (vt) "He is smoking."

ᎪᎩᏍᎦ [gogịʔsga]

ᎤᏬᎩᎩᏒᎢ [uwogị^{3}gịsv^{23}ʔi]

ᎪᎩᏍᎪᎢ [gogih^{3}sgo^{3}ʔi]

ᎰᎩ [hogị]

ᎤᏬᎩᏍᏗ [uwogih^{3}sdi]

ᎪᎯ [gohi] (pt) "After a while.; A while ago."

... ᎾᏍᎩᏃ ᎪᎯ ᎢᏴᏛ ᎤᎷᏤᎸᎩ ᏧᏁᏩᏗ, ᎠᎴ ᎢᏳᏍᏗ ᎤᎸᏏᎸ ᎤᏛᏛᏅᎩ.
... who after a little time came to *Christian*, and asked him what he would have?
[ᏧᏁᏩᏗ ᏚᏂᎩᏒᏒᎢ]

ᎪᎯ [kohi] (n) "Butternut.; White walnut.; biol. *Juglans cinerea.*"

ᎪᎯᎩᎳ [gọhigịla] (pt) "After a while."

ᎪᎯᏳ [gọhiyu] (pt) "Later."

ᎪᎯᏳᎲᏍᎦ [gọhi^{3}yụhvsga] (vt) "He agrees.; He believes."

ᎪᎢᏳᎲᏍᎦ [gọʔi^{3}yụhvsga]

ᎤᏬᎯᏳᏅᎢ [uwọhi^{3}yụʔhnv^{23}ʔi]

ᎪᎯᏳᎲᏍᎪᎢ [gọhi^{3}yụhvsgo^{3}ʔi]

ᎰᎯᏳᎲᎦ [họhi^{3}yụhvga]

ᎤᏬᎯᏳᏗ [uwọhi^{3}yhdi]

ᎾᏍᎩᏰᏃ ᏂᎦᎥᎩ ᎤᏁᎳᏅᎯ ᎤᎨᏳᏒᎩ ᎡᎶᎯ, ᎦᎤᏲᏒᎩ ᎤᏤᎵᎦ ᎤᏪᏥ ᎾᏍᎩ ᎤᏩᏒᎯᏳ ᎤᎦᏁᎸᎯ, ᎩᎶ ᎾᏍᎩ ᏱᎪᎯᏳᎲᏍᎦ ᎤᏲᎱᎯᏍᏗᏱ ᏂᎨᏒᎾ, ᎬᏂᏛᏉᏍᎩᏂ ᎤᏩᏛᏗ.
for God did so love the world, that His Son — the only begotten — He gave, that every one who is believing in him may not perish, but may have life age-during.
[ᏣᏂ 3:16]

ᎪᎰᎾᏗᎭ [gohọ³hndịha] (vt) "He is dropping it (a solid).; He is knocking it (a solid) off."

ᎪᎣᎾ>;ᏗᎭ [gọʔọ³hndịha]

ᎤᏬᎰᎾᏔᏅᎢ [uwohọ³hntạnv²³ʔi]

ᎪᎰᎾᏗᏍᎪᎢ [gohọ³hndịsgo³ʔi]

ᎰᎰᎾᏓ [hohọ³hnda]

ᎤᏬᎰᎾᏙᏗ [uwohọ³hndohdi]

ᎪᎰᏍᎦ [gohosga] (vi) "He is falling.; It (a solid) is falling."

ᎪᎣᏍᎦ [gọʔosga]

ᎤᏬᎰᏒᎢ [uwohosv²³ʔi]

ᎪᎰᏍᎪᎢ [gohosgo³ʔi]

ᎰᎰᎯ [hohohi]

ᎤᏬᎰᎯᏍᏗ [uwohohịsdi]

ᎿᏉᏃ ᎠᏂᏯᏫᏍᎩ ᏚᏂᎦᎵᏒᎩ ᎠᏍᎦᏱᏛ ᎤᏍᏗ ᏥᏳ ᎦᏙᏌᏗᏍᏛᎢ, ᎠᎴ ᎾᏍᎩ <u>ᎤᏬᎰᏒᎩ</u>.
then the soldiers did cut off the ropes of the boat, and <u>suffered it to fall off</u>.
[ᎨᏥᏅᏏᏛ ᏄᎾᏛᏁᎵᏙᎸᎢ 27:32]

ᎪᎲᎾᏗᎭ [gohvhndịha] (vt) "He is dropping it (a liquid).; He is knocking it (a liquid) off."

ᎪᎥᎾᏗᎭ [gọʔvhndịha]

ᎤᏬᎲᎾᏔᏅᎢ [uwohvhntạnv²³ʔi]

ᎪᎲᎾᏗᏍᎪᎢ [gohvhndịsgo³ʔi]

ᎰᎲᎾᏓ [hohvhnda]

ᎤᏬᎲᎾᏙᏗ [uwohvhndohdi]

ᎪᎲᏓᏓᎳ [kọhỵdadahla] (n) "Knoxville, TN."

ᎪᎳ [gola] (n) "Winter."

ᎠᎴ ᎢᏣᏓᏙᎵᏍᏗᏍᎨᏍᏗ ᎢᏥᏔᏲᎯᎮᏍᏗ <u>ᎪᎳ</u> ᎠᎴ ᎤᎾᏙᏓᏆᏍᎬ ᎢᏣᎵᏍᏗᏱ ᏂᎨᏒᎾ ᎢᏳᎵᏍᏙᏗᏱ.
and pray ye that your flight may not be <u>in winter</u>, nor on a sabbath;
[ᎹᏚ 24:20]

Note: 1st new moon in October to the 1st new moon in April.

ᎪᎳ [kola] (n) "A bone."

ᎴᏆᏂᏃ ᎯᎠ ᏄᏪᏎᎴᎢ, ᎤᏙᎯᏳᎯᏯ ᏂᎯ ᎠᏴ <u>ᏗᎩᎪᎳ</u> ᎠᎴ ᎠᏴ ᎠᎩᏇᏓᎸᎢ ...
and Laban saith to him, 'Only <u>my bone</u> and my flesh [art] thou;' ...
[ᎼᏏ ᎢᎬᏱᏱ 29:14]

ᎪᎳᎧᎩᏍᏗ [kolạkạgisdi] (n) "Boneset (plant).; Snakeroot.; biol. *Eupetorium spp.*"

ᎪᎵᎧ [golka] (vt) "He is acquainted with him.; He is understanding it.; He is recognizing it."

ᏥᏲᎵᎦ, ᎪᎵᎦ [tsiyolịga, golịga]

ᎤᏬᎵᏨᎢ [uwolhtsv²³ʔi]

ᎪᎵᎪᎢ [golko³ʔi]

ᎯᏲᎩ, ᎰᎵᎩ [hịyogi, holki]

ᎤᏬᎵᏍᏗ [uwolisdi]

... ᎥᏝ ᎠᎴ <u>ᏱᎪᎵᎦ</u> ᏂᏪᏍᎬᎢ. ...
... neither do <u>I understand</u> what thou sayest ...
[ᎹᎦ 14:68]

ᎪᎵᏍᏓᏴᎢ [gọlịsdayỵʔi] (n) "Swift water.; Water that is moving swiftly."

ᎪᎸᎲ [kọlỵhv] (adj) "Boney."

ᎪᎸᏅ [kolỵnv] (n) "Raven."

ᎪᎸᏅ ᎠᏰᎵᏍᎩ [kolỵnỵ ahyelisgi] (n) "Raven mocker."

ᎪᎸᏅᏱ [kolỵnvyi] (n) "Raven's Place (Big Cove)."

ᎪᏍᏓ [kọsda] (n) "Ashes."

ᎪᏍᏓᏂᏍᏗ [gosda³nịsdi] (n) "Narrowleaf plantain.; biol. *Plantago lanceolata.*"

ᎪᏍᏗᏳᎵ [gọsdiyuhli] (adj) "Blunt."

ᎪᏍᏗᏳᏍᏗ [kọsdiyụsdi] (n) "Rabbit tobacco.; biol. *Pseudognaphalium obtusifolium.*"

ᎪᏍᏙᎯ [kosdọhi] (n) "In ashes."

ᎪᏒᎦ [gosvʔga] (n) "Elderberry.; American black elderberry.; biol. *Sambucus canadensis.*"

ᎪᏒᎾᎳᏗᏍᏗᏳ [gọsvhnạldịsdiyu] (n) "Window lock."

ᎪᏒᏅ [gọsvnv] (n) "Butter.; Margarine."

ᎪᏒᏍᎦ [gọ³svsga] (vt) "He is creating.; He is forming."

ᎪᏒᏍᎦ [gọsvsga]

ᎤᏬᏒᏅᎢ [uwọ³svhnv²³ʔi]

ᎪᏒᏍᎪᎢ [gọ³svsgo³ʔi]

ᎰᏒᎾ [họ³svna]

ᎤᏬᏒᏗ [uwọ³svhdi]

ᎪᏕᏍᎩ [kodẹsgi] (n) "Shovel.; Spade."

ᎪᏕᏍᎩ [kọdesgi] (n) "Shovel.; Spade."

ᎪᏘᏍᎦ [ktisga] (vi) "He is swelling."

ᎪᏘᏍᎦ [gọʔtisga]

ᎤᏬᏘᏒᎢ [uwhtisv²³ʔi]

ᎪᏘᏍᎪᎢ [ktisgo³ʔi]

ᎰᏘᎯ [hohtihi]

ᎤᏬᏘᏏ [uwhtisi]

ᎪᏪᎳᎩᎠ [kọwelạgịʔa] (vt) “He is erasing.”

ᎪᏪᎳᎩᎠ [gọʔwelạgịʔa]

ᎤᏬᏪᎳᎩᏒᎢ [uhwọwelạgịsv^{23}ʔi]

ᎪᏪᎳᎩᏍᎪᎢ [kọwelạgịsgo^{3}ʔi]

ᎰᏪᎳᎩ [hohwelạgi]

ᎤᏬᏪᎳᎩᏍᏗ [uhwọwelạgịsdi]

ᎪᏪᎵ [gohweli] (n) “Paper.; Book.; Letter.”

ᏂᎦᏓ ᏦᏣᏕᎶᏆᏍᎩ ᏙᏥᎪᎵᏰᏍᎪ ᏗᎪᏪᎵ.
All who are learning are studying the book.
[ᏣᎳᎩ ᏔᎵᏁ ᏗᏂᏂᏙᎯ ᏗᎦᏂᏙᏗ]

ᎪᏪᎵᎠ [gohwelịʔa] (vt) “He is writing.”

ᎪᏪᎵᎠ [gọwelịʔa]

ᎤᏬᏪᎳᏅᎢ [uwohwelạʔnv^{23}ʔi]

ᎪᏪᎳᏍᎪᎢ [gohwelʔsgo^{3}ʔi]

ᎰᏪᎳᎦ [hohwelaga]

ᎤᏬᏪᎶᏗ [uwohwelodi]

… ᎠᏎᏃ ᏥᏌ ᎤᏗᏌᏓᏛᎩ, ᎦᏰᏌᏛᏃ ᎤᏩᏔᏅᎩ ᎤᏬᏪᎳᏅᎩ ᎦᏙᎯ.
… And Jesus, having stooped down, with the finger he was writing on the ground,
[ᏣᏂ 8:6]

ᎪᏪᎵ ᎠᏕᎳ ᏤᎦ [gohwelị ạdelạ tsega] (n) “Check (written payment document).”

ᎪᏪᎵ ᎦᎸᏉᏗ [gohweʔlị gạlvkwdi] (n) “Bible.”

ᎪᏪᎵᏗᎦᏂᏙᎯ

ᎪᏪᎵᏗᎦᏂᏙᎯ [gohwelịdigahnịdohi] (n) “Mailman.”

ᎪᏪᎵ ᏗᎧᏃᎩᏍᏗ [gohwelị dịkạnogisdi] (n) “Songbook.; Hymnal.”

ᎪᏪᎵ ᏧᏍᏗ [gohwelị tsusdi] (n) “Vote.; Ballot.”

ᎪᏫ [kowi] (n) “Coffee.”

English borrowing.

ᎪᏯᏛᎢ [gohyạdṿʔi] (n) “Sleeve.”

Ꭻ

ᎫᎢᎶᎠ [gụʔilọʔa] (vt) “He is washing it (something long).”

ᎫᎢᎶᎠ [gụʔilọʔa]

ᎤᏭᎢᎶᎥᎢ [uwụʔilọv^{23}ʔi]

ᎫᎢᎶᏍᎪᎢ [gụʔilọsgo^{3}ʔi]

ᎱᎢᎶᏣ [hụʔilọtsa]

ᎤᏭᎢᎶᏍᏗ [uwụʔilọsdi]

ᎫᎩᎠ [gugiʔa] (vt) “He is taking it (a solid) from a liquid.”

ᎫᎩᎠ [gugịʔa]

ᎤᏭᎩᏒᎢ [uwugịsv^{23}ʔi]

ᎫᎩᏍᎪᎢ [gugịsgo^{3}ʔi]

ᎱᎩ [hugi]

ᎤᏭᎩᏍᏗ [uwugịsdi]

ᎫᎫ [gugu] (n) “Bottle.; Tick.; Vial.”

ᎠᏏᏴᏫᏃ ᎾᏍᎩ Ꮎ ᏅᎩ ᎢᏯᏂᏛ ᎨᏒ ᏗᏅᏃᏛ ᎦᎵᏉᎩ ᎢᏯᏂᏛ ᏗᏂᎧᎿᏩᏗᏙᎯ ᏚᏁᎸᎩ ᎦᎵᏉᎩ ᎫᎫ ᎠᏕᎸᏓᎶᏂᎨ ᏗᎪᏢᏔᏅᎯ, …
and one of the four living creatures did give to the seven messengers seven golden vials, …
[ᎠᏥᎾᏄᎪᏫᏎᎸᎢ 15:7]

ᎫᎭ [gụha] (vi) “He is in a liquid.; It (a solid) is in a liquid.”

ᎫᎠ [gụʔa]

ᎤᏭᎮᏍᏛᎢ [uwụhesdv^{23}ʔi]

ᎫᎰᎢ [gụho^{3}ʔi]

ᎱᎮᏍᏗ [hụhesdi]

ᎤᏭᎮᏍᏗ [uwụhesdi]

ᎫᎯᎶᎠ [gụ^{3}hiloʔa] (vt) “He is washing it (a solid).”

ᎫᎢᎶᎠ [gụʔiloʔa]

ᎤᏭᎯᎶᎥᎢ [uwụ^{3}hiloʔv^{23}ʔi]

ᎫᎯᎶᏍᎪᎢ [gụ^{3}hilosgo^{3}ʔi]

ᎱᎯᎶᏣ [hụ^{3}hilotsa]

ᎤᏭᎯᎶᏍᏗ [uwụ^{3}hilosdi]

ᎫᎴ [gule] (n) “Acorn.”

ᎯᏍᏕᎳ ᏌᎶᎵ ᎫᎴ ᏗᏜᎢ ᏭᎷᎯᏍᏗᎢ.
Help the squirrel walk his acorns to where they go.
[ᏣᎳᎩ ᏔᎵᏁ ᏗᏂᏂᏙᎯ ᏗᎦᏂᏙᏗ]

ᎫᎴᏗᏍᎪᏂᎯ [gulehdịsgohnịhi] (n) “Mourning dove.; Turtle dove.; biol. *Zenaida macroura.*”

… ᎠᎴ ᎠᏓᏅᏙ ᎫᎴᏗᏍᎪᏂᎯ ᎾᏍᎩᏯᎢ, ᏧᏠᎠᏏᏗᏎ ᎾᏍᎩ ᎤᏪᏯᎸᏤᎢ.
… and the Spirit as a dove coming down upon him;
[ᎹᎦ 1:10]

ᎫᎴᏧᎾᏍᏗ [gulẹtsunsdi] (n) “Red oak.; biol. *Quercus falcata.*”

ᎫᏇ ᏗᎦᎾᏌᎢ [gugwẹ diganạsạʔi] (n) “Guineafowl.; biol. *Numida meleagris.*”

ᎫᏌᎥᏍᎦ [gu^{3}sạʔvsga] (vt) “He is covering it.”

ᎫᏌᎥᏍᎦ [gu^{3}sạʔṿʔsga]

ᎤᏭᏌᏅᎢ [uwu^{3}sạʔnv^{23}ʔi]

ᎫᏌᎥᏍᎪᎢ [gu^{3}sạʔvsgo^{3}ʔi]

ᎱᏌᎥᎦ [hu^{3}sạʔvga]

ᎤᏭᏌᏗ [uwu^{3}sadi]

ᎫᏌᎩᎠ [gusạgị^{3}ʔa] (vt) “He is uncovering it.”

ᎫᏌᎩᎠ [gusạgị^{3}ʔa]

ᎤᏭᏌᎩᏒᎢ [uwusạgị^{3}sv^{23}ʔi]

ᎫᏌᎩᏍᎪᎢ [gusạgị^{3}sgo^{3}ʔi]

ᎱᏌᎩ [husạgị]

ᎤᏭᏌᎩᏍᏗ [uwusạgị^{3}sdi]

ᎫᏍᏗ [kusd] (n) “Beech.; American beech.; biol. *Fagus grandifolia.*”

ᎫᏍᏗᎭ [gụ^{3}sdịha] (vt) “He is mixing liquids.”

ᎫᏍᏗᎭ [gụsdịha]

ᎤᏭᏍᏓᏅᎢ [uwụ^{3}sdạʔnv^{23}ʔi]

ᎫᏍᏗᏍᎪᎢ [gụ^{3}sdịsgo^{3}ʔi]

ᎱᏍᏓ [hụ^{3}sda]

ᎤᏭᏍᏙᏗ [uwụ^{3}sdohdi]

ᎫᏓᎳᎩᎠ [gụdalạgiʔa] (vt) “He is unplugging it.”

ᎫᏓᎳᎩᎠ [gụdalạgiʔa]

ᎤᏭᏓᎳᎩᏒᎢ [uwụdalạgisv^{23}ʔi]

ᎫᏓᎳᎩᏍᎪᎢ [gụdalạgisgo^{3}ʔi]

ᎱᏓᎳᎩ [hụdalạgi]

ᎤᏭᏓᎳᎩᏍᏗ [uwụdalạgisdi]

ᎫᏓᎸᎥᏍᎦ [gudalvʔvsga] (vt) “He is plugging it in.”

ᎫᏓᎸᎥᏍᎦ [gudalvʔṿʔsga]

ᎤᏭᏓᎸᏅᎢ [uwudalvʔnv^{23}ʔi]

ᎫᏓᎸᎥᏍᎪᎢ [gudalvʔvsgo^{3}ʔi]

ᎱᏓᎸᎥᎦ [hudalvʔvga]

ᎤᏭᏓᎸᏗ [uwudalhdi]

ᎫᏔᎩᎠ [guʔtạgiʔa] (vt) “He is picking it (something long) up from the ground.”

ᎫᏓᎩᎠ [guʔdʔạgiʔa]

ᎤᏭᏔᎩᏒᎢ [uwuʔtạgisv^{23}ʔi]

ᎫᏔᎩᏍᎪᎢ [guʔtạgisgo^{3}ʔi]

ᎱᏔᎩ [huʔtạgi]

ᎤᏭᏔᎩᏍᏗ [uwuʔtạgisdi]

ᎫᏘᎭ [gutịha] (vt) “It is snowing.”

—

ᎤᏭᏔᎭᏅᎢ [uwuthạnv^{23}ʔi]

ᎫᏘᏍᎪᎢ [gutịsgo^{3}ʔi]

ᏫᎫᏔ [wịguta]

ᎤᏭᏙᏗ [uwutohdi]

ᎫᏩ [kuwa] (n) “Mulberry.; Red mulberry.; biol. *Morus rubra.*”

ᎫᏫᏳᎦᏍᏗ [kuhwiyụgsdi] (n) “Sycamore.; American sycamore.; biol. *Platanus occidentalis.*”

ᎫᏯᎩᎠ [gụyạgiʔa] (vi) “He is plucking a chicken.”

ᎫᏯᎩᎠ [gụyạgiʔa]

ᎤᏭᏯᎩᏒᎢ [uwụyạgisv^{23}ʔi]

ᎫᏯᎩᏍᎪᎢ [gụyạgisgo^{3}ʔi]

ᎱᏯᎦ [hụyạga]

ᎤᏭᏯᎩᎢᏍᏗ [uwụyạgiisdi]

ᎫᏰᏉᏂ [gụyẹgwoni] (n) “July.”

E

ᎬᎦ [gvʔga] (vi) “It (something flexible) is in a liquid.”

—

ᎤᏩᏅᎢ [uwaʔnv^{23}ʔi]

ᎬᎪᎢ [gvʔgo^{3}ʔi]

ᏫᎬᎨᏍᏗ [wịgvʔgẹsdi]

ᎤᏩᏗ [uwaʔhdi]

ᎬᎩᎠ [gvgị^{3}ʔa] (vt) “He is unravelling it.”

ᎬᎩᎠ [gvgị^{3}ʔa]

ᎤᏩᎩᏒᎢ [uwạgị^{3}sv^{23}ʔi]

ᎬᎩᏍᎪᎢ [gvgị^{3}sgo^{3}ʔi]

ᎲᎩ [hvgị]

ᎤᏩᎩᏍᏗ [uwạgị^{3}sdi]

ᎡᎭᏙᏯᏅᎯᏓ, ᎠᏧ ᏭᏙᏯᏅᎯᏁᎩ, ᎠᏧ ᎤᏩᎩᏒᎩ, …
Give me thy hand: so he gave him his hand, and he drew him out, …
[ᏧᎫᏁᎶᏗ ᎦᏂᎩᏒᏒᎢ]

ᎬᎩᎶᎠ [kgiloʔa] (vt) “He is washing it (something flexible).”

ᎬᎩᎶᎠ [gvʔgiloʔa]

ᎤᎩᎶᎥᎢ [uwkiloʔv^{23}ʔi]

ᎬᎩᎶᏍᎪᎢ [kgilosgo^{3}ʔi]

ᎲᎩᎶᏣ [hv^{3}kilotsa]

ᎤᎩᎶᏍᏗ [uwkilosdi]

ᎬᎩᎶᎠ [gvgilọʔa] (vt) “He is washing it (something alive).”

ᏥᏴᎩᎶᎠ [tsiyvgilọʔa]

ᎤᏩᎩᎶᎥᎢ [uwạgilọʔv^{23}ʔi]

ᎬᎩᎶᏍᎪᎢ [gvgilọsgo^{3}ʔi]

ᎯᏴᎩᎶᏣ [hiyvgilọtsa]

ᎤᏩᎩᎶᏍᏗ [uwạgilọsdi]

ᎬᎩᏍᏗ [gvgisdi] (n) “Watermelon.; biol. *Citrullus lanatus.*”

ᎬᏴᎪᏦᏘ [gv³gitsa̱le?a] (vi) "He is itching.; He is having an itch."

ᎬᏴᎪᏦᏘ [gv³gitsa̱le?a]

ᎣᏩᏴᎪᏦᎢᎢ [uwa³gitsa̱le?v²³?i]

ᎬᏴᎪᏦᎣᎠᎢ [gv³gitsa̱lesgo³?i]

ᎭᏴᎪᏦᏥ [hv³gitsa̱letsa]

ᎣᏩᏴᎪᏦᎣᏒ [uwa³gitsa̱lesdi]

ᎬᎠᎣᏒ [gv̱gosdi] (n) "Sifter."

ᎬᏇ [kvhe] (n) "Bobcat.; biol. *Lynx rufus.*"

ᎬᏫᎵ [gvhv̱li] (n) "Raccoon.; biol. *Procyon lotor.*"

ᎬᎾ [kvna] (n) "Turkey.; biol. *Meleagris gallopavo.*"

ᎬᎾ ᎢᏙᎢᏛᏆ [kvna̱ ina̱gee̱hi] (n) "Wild turkey.; biol. *Meleagris gallopavo.*"

ᎬᎾᏫᏥᏬ [gvhna̱wo̱³hdi̱ha] (vt) "He is frying it."

ᎬᎾᏫᏥᏬ [gvna̱?wo̱³hdi̱ha]

ᎣᏩᎬᎾᏫᏬᎣᎢ [uwahna̱wo̱³ta̱nv²³?i]

ᎬᎾᏫᏥᎣᎠᎢ [gvhna̱wo̱³hdisgo³?i]

ᎭᎬᎾᏫᏣ [hvhna̱wo̱³hda]

ᎣᏩᎬᎾᏫᎣᏙᏥ [uwahna̱wo̱³hdohdi]

ᎬᏞᏣ [gv̱nehi] (n) "Ink pen."

ᎬᎾᏫᎢ [gvni̱ge?i] (adj) "Black."

ᎬᎾᏫ ᏅᏥ [gvni̱ge̱ seti] (n) "Black walnut, eastern.; biol. *Juglans nigra.*"

ᎬᎾᏟᎣᏙᏥ [gvni̱lidasdo?di] (n) "Hammer."

ᎬᎾᏍᏒ [gv̱nhsga] (vi) "It is cooking."

———

ᎣᏩᎭᏒᎢ [uwa̱nhsv²³?i]

ᎬᎾᏒᎠᎢ [gv̱nhsgo³?i]

ᎾᎬᎾᏫ [wi̱gvnhi]

ᎣᏩᎭᏒᏥ [uwa̱nhisdi]

ᎠᏫᎣᏞᏗᏎ ᎬᎾᏒ.
The food is cooking.
[King pg 113]

ᎬᏃᏞᏍᏒ [gv̱nosasga] (vt) "He is sweeping."

ᎬᏃᏞᏒ [gv̱nosa̱?sga]

ᎣᏩᏃᏬᎭᎢ [uwa̱nosahv²³?i]

ᎬᏃᏞᎠᎢ [gv̱nosasgo³?i]

ᎭᏃᏬ [hv̱nosa]

ᎣᏩᏃᏬᏥ [uwa̱nosasdi]

ᎬᏃᏬᏥ [gv̱nosa̱sdi] (n) "A broom."

ᏍᎥ ᎣᏥ ᎠᏞᏬᏥ? ᏲᏣᏫᏴ. ᎤᏞᏫᎣᏂᎬ: Ꭰ) ᎬᏃᏬᏥ, ᎡᎵ) ᏍᏥ, Ꭲ) ᏂᏬᏍᏀ.
What is seen? Choose. Give him them: a) Brooms, b) Dirt, c) Rats.
[ᏣᏫᏴ ᎣᏳᏁ ᏥᏂᏴᏙᏫ ᏥᎦᏛᎢ]

ᎬᏅᏳᏴᏛ [gvnuya̱gi?a] (vt) "He is pulling up weeds."

ᎬᏅᏫᏴᏛ [gvnuya̱gi?a]

ᎣᏩᏅᏬᎡᎢᎢ [uwanuya̱gv?v²³?i]

ᎬᏅᏴᏬᎠᎢ [gvnuya̱gisgo³?i]

ᎭᏅᏫᏍ [hvnuya̱ga]

ᎣᏩᏅᏬᎬ [uwanuya̱kdi]

ᎡᎣᏴᎱᏳ [kvnv̱gihlgi] (n) "Honeysuckle bush.; biol. *Lonicera spp.*"

ᎡᎣᏍᏳ [kvndv̱gi] (n) "Kentucky."

ᎬᏒᏍ [gvsga] (vt) "He is weaving."

ᎬᏒᏍ [gv̱?sga]

ᎣᏩᎣᎢ [uwa̱?nv²³?i]

ᎬᏫᎠᎢ [gvsgo³?i]

ᎭᎾ [hv̱na]

ᎣᏩᏥ [uwhdi]

ᎬᏒᏌᏬᏒ [gvsgahlah³sga] (vt) "He is hiding it (a solid)."

ᎬᏒᏌᏬᏒ [gv̱?sgahlah³sga]

ᎣᏩᏍᏌᏬᎣᎢ [uwasgahla̱³nv²³?i]

ᎬᏒᏌᏬᎠᎢ [gvsgahlah³sgo³?i]

ᎭᏍᏒᏌᏍ [hvsgahla̱³ga]

ᎣᏩᏍᏌᏍᏥ [uwasgahldi]

ᎬᏒᏌᏥᎠ [gvsgaldi̱?a] (vt) "He is hiding it (something long)."

ᎬᏒᏌᏥᎠ [gv̱?sgaldi̱?a]

ᎣᏩᏍᏌᏬᎢᎢ [uwasgald?v²³?i]

ᎬᏒᏌᏥᎣᎠᎢ [gvsgaldi̱sgo³?i]

ᎭᏍᏒᏌᏝ [hvsgalda]

ᎣᏩᏍᏒᏌᏥᎣᏥ [uwasgaldi̱sdi]

ᎬᏒᏌᎵᎣᏒ [gvsga̱lv³?vsga] (vt) "He is hiding it (something flexible)."

ᎬᏒᏌᎵᎣᏒ [gv̱?sga̱lv³?vsga]

ᎣᏩᏍᏌᎵᎣᎢ [uwasga̱lv³?nv²³?i]

ᎬᏒᏌᎵᎣᎠᎢ [gvsga̱lv³?vsgo³?i]

ᎭᏒᏌᎵᏍ [hvsga̱lv³?vga]

ᎣᏩᏒᏌᎵᏥ [uwasga̱lv³?di]

ᎬᏒᎢᎬᏛ [gvsgwa̱lo³?a] (vt) "He is cracking it."

ᎬᏒᎢᎬᏛ [gv̱?sgwa̱lo³?a]

ᎣᏩᏒᎢᎬᎢᎢ [uwasgwa̱lo³?v²³?i]

ᎬᏒᎢᎬᎣᎠᎢ [gvsgwa̱lo³sgo³?i]

ᎭᏒᎢᎬᎬ [hvsgwa̱lo³tsa]

ᎣᏩᏒᎢᎬᎣᏥ [uwasgwa̱lo³sdi]

ᎬᏝ [gvda] (pt) "In a fire."

91

ELYD [gvdạgiʔa] (vt) "He is taking it (a solid) off of a fire."

  ELYD [gvdạgiʔa]

  OꞋGLYRT [uwadạgisv^{23}ʔi]

  ELYꙍAT [gvdạgisgo^{3}ʔi]

  ᏫLY [hvdạgi]

  OꞋGLYꙍᎯ [uwadạgisdi]

ELᏢᎠD [gvdạ^{3}ʔldịʔa] (vt) "He is turning off a light."

  ELᏢᎠD [gvdạ^{3}ʔldịʔa]

  OꞋGLᏢᏬT [uwhdạ^{3}ʔldv^{23}ʔi]

  ELᏢᎠꙍAT [kdạ^{3}ʔldịsgo^{3}ʔi]

  ᏫLᏢL [hvhdạ^{3}ʔlda]

  OꞋGLᏢᎠꙍᎯ [uwhdạ^{3}ʔldịsdi]

ELGꙍS [gvdạlosga] (vi) "A light going out."

———

  OꞋGLGRT [uwạdạlosv^{23}ʔi]

  ELGꙍAT [gvdạlosgo^{3}ʔi]

  ΘELGꙍ [wịgvdạlohi]

  OꞋGLGꙍᎯ [uwạdạlohịsdi]

EWꙍS [gvtah^{3}sga] (vt) "He is placing it (a solid) in a fire."

  ELꙍS [gvdʔah^{3}sga]

  OꞋGWOT [uwata^{3}nv^{23}ʔi]

  EWꙍAT [gvtah^{3}sgo^{3}ʔi]

  ᏫWS [hvta^{3}ga]

  OꞋGᎫᎠ [uwatdi]

EᎠ [gvhdi] (pt) "With.; In (a language).; Using."

  ꙍGꙍᎠ EᎠ ꮨOᴜᎾT SᏒᎠ Zꝥ ꙍᏘᎻhꙍᎠ.
  They made a wedge and maul <u>from</u> locust.
  [King pg 122]

EᎠᕼ [gvhdịha] (vt) "He is using it."

  EᎠᕼ [gvdịha]

  OꞋGWOT [uwạtạnv^{23}ʔi]

  EᎠꙍAT [gvhdịsgo^{3}ʔi]

  ᏫL [hvhda]

  OꞋGVᎠ [uwahdohdi]

EVYD [gvtokị^{3}ʔa] (vt) "He is shelling (peas)."

  EVYD [gvʔdokị^{3}ʔa]

  OꞋGVYRT [uwhtokị^{3}sv^{23}ʔi]

  EVYꙍAT [gvtokị^{3}sgo^{3}ʔi]

  ᏫVY [hvhtokị]

  OꞋGVYꙍᎠ [uwhtokị^{3}sdi]

EᏦʼiꙍS [gvhdv^{3}ʔvsga] (vt) "He is putting it (something flexible) into a fire."

  EᏦʼiꙍS [gvdv^{3}ʔvsga]

  OꞋGᏦOT [uwahdv^{3}ʔnv^{23}ʔi]

  EᏦʼiꙍAT [gvhdv^{3}ʔvsgo^{3}ʔi]

  ᏫᏦʼiS [hvhdv^{3}ʔvga]

  OꞋGᏦᎠ [uwahdv^{3}ʔdi]

EᏦʼYD [kdvgiʔa] (vt) "He is taking it (something flexible) from a fire."

  EᏦʼYD [gvʔdvgiʔa]

  OꞋGᏦʼYRT [uwhdvgisv^{23}ʔi]

  EᏦʼYꙍAT [kdvgisgo^{3}ʔi]

  ᏫᏦʼY [hvhdvgi]

  OꞋGᏦʼYꙍᎠ [uwhdvgisdi]

EGᏭWꙍS [gvʔhwạlah^{3}sga] (vt) "He is soaking it."

  EGᏭWꙍS [gvwạʔlah^{3}sga]

  OꞋGᏭWOT [uwaʔhwạlạ^{3}nv^{23}ʔi]

  EGᏭWꙍAT [gvʔhwạlah^{3}sgo^{3}ʔi]

  ᏫᏭWS [hvʔhwạla^{3}ga]

  OꞋGᏭWᎠ [uwaʔhwạldi]

Ꮀ

ᎰΘ [hạna] (pt) "There."

Ꮀh [hạni] (pt) "Here, this."

  ... TꞬ Dꝩ DB ꙍYWbᎠꙍᎢꙍᎠ, <u>Dh</u> ᎠD AꙍᏢᴕ ᴕAᏢꙍ ...
  ... If you believe not me, read <u>here</u> in this Book ...
  [ᎫᏁGᎠ ShYRRT]

ᎰZ [hahno] (pt) "Never."

ᎰᎠ [hạdi] (pt) "No."

ᎰP [hạdlv] (pt) "Where?"

  Oklahoma Dialect.

ᎰKGᏦʼ [hạtsowadv] (n) "Pocket."

ᎰG [hạwa] (pt) "Alright.; Okay."

  "ᎰG!", OꙍᏜᏫᏝ DᏢ.
  "Alright!", yelled Al.
  [GWY KTᏁ ᏥhhVꙍ ᎠᏏᏓVᎠ]

ᎰGS [hạwaga] (pt) "Isn't that right?"

ᎰGᏉ [hạwagwo] (pt) "So long for now (idiom)."

ᎰΘh [hạwini] (pt) "Deep.; Inside."

  Z OꞋᎶᎵL DL ᎰΘh ShᏢST.
  Then they put dry wood <u>inside</u>.
  [King pg 122]

ᎤᎭᏫᏯ [hạwiya] (n) "Meat."

ᎤᏍᏗ ᎤᏓᎨ ᎤᎭᏫᏯ ᎠᏰᎸᏗ ᏂᎦᏙ, ᎠᎴ ᎤᏍᎦ-ᏗᎠᏬᎸᏗ ᏗᎠᏬᎸᏗ ᏂᎦᏙ, …
Right [it is] not to eat flesh, nor to drink wine, …
[GH 14:21]

ᎤᎭᏫᏯ ᎠᏍᏙᏓ [hạwiya ạsdoda] (n) "Sausage."

ᎤᏯᎦᎸᏗᏫ [hạyagalvdvɂi] (n) "Wall paper.; Jacket lining."

ᎤᏯᏣᎪᎯ [hạyatsohi] (n) "Handkerchief."

ᎤᏰᎳᏍᏗ [hạyelạsdi] (n) "Knife."

ᎡᏘᎤᎲᏃ ᎤᏙᏫᏍᏕ ᎠᎴ ᎤᏰᎳᏍᏗ ᎤᏰᎵ ᎤᏍᏙᏗ ᎤᏫᎩ.
and Abraham putteth forth his hand, and taketh the knife – to slaughter his son.
[ᏣᏈ ᎡᏈᏍᏆ 22:10]

Ꭿ

ᎯᏗ [hiɂa] (pt) "This.; This one."

ᎾᏍ�YᏃ ᎯᏗ ᏂᏍᏫᏄᏐ ᎠᎢᏍᏗ ᏣᏝᏕ Ꭴ�horᏍᏘᎮᎡᏋ, …
At this his Relations were sore amazed; …
[ᏣᏁᎦᏗ ᏎᎯᏯᎡᎡᏘ]

ᎯᏗᏃᏍᏆᏍᏗ [hiɂahnoɂnụsdi] (pt) "This is."

ᎯᏘᏨ [hiɂitsv] (pt) "This way."

ᎯᏍ [hiɂga] (pt) "This much."

ᎯᏴᏍᎠᎯ [hiksgohi] (adj) "Fifty."

ᎠᎴ ᏎᏁᎦᏴᏍᎬ ᎤᏁᎢᎲᏗ ᎡᏣᏗ ᎠᏰᎠᏌᏆ ᎠᎾᏍᏍᎠᎯ ᏗᎡᏏᎾ.
and the waters are mighty on the earth a hundred and fifty days.
[ᏣᏈ ᎡᏈᏍᏆ 7:24]

ᎯᎠ ᎤᎡᏛᎯ [higọ ụsvhi] (n) "Tonight."

ᎯᎶᏍᏆᎤᏨ [hilsdvwotsv] (n) "Pull (corn fodder or blades)."

ᎠᏍᏩᏍᏍᎠ [hisgạdụhi] (adj) "Fifteen."

ᎠᏍᏪ [hisgi] (adj) "Five."

ᎠᎡᎶᎤᏃᎤ ᎢᏍᎾ ᏎᏯᏐᎤᏘ, ᎠᏍᏪ ᎢᏫᎲᎾ ᏗhᏍᏍᎲ, …
And out of his brethren he hath taken five men, …
[ᏣᏈ ᎡᏈᏍᏆ 47:2]

ᎠᏍᏪᏉ [hisgwo] (pt) "Him too."

Ᏺ

ᏺᎤᎵ [howini] (pt) "Deep.; Inside."

ᏺᎤᎵᏣ [howinitsa] (pt) "Under."

Ꭸ

ᎦᎦ [huhu] (n) "Yellow-breasted chat.; Yellow breasted mockingbird.; biol. *Icteria virens.*"

ᎦᎶᏌᎬᏘ [huhlsigvɂi] (pt) "In the dark."

ᎦᎤᎵᎮᎬ [hundadsgv] (n) "Group."

ᎦᎻᎯᎥ [hunihiv] (n) "Stream.; Small river."

ᎦᏛ [huda] (pt) "Vine, to be on."

ᎦᎬᏳ [huhyugi] (n) "Disease."

Ꮺ

ᏭᏍ [hvga] (pt) "How."

ᏭᏍᏗᎥ [hvgaɂiyv] (pt) "When."

ᏭᏍᏗᎥ ᏉᎠᎻᎮ?
"When are you coming back?"
[King pg 120]

Ꮎ

ᎾᏂᎮ [naɂy'ni] (pt) "Near.; Close by."

… ᎾᏍᏳ ᎯᏗ ᎤᏫᎠᎦᏆ ᏄᎸᏗ, ᏓᏉᏃ ᎠᎠᏫ ᎢᎡ ᎣᎤᎾᎵ ᎤᎳᎥᏃ ᏘᏍᏍᏆᏗ ᎢᎡ ᎾᎻ ᏂᏍᏆᏏ; ᎠᎴ …
… But though this be so, yet since things present and our fleshly appetite are such near neighbors one to another; and, …
[ᏣᏁᎦᏗ ᏎᎯᏯᎡᎡᏘ]

ᎾᎨᏘ [nageɂi] (n) "Balsam poplar.; biol. *Populus sect. Tacamahaca.*"

ᎾᎾ ᎤᏍᏫᏗ [nan ụdehyti] (n) "Plantain, broadleaf.; biol. *Plantago major.*"

ᎾᏬ [nagwo] (pt) "Now.; There."

ᎾᏬ ᏗᎢᎤᏫ ᏄᎾᏫ ᏎᏍᎤᏝᏫᎬᎬ ᎤᏅᎯᎥᏩᏆ ᏗᎵᏌᎴᎦᏆ ᎢᎡᏘ.
Now I begin to reap the benefits of my hazards.
[ᏣᏁᎦᏗ ᏎᎯᏯᎡᎡᏘ]

ᎾᏛᏂᎤ [nadyneha] (vt) "He is doing it."

ᏂᏍᏛᏂᏗ [nigadynęɂa]

ᏄᏛᏂᎦᏘ [nudynęlv²³ɂi]

ᎾᏛᏂᏺᏘ [nadyneho³ɂi]

ᏮᏛᏂᏍ [hnadynega]

ᎢᏳᏛᏗ [iyudɂdi]

… ᎠᎴ ᎡᏴᎤᏬ ᏗhᎠᏍ ᎾᏍᏳ ᏎᎡᎢᏁᎬᏘ, �YᎬᏃ ᏐᎾ ᏮᏂᏌ, ᎡᎠᏘ; ᎤᎬᎶᎤᏃ ᎡᏬᎾ ᏮᏂᏌ, ᏗᎡᎠᏘ; ᏮᎤᏂᏗᎠᏗᏃ, ᎯᏗ ᏮᏛᏍ ᏮᏂᏌ, ᎾᏍᏳ ᎾᏛᏂᏺᏘ.
… having under myself soldiers, and I say to this one, Go, and he goeth, and to another, Be coming, and he cometh, and to my servant, Do this, and he doth [it].'
[ᎠᏒ 8:9]

Ꭲ

ᎢᎳᏍᎪᎯ [nelsgohi] (adj) "Eighty."

> … ᎠᏍᏗ ᏅᎾᏫᏘᎢ, ᎠᎾᏳ ᎠᎼᎵ ᏓᎩᏎᎢ, ᎠᎴ ᎢᎳᏍᎪᎯ ᎩᏩᎧᏍ.
> … and he saith to him, Take thy bill, and write <u>eighty</u>. [ᎹᏍ 16:7]

ᎢᎤᏎᎯ [neladuhi] (adj) "Eighteen."

Ꮒ

Ꮒ [ni] (pt) "Look!"

ᏂᎦᎵᏍᏬᏘᎯ [nigalsgwe³tuiha] (vi) "It is because of.; It happens."

> ᏂᏥᎠᎵᏍᏬᏍᏘᎯ [nitsialsgwe³dɂuiha]
> ᏄᎵᏍᏬᏍᏙᎥᎢ [nulsgwe³tuanv²³ɂi]
> ᏂᎦᎵᏍᏬᏍᏘᎥᎠᎢ [nigalsgwe³tuisgo³ɂi]
> ᏅᎾᎵᏍᏬᏍᏚ [hnalsgwe³tua]
> ᎢᏳᎵᏍᏬᏍᏚᏗ [iyulsgwe³tuudi]

ᏂᎦᏓ [nigada] (adj) "All."

> ᏙᏂᏃ, ᏂᎦᏓ ᎤᏂᎬ ᎤᏍᎪᎦ ᎤᎦ ᏍᏎ.
> And last, <u>everyone</u> ate warm sliced bread. [ᏣᏫᏯ ᏫᎵᏂ ᏗᎯᎯᏫᎠ ᎷᏍᏂᎥᏗ]

ᏂᎦᏫᏓ [nigawęɂa] (vt) "He is saying it.; He is uttering it."

> ᏂᏥᏫᏓ [nitsiwęɂa]
> ᏄᏫᏒᎢ [nuwęsv²³ɂi]
> ᏂᎦᏫᏍᎠᎢ [nigawęsgo³ɂi]
> ᏅᏫ [hniwe]
> ᎢᏳᏫᏍᏗ [iyuwęsdi]
>
> … ᏄᏫᏯᎩ, "ᏍᏙᏃ ᏞᏍᏘᏂᎵ?"
> … <u>saying</u> "What shall I do?" [ᏚᏂᎦᎵ ᏍᏂᎩᏒᎥᎢ]

ᏂᎨᎢ [nigei] (pt) "At a distance.; Way off.; Over yonder.; Over there."

ᏂᎨᎢᏘᎷ [nigeɂiyvda] (pt) "Something or things way off in the distance."

ᏂᎪᎯᎵᏴᎢ [nigohilvɂi] (pt) "Always."

> ᏙᎢ ᏥᏍᏩᏘ ᏂᎪᎯᎵᏴᎢ ᏫᏘᎤᏍᎵᏫᎢ; …
> and I knew that Thou <u>always</u> dost hear me, … [ᏣᏂ 11:42]

ᏂᎩᎥᎢ [nikvɂi] (pt) "Everywhere."

> … ᏙᎢ ᎤᏃᏟᎲᏚ ᏂᎩᎥᎢ ᏍᏎᏬ ᏂᏏ ᎤᏫᏘᏂᎠᎵ ᏄᎵᏂᎦ ᏥᎤ.
> … and he went away <u>through all</u> the city proclaiming how great things Jesus did to him. [ᎹᏍ 8:39]

ᏂᎬᏁᎯ [nigvneha] (vt) "He is making it."

> ᏂᎬᏁᎠ [nigvnęɂa]
> ᏄᏩᏁᎥᎢ [nuwanęlv²³ɂi]
> ᏂᎬᏁᎰᎢ [nigvneho³ɂi]
> ᎤᏁᎦ [hnvnega]
> ᎢᏳᏫᏗ [iyuwhdi]

ᏂᎬᏂᎯᎳᎩ [nigv³hneha] (vt) "He is making something for him."

> ᏂᏥᏰᏁᎯ [nitsiyyɂneha]
> ᏄᏩᏂᎦᎥᎢ [nuwa³hnęlv²³ɂi]
> ᏂᎬᏂᎰᎢ [nigv³hneho³ɂi]
> ᏂᏰᏁᏏ [hniyyɂnęsi]
> ᎢᏳᏩᏂᎰᏗ [iyuwa³hnesdi]

ᏂᎬᏫᎰᏗ [nigvwhsdi] (pt) "Appears as.; Looks like."

ᏂᎵᏛᏱ [nildvyi] (n) "River (small)."

Ꮓ

ᏃᎢ [noɂi] (pt) "Now."

ᏃᎴ [nole] (pt) "And."

> ᏩᎦᏗ ᎡᎵ ᏊᏟᏘ ᏍᏛᏗ ᏃᎴ ᏫᏘᎯᎰᏗ.
> They made a wedge <u>and</u> maul from locust. [King pg 122]

ᏃᏄ [nonu] (n) "Hemlock (tree).; biol. *Tsuga caroliniana*."

ᏃᎩᏏ [nokwisi] (n; gn) "A star.; Meadowlark, eastern.; biol. *Sturnella magna*."

> ᏔᏥᎵ ᏬᎠᎠ ᏃᎩᏏ ᏌᎵᏘ ᏃᎴ ᎡᎵᎵ ᎤᏎᎵᎠ. ᏆᏛᏓᏍ ᏃᎩᏏ ᏌᎵᏘ?
> Lejili saw ten <u>meadowlarks</u> and then she saw six went away. How many <u>meadowlarks</u> does she see? [ᏣᏫᏯ ᎤᏳᏂ ᏗᎯᎯᏫᎠ ᎷᏍᏂᎥᏗ]

ᏃᎩᏏ ᎤᏍᏗ [nokwisi usdi] (n) "Puffball (fungus).; biol. *Gasteroid fungi*."

ᏃᏛᏥ [nohdatsi] (n) "Wild allspice.; Spicebush.; Spicewood.; biol. *Lindera benzoin*."

ᏃᏗ [nodi] (pt) "Now."

ᏃᏥ [notsi] (n) "Pine tree (all varieties).; biol. *Pinus spp*."

ᏃᏥ ᎢᏳᏗ [notsi iyusdi] (n) "Spruce.; biol. *Picea rubra*."

ᏃᏯ [noya] (n) "Sand."

> ᎧᎳᏃ ᎤᏣᏗᏗ ᎤᏫᏓᎵᏂ ᏃᎦ ᏙᎯᏴᎠ ᏥᏍᏫᏟ ᏐᏓ�YᎥᎢ, …
> and Joseph gathereth corn as <u>sand</u> of the sea, multiplying exceedingly, … [ᏚᏆ ᏔᎥᎶᎥ 41:49]

ᏃᏯᎯ [noyaha] (n) "Sandy."

Ꮕ

ᏄᎦᎵ [nugahli] (n) "Blackberries.; biol. *Rubus spp*."

ᏄᎦᎵ [nugahlv] (n) "Sawbrier.; Cat greenbriar.; Catbriar.; biol. *Smilax glauca.*"

ᏄᎾ [nuna] (n) "Potato(es).; biol. *Solanum tuberosum.*"

ᏄᎾ ᎤᏂᎦᎾᏍᏗ [nuna uniganasda] (n) "Sweet potato(es).; biol. *Ipomoea batatas.*"

ᏄᏓᎴᎯ [nudalehi] (n) "The other one."

ᏄᎭᏩᎾᏕᎦ [nuhwanadega] (vt) "He is treating him (specify: bad or good)."

ᏂᎦᏬᏩᎾᏕᎦ [na¹gwynadega]

ᏄᎭᏩᎾᏙᎸᎢ [nuhwanado?lv²³?i]

ᏄᎭᏩᎾᏕᎪᎢ [nuhwanadego³?i]

ᏂᏘᏍᏩᎾᏕᎨᏍᏗ [nitsvnadegesdi]

ᎢᏳᎭᏩᎾᏕᎯᏗ [iyuhwanadehdi]

ᏄᏯᎩ [nuyagi] (n) "New York."

Ꭴ

ᎤᎦᏚᎯ [nvgaduhi] (adj) "Fourteen."

ᎤᎩ [nvki] (adj) "Four."

... ᎤᎩ ᎦᎦᏛ ᏂᎦᏘᏩᏐᏅᎢᏘ.
... hath become <u>four</u> chief [rivers];
[ᏃᏏ TEᏒᏅᏊ 2:10]

ᎤᎩᏅ ᎢᎦ [nvgine iga] (n) "Thursday."

ᎤᎩᏍᎪᎯ [nvksgohi] (adj) "Forty."

ᎤᏃ ᏓᏍᎪᎠᏍᎩ [nvno asdvgosgi] (n) "Bull dozer."

ᎤᏃᎯ [nvnohi] (n) "Road."

... Ꮥ ᏦᏐᏗᏅᎬ ᎤᏃᎯ ᏗᎦᏯᏍᏗ ᏂᎦᏘᏩᏐᏁᏴ ...
... and their hap was to meet just as they were crossing <u>the way</u> of each other ...
[ᏙᏂᎬᏗ ᏍᎭᏴᏏᏘ]

ᎤᏓᏕᎦᏔ [nvdadegwa] (n) "November."

ᎤᏓᏗᎧᏂ [nvdadikani] (n) "Sunflower.; biol. *Helianthus.*"

ᎤᏙᏆᏪᏯ [nvdokwehya] (n) "Sourwood.; Sorrel tree.; biol. *Oxydendrum arboreum.*"

ᎤᏙᏆᏪᏯ ᏗᎤᏍᏗ [nvdogwehya iyusdi] (n) "Like sourwood (plant)."

ᎤᏙᏗᏍᎡᏍᏗ [nvdodisesdi] (n) "Calendar."

ᎤᏣᏛ [nvchadv] (n) "Breast."

ᎤᏬᎯᏗ [nvwohdi] (n) "Medicine."

"ᏗᏣᏙᏟᏍᎦᏚᏗ ᏗᏂᎣᏪ ᎤᏬᎯᏗ ...
"You should be learning doctoring <u>medicine</u> ...
[King pg 122]

ᎤᏯ [nvya] (n) "Rock."

ᎤᏍᏔ Ꮥ ᏦᏍᏗ ᎤᏯ ᏗᎫᎦ.
Put inside seeds or little <u>rocks</u>.
[ᏇᏯ ᎿᏘᏂ ᏗᏂᎭᏫᎠ ᏗᏍᎯᎥᏗ]

ᎤᏯ ᎤᎿᏬ [nv?ya uhnuwo] (n) "Rock armor."

ᎦᎵᎥᏥᏘ ᎤᏅ ᎤᎤᎦᏘ.
The <u>rock armor</u> was ripped.
[King pg 122]

ᎤᏥᎠ [nv?yohi] (n) "Rocky."

Ꮹ

ᎬᎳᎪᎦ [gwaloga] (n) "Sumac.; biol. *Rhus spp.*"

ᎬᎹᎵᏏ [kwalu³si] (n) "Muscadine grapes.; biol. *Vitis rotundifolia.*; Summer grapes.; Pigeon grapes.; biol. *Vitis aestivalis.*"

ᎬᎾ [kwana] (n) "Peach.; biol. *Prunus persica.*"

ᎦᎥ ᎤᏒᏗ ᏓᎵᏁ? ᏛᎴᏪᏯ. ᎾᏍᎠᎥᏓ: D) ᎯᏂᏍᎿᏐ, R) ᏩᏫ, T) ᎬᎾ.
What was he handed? Choose. Hand him them: a) Crayfish, b) Beaver, c) <u>Peaches</u>.
[ᏇᏯ ᎤᎩᏂ ᏗᏂᎭᏫᎠ ᏗᏍᎯᎥᏗ]

ᎬᎾᏗᏯ [gwandiya] (n) "Stretch mouth snake."

ᎬᎾᎾᏍᏗᎢᎢ [gwanunsdi?i] (n) "Plum.; biol. *Prunus domestica.*"

Ꮜ

ᏌᎧ [saka] (adj) "Lightweight."

ᏌᎧ ᎦᏌᎴᏂ [saka gasaleni] (n) "Jacket."

ᏌᎪᏂᎨᎢᎢ [sagonige?i] (adj) "Blue."

ᏌᎪᏂᎨ ᎤᏍᎪᎸᎢ [sakonige usgolv?i] (adj) "Gray."

ᏌᎵ [sali] (n) "Persimmon.; biol. *Diospyros virginiana.*"

ᏌᎵᏥᎩ [sali³gu³gi] (n) "Snapping turtle.; biol. *Chelydra serpentina.*; Mud turtle (eastern).; biol. *Kinosternon subrubrum.*"

ᏌᎶᎵ [saloli] (n) "Gray squirrel.; biol. *Sciurus carolinensis.*; Squirrel.; biol. *Sciurus spp.*"

ᎦᎥ ᎤᏒᏗ ᏓᎵᏁ? ᏛᎴᏪᏯ. ᎣᎯᏒᎦ: D) ᎯᏒᏍ, R) ᏌᎶᎵ, T) ᎤᏪᎯ.
What is being handed? Choose. I am handing it to him: a) A rabbit, b) <u>A squirrel</u>, c) An egg.
[ᏇᏯ ᎤᎩᏂ ᏗᏂᎭᏫᎠ ᏗᏍᎯᎥᏗ]

ᏌᎶᎵ ᎠᎦᏔ [saloli akta] (n) "Dewberries.; biol. *Rubus spp.*"

ᏌᎶᎵ ᏬᎯᏗ [saloli wohdi] (n) "Fox squirrel.; biol. *Sciurus niger.*"

ᏌᎷᏱ [saluyi] (n) "Thicket."

ᏌᎾᏋ [sanawa] (n) "Pigeon hawk.; Merlin (bird).; biol. *Falco columbarius.*"

ᏌᎾᏬ [sanywo] (n) "Mythical hawk like bird."

ᏌᏌ [sasa] (n) "Goose.; biol. *Branta canadensis.*"

Ꮝ

ᏍᎦᏎᎲ [sgasehnv] (adj) "Bold, to be.; Fearless."

ᏂᏍᎦᏎᎲᎾ [nasgasehnvna]

ᏍᎦᏁᎬᏍᏗ [sgayegvsdi] (n) "Boss.; Manager."

ᏍᎧᎳ ᎦᎶᎬᎯ [skala galogwehi] (n) "Pistol (gun)."

ᏍᎩ [sgi] (pt) "Thanks.; That."

ᏍᎩᎦ [sgiga] (pt) "That much."

ᏍᎩᎾᏂ [sg̣inahni] (pt) "That's the one."

ᏍᎩᏄᏍᏗ(Ꭲ) [sgịʔnụsd(ị)] (pt) "Is that?"

ᏍᎩᏈᏳᏍᏗ [sgịgwiyụsdi] (pt) "It's just like that."

ᏍᎩᏊᏩᏌ [sgịgwụwạsa] (pt) "The only thing."

ᏍᎩᏕᎦ [sgidẹga] (pt) "Is that so?"

ᏍᎪᎯ [sgohi] (adj) "Ten."

ᏍᎪᎯᏥᏆ [sgohitsgwa] (adj) "One hundred."

ᏍᎪᏂᏎᎾᏏ [sgonịsensi] (n) "A dime."

ᏍᏆᎳᎯ [sgwalạhi] (adj) "Short."

ᏍᏉᎵ [sgwohli] (n) "Stomach."

ᏍᏓᏯ [sdaya] (adj) "Hard."

> ᏍᏓᏯ ᏧᏄᎾ ᏗᎪᏪᎵ $2.25, ᏩᏂᎮ ᏧᏄᎾ ᏗᎪᏪᎵ $0.75.
> A hard-back book $2.25, A soft-back book. $0.75.
> [ᏣᎳᎩ ᎤᎩᏁ ᏗᏂᏂᏙᎯ ᏗᎦᏲᏙᏗ]

ᏍᏓᏱ [sdahyi] (adj) "Too hard."

ᏍᏓᏴᎲᏍᎩ [sdayṿhṿsgi] (n) "Wife.; Cook."

ᏍᏕᏯᏗ [sdeyadi] (n) "Rope."

ᏍᏗᎧᏓ [sdikạda] (pt) "Just a little."

ᏍᏗᏯᎯ [sdiyạhi] (n) "Sick."

ᏍᏗᏰᎬᎢ [sdịyẹkvʔi] (n) "Hair on the head."

ᏍᏙᏍᏗ [sdosdi] (n) "Pestle."

ᏍᏚᎩᏍᏗ [sdụgisdi] (n) "Key."

Ꮞ

ᏎᎦ [sega] (pt) "Awhile.; A little while."

> "ᎮᎾ ᏎᎦ …
> "Come here awhile …
> [King pg 121]

ᏎᎦᏨ [segatsv] (pt) "Almost."

ᏎᎵᎦᏍᏉ [seliksgwo] (n) "Muskrat.; biol. *Ondatra zibethicus.*"

ᏎᎷ [selu] (n) "Corn.; biol. *Zea Mays.*"

ᏎᎷ ᎤᏁᏄᏗ [selụ ụnenuhdi] (n) "Cornsilk."

ᏎᎷ ᎤᏂᏥ [selụ ụnitsi] (n) "Job's tears.; biol. *Coix lacryma*-jobi."

ᏎᎷ ᎦᏚ [sẹlụ gadu] (n) "Corn bread."

ᏎᎷᏉᏯ [selụgwọya] (n) "Adam's needle.; biol. *Yucca flaccida.*"

ᏎᎷᏯᎯ [seluyạhi] (n) "Flour corn."

ᏎᎼᏂ [semoni] (n) "Salmon.; biol. *Salmo salar.*"

ᏎᏅᏏ [senhsi] (n) "Cent."

> *English borrowing.*

ᏎᏗ [sedi] (n) "Walnut.; biol. *Juglans nigra.*"

ᏎᏗᏳᏍᏗ [sedịyụsdi] (n) "Pear.; biol. *Pyrus communis.*"

ᏎᏩᏓ [sehwạda] (n) "Hornet.; biol. *Dolichovespula maculata.*"

Ꮟ

Ꮟ [sịh] (pt) "Wait."

ᏏᎦᏓᏍᎩ [sigạdasgi] (n) "Carrion flower.; Smooth carrion-flower.; Smooth herbaceous greenbrier.; biol. *Smilax herbacea.*"

ᏏᎳᏉ [silạgwo] (n) "Sylva, NC."

ᏏᎸᎢ [sịlvʔi] (pt) "Wait a minute.; A moment."

ᏏᏅᏓ [sinvda] (n) "Month."

ᏏᏆ [sịkwa] (n) "Pig.; Hog.; biol. *Sus.*"

> ᎮᎯᏃ ᎢᏴᏛ ᏗᏁᏙᎲ ᎤᏂᏣᏘ ᏑᎾᏓᏡᎩ ᏏᏆ ᎠᎾᎵᏍᏓᏴᏂᏙᎲᎢ.
> And there was far off from them a herd of many swine feeding,
> [ᎹᏚ 8:30]

ᏏᏈᏲ [sịgwiyo] (n) "Sevierville, TN."

ᏏᏉ [sịgwo] (pt) "More.; Again."

ᏏᏎᎦ [sịsega] (pt) "Wait a while."

ᏏᏲ (ᎣᏏᏳ) [siyọ (ọsiyụ)] (pt) "Hello."

Ꮠ

ᏐᎣᏁᎳ [soʔọnela] (adj) "Nine."

> … ᏝᏍᎪ ᎠᏍᎪᎯ ᏧᎮᏥᎤᏕᏄᎡᎢ? ᎠᏎᏃ ᏐᎣᏁᎳ ᎢᏯᏂᏛ ᎭᏢ?
> … 'Were not the ten cleansed, and the nine — where?
> [ᎷᎦ 17:17]

ᏐᎣᏁᎳᏍᎪᎯ [soʔọnelsgohi] (adj) "Ninety."

> ᎦᏙ ᎢᏤᎵᎭ; ᎢᏳᏃ ᎩᎶ ᎠᏍᎦᏯ ᎠᏍᎪᎯᏧᏈ ᎠᏫ ᏧᏚᎾᏝᎠ, ᏌᏉᏃ ᏳᎴᏲᏒᏄ, ᏝᏍᎪ ᏐᎣᏁᎳᏍᎪᎯ ᏐᎣᏁᎳᏕᎵ ᎢᏯᏂᏛ ᏧᏗᎬᎦᎪᎢ, ᎠᎴ ᏧᏗᎧᎾᎷᏏᏙᎮ ᎦᏚᏏ ᏳᏲᎮ ᎤᎴᏲᏒᏄᎯ?
> 'What think ye? if a man may have an hundred sheep, and there may go astray one of them, doth he not — having left the ninety-nine, having gone on the mountains — seek that which is gone astray?
> [ᎹᏚ 18:12]

ᏐᎣᏁᎳᏚᎯ [soʔọnelạduhi] (adj) "Nineteen."

ᏐᎩ [soʔgi] (n) "Waynesville, NC."

ᏐᎯ [sohi] (n) "Hickory nut.; biol. *Carya spp.*"

ᏐᏈᎢ ᎤᏂᎩᏍᏗ [sogwịʔị unịgịsdi] (n) "Oatmeal."

ᏐᏈᎵ [sogwịli] (n) "Horse.; biol. *Equus ferus caballus.*"

> ᎦᏙ ᎤᏍᏗ ᎠᏓᏁᎭ? ᎭᏑᏯᏍᎩ. ᏙᏗᏍᎩᏂᎥᏏ: Ꭰ) ᏪᏌ, Ꭱ) ᏅᏯ, Ꭲ) ᏐᏈᎵ.
> What is he giving? Choose. He will hand them to him: a) Cats, b) Rocks, c) Horses.
> [ᏣᎳᎩ ᎤᎩᏁ ᏗᏂᏂᏙᎯ ᏗᎦᏲᏙᏗ]

ᏐᏈᎵ ᎠᎩᎾ [sọgwịli ạgina] (n) "Colt."

ᏐᏊ [sogwu] (adj) "One."

> ᎤᎾᎦᏯᎳᏁᎴᎢ ᎠᏂᏍᎦᏯ ᏐᏊ ᎠᎪᏣᏍᎬᎢ.
> The men became antagonized (as their number) became one less.
> [King pg 121]

ᏐᏚᎯ [soʔdụhi] (adj) "Eleven."

ᏐᏤᎾ [sotsena] (n) "Coneflower.; Black-eyed-susan.; Sochana.; biol. *Rudbeckia hirta.*"

Ꮡ

ᏑᎵ [suli] (n) "Buzzard.; Turkey vulture.; biol. *Cathartes aura.*"

ᏑᎾᎴᎢ [sunalẹʔi] (pt) "Tomorrow."

… ᎪᎯ ᎢᎦ ᎠᎴ ᏑᎾᎴᎢ ᏓᏲᏤᏏ ᎨᎯ ᏗᎦᏚᎲᎢ, ᏑᏕᏘᏴᏛᏃ ᏬᏙᏢᏍᏗ …
… 'To-day and to-morrow we will go on to such a city, and will pass there one year, …
[ᏥᎻ: 4:13]

ᏑᎾᎴᎢᏣ [sunaleʔitsa] (pt) "Dawn."

ᏑᎾᎴ ᎤᏒᎯ [sunalẹ ụsvhi] (n) "Tomorrow night."

ᏑᎾᏙᏓᏆᏍᏗ [sundodagwasdi] (n) "A week."

ᏤᎦᏈᏃ ᎾᏍᎩ ᏄᏛᏁᎴᎢ, ᎠᎴ ᎾᏍᎩ ᎤᏤᎵ ᏑᎾᏙᏓᏆᏍᏗ ᎨᏒ ᎤᏍᏆᎦᎴᎢ; …
And Jacob doth so, and fulfilleth the week of this one, …
[ᎼᏏ ᎢᎬᏱᏱ 29:28]

ᏑᏒᎯᏓ [sụsvhida] (pt) "Overnight."

ᏑᏓᎴᎦ [sudạlega] (pt) "One thing."

ᏑᏓᎵ [sudạli] (adj) "Six."

… ᎤᏗᎦᎵᏍᏙᏗᎭ ᏑᏓᎵ ᏕᏥᎾᏄᎪᏫᏎᎸ ᎠᏂᏧᏣ; ᏤᏆᎳᏂᏃ ᏚᏬᎡᎢ.
… for I have borne to him six sons;' and she calleth his name Zebulun;
[ᎼᏏ ᎢᎬᏱᏱ 30:20]

ᏑᏓᎵᏍᎪᎯ [sudahlsgohi] (adj) "Sixty."

… ᎠᎴ ᎤᎵᏰᏁᎢ, ᎠᎴ ᎠᏛᏍᎨᎢ, ᎠᎴ ᎧᏁᏉᎨᎢ, ᎠᎴ ᎤᎦᏔᏔᏁᎢ, ᎢᎦᏛ ᏦᎠᏍᎪᎯ ᎢᏳᏩᎫᏗ, ᎢᎦᏛᏃ ᏑᏓᎵᏍᎪᎯ, ᎢᎦᏛᏃ ᎠᏍᎪᎯᏧᏈ.
and other fell to the good ground, and was giving fruit, coming up and increasing, and it bare, one thirty-fold, and one sixty, and one an hundred.'
[ᎹᎦ 4:8]

ᏑᏕᏘᏴᏓ [sudẹtiyvda] (n) "Year."

ᏑᏥᎶᏓ [sụtsịloda] (n) "A mile.; A gallon.; A yard (measurement).; An acre."

Ꮢ

ᏒᎦᏔ [svkta] (n) "Apple (all varieties)."

ᏒᎦᏛ ᎢᎾᎨᎠᏁᎵ [svgdỵ inạgeanehl] (n) "Crab apple.; biol. *Malus spp.*"

ᏒᎩ [svgi] (n) "Onion.; biol. *Allium cepa.*"

ᏒᎩ [svki] (n) "Mink.; biol. *Neovison vison.*"

ᏒᎯᏰᏱᏗᏣ [svhịyẹyhdịtsa] (pt) "Afternoon."

ᏒᏃ ᎡᏙ ᏅᏓ [svnọ edo nvda] (n) "Moon."

ᏒᏓᎷᎩ [svdạlugi] (n) "A shingle."

ᏒᏗᏩᎵ [svdịwạʔli] (n) "Raspberries.; biol. *Rubus spp.*"

ᏒᏙᏂ [svdoʔni] (n) "Barrel."

Ꮣ

ᏓᎦᎩ [dagki] (n) "Curled dock.; Yellow dock.; biol. *Rumex crispus.*"

ᏓᎦᎴᏂᎠ [dagạlenịʔa] (vi) "He is separating."

ᏕᎦᎦᎴᏂᎠ [degagạlenịʔa]

ᏚᎦᎴᏅᎥᎢ [dugạlenỵʔv23ʔi]

ᏓᎦᎴᏂᏍᎪᎢ [dagạlenisgo3ʔi]

ᏔᎦᎴᎾ [tagạlena]

ᏧᎦᎴᏂᏗ [tsugạlenhdi]

ᏓᎦᏏ [dagsi] (n) "Box turtle.; Terrapin.; biol. *Terrapene carolina.*; Padlock."

"ᏓᎦᏏ, ᎭᏢ ᏣᎩᏎ ᎤᏬᏚᎯ ᎤᏃᏴᎩ?"
"Turtle, where is that pretty sound coming from?"
[ᏣᎳᎩ ᏔᎵᏁ ᏗᏂᏂᏙᎯ ᏗᏕᏲᏙᏗ]

ᏓᎦᏒᏍᏗᎭ [daksvsdịha] (vt) "He is making smoke. It is smoking."

ᏕᏥᎦᏒᏍᏗᎭ [dejịgasvsdiha]

ᏚᎦᏒᏍᏓᏅᎢ [duksvstạʔnv23ʔi]

ᏓᎦᏒᏍᏗᏍᎪᎢ [daksvsdịsgo3ʔi]

ᏘᎦᏒᏍᏓ [tiksvsda]

ᏧᎦᏒᏍᏙᏗ [tsuksvsdohdi]

ᏓᎦᏔᎵᎭ [daktạlịha] (vi) "He is shelling corn."

ᏕᏥᎦᏓᎵᎭ [detsịkdạlịha]

ᏚᎦᏔᎸᎲᎢ [duktạlvhv23ʔi]

ᏓᎦᏔᎵᏍᎪᎢ [daktạlịsgo3ʔi]

ᏘᎦᏔᎳ [tịktạla]

ᏧᎦᏔᎵᏗ [tsuktahldi]

ᏓᎧᎾ [dakahna] (vt) "He is looking at it."

ᏕᏥᎧᎾ [detsịkaʔna]

ᏚᎧᎾᏅᎢ [dukahnanv23ʔi]

ᏓᎧᏃᎢ [dakahno3ʔi]

ᏘᎧᎾᎦ [tịkahnaga]

ᏧᎧᎾᏗ [tsukahndi]

ᏓᎧᏁᎦ [dakạnẹga] (vt) "He is placing living things in a row."

ᏕᏥᎧᏁᎦ [detsịkạnẹga]

ᏚᎧᏁᏒᎢ [dukạnẹsv23ʔi]

ᏓᎧᏁᎪᎢ [dakạnẹgo3ʔi]

ᏘᎧᏄᎾ [tịkạnụʔna]

ᏧᎧᏁᎥᏍᏗ [tsukạnẹvsdi]

ᏓᎧᏂᎭ [dakąnįha] (vi) "He is opening eyes.; He is looking."

ᏕᎦᎧᏂᎠ [degakąnį?a]

ᏚᎧᎾᏅᎢ [dukąnąnv²³?i]

ᏓᎧᏂᏍᎪᎢ [dakąnhsgo³?i]

ᏔᎧᏂᎦ [takąn?ga]

ᏧᎧᏅᏗ [tsukąnhdi]

... ᎩᎶ ᎠᎨᏴ ᏓᎧᏂᏍᎨᏍᏗ ᏧᎾᏂᏏᏗᏱ ᎤᏚᎵᏍᎨᏍᏗ, ...
... every one who is looking on a woman to desire her, ...
[ᎹᏚ 5:28]

ᏓᎧᏂᎭ [dakąnhįha] (vt) "He is tying."

ᏕᏥᎦᏂᎭ [detsįgą?nhįha]

ᏚᎧᏂᎸᎢ [dukąnhlv²³?i]

ᏓᎧᏂᎰᎢ [dakąnhįho³?i]

ᏘᎧᏂᏣ [tįkąntsa]

ᏧᎧᏂᏍᏗ [tsukąnhsdi]

ᏓᎨᏬᎦ [dakewoga] (vi) "He is becoming blind."

ᏕᏥᎨᏬᎦ [detsįkewoga]

ᏚᎨᏬᏨᎢ [dukewotsv²³?i]

ᏓᎨᏬᎪᎢ [dakewogo³?i]

ᏘᎨᏬᎩ [tįkewogi]

ᏧᎨᏬᎢᏍᏗ [tsukewǫ?įsdi]

ᏓᎬᏓᎳᎩᎠ [dakvdąlągi³?a] (vt) "He is pulling rocks from the ground."

ᏕᏥᎬᏓᎳᎩᎠ [detsį?kvdąlągi³?a]

ᏚᎬᏓᎳᎩᏒᎢ [dukvdąlągi³sv²³?i]

ᏓᎬᏓᎳᎩᏍᎪᎢ [dakvdąlągi³sgo³?i]

ᏘᎬᏓᎳᎩ [tįkvdąlągi]

ᏧᎬᏓᎳᎩᏍᏗ [tsukvdąlągi³sdi]

ᏓᎬᏩᎳᏍᎦ [dagy?hwąlasga] (vt) "He is betting."

ᏕᏥᎬᏩᎳᏍᎦ [detsįgywą?lasga]

ᏚᎬᏩᎳᏅᎢ [dugy?hwąląnv²³?i]

ᏓᎬᏩᎳᏍᎪᎢ [dagy?hwąlasgo³?i]

ᏘᎬᏩᎳᎦ [tįgy?hwąlaga]

ᏧᎬᏩᎳᏗ [tsugy?hwąlhdi]

ᏓᎳᎳ [dąlala] (n) "Red-headed woodpecker.; biol. *Melanerpes erythrocephalus.*"

ᏓᎳᏍᎨᏫ [dahlsgewi] (n) "Shrew.; biol. *Family Soricidae.*"

ᏓᎳᏍᏙᎬ [dahlsdogv] (n) "Night hawk.; biol. *Chordeiles minor.*"

ᏓᎳᏑᎳᎩᎠ [dalasulągi³?a] (vt) "He is taking off shoes."

ᏕᎦᎳᏑᎳᎩᎠ [degalą?sulągi³?a]

ᏚᎳᏑᎳᎩᏒᎢ [dulasulągi³sv²³?i]

ᏓᎳᏑᎳᎩᏍᎪᎢ [dalasulągi³sgo³?i]

ᏔᎳᏑᎳᎩ [talasulągi]

ᏧᎳᏑᎳᎩᏍᏗ [tsulasulągi³sdi]

... "ᏔᎳᏑᎳᎩ, ᎾᎿᏰᏃ ᏥᏙᎦ ᎦᎸᏉᏗᏳ ᎦᏙᎯ.
... Loose the sandal of thy feet, for the place in which thou hast stood is holy ground;
[ᎨᏥᏅᏏᏛ ᏄᎾᏛᏁᎵᏙᎸᎢ 7:33]

ᏓᎳᏑᎳᏍᎦ [dalą³suhlasga] (vt) "He is putting on shoes."

ᏕᎦᎳᏑᎳᏍᎦ [degaląsuhlasga]

ᏚᎳᏑᎳᏅᎢ [dulą³suhląnv²³?i]

ᏓᎳᏑᎳᏍᎪᎢ [dalą³suhlasgo³?i]

ᏔᎳᏑᎳᎦ [talą³suhlaga]

ᏧᎳᏑᎳᏗ [tsulą³suhldi]

ᏓᎳᏚᎯ [dąladųhi] (adj) "Sixteen."

ᏓᎴᎲᏍᎦ [dalehvsga] (vi) "He is rising from sitting."

ᏕᎦᎴᎥᏍᎦ [degalę?vsga]

ᏚᎴᏅᎢ [dulę?hnv²³?i]

ᏓᎴᎲᏍᎪᎢ [dalehvsgo³?i]

ᏔᎴᎲᎦ [talehvga]

—

ᏔᎴᎲᎦ, ᎮᏓ ᏂᎦᏅᎯᏒ ᎠᎴ ᎾᏯᏛᎥ ᎯᎠ ᎦᏙᎯ; ᏂᎯᏰᏃ ᏓᎬᏁᎵ.
rise, go up and down through the land, to its length, and to its breadth, for to thee I give it.'
[ᎼᏏ ᎢᎬᏱᏱ 13:17]

ᏓᎴᏍᎩᏍᎩ [dąlesgisgi] (n) "Monkey."

ᏓᎴᏴᏍᎩ [dąleyvsgi] (n) "Eastern newt.; Salamander.; biol. *Notophthalmus viridescens.*"

ᏓᎵᎷᎨᏍᎦ [dahlįlųkesga] (vi) "He is rocking a chair."

ᏕᎦᎵᎷᎨᏍᎦ [degą?lįlųkesga]

ᏚᎵᎷᎨᎲᎢ [duhlįlųkehv²³?i]

ᏓᎵᎷᎨᏍᎪᎢ [dahlįlųkesgo³?i]

ᏔᎵᎷᎬᎵ [tahlįlųkvli]

ᏧᎵᎷᎨᏗ [tsuhlįlųkehdi]

ᏓᎵᎾᏒᏍᏗᎭ [dahlįnąsvsdįha] (vi) "He is skating."

ᏕᎦᎵᎾᏒᏍᏗᎭ [degą?lįnąsvsdįha]

ᏚᎵᎾᏒᏍᏓᏅᎢ [duhlįnąsvsdąnv²³?i]

ᏓᎵᎾᏒᏍᏗᏍᎪᎢ [dahlįnąsvsdįsgo³?i]

ᏔᎵᎾᏒᏍᏓ [tahlįnąsvsda]

ᏧᎵᎾᏒᏍᏙᏗ [tsuhlįnąsvsdohdi]

ᏝᎻᏲᎥᏍᎦ [dahlini³gwanɂvsga] (vi) "He is kneeling."

ᏍᏍᏞᎻᏲᎥᏍᎦ [degaɂlini³gwanɂvsga]

ᏍᏞᎻᏲᎣᎢ [duhlini³gwanɂnv²³ɂi]

ᏝᎻᏲᎥᏍᎪᎢ [dahlini³gwanɂvsgo³ɂi]

ᏪᏞᎻᏲᎥᏍ [tahlini³gwanɂvga]

ᏗᏞᎻᏲᎯ [tsuhlini³gwanvdi]

ᎤᏬᏯᏃ ᎠᏗ ᏋᏬᏣ, ᏍᏞᎻᏲᎣᏱ ᏓᏍ ᎻᏍᏙ ᎠᎲᏍᏪᏬ ᎤᎵᏫᏫᏬᎣᏱ.
And these things having said, having bowed his knees, with them all, he did pray,
[ᏇᎶᏏᏙᏛ ᏋᏆᎵᏇᏉᎢ 20:36]

ᏝᏈᏃᏇ [dahlinoheha] (vt) "He is telephoning."

ᏍᏍᏈᏃᏇ [degaɂlinoheha]

ᏍᏈᏃᏇᎢ [duhlinohehlv²³ɂi]

ᏝᏈᏃᏇᎪᎢ [dahlinohesgo³ɂi]

ᏪᏈᏃᏌᏈ [tahlinoɂhvli]

ᏗᏈᏃᏇᎯ [tsuhlinohehdi]

ᏝᏈᏪᏍᏍ [dalitadega] (vi) "He is jumping up and down."

ᏍᎬᏈᏪᏍᏍ [degvlitadega]

ᏍᏈᏪᏍᎡᎢ [dulitadesv²³ɂi]

ᏝᏈᏪᏍᎪᎢ [dalitadego³ɂi]

———

———

ᏝᏈᏫᏯᎠ [daliyagi³ɂa] (vt) "He is taking off a sock."

ᏍᏍᏈᏫᏯᎠ [degaliyagi³ɂa]

ᏍᏈᏫᏯᎡᎢ [duliyagi³sv²³ɂi]

ᏝᏈᏫᏯᎪᎢ [daliyagi³sgo³ɂi]

ᏪᏈᏫᏯ [taliyagi]

ᏗᏈᏫᏯᎡᎯ [tsuliyagi³sdi]

ᏝᏈᎯᏲ [dalihyoha] (vt) "He is putting on a sock."

ᏍᏍᏈᎯᏲ [degaliɂyoha]

ᏍᏈᎯᏋᎢ [dulihyolv²³ɂi]

ᏝᏈᎯᏇᎢ [dalihyoho³ɂi]

ᏪᏈᎯᏍ [talihyoga]

ᏗᏈᎯᏲᎡᎯ [tsulihyosdi]

ᏝᎷᎨ [daloge] (n) "Hog sucker (plant).; biol. *Hypentelium nigricans.*"

ᏝᎷᎬ [dalogv] (n) "Rain crow.; Rain raven.; Storm crow.; Yellow-billed cuckoo.; biol. *Coccyzus Americanus.*"

ᏝᎷᎻ [daloni] (n) "Gall bladder."

ᏝᎶᎻᎮ ᎣᎤᎶᏍᏔ [dalonige unasdetsi] (n) "Yellow root.; Carolina yelloweyed grass.; biol. *Xyris caroliniana.*"

ᏝᎶᎻᎮ ᎣᏫᎠᎦᎢ [dalonige usgolvɂi] (adj) "Orange (color)."

ᏝᎶᎻᎮ ᏍᏪᎷᏫᏯ [dalonige galadisgi] (n) "Carrots."

ᏝᎶᎻᎮ ᏂᎶᏍᏉ [dalonige tsisdetsi] (n) "Weasel.; Long-tailed weasal.; Big stoat.; biol. *Mustela frenata.*"

ᏝᎧᏬᎠ [dahnawoɂa] (vt) "He is dressing."

ᏍᏍᎧᏬᎠ [degaɂnawoɂa]

ᏍᎧᏬᎢᎢ [duhnawoɂv²³ɂi]

ᏝᎧᏬᎪᎢ [dahnawosgo³ɂi]

ᏪᎧᏬᏨ [tahnawotsa]

ᏗᎧᏬᎡᎯ [tsuhnawosdi]

ᏝᏁᎦ [danega] (vt) "He is placing solid things in a row."

ᏍᏂᏁᎦ [detsinega]

ᏍᏁᏒᎢ [dunesv²³ɂi]

ᏝᏁᎪᎢ [danego³ɂi]

ᏂᏁᎦ [tinuga]

ᏗᏁᎡᎯ [tsuneysdi]

ᏝᏁᎶᏫᏲᏍ [daɂnelohvsga] (vt) "He is playing a game."

ᏍᏍᏁᎶᎢᏲᏍ [degaɂneloɂvsga]

ᏍᏁᎶᎣᎢ [duɂneloɂhnv²³ɂi]

ᏝᏁᎶᏫᏲᎪᎢ [daɂnelohvsgo³ɂi]

ᏪᏁᎶᏫᏍ [taɂnelohvga]

ᏗᏁᎶᎯ [tsuɂneldi]

ᏝᏁᎶᎯᏲ [daɂne³hldiha] (vt) "He is playing with."

ᏍᏍᏁᎶᎯᏲ [degaɂneɂldiha]

ᏍᏁᎶᏪᎣᎢ [duɂne³hltanv²³ɂi]

ᏝᏁᎶᎯᎪᎢ [daɂne³hldisgo³ɂi]

ᏪᏁᎶᏢ [taɂne³hlda]

ᏗᏁᎶᎥᎯ [tsuɂne³hldohdi]

ᏝᏁᏏᎯᏲ [danehdsdiha] (vt) "He is including."

ᏍᏍᏁᏏᎯᏲ [deganeɂdsdiha]

ᏍᏁᏏᎣᎢ [dunehdsdanv²³ɂi]

ᏝᏁᏏᎯᎪᎢ [danehdsdisgo³ɂi]

ᏪᏁᏏᏢ [tanehdsda]

ᏗᏁᏏᎥᎯ [tsunehdsdohdi]

ᏝᎻᏪᏫᏝᎾᎢ

ᏝᎻᏪᏫᏝᎾᎢ [danilasdadyɂi] (n) "Clan members."

ᏝᎣᏂᎦ [danynega] (vt) "He is placing flexible things into a row."

ᏍᏂᎣᏂᎦ [detsinynega]

ᏍᎣᏂᏒᎢ [dunynesv²³ɂi]

ᏝᎣᏂᎪᎢ [danynego³ɂi]

ᏂᎣᏋᏍ [tinynuga]

ᏗᎣᏂᎡᎥᎯ [tsunynysdi]

ᏓᏆᎳᎩᎠ [dakwąlagi^{3}ʔa] (vi) "He is snoring."

ᏕᏥᏆᎳᎩᎠ [detsįʔkwąlagi^{3}ʔa]
ᏚᏆᎳᎩᏒᎢ [dukwąlagi^{3}sv^{23}ʔi]
ᏓᏆᎳᎩᏍᎪᎢ [dakwąlagi^{3}sgo^{3}ʔi]
ᏘᏆᎳᎩᏣ [tįkwąlagi^{3}tsa]
ᏧᏆᎳᎩᏍᏗ [tsukwąlagi^{3}sdi]

ᏓᏆᎴᎷ [dagwąlelu] (n) "Car.; Automobile."

... ᏦᏩᏃ ᏚᏁᎴ ᏓᏆᎴᎷ ᎾᏍᎩᏯ ᏄᏪᏒ ᎤᏁᏨ ᏇᎵᏲ, ...
... and Joseph giveth waggons to them by the command of Pharaoh, ...
[ᎼᏏ ᎢᎬᏱᏱ 45:21]

ᏓᏍᎪᎸᎢᏍᏗᎭ [dasgǫlvʔįsdįha] (vt) "He is fading clothes."

ᏕᏥᏍᎪᎸᎢᏍᏗᎭ [detsįʔsgǫlvʔįsdįha]
ᏚᏍᎪᎸᎢᏍᏓᏅᎢ [dusgǫlvʔįsdąnv^{23}ʔi]
ᏓᏍᎪᎸᎢᏍᏗᏍᎪᎢ [dasgǫlvʔįsdįsgo^{3}ʔi]
ᏘᏍᎪᎸᎢᏍᏓ [tisgǫlvʔįsda]
ᏧᏍᎪᎸᎢᏍᏙᏗ [tsusgǫlvʔįsdohdi]

ᏓᏍᏆᎵᏗᎭ [dasgwahldįha] (vi) "He is running."

ᏕᏥᏍᏆᎵᏗᎭ [detsįʔsgwahldįha]
ᏚᏍᏆᎵᏔᏅᎢ [dusgwahltąnv^{23}ʔi]
ᏓᏍᏆᎵᏗᏍᎪᎢ [dasgwahldįsgo^{3}ʔi]
ᏘᏍᏆᎵᏓ [tisgwahlda]
ᏧᏍᏆᎵᏙᏗ [tsusgwahldohdi]

ᏓᏍᏆᏄᏥᎦ [dasgwąnuʔtsga] (vt) "He is sucking something. (Continously, like his thumb.)."

ᏕᏥᏍᏆᏄᏥᎦ [detsįʔsgwąnuʔtsga]
ᏚᏍᏆᏄᏨᎢ [dusgwąnuʔtsv^{23}ʔi]
ᏓᏍᏆᏄᏥᎪᎢ [dasgwąnuʔtsgo^{3}ʔi]
ᏘᏍᏆᏄᏣ [tisgwąnuʔtsa]
ᏧᏍᏆᏄᏥᏗ [tsusgwąnuʔtsdi]

ᏓᏍᏆᏗᎠ [dasgwadį^{3}a] (vt) "He is graduating.; He is ending it."

ᏕᏥᏍᏆᏗᎠ [detsįʔsgwadį^{3}a]
ᏚᏍᏆᏛᎢ [dusgwadv^{23}ʔi]
ᏓᏍᏆᏗᏍᎪᎢ [dasgwadįsgo^{3}ʔi]
ᏘᏍᏆᏓ [tisgwada]
ᏧᏍᏆᏗᏍᏗ [tsusgwatsdi]

ᏓᏐᎧ [dasǫka] (vt) "He is crossing."

ᏕᏥᏐᎧ [detsįsʔǫka]
ᏚᏐᏨᎢ [dusohtsv^{23}ʔi]
ᏓᏐᎪᎢ [dasǫko^{3}ʔi]
ᏘᏐᎩ [tįsǫki]
ᏧᏐᎯᏍᏗ [tsusǫhįsdi]

ᏓᏑᎴᎭ [dasu^{3}leha] (vt) "He is washing hands."

ᏕᎦᏑᎴᎭ [degąsu^{3}leha]
ᏚᏑᎴᎲᎢ [dusu^{3}lehv^{23}ʔi]
ᏓᏑᎴᏍᎪᎢ [dasu^{3}lesgo^{3}ʔi]
ᏔᏑᎴᎠ [tąsu^{3}lęa]
ᏧᏑᎴᏗ [tsusu^{3}lhdi]

ᏓᏑᏓᏆᎴᏆ [dąsudągwąlegwa] (n) "Chestnut.; Mountain oak.; biol. *Castanea*."

ᏓᏑᏫᏍᎦ [dasųhwį^{3}sga] (vi) "He is barking."

ᏕᎦᏑᏫᏍᎦ [degasųhwį^{3}sga]
ᏚᏑᏫᏒᎢ [dusųhwį^{3}sv^{23}ʔi]
ᏓᏑᏫᏍᎪᎢ [dasųhwį^{3}sgo^{3}ʔi]
ᏔᏑᏫ [tąsų^{3}hwi]
ᏧᏑᏫᏍᏗ [tsusųhwį^{3}sdi]

ᏓᏑᏫᏍᎦ [dasų^{3}hwisga] (vt) "He is painting."

ᏕᏥᏑᏫᏍᎦ [detsįʔsų^{3}hwisga]
ᏚᏑᏫᏒᎢ [dusų^{3}hwisv^{23}ʔi]
ᏓᏑᏫᏍᎪᎢ [dasų^{3}hwisgo^{3}ʔi]
ᏘᏑᏫ [tisų^{3}hwi]
ᏧᏑᏫᏍᏗ [tsusų^{3}hwisdi]

ᏓᏑᏯᎩᎠ [dasuyągį^{3}ʔa] (vt) "He is selecting."

ᏕᎦᏑᏯᎩᎠ [degąsuyągį^{3}ʔa]
ᏚᏑᏯᎩᏒᎢ [dusuyągį^{3}sv^{23}ʔi]
ᏓᏑᏯᎩᏍᎪᎢ [dasuyągį^{3}sgo^{3}ʔi]
ᏔᏑᏯᎩ [tąsuyągį]
ᏧᏑᏯᎩᏍᏗ [tsusuyągį^{3}sdi]

ᏓᏓᎴᎦ [dadąleʔga] (vi) "He is different from."

ᏕᎦᏓᎴᎦ [degadąleʔga]
ᏚᏓᎴᏨᎢ [dudąleʔtsv^{23}ʔi]
ᏓᏓᎴᎪᎢ [dadąleʔgo^{3}ʔi]
ᏔᏓᎴᎩ [tadąleʔgi]
ᏧᏓᎴᎢᏍᏗ [tsudąleʔisdi]

ᏓᏓᎾᎩᎠ [dada^{3}nągį^{3}ʔa] (vt) "He is picking up things that are alive."

ᎦᏥᏯᏓᎾᎩᎠ [gajiyada^{3}nągį^{3}ʔa]
ᏚᏓᎾᎩᏒᎢ [duda^{3}nągį^{3}sv^{23}ʔi]
ᏓᏓᎾᎩᏍᎪᎢ [dada^{3}nągį^{3}sgo^{3}ʔi]
ᎦᎯᏯᏓᎾᎩ [gahiyada^{3}nągį]
ᏧᏓᎾᎩᏍᏗ [tsuda^{3}nągį^{3}sdi]

ᏓᏓᎾᎩᎠ [dadạnạgi^{3}ʔa] (vi) "He is stretching."

ᏕᎦᏓᎾᎩᎠ [degadạnạgi^{3}ʔa]
ᏚᏓᎾᎩᏒᎢ [dudạnạgi^{3}sv^{23}ʔi]
ᏓᏓᎾᎩᏍᎪᎢ [dadạnạgi^{3}sgo^{3}ʔi]
ᏔᏓᎾᎩ [tadạnạgi]
ᏧᏓᎾᎩᏍᏗ [tsudạnạgi^{3}sdi]

ᏓᏓᏂᎸᎦ [dadạni^{3}lvga] (vt) "He is welcoming.; He is receiving."

ᏕᎦᏓᏂᎸᎦ [degadạni^{3}lvga]
ᏚᏓᏂᎸᏨᎢ [dudạni^{3}lvʔtsv^{23}ʔi]
ᏓᏓᏂᎸᎪᎢ [dadạni^{3}lvgo^{3}ʔi]
ᏔᏓᏂᎸᎩ [tadạni^{3}lvʔgi]
ᏧᏓᏂᎸᎢᏍᏗ [tsudạni^{3}lvʔisdi]

… ᎠᏎᏃ ᎥᏝ ᎩᎶ ᏱᏓᏓᏂᎸᎦ ᎾᏍᎩ ᎤᏃᎮᎸᎢ.
… and his testimony none receiveth;
[ᏣᏂ 3:32]

ᏓᏓᏄᎪᏍᎦ [dadahnugoh^{3}sga] (vt) "He is performing the scratching ritual.; He is receiving a vaccine."

ᏕᎦᏓᏄᎪᏍᎦ [degadạʔnugoh^{3}sga]
ᏚᏓᏄᎪᏒᎢ [dudahnugoh^{3}sv^{23}ʔi]
ᏓᏓᏄᎪᏍᎪᎢ [dadahnugoh^{3}sgo^{3}ʔi]
ᏔᏓᏄᎪᎵ [tadahnugọ^{3}li]
ᏧᏓᏄᎪᏍᏗ [tsudahnugoh^{3}sdi]

ᏓᏓᏑᎧᎵᎭ [dadasụ^{3}kạlịha] (vt) "He is cutting his nails."

ᏕᎦᏓᏑᎦᎵᎭ [degadasụʔgạlịha]
ᏚᏓᏑᎧᎸᎲᎢ [dudasụ^{3}kạlṿhv^{23}ʔi]
ᏓᏓᏑᎧᎵᏍᎪᎢ [dadasụ^{3}kạlịsgo^{3}ʔi]
ᏔᏓᏑᎧᎳ [tadasụ^{3}kạla]
ᏧᏓᏑᎧᎵᏗ [tsudasụ^{3}kahldi]

ᏓᏓᏛᏂᎭ [dadadvhnịha] (vi) "He is boxing.; He is fist fighting."

ᏕᎦᏓᏛᏂᎭ [degadadṿʔnịha]
ᏚᏓᏛᏂᎸᎢ [dudadvhnịlv^{23}ʔi]
ᏓᏓᏛᏂᎰᎢ [dadadvhnịho^{3}ʔi]
ᏔᏓᏛᎱᎦ [tadadṿhụga]
ᏧᏓᏛᏂᏍᏗ [tsudadvhnsdi]

ᏓᏕᎦ [dadega] (vt) "He is placing long things into a row."

ᏕᏥᏕᎦ [detsịdega]
ᏚᏕᏒᎢ [dudesv^{23}ʔi]
ᏓᏕᎪᎢ [dadego^{3}ʔi]
ᏘᏚᎦ [tịduga]
ᏧᏕᎥᏍᏗ [tsudeṿsdi]

ᏓᏕᏲᎲᏍᎦ [dadehyohvsga] (vt) "He is teaching."

ᏕᎦᏕᏲᎲᏍᎦ [degadẹʔyohvsga]
ᏚᏕᏲᏅᎢ [dudehyohnv^{23}ʔi]
ᏓᏕᏲᎲᏍᎪᎢ [dadehyohvsgo^{3}ʔi]
ᏔᏕᏲᎲᎦ [tadehyohvga]
ᏧᏕᏲᏗ [tsudehyohdi]

… ᎠᎴ ᎾᏍᎩ ᏄᏍᏕᏍᏗ ᏓᏕᏲᎲᏍᎨᏍᏗ, ᎦᎸᏉᏗᏳ ᎠᎪᏎᎮᏍᏗ ᎦᎸᎳᏗ ᎡᎯ ᎤᎬᏫᏳᎯ ᎨᏒᎢ.
… but whoever may do and may teach [them], he shall be called great in the reign of the heavens.
[ᎹᏚ 5:19]

ᏓᏖᏍᏗᎭ [dahtesdịha] (vt) "He is ironing clothes."

ᏕᏥᏖᏍᏗᎭ [detsịʔtesdịha]
ᏚᏖᏍᏓᏅᎢ [duhtesdạnv^{23}ʔi]
ᏓᏖᏍᏗᏍᎪᎢ [dahtesdịsgo^{3}ʔi]
ᏘᏖᏍᏓ [tihtesda]
ᏧᏖᏍᏙᏘ [tsuhtesdọti]

ᏓᏗᎦᏍᎦ [dadiksga] (vi) "He is defecating."

ᏕᎦᏗᎦᏍᎦ [degadiksga]
ᏚᏗᎦᏒᎢ [dudiksv^{23}ʔi]
ᏓᏗᎦᏍᎪᎢ [dadiksgo^{3}ʔi]
ᏔᏗᎦ [tadiga]
ᏧᏗᎦᏍᏗ [tsudiksdi]

ᏓᏙᏂᎭ [dadoniha] (vi) "He is conjuring.; He is witching."

ᏕᎦᏙᏂᎠ [degadonịʔa]
ᏚᏙᏅᎥᎢ [dudonṿʔv^{23}ʔi]
ᏓᏙᏂᏍᎪᎢ [dadonisgo^{3}ʔi]
ᏔᏙᎾ [tadona]
ᏧᏙᏂᏗ [tsudonhdi]

ᏓᏛᎯᏍᏗᎭ [datvhịsdịha] (vt) "He is raising children.; He is rearing them."

ᏕᎦᏛᎯᏍᏗᎭ [degadʔvhịsdịha]
ᏚᏛᎯᏍᏔᏅᎢ [dutvhịstạnv^{23}ʔi]
ᏓᏛᎯᏍᏗᏍᎪᎢ [datvhịsdịsgo^{3}ʔi]
ᏔᏛᎯᏍᏓ [tatvhịsda]
ᏧᏛᎯᏍᏙᏗ [tsutvhịsdohdi]

ᏓᏣᎪᏍᎦ [datsạgosga] (vt) "He is scratching."

ᏕᎦᏣᎪᏍᎦ [degatsạgọʔsga]
ᏚᏣᎪᏒᎢ [dutsạgosv^{23}ʔi]
ᏓᏣᎪᏍᎪᎢ [datsạgosgo^{3}ʔi]
ᏔᏣᎪᎳ [tatsạgola]
ᏧᏣᎪᏍᏗ [tsutsạgosdi]

ᏓᏥᎶᏍᏗᎭ [da?tsilo³sdiha] (vt) "He is drawing."

ᏕᎦᏥᎶᏍᏗᎠ [dega?tsilo³sdi?a]

ᏚᏥᎶᏍᏓᏅᎢ [du?tsilo³sdạnv²³?i]

ᏓᏥᎶᏍᏗᏍᎪᎢ [da?tsilo³sdisgo³?i]

ᏔᏥᎶᏍᏗᏍᏓ [ta?tsilo³sdisda]

ᏧᏥᎶᏅᏗ [tsu?tsilo³stdi]

�джᎶᏍᏓᎣᏍ ᏓᏥᎶᏍᏗᎭ Ꮓ ᎠᎦᏟᏍ ᎠᏁᏍᏫ.
The man is drawing and painting the picture.
[King pg 112]

ᏓᏨᏍᏗᎭᏍᎦ [datsvstah³sga] (vt) "He is turning on a light."

ᏕᏥᏨᏍᏗᎭᏍᎦ [detsịtsvstah³sga]

ᏚᏨᏍᏬᎣᎢ [dutsvsta³nv²³?i]

ᏓᏨᏍᏗᎭᏍᎪᎢ [datsvstah³sgo³?i]

ᏗᏨᏍᏗᎦ [tịtsvsta³ga]

ᏧᏨᏍᏬᏗ [tsutsvstdi]

ᏓᎤᏍᎦ [dawisga] (vt) "He is planting seeds."

ᏕᏥᎤᏍᎦ [detsịwị?sga]

ᏚᎣᏏᎢ [duwisv²³?i]

ᏓᎤᏍᎪᎢ [dawisgo³?i]

ᏗᎤᎯ [tịwihi]

ᏧᎤᏬᏗ [tsuwisdi]

… ᏲᎦ ᎢᏣᏬᏗ, ᏰᏍᏫ-ᎢᏣᏬᏗ �‎Ꭱ ᎤᎣᏔ ᏔᎯᏫᏗ ᏚᎣᏏᎢ; …
…'A certain one had a fig-tree planted in his vine-yard, …
[MᏍ 13:6]

ᏓᏯᎨᎩᏍᎦ [dayakeksga] (vt) "He is peeling."

ᏕᏥᏯᎨᎩᏍᎦ [detsịyakeksga]

ᏚᏯᎨᏍᏛᎢ [duyakeksv²³?i]

ᏓᏯᎨᎩᏍᎪᎢ [dayakeksgo³?i]

ᏗᏯᎨᏣ [tịyakegtsa]

ᏧᏯᎨᏍᏗ [tsuyakeksdi]

ᏓᏯᎧᎳᏍᎦ [daykahlasga] (vt) "He is assembling.; He is stacking."

ᏕᏥᏤ?ᎦᎳᏍᎦ [detsiyẹ?gahlasga]

ᏚᏯᎧᎳᏅᎢ [duykahlạnv²³?i]

ᏓᏯᎧᎳᏍᎪᎢ [daykahlasgo³?i]

ᏗᏯᎧᎳᎦ [tịykahlaga]

ᏧᏯᎧᎵᏗ [tsuykahldi]

Ꮣ�yᎥᎩᎠ [da¹yv³gị?a] (vt) "He is tickling him."

ᏕᏥ?ᎤᎥᎩᎠ [detsi¹?yv³gị?a]

ᏚᏯᎥᎩᏍᎢ [du¹yv³gịsv²³?i]

ᏓᏯᎥᎩᏍᎪᎢ [da¹yv³gịsgo³?i]

ᏗᏯᎥᎩ [ti¹?yv³gi]

ᏧᏯᎥᎩᏍᏗ [tsu¹yv³gịsdi]

W

ᏩᏩ [tạla] (n) "Oak.; biol. *Quercus L.*"

ᏩᏩᏚ [tạladu] (n) "Cricket.; biol. *Gryllus assimilis.*"

ᏩᏩᏚᎠ [tahldụhi] (adj) "Twelve."

ᏩᎵ [tali] (adj) "Two."

ᏩᎵ ᏔᏍ ᎤᎤ Ꭴ?ᎤᎵᏍᎣ ᏴᏐ ᏕᏎᏴᏬᎵᎠE,
Two geese are hearing the dog making music,
[ᏳᏯ ᏩᎵᏗ ᏗᎯᎮᏙᎠ ᎴᏍᏝᏙᏗ]

ᏩᎵᏗ [talịne] (n) "Tuesday."

ᏩᎵᏍᎪᎯ᎐ [tahlsgohi] (adj) "Twenty."

ᏩᎵᏍᎪᎯ Ꭽ᎐ [tahlsgo sogwu] (adj) "Twenty-one."

ᏩᎵᏥᏩ [talịtsgwa] (adj) "Two hundred."

ᏩᎷᎩᏍᎩ [tạlugisgi] (n) "Tin.; Tin can.; Bucket."

ᏩᎷᏣ [tạlutsa] (n) "Basket."

… ᎠᏓ ᎣᏬᏴ ᏕᏬᏯᎳᎠᎬᏴ, Ꭰ ᎡᎯᏫ? ᎨᎢ ᏩᎷᏣ ᏕᏍ ᎤᎯᎴᎬ ᎴᏍᏣᏗ ᏝᏘᏃᎲᏛᏴ;
… 'I also [am] in a dream, and lo, three baskets of white bread [are] on my head,
[ᏛᏏ ᎢᎬᎥᎰ 40:16]

ᏩᎾᏏ [tansi] (n) "Tennessee."

ᏩᏁᎦ�wᎢ [tạnegwa] (n) "Mule (animal).; biol. *Equus asinus x Equus caballus.*"

ᏩᏘᎵ [tagwali] (n) "Bear grass.; Spiderwort.; Virginia spiderwort.; biol. *Tradescantia virginiana.*"

ᏩᎤᏗ [tạwodi] (n) "Hawk.; biol. *Buteo spp.*"

ᏩᎤᏗ ᎡᏘ [tạwod? egwa] (n) "Red-tailed hawk.; biol. *Buteo jamaicensis.*"

ᏩᏯ [taya] (n) "Cherry.; biol. *Prunus spp.*"

ᏩᏯ ᎢᏃᎮᏘ [tayạ ịnạge?i] (n) "Wild cherry.; biol. *Prunus pensylvanica.*"

ᏩᎦᎤᎵᎵ [tạyuhali] (n) "Fence lizard.; Pine lizard.; biol. *Sceloporus undulatus.*"

Ꮝ

ᏕᎦᎵᏗ [dẹgahldi] (n) "Bag.; Cloth sack."

ᏍᏆᎬᎨᎵ [degalokeli] (vi) "He is going across a hill."

ᏛᎢᎬᎨᎵ [detsilokeli]

ᏕᎬᎨᎣᏘ [dulokelęsv²³ʔi]

ᏍᏆᎬᎨᎵᏐᎢᎢ [degalokeliso³ʔi]

ᏠᎬᎨᎷᏍ [tilokeluʔga]

ᏧᎬᎨᎠᏍᎠ [tsulokelysdi]

ᏍᏍᎾᎪᏍᎠᎶ [degantsosdiha] (vt) "He is pickling."

ᏛᎢᎾᎪᏍᎠᎠᎠ [detsintsosdiʔa]

ᏎᎾᎪᏍᎳᎣᎢ [duntsostanv²³ʔi]

ᏍᏍᎾᎪᏍᎠᎠᏍᎪᎢ [degantsosdisgo³ʔi]

ᏠᎾᎪᏍᎳ [tintsosda]

ᏧᎾᎪᏍᎠᏫᎠ [tsuntsostdi]

ᏍᏍᏁᎥᏙᏍᏰᎶ [deganeh³sgwatdiha] (vt) "He is tumbling it end over end."

ᏛᎢᏁᎥᏙᏍᏰᎶ [detsineʔsgwatdiha]

ᏎᎥᏙᏍᏏᎣᎢ [duneh³sgwattanv²³ʔi]

ᏍᏍᏁᎥᏙᏍᏰᎠᏍᎪᎢ [deganeh³sgwatdisgo³ʔi]

ᏠᎥᏙᏍᏰᎳ [tineh³sgwatda]

ᏧᏁᎥᏙᏍᏰᏫᎠ [tsuneh³sgwatdohdi]

ᏍᏍᎯ [dega³ni] (vt) "He is carrying it (something long)."

ᏛᎢᎯ [detsi³ni]

ᏎᎾᏘ [du³nęsv²³ʔi]

ᏍᏍᎯᏐᎢ [dega³niso³ʔi]

ᏠᎾᏍ [ti³nuʔga]

ᏧᎣᎠᎠ [tsu³nysdi]

Ꮎ, ᏠᎾᏍ ᏧᎬᏈᏐᎠᏫᎠᎠ, ᏏᏃᏟ ᎠᎠ ᏍᎬᏟᎠ, ᎠᎠ ᎢᎾᎢ ᎣᎬᎠ, ᎠᎣᏃ ᎣᏍᎣᎠ ᎠᏯᏂᎦᏍᎷᏍ;
and now, take up, I pray thee, thy instruments, thy quiver, and thy bow, and go out to the field, and hunt for me provision,
[ᎦᏅ TEᎥᏍ 27:3]

ᏍᏍᏄᎳᏏᎳ [deganulagdʔa] (vt) "He is shucking corn."

ᏛᎢᏄᎳᏏᎳ [detsinulagdʔa]

ᏎᏄᎳᏏᏨᎢ [dunulagtsv²³ʔi]

ᏍᏍᏄᎳᏏᎳᏍᎪᎢ [deganulagdsgo³ʔi]

ᏠᏄᎳᏏᎠ [tinulagd³i]

ᏧᏄᎳᏏᎠᏫᎠ [tsunulagdʔsdi]

ᏍᏍᏫᎯᎣᎠᏰᎶ [degasu³ʔyohonhdiha] (vt) "He is sliding it."

ᏛᎢᏫᎯᎣᎠᏰᎶ [detsisʔu³yohonhdiha]

ᏎᏫᎯᎣᎣᎢ [dusu³yohonhtanv²³ʔi]

ᏍᏍᏫᎯᎣᎠᏰᎠᏍᎪᎢ [degasu³yohonhdisgo³ʔi]

ᏠᏫᎯᎣᏤ [tisu³yohonhda]

ᏧᏫᎯᎣᏫᎠ [tsusu³yohonhdohdi]

ᏍᏍᏞᏛᏫᎩᎠ [dega³danolagiʔa] (vt) "He is stringing beans."

ᏛᎢᏞᏛᏫᎩᎠ [detsi³danolagiʔa]

ᏎᏞᏛᏫᎩᏘ [du³danolagisv²³ʔi]

ᏍᏍᏞᏛᏫᎩᏍᎪᎢ [dega³danolagisgo³ʔi]

ᏠᏞᏛᏫᎩ [ti³danolagi]

ᏧᏞᏛᏫᎩᏍᎠ [tsu³danolagisdi]

ᏍᏍᏫᏚᎤᎣᏍ [dektą³gwalesga] (vt) "He is making pottery."

ᏛᎢᏫᏚᎤᎣᏍ [detsiʔtą³gwalesga]

ᏎᏫᏚᎤᎢᎢ [duhtą³gwalehlv²³ʔi]

ᏍᏍᏫᏚᎤᎣᎠᎢ [dektą³gwalesgo³ʔi]

ᏠᏫᏚᎤᏍ [tihtą³gwalega]

ᏧᏫᏚᎤᎣᎠ [tsuhtą³gwalesdi]

ᏍᏍᏎᏚᎥᎠᏍ [degaduhvsga] (vt) "He is baking bread."

ᏛᎢᏏᎢᎥᎠᏍ [detsiduʔvsga]

ᏎᏎᎣᎢ [duʔduhnv²³ʔi]

ᏍᏍᏎᏚᎥᎠᎢ [degaduhvsgo³ʔi]

ᏠᏎᏚᎥᏍ [tiduhvga]

ᏧᏎᎠ [tsuʔtdi]

ᏍᏍᎬᎯᎣᎲᏰᎶ [degayuyohohndiha] (vi) "He is driving recklessly fast on dangerous rural or mountain roads.; He is rolling or skidding logs downhill.; He is ball-hooting."

ᏛᎢᎬᎯᎣᎲᏰᎶ [detsiyuyoʔohndiha]

ᏎᎬᎯᎣᎣᎢ [duyuyohohntanv²³ʔi]

ᏍᏍᎬᎯᎣᎲᏰᎠᎢ [degayuyohohndisgo³ʔi]

ᏠᎬᎯᎣᏤ [tiyuyohohnda]

ᏧᎬᎯᎣᏫᎠ [tsuyuyohohndohdi]

ᏎᎠ [deka] (n) "Frog."

ᏎᎠᏃᎩᎠ [dekąnogiʔa] (vt) "He is singing."

ᏛᎢᏃᎩᎠ [detsiʔnogiʔa]

ᏎᏃᎩᏘ [duhnogisv²³ʔi]

ᏎᎠᏃᎩᏍᎪᎢ [dekąnogisgo³ʔi]

ᏠᏃᎩ [tihnogi]

ᏧᏃᎩᏍᎠ [tsuhnogisdi]

… ᏯᎬ ᎣᏍᎰᏍᎠ ᎣᎵᎣᏖᏍᎠ ᏎᎠᏃᎩᏫᎰᏍᎠ.
… is any of good cheer? let him sing psalms;
[ᎯᎲ 5:13]

103

ᏕᎨᏲᎲᏍᎦ [dekẹyọhvsga] (vt) "He is teaching (ehyohv)."

ᏕᎨᏲᎲᏍᎦ [degẹʔyọhvsga]

ᏚᏪᏲᏅᎢ [duhwẹyọʔhnv²³ʔi]

ᏕᎨᏲᎲᏍᎪᎢ [dekẹyọhvsgo³ʔi]

ᏖᏲᎲᎦ [tehyọhvga]

ᏧᏪᏲᏗ [tsuhwẹyọʔhdi]

ᎿᏉᏃ ᎤᏩᏒ ᎤᏤᎵᎪᎯ ᎤᎷᏨ ᏧᏂᎳᏫᏍᏗᏱ ᏚᏪᏲᏅᎩ; ᎾᏍᎩ ᎢᏳᏍᏗ ᎤᏂᏍᏆᏂᎪᏒᎩ, …
and having come to his own country, he was teaching them in their synagogue, so that they were astonished, …
[ᎹᏚ 13:54]

ᏕᎪᎠ [degoʔa] (vt) "He is naming him."

ᏕᏥᏲᎠ [detsiyoʔa]

ᏚᏬᎥᎢ [duwoʔv²³ʔi]

ᏕᎪᏍᎪᎢ [degosgo³ʔi]

ᏘᏲᏣ [tiyotsa]

ᏧᏬᏍᏗ [tsuwosdi]

ᏕᎫᏣᎾᎩᎠ [degutsąngį³ʔa] (vi) "He is stretching."

ᏕᎫᏣᎾᎩᎠ [degutsąngį³ʔa]

ᏚᏭᏣᎾᎩᏒᎢ [duwutsąngį³sv²³ʔi]

ᏕᎫᏣᎾᎩᏍᎪᎢ [degutsąngį³sgo³ʔi]

ᏚᏣᎾᎩ [tutsąngį]

ᏧᏭᏣᎾᎩᏍᏗ [tsuwutsąngį³sdi]

ᏕᎬᎾᎦᎳᏬᎣᎠ [degvnągąląwọoʔa] (vt) "He is pruning a tree."

ᏕᎬᎾᎦᎳᏬᎣᎠ [degvnągąląwọoʔa]

ᏚᏩᎾᎦᎳᏬᎣᎥᎢ [duwanągąląwọoʔv²³ʔi]

ᏕᎬᎾᎦᎳᏬᎣᏍᎪᎢ [degvnągąląwọosgo³ʔi]

ᏛᎾᎦᎳᏬᎣᏣ [tvnągąląwọotsa]

ᏧᏩᎾᎦᎳᏬᎣᏍᏗ [tsuwanągąląwọosdi]

ᏕᎬᏍᎦ [degvhsga] (vt) "He is putting it (something flexible) into a liquid."

ᏕᎬᏍᎦ [degvʔhsga]

ᏚᏩᏅᎢ [duwahʔnv²³ʔi]

ᏕᎬᏍᎪᎢ [degvhsgo³ʔi]

ᏛᎲᎦ [tvhvʔga]

ᏧᏩᏗ [tsuwahdi]

ᏕᎬᏗᏰᎠ [degvdi³yẹʔa] (vt) "He is washing dishes."

ᏕᎬᏗᏰᎠ [degvdi³yẹʔa]

ᏚᏩᏗᏰᎥᎢ [duwadi³yẹʔv²³ʔi]

ᏕᎬᏗᏰᏍᎪᎢ [degvdi³yẹsgo³ʔi]

ᏛᏗᏯ [tvdi³ya]

ᏧᏩᏗᏰᏗ [tsuwadi³yedi]

ᏕᎬᏣᎳᏍᎦ [degvchąlah³sga] (vt) "He is frying meat."

ᏕᎬᏣᎳᏍᎦ [degvtsąʔlah³sga]

ᏚᏩᏣᎳᏅᎢ [duwachąlą³nv²³ʔi]

ᏕᎬᏣᎳᏍᎪᎢ [degvchąlah³sgo³ʔi]

ᏛᏣᎳᎦ [tvchąla³ga]

ᏧᏩᏣᎳᏗ [tsuwachąldi]

ᏕᎷᎨ [dehlụge] (adj) "Purple."

ᏕᎷᏱ [dehluyi] (n) "June."

ᏕᏣᎵᏗᎾᎢ [detsahldihnąʔi] (n) "Your family."

ᏕᏩ [dewa] (n) "Flying squirrel.; biol. *Glaucomys volans.*"

Ꮦ

ᏖᎸᎳᏗ [tẹlṿ³ladi] (n) "Fox grapes.; Wild grapes.; biol. *Vitis labrusca.*"

… ᎠᎴ ᎠᏥᎸᏍᎬᎩ; ᎠᎴ ᏖᎸᎳᏗ ᎤᏅᎾᏏᏛ ᎤᎾᏓᏛᏅᎩ;
… gone up hath its blossom, its clusters have ripened grapes;
[ᎼᏏ ᎢᎬᏱᏱ 40:10]

Ꮧ

ᏗᎤᏓᏍᎦ [dįʔụdasga] (n) "A bush."

ᏗᎦᎦᎸᏅᎯᏓ [digaʔgąlvnṿhida] (n) "Weeping willow.; biol. *Salix babylonica.*"

ᏗᎦᎦᏛᎾᎯᏛ [digagdṿnąhidv] (n) "Sharp-shinned hawk.; Long tailed sharp-shinned hawk.; biol. *Accipiter striatus.*"

ᏗᎦᎳᏫᎢᏍᏗ [dįgąlawį'isdi] (n) "Meeting."

ᏗᎦᎳᏫᎢᏍᏗ [dįgąlawįʔįsdi] (n) "Church.; Council house."

ᏗᎦᎸᏌᏓᏗᏍᏗᎯᏍᎩ [dįgąlṿsądądįsdįhįsgi] (n) "Movie projector."

ᏗᎦᎸᏫᏍᏓᏁᏗ [dįgąlvhwįsdąndi] (n) "A place of work.; A business."

ᏗᎦᏅᏐᏍᏙᏗ [dįganṿsọsdohdi] (n) "Brake (on a vehicle)."

ᏗᎦᏘ [dikti] (n) "Shepherd."

ᏗᎦᏚᎲᏱ [digadụhvʔy] (n) "Town at a distance."

ᏗᎧᏃᎩᏍᏙᏗ [dįkąnọgisdohdi] (n) "Hymn book."

ᏗᎨᏛᏍᏗ [dįgedvsdi] (n) "Post."

ᏗᎩᏥ [dįgįtsi] (n) "Tadpole.; Pollywog."

ᏗᎪᏓᎳᏗ [dįkodąldi] (n) "Pepper (black)."

ᏗᎪᏪᎵᏍᎩ [dịgohwelisgi] (n) "Writer."

> ᏴᏃᏁ ᎢᎦᏃᏗ ᏗᎪᏪᎵᏍᎩ ᎤᎷᏅᎥᏔ, ᎠᏗ ᏓᏉᎳᏕᎢᎢ; ᏪᏍᏫᏬᏬᏯ ᏞᎪᏥᏣᏆᏉ ᏂᏏ ᏈᏉᏔ.
> and a certain <u>scribe</u> having come, said to him, 'Teacher, I will follow thee wherever thou mayest go;' [ᎦᏍ 8:19]

ᏗᎪᏪᎶᎥᏗ [dịgohwelo?di] (n) "Pencil.; Pen."

ᏗᎫᏦᏴᎪᏗ [dịgutsạnagisdi] (n) "Accordian."

ᏗᎬᏴᏍᎪᏯ [dịgki?osgi] (n) "Washing machine."

ᏗᎬᏓꞪᎪᏗ [dịgvleyọsdi] (n) "Patchwork (for quilt)."

ᏗᎬᏂᎨᎢᎢ [dịgvnịge?i] (n) "Black oak.; biol. *Quercus velutina.*"

ᏗᏪᏏᎶᎪᏯ ᎡᎬᎢ [dịlagạlisgi egwa] (n) "White willow.; biol. *Salix alba.*"

ᏗᏪᏏᎶᎪᏯ ᎤᏍᏗ [dịlagạlịsgi usdi] (n) "Mountain willow.; biol. *Salix eastwoodiae.*"

ᏗᏪᏬᏚᏈᏗ [dihlsgahldi] (n) "Ball sticks."

ᏗᏓᎢ [dịlegwa] (n) "Kingbird.; Eastern kingbird.; biol. *Tyrannus tyrannus.*"

ᏗᏓᎬꞪᎬ [dileyesụ?lo] (n) "Gloves."

ᏗᎵ [dili] (n) "Skunk.; Striped skunk.; biol. *Mephitis mephitis.*"

> ᎠᎦᎪᏗ ᏑᏁᎪ. ᏅᏆᎪᏯ. ᏰᏌᏁᎥᏛ: Ꭰ) ᏬᏬ, Ꮳ) ᎭᎬᎵ, Ꮤ) ᏗᎵ.
> He is holding something. Choose it. Hand him: a) Coffee, b) Squirrels, c) <u>Skunks</u>.
> [ᎬᏪᏯ ᎤᏰᏁ ᏗᎭᎭᏉᎠ ᏗᏍᎭᏉᏗ]

ᏗᎵᏏᎶᎪᏯ [dilịgalịsgi] (n) "Pussywillow.; American willow.; biol. *Salix discolor.*"

ᏗᎵᏃᏓᏗ [dihlịnohehdi] (n) "Telephone."

ᏗᎵᏬᏙᏗ [dihlsdohdi] (n) "Scissors."

ᏗᎵᏪᏬᎪᏙᏗ [dihltạwosdodi] (n) "Comb."

ᏗᎾᎵᎥᏥ [dịnahlịnvtsi] (n) "Brothers."

> ᏅᏬᏓᎵᎥᏥ [ọsdahlịnvtsi]

ᏗᎾᏓᏍᎪᏯ [dihndasdasgi] (n) "Blue violet.; biol. *Viola sororia.*"

ᏗᎾᏓᏍᎪᏯ ᎤᎯᏁᏓ [dihndasdasgị ụnịnega] (n) "White violet.; Sweet white violet.; biol. *Viola blanda.*"

ᏗᎾᏛᏁᎵᏍᎬᎢᏔ [dinạdvnelịsgv?i] (n) "Festival.; Show.; Drama."

ᏗᎵᎳᏫ [dịnihlọwi] (n) "Twins."

ᏗᏂᏬᏍᏙᏗ [dihnỵwo³sdohdi] (n) "Bed clothes."

ᏗᏂᏬ ᏗᎧᎭᏲᏗᏍᎪᏯ [dihnỵwọ dịkahyọdịhsgi] (n) "Clothes dryer."

ᏗᏎᏍᏗ [dịsesdi] (n) "Numbers."

ᏗᏓᏂᏏᏁᎩ [dịdansịnegi] (n) "Sled."

ᏗᏓᎾᏫᏓ [dịdanạwida] (n) "Cross."

ᏗᏓᏂᏐᏗᏳ

ᏗᏓᏂᏐᏗᏳ [dịdanịsodiyu] (n) "Cemetary."

ᏗᏓᏂᏐᏗᏳ [dịdanịsohdiyu] (n) "Cemetary."

ᏗᏓᏂᏨᏍᎩ [dịdahnịtsịsgi] (n) "Policeman."

ᏗᏓᏅᎢᏔ [dịdanv?i] (n) "Store at a distance."

ᏗᏓᏛᏅᏬᏬᏙᏗ [dịdahnỵwohdohdi] (n) "Treatment (medical)."

ᏗᏓᏍᏙᏰᏍᎩ [dịdạsdoyẹsgi] (n) "Barber."

ᏗᏓᏍᏚᏗᏳ [dịdạsdudiyu] (n) "Jail."

ᏗᏓᏥᎶᏍᏗᏍᎩ [dịdạtsilosdisgi] (n) "Camera.; Photographer."

ᏗᏓᏬᏍᎩ [dịdạwosgi] (n) "Baptist."

> ᏪᎠᎦ ᎤᎷᏛ ᎨᏂ ᏗᏓᏬᏍᎩ ᎠᏈᏥᏘᏬᏚᏄ ᏔᏈ ᏧᏗᏅ,
> And in those days cometh John the <u>Baptist</u>, proclaiming in the wilderness of Judea,
> [ᎦᏍ 3:1]

ᏗᏕᎶᎬᏪᏍᎩ [didẹlogwasgi] (n) "Student.; Disciple."

> ᏗᏕᎶᎬᏪᏍᎩ ᎥᏂ ᎤᏟ ᏴᏫᎯᏋᏬᏘ ᏸᏅᏑᏫ ᏧᏪᏂᏬᏬᏯ, ᏗᏤ ᎠᏈᎤᏊᎳᎪᏗ ᎥᏂ ᎤᏟ ᏴᏫᎯᏋᏬᏘ ᏸᏅᏑᏫ ᎤᏬᏅᏚᏫᎠ.
> 'A <u>disciple</u> is not above the teacher, nor a servant above his lord;
> [ᎦᏍ 10:24]

ᏗᏕᎶᎬᏬᏗ [didẹlkwạsdi] (n) "School."

ᏗᏕᏍᏗᏓᏁᎬᎢ [dịdesdịdạnegwa] (n) "Castor oil beans."

ᏗᏕᎯᏬᏍᎩ [didehyọhỵsgi] (n) "Teacher."

> … ᏑᏴᏃ ᏗᏴᏆᏬᏍᎩ ᎠᏍᏊ ᏕᎭᏯᏏᏬᎠ ᏗᏤ ᏕᎭᏅᏚ ᏔᏨᏫ ᏘᏗᏋᎶᏏᏚᏬᏅᏑ?
> … 'Wherefore with the tax-gatherers and sinners doth <u>your teacher</u> eat?'
> [ᎦᏍ 9:11]

ᏗᏖᏍᏗ [ditẹsdi] (n) "Iron (to iron clothes with)."

ᏗᏘᏲᎯᎯ [dịtiyohịhi] (n) "Lawyer."

ᏗᏙᎵᏍᎩ [dịdolesgi] (n) "Arthritis.; Rheumatism."

ᏗᏥᎶᏍᏓᏄᎠ [dịtsịlosdạnvhi] (n) "Picture.; Photograph."

ᏗᏪᏓᎶᎯ [dịwedạlohi] (n) "White-breasted nuthatch.; biol. *Sitta carolinensis.*"

ᏗᎭᏴᎩᏍᏗ [dihyvgịsdi] (n) "Banjo."

Ꮖ

ᏆᎵ [tili] (n) "Chestnut.; American chestnut.; biol. *Castanea dentata.*"

ᏆᎵ ᎠᏇᏍ ᏍᏍ [tịlị ạsuyị gadu] (n) "Chestnut bread."

ᎢᏅ [tina] (n) "Lice.; biol. *Family Aphididae.*"

> "ᎢᏅ ᎻᏍ ᎢᏅ ᏗᎬᏔᏈ".
> "Come here awhile, let me kill the <u>lice</u>".
> [King pg 121]

Ꮣ

ᏙᏘᎪᏗ [do?iyụhsdi] (pt) "What."

ᏙᎩᏏ [dogsi] (n) "Muscovy duck.; biol. *Cairina moschata.*"

ᏙᎩᎠᏍᏗ [togiyasdi] (n) "Asheville, N.C."

ᏙᎯᏥᏆ [tohịtsgwa] (n) “Grasshopper.; biol. *Order Orthoptera.*”

ᏙᎳᏗᏳᏍᏗ [tohldịyụsdi] (n) “Spiny amaranth.; biol. *Amaranthus spinosus.*”

ᏙᎳᏥ [dolạtsi] (n) “Water oak.; biol. *Quercus nigra.*”

ᏙᎳᏥ [tolạtsi] (n) “Grasshopper.; biol. *Order Orthoptera.*”

ᏙᎴᏓ [toleda] (n; gn) “Burlap sack.; Bear nettle.”

ᏙᏂ [doni] (pt) “Why.”

ᏙᏌ [dọsa] (n) “Gnats.; biol. *Simulium meridionale.*”

> “ᏙᏌ ᎤᏂᏣᏔ” ᎠᏗᏍᎨᎢ ᎦᎾ ᎡᏩᏂᎸᎢ.
> “Lots of gnats”, she was saying as she was being hit by the bullets.
> [King pg 121]

ᏙᏌᎾ [dọsạna] (n) “Turnip.; biol. *Brassica rapa.*”

ᏙᏒᎾ ᎢᎾᎨ ᎡᎯ [dosṿnạ ịnạge ẹhi] (n) “Jack-in-the-pulpit.; Wild turnip.; biol. *Arisaema triphyllum.*”

ᏙᏒᏓᎵ [dosṿdali] (n) “Ant.”

ᏙᏓᏆᏍᎬᎢ [dodạgwasgvʔi] (n) “Sunday.”

ᏙᏓᏈᏕᏂ [dọdạgwịdeni] (n) “Saturday.”

ᏙᏓᏉᏅᎯ [dodạgwonṿhi] (n) “Monday.”

ᏙᏗ [dodi] (pt) “Maybe.”

ᏙᏗ ᎢᏳᏍᏗ [dodi iyụsdi] (pt) “What can it be.”

ᏙᏥ [doʔtsi] (n) “White pine.; biol. *Pinus Strobus L.*”

ᏙᏧᏩ [totsuwa] (n) “Red bird.; Cardinal.; biol. *Cardinalis cardinalis.*”

ᏙᏯ [doya] (n) “Beaver.; biol. *Castor canadensis.*”

ᏙᏱ [doyi] (pt) “Outside.”

> ᎯᎠᏃ ᏄᎵᏍᏔᏁᎢ, ᎾᏍᎩ [ᎠᎨᏴ] ᏏᏉ ᎤᏙᎴᎰᏒ ᎤᏂᏴ ᎤᏄᏬ ᎤᏒᎦᏄᎢ, ᎠᎴ ᏙᏱ ᏮᏗᎵᏍᏔᏅᎢ,
> And it cometh to pass when she seeth that he hath left his garment in her hand, and fleeth without,
> [ᎼᏏ ᎢᎬᏱᏱ 39:13]

ᏙᏱᏨ [dọyitsv] (pt) “Outside of.”

ᏙᏱᏨᎯ ᎠᏲᏓᏒᎢ [doyitsṿhị ạyọdạsṿʔi] (n) “Porch.”

ᏙᏳᏂᏏ [doyụnisi] (n) “Water beetle.; Mellow bug.; biol. *Gyrinus spp.*”

S

ᏚᎵᎢᏍᏗ [dụlịʔisdi] (n) “September.”

ᏚᎵᏍᏆᎵᏒᎯᎠ [dulsgwạlị^{3}sṿhia] (vi) “He is broke.; He is bankrupt.”

> **ᏓᏆᎵᏍᏆᎵᏒᎢᎠ** [da^{1}gwalsgwạlị^{3}sṿʔia]
> **ᏚᎵᏍᏆᎵᏒᏒᎢ** [dulsgwạlị^{3}svsv^{23}ʔi]
> **ᏚᎵᏍᏆᎵᏒᏍᎪᎢ** [dulsgwạlị^{3}sṿsgo^{3}ʔi]
> **ᏗᏣᎵᏍᏆᎵᏒᎠᎦ** [dịtsalsgwạlị^{3}sṿaga]
> **ᏧᎵᏍᏆᎵᏒᏍᏗ** [tsulsgwạlị^{3}svsdi]

ᏚᎵᏗᎾᎥᎢ [duldinaʔṿʔi] (n) “Family.”

> **ᏓᏆᎵᏗᎾᎥᎢ** [dạgwạldinaʔṿʔi]

ᏚᎵᏘᎾᎠ [dultihnạʔa] (vi) “He has a family.”

> **ᏓᏆᎵᏗᎾᎠ** [da^{1}gwaldʔihnạʔa]
> **ᏚᎵᏘᏅᏅᎢ** [dultihnvnv^{23}ʔi]
> **ᏚᎵᏘᎾᎣᎢ** [dultihnạʔo^{3}ʔi]
> —
> **ᏧᎵᏘᏅᏗ** [tsultihnvʔdi]

ᏚᎶᏒᎯ [dulosvhi] (vi) “He is from ….”

> **ᏓᎩᎶᏒᎢ** [da^{1}gịlosṿʔi]
> **ᏚᎶᎡᏍᏛᎢ** [duloesdv^{23}ʔi]
> **ᏚᎶᏒᎯ** [dulosvhi]
> **ᏗᏣᎶᎯ** [dịtsạlohi]
> **ᏧᎶᎯᏍᏗ** [tsulohịsdi]

ᏚᎸᏫᏍᏓᏁᎭ [duhlṿwisdạʔneha] (vi) “He is working.; He is laboring.”

> **ᏓᎩᎸᏫᏍᏓᏁᎭ** [da^{1}gịlṿʔwisdạʔneha]
> **ᏚᎸᏫᏍᏓᏁᎸᎢ** [duhlṿwisdạʔnẹlv^{23}ʔi]
> **ᏚᎸᏫᏍᏓᏁᎰᎢ** [duhlṿwisdạʔneho^{3}ʔi]
> **ᏗᏣᎸᏫᏍᏓᏏ** [dịtsahlṿwisdạsi]
> **ᏧᎸᏫᏍᏓᏁᏗ** [tsuhlṿwisdạʔnhdi]
>
> ᏗᏊᎤᏒᏃ ᏗᎩᎸᏫᏍᏓᏁᏗ ᏃᎴ ᎠᏆᏙᏬᏐᎸᏍᏙᏗ.
> “I want to work and rest at home.”
> [King pg 116]

ᏚᏂᏅᏗ [dụninṿdi] (n) “October.”

ᏚᏃᎸᏓᏂ [dụnọlvdạni] (n) “January.”

ᏚᏇᏍᏗ [tugwẹsdi] (n) “Blow gun.”

ᏚᏐᎦ ᏨᏁᏆ [dụsog tsṿnegwa] (n) “Rhododendron.; biol. *Rhododendron ferrugineum L.*”

ᏚᏘ [tuti] (n) “Dark-eyed junco.; Snowbird.; biol. *Junco hyemalis.*”

ᏚᏘᏱ [tutiyi] (n) “Snowbird Community.”

ᏚᏙᎨᎯᏙᎭ [dudogehidoha] (vi) “He is stumbling.”

> **ᏓᏆᏙᎨᎢᏙᎭ** [da^{1}gwạdogẹʔidoha]
> **ᏚᏙᎨᎯᏙᎸᎢ** [dudogehidọʔlv^{23}ʔi]
> **ᏚᏙᎨᎯᏙᎰᎢ** [dudogehidoho^{3}ʔi]
> **ᏗᏣᏙᎨᎯᏓ** [dịtsadogehida]
> **ᏧᏙᎨᎯᏓᏍᏗ** [tsudogehidạsdi]

ᏚᏪᎧ [dụweka] (n) “Salamander.; North American newt.; biol. *Notophthalmus spp.*”

ᏚᏫᏍᎦᎵ [dụwịsgạli] (n) “Flint.; Arrowheads.”

ᏚᏬᎵ [dụwohli] (n) “Mushroom.; Cork.; Stopper.”

ᏚᏯ [duya] (n) “Chestnut-sided warbler.; biol. *Setophaga pensylvanica.*”

ᏚᏯ [tụya] (n) “Beans.; biol. *All Varieties.*”

> ᏎᎷ ᏃᎴ ᏚᏯ ᎨᎬᏂᏍᏓᏁ ᏗᏂᏲᎵ ᎡᏥᏂ.
> Rachel is cooking beans and corn for the children.
> [King pg 115]

ᏑᏧ ᎠᎯᏩᏗᏍᎩ [tuya aniladisgi] (n) "Peanuts."

ᏑᏧ ᎠᏑᏴ ᎦᏚ [tuya asuyi gadu] (n) "Bean bread."

ᏑᏧ ᎢᎾᎨᎥ [tuya inageʔi] (n) "Hog-peanut.; Ground bean.; Literally: {|Wild bean|}.; biol. *Amphicarpaea bracteata.*"

ᏑᎧᏁᏥ [tuyanegwa] (n) "Lima bean.; Butter bean.; biol. *Phaseolus lunatus.*"

ᏑᏩᏍᏗ [duyasdi] (n) "Jack-in-the-pulpit.; Wild turnip.; biol. *Arisaema triphyllum.*"

ᏍᏇᏒᏩ [duyukta] (adj) "Proper.; Correct.; Just."

ᏍᏇᏒᏉᏫᎣᏍᎦ [du¹ysdo³yhsga] (vi) "He is sneezing."

   ᏝᎩᏇᏒᏉᏫᎣᏍᎦ [da¹gi¹ʔysdo³yhsga]

   ᏍᏇᏒᏙᏴᎢ [du¹ysdo³yhv²³ʔi]

   ᏍᏇᏒᏉᏫᏪᎣᎢ [du¹ysdo³yhsgo³ʔi]

   ᏥᏣᏇᏒᏉᏨ [ditsa¹ysdo³ytsa]

   ᏧᏇᏒᏉᏫᎣᏍᏗ [tsu¹ysdo³yhsdi]

Ꮧ

ᏛᎧ [dvka] (n) "Housefly.; biol. *Musca domestica.*"

ᏛᎬᎾ [dvgvna] (n) "Oyster.; Acne."

ᏛᏁᎬᏫᏳᏍᏗ ᎠᎾᏬ [tvnegwiyusdi ahnawo] (n) "Velvet."

ᏛᏐᏥᏤᏍ [dvsotsvcheha] (vt) "He is ridiculing.; He is making fun of."

   ᏕᎩᏐᏨᏫᏤᏍ [degysotsvdsʔeha]

   ᏚᎤᏐᏥᏤᏩᎢ [duwasotsvcheʔlv²³ʔi]

   ᏛᏐᏥᏤᏬᎢ [dvsotsvcheho³ʔi]

   ᏛᏐᏥᏤᏏ [tysotsvchʔsi]

   ᏧᎤᏐᏥᏤᏗ [tsuwasotsvchehdi]

ᏛᏗᏍᏗ [tvdisdi] (n) "Ruffed grouse.; Pheasant.; biol. *Bonasa umbellus.*"

ᏛᏯᏥ [tvyegwa] (n) "Eel.; biol. *Anguilla rostrata.*"

Ꮳ

ᏣᎦᏴ [tsgayʔi] (n) "Yellow jacket.; biol. *Vespula maculifrons.*"

ᏣᎸᏍᏙᏂ [tsahlsdoni] (n) "Bryson City, North Carolina."

ᏣᎶᎯ [tsalohi] (n) "Kingfisher.; Belted kingfisher.; biol. *Megaceryle alcyon.*"

ᏣᎹᎭ [tsamaha] (n) "Bat.; biol. *Family Vespertilionidae.*"

ᏣᏁᎳ [tsanela] (adj) "Eight."

ᏣᏁᏅ [tsanenv] (n) "Skink.; biol. *Family Scincidae.*"

ᏣᏃ [tsahno] (pt) "No."

ᏣᏃᏏ [tsanosi] (n) "Rhinoceros."

ᏣᏄᏏ [tsanusi] (n) "Leech.; biol. *Class Hirudinea.*"

ᏣᏄᏏ [tsanusi] (n) "Murphy, N.C."

ᏣᎺᏬᏍ [tsagwolde] (n) "Bluebird.; Eastern bluebird.; biol. *Sialia sialis.*"

ᏣᎦᏄᎩ [tsadanugi] (n) "Chattanooga."

ᏣᏘᏏᏩ [tsatsiya] (n) "Georgia."

ᏣᏴᎦ [tsahyiga] (n) "Poke salad.; Pokeweed.; Poke.; biol. *Phytolacca americana.*"

ᏣᏴᎦ [tsayga] (n) "Blue jay.; biol. *Cyanocitta cristata.*"

Ꮵ

ᏥᏣ [tsigtsa] (n) "Song sparrow.; biol. *Melospiza melodia.*"

ᏥᎩᎩ [tsigigi] (n) "Katydid.; biol. *Family Tettigoniidae.*"

ᏥᎵ [tsgili] (n) "Long-eared owl.; biol. *Asio otus.*; Witch.; Ghost.; Night traveler."

ᏥᎵᎵ [tsigilili] (n) "Chickadee.; biol. *Poecile carolinensis.*"

ᏥᎪᏴ [dsgoyi] (n) "Worm.; Bug.; Insect."

ᏥᎪᏴ ᎠᏁᏍᎩᎸᎥᏍᎩ [tsgoyi anesgilvʔvsgi] (n) "Caterpillar."

ᏥᎪᏴᏙᏍᏗ [dsgoyiʔdosdi] (n) "Pee wee (bird).; Least flycatcher (bird).; Chebecker (bird).; biol. *Empidonax minimus.*"

ᏥᏍᎪᎠᎩᎵ [tsisgogili] (n) "Crayfish, red."

ᏥᏍᏩ [tsisgwa] (n) "Bird."

   ᎡᏗ ᎢᏣᎲᏫᏍᏗ ᏥᏝ ᏔᎵ ᏥᏍᏩ ᏂᎡᏍᏓ ᎤᏥ ᏔᏍ ᏧᎬᎦᏗ …
   That proverb, *A Bird in the Hand is worth two in the Bush* …
   [ᏧᏂᎬᎦᏗ ᏐᏴᎡᎡᏘ]

ᏥᏍᏩᎦᏬᏂᏍᎩ [tsisgwagawoʔnisgi] (n) "Parrot."

ᏥᏍᏩᎸᎾ [tsisgwalvna] (n) "Humblehead (fish).; biol. *Cottus spp.*"

ᏥᏍᏩᏯ [tsisgwaya] (n) "Sparrow.; House sparrow.; biol. *Passer domesticus.*"

   ᎥᏍᎠ ᎠᎲᏪᎵ ᏥᏍᏩ ᎤᏥᏴ ᏔᏬᏗᎥᏗ ᏧᎬᎬᎦᏗ ᏒᏴ, …
   'Are not two sparrows sold for an assar? …
   [ᏈᏍ 10:29]

ᏥᏍᏩᏬᎾᏨ [tsisgwenutsv] (n) "Downy woodpecker.; biol. *Dryobates pubescens.*"

ᏥᏍᎹᏬᎦᏗ [tsgwisda] (adj) "A great deal of.; A lot.; Many."

ᏥᏍᎹᏬᏬᎠ [tsisgwohi] (n) "Birdtown."

ᏥᏍᎹᏬᏬ [tsisgwogwo] (n) "Robin.; American robin.; biol. *Turdus migratorius.*"

ᏥᏍᎦᏥ [tsisdetsi] (n) "Mouse.; Rat.; biol. *Rattus spp.*"

ᏥᏍᏚ [tsisdu] (n) "Rabbit.; Eastern cottontail.; biol. *Sylvilagus floridanus.*"

   ᎤᏝ ᏥᏍᏚ ᎤᏫᏌ ᏯᏨ ᏍᏍᏃᏴᏬᏍᎦᎬ.
   One rabbit is listening to the dog making music.
   [ᏣᏬᏯ ᏪᎵᏧ ᏂᎲᏂᏙᏥ ᏧᏏᏫᏥ]

ᏥᏍᏚ ᏍᎩᏓᏘ [tsisdu sgidati] (n) "Cotton grass.; Rabbit's tail.; biol. *Eriophorum spp.*"

ᏥᏍᏛᎾ [tsisdvna] (n) "Crayfish, green.; Crayfish, brown."

ᏥᏓᎦ [tsịdaga] (n) “Chicken.; biol. *Gallus gallus domesticus.*”

English borrowing.

ᏥᏥ [tsitsi] (n) “Cotton thistle.; Scotch thistle.; Dart (for a blow gun).; biol. *Onopordum acanthium.*”

ᏥᏲ [tsiyo] (n) “Otter.; biol. *Lontra canadensis.*”

ᏥᏲᎯ [tsiyọhi] (n) “Robbinsville.”

ᏥᏳ [tsiyu] (n) “Canoe.; Boat.; Airplane.; Yellow poplar.; biol. *Populus spp.*; Tulip tree.; biol. *Liriodendron tulipifera.*”

Ꮶ

ᏦᎢ [tsoʔi] (adj) “Three.”

ᏦᎾᏰᏃ ᏦᎢ ᎢᎦ ᎠᎴ ᏦᎢ ᏒᏃᏱ ᎠᏣᏗ ᎡᏆ ᎤᏍᏠᎵᏱ ᏩᏯᎡᎢ, …
for, as Jonah was in the belly of the fish three days and three nights, …
[ᎹᏚ 12:40]

ᏦᎢᏁ ᎢᎦ [tsoʔịnẹ iga] (n) “Wednesday.”

ᏦᎣᏍᎪᎯ [tsoʔọsgohi] (adj) “Thirty.”

ᏦᎦᏚ ᎢᏯᏅᏓ [tsọgạdụ ịyạnvda] (n) “Thirteen months (a traditional year).; Year, traditional.”

ᏦᎦᏚᎯ [tsogạdụhi] (adj) “Thirteen.”

ᏦᎨᏏ [tsọgesi] (n) “Field.”

ᏦᎩ [tsogi] (pt) “Upstream.”

ᏦᎳ [tsohla] (n) “Scarlet tanager.; biol. *Piranga olivacea.*”

ᏦᎳ [tsola] (n) “Tobacco.; biol. *Nicotiana tabacum.*”

ᏦᎳ ᎠᎦᏴᎵ [tsolạ ạgạyvli] (n) “Booger tobacco.; Aztec tobacco.; biol. *Nicotina rustica.*”

ᏦᎳ ᎠᏍᏓᏯᏔᏅᎯ [tsolạ ạsdạyhtạnỵhi] (n) “Tobacco, plug of.”

ᏦᎳ ᎤᏬᏍᎩᎵ [tsolạ ụwosgịli] (n) “Snuff.”

ᏦᎳ ᎦᏄᏕᏲᎸᎯ [tsolạ gạnudeyohlỵhi] (n) “Tobacco, twist of.”

ᏦᎳᏂ [tsolạni] (n) “Window pane.”

ᏦᏍᏓᎵᏅᏥ [tsọsdahlịnvtsi] (n) “Brothers, we are.”

ᏦᏓᎸ ᏅᏯ [tsodạlỵ nỵʔya] (n) “Stone Mountain, GA.”

ᏦᏯᎦ [tsoyạga] (n) “Bank swallow.; biol. *Riparia riparia.*”

Ꮷ

ᏧᎦᏃᏅ [tsugạnonv] (n) “Ash (tree).; biol. *Fraxinus L.*”

ᏧᎦᏃᏮᎢ [tsụganọwvʔi] (n) “Florida.”

ᏧᎦᏃᏮᎢ, ᏧᎦᎾᏮᎢ [tsuganọwvʔi, tsuganạwvʔi] (n) “South.”

ᏗᎧᎸᎬᏃ ᎢᏗᏢ ᏗᏂᎶᏍᎨᏍᏗ, ᎠᎴ ᏭᏕᎵᎬᎢ, ᎠᎴ ᏧᏴᏢᎢ, ᎠᎴ ᏧᎦᎾᏮᎢ, …
and they shall come from east and west, and from north and south, …
[ᎷᎦ 13:29]

ᏧᎦᏅᏍᏓᎵ [tsugạnvsdahli] (n) “Bull.; Boar.”

ᏧᎦᏍᏆᎾᎩᏓ [tsuksgwạnạgida] (n) “Goat.; biol. *Capra spp.*”

ᏧᎧ [tsuka] (n) “Flea.; biol. *Order Siphonaptera.*”

ᏧᎩᏅ [tsuʔginv] (n) “Elm.; biol. *Ulmus spp.*”

ᏧᎫ ᏧᎾᏍᏗ [tsug tsunsdi] (n) “Laurel.; biol. *Kalmia angustifolia.*”

ᏧᎬᏩᎶᏗ [tsugvwahldi] (n) “Value.; Worth.; Cost.”

… ᎠᎴ ᎤᏲᎸᎩ ᎦᏕᎶᏗ ᎠᎧᎵ ᏧᎬᏩᎶᏗ.
… and brought him a bag of treasure.
[ᏧᏁᎶᏗ ᏕᏂᎩᏒᏒᎢ]

ᏧᎯᏥᏆ [tsuhitsgwa] (n) “Bean salad (food).; Rose twisted stalk.; biol. *Streptopus lanceolatus.*”

ᏧᎳ [tsula] (n) “Fox.; biol. *Vulpes spp.*”

ᏧᎳ ᏕᏂᏔᎴᏐᎢ, ᏥᏍᏆᏃ ᎦᎸᎶ ᎠᏁᎯ ᏕᎾᏁᏍᏓᏝᎨᎢ, …
‘The foxes have holes, and the birds of the heaven places of rest, …
[ᎹᏚ 8:20]

ᏧᎳ ᎩᎦᎨ [tsulạ gigạge] (n) “Red fox.; biol. *Vulpes vulpes.*”

ᏧᎳ ᏌᎪᏂᎨ [tsulạ sạkonịge] (n) “Gray fox.; Blue fox.; biol. *Urocyon cinereoargenteus.*”

ᏧᎳᏍᎩ [tsulạsgi] (n) “Alligator.; Iron pot.; biol. *Alligator mississippiensis.*”

ᏧᎳᏍᎩ ᎬᏂᏍᎦ ᎠᎵᏍᏓᏴᏗ.
The food is cooking in the pot.
[King pg113]

ᏧᎵᎡᎾ [tsulịʔena] (n) “Yellow-bellied sapsucker.; biol. *Sphyrapicus varius.*”

ᏧᎵᎡᏂ [tsulịʔeni] (n) “Deaf (in both hears).”

ᏧᎵᏍᏓᎾᎵ [tsụlisdạnali] (n) “Catfish.; biol. *Ictaluridae spp.*”

ᏧᎾᏥᎠᏙᎯ [tsunạtsiʔạdohi] (n) “Ear rings.”

ᏧᏁᎸᏗ [tsụnehldi] (n) “Christian.”

ᏧᏁᏍᏓᎳ ᏗᏗᏳ [tsunẹsdạlạ dihdiyu] (n) “Can house.”

ᏧᏂᎩᎶᏍᏗ [tsuhnịgịlosdi] (n) “Friday.”

ᏧᏂᎩᏥᏴᏍᏗ [tsụnigitsịyvsdi] (n) “Mud flutter fish.”

ᏧᏂᎶᎩ [tsụnihlọgi] (n) “Honey mushroom.; Slicky mushroom.”

ᏧᏂᎶᎸᏗ [tsunilohldi] (n) “Rainbow trout.; biol. *Oncorhynchus mykiss.*”

ᏧᏂᎶᏪ [tsunihlogwe] (n) “Honey mushroom.; Slicky mushroom.; biol. *Armillaria mellea.*”

ᏧᏂᎶᏗ ᏐᏈᎵ [tsunilohdị sogwịli] (n) “Zebra.; Striped horse.; biol. *Equus spp.*”

ᏧᏂᏦᏍᏗ [tsuhnịtsosdi] (adj) “Sour.”

ᏧᏂᏦᏴᏍᏗ [tsuhnịtsohysdi] (n) “False rhubarb.; biol. *Rheum rhaponticum.*”

ᏧᏂᏲᎱᏒ ᏗᎦᎾᎩᏏᏙᎯ [tsụniyọhụsỵ dịgạnạgisidohi] (n) “Hearse.”

ᏧᏃᏪᎶᏗᏳ [tsunohwelodiyu] (n) “Office.”

ᏧᏆᎶᎦ ᏤᏆ [tsugwạlogạ tsegwa] (n) “Cucumber tree.; biol. *Magnolia acuminata.*”

ᏧᏆᏆ [tsugwagwa] (n) "Red buckeye.; biol. *Aesculus pavia.*"

ᏧᏍᎦ ᏓᎶᏗ [tsusgą dąlo³hdi] (n) "Sessile bellwort. Wild oats.; biol. *Uvularia sessilifolia.*"

ᏧᏍᎪ [tsusgo] (n) "Post oak.; biol. *Quercus stellata.*"

ᏧᏍᏓᏱ [tsụsdayi] (n) "Hard corn (past roasting stage)."

ᏧᏔᎾᎶ [tsutąnalo] (n) "Bridle."

ᏧᏕᎩ [tsụdegi] (n) "Pitcher (baseball)."

ᏧᏕᏒᎾᎵ [tsụdesvnali] (n) "Vireo.; Red-eyed vireo.; biol. *Vireo olivaceus.*"

ᏧᏗᏆᏅᏥ [tsudịgwantsi] (n) "Barn swallow.; biol. *Hirundo rustica.*"

ᏧᏗᏆᏍᏗ [tsụdịgwasdi] (n) "Peacock."

ᏧᏚᎶᏗ

ᏧᏚᎶᏗ [tsụdulodi] (n) "Harelip.; Split lip."

ᏧᏛᏃᎯᏛ [tsudvnohịdv] (n) "Sheets."

ᏧᏤᏲᏍᏗ [tsutsẹyosdi] (adj) "Sticky."

ᏧᏦᎵᏛ [tsụtsoldv] (n) "Oven bird.; biol. *Seiurus aurocapilla.*"

ᏧᏧ [tsutsu] (n) "Purple martin.; biol. *Progne subis.*"

ᏧᏩ [chuwa] (n) "Waterdog.; Mudpuppy.; biol. *Necturus spp.*"

ᏧᏩᎩ [tsuwagi] (n) "Sugar maple.; Rock maple.; Maple.; biol. *Acer saccharum.*"

ᏧᏩᏂᎨᎢ [tsụwạnigeʔi] (n) "Soft corn (roasting stage)."

ᏧᏩᏚᏂ [tsụwạduni] (n) "Veins."

ᏓᏆᏚᏂ [dạgwạduni]

ᏧᏪᏥ ᏓᏂᏑᏫᏍᎬᎢ [tsụwetsị dạnịsuwịsgvʔi] (n) "Easter."

ᏧᏬᏍᎦ [tsụwosga] (n) "Towhee.; Eastern towhee.; biol. *Pipilo erythrophthalmus.*"

ᏧᏲᏂ [tsuhyoni] (n) "Antlers."

ᏧᏴᏨᎢ [tsuhyvtsvʔi] (n) "North."

ᏗᎧᏄᎬᏃ ᎢᏗᏢ ᏗᏂᎶᏍᎨᏍᏗ, ᎠᎴ ᏭᏕᎵᎬᎢ, ᎠᎴ ᏧᏴᏢᎢ, ᎠᎴ ᏧᎦᎾᏮᎢ, …
and they shall come from east and west, and from north and south, …
[ᎷᎦ 13:29]

Ꮸ

ᏨᏓᏥ [tsvdạtsi] (n) "Panther.; Mountain lion.; biol. *Puma concolor.*"

Ꮹ

ᏩᎦᏘ [wạkti] (vi) "He is going somewhere."

ᏫᏥᎦᏘ [wịtsịgạʔti]

ᏭᎦᏖᏍᏛᎢ [wuktesdv²³ʔi]

ᏩᎦᏙᎢ [wạkto³ʔi]

ᏫᎦᏖᏍᏗ [hwịktesdi]

ᏭᎦᏖᏍᏗ [wuktesdi]

ᏓᎬᏃᏁᎵᏎʼ, ᎾᏍᎩᏂ ᎤᏍᏗ ᎦᎶᎯᏍᏗᏱ ᏗᎪᏢᏒ ᏫᏥᎦᏘ; …
I tell you, Sir, I am going to yonder Wicket-gate before me; …
[ᏧᏁᎶᏗ ᏚᏂᎩᏒᏒᎢ]

ᏩᎧ [wạka] (n) "Cow."

Spanish borrowing.

ᏩᎧ ᎠᎩᎾ [wạkạ ạgina] (n) "Calf."

ᏩᎧ ᎤᎳᏏᏗ [wạkạ ụlạsidi] (n) "Crow bar.; Cow's foot."

ᏩᎧ ᎭᏫᏯ [wạkạ hạwiya] (n) "Beef."

ᏩᎩᎦ [wagiga] (n) "Squash.; biol. *Cucurbita spp.*"

ᏩᎫᎵ [wạguli] (n) "Eastern whip-poor-will. Whip-poor-will.; biol. *Antrostomus vociferus.*"

ᏩᎱᎱ [wạhụhu] (n) "Screech owl.; biol. *Megascops asio.*"

ᏩᎴᎳ [walẹla] (n) "Hummingbird.; biol. *Archilochus colubris.*"

ᏩᎴᎷ ᎤᏂᎦᎴᎩᏍᏗ [wạlelụ ụnịgạlẹgịsdi] (n) "Jewelweed.; Spotted touch-me-not.; biol. *Impatiens capensis.*"

ᏩᎴᎷ ᎤᏂᏣᎩᏍᏗ [wạlelụ ụnịtsạgisdi] (n) "Red horsemint.; Crimson beebalm.; biol. *Monarda didyma.*"

ᏩᎶᏏ [wạlosi] (n) "Toad.; Warts.; biol. *Bufu spp.*"

ᏩᎾ [wana] (adj) "Soft."

ᏩᏁᎢ [wạnẹʔi] (n) "Hickory.; biol. *Carya spp.*"

ᏩᏁᎩᏓ [wạnegịda] (n) "Angelico.; Lovage.; biol. *Ligusticum canadense.*"

ᏩᏓ [wạda] (pt) "Thanks."

ᏩᏓᎬ [wạdagv] (n) "Goldfinch.; biol. *Spinus tristis.*"

ᏩᏘᏰᎵ [watịyeli] (n) "Magpie."

ᏩᏚᎵᏏ [wadulisi] (n) "Honey.; Bee.; Molasses."

… ᎠᎴ ᎤᏍᏗ ᏩᏚᎵᏏ, ᎠᎴ ᏗᎦᏩᏒᎩ, ᎠᎴ ᎻᎳ, ᎠᎴ ᎤᏅᏙᎩ ᎠᎾᏓᏛᏍᎩ, ᎠᎴ ᎠᏪᏂ.
… and a little honey, spices and myrrh, nuts and almonds;
[ᎼᏏ ᎢᎬᏱᏱ 43:11]

ᏩᏚᏰᎳ [wạdụyela] (n) "Mockingbird.; Imitator bird.; Brown thrasher.; biol. *Toxostoma rufum.*"

ᏩᏥ [watsi] (n) "Wristwatch."

English borrowing.

ᏩᏥᎦ [wạtsga] (n) "Green amaranth.; biol. *Amaranthus viridis.*"

ᏩᏥᏂ [watsịni] (n) "Virginia."

ᏩᏯ [wahya] (n) "Wolf.; biol. *Canis lupus.*"

ᏇᏂ ᏕᏓᏕᎸᎥᏍᎨᏍᏗ ᏩᏯ ᎾᏍᎩᏯᎢ; ᏑᎾᎴ ᏕᏰᏍᎨᏍᏗ ᎤᏂᏴᏛ, …
Benjamin! a wolf teareth; In the morning he eateth prey, …
[ᎼᏏ ᎢᎬᏱᏱ 49:27]

ᏩᏯᏂᎭ [wa¹yanịha] (vt) "He is calling out for him."

ᏫᏥᏯᏂᎭ [wịtsi¹ʔyanịha]

ᏭᏯᏅᎲᎢ [wu¹yanvhv²³ʔi]

ᏩᏯᏂᏍᎪᎢ [wa¹yanịsgo³ʔi]

ᏫᏯᎾ [hwi¹ʔyana]

ᏭᏯᏅᏗ [wu¹yanhdi]

ᎾᏉᏃ ᎦᎶᎯᏍᏗᏱ ᏓᏳᎷᏨᎯ ᎦᏁᎳ ᏭᏯᏅᎲᎩ, ᎾᏍᎩᏃ ᎪᎯ ᎢᏴᏛ ᎤᎷᏤᎸᎩ ᏧᏁᎶᏗ, ᎠᎴ ᎢᏳᏍᏗ ᎤᎸᏏᎸ ᎤᏛᏛᏅᎩ.
So he called for the Master of the house, who after a little time came to *Christian*, and asked him what he would have?
[ᏧᏁᎶᏗ ᏚᏂᎩᏒᏒᎢ]

ᏩᏲᎯ [wahyohi] (n) "Wolftown."

Ꮺ

ᏪᏌ [wehsa] (n) "Cat.; biol. *Felis silvestris catus.*"

ᎦᏙ ᎤᏍᏗ ᎠᏓᏁᎭ? ᎭᏑᏯᎩ. ᏙᏗᏍᎩᏂᎥᏏ: Ꭰ) ᏪᏌ, Ꭱ) ᏅᏯ, Ꭲ) ᏐᏈᎵ.
What is being given? Choose. I will hand you them: a) Cats, b) Rocks, c) Horses.
[ᏣᎳᎩ ᏅᎩᏁ ᏗᏂᏂᏙᎯ ᏗᎦᏲᏙᏗ]

Spanish borrowing.

ᏪᏌ ᎠᏓᎯ [wẹsạ ạdạhi] (n) "Kitten."

Ꮻ

ᏫᏍᎩ [hwisgi] (n) "Whiskey."

English borrowing.

ᏫᏏ [wisi] (n) "Wishi mushroom.; Hen-of-the-woods.; biol. *Grifola frondosa.*"

ᏫᏥᎨᏆ [wịtsiʔgẹ³gwa] (adj) "Bigger."

ᏫᏥᎸᏬᏚᎭ [wịtsinuwodụha] (adj) "Prettier.; Prettiest."

Ꮼ

ᏬᏗ [wodi] (n) "Indian Paint."

ᏬᏗᎨᎠᏍᎪᎵ [wodịgeạsgoli] (n) "Copperhead.; biol. *Agkistrodon contortrix.*"

ᏬᏗᎨᎢ [wodịgeʔi] (adj) "Brown."

ᏬᏰ [woye] (n) "Foul ball (stickball)."

ᏬᏱ [woyi] (n) "Passenger pigeon.; biol. *Ectopistes migratorius.*"

… ᎠᏂᏔᎵ ᏧᎴᏗᏂᏍᎪᏂᎯ, ᎠᎴ ᎠᏂᏔᎵ ᎠᏂᏛ ᏬᏱ.
…'A pair of turtle-doves, or two young pigeons.'
[ᎷᎦ 2:24]

Ꮽ

ᏭᏕᎵ [wudeʔli] (pt) "Out of sight."

ᏭᏕᎵᎬ [wudeligv] (n) "Oklahoma."

ᏭᏕᎵᎬ ᎠᏁᎯ ᎠᏂᏴᏫᏯ [wudeligv ạnẹhị ạniyvwịya] (n) "Western Indians."

ᏭᏕᎵᎬᎢ [wudeligvʔi] (n) "West."

ᏗᎧᎸᎬᏃ ᎢᏗᏢ ᏗᏂᎶᏍᎨᏍᏗ, ᎠᎴ ᏭᏕᎵᎬᎢ, ᎠᎴ ᏧᏴᏢᎢ, ᎠᎴ ᏧᎦᎾᏮᎢ, …
and they shall come from east and west, and from north and south, …
[ᎷᎦ 13:29]

Ᏸ

ᏰᎵᏉ [yeligwo] (pt) "Enough.; To be able to."

… ᏰᎵᏉ ᎤᏲ ᎢᎦ ᎤᏪᎲᎢ.
… sufficient for the day [is] the evil of it.
[ᎹᏚ 6:34]

Ᏺ

ᏲᎾ [yona] (n) "Bear.; American black bear.; biol. *Ursus americanus.*"

ᎭᏢ ᏲᎾ ᎠᏓ?
Where is bear cub?
[ᏣᎳᎩ ᏔᎵᏁ ᏗᏂᏂᏙᎯ ᏗᎦᏲᏙᏗ]

ᏲᎾ ᎤᏤᏍᏓ [yonạ ụtsesda] (n) "Wood-fern.; biol. *Dryopteris spp.*"

Ᏼ

ᏴᎩ [yvgi] (n) "Fork.; Nail.; Pin.; Pitchfork.; Spear."

ᏦᎢᏯᏂ ᏚᎴᎢ ᏴᎩ ᎤᏩᏑᎦᎵ.
Spear Finger killed three of them.
[King pg 121]

ᏴᎩ ᎤᏩᏑᎧᎵ [yvgị ụwasụkahli] (n) "SpearFinger (Mythological)."

ᎡᏘᏴᏃ ᏥᎨᏐᎢ ᎡᎮᎢ ᎠᎦᏴᎵᎨᎢ ᏴᎩ ᎤᏩᏑᎦᎵ ᏚᏙᎡᎢ.
"Long ago lived an old woman name Spear Finger."
[King pp 121-123]

ᏴᎾᏌ [yṿnsa] (n) "Buffalo.; biol. *Bison Bison.*"

BᎾ [yvwi] (n) "A person."

> ... ᏣᏂᎬᎵ ᎦᎠᏫᏴ <u>BᎾ</u> ᎤᎥᏙᎿᏙᎮᎷ ᎠᏟᏋᏺᏔᎤᏗ, ᎾᏘ ᎾᎤᏏᎩ ᏓᎷᎩ; ...

> ... *Christian* saw the Picture of a very grave <u>Person</u> hang up against the wall; ...

> [ᏣᏂᎬᎵ ShᏴᏒᏒᎢ]

BᎾ ᏓᎾᏗᏟ [yvwį tsunsdiʔi] (n) "The little people (mythological)."

English to Cherokee Lookup

A

A lot: ᏥᏍᏇᏍᏓ [tsgwịsda] pg 107)

Abdomen (his): ᎠᏍᏆᏁᎦᎸᎢ [ąsgwąnegąlv̨ʔi] pg 31)

Above: ᎦᎸᎳᏗᏣ [gạlvlạdịtsa] pg 72)

Accipiter striatus: ᏗᎦᎦᏛᎾᎯᏛ [dịgagdv̨nạhidv] pg 104)

Accordian: ᏗᎫᏣᎾᎩᏍᏗ [dịgutsạnạgisdi] pg 105)

Acer rubrum: ᎩᎦᎨᏨᏩᎩ [gịgạgetsvhwạgi] pg 87)

Acer saccharum: ᏧᏩᎩ [tsuwagi] pg 109)

Aching: ᎤᏪᎯᏍᏓᏁᎭ [uwẹhịsdaneha] pg 65)

Acne: ᏛᎬᎾ [dv̨gvna] pg 107)

Acorn: ᎫᎴ [gule] pg 89)

Acorus calamus: ᎤᏲᏓᎵ [ụyodahli] pg 67)

Acquainted with him: ᎪᎵᎧ [golka] pg 88)

Acre: ᏑᏥᎶᏓ [sụtsịloda] pg 97)

Acting: ᎠᏛᏁᎵᎭ [advneliha] pg 43)

Acting up: ᎠᏛᏁᎵᎭ [advnẹliha] pg 43)

Actor: ᎠᏛᏁᎵᏍᎩ [ạdvnelịsgi] pg 43)

Adam's needle: ᏎᎷᏉᏯ [selụgwọya] pg 96)

Adding: ᎠᏌᏂᏙᎭ [asạnidoha] pg 28)

Admiring it: ᎠᏍᏆᏂᎪᏍᎦ [asgwạ^{3}nịgosga] pg 31)

Aesculus pavia: ᎤᏍᏆᏙ [ụsgwạdo] pg 60), ᏧᏆᏆ [tsug-wagwa] (pg 109)

Affadavit: ᎠᏎᎵᏓᏅ [ạsẹlịdanv] pg 33)

Afraid of: ᎠᏍᎦᎢᎭ [asgạʔịha] pg 29)

After a while: ᎪᎯ [gohi] pg 87), ᎪᎯᎩᎳ [gọhịgịla] (pg 87)

Afternoon: ᏒᎯᏰᏽᏗᏣ [sv̨hịyẹyhdịtsa] pg 97)

Afterwards: ᎤᎶᏐᏅ [ụlosọnv] pg 56)

Again: ᏏᏉ [sịgwo] pg 96)

Agkistrodon contortrix: ᏬᏗᎨᎠᏍᎪᎵ [wodịgeạsgoli] pg 110)

Agkistrodon piscivorus: ᎧᏁᏉᏓ [kạnegwoda] pg 84)

Agony, suffering (in): ᎠᎯᎵᏲᎦ [ahihlịyoga] pg 19)

Agrees: ᎪᎯᏳᎲᏍᎦ [gọhi^{3}yụhvsga] pg 87)

Airplane: ᏥᏳ [tsiyu] pg 108)

Alive: ᎡᎭ [ẹha] pg 51)

All: ᏂᎦᏓ [nịgada] pg 94)

Allegheny serviceberry: ᎤᏙᎳᏂ [ụdolạni] pg 62)

Alligator: ᏧᎳᏍᎩ [tsulạsgi] pg 108)

Alligator mississippiensis: ᏧᎳᏍᎩ [tsulạsgi] pg 108)

Allium cepa: ᏒᎩ [svgi] pg 97)

Allium tricoccum: ᎤᏩᏍᏗ [ụwạsdi] pg 64)

Almost: ᏎᎦᏨ [segatsv] pg 96)

Alnus serrulata: ᎠᏤᏓ [ahtsehd] pg 44)

Alone: ᎤᏩᏌ [uwạsa] pg 64)

Already: ᎦᏳᎳ [gayula] pg 84)

Alright: ᎭᏩ [hạwa] pg 92)

Always: ᏂᎪᎯᎸᎢ [nịgohịlv̨ʔi] pg 94)

Amaranthus spinosus: ᏙᎳᏗᏳᏍᏗ [tohldịyụsdi] pg 106)

Amaranthus viridis: ᏩᏥᎦ [wạtsga] pg 109)

Ambrosia trifida: ᎤᏆᏍᏓᎷᏽᏓ [ụgwạsdaluhyda] pg 60)

Amelanchier laevis: ᎤᏙᎳᏂ [ụdolạni] pg 62)

American beech: ᎫᏍᏗ [kusd] pg 90)

American black bear: ᏲᎾ [yona] pg 110)

American black elderberry

American black elderberry: ᎪᏒᎦ [gosvʔga] pg 88)

American chestnut: ᏘᎵ [tili] pg 105)

American chinquapin: ᎤᏅᎩᏅ [uhnv̨ginv] pg 59)

American eagle: ᎠᏬᎯᎵ [ạwọhịli] pg 47)

American hazelnut: ᎠᏳᎩᏓ [ahyụgida] pg 49)

American kestrel: ᎩᎩ [gigi] pg 87)

American robin: ᏥᏍᏉᏉ [tsisgwogwo] pg 107)

American sycamore: ᎫᏫᏳᎦᏍᏗ [kuhwiyụgsdi] pg 90)

American tiger lily: ᎧᎾᎫᏣᏘ [kahngutsạti] pg 84)

American walking fern: ᎢᎾᏓ ᎦᏁᎦ [inạdạ gahnga] pg 52)

American willow: ᏗᎵᎦᎵᏍᎩ [dilịgạlịsgi] pg 105)

American witch-hazel: ᎦᎾᏑᏛᎶ [gạnsudv̨lo] pg 74)

Amphicarpaea bracteata: ᏚᏯ ᎢᎾᎨᎢ [tuyạ ịnageʔi] pg 107)

Amusing himself: ᎠᏍᏆᏂᎪᏒᎥᏍᎦ [ạsgwanịgọsv̨ʔvsga] pg 31)

And: ᎠᎴ [ạle] pg 21), ᏃᎴ [nole] (pg 94)

Andropogon virginicus: ᎧᏁᏍᎦ ᏬᏗ [kạnesgạ wodi] pg 85)

Angelico: ᏩᏁᎩᏓ [wạnegịda] pg 109)

Angry: ᎤᎾᎦᎸᎭ [uhnạgạlvha] pg 57)

Angry (becoming): ᎤᎾᎦᎸᎦ [uhnạgạlvga] pg 57)

Anguilla rostrata: ᎬᎾᎫ [tvyegwa] pg 107)

Ankle (his): ᎦᏅᏍᏨᎢ [gạnvsỵtsv?i] pg 80)

Ant: ᎥᏛᏓᎵ [dosỵdali] pg 106)

Antlers: Ꮷ�f̣Ꮒ [tsuhyoni] pg 109)

Antrostomus vociferus: ᏩᎫᎵ [wạguli] pg 109)

Anus (his): ᎤᏍᏇᏂ [ukseni] pg 53)

Anxious: ᎤᎶᏅᏟᏌ [ulonv³tseha] pg 56)

Any: ᎢᏳᏍᏗᏈᏫ [iyụsdigwo] pg 53)

Anything: ᎦᎲᏍᏗ [gạhụsdi] pg 69)

Anytime: ᎢᏳᎬ [iyugwo] pg 53)

Appears as: ᏂᎬᎮᏍᏗ [nigvwhsdi] pg 94)

Apple (all varieties): ᏍᎦᏔ [svkta] pg 97)

Applying brakes: ᎦᏅᏍᎣᎯᎭ [gạnvso³hịha] pg 80)

Approving it: ᎠᏍᏓᎥᏱᏗᎠ [asdạ?yi³dị?a] pg 32)

April: ᎧᏬᏄ [kạwonu] pg 86)

Apron: ᎠᏤᏎᏙ [ạtsesạdo] pg 44)

Archilochus colubris: ᏩᎴᎳ [wạlẹla] pg 109)

Ardea herodias: ᎧᏂᏍᎦᏩ [kạnịsgạwa] pg 85)

Arguing: ᎠᏘᏲᎯᎭ [atiyọ³hịha] pg 41)

Arisaema triphyllum: ᎥᏛᏯᏁ ᎢᎾᎨ ᎡᎯ [dosvnạ ịnạge ẹhi] pg 106), ᏚᏯᏍᏗ [dụyạsdi] (pg 107)

Arising from lying: ᎠᏗᏗᎠ [adidị?a] pg 41)

Arm (his): ᎦᏃᎨᏂ [gạhnogeni] pg 77)

Armillaria mellea: ᎤᏂᎶᎦ [ụnịlogwe] pg 58), ᏧᏂᎶᎦ [tsunịhlogwe] (pg 108)

Armpit (his): ᎦᏍᎨᏂ [gạsgeni] pg 81)

Arriving: ᎢᎦᎵᎧ [igạ?lka] pg 52)

Arrow: ᎦᏓᎵᏗ [gadahlịda] pg 81)

Arrowheads: ᏚᏫᏍᎦᎵ [dụwịsgali] pg 106)

Arthritis: ᏗᏙᎴᏍᎩ [dịdolesgi] pg 105)

Arundinaria spp: ᎢᏯ [ihya] pg 52)

As long as: ᎢᎪᎯᏛ [igọhidv] pg 52)

Ash (tree): ᏧᏣᏃᏅ [tsugạnonv] pg 108)

ASHAMED

Ashamed: ᎠᏕᎰᏍᎦ [adẹhoh³sga] pg 39)

Ashes: ᎪᏍᏓ [kọsda] pg 88)

Ashes (in): ᎪᏍᏙᎯ [kosdọhi] pg 88)

Asheville, N.C: �normᏉᎩᏯᏍᏗ [togiyasdi] pg 105)

Asio otus: ᏥᎩᎵ [tsgili] pg 107)

Asking: ᎠᏂᏔᏯᎰᎯᎭ [ahtạyohịha] pg 39)

Asking a question: ᎠᏓᏂᎠᏛᎲᏍᎦ [adatv³dvhvsga] pg 37)

Asking for: ᎠᏂᏔᏯᎰᎯᎭ [ahtạyohịha] pg 39)

Asking him for it: ᎠᏂᏔᏯ᱓ᎡᎭ [ahtạyo³seha] pg 39)

Asking him to do ...: ᎦᏅᏍᎦ [gạnvsga] pg 80)

Asleep: ᎦᎵᎯᎭ [gahlịha] pg 70)

Asplenium rhizophyllum: ᎢᎾᏓ ᎦᎲᎦ [inạdạ gahnga] pg 52)

Assaulting him: ᎦᎵᎥᏂᎭ [gạli?vniha] pg 70)

Assembling: ᏓᏲᎧᎳᏍᎦ [daykahlasga] pg 102)

Assembling together: ᎠᏅᏓᏓᏍᎩᎭ [ạnạdạdsgiha] pg 25)

Attached to it: ᎦᏯᎸᏅᎦ [gạyạlvnga] pg 83)

Attaching it to something: ᎠᏯᎸᎥᏍᎦ [ạyạlv?vsga] pg 47)

Attending: ᎨᎳᏗᏙᎭ [kẹlạdi³dọha] pg 86)

Attractive: ᎤᏬᏚᎭ [uwodụha] pg 66)

Auctioneer: ᎦᏅᏚᏍᎩ [gạndụsgi] pg 74)

August: ᎦᎶᏂ [galoni] pg 72)

Automobile: ᏓᏆᎳᎴᎷ [dagwạlelu] pg 100)

Autumn: ᎤᎶᎪᎲᏍᏗ [ụlogọhọsdi] pg 56)

Awhile: ᏎᎦ [sega] pg 96)

Axe: ᎦᎶ?ᏰᎯᏍᏗ [galọ?yhsdi] pg 72)

Aztec tobacco: ᏦᎳ ᎠᎦᏰᎵ [tsolạ ạgạyvli] pg 108)

B

Baby: ᎤᏍᏗᎢ [ụsdi?i] pg 60)

Baby sitting: ᎠᏓᏛ꟥ᏰᎭ [ạdaktị?yeha] pg 36)

Back: ᎢᎦᎵᎧ [igạ?lka] pg 52)

Back, the lower part (his): ᎦᏤᏍᎨᏂ [gạtesgeni] pg 82)

Bad: ᎤᏲ?Ꭲ [uyo?i] pg 67)

Bad (becoming): ᎠᏲᎦ [ạyọ³ga] pg 48)

Baeolophus bicolor: ᎤᏧᎩ [ụtsugi] pg 64)

Bag: ᏕᎦᎵᏗ [dẹgahldi] pg 102)

Baking bread: ᏕᎦᏓᎲᏍᎦ [degadụhvsga] pg 103)

Bald: ᎤᎨᏬᏗ [ugewodi] pg 54)

Bald eagle: ᎠᏬᎯᎵ [ạwọhịli] pg 47)

Ball: ᎠᎵᏍᎦᏗ [alsgahdi] pg 22)

Ball game (stickball): ᎠᏁᏣ [ạnetsa] pg 26), ᎠᏁᏦᏗ [ạnetsodi] (pg 26)

Ball player: ᎠᏁᏦ?ᎥᏍᎩ [ạnetso?vsgi] pg 26)

Ball sticks: ᏗᎳᏍᎦᎵᏗ [dihlsgahldi] pg 105)

Ball-hooting: ᎠᏳᏲᎰᏍᎦ [ayuyohosga] pg 50), ᏕᎦᏳᏲᎰᎲᏗᎭ [degayuyohohndịha] (pg 103)

Ballot: ᎪᏪᎵ ᏧᏍᏗ [gohwelị tsusdi] pg 89)

Balsam poplar: ᎾᎨ?Ꭲ [nạgẹ?i] pg 93)

Bandaging: ᎠᎸᎢᎭ [ahlv³ịha] pg 25)

Banjo: ᏗᎲᏴᎩᏍᏗ [dihyvgịsdi] pg 105)

Bank swallow: ᏦᏯᎦ [tsoyạga] pg 108)

Bankrupt: ᏚᎵᏍᏆᎵ᱓ᏏᎭᎠ [dulsgwạli³syhia] pg 106)

Baptist: ᏗᏓᏬᏍᎩ [dịdạwosgi] pg 105)

Barber: ᏗᏓᏙᏰᏍᎩ [dịdạsdoyẹsgi] pg 105)

Bark of a tree: ᎤᏯᎷᎦ [uhyạluga] pg 66)

Barking: ᏓᏑᏪ?ᏍᎦ [dasụhwị³sga] pg 100)

Barn swallow: ᏧᏗᎦᏬᏂ [tsudịgwantsi] pg 109)

Barred owl: ᎤᎫᎫ [ụguku] pg 54)

Barrel: RVh [svdo?ni] pg 97)

Bashful: O'ЅІꚈꙆ [udẹhọsati] pg 62)

Basket: WMG [tạlutsa] pg 102)

Bat: GꙆ°Ꮋ [tsamạha] pg 107)

Bathing: DLꙀD [adạwo³?a] pg 38)

Batter: DꝞꝞꝰꙆ [ạsugelyhi] pg 35)

Battery: DOЅꝞꙀУ [ạnagạlịsgi] pg 25)

Beach: DꝞ° DꙀꝞ°T [ạm ạsdv?i] pg 25)

Bean bread: Sꙅ DꝞꙄ ЅS [tuyạ ạsuyị gadu] pg 107)

Bean salad (food): ꓮꙊꞪꓓ [tsuhitsgwa] pg 108)

Beans: Sꙅ [tụya] pg 106)

Bear: ꓮΘ [yona] pg 110)

Bear grass: WꓓꝞ [tagwali] pg 102)

Bear huckleberry: RGꙆꙀУ [ẹlotịsgi] pg 51)

Bear nettle: VꙊL [toleda] pg 106)

Bearing false witness: DꞪAiꙀS [atsgọ?vsga] pg 44)

Beating him in a game: DGꙀS [a?hlosga] pg 24)

Beating him up: ЅꝞihᎻ [gạli?vniha] pg 70)

Beating it: ЅOꝞGD [gạnvgwạlọ³?a] pg 80)

Beaver: Vꙅ [doya] pg 106)

Because of: hЅꝞꙀꙀSTᎻ [nịgalsgwe³tụịha] pg 94)

Bed: Ꮝhꖬ [gạnịsi] pg 77)

BED CLOTHES

Bed clothes: ꙆOꙀꙀVꙆ [dihnywo³sdohdi] pg 105)

Bed cover: DꝞꙀO°Ꙇ [algwehnvhdi] pg 22)

Bee: GꙅЅꝞꖬ [wadulisi] pg 109)

Beech: ꓓꙀꙆ [kusd] pg 90)

Beef: Gꙅ ᎻⵔꙀ [wạkạ hạwiya] pg 109)

Beer: O'ꙀУꝞ [ụwogịli] pg 65)

Beet, red: УЅꝞ ЅWꙀУ [gigạgẹ gahlasgi] pg 87)

Before: DEꙅꙆG [ạgvyịditsa] pg 19)

Begging him: DꙀꙆЅꙆᎻ [asdiyedịha] pg 32)

Beginning it: DꙊhD [alenị?a] pg 21)

Beginning with: DꙊO°ꙆᎻ [alẹnhdịha] pg 21)

Behind: ꙅhꙆG [ohnịditsa] pg 53)

Being bad: O'ꝞTꙀ [uyọ°?iya] pg 67)

Being born: DЅꙀꙀS [ạdẹhvh³sga] pg 39)

Being carried by it (a liquid): ЅOꙄꙀꙆᎻ [gạntsvsdiha] pg 74)

Being carried by it (a solid): DBꙀꙆᎻ [ạyvsdiha] pg 50)

Being carried by it (something alive) or it (something flexible): ЅO°ꙀꙆᎻ [gạnysdiha] pg 80)

Being carried by it (something long): ЅO°ꙀꙆᎻ [gạnysdịha] pg 80)

Being good: ꙀꙀL [ọsda] pg 53)

Being hanged: ЅLD [gạda?a] pg 81)

Being rained on: O'ЅꙀS [ugah³sga] pg 53)

Being spilled on: O'ꙀЅꝞD [usdutsị?a] pg 60)

Being troublesome: DЅꙀVꙆᎻ [adehytohdịha] pg 40)

Belching: O'ꙆꙍS [ugulega] pg 54)

Believes: AꙀGꙀꙀS [gọhi³yụhvsga] pg 87)

Believing in: O'ꙀꙆGᎻ [uwohị³yuha] pg 65)

Belonging to a group: O'ꝞAᎻ [uligoha] pg 55)

Below: RꙆꙆ [ẹlvdi] pg 51)

Belt: DLKꙀꙆ [ạdatsosdi] pg 37)

Belted kingfisher: GGꙆ [tsalọhi] pg 107)

Bending: DBꝞꝞ°iꙀS [ạyvgwịdv³?vsga] pg 50)

Berry: O'LWO°Ꙇ [uḍạtanyhi] pg 61)

Beside: O'ꝞꙆꓚ̈ [ulditsv] pg 56)

Beta vulgaris: УЅꝞ ЅWꙀУ [gigạgẹ gahlasgi] pg 87)

Betting: LEGWꙀS [dagy?hwạlasga] pg 98)

Betula nigra: ЅꙆꙆꙀУ [ganedi³sgi] pg 76)

Between: DβꝞ [ayehli] pg 48)

Bible: AꙀꝞ Ѕ꙲ꙊꙆ [gohwe?lị galykwdi] pg 89)

Big: Rꓓ [egwa] pg 51), O'WΘ [utạna] (pg 62)

Big (becoming): DWZꙀS [atạnoh³sga] pg 38)

Big stoat: LGhꝞ ꞪꙀЅꞪ [dạlonịgẹ tsịsdetsi] pg 99)

Bigger: ΘꞪꝞꓓ [wịtsi?gẹ³gwa] pg 110)

Bigmouth bass: O'ZΘ [uhnọka] pg 59)

Bird: ꞪꙀꓓ [tsisgwa] pg 107)

Bird clan: DhꞪꙀꓓ [ạnitsisgwa] pg 26)

Birdtown: ꞪꙀ꙲°Ꙁ [tsịsgwohi] pg 107)

Birth: O'ЅO° [udenv] pg 62)

Birth mark: O'VꙀ꙲T [uḍowelv?i] pg 63)

Birthplace: O'ЅO° [ụdenv] pg 62)

Bison Bison: BΘꙌ [yvnsa] pg 110)

BITING IT

Biting it: DꙀЅꝞS [asga³hlga] pg 29)

Bitter: O'BꙀꙆ [uhyvsdi] pg 68)

Black: EhꝞT [gvnige?i] pg 91)

Black birch: ЅꙆꙆꙀУ [ganedi³sgi] pg 76)

Black Fox (Surname): TZꝞ [ịnoli] pg 52)

Black gum: O'hꓓ [unịkwa] pg 58)

Black huckleberry: ꙀGꙀ [kawạya] pg 86)

Black locust: ꙀGꙀꙆ [kạlọgwedi] pg 84)

Black oak: ꓓEhꝞT [digvnige?i] pg 105)

Black people: DhEΘꝞT [ạnigvnage?i] pg 26)

Black rat snake: ЅꝞУ [ga?legi] pg 69)

Black walnut, eastern: EhꝞ ꝟꙆ [gvnigẹ seti] pg 91)

Black-eyed-susan: ꝞVΘ [sotsena] pg 97)

Blackberries: ᏄᎦᎵ [nugahli] pg 94)

Blackburnian warbler: ᎦᏅᎩ [gąnvgi] pg 79)

Blacksnake: ᎦᎴᎩ [gąʔlegi] pg 69)

Blaming him: ᎠᏚᎯᏍᏗᎭ [ądụhịsdịha] pg 42)

Bleeding: ᎠᏔᏍᎩᎠ [ątasgį^{3}ʔa] pg 38)

Blind (becoming): ᏓᎨᏬᎦ [dakewoga] pg 98)

Blood: ᎩᎦ [giga] pg 87)

Blow gun: ᏚᏇᏍᏗ [tugwęsdi] pg 106)

Blowing on him: ᎠᏦᏖᎭ [atsoteha] pg 45)

Blue: ᏌᎪᏂᎨᎢ [sagonịgeʔi] pg 95)

Blue clan: ᎠᏂᏌᎰᏂ [ąnịsąhoni] pg 26)

Blue fox: ᏧᎳ ᏌᎪᏂᎨ [tsulą sąkonįge] pg 108)

Blue houndstongue: ᎤᏂᏍᏕᎴᏍᏗ [ụnịsdẹlesdi] pg 58)

Blue jay: ᏣᏱᎦ [tsąyga] pg 107)

Blue racer (snake): ᎤᎦᏑᎯ [ugsụhi] pg 53)

Blue violet: ᏗᎾᏓᏍᏓᏍᎩ [dihndasdasgi] pg 105)

Blueberry: ᎧᏩᏯ [kawąya] pg 86)

Bluebird: ᏣᏉᎳᏕ [tsagwolde] pg 107)

Blunt: ᎪᏍᏗᏳᎵ [gọsdiyuhli] pg 88)

Boar: ᏧᎦᏅᏍᏓᎵ [tsugąnvsdahli] pg 108)

Board: ᎠᏯᏖᎾ [ąyąte^{3}na] pg 48)

Boasting: ᎠᏨᏮᏍᎦ [atsỵ^{3}k-whsga] pg 46)

Boat: ᏥᏳ [tsiyu] pg 108)

Bobcat: ᎬᎮ [kvhe] pg 91)

Body (his): ᎠᏰᎸᎢ [ahyelv^{3}ʔi] pg 48)

Boiling: ᎠᎵᏥᎭ [altsiha] pg 23)

Boiling it: ᎠᎵᏥᏗᎭ [ahlidsdịha] pg 23)

Bold, to be: ᏍᎦᏎᏅ [sgąsehnv] pg 95)

Bombycilla cedrorum: ᎤᏃᏴ [unoyv] pg 59)

Bonasa umbellus: ᏛᏗᏍᏗ [tvdịsdi] pg 107)

Bone: ᎪᎳ [kola] pg 88)

Boneset (plant): ᎪᎳᎧᎩᏍᏗ [koląkągisdi] pg 88)

Boney: ᎪᎸᎲ [kọlỵhv] pg 88)

Bonnet: ᎠᎵᏍᏚᎶᎯ [alsdulọhi] pg 23)

Booger tobacco: ᏦᎳ ᎠᎦᏴᎵ [tsolą ągąyvli] pg 108)

Book: ᎪᏪᎵ [gohweli] pg 89)

Born: ᎤᏕᏅ [ụdenv] pg 62)

Borrowing it

Borrowing it: ᎠᏙᎵᏍᎦ [ątohlsga] pg 42)

Boss: ᏍᎦᏰᎬᏍᏗ [sgąyegvsdi] pg 95)

Both: ᎢᏧᎳ [ịtsula] pg 52)

Bothering someone: ᎠᏕᏯᏙᏗᎭ [adehytohdịha] pg 40)

Botrypus virginianus: ᎤᏎᎳᏘ [usẹlati] pg 60)

Bottle: ᎫᎫ [gugu] pg 89)

Bottle groud: ᎦᎸᎾ [gąlvʔna] pg 72)

Bow: ᎦᎵᏣᏗ [gahltsadi] pg 71)

Bowing: ᎠᏗᏍᏚᏍᎦ [adį^{3}sdusga] pg 41)

Bowl: ᎤᏅᏪᏓ [ụnỵweda] pg 60)

Box: ᎧᏁᏌ [kąnesa] pg 85)

Box turtle: ᏓᎦᏏ [dagsi] pg 97)

Boxing: ᏓᏓᏛᏂᎭ [dadadvhnịha] pg 101)

Boy: ᎠᏧᏣ [ąchutsa] pg 45)

Boy, teenage: ᎠᏫᎾ [ąwina] pg 46)

Bragging: ᎠᏨᏮᏍᎦ [atsỵ^{3}k-whsga] pg 46)

Braiding hair: ᎠᏍᏕᏲᏎᎭ [ąsdẹyoseha] pg 32)

Brains: ᎤᏅᏥᏓ [unvtsida] pg 59)

Brake (on a vehicle): ᏗᎦᏅᏐᏍᏙᏗ [digąnỵsọsdohdi] pg 104)

Branch: ᎠᎹᎨᏴᎢ [ąmageyvʔi] pg 25)

Branch lettuce: ᎠᎪᏍᏚᎩᏍᏗ [ągosdụgisdi] pg 18)

Branch of a tree: ᎤᏩᏂᎦᎳᏅ [ụwanịgahląnv] pg 64)

Branta canadensis: ᏌᏌ [sąsa] pg 95)

Brassica oleracea: ᎣᏍᎨᏫ [ọsgewi] pg 53)

Brassica rapa: ᏙᏌᎾ [dọsąna] pg 106)

Bread: ᎦᏚ [gadu] pg 82)

Breaking (becoming): ᎠᏲᎦ [ąyo^{3}ga] pg 48)

Breaking his bone: ᎠᏛᎳᎦ [advlagʔa] pg 43)

Breaking it (a solid): ᎦᎶᎠ [gąlọʔa] pg 71)

Breaking it (something long): ᎠᏍᏆᎵᏍᎦ [asgwąʔlih^{3}sga] pg 31)

Breast: ᏅᏣᏛ [nvchądv] pg 95)

Breathing: ᎠᏛᎵᎭ [advliha] pg 43)

Briar: ᎧᏄᎦᎵ [kąnugali] pg 85)

Brick: ᎠᏛᏓᎾ [ądvdaʔna] pg 43)

Bridge: ᎠᏒᏨ [ąsvtsv] pg 35)

Bridging it: ᎠᏒᏣᏗᎠ [asvhtsą^{3}dịʔa] pg 35)

Bridle: ᏧᏔᎾᎶ [tsutąnalo] pg 109)

Bringing it (a liquid): ᎦᏁᏤᎭ [gąnhtseha] pg 76)

Bringing it (a solid): ᎠᏲᎯᎭ [ąhyohịha] pg 49)

Bringing it (something alive): ᎧᏂ [kąni] pg 85)

Bringing it (something flexible): ᎦᏃᎯᎭ [gąnhohịha] pg 77)

Broadcasting (seed or similar in concept): ᎦᎳᎨᏴᏛᎥᏍᎦ [gąlągẹ^{3}hydvʔvsga] pg 69)

Broke: ᏚᎵᏍᏆᎵᏒᎯᎠ [dulsgwąlį^{3}sỵhia] pg 106)

Broken bone: ᎤᏛᎳᎦᏍᏛᏅ [udvlągsdỵnv] pg 63)

Brooding: ᎠᎵᏲᏪᏗᎭ [ahlịyowẹ^{3}hdịha] pg 24)

Broom: ᎬᏃᏌᏍᏗ [gỵnosąsdi] pg 91)

Broomsedge bluestem: ᎧᏁᏍᎦ ᏬᏗ [kąnesgą wodi] pg 85)

Brother's older brother: ᎤᏂᎵ [unịli] pg 58)

Brother's sister (male ego): ᎤᏙᎯ [udohi] pg 62)

Brother's sister's son: ᎤᏫᎾ [uwina] pg 65)

Brother's younger brother

Brother's younger brother: ᎤᏄᏥ [unutsi] pg 59)

Brothers: ᏗᎾᎵᏅᏥ [dịnahlịnvtsi] pg 105)

Brothers, we are: ᏦᏍᏓᎵᏅᏥ [tsọsdahlịnvtsi] pg 108)

Brown: ᏬᏗᎨᎢ [wodịgeʔi] pg 110)

Brown thrasher: ᏩᏚᏰᎳ [wạdụyela] pg 109)

Bruise, to have a: ᎤᏲᏃᎪᏍᏓᎯ [uyonọgosdạhi] pg 67)

Bryson City, North Carolina: ᏣᎵᏍᏙᏂ [tsahlsdoni] pg 107)

Buck: ᎦᎳᎩᎾ [gạlạgina] pg 69)

Bucket: ᏔᎷᎩᏍᎩ [tạlugisgi] pg 102)

Budding: ᎠᏍᎫᏓᏔᏍᎦ [ạsgudạtasga] pg 30)

Buffalo: ᏴᎾᏌ [yṿnsa] pg 110)

Bufu spp: ᏩᎶᏏ [wạlosi] pg 109)

Bug: ᏥᎪᏱ [dsgoyi] pg 107)

Bugle: ᎦᏤᎷᎩᏍᏙᏗ [gatsehlụkisdohdi] pg 83)

Building: ᎠᏓᏁᎸᎢ [adanelvʔi] pg 36)

Building it: ᎠᏁᏍᎨᎭ [ahnesgeha] pg 26)

Bull: ᏧᎦᏅᏍᏓᎵ [tsugạnvsdahli] pg 108)

Bull dozer: ᏅᏃ ᎠᏍᏛᎪᏍᎩ [nvnọ ạsdvgọsgi] pg 95)

Bullet: ᎦᏂ [gạʔni] pg 77)

Bullfrog: ᎧᏄᏄ [kạnunu] pg 85)

Bullsnake: ᎢᎾᏓ ᏐᎸᎨᎢ [inạdạ sọlṿgẹʔi] pg 52)

Bullying: ᎦᏁᏄᎵᎠ [gạnenụ^{3}lịʔa] pg 76)

Bumping his elbow: ᎤᎫᏍᏆᎶᎠ [ukụsgwạlo^{3}ʔa] pg 55)

Bumping his head: ᎠᏓᏍᏆᎶᏍᏗᎭ [adasgwạlosdiha] pg 37)

Bumping someone's head: ᎠᏍᏆᎶᎠ [asgwạlọʔa] pg 31)

Bundle: ᎠᏓᎳᏒᎯ [ạdahlsṿhi] pg 36)

Burial: ᎦᏂᏌᎲᎢ [gạnisạhvʔi] pg 77)

Burlap sack: ᏙᎴᏓ [toleda] pg 106)

Burner on a stove: ᎤᏓᏪᎳᎩᏍᏗ [udạwelạgịsdi] pg 61)

Burning: ᎠᎪᎲᏍᎦ [ạgọhvsga] pg 17), ᎠᏙᏪᎳᎩᎠ [ạdọwe-lagịʔa] (pg 42)

Burning himself with hot food: ᎠᎱᎴᏴᏍᎦ [ahụleyvsga] pg 20)

Burning it: ᎠᎪᎲᏍᏗᎭ [agohṿsdịha] pg 17), ᎦᎴᏗᎭ [gạl-hdịha] (pg 70)

Burning up: ᎠᎪᎲᏍᎦ [ạgohvh^{3}sga] pg 17)

Burying him: ᎦᏂᏌᎲᏍᎦ [gạʔnisạ^{3}hvsga] pg 77)

Burying it: ᎦᏄᎳᏒᎥᏍᎦ [gạnulah^{3}sṿʔvsga] pg 79)

Bush: ᎤᏓᏁᎶᎲ [udạnelọhv] pg 61), ᏗᎤᏓᏍᎦ [dịʔụdasga] (pg 104)

Business: ᏗᎦᎸᏫᏍᏓᏁᏗ [dịgạlvhwịsdạndi] pg 104)

But yet: ᎠᏎᏃ [ạsehno] pg 34)

Butcher knife: ᎡᏆ ᎭᏰᎳᏍᏗ [egwạ hạyelạsdi] pg 51)

Buteo jamaicensis: ᏔᏬᏗ ᎡᏆ [tạwodʔ egwa] pg 102)

Buteo spp: ᏔᏬᏗ [tạwodi] pg 102)

Butter: ᎪᏒᏅ [gọsvnv] pg 88)

Butter bean: ᏚᏯᏁᏆ [tuyạnegwa] pg 107)

Butterfly: ᎧᎹᎹ [kạmama] pg 84)

Butternut: ᎪᎯ [kohi] pg 87)

Button: ᎠᎦᏁᏍᏗ [agạnesdi] pg 13)

Buying it: ᎤᏩᏍᎦ [uhwasga] pg 64)

Buying things: ᎤᏩᏒᎥᏍᎦ [uhwạ^{3}sṿʔvsga] pg 64)

Buzzard: ᏑᎵ [suli] pg 97)

Buzzards (they are): ᎠᏂᏑᎵ [ạnịsuli] pg 26)

By oneself

By oneself: ᎤᏩᏌ [uwạsa] pg 64)

C

Cabbage: ᎣᏍᎨᏫ [ọsgewi] pg 53)

Cairina moschata: ᏙᎦᏏ [dogsi] pg 105)

Calendar: ᏅᏙᏗᏎᏍᏗ [nṿdọdịsẹsdi] pg 95)

Calf: ᏩᎧ ᎠᎩᎾ [wạkạ ạgina] pg 109)

Calf of the leg (his): ᎦᏍᏓᎨᏂ [gạsdgeni] pg 81)

Calling (idiom): ᎦᎸᏛᏂᎭ [gạlvdv^{3}ʔniha] pg 73)

Calling out for him: ᎠᏯᏂᎭ [a^{1}yạ^{3}nịha] pg 47), ᏩᏯᏂᎭ [wa^{1}yanịha] (pg 110)

Camel: ᎨᎻᎵ [kemịli] pg 86)

Camera: ᏗᏓᏥᎶᏍᏗᏍᎩ [dịdạtsilosdisgi] pg 105)

Can house: ᎦᎵᏔᏅᏔᏅ ᎠᏗ [gahltạnvtạnvʔ ahdi] pg 71), ᏧᏁᏍᏓᎳ ᏗᏗᏳ [tsunẹsdạlạ dihdiyu] (pg 108)

Canadian lousewort: ᎤᎫᎫᏍᏙ [ụgukusdo] pg 54)

Cancer: ᎠᏓᏰᏍᎩ [ạdayesgi] pg 38)

Candy roaster squash: ᎤᎾᏤᏥᏗ [ụntsetsdi] pg 57)

Canis lupus: ᏩᏯ [wahya] pg 110)

Canis lupus familiaris: ᎩᎵ [gihli] pg 87)

Canning it: ᎦᎶᏔᏅᎥᏍᎦ [gạlhtạnṿ^{3}ʔvsga] pg 72)

Canoe: ᏥᏳ [tsiyu] pg 108)

Cantaloupe: ᎦᏩᏒᎩ [gawhsvgi] pg 83)

Cap over a stove pipe: ᎠᏍᏇᏚᏍᏗ [ạsgwetụsdi] pg 31)

Capra spp: ᏧᎦᏍᏆᎾᎩᏓ [tsuksgwạnạgida] pg 108)

Car: ᏓᏆᎴᎷ [dagwạlelu] pg 100)

Cardinal: ᏙᏧᏩ [totsuwa] pg 106)

Cardinalis cardinalis: ᏙᏧᏩ [totsuwa] pg 106)

Carolina wren: ᎠᎵᏔᎹ [ạlịtạma] pg 23)

Carolina yelloweyed grass: ᏓᎶᏂᎨ ᎤᎾᏍᏕᏥ [dạlonịge ụnạsdetsi] pg 99)

Carpenter: ᎠᏲᎳᏅᏅ [ạyohlạnvnv] pg 49)

Carrion flower: ᏏᎦᏓᏍᎩ [sigạdasgi] pg 96)

Carrots: ᏓᎶᏂᎨ ᎦᎳᏗᏍᎩ [dạlonịgẹ galạdisgi] pg 99)

Carrying it (a liquid): ᎦᎾᏥ [gạnhtsi] pg 74)

Carrying it (a liquid) off: ᎦᏁᏫᏗᎭ [gąnẹwidiha] pg 76)

Carrying it (a solid): ᎠᏱ [ąhyi] pg 48)

Carrying it (a solid) off: ᎠᏫᏗᎭ [ąwidiha] pg 47)

Carrying it (something alive) or it (something flexible) off: ᎦᎾᏫᏗᎭ [gąnąwidiha] pg 74)

Carrying it (something flexible): ᎦᏁᎧ [gąnẹka] pg 75), ᎦᏁᎭ [gąnheha] (pg 75)

Carrying it (something long): ᏕᎦᏂ [dega³ni] pg 103)

Carrying it (something long) off: ᎦᏯᏫᏗᎭ [gąyąwidiha] pg 83)

Carrying it on his back: ᎠᎵᏎᎭ [aliseha] pg 23)

Carving it: ᎠᏲᎳᏅᎥᏍᎦ [ąyo³ʔląnvʔvsga] pg 49)

Carya spp: ᏐᎯ [sohi] pg 96), ᏩᏁᎢ [wąnẹʔi] (pg 109)

Castanea: ᏓᏑᏓᏆᎴᏆ [dąsudągwąlegwa] pg 100)

Castanea dentata: ᏘᎵ [tili] pg 105)

Castanea pumila: ᎤᏅᎩᏅ [uhnvginv] pg 59)

Castor canadensis: ᏙᏯ [doya] pg 106)

Castor oil beans: ᏗᏕᏍᏗᏓᏁᏆ [dįdesdįdąnegwa] pg 105)

Cat: ᏪᏌ [wehsa] pg 110)

Cat greenbriar: ᏄᎦᎸ [nugahlv] pg 95)

Catawba: ᎠᏂᏔᏘ [ąnitagwi] pg 26)

Catberry: ᎤᏍᏓᏍᏗ [ųsdąsdi] pg 60)

Catbriar: ᏄᎦᎸ [nugahlv] pg 95)

Catcher, hind (baseball): ᎣᏁᎦᏂᏱᏍᎩ [ohnegąniyįsgi] pg 53)

Catching fire

Catching fire: ᎠᏥᏍᏓᎵᎦ [atsi³sdahlga] pg 45)

Catching something thrown or chased: ᎦᏂᏱᎭ [gąʔni³yiha] pg 77)

Caterpillar: ᏥᎪᏱ ᎠᏁᏍᎩᎸᎥᏍᎩ [tsgoyį ąnesgįlvʔvsgi] pg 107)

Catfish: ᏧᎵᏍᏓᎾᎵ [tsųlisdąnali] pg 108)

Cathartes aura: ᏑᎵ [suli] pg 97)

Causing it to flow: ᎨᏴᎯᏍᏗᎭ [geʔyvhisdįha] pg 87)

Cave: ᎤᏍᏓᎦᎸᎢ [ųsdagąlvʔi] pg 60)

Cavern: ᎤᏍᏓᎦᎸᎢ [ųsdagąlvʔi] pg 60)

Ceasing: ᎠᏲᎯᏍᏗᎭ [ąyohisdįha] pg 49)

Cedar: ᎠᏥᏂ [atsini] pg 44)

Cedar waxwing: ᎤᏃᏴ [unoyv] pg 59)

Cemetary: ᏗᏓᏂᏐᏗᏳ [dįdanįsodįyu] pg 105), ᏗᏓᏂᏐᏗᏳ [dįdąnįsohdįyu] (pg 105)

Cent: ᏎᏅᏏ [senhsi] pg 96)

Cervus canadensis: ᎠᏩ ᎤᏔᎾ [ahwą utąna] pg 46)

Chaetura pelagica: ᎠᏂᎪᏍᏓᏯ [ąnigọsdahya] pg 26)

Chair: ᎦᏍᎩᎶᎯ [gąsgįlọhi] pg 81)

Challenging: ᎦᏁᏄᎵᎠ [gąnenų³lįʔa] pg 76)

Chapter: ᎠᏯᏙᎸᎢ [ąyadohlvʔi] pg 48)

Charcoal: ᎧᏃᏍᎬ [kąnosgv] pg 85)

Chasing him/it: ᎠᎨᎯ [ąkẹhi] pg 16)

Chattanooga: ᏣᏓᏄᎩ [tsądąnugi] pg 107)

Cheating: ᎦᎶᏅᎮᎭ [gąlonvheha] pg 72)

Chebecker (bird): ᏥᎪᏲᏙᏍᏗ [dsgoyiʔdọsdi] pg 107)

Check (written payment document): ᎪᏪᎵ ᎠᏕᎳ ᏤᎦ [go-hwelį ądelą tsega] pg 89)

Cheek (his): ᎦᎦᏆᎴᏂ [gąkgwąleni] pg 68)

Chelone spp: ᎠᏫ ᎦᏁᎪᎢ [ahwį gahngoʔi] pg 46)

Chelydra serpentina: ᏌᎵᎫᎩ [sąlį³gu³gi] pg 95)

Cheraw or sera: ᎠᏂᏑᏩᎵ [ąnisųwali] pg 26)

Cherokee: ᎠᏴᏫᏯ [ąyvwįya] pg 51)

Cherry: ᏔᏯ [taya] pg 102)

Chest (of the body): ᎦᏁᏥᎢ [gąnetsiʔi] pg 76)

Chestnut: ᏓᏑᏓᏆᎴᏆ [dąsudągwąlegwa] pg 100), ᏘᎵ [tili] (pg 105)

Chestnut bread: ᏘᎵ ᎠᏑᏱ ᎦᏚ [tįlį ąsuyį gadu] pg 105)

Chestnut-sided warbler: ᏚᏯ [duya] pg 106)

Chewing gum: ᎠᏣ ᎠᎩᏍᏙᏍᏗ [atsą ągįsdosdi] pg 43)

Chewing it: ᎠᎩᏍᏙᎠ [ągisdo³ʔa] pg 17)

Chickadee: ᏥᎩᎵᎵ [tsigįlili] pg 107)

Chickasaw: ᎠᏂᏥᎧᏌ [ąnitsikąsa] pg 26)

Chicken: ᏥᏓᎦ [tsįdaga] pg 108)

Chief: ᎤᎬᏫᏳᎯ [ugvwįyųhi] pg 55)

Child: ᎠᏲᎵ [ąyohli] pg 49)

Child (his): ᎤᏪᏥ [ųwetsi] pg 65)

Chimaphila maculata: ᎠᏨᎩ ᎢᎾᎨᎡᎯ [ahtsvgį įnągeẹhi] pg 45)

Chimney: ᎠᎱᏣᏬᎳᏛᎢ [ąhutsąwolądvʔi] pg 20)

Chimney swift: ᎠᏂᎪᏍᏓᏯ [ąnigọsdahya] pg 26)

Chin: ᎠᏳᎨᏂ [ąyųkeni] pg 49)

Chipmunk, eastern: ᎩᏳᎦ [kįyuga] pg 87)

Choctaw: ᎠᏂᏣᎧᏔ [ąnitsakta] pg 26)

Choking him: ᎥᏍᎩᏱᎭ [vsgiyįha] pg 68)

Chopping it: ᎦᎷᏴᏍᎦ [gąlu³ʔyhsga] pg 72)

Chordeiles minor

Chordeiles minor: ᏓᎳᏍᏙᎬ [dahlsdogv] pg 98)

Christian: ᏧᏁᎸᏗ [tsųnehldi] pg 108)

Christmas: ᎤᎾᏕᏘᏱᏍᎬᎢ [ųnądetįyįsgvʔi] pg 57)

Church: ᏗᎦᎳᏫᎢᏍᏗ [digąlawįʔįsdi] pg 104)

Churn: ᎦᏓᎫᎦ [gadąguga] pg 81)

Churning: ᎠᏍᏙᎠ [asdoʔa] pg 32)

Cigar: ᎪᎦᏍᏗ [goksdi] pg 87)

Cigarette: ᎪᎦᏍᏗ [goksdi] pg 87)

Circus hudsonius: ᎠᎪᏕᎯ [ągọdẹhi] pg 18)

Citrullus lanatus: ᎬᎩᏍᏗ [gṿgisdi] pg 90)

Clan: ᎤᏍᏓᎸᎢ [usdahlvʔi] pg 60)

Clan members: ᏓᏂᎳᏍᏓᏛᎢ [dạnịlasdạdṿʔi] pg 99)

Clarinet: ᎦᏤᎷᎩᏍᏙᏗ [gatsehlụkisdohdi] pg 83)

Class Hirudinea: ᏣᏄᏏ [tsanusi] pg 107)

Clay: ᎦᏓᏆᎵ [gạdạgwali] pg 82)

Cleaning (1): ᎦᏅᎦᎵᎠ [gạnvgạ^{3}lịʔa] pg 79)

Cleaning (2): ᎦᏅᎦᎵᎭ [gạnvgạ^{3}liha] pg 79)

Clearing a field: ᎦᎶᎨᏗᎠ [gạlọgedịʔa] pg 71)

Clearing a path: ᎠᏣᎦᏍᎦ [ahtsạ^{3}ksga] pg 43)

Clearing it (something alive) away: ᎠᎧᎲᎠ [ạkạhṿʔa] pg 15)

Clearing it (something flexible) off: ᎦᎾᎬᎠ [gạna^{3}ʔgṿʔa] pg 74)

Clearing it (something long) away: ᎠᏏᏴᎠ [asi^{3}yṿʔa] pg 34)

Clearing stuff away: ᎧᏅᎠ [kạnvʔa] pg 85)

Climbing (up): ᎦᎳᎯ [gạʔlahi] pg 69)

Climbing a hill: ᎧᎾᎷᏍᎦ [kạnạluh^{3}sga] pg 84)

Climbing over: ᎠᏓᏬᎯᎵᏗᎠ [adạwohịldịʔa] pg 38)

Clock: ᎦᎾᏁᏍᎩ [gaʔnạnẹsgi] pg 74)

Close by: ᎾᎥᏂ [nạʔṿ'ni] pg 93)

Closing it: ᎠᏍᏚᎲᏍᎦ [asduhvh^{3}sga] pg 33)

Cloth: ᎠᏅᏬ [ahnṿwo] pg 27)

Cloth sack: ᏕᎦᎵᏗ [dẹgahldi] pg 102)

Clothes dryer: ᏗᏅᏬ ᏗᎧᏲᏗᏍᎩ [dihnṿwọ dịkahyọdịhsgi] pg 105)

Cloud: ᎤᎶᎩᎸ [ulogịlv] pg 56)

Coaching: ᎠᏏᏅᏍᏗᎭ [asị^{3}nhṿsdịha] pg 34)

Coal: ᎧᏃᏍᎬ [kạnosgv] pg 85)

Coat: ᎤᏌᎴᏂ [usạleni] pg 60), ᎦᏌᎴᎾ [gasạlena] (pg 81)

Coccyzus Americanus: ᏓᎶᎬ [dạlogv] pg 99)

Coffee: ᎪᏫ [kowi] pg 89)

Coix lacryma-jobi: ᏎᎷ ᎤᏂᏥ [selụ ụnitsi] pg 96)

Colaptes auratus auratus: ᎤᏁᎦᏓ [ụnegada] pg 57)

Cold: ᎤᏴᏣ [uhyvtsa] pg 68), ᎧᎾᏬᎦ [kạnạwo^{3}ga] (pg 84)

Cold water: ᎠᎹ ᎤᏯᏥ [ạm uhyatsi] pg 25)

Colinus virginianus: ᎤᏊᏪᎯ [ụgkwehi] pg 55)

Collander: ᎦᏁᏐᎸᏍᏙᏗ [gạnẹsolṿsdoʔdi] pg 76)

Collar: ᎠᏯᏨᏗ [ahyạtsvhdi] pg 48)

Colt: ᏐᏈᎵ ᎠᎩᎾ [sọgwịli ạgina] pg 96)

Coluber constrictor: ᎤᎦᏑᎯ [ugsụhi] pg 53)

Comb: ᏗᎵᏔᏬᏍᏙᏗ [dihltạwosdodi] pg 105)

Combing it: ᎠᏔᏬᎠ [ahtạwo^{3}ʔa] pg 38)

Come in: ᎦᎵᏦᏕ [gahltsode] pg 71)

Come to a point ...: ᎠᎵᏰᎶᏍᎦ [ahlịyẹ^{3}hlosga] pg 24)

Coming back to life: ᎠᏛᏂᏗᎠ [advhnidịʔa] pg 43)

Coming to an end: ᎠᏍᏛᏍᎦ [astvsga] pg 33)

Common evening-primrose: ᎠᎾᏓᏥ [ạndatsi] pg 25)

Common greenbrier: ᎠᏂᏍᎩᎾ ᎤᎾᏁᏌᏓ [ạnisgịnạ ụnạnẹsạda] pg 26)

Coneflower: ᏐᏤᎾ [sotsena] pg 97)

Congaree (the dog people), see Mooney pg 508: ᎠᏂᎩᎵ [ạnigihli] pg 26)

Congregating (they are) (they are): ᎠᎾᏓᏥᎩᎭ [ạnạdạdsgiha] pg 25)

Conjuring: ᎠᏓᏁᏌᎩᎠ [adahnẹsagịʔa] pg 36), ᏓᏙᏂᎭ [dadoniha] (pg 101)

Conserving: ᎠᎵᏏᏂᏗᎭ [alsị^{3}hndịha] pg 23)

Considering: ᎠᏓᏅᏖᏏᎭ [adante^{3}sịha] pg 37)

Constitution: ᎠᏓᎶᏍᏗ [ạdaʔlosdi] pg 36)

Container for it (a liquid): ᎠᏥᏍᏙᏗ [ạtsị^{3}sdohdi] pg 45)

Container for it (something flexible): ᎦᎸᏙᏗ [gahlvdohdi] pg 73)

Container for solid items: ᎦᎵᏔᏅᏙᏗ [gahltạnvdohdi] pg 71)

Container for something long: ᎦᎳᏗᏍᏙᏗ [gahlạdịsdohdi] pg 69)

Cook: ᏍᏓᏯᎲᏍᎩ [sdayṿhṿsgi] pg 96)

Cooking: ᎬᏂᏍᎦ [gṿnhsga] pg 91)

Copperhead: ᏬᏗᎨᎠᏍᎪᎵ [wodigeạsgoli] pg 110)

Cork: ᏚᏬᎵ [dụwohli] pg 106)

Corn: ᏎᎷ [selu] pg 96)

Corn beer: ᎠᎹᎨᎢ [ạmagẹʔi] pg 25)

Corn bread: ᏎᎷ ᎦᏚ [sẹlụ gadu] pg 96)

Corn cob: ᎤᏗ [udi] pg 62)

Corn tassel: ᎤᏥᏣᏗ [ụtsitsạdi] pg 64)

Corn tassel is falling off: ᎠᏥᎳᏙᎣᏍᎦ [ạtsilạdọʔosga] pg 44)

Corner: ᎤᏅᏏᏴᎢ [ụnvsiyvʔi] pg 59)

Cornsilk: ᏎᎷ ᎤᏁᏄᏗ [selụ ụnenuhdi] pg 96)

Corpse: ᎤᏴᏐᏒᎯ [uyṿhosṿhi] pg 67)

Correct: ᏚᏳᎦᏔ [dụyukta] pg 107)

Corvus brachyrhynchos: ᎪᎦ [koga] pg 87)

Corylus americana: ᎠᏳᎩᏓ [ahyụgida] pg 49)

Cost: ᏧᎬᏩᎶᏗ [tsugvwahldi] pg 108)

Cotton: ᎤᏥᎸ [utsịʔlv] pg 64)

Cotton grass: ᏥᏍᏚ ᏍᎩᏓᏘ [tsisdụ sgidạti] pg 107)

Cotton thistle: ᏥᏥ [tsitsi] pg 108)

Cottonmouth: ᎧᏁᏇᏓ [kạnegwoda] pg 84)

Cottonwood: ᎠᏓ ᎬᏂᎯᏛ [adạ gṿnịhidv] pg 36)

Cottus spp: ᏥᏍᏆᎸᎾ [tsịsgwạlvna] pg 107)

Coughing: ᎤᏏᏩᏍᎦ [usihwah^{3}sga] pg 61)

Council house: ᎫᏆᎳᏫᎢᎢᏍ [digalawi?isdi] pg 104)

Counting: D┼ᎮᎱ [ase³hiha] pg 33)

County: ᎦᏚᎩ [gadugi] pg 82)

Covered with dirt: ᎦᏄᎳᏍᎠ [ganulah³sa?a] pg 78)

Covering it: ᏙᎠᏴᏗᎾᏍ [ado³sv?vsga] pg 42), ᏻᏈᎾᏍ [gu³sa?vsga] (pg 89)

Covering it with dirt: ᎦᏄᎳᏴᏗᎾᏍ [ganulah³sv?vsga] pg 79)

Cow: ᏆᎠ [waka] pg 109)

Cow's foot: ᏆᎠ ᎤᏢᏍᏗ [waka ulasidi] pg 109)

Coward: ᎤᏍᎦᎴᏂ [usga?eni] pg 60)

Crab apple: ᏒᎦᏓᏛ ᎢᎾᎦᎠᏁᎵ [svgdy inageanehl] pg 97)

CRACKING

Cracking: DᏍᎾᏥᎦᏛ [adysgwalo?a] pg 43)

Cracking it: EᎾᏥᎦᏛ [gvsgwalo³?a] pg 91)

Crane: ᎧᏅᏍᎦᏫ [kansgawi] pg 84)

Craving it: DᎠᏴᎾᏍ [asgwoh³sga] pg 31)

Crawling: DᏙᏟᏂᏛ [adahnsi³nidoha] pg 37)

Crayfish, brown: ᏨᏍᏛᎾ [tsisdvna] pg 107)

Crayfish, green: ᏨᏍᏛᎾ [tsisdvna] pg 107)

Crayfish, red: ᏥᏍᎪᎩᎵ [tsisgogili] pg 107)

Crazy: ᎤᎸᏗᏱ [ulvdiha] pg 56)

Creating: ᎠᏒᎾᏍ [go³svsga] pg 88)

Creek: DᎻᎢᏴᏔ [amageyv?i] pg 25)

Creek (lower): DᏂᎧᏫᏔ [anikawita] pg 26)

Creek (upper): DᏂᏧᏏ [anikusi] pg 26)

Crested iris: ᎤᎾᏍᏔ [usga?hi] pg 60)

Cricket: ᏩᏩᏚ [taladu] pg 102)

Crimson beebalm: ᏩᎴᎷ ᎤᏂᏣᎩᏍᏗ [walelu unitsagisdi] pg 109)

Crippled: DᏟᏒᏂD [ali?enia] pg 21)

Cross: ᏗᏓᎾᏩᎳ [didanawida] pg 105)

Crossing: ᏓᏐᎧ [dasoka] pg 100)

Crotalus horridus: DᏨᏯ ᎤᏒᏃᏗ [atsyya utsonydi] pg 46), ᎤᏒᏃᏗ [utsonadi] (pg 64)

Crow: ᎠᎦ [koga] pg 87)

Crow bar: ᏆᎠ ᎤᏢᏗ [waka ulasidi] pg 109)

Crown of his head: DᏣᏍᎢᏂ [ayhsgeni] pg 47)

Crowsfoot: DᏂᎠᎸᏍᎦᎸᏯ [anahlsgwalysgi] pg 25)

Crying: DᎨᏲᏱ [atsohyiha] pg 45)

Crying out: ᎤᏌᎷᎧ [uhweluka] pg 65)

Cucumber: ᎦᎦᎻ [gagama] pg 68)

Cucumber tree: ᏧᏍᎦᏍ ᏤᏆ [tsugwaloga tsegwa] pg 108)

Cucumis melo: ᎦᏆᏒᏱ [gawhsvgi] pg 83)

Cucumis sativus: ᎦᎦᎻ [gagama] pg 68)

Cucurbita maxima: ᎤᏁᏒᏥᏗ [untsetsdi] pg 57)

Cucurbita spp: ᏆᏱᏍ [wagiga] pg 109)

Cullowhee, NC: ᎦᎸᎯ [gahlohi] pg 71)

Cup: ᎦᏄᎱᎳᏗ [ganuhuhldi] pg 78)

Curled dock: ᏔᎦᎩ [dagki] pg 97)

Cutting a tree: ᎦᎴᏴᏗᏱ [galeyvsdiha] pg 70)

Cutting hair: DᏍᏙᏴᏱ [asdo³yeha] pg 32)

Cutting his nails: ᏓᏓᏑᎷᎧᎵᏱ [dadasu³kaliha] pg 101)

Cutting into strips: ᎦᎷᏓᏍᎦ [galvdasga] pg 73)

Cutting it (a solid) off: DᎬᏆᎳᎵᏱ [agy³haliha] pg 19)

Cutting it (something flexible) off: DᎦᎸᏍᎦ [aga?lisga] pg 13)

Cutting it (something long) off: DᏌᏥᎸᏍᎦ [asgwa³?lisga] pg 30)

Cutting it with a knife: DᏰᎦᎸᏱ [a¹yehloha] pg 48)

Cutting it with an axe: ᎦᎷᏴᏍᎦ [galu³?yhsga] pg 72)

Cutting off a head of cabbage: DᏌᏧᎳᏱD [asgudagi?a] pg 30)

Cutting weeds: DᎦᏓᎾᏍ [ahtsa³ksga] pg 43)

Cyanocitta cristata: ᏣᏯᎦ [tsayga] pg 107)

Cynoglossum virginianum: ᎤᏂᏍᏕᎴᏍᏗ [unisdelesdi] pg 58)

Cypripedium spp: ᎤᎫᏆ ᎤᏢᏑᏩ [ugkwe ulasula] pg 55)

D

Dancing: DᎵᏍᎩᎠD [alsgi³?a] pg 22)

Dark (in the): ᎷᎸᏏᎦᏴᎢ [huhlsigv?i] pg 93)

Dark-eyed junco: ᏚᏗ [tuti] pg 106)

Dart (for a blow gun): ᏨᏟ [tsitsi] pg 108)

Daughter-in-law: ᎤᏦᎢ [utso?i] pg 64)

Dawn: ᏴᎾᎴᏥᎦ [sunale?itsa] pg 97)

Day: ᏔᎦ [iga] pg 52), ᎤᏙᏗᎬᏛ [udodygwadv] (pg 63)

Dead: ᎤᎵᏬᏨᎭ [uliwotsvhi] pg 56), ᎤᎯᏒᎭ [uyhosvhi] (pg 67)

Deaf (in both hears): ᏧᎵᏒᏂ [tsuli?eni] pg 108)

December: ᎢᎾᏱᏉ [vsgiyi] pg 68)

Deep: DᏍᏛᎧᎠ [asdv³ka] pg 33), ᎱᏂ [hawini] (pg 92), ᎰᏂ [howini] (pg 93)

Deer: DᎥᎢ [ahwi] pg 46)

Deer clan: DᏂᎧᎥᎢ [anikawi] pg 26)

Deer tongue: DᎥᎢ ᎦᎾᏃᎢ [ahwi gahngo?i] pg 46)

Deer-eye (black eyed susan): DᎥᎢ DᎦᏔ [ahwi akta] pg 46)

Defecating: ᏓᏗᎩᏍᎦ [dadiksga] pg 101)

Degenerant: ᎤᎸᎾᏥᏍᎩ [ulvntisgi] pg 56)

Delaware Indians: DᎾᎧᏫᎾᎩ [anakwanki] pg 25)

Delegating him to do …:: ᎦᏅᏍᎦ [ganvsga] pg 80)

Denying it: DᏎᏲᏱ [adehyiha] pg 40)

Devil: DᏍᎩᎾ [asgina] pg 30)

Dew on the ground: ᎤᏰᏌᏛ [uhyesadv] pg 66)

120

Dewberries: ᎤᏔᎸ ᎠᏚᏫ [saloli akta] pg 95)

Diaper: ᎠᏐᏍᏗ [asosdi] pg 34)

Didelphis virginiana: ᎤᏪᏕᏍᏗ [utsedsdi] pg 63)

Different: ᎤᏓᎴᎯ [udalehi] pg 61)

Different from: ᏓᏓᎴᎦ [dadale?ga] pg 100)

Digging it: ᎠᏍᎪᏍᎦ [asgosga] pg 30)

Dime: ᏍᎪᏂᏎᏏ [sgonisensi] pg 96)

Diospyros virginiana: ᏌᎵ [sali] pg 95)

Dipping a liquid: ᎠᎫᎩᎠ [akugi?a] pg 18)

Dirt: ᎦᏓ [gahda] pg 81)

Dirty: ᎦᏓᎭ [gahdaha] pg 81)

Disciple: ᏗᏕᎶᎦᏍᎩ [didelogwasgi] pg 105)

Disease: ᎲᏳᎩ [huhyugi] pg 93)

Dish: ᎤᎾᏩ [uhnawa] pg 57)

Dislikes him: ᎦᏁᎵᎭ [gane³liha] pg 76)

Disposing of a body: ᎦᏂᏌᎲᏍᎦ [ga?nisa³hvsga] pg 77)

Distance: ᏂᎨᎢ [nigei] pg 94)

Distress: ᎡᎯᏍᏗ [ehisdi] pg 51)

Diving: ᎠᎵᎩᏴᏍᎦ [aligvyhsga] pg 21)

Doctor: ᎦᎾᎩᏗ [ga?nakdi] pg 73)

Doctoring him: ᎧᏅᏫᎠ [kanvwi?a] pg 86)

Dog: ᎩᎵ [gihli] pg 87)

Doing it: ᎾᏛᏀᎭ [nadvneha] pg 93)

Dolichovespula maculata: ᏎᎾᏓ [sehwada] pg 96)

Dollar: ᎠᏕᎵᎯ [adely?hi] pg 39)

Door: ᎠᏍᏙᎯᏗ [asdohdi] pg 32)

Doorway: ᎦᎶᎯᏍᏗ [galohisdi] pg 71)

Dotted: ᎤᏚᎢᏍᎦ [udu?isga] pg 63)

Dough

Dough: ᎦᏚᎳᏍᏗ [gadulasdi] pg 82)

Down: ᎡᎸᏗ [elvdi] pg 51)

Down below: ᎡᎳᏗ [eladi] pg 51)

Downhill: ᎨᏓᎵ [kedali] pg 86)

Downy woodpecker: ᏥᏍᏇᏄᏨ [tsisgwenutsv] pg 107)

Dragging it: ᎦᏂᏏᏂ [gansi³ni] pg 74)

Drama: ᏗᎾᏛᏁᎵᏍᎬᎢ [dinadvnelisgv?i] pg 105)

Drawing: ᏓᏟᏍᏗᎭ [da?tsilo³sdiha] pg 102)

Dreaming about it: ᎠᏍᎩᏥᏍᎦ [asgi³tsga] pg 30)

Dreaming of many things: ᎠᏍᎩᏨᎥᏍᎦ [asgichy?vsga] pg 30)

Dress: ᎠᏌᎾ [asano] pg 28)

Dressing: ᏓᎾᏩᎠ [dahnawo?a] pg 99)

Drinking: ᎠᏗᏣᏍᎦ [adi³tsga] pg 41)

Dripping: ᎤᏍᏚᏥᎠ [usdutsi?a] pg 60), ᎦᏍᎪᎳᏍᎦ [gasgwolvsga] (pg 81)

Driving a car: ᎠᏲᎵ [ahyeli] pg 48)

Driving it: ᎦᎾᏅᏍᏗᎭ [gahnvwsdiha] pg 80)

Driving it in: ᎠᎭᏔᏍᎦ [ahatasga] pg 19)

Driving recklessly fast on dangerous rural or mountain roads: ᎠᏳᏲᎰᏍᎦ [ayuyohosga] pg 50), ᏕᎦᏳᏲᎰᎲᏗᎭ [degayuyohohndiha] (pg 103)

Dropping accidentally it (a solid): ᎤᏬᎰᏎᎭ [uwoho³seha] pg 65)

Dropping it (a liquid): ᎪᎲᏅᏗᎭ [gohvhndiha] pg 88)

Dropping it (a solid): ᎪᎰᏅᏗᎭ [goho³hndiha] pg 88)

Dropping it (something alive): ᎠᏙᎥᎲᏅᏗᎭ [ado?vhndiha] pg 41)

Dropping it (something flexible): ᎠᏙᎥᎲᏅᏗᎭ [ado?vhndiha] pg 41)

Dropping it (something long): ᎠᏐᎰᎲᏅᏗᎭ [aso?ohndiha] pg 34)

Drowning: ᎠᎩᎦ [agvga] pg 19), ᎦᏃᏴᎦ [ganoyv³ga] (pg 78)

Drowning him: ᎠᎩᏯᎲᏍᎦ [agv?yhsga] pg 19)

Drum: ᎠᎱᎵ [ahu?li] pg 20)

Drying it out: ᎠᎧᎰᎯᏅᏗᎭ [akahyoh³diha] pg 16)

Drying out: ᎠᎧᎯᏲᏍᎦ [akahyosga] pg 15)

Dryobates pubescens: ᏥᏍᏇᏄᏨ [tsisgwenutsv] pg 107)

Dryocopus pileatus: ᎨᎬᎪᎬ [ge?gwogv] pg 86)

Dryopteris spp: ᏲᎾ ᎤᏤᏍᏓ [yona utsesda] pg 110)

Duck: ᎧᏬᏄ [kawonu] pg 86)

Dumetella carolinensis: ᎤᏥᎹ [utsi?ma] pg 64)

During the year (in the): ᎤᏕᎯᏗᏴᏌᏗᏍᎥᎢ [udehdiyvsadisv?i] pg 62)

Dwarf chestnut: ᎤᎾᏱᎾ [uhnyginv] pg 59)

Dwarf crested iris: ᎤᏍᎦᎯ [usga?hi] pg 60)

Dwelling: ᎡᎯ [ehi] pg 51)

E

Eager: ᎤᎵᏔᏅᏀᎭ [uhlita³?neha] pg 56)

Eagle: ᎠᏬᎯᎵ [awohili] pg 47)

Ear: ᎦᎴᏂ [gale?ni] pg 70)

Ear rings: ᏧᎾᏥᎠᏙᎯ [tsunatsi?adohi] pg 108)

Earache: ᎤᎵᏍᏆᏗᏍᎬᎢ [ulisgwadisgv?i] pg 55)

Earth: ᎡᎶᎯ [elohi] pg 51)

East: ᎧᎸᎬᎢ [kalvgv?i] pg 84)

Easter: ᏧᏪᏥ ᏓᏂᏑᏫᏍᎬᎢ [tsuwetsi danisuwisgv?i] pg 109)

Eastern bluebird: ᏣᎪᎳᏕ [tsagwolde] pg 107)

Eastern cottontail: ᏥᏍᏚ [tsisdu] pg 107)

Eastern kingbird: ᏗᎵᎦᏩ [dilegwa] pg 105)

Eastern newt: ᏓᎴᏴᏍᎩ [daleyvsgi] pg 98)

Eastern racer: ᎤᎦᏑᎯ [ugsuhi] pg 53)

Eastern towhee: ᏧᏬᏍᎦ [tsuwosga] pg 109)

121

Eastern whip-poor-will. Whip-poor-will: ᏩᏊᎵ [wạguli] pg 109)
Eating a meal: ᎠᎵᏍᏓᏴᎲᏍᎦ [alsda³ʔyvhvsga] pg 22)
Eating it (a solid): ᎠᎩᎠ [ạgịʔa] pg 16)
Eating it (something flexible): ᎠᏯᎩᎠ [ạyạ³gịʔa] pg 47)
Eating it (something long): ᎠᏍᏗᎩᎠ [asdi³gịʔa] pg 32)
Ectopistes migratorius: ᏬᏱ [woyi] pg 110)
Edge of: ᎠᏍᏛᎢ [ạsdvʔi] pg 33)
Eel: ᏛᏰᏆ [tvyegwa] pg 107)
Egg (his): ᎤᏪᏥ [ụwetsi] pg 65)
Eight: ᏧᏁᎳ [tsanela] pg 107)
Eighteen: ᏁᎳᏚᎯ [neladụhi] pg 94)
Eighty: ᏁᎳᏍᎪᎯ [nelsgohi] pg 94)
Elastic: ᎠᏣ ᏗᏓᏅᎩᏍᎩ [atsạ didạnạgisgi] pg 44)
Elbow (his): ᎠᎫᏍᎨᏂ [ạkụsgeni] pg 18)
Elbowing it: ᎠᎪᏍᎩᏍᏗᎭ [akọsgisdịha] pg 18)
Elderberry: ᎪᏒᎦ [gosvʔga] pg 88)
Electricity: ᎠᎾᎦᎵᏍᎩ [ạnagạlịsgi] pg 25)
Elephant: ᎧᎹᎹ [kạmama] pg 84)
Eleven: ᏐᏚᎯ [soʔdụhi] pg 97)
Elk: ᎠᏩ ᎤᏔᎾ [ahwạ utạna] pg 46)
Elm: ᏧᎩᏅ [tsuʔginv] pg 108)
Emitting body gas: ᎠᏌᎩᎠ [asạkiʔa] pg 28)
Empidonax minimus: ᏥᎪᏱᏙᏍᏗ [dsgoyiʔdọsdi] pg 107)
End: ᎣᏂ [ohni] pg 53)
End (at the): ᎠᏍᏛᎢ [ạsdvʔi] pg 33)
Ending it: ᏓᏍᏆᏗᎠ [dasgwadị³a] pg 100)
Enemy (his): ᎤᏍᎦᎩ [usgagi] pg 60)
Englishmen: ᎠᏂᎩᎵᏏ [ạnigịlịsi] pg 26)
Enough: ᏰᎵᏉ [yeligwo] pg 110)
Entering it: ᎠᏴᎯᎭ [ạyvhịha] pg 50)
Equus asinus x Equus caballus: ᏔᏁᏆ [tạnegwa] pg 102)
Equus ferus caballus: ᏐᏈᎵ [sogwịli] pg 96)
Equus spp: ᏧᏂᎶᏗ ᏐᏈᎵ [tsunilohdị sogwịli] pg 108)
Erasing: ᎪᏪᎳᎩᎠ [kọwelạgịʔa] pg 89)
Eriophorum spp: ᏥᏍᏚ ᏍᎩᏓᏘ [tsisdụ sgidạti] pg 107)
Eupetorium spp: ᎪᎳᎧᎩᏍᏗ [kolạkạgisdi] pg 88)

EVAPORATED

Evaporated: ᎤᎶᏐᏅ [ụlọsohnv] pg 56)
Evening: ᎤᏏᏂᏕᎾ [ulsihnidena] pg 56)
Evening star: ᎠᎾᏓᏥ [ạndatsi] pg 25)
Everywhere: ᏂᏆᎢ [nịkvʔi] pg 94)
Examining it: ᎠᎪᎵᏰᎠ [ạgoli³yẹʔa] pg 17)
Exiting: ᎦᏄᎪᎦ [gạnugo³ga] pg 78)

Eye (his): ᎠᎦᏙᎵ [ạktoli] pg 14), ᎠᎧᏅᎢ [ạkanvʔi] (pg 15)
Eye ball: ᎠᎦᏔ [ạkta] pg 13)
Eyebrow (his): ᎤᎦᏘᏳᏩᏅᎢ [uktiyuwạnvʔi] pg 54)
Eyelash (his): ᎤᎧᏛᎢ [ukạdvʔi] pg 54)
Eyelid (his): ᎤᎦᏔᏄᎶᏓ [uktạnuloda] pg 54)

F

Face (his): ᎤᎧᏛᎢ [ukạdvʔi] pg 54)
Fading: ᎠᏍᎪᎸᎦ [asgolvga] pg 30)
Fading clothes: ᏓᏍᎪᎸᎢᏍᏗᎭ [dasgọlvʔịsdịha] pg 100)
Fagus grandifolia: ᎫᏍᏗ [kusd] pg 90)
Failing: ᎤᏄᏞᎲᏍᎦ [unu³lvhvsga] pg 59)
Fainting: ᎤᎸᏖᎭ [ulvteha] pg 56)
Falco columbarius: ᏌᎾᏩ [sanạwa] pg 95)
Falco sparverius: ᎩᎩ [gigi] pg 87)
Fall (season): ᎤᎶᎪᎰᏍᏗ [ụlogọhọsdi] pg 56)
Falling: ᎦᎶᎰᏍᎦ [gạloʔoh³sga] pg 71), ᎪᎰᏍᎦ [gohosga] (pg 88)
Falling (a solid): ᎪᎰᏍᎦ [gohosga] pg 88)
Falling (multiple falls): ᎦᏄᎪᎰᏍᎦ [gạnugoʔọsga] pg 78)
Falling (something long): ᎠᏐᎰᏍᎦ [asọʔosga] pg 34)
Falling to the ground: ᎦᏅᎦ [gạnv³ga] pg 79)
False hellebore: ᎠᏍᏇᏁᏓ [ạsgwyneda] pg 31)
False rhubarb: ᏧᏂᏦᏴᏍᏗ [tsuhnịtsohysdi] pg 108)
False solomon's seal: ᎤᏗᎵᏍᏗ [ụdihlịsdi] pg 62)
Family: ᏚᎵᏗᎾᏴᎢ [duldinaʔyvʔi] pg 106)
Family Anatidae: ᎧᏬᏄ [kạwonu] pg 86)
Family Aphididae: ᏘᎾ [tina] pg 105)
Family Scincidae: ᏣᏁᏅ [tsạnenv] pg 107)
Family Soricidae: ᏓᏥᏍᎨᏫ [dahlsgewi] pg 98)
Family Tettigoniidae: ᏥᎩᎩ [tsigigi] pg 107)
Family Vespertilionidae: ᏣᎹᎭ [tsamạha] pg 107)
Family: Acrididae: ᎢᏞ [vle] pg 68)
Far: ᎢᎾ [ina] pg 52)
Far far away: ᎢᏅᎯᏳ [invhiyu] pg 52)
Fast: ᎤᎵᏍᏓ [uhlịsda] pg 55), ᎦᏨᏄᎳ [gatsvnula] (pg 83)
Fastening: ᎠᏍᏓᏱᏗᎠ [asda³ʔyidịʔa] pg 32)
Fat: ᎦᎵᏦᎯᏓ [gahltsohida] pg 71)
Father: ᎤᏙᏓ [udoda] pg 62)
Father's brother: ᎤᏙᏓ [udoda] pg 62)
Father's brother's wife: ᎤᏘᎾᎢ [utịnạʔi] pg 62)
Father's father: ᎤᏂᏏ [unisi] pg 58)
Father's sister: ᎤᎶᎩ [uhlogi] pg 56)
Fearless: ᏍᎦᏎᏅ [sgạsehnv] pg 95)
Feather: ᎤᎩᏓᎵ [ụgidahli] pg 54)
February: ᎦᎵᎦᎵ [gahlgali] pg 70)

Federal government officials: DhᏉᏐᏋ [aniwatsini] pg 26)

Feeding: ᏝᏘᏬ [keloha] pg 86)

Feeling it: DRhᏬ [asy³hniha] pg 35)

Felis silvestris catus: ᏉᎱ [wehsa] pg 110)

Fen orchid: ᎣᏟᏞᏝᏎᎯᎫ [uyodahliyusdi] pg 67)

Fence: DKBT [atsohyvʔi] pg 45)

Fence lizard: WᏪᏬᏞ [tayuhali] pg 102)

Festival: ᎫᎧᏒᏝᏞᎪET [dinadvnelisgvʔi] pg 105)

Fetching it (a liquid): ᎤᏑᏴᏴ [ganegisi] pg 75)

Fetching it (a solid): DᎩᏴ [agisi] pg 17)

Fetching it (something alive) or it (something flexible): ᎤᎾᎩᏴ [ganagisi] pg 74)

Fetching it (something long): DᎥD [ayi³ʔa] pg 48)

Fever

Fever: ᎣᎫᏟᎩ [udilegi] pg 62)

Field: KᏝᏴ [tsogesi] pg 108)

Fifteen: ᎯᎾᎦᎦᎯ [hisgaduhi] pg 93)

Fifty: ᎯᎩᎾᎠᎯ [hiksgohi] pg 93)

Fighting: DᏞᏬ [ahliha] pg 21)

Filling it: DᎧᏞTᏬ [akaliʔiha] pg 15)

Finding it (a liquid): ᎤᎫᎣᎫᏬ [gane³hwdiha] pg 77)

Finding it (a solid): DᎩᎫᏬ [ahwa³tiha] pg 46)

Finding it (something alive) or it (something flexible): ᎤᎾᎣᎫᏬ [gana³whtiha] pg 75)

Finding it (something long): DBᎣᎫᏬ [ayy³hwtiha] pg 51)

Finger: DᏏᎱᏒᎢT [a³hyesadvʔi] pg 48)

Fingernail (his): ᎤᎰᏐᎧᏁT [uhyesukahlvʔi] pg 66)

Finishing: DᏍᎥᎤᎾ [astvsga] pg 33)

Fire: DᏐW [atsila] pg 44)

Fire (in a): EᏝ [gvda] pg 91)

Fire, uncontrolled: ᎤᏞE [galigv] pg 70)

Firecracker plant: ᎣᎾᏓᎡ [usgwado] pg 60)

Fireplace: DᏐWᎯ [atsilahi] pg 44)

Fireside: DᏐWᎦᎫᎯ [atsilayuhldi] pg 44)

Firing a gun: DᏍᎩᎦᏬ [asdayohiha] pg 32)

First: DEᎥᏏ [agvyi] pg 19)

Fish: DᎩᎫ [atsadi] pg 44)

Fish hawk: ᎪᎣᏙᎬ [kanvtsuhwa] pg 85)

Fish hook: DᏐᏙ [atsu³di] pg 45)

Fishing: DᏓᎳᎾᎤ [ahchu³hvsga] pg 45)

Fishing pole: ᎤᏓᎫ [gadvdi] pg 82)

Fist (his): ᎣᎾᎤᏬ [usgwenyhi] pg 60)

Fist fighting: ᏝᏝᏒhᏬ [dadadvhniha] pg 101)

Five: ᎯᎾᎩ [hisgi] pg 93)

Flag: ᎤᏝᎫ [gadati] pg 82)

Flashlight: DᏟᎾVᏝ [atsystdi] pg 46)

Flat: DᏉᏔᎾ [ayate³na] pg 48)

Flea: ᏙᏔ [tsuka] pg 108)

Flesh (his): ᎣᏬᎶᏓT [ugwedahlvʔi] pg 60)

Flint: ᎤᏩᎤᏞ [duwisgali] pg 106)

Flipping it: ᎤᎿhᏬ [galvdv³ʔniha] pg 73)

Flipping it (something alive) with his finger: DᏔᎯᎥᏬ [agwayohiha] pg 27)

Flirting with her: DᏐSiᎾᎤ [atstuʔvsga] pg 45)

Floating: ᎧᎬᎯ [kanuhi] pg 85)

Floating it: ᎧᎬᏫᎥᏬ [kanuhv³hdiha] pg 85)

Flooding: ᎤᎣᎦᎩD [ganvhugiʔa] pg 79)

Floor: DᏏᏝᎱᏔT [ayodasahvʔi] pg 49)

Floor (on the): RWᎫ [eladi] pg 51)

Florida: ᏙᎤZᎶT [tsuganowvʔi] pg 108)

Flour: ᎣᎤᎤᎯ [utsalesdi] pg 63)

Flour corn: ᏠMᏫᎯ [seluyahi] pg 96)

Flower: DᏐᎦᎥᎩ [atsilvsgi] pg 44)

Flowers is falling off: DᏐWVᏯᎤᎤ [atsiladoʔosga] pg 44)

Flowing: DᏐᏫ [ageʔya] pg 16), ᏝᏫ [geʔya] (pg 87)

Flute: ᎤᏙMᎩᏫVᎫ [gatsehlukisdohdi] pg 83)

Flying

Flying: DWᎧᎫᏬ [ahlawi³diha] pg 21), ᎤZᎯᏞ [ganohi³li] (pg 78)

Flying squirrel: ᎤᎬ [dewa] pg 104)

Foam: ᎣᏬᎩᏞ [uwogili] pg 65)

Foaming: ᎤᏬᎩWᎾᎤ [gawo³kilasga] pg 83)

Fog: ᎣᏔᎯᎫ [ukahadi] pg 54)

Following: DᏫᏝᎩᎫ [asda³wadi] pg 31)

Food: ᎣᏞᏫᏝBᎫ [ulsdahydi] pg 55)

Foot (his): ᎣWᏴᎤh [uhlasihdeni] pg 55)

For the duration of: TAᎦᏒ [igohidv] pg 52)

Forehead (his): DEᏝᎯh [agvdigeni] pg 19)

Forgetting it: ᎣᎬᏝᎤᎾ [uwke³whsga] pg 64)

Fork: BᎩ [yvgi] pg 110)

Fork in the branch of a tree: ᎣᎬᏝE [ulodskv] pg 56)

Forming: ARᎾᎤ [go³svsga] pg 88)

Forty: ᎣᎩᏫᎠᎯ [nvksgohi] pg 95)

Foul ball (stickball): ᏫᏰ [woye] pg 110)

Four: ᎣᎩ [nvki] pg 95)

Fourteen: ᎣᎤᎦᎯ [nvgaduhi] pg 95)

Fox: ᏙW [tsula] pg 108)

Fox grapes: ᎣᎻᏔᏋWᎫ [unitelvlahdi] pg 58), ᏔᏋWᎫ [tely³ladi] (pg 104)

Fox squirrel: ᎱᎬᏞ ᏬᎫ [saloli wohdi] pg 95)

Fragaria virginiana: ᎠᏂ [ani] pg 26)

Fraxinus L: ᏧᎦᏃᏅ [tsugạnonv] pg 108)

Freckles: ᎤᏁᏘ [ụneti] pg 58)

Free labor company: ᎦᏚᎩ [gadugi] pg 82)

Freeing: ᎤᏲᏍᎦ [uyosga] pg 67)

Freezer: ᎠᏴᏣᏗᏍᏗᏍᎩ [ahyvtsạdịsdịsgi] pg 50), ᎤᏁᏍᏓᎵ ᎪᏒᏍᎩ [ụnẹsdahl gọsvsgi] (pg 58)

Freezing: ᎤᏁᏍᏓᎳᏗᎠ [unesdaldịʔa] pg 58)

Frenchmen: ᎠᏂᎦᎸᏥ [ạnigạlvhtsi] pg 26)

Friday: ᏧᏂᎩᎶᏍᏗ [tsuhnigịlosdi] pg 108)

Friend: ᎤᎾᎵᎢ [unali^{4}ʔi] pg 57)

Friends (his) (they are): ᎤᎾᎵᎢ [unali^{4}ʔi] pg 57)

Friendship: ᎠᎵᎢ [alịʔi] pg 21)

Frightening him: ᎠᏖᏍᏗᎭ [ạtesdiha] pg 40)

Frog: ᎦᎵᏉᎩ [gahlgwogi] pg 70), ᏕᎧ [deka] (pg 103)

From ...: ᏚᎶᏒᏫ [dulosvhi] pg 106)

Frost on ground (white): ᎤᏯᏛᎲ [uhyạtvhv] pg 66)

Frost on the ground (ice): ᎤᎾᏄᏍᏗ [unaʔnụsdi] pg 57)

Frying it: ᎬᎾᏬᏗᎭ [gvhnạwọ^{3}hdịha] pg 91)

Frying meat: ᏕᎬᏣᎳᏍᎦ [degvchạlah^{3}sga] pg 104)

Full: ᎤᏑᎵᎭ [usulịha] pg 61)

Full moon: ᎧᎵ ᏅᏓ [kạli nvda] pg 84)

Funny: ᎤᏬᏥᏗ [uwotsdi] pg 66)

G

Gall bladder: ᏓᎶᏂ [dạloni] pg 99)

Gallon: ᎢᏳᏥᎶᏓ [iyutsiloda] pg 53), ᏑᏥᎶᏓ [sụtsịloda] (pg 97)

Gallus gallus domesticus: ᏥᏓᎦ [tsịdaga] pg 108)

Gap in the mountain: ᎤᏴᎳᏛ [ụyvlạtv] pg 67)

Garden: ᎠᏫᏒᏗᏳ [ahwisvdiyu] pg 47)

Garden hose: ᎠᎻ ᎤᏪᏓᏍᏗ [ạm ụwẹdạsdi] pg 25)

Garden snake: ᎣᏛᎳᏘᎢ [ọdvhlaʔtịʔi] pg 53)

Garter snake: ᎣᏛᎳᏘᎢ [ọdvhlaʔtịʔi] pg 53)

Gasoline: ᎪᎢ [goʔi] pg 87)

Gasteroid fungi: ᏃᏈᏏ ᎤᏍᏗ [nokwịsi usdi] pg 94)

Gathering things: ᎦᎩᏍᎭ [gạgisha] pg 68)

Gathering together (they are): ᎠᎾᏓᏥᎩᎭ [ạnạdạdsgiha] pg 25)

Gaylussacia baccata: ᎧᏩᏯ [kawạya] pg 86)

Gaylussacia ursina: ᎡᎶᏗᏍᎩ [ẹlotịsgi] pg 51)

Georgia: ᏣᏥᏯ [tsạtsịya] pg 107)

Germans: ᎠᏂᏓᏥ [ạnidatsi] pg 26)

Getting into it: ᎠᎩᎸᎥᏍᎦ [ạkịʔlyʔvsga] pg 17)

Getting it (a solid): ᎠᎩᎠ [ạgi^{3}ʔa] pg 16)

Getting onto it: ᎠᎩᎸᎥᏍᎦ [ạkịʔlyʔvsga] pg 17)

Getting ready: ᎠᏛᏅᎢᏍᏗᎭ [advnvʔisdịha] pg 43)

Getting shallow: ᎦᏅᏬᎦ [gạnvwoʔga] pg 80)

Getting something in his eye: ᎤᎦᏑᎲᏍᎦ [uksuhvsga] pg 53)

Getting well: ᎠᏗᏫᏍᎦ [adi-whsga] pg 41)

Ghost: ᏥᎩᎵ [tsgili] pg 107)

Giant ragweed: ᎤᏆᏍᏓᎷᏯᏓ [ụgwạsdaluhyda] pg 60)

Ginseng, American: ᎣᏓᎵᎦᎵ [odạlịgạʔli] pg 53)

Girl, preteen: ᎠᏲᏣ [ahyọtsa] pg 49)

Girl, teenage: ᎠᏔ [ata] pg 38)

Giving birth: ᎠᎷᎸᎥᏍᎦ [alulv^{3}ʔvʔhsga] pg 24), ᎦᎧᎲᏍᎦ [gạkạhvh^{3}sga] (pg 68)

Giving it (a liquid) to him: ᎦᏁᏁᎭ [gạneneha] pg 76)

Giving it (a solid): ᎠᏓᏁᎭ [adahneha] pg 36)

Giving it (something alive) to him: ᎠᎧᏁᎭ [ạkaneha] pg 15)

Giving it (something flexible) to him: ᎦᏅᏁᎭ [gạnvneha] pg 79)

Giving it (something long) to him: ᎠᏕᎭ [ạdeha] pg 39)

Giving thanks: ᎠᎵᎮᎵᎦ [alihe^{3}liga] pg 22)

Giving up: ᎠᏓᏲᏍᎦ [ạdahyosga] pg 38)

Glass: ᎤᏁᏍᏓᎵ [unẹsdahli] pg 58)

Glaucomys volans: ᏕᏩ [dewa] pg 104)

Gleditsia triacanthos: ᎧᎵᏎᏥ [kahlsetsi] pg 84)

Glorifying it: ᎦᎸᏉᏗᎭ [gạlvkwohdịha] pg 72)

Gloves: ᎠᎵᏰᏑᎶ [ạliyẹ^{3}sụlo] pg 24), ᏗᎴᏰᏑᎶ [dileyesụʔlo] (pg 105)

Gnats: ᏙᏌ [dọsa] pg 106)

Gnawing: ᎠᏍᎪᎩᎠ [asgogịʔa] pg 30)

Goat: ᏧᎦᏍᏆᎾᎩᏓ [tsuksgwạnạgida] pg 108)

Gobbler: ᎦᎳᎩᎾ [gạlạgina] pg 69)

God: ᎤᏁᎳᏅᎯ [ụnehlạnvhi] pg 58)

Going: ᎡᎦ [ega] pg 51)

Going across a hill: ᏕᎦᎶᎨᎵ [degạlokeli] pg 103)

Going after: ᎤᏯᎵ [uyhạli] pg 66)

Going back: ᎢᎡᎦ [ịʔega] pg 52)

Going down hill

Going down hill: ᎠᎦᏐᏗᎭ [agạsoh^{3}dịha] pg 13)

Going in a circle: ᎠᏕᏲᎭ [adehyoha] pg 40)

Going on a trip: ᎠᏁᎳᏗᎠ [ahnelạdịʔa] pg 26)

Going out of it: ᎦᏄᎪᎦ [gạnugo^{3}ga] pg 78)

Going out of sight: ᎤᏕᎵᎦ [udelịga] pg 62)

Going over a hill: ᎦᏬᎯᎶᏍᎦ [gạwọhịlosga] pg 83)

Going somewhere: ᏩᎦᏘ [wạkti] pg 109)

Going then turning and coming back: ᎠᎪᎸᎠ [agoʔlvʔa] pg 18)

Going there and lying down: ᎠᏏᏂ [ạsi^{3}hni] pg 34)

Going through: ᎠᎦᏛᎴᎭ [ạktṿ³ʔleha] pg 14)

Going to eat: ᎠᎵᏍᏓᏴᏍᎦ [alsdahyṿhsga] pg 22)

Going to go visit someone: ᎠᏩᏛᎯ [ahwạtvhi] pg 46)

Going to the bathroom: ᎠᏨᎠ [atsvʔa] pg 45)

Going up a hill: ᎧᎾᎷᏍᎦ [kạnạluh³sga] pg 84)

Golden-club: ᎦᏁᏏ [gạnesi] pg 76)

Goldfinch: ᏩᏓᎬ [wạdagv] pg 109)

Good: ᎣᏍᏗ [osdi] pg 53), ᎣᏏ [osi] (pg 53)

Goose: ᏌᏌ [sạsa] pg 95)

Gourd: ᎦᎸᎾ [gạlvʔna] pg 72)

Gourd dipper: ᎦᎸᎾ [gạlvʔna] pg 72)

Graduating: ᏓᏍᏆᏗᎠ [dasgwadị³a] pg 100)

Granddaughter: ᎤᎵᏏ [ulisi] pg 56)

Grandmother: ᎤᎵᏏ [ulisi] pg 56)

Grandson: ᎤᏂᏏ [unisi] pg 58)

Grass: ᎦᏄᎸᎯ [gạnulṿhi] pg 79)

Grasshopper: ᏙᎯᏥᏆ [tohịtsgwa] pg 106), ᏙᎳᏥ [tolạtsi] (pg 106)

Graty blue heron: ᎧᏂᏍᎦᏩ [kạnịsgạwa] pg 85)

Grave: ᎦᏂᏌᎲᎢ [gạnisạhvʔi] pg 77)

Gravy: ᎤᎦᎹ [ugạma] pg 53)

Gray: ᏌᎪᏂᎨ ᎤᏍᎪᎸᎢ [sạkonige ụsgolvʔi] pg 95)

Gray catbird: ᎤᏥᎹ [utsịʔma] pg 64)

Gray fox: ᏧᎳ ᏌᎪᏂᎨ [tsulạ sạkonịge] pg 108)

Gray squirrel: ᏌᎶᎵ [sạloli] pg 95)

Grazing: ᎠᏂᏛᎾᏗᎠ [andvhnạdịʔa] pg 26)

Grease: ᎪᎢ [goʔi] pg 87)

Great bulrush: ᎦᎾᎦᏥ ᎤᏔᎾ [gạnagạtsị ụtạna] pg 73)

Great deal of: ᏥᏍᏈᏍᏓ [tsgwịsda] pg 107)

Green (of plants): ᎠᏤᎯ [ạtsehi] pg 44)

Green amaranth: ᏩᏥᎦ [wạtsga] pg 109)

Greeting him: ᎠᏲᎵᎭ [ạyo³ʔliha] pg 49)

Grifola frondosa: ᏫᏏ [wisi] pg 110)

Grinding: ᎠᏍᏙᎠ [asdoʔa] pg 32)

Gritter: ᎠᏑᎪᏍᏗ [ạsugọsdi] pg 35)

Ground (on the): ᎡᎳᏗ [elạdi] pg 51)

Ground bean: ᏚᏯ ᎢᎾᎨᎢ [tuyạ ịnạgeʔi] pg 107)

Ground lemon: ᎤᏂᏍᏇᏚᎦ [ụnịsgweduga] pg 58)

Ground snake: ᎪᎢ [goʔi] pg 87)

Groundcherry: ᎤᏅᏚᎯᏍᏓ [ụnvdụhisda] pg 59)

Groundhog: ᎣᎦᏅ [ogạnv] pg 53)

Group: ᎤᏂᏣᏛ [unitsạdv] pg 58), ᎱᎾᏓᏥᎬ [hundadsgv] (pg 93)

Group

Group (in a): ᎡᎳ [ehla] pg 51)

Growing: ᎠᎵᏰᎲᏍᎦ [aliyẹhvsga] pg 24), ᎠᏛᏍᎦ [atvsga] (pg 43)

Grown-up: ᎤᏔᎾ [utạna] pg 62)

Grus americana: ᎧᎾᏍᎦᏫ [kạnsgạwi] pg 84)

Gryllus assimilis: ᏔᎳᏚ [tạladu] pg 102)

Guineafowl: ᎫᏇ ᏗᎦᎾᏌᎢ [gugwẹ dịganạsạʔi] pg 89)

Gun: ᎧᎶᏇᏗ [kạlọgwedi] pg 84)

Gyrinus spp: ᏙᏳᏂᏏ [doyụnisi] pg 106)

H

Haemorhous purpureus: ᎤᏦᏁᏗ [ụtsonedi] pg 64)

Hailing: ᎦᏁᏐᎣᏍᎦ [gạnesọʔọsga] pg 76)

Hair on the head: ᏍᏗᏰᎬᎢ [sdịyẹkvʔi] pg 96)

Hairy: ᎤᏳᏩᎾ [uyụwạʔna] pg 67)

Half: ᎠᏰᎵ [ạyehli] pg 48)

Haliaeetus leucocephalus: ᎠᏬᎯᎵ [ạwọhịli] pg 47)

Ham (whole): ᎦᎦᎶ [gagạlo] pg 68)

Ham, portion of: ᎦᎦᎶ ᎠᎦᎭᎸᏓ [gagạlo ạgạhạlvda] pg 68)

Ham, sliced: ᎦᎦᎶ ᎠᎦᎭᎸᏓ [gagạlo ạgạhạlvda] pg 68)

Hamamelis virginiana: ᎦᎾᏑᏛᎶ [gạnsudṿlo] pg 74)

Hammer: ᎦᏅᏆᎶᏍᏗ [gạnvgwạlosdi] pg 80), ᎦᏅᏆᎶᏍᏗ [gạnvkwạlọsdi] (pg 80), ᎬᏂᎵᏓᏍᏙᏗ [gvnịlidasdoʔdi] (pg 91)

Hammering it in: ᎠᎭᏔᏍᎦ [ahạtasga] pg 19)

Hand (his): ᎤᏬᏰᏂ [uwọʔyeni] pg 66)

Handing it (a solid) to him: ᎠᎥᏏ [ạʔvsi] pg 13)

Handkerchief: ᎭᏯᏦᎯ [hạyatsohi] pg 93)

Hanging it (a solid) up: ᎠᏔᏍᎦ [atah³sga] pg 38)

Hanging it (something flexible) up: ᎦᏛᎥᏍᎦ [gạdv³ʔvsga] pg 82)

Hanging it (something long) up: ᎠᏙᏌᏗᎠ [ạtosạ³dịʔa] pg 42)

Happens: ᏂᎦᎵᏍᏇᏚᎢᎭ [nịgalsgwe³tụịha] pg 94)

Happy: ᎠᎵᎮᎵᎦ [alihe³liga] pg 22)

Hard: ᎠᏍᏓᏱ [ạsdayi] pg 31), ᏍᏓᏯ [sdaya] (pg 96)

Hard corn (past roasting stage): ᏧᏍᏓᏱ [tsụsdayi] pg 109)

Harelip: ᏧᏚᎶᏗ [tsụdulodi] pg 109)

Harness: ᎠᏯᏨᏗ [ahyạtsvhdi] pg 48)

Has a birthday: ᎤᏕᏘᏱᎭ [udẹtịyịha] pg 62)

Has a family: ᏚᎵᏘᎾᎠ [dultihnạʔa] pg 106)

Has a fever: ᎤᏗᎴᎲᏍᎦ [udịlẹhvsga] pg 62)

Has a headache: ᎤᏍᎫᏩᏗᎠ [usgu³wạdịʔa] pg 60)

Has a holiday: ᎤᏙᏓᏆᎠ [udo^{3}dạgwạʔa] pg 63)

Has a sore: ᎤᏥᏓᎳᏗᎠ [utsdạlạdịʔa] pg 64)

Has a tail: ᎦᏂᏓᏓ [gạnidạda] pg 77)

Has a toothache: ᎤᏳᏆᏗᎠ [u^{1}yụ^{3}gwạdịʔa] pg 67)

Has an earache: ᎤᎵᏍᏆᏗᎠ [uli^{3}sgwạdịʔa] pg 55)

Has an inclination to: ᎤᏚᎵᏗᎭ [uduhldịha] pg 63)

Has chills: ᎤᏅᏩᏍᏗᎭ [unvwasdịha] pg 60)

Has diarrhea: ᎤᏍᏉᎳᏗᎠ [usgwolạdịʔa] pg 60)

Has his mouth open: ᎤᏔᎶᎦ [utạloga] pg 61)

Has it (a liquid): ᎤᏁᎭ [uneha] pg 58)

Has it (a solid): ᎤᎭ [uha] pg 55)

Has it (something alive): ᎤᎧᎭ [uʔkạha] pg 54)

Has it (something flexible): ᎤᎾᎠ [unạʔa] pg 57)

Has it (something long): ᎤᏩᏯ [uwaya] pg 65)

Has livestock or animals: ᎤᎧᎾᎠ [ukạ^{3}hnạʔa] pg 54)

Hat: ᎤᎵᏍᏇᏔᏬᎯ [ulsgwetạwọhi] pg 55)

Hating him: ᎦᏂᏆᏘᎭ [gạnịgwạ^{3}tiha] pg 77)

Having an itch: ᎬᎩᏣᎴᎠ [gv^{3}gịtsạleʔa] pg 91)

Hawk: ᏔᏬᏗ [tạwodi] pg 102)

Hay: ᎧᏁᏍᎦ [kạnesga] pg 85)

Hazel alder: ᎠᏤᏓ [ahtsehd] pg 44)

Hazelnut: ᎠᏳᎩᏓ [ahyụgida] pg 49)

HEAD

Head (his): ᎠᏍᎪᎵ [ạsgoli] pg 30)

Healing up: ᎠᏗᏫᏍᎦ [adi-whsga] pg 41)

Hearing it: ᎠᏛᎩᎠ [ạtvgịʔa] pg 42)

Hearse: ᏧᏂᏲᎱᏒ ᏗᎦᎾᎩᏏᏙᎯ [tsụniyọhụsṿ dịgạnagisidohi] pg 108)

Heart: ᎦᎾᏫᎯ [gạnahwịhi] pg 74)

Heart (his): ᎤᏓᏅᏙ [udando] pg 61)

Heartleaf: ᎤᏂᏍᏆᎵ [ụnisgwali] pg 58)

Heat: ᎤᏗᎴᎬᎢ [ụdịlegṿʔi] pg 62)

Heater: ᎠᎦᎾᏬᎯᏍᏗ [ạganạwọhịsdi] pg 13)

Heaven: ᎦᎸᎳᏗ [gạlv^{3}lạdi] pg 72)

Heavy coat: ᎤᎭᎨᏗ ᎦᏌᎴᎾ [uhạgedị gasạlena] pg 55)

Heel of the foot (his): ᎦᏗᎨᏂ [gạdigeni] pg 82)

Height: ᎢᎦᏗ [igạdi] pg 52)

Held erect: ᎤᏎᎳᏘ [usẹlati] pg 60)

Helianthus: ᏅᏓᏗᎧᏂ [nvdadikani] pg 95)

Hello: ᎣᏏᏳ [osiyu] pg 53), ᏏᏲ (ᎣᏏᏳ) [siyọ (ọsiyụ)] (pg 96)

Helmitheros vermivorum: ᎩᏳᎬ [kịyugv] pg 87)

Helping: ᎠᏍᏕᎵᎭ [asde^{3}lịha] pg 32)

Hemlock (tree): ᏃᏄ [nonu] pg 94)

Hemming: ᎠᏴᏈᏛᎥᏍᎦ [ạyṿgwịdv^{3}ʔvsga] pg 50)

Hen Harrier: ᎠᎪᏕᎯ [ạgọdẹhi] pg 18)

Hen-of-the-woods: ᏫᏏ [wisi] pg 110)

Here, this: ᎭᏂ [hạni] pg 92)

Hers: ᎤᏤᎵ [utseli] pg 63)

Herself: ᎤᏩᏌ [uwạsa] pg 64)

Hiccup: ᎤᏩᎫᏩᏍᏗ [ụwagụwạsdi] pg 64)

Hickory: ᏩᏁᎢ [wạnẹʔi] pg 109)

Hickory nut: ᏐᎯ [sohi] pg 96)

Hickory nut soup: ᎧᏅᏥ [kạnvtsi] pg 85)

Hiding: ᎠᏗᏍᎦᎳᏍᎦ [adịsgahlah^{3}sga] pg 40)

Hiding it (a solid): ᎬᏍᎦᎳᏍᎦ [gvsgahlah^{3}sga] pg 91)

Hiding it (something flexible): ᎬᏍᎦᎸᎥᏍᎦ [gvsgạlv^{3}ʔvsga] pg 91)

Hiding it (something long): ᎬᏍᎦᎳᏗᎠ [gvsgaldịʔa] pg 91)

Him too: ᎯᏍᏉ [hisgwo] pg 93)

Himself: ᎤᏩᏌ [uwạsa] pg 64)

Hinge, hinges: ᎦᏙᏌᏗᏍᏙᏗ [gatosạdịsdohdi] pg 82)

Hip (his): ᎠᎧᏍᎨᏂ [ạkasgeni] pg 15)

Hirundo rustica: ᏧᏗᏆᏅᏥ [tsudịgwantsi] pg 109)

His: ᎤᏤᎵ [utseli] pg 63)

Hitting someone in the head with it (something long): ᎠᏍᏆᎸᎢᎭ [asgwạlv^{3}ʔịha] pg 31)

Hoar frost: ᎤᎾᏄᏍᏗ [unaʔnụsdi] pg 57)

Hoe: ᎦᎶᎪᏗ [gạlogohdi] pg 71)

Hoeing: ᎦᎶᎩᎠ [gạlo^{3}gịʔa] pg 71)

Hog: ᏏᏆ [sịkwa] pg 96)

Hog sucker (plant): ᏓᎶᎨ [dạloge] pg 99)

Hog-peanut: ᏚᏯ ᎢᎾᎨᎢ [tuyạ ịnageʔi] pg 107)

Holding it (a liquid): ᎦᎾᏤᎭ [gạ^{3}nhtsẹha] pg 74), ᎦᏁᏤᎭ [gạnhtseha] (pg 76)

Holding it (a solid): ᎦᏰᎭ [ga^{1}yeha] pg 83)

Holding it (something alive) in hand: ᎤᏂᏯ [uʔni^{3}yha] pg 59)

Holding it (something flexible): ᎦᏁᎭ [gạ^{3}hnẹha] pg 75)

HOLDING IT

Holding it (something long): ᎦᏁᎭ [gạneha] pg 75)

Hole: ᎠᏔᎳᎦᏒᎢ [ạtạlạksṿʔi] pg 38)

Hollering: ᎠᏙᎯᎠ [ạtohị^{3}ʔa] pg 41), ᎤᏪᎷᎧ [uhwẹlụka] (pg 65)

Hollow: ᎤᏒᏙᏂ [ụsṿdoni] pg 61)

Hollow (they are): ᎤᏂᏒᏙᏂ [unịsvdọni] pg 58)

Hollow mushrooms: ᎤᏂᏒᏙᏂ [unịsvdọni] pg 58)

Home (at): ᎤᏬᎳ [uwohla] pg 66)

Home (his): ᎤᏪᏅᏒᎢ [uwenvsvʔi] pg 65)

Homesick: ᎠᎱᎳᎨᎦ [ahulạgẹga] pg 20)

Hominy grits: ᏍᏖᏈᏂ [ganoheni] pg 77)

Hominy soup: ᎠᏥᎢᎢᎢ [amage?i] pg 25)

Honey: ᏇᏚᏈᏓ [wadulisi] pg 109)

Honey locust: ᎤᎵᏎᎢᏓ [kahlsetsi] pg 84)

Honey mushroom: ᎤᏂᏣᏫ [unilogwe] pg 58), ᏧᏂᎦᏫ [tsunihlogi] (pg 108), ᏧᏂᏣᏫ [tsunihlogwe] (pg 108)

Honeysuckle bush: ᎬᏂᏲᎵᏟ [kvnygihlgi] pg 91)

Hoot howl: ᎤᎫᎫ [uguku] pg 54)

Horn: ᏍᎥᎷᏲᏫᎥᏗ [gatsehlukisdohdi] pg 83)

Horn of an animal: ᎤᎯᎧ [uhyona] pg 67)

Hornet: ᏎᏆᎵ [sehwada] pg 96)

Horse: ᎢᎢᏈᏈ [sogwili] pg 96)

Horse (on a): ᎤᏲᏔ [uki?la] pg 54)

Horse corn: ᎠᏂᏍᎣᎡᎵ [anisynyhida] pg 26)

Hospital: ᏍᎾᏍᎥ [ga?nakdo] pg 73)

Hot: ᎤᏗᎸᎡᎢ [udilegv?i] pg 62), ᏍᎣᏰᎾᏍ [gale³yvsga] (pg 70)

Hot pepper: ᎤᏟᎶᏈ [utsi?lv] pg 64)

Hot water: ᎠᎢᎥ ᎤᏗᎶᏰ [am udihleki] pg 25)

Hour: ᏔᏥᏫᎤᎡᎵ [iyuwenvsdi] pg 53)

House: ᏍᏈᎩᏍ [gahltsode] pg 71)

House (his): ᏍᎾᏲᏗᎢ [ganagilv?i] pg 74)

House sparrow: ᏥᏎᏌᏫ [tsisgwaya] pg 107)

Housefly: ᎧᎥ [dvka] pg 107)

How: ᎲᏍ [hvga] pg 93)

Huckleberry: ᎧᏇᏫ [kawaya] pg 86)

Huckleberry bread: ᎧᏇᏫ ᎠᏈᎥᏸ [kawaya asu?yi] pg 86)

Hugging him: ᎠᏄᎩᏣᏍ [ahnugichasga] pg 27)

Humblehead (fish): ᏥᏎᏌᎸᎾ [tsisgwalvna] pg 107)

Hummingbird: ᏇᏖᏫ [walela] pg 109)

Hungry: ᎤᎯᏏᎭ [uyo³siha] pg 67)

Hunting animals: ᏍᏖᏈᎥᎠ [gano³hlido?ha] pg 78)

Hurry: ᎤᏟᏍᎵ [uhlisda] pg 55), ᎤᏇᎤᏍ [uwanvga] (pg 64)

Hurry (in a): ᏍᏥᏄᏔ [gatsynula] pg 83)

Hurrying: ᎤᎤᏍ [unvga] pg 59)

Hurrying (in a): ᎤᏇᎤᏍ [uwanvga] pg 64)

Husband (her): ᎤᎦᎠ [uhyehi] pg 66)

Hydrangea arborescens: ᏍᏈᏩᏯ ᏧᏫᏍ [gahlkwogi tsuyasdu] pg 71)

Hylocichla mustelina: ᎧᏫᎬ [kawogv] pg 86)

Hymn book: ᏗᎧᏃᏥᏫᎥᎵ [dikanogisdohdi] pg 104)

Hymnal: ᎠᏪᏟ ᏗᎧᏃᏥᏫᎵ [gohweli dikanogisdi] pg 89)

Hypentelium nigricans: ᎵᏍᏆ [daloge] pg 99)

I

I: ᎠᎥ [ayv] pg 50)

Ice: ᎤᏁᏍᏓᎵᎵ [unesdahli] pg 58)

Ice plant: ᎤᏁᏍᏓᎵᎵ ᎠᎶᏍᏱᎩ [unesdahl gosysgi] pg 58)

Ictaluridae spp: ᏧᎵᏍᏓᎾᎵᎵ [tsulisdanali] pg 108)

Icteria virens: ᎦᎦ [huhu] pg 93)

Igniting it: ᎠᏟᏍᏓᏟᎦᏍ [atsi³sdahlasga] pg 45)

Ilex mucronata: ᎤᏍᏓᏍᏗ [usdasdi] pg 60)

Imitator bird: ᏇᏍᎦᏪ [waduyela] pg 109)

Impatiens capensis: ᏇᎶᎷ ᎤᏂᎦᎮᎩᏍᏗ [walelu unigalegisdi] pg 109)

Imposed restriction: ᏍᏍᎶᎵ [gaktvda] pg 68)

In (a language): ᎬᏗ [gvhdi] pg 92)

In a container (a solid): ᏍᏩᏗ [gahlaa] pg 69)

In a container (something alive): ᎠᏯᎠᏗ [aya?a] pg 47)

In a container (something flexible): ᏍᏩᏗ [gala?a] pg 69)

In a container (something long): ᏍᏩ [gala] pg 69)

In a liquid (in a) (a solid): ᏦᎯ [guha] pg 89)

In a liquid (something alive): ᎠᏯᎠᏗ [aya?a] pg 47)

In a liquid (something flexible): ᎬᏍ [gv?ga] pg 90)

Inch: ᏔᏯᏏᏔᏛᎯ [iyasitadvhi] pg 53)

Including: ᎵᏂᏟᏗᎭ [danehdsdiha] pg 99)

Income: ᎤᎵᎶᏒ [udalosv] pg 61)

Indian beads: ᎠᏕᏗᏯᏍᏗ [adediyasdi] pg 39)

Indian hellebore: ᎠᏍᎬᏂᏕᎵ [asgwyneda] pg 31)

Indian Paint: ᏬᏗ [wodi] pg 110)

Indian poke: ᎠᏍᎬᏂᏕᎵ [asgwyneda] pg 31)

Indigo bunting: ᎠᏟᏣᏃᏍᏍ [alitsanosga] pg 23)

Infection: ᎤᏰᎶᎯᏎᎥᎢᎢ [uyelohisehy?i] pg 66)

Initially: ᎠᎬᏴ [agvyi] pg 19)

Ink pen: ᎬᏂᎮᎯ [gynehi] pg 91)

Insect: ᏥᎠᏴ [dsgoyi] pg 107)

Inside: ᎠᏯᎠᏗ [aya?a] pg 47), ᎭᏫᏂ [hawini] (pg 92), ᎰᏫᏂ [howini] (pg 93)

Intending: ᎤᏰᎯᎸᎭ [uyeh³lvha] pg 66)

Interpreter: ᏍᏂᏟᏗᏍᎩ [gahnetsdisgi] pg 76)

Interpreting it: ᎠᏂᏁᏍᏗᎭ [ahnesdiha] pg 26)

Intoxicated: ᎤᏴᏯᏍᏓᎩᎠ [u¹yysda³gi?a] pg 68)

Investigating it: ᎠᎧᏛᎭᏍᏍ [akdv³hvsga] pg 14)

Ipomoea batatas: ᏄᎾ ᎤᏂᎦᎾᏍᎵ [nuna uniganasda] pg 95)

Iris cristata: ᎤᏍᎦᎯᎢ [usga?hi] pg 60)

Iron (to iron clothes with): ᏗᏖᏍᏗ [ditesdi] pg 105)

Iron pot: ᏧᎷᏍᎩ [tsulasgi] pg 108)

Ironing clothes: ᎵᏛᏍᏗᎭ [dahtesdiha] pg 101)

Iroquois: ᎠᏂᏅᏛᏇᎩ [aninvdawegi] pg 26)

Island: ᎠᎢᎥ ᎠᏰᏟ [am ayehli] pg 25)

Isn't that right?: ᎭᏇᏍ [hawaga] pg 92)

Itching: ᎤᎯᎵᏯᏗ [uyo³dagi?a] pg 67), ᎬᏯᎦᏕᎠ [gv³gitsale?a] (pg 91)

127

J

Jack-in-the-pulpit: ᏙᏒᎾ ᎢᎾᎨ ᎡᎯ [dosṿnạ ịnage ẹhi] pg 106), ᏚᏯᏍᏗ [dụyạsdi] (pg 107)

Jacket: ᎦᏌᎴᎾ [gasạlena] pg 81), ᏌᎧ ᎦᏌᎴᏂ [sạkạ gạsạleni] (pg 95)

Jacket lining: ᎭᏯᎦᎸᏛᎢ [hạyagạlvdvʔi] pg 93)

Jail: ᏗᏓᏍᏚᏗᏳ [dịdạsdudịyu] pg 105)

January: ᏚᏃᎸᏓᏂ [dụnọlvdạni] pg 106)

Jaw: ᎠᏳᎪᎢ [ahyụgọʔi] pg 49)

Jewelweed: ᏩᎴᎷ ᎤᏂᎦᎴᎩᏍᏗ [wạlelụ ụnịgạlẹgịsdi] pg 109)

Job's tears: ᏎᎷ ᎤᏂᏥ [selụ ụnitsi] pg 96)

Joining: ᎠᏖᎳᏕᎭ [atẹ^{3}ldeha] pg 40)

Jug: ᎦᏓᎫᎦ [gạdạguga] pg 81)

Juglans cinerea: ᎪᎯ [kohi] pg 87)

Juglans nigra: ᎬᏂᎨ ᏎᏗ [gvnịgẹ seti] pg 91), ᏎᏗ [sedi] (pg 96)

July: ᎫᏰᏉᏂ [gụyẹgwoni] pg 90)

Jumping: ᎠᏢᏔᏕᎦ [ahltạde^{3}ga] pg 23)

Jumping forward: ᎠᏓᎾᏫᏗᎭ [adạna^{3}wịdiha] pg 36)

Jumping up and down: ᏓᏢᏔᏕᎦ [dalịtạdẹga] pg 99)

Junco hyemalis: ᏚᏘ [tuti] pg 106)

Juncus tenuis: ᎧᏁᏍᎦ [kạnesga] pg 85)

June: ᏕᎷᏱ [dehluyi] pg 104)

Jury: ᎠᏂᏑᎵ [ạnịsuli] pg 26)

Just: ᏚᏳᎦᏔ [dụyukta] pg 107)

Just a little: ᏍᏗᎧᏓ [sdikạda] pg 96)

Just like that: ᏍᎩᏈᏳᏍᏗ [sgịgwiyụsdi] pg 96)

K

Kalmia angustifolia: ᏧᎫ ᏧᎾᏍᏗ [tsug tsunsdi] pg 108)

Katydid: ᏥᎩᎩ [tsịgigi] pg 107)

Kentucky: ᎬᏅᏛᎩ [kvndvgi] pg 91)

Kettle: ᎤᏔᎶᎩ [ụtạlogi] pg 61)

Key: ᏍᏚᎩᏍᏗ [sdụgisdi] pg 96)

Kicking him: ᎠᎶᏕᎯᎭ [alo^{3}ʔdehịha] pg 24)

Kicking up his leg: ᎠᏣᏯᎩᎠ [atsạʔyạkiʔa] pg 44)

Killer: ᎠᏓᎯ [ạdạ^{3}hi] pg 36)

Killing him: ᎠᎯᎭ [ahịha] pg 19)

King: ᎤᎬᏫᏳᎯ [ugvwịyụhi] pg 55)

Kingbird: ᏗᎴᏆ [dịlegwa] pg 105)

Kingfisher: ᏣᎶᎯ [tsalọhi] pg 107)

Kinosternon subrubrum: ᏌᎵᎫᎩ [sạlị^{3}gu^{3}gi] pg 95)

Kissing (sucking): ᎠᏍᏆᏄᏥᎦ [asgwạnu^{3}tsga] pg 31)

Kissing her: ᎠᏔᏪᏙᏍᎦ [atạwe^{3}dosga] pg 38)

Kitchen: ᎠᏓᏍᏓᏴᏗ [ạdạsdahydi] pg 37)

Kitten: ᏪᏌ ᎠᏓᎯ [wẹsạ ạdạhi] pg 110)

Knee: ᎦᏂᎨᏂ [gạnigeni] pg 77)

Kneeling: ᏓᏢᏂᏆᏅᎥᏍᎦ [dahlịni^{3}gwạnṿʔvsga] pg 99)

Knife: ᎭᏰᎳᏍᏗ [hạyelạsdi] pg 93)

Knocking it (a liquid) off: ᎪᎲᎾᏗᎭ [gohvhndịha] pg 88)

Knocking it (a solid) off: ᎪᎰᎾᏗᎭ [gohọ^{3}hndịha] pg 88)

Knocking over a stack of objects: ᎠᏌᏙᎥᏗᎭ [asạdoʔṿdịha] pg 29)

Knowing it: ᎠᎦᏔᎭ [ạktaha] pg 14)

Knoxville, TN: ᎪᎲᏓᏓᎳ [kọhṿdadahla] pg 88)

L

Laboring: ᏚᎸᏫᏍᏓᏁᎭ [duhlṿwisdạʔneha] pg 106)

Lace: ᎠᎦᏖᎾ [ạgạtena] pg 14)

Lacking: ᎤᎶᎳ [uloʔla] pg 56), ᎤᏂᎬᎦ [uhnigvga] (pg 58)

Lactuca sativa: ᎠᎪᏍᏓᎩᏍᏗ [ạgosdạkịsdi] pg 18)

Lady's slipper orchids: ᎤᎫᏇ ᎤᎳᏑᎳ [ụgkwẹ ụlạsụla] pg 55)

Lagenaria siceraria: ᎦᎸᎾ [gạlvʔna] pg 72)

Lake: ᎠᎹ ᏗᏍᏚᎲᎢ [ạm dịsdụhvʔi] pg 25)

Lamp: ᎠᏨᏍᏙᏗ [ạtsṿstdi] pg 46)

Lard: ᎪᎢ [goʔi] pg 87)

Large: ᎡᏆ [egwa] pg 51)

Largemouth bass: ᎤᏃᎧ [uhnọka] pg 59)

Last: ᎣᏂ [ohni] pg 53)

Late: ᎤᎪᏂᏲᎦ [ugoniyoga] pg 54), ᎤᎪᏂᏲᎦ [ugọ^{3}hniyoga] (pg 54)

Later: ᎪᎯᏳ [gọhiyu] pg 87)

Laurel: ᏧᎫ ᏧᎾᏍᏗ [tsug tsunsdi] pg 108)

Lawyer: ᏗᏘᏲᎯᎯ [dịtịyohịhi] pg 105)

Laying down it (a liquid): ᎦᎮᎲᏍᎦ [gahẹhvsga] pg 69)

Laying it (something long) down: ᎠᏗᎠ [adịʔa] pg 40)

Lazy: ᎠᏓᏄᎸᎭ [adanu^{3}lvha] pg 36)

Lead: ᎦᏂ [gạʔni] pg 77)

Leading him: ᎨᎵᏏᏂ [gelịsini] pg 86)

Leaf: ᎤᏆᎶᎦ [ugwạloga] pg 60)

Learning: ᎠᏕᎶᏆᎠ [adehlọ^{3}kwạʔa] pg 39), ᎠᏙᎴᏈᎠ [adohlẹkwịʔa] (pg 42)

Least flycatcher (bird): ᏥᎪᏱᏙᏍᏗ [dsgoyiʔdọsdi] pg 107)

Leaves are falling: ᎦᏍᏗᏭᎣᏍᎦ [gạsdịwụʔosga] pg 81)

Leaves are turning: ᎦᎳᎪᎰᏍᎦ [gạlagohosga] pg 69), ᎦᎶᎪᎰᏍᎦ [gạlọgọhosga] (pg 71)

Leaving it (a solid) or it (a liquid): ᎠᎯᏱᎠ [ahiyịʔa] pg 20)

Leaving it (something alive): ᎠᎧᎯᏱᎠ [ạkạhiyịʔa] pg 14)

Leaving it (something flexible): ᏚᎿᎥD [gạ?ni³yị?a] pg 77)

Leaving it (something long): ᎠᏆᏏ [ạd?siya] pg 41)

Leech: ᏣᏄᏏ [tsanusi] pg 107)

Left: ᎠᏍᎥᎬᎵ [ạksgỵnida] pg 13)

Left-handedness (his): ᎠᏍᎥᎬᎵ [ạksgỵnida] pg 13)

Leg (his): ᏲᎤᎥᏂ [gạnvsgeni] pg 80)

Lending: ᎠᏗᎩᏏᏗ [adạtolsdịha] pg 37)

Letter: ᎪᏪᎵ [gohweli] pg 89)

Lettuce: ᎠᎪᏍᏓᎩᏍᏗ [agosdạkịsdi] pg 18)

Lice: ᏗᏁ [tina] pg 105)

Lichen(s): ᎤᏣᎳ [utsạla] pg 63)

Lifting it: ᎠᏎᎳᏓ [asạlad?a] pg 28), ᎠᏎᎳᎫᎢᏗ [asạ³?ldị?a] (pg 28)

Light: ᎠᏨᏍᏗᏫᏗ [ạtsỵstdi] pg 46)

Light going out: ᎬᏓᎶᏍᎦ [gỵdạlosga] pg 92)

Lightening: ᎠᎾᎦᎵᎭ [ạna³galiha] pg 25), ᎠᎾᎦᎵᏍᎩ [ạnagạlịsgi] (pg 25)

Lightweight: ᎠᏎᎦᎠ [asakaa] pg 28), ᏎᎦ [sạka] (pg 95)

Ligusticum canadense: ᏩᏁᎩᏓ [wạnegịda] pg 109)

Like: ᎢᏳᏍᏗ [iyụsdi] pg 53)

Like sourwood (plant): ᏅᏙᎨᏯ ᎢᏳᏍᏗ [nvdogwe-hyạ iyụsdi] pg 95)

Lilium superbum: ᎧᏂᎫᏣᏘ [kahngutsạti] pg 84)

Lima bean: ᏚᏯᏁᏆ [tuyạnegwa] pg 107)

Limb: ᎤᏩᏂᎦᏝᎥ [ụwanịgahlạnv] pg 64)

LINDERA BENZOIN

Lindera benzoin: ᏃᎭᏓᏥ [nohdạtsi] pg 94)

Linen: ᎠᎧᏱᎯᏓ [ạkỵhịda] pg 19)

Liparis loeselii: ᎤᏲᏓᎵᏳᏍᏗ [ụyọdahlịyụsdi] pg 67)

Liquid: ᎫᎭ [gụha] pg 89)

Liriodendron tulipifera: ᏥᏳ [tsiyu] pg 108)

Listening: ᎠᏛᏓᏍᏗᎭ [atvdasdịha] pg 43)

Literally: {|Wild bean|}: ᏚᏯ ᎢᎾᎨᎢ [tuyạ ịnage?i] pg 107)

Little: ᎤᏍᏗ [ụsdi] pg 60), ᎦᏲᎵ [gayohli] (pg 84)

Little people (mythological): ᏴᏫ ᏧᏂᏍᏗᎢ [yvwị tsunsdi?i] pg 111)

Little while: ᏎᎦ [sega] pg 96)

Liver: ᎤᏌᎳ [ụwela] pg 65)

Living: ᎡᎭ [ẹha] pg 51)

Living at: ᎡᎯ [ẹhi] pg 51)

Loafing: ᎡᏙᎵᏙᎭ [edọ?li³doha] pg 52)

Loft: ᎦᎸᎳᏗ [galv³lạdi] pg 72)

Log: ᎠᏍᏛᏓᎦᏬᎳᏍᏗ [asỵdạgwạlosdi] pg 35)

Lonesome: ᎤᏑᎳᎪᎦ [usulạgoga] pg 61)

Long: ᏲᎤᎸᎵ [gạnyhida] pg 79)

Long hair clan (twister): ᎠᏂᎩᎶᎯ [ạnigịlọhi] pg 26)

Long tailed sharp-shinned hawk: ᏗᎦᎦᏛᎾᎯᏛ [dị-gagdỵnạhidv] pg 104)

Long-eared owl: ᏥᎩᎵ [tsgili] pg 107)

Long-tailed weasal: ᏓᎶᏂᎨ ᏥᏍᏕᏥ [dạlonigẹ tsịsdetsi] pg 99)

Lonicera spp: ᎬᏅᎩᎯᎵᎩ [kvnỵgihlgi] pg 91)

Lontra canadensis: ᏥᏲ [tsiyo] pg 108)

Look!: Ꮒ [ni] pg 94)

Looking: ᏓᎧᏂᎭ [dakạnịha] pg 98)

Looking at it: ᎠᏥᏙᏍᏗᎭ [aktosdịha] pg 14), ᏓᎧᎾ [dakahna] (pg 97)

Looking for: ᎤᏯᎵ [uyhạli] pg 66)

Looks like: ᏂᎬᏎᏍᏗ [nịgvwhsdi] pg 94)

Losing it: ᎤᏲᎱᏎᎭ [uyohụ³seha] pg 67)

Lost (die): ᎠᏲᏒᏍᎦ [ayọ?osga] pg 48)

Lots: ᎤᏂᏣᏛ [unitsạdv] pg 58)

Lovage: ᏩᏁᎩᏓ [wạnegịda] pg 109)

Loving: ᎤᏓᎨᏳᎭ [udage³yuha] pg 61)

Loving it: ᎦᎸᎬᏗᎭ [galvgwdiha] pg 72)

Lower: ᎡᎳᏗ [elạdi] pg 51)

Lower back: ᎠᏕᏍᎨᏂ [ạtẹsgeni] pg 40)

Loyal: ᎤᏬᎯᏳᏂ [ụwohịyụni] pg 65)

Lumbricus terrestris: ᎤᏂᏥᏯ [ụnịtsiya] pg 58)

Lunatic: ᎤᎵᏅᏗᏍᎩ [ulỵntịsgi] pg 56)

Lycopus virginicus: ᎠᏂᏬᏂᏍᎩ [ạniwọ?nịsgi] pg 26)

Lying: ᎠᏥᏍᎣᏒᏍᎦ [atsgọ?vsga] pg 44)

Lying down: ᎦᏁᎠD [gạnạ?a] pg 73)

Lynx rufus: ᎬᎮ [kvhe] pg 91)

M

Magnolia acuminata: ᏧᏆᎶᎦ ᎤᎦ [tsugwạlogạ tsegwa] pg 108)

Magpie: ᏩᏗᏱᎵ [wạtiyeli] pg 109)

Maianthemum racemosum: ᎤᏗᎵᏍᏗ [ụdihlịsdi] pg 62)

Mailman: ᎪᏪᎵᏗᎦᎲᎠᏙ [gohwelịdigahnịdohi] pg 89)

Making a noise: ᎤᏃᏴᏃᎮᏣ [uhnọyỵ?nohyvhlga] pg 59)

Making fast: ᎠᏍᏓ?ᏱᏗᎠ [asda³?yidị?a] pg 32)

Making fun of: ᏛᏐᏨᎮᎭ [dvsọtsvcheha] pg 107)

Making fun of him: ᎠᏙᏥᏗᎭ [ado³tsdịha] pg 42)

Making him fall: ᎦᎶᏒᏙᎭ [gạlọ?ohndịha] pg 71)

Making himself attractive: ᎠᏓᏙᏚ?ᎢᏍᏗᎭ [adạdoduᴗᵢs-diha] pg 37)

Making it: ᏂᎬᏁᎭ [nịgvneha] pg 94)

Making it deep: ᎠᏍᏛ³ᎯᏍᏗᎭ [asdv³hisdịha] pg 33)

Making it shallow: ᏲᏬᏗᎭ [gạnywo³diha] pg 81)

Making pottery: ᏕᏛᏗᎦᏩᎴᏍᎦ [dektạ³gwạlesga] pg 103)

Making smoke. It is smoking: ᏓᎦᏒᏍᏗᎭ [daksvsdịha] pg 97)

Making something for him: ᏂᎬᏁᎭ [nịgỵ³hneha] pg 94)

Malus spp: ᏒᎦᏛ ᎢᎾᎨᎠᏁᎵ [svgdỵ inạgeanehl] pg 97)

Man: ᎠᏍᎦᏯ [ạsgaya] pg 29)

Man, elderly: ᎤᏛᏐᏅ [utvsọnv] pg 63)

Manager: ᏍᎦᏰᎬᏍᏗ [sgạyegvsdi] pg 95)

Many: ᎤᏂᏣᏛ [unitsạdv] pg 58), ᏥᏍᏈᏍᏓ [tsgwịsda] (pg 107)

Maple: ᏧᏩᎩ [tsuwagi] pg 109)

Marble: ᎦᏓᏲᏍᏗ [gạdayọsdi] pg 82)

March (month): ᎠᏅᏱ [ạnvhyi] pg 27)

Margarine: ᎪᏒᏅ [gọsvnv] pg 88)

Marmota monax: ᎣᎦᏅ [ogạnv] pg 53)

Marsh hawk: ᎠᎪᏕᎯ [ạgọdẹhi] pg 18)

Maryville, TN: ᎤᎾᏆᏢ [ụnạgwahlv] pg 57)

Mashing it: ᎦᏙᏫᏗᎭ [gạdọwidiha] pg 82)

Mask: ᎠᎬᏚᎶ [ạgvdụʔlo] pg 19)

Mass of people: ᎤᏂᏣᏘ [unitsạti] pg 58)

Matches: ᎠᏨᏍᏙᏗ [ạtsỵstdi] pg 46)

Mattress: ᎠᏤᏍᏙ [ạtsẹsdo] pg 44)

May: ᎠᏂᏍᎬᏘ [ahnsgvti] pg 26)

Mayapple: ᎤᏂᏍᏇᏚᎦ [ụnịsgweduga] pg 58)

Maybe: ᏙᏗ [dodi] pg 106)

Maypop: ᎤᏩᎦ [uwạga] pg 64)

Me too: ᎠᏴᏍᏉ [ạyhsgwo] pg 50)

Meadowlark, eastern: ᏃᏈᏏ [nọkwịsi] pg 94)

Mean: ᎤᏁᎫᎭ [uneguha] pg 57)

Meander: ᎤᏪᏛᎢ [ụwedvʔi] pg 65)

Meaning: ᎤᏰᎸᎭ [uyeh³lvha] pg 66)

Measles: ᎦᏁᏃᏗᏍᎩ [gạnenọdịsgi] pg 76)

Measuring it: ᎠᏥᎶᎠ [atsihlọ³a] pg 44)

Meat: ᎭᏫᏯ [hạwiya] pg 93)

Medicine: ᏅᏬᏗ [nỵwohdi] pg 95)

Meeting: ᏗᎦᎳᎾ'ᎢᏍᏗ [digạlawị'ịsdi] pg 104)

Megaceryle alcyon: ᏣᎶᎯ [tsalọhi] pg 107)

Megascops asio: ᏩᎱᎱ [wạhụhu] pg 109)

Melanerpes erythrocephalus: ᏓᎳᎳ [dạlala] pg 98)

Meleagris gallopavo

Meleagris gallopavo: ᎬᎾ [kvna] pg 91), ᎬᎾ ᎢᎾᎨᎡᎯ [kvnạ inạgeẹhi] (pg 91)

Mellow bug: ᏙᏳᏂᏏ [doyụnisi] pg 106)

Melospiza melodia: ᏥᎦᏣ [tsigtsa] pg 107)

Mephitis mephitis: ᏗᎵ [dili] pg 105)

Merlin (bird): ᏌᎾᏩ [sanạwa] pg 95)

Micropterus salmoides: ᎤᏃᎧ [uhnọka] pg 59)

Middle (in the): ᎠᏰᎵ [ạyehli] pg 48)

Mile: ᎢᏳᏥᎶᏓ [iyutsiloda] pg 53), ᏑᏥᎶᏓ [sụtsịloda] (pg 97)

Milk: ᎤᏅᏗ [ụnvdi] pg 59)

Milking it: ᎦᏁᎩᏒᎭ [gạnegi³ʔeha] pg 75)

Mingling: ᎨᎳᏗᏙᎭ [kẹlạdi³dọha] pg 86)

Mink: ᏒᎩ [svki] pg 97)

Minnow: ᎠᏨᏗᏯ [ạtsvdiya] pg 46)

Minute(s): ᎢᏯᏔᏬᏍᏓᏅᎯ [ịyhtạwosdạnỵhi] pg 53)

Mirror: ᎠᏓᎨᏗ [ạdakehdi] pg 36), ᎠᏓᎨᏙᏗ [ạdạkẹdọdi] (pg 36)

Misbehaving: ᎠᏍᎦᏅᎦ [asgạnvga] pg 29)

Mischievious: ᎤᏁᎫᏣᏔ [unektsạta] pg 58)

Mistletoe: ᎤᏓᎵ [ụdahli] pg 61)

Mixing it: ᎠᏑᎨᎭ [ạsu³geha] pg 35)

Mixing liquids: ᎫᏍᏗᎭ [gụ³sdịha] pg 90)

Mixing stuff together: ᎠᏑᏰᎭ [ạsụ³ʔyeha] pg 35)

Moccasin: ᎤᏧᏬᏗ [ụtsuwọdi] pg 64)

Moccasin flower: ᎤᎫᏇ ᎤᎳᏑᎳ [ụgkwẹ ụlạsụla] pg 55)

Mocking him: ᎠᏰᎵᎠ [a¹yelịʔa] pg 48)

Mockingbird: ᏩᏚᏰᎳ [wạdụyela] pg 109)

Molasses: ᏩᏚᎵᏏ [wadulisi] pg 109)

Mole (on the flesh): ᎤᏪᏘ [ụweti] pg 65)

Moment: ᏏᎸᎢ [sịlvʔi] pg 96)

Monarda didyma: ᏩᎴᎷ ᎤᏂᏣᎩᏍᏗ [wạlelụ ụnịtsạgisdi] pg 109)

Monday: ᏙᏓᏉᏅᎯ [dodạgwonỵhi] pg 106)

Money: ᎠᏕᎳ [ạdela] pg 39)

Monkey: ᏓᎴᏍᎩᏍᎩ [dạlesgisgi] pg 98)

Month: ᏏᏅᏓ [sinvda] pg 96)

Moon: ᏒᏃ ᎡᏙ ᏅᏓ [svnọ edo nvda] pg 97)

Morchella esculenta: ᎤᏂᏒᏙᏂ [unịsvdọni] pg 58)

More: ᏏᏉ [sigwo] pg 96)

Morel: ᎤᏂᏒᏙᏂ [unịsvdọni] pg 58)

Morus rubra: ᎫᏩ [kuwa] pg 90)

Moth: ᎠᏛᏙᏩ [ạdvtọwa] pg 43)

Mother: ᎤᏥ [utsi] pg 64)

Mother's brother: ᎤᏚᏥ [udutsi] pg 63)

Mother's brother's wife: ᎤᎳᎾ [ulạna] pg 55)

Mother's father: ᎤᏚᏚ [ududu] pg 63)

Mother's sister: ᎤᏥ [utsi] pg 64)

Mountain: ᎣᏓᎵ [odali] pg 53), ᎤᏅᏓᏒᎢ [unvdạsvʔi] (pg 59)

Mountain cane: ᎦᏂ [gạʔni] pg 77)

Mountain holly: ᎤᏍᏓᏍᏗ [ụsdạsdi] pg 60)

Mountain lion: ᏨᏓᏥ [tsvdạtsi] pg 109)

Mountain oak: ᏓᏑᏓᏆᎴᏆ [dạsudạgwạlegwa] pg 100)

Mountain willow: ᏗᎳᎦᎵᏍᎩ ᎤᏍᏗ [dịlagạlịsgị usdi] pg 105)

Mounting it: ᎠᎩᎸᏍᎦ [ąkįʔlvʔvsga] pg 17)

Mourning dove: ᎫᎴᏗᏍᎪᏂᎯ [gulehdįsgohnįhi] pg 89)

Mouse: ᏥᏍᏕᏥ [tsisdetsi] pg 107)

Mouth (his): ᎠᎰᎵ [ąholi] pg 20)

Movie projector: ᏗᎦᎸᏌᏓᏗᏍᏗᎯᏍᎩ [dįgąlvsądądįsdįhįsgi] pg 104)

Moving: ᎠᎵᏰᎵ [ahlįye³li] pg 24)

Moving his household from ...: ᎠᏓᏅᎠ [adą³ʔnvʔa] pg 36)

Moving it (a solid): ᎠᎧᏴᎠ [ąkąhvʔa] pg 15), ᎠᎬᎠ [ąkv³ʔa] (pg 18)

Moving it (something alive): ᎠᎧᏴᎠ [akąhvʔa] pg 15), ᎠᎬᎠ [ąkv³ʔa] (pg 18)

Moving it (something flexible) off: ᎦᎾᎬᎠ [gąna³ʔgvʔa] pg 74)

Mowing: ᎠᏣᎦᏍᎦ [ahtsą³ksga] pg 43)

Much: ᎠᎦᏓ [ągada] pg 13), ᎤᏣᏘ [ụtsati] (pg 63)

Mud flutter fish: ᏧᏂᎩᏥᏴᏍᏗ [tsụnigitsįyvsdi] pg 108)

Mud turtle (eastern): ᏌᎵᎫᎩ [sąlį³gụ³gi] pg 95)

Mudpuppy: ᏧᏩ [chuwa] pg 109)

Mulberry: ᎫᏩ [kuwa] pg 90)

Mule (animal): ᏔᏁᏆ [tąnegwa] pg 102)

Mulligan blanket: ᎤᏍᏆᏅᏂ [ụsgwąnvhni] pg 60)

Mumps: ᎠᏓᏴᏦᏗᏍᎩ [ądąyvtsọdįsgi] pg 38)

Murphy, N.C: ᏣᏄᏏ [tsąnusi] pg 107)

Musca domestica: ᏛᎧ [dvka] pg 107)

Muscadine grapes: ᏆᎷᏏ [kwąlụ³si] pg 95)

Muscovy duck: ᏙᎦᏏ [dogsi] pg 105)

Mushroom: ᏚᏬᎵ [dụwohli] pg 106)

Musical instrument (of any kind): ᎧᏃᎩᏍᏙᏗ [kąnogisdohdi] pg 85)

Muskrat: ᏎᎵᎦᏍᏉ [seliksgwo] pg 96)

Mussel: ᎤᏯᏍᎦ [uhyasga] pg 66)

Mustard: ᎠᏥᎳ [atsila] pg 44)

Mustard greens: ᎠᏲᏍᎩ [ąʔyọsgi] pg 49)

Mustela frenata: ᏓᎶᏂᎨ ᏥᏍᏕᏥ [dąlonigẹ tsįsdetsi] pg 99)

Mythical hawk like bird: ᏌᏅᏬ [sąnvwo] pg 95)

N

Nail: ᏴᎩ [yvgi] pg 110)

Naked: ᎤᏰᎳᎭ [ụyeląha] pg 66)

Naming him: ᏕᎪᎠ [degoʔa] pg 104)

Narrowleaf plantain: ᎪᏍᏓᏂᏍᏗ [gosda³nįsdi] pg 88)

Nasturtium officinale: ᎠᎼ ᎤᎵᏏ [ąmọ ụlisi] pg 25)

Natchez: ᎠᏂᏃᏥ [ąninotsi] pg 26)

Native American: ᎠᏴᏫᏯ [ąyvwįya] pg 51)

Near: ᎾᎥᏂ [nąʔv'ni] pg 93)

Neck, front of (his): ᎠᏴᏤᏂ [ąyvhtseni] pg 50)

Neck, the back of (his): ᎦᎩᎵᎨᏂ [gągihlgeni] pg 68)

Necklace: ᎠᏯᏨᏗ [ahyątsvhdi] pg 48)

Necktie: ᎠᏯᏨᏗ [ahyątsvhdi] pg 48)

Necturus spp: ᏧᏩ [chuwa] pg 109)

Need (in): ᎤᏂᎬᎦ [unigvga] pg 58)

Needing: ᎤᏂᎬᎦ [uhnigvga] pg 58)

Neovison vison: ᏒᎩ [svki] pg 97)

Nest: ᎤᏁᏍᎩᎸᎢ [uhnesgįlvʔi] pg 58)

Net: ᎠᎦᏳᎳᏗ [ągahyụladi] pg 14)

Never: ᎭᏃ [hahno] pg 92)

New: ᎠᏤᎯ [ątsehi] pg 44)

New moon: ᎠᏤ ᏅᏙ [ątse nvdo] pg 44)

New year: ᎠᏤ ᎤᎾᏕᏘᏱᏍᎬᎢ [ątse ụnądetįyįsgvʔi] pg 44)

New York: ᏄᏯᎩ [nụyagi] pg 95)

Next to: ᎤᎵᏗᏨ [ulditsv] pg 56)

Nicotiana tabacum: ᏦᎳ [tsola] pg 108)

Nicotina rustica: ᏦᎳ ᎠᎦᏴᎵ [tsolą ągąyvli] pg 108)

Night (at): ᎤᏒᎯ [ụsv³hi] pg 61)

Night hawk: ᏓᎳᏍᏙᎬ [dahlsdogv] pg 98)

Night traveler: ᏥᎩᎵ [tsgili] pg 107)

Nightcrawlers: ᎤᏂᏥᏯ [ụnįtsįya] pg 58)

Nine: ᏐᎣᏁᎳ [soʔọnela] pg 96)

Nineteen: ᏐᎣᏁᎳᏚᎯ [soʔọnelądụhi] pg 96)

Ninety: ᏐᎣᏁᎳᏍᎪᎯ [soʔọnelsgohi] pg 96)

No: ᎭᏗ [hądi] pg 92), ᏣᏃ [tsahno] (pg 107)

Nodding his head: ᎠᎵᏍᎫᏩᏍᎦ [ąhlsgụ³whsga] pg 22)

None: ᎧᏂᎩᏓ [kąnigįda] pg 85), ᎧᏂᎩᏓ [kąnigįda] (pg 85)

Noon: ᎢᎦ [iga] pg 52)

North: ᏧᏴᏨᎢ [tsuhyvtsvʔi] pg 109)

North American bamboo: ᎢᏯ [ihya] pg 52)

North American newt: ᏚᏪᎧ [dụweka] pg 106)

North Carolina: ᎦᏯᎴᎾ [gayąlena] pg 83)

Northern bobwhite: ᎤᎫᏇᎯ [ụgkwehi] pg 55)

Nose (his): ᎠᏴᏐᎵ [ąyvsoli] pg 50)

Not: ᎨᏍᏗ [gẹsdi] pg 86)

Not any: ᎧᏂᎩᏓ [kąnigįda] pg 85), ᎧᏂᎩᏓ [kąnigįda] (pg 85)

Nothing: ᎧᏂᎩᏓ [kąnigįda] pg 85), ᎨᏍᏗ ᎪᎱᏍᏗ [gẹsd gọhụsdi] (pg 86)

Noticing it: ᎠᏕᎶᎣᏍᎦ [adeloʔosga] pg 39)

Notophthalmus spp: ᏚᏪᎧ [dụweka] pg 106)

Notophthalmus viridescens: ᏓᎴᏴᏍᎩ [dąleyvsgi] pg 98)

November: ᏅᏓᏕᏆ [nvdądegwa] pg 95)

Now

Now: ᎾᏉ [nagwo] pg 93), ᏃᎢ [noʔi] (pg 94), ᏃᏗ [nodi] (pg 94)
Nude: ᎤᏰᎳᎭ [ụyelạha] pg 66)
Nudging it with his elbow: ᎠᎫᏍᎩᎠ [ạkusgiʔa] pg 18)
Numbers: ᏗᏎᏍᏗ [dịsesdi] pg 105)
Numida meleagris: ᎫᏇ ᏗᎦᎾᏌᎢ [gugwẹ dịganạsạʔi] pg 89)

O

Oak: ᎠᏓᏯᎯ [ạdạyạhi] pg 38), ᏔᎳ [tạla] (pg 102)
Oarlock: ᎤᎶᏥᎬ [ulodskv] pg 56)
Oatmeal: ᏐᏘᎢ ᎤᏂᎩᏍᏗ [sogwịʔị unịgịsdi] pg 96)
Obedient: ᎤᏬᎯᏳᏂ [ụwohịyụni] pg 65)
Obtaining it (a solid): ᎠᎩᎠ [ạgi³ʔa] pg 16)
Ocean: ᎠᎼ ᎡᏉᎯ [ạm egwohi] pg 25)
October: ᏚᏂᏅᏗ [dụninṿdi] pg 106)
Odocoileus virginianus: ᎠᏫ [ahwi] pg 46)
Oenothera biennis: ᎠᎾᏓᏥ [ạndatsi] pg 25)
Office: ᏧᏃᏪᎶᏗᏳ [tsunohwelodiyu] pg 108)
Offspring: ᎤᏪᏥ [ụwetsi] pg 65)
Okay: ᎭᏩ [hạwa] pg 92)
Oklahoma: ᏭᏕᎵᎬ [wudelịgv] pg 110)
Old (inanimate only): ᎤᏪᏗ [ụwedi] pg 65)
Old (something alive): ᎠᎬᏴᎵᎨᎢ [ạkyvligẹʔi] pg 19)
Oncorhynchus mykiss: ᏧᏂᎶᎸᏗ [tsunilohldi] pg 108)
Ondatra zibethicus: ᏎᎵᎩᏍᏉ [seliksgwo] pg 96)
One: ᏐᏊ [sogwu] pg 96)
One foot (12 inches): ᎢᏯᎳᏏᏅᎯ [iyạʔlạsihnṿhi] pg 52)
One hundred: ᏍᎪᎯᏥᏆ [sgohitsgwa] pg 96)
One thing: ᏑᏓᎴᎦ [sudạlega] pg 97)
One thousand: ᎠᎦᏴᎵ [ạgạyvli] pg 14)
One who sews: ᎦᏰᏫᏒᏱᏍᎩ [gayewhsvʔỵsgi] pg 83)
Onion: ᏒᎩ [svgi] pg 97)
Only thing: ᏍᎩᏊᏩᏌ [sgịgwụwạsa] pg 96)
Onopordum acanthium: ᏥᏥ [tsitsi] pg 108)
Open mouth (his): ᎤᏔᎶᎩ [ụtạlogi] pg 61)
Opening a door: ᎠᏍᏚᎩᎠ [asdụ³giʔa] pg 33)
Opening eyes: ᏓᎧᏂᎭ [dakạnịha] pg 98)
Opossum: ᎤᏤᏥᏍᏗ [utsedsdi] pg 63)
Or: ᎠᎴ [ạle] pg 21)
Or it (a liquid) is falling (something flexible): ᎦᏙᎣᏍᎦ [gạdoʔosga] pg 82)
Orange (color): ᏓᎶᏂᎨ ᎤᏍᎪᎸᎢ [dạlonige ụsgolṿʔi] pg 99)
Order Hymenoptera: ᎧᎾᏥᏍᏕᏥ [kantsịsdetsi] pg 84)
Order Orthoptera: ᏙᎯᏥᏆ [tohịtsgwa] pg 106), ᏙᎳᏥ [tolạtsi] (pg 106)
Order Siphonaptera: ᏧᎧ [tsuka] pg 108)
Orontium aquaticum: ᎦᏁᏏ [gạnesi] pg 76)
Osage: ᎠᏂᏆᏌᏏ [ạnikwasasi] pg 26)
Osprey: ᎧᏅᏧᏩ [kạnvtsuhwa] pg 85)
Other one: ᏄᏓᎴᎯ [nudạlẹhi] pg 95)
Otter: ᏥᏲ [tsiyo] pg 108)
Out of sight: ᏭᏕᎵ [wudeʔli] pg 110)
Outside: ᏙᏱ [doyi] pg 106)
Outside of: ᏙᏱᏨ [dọyitsv] pg 106)
Outwitting him: ᎦᎶᏅᎡᎭ [gạlonṿʔeha] pg 72)
Oven bird: ᏧᏦᎵᏛ [tsụtsoldv] pg 109)
Over there (at a): ᏂᎨᎢ [nịgei] pg 94)
Over yonder: ᏂᎨᎢ [nịgei] pg 94)
Overalls: ᎤᏤᏌᏗ [ụtsesadi] pg 63)
Overeating: ᎤᏯᎶᏘᎭ [uyạlotịha] pg 66)

Overnight

Overnight: ᏑᏒᎯᏓ [sụsṿhida] pg 97)
Ovis aries: ᎤᏃᏕᎾ [ụnọdena] pg 59)
Owes someone: ᎤᏚᎦ [utuga] pg 63)
Ownership: ᎤᏤᎵ [utseli] pg 63)
Oxydendrum arboreum: ᏅᏙᏇᏯ [nvdọkwehya] pg 95)
Oyster: ᏛᎬᎾ [dṿgvna] pg 107)

P

Pacing back and forth: ᎠᏨᏏᏰᎠ [atsvsiyeʔa] pg 46)
Paddling him: ᎠᏆᎸᏂᎭ [agwạlvʔnị³ha] pg 27)
Padlock: ᏓᎦᏏ [dagsi] pg 97)
Pain: ᎡᎯᏍᏗ [ẹhịsdi] pg 51)
Paint clan: ᎠᏂᏬᏗ [ạniwodi] pg 27)
Painting: ᏓᏑᏫᏍᎦ [dasụ³hwisga] pg 100)
Pair of pants: ᎠᏑᎶ [asulo] pg 35)
Pale: ᎤᏍᎪᎸ [ụsgolv] pg 60)
Panax quinquefolius: ᎣᏓᎵᎦᎵ [odạlịgạʔli] pg 53)
Pandion haliaetus: ᎧᏅᏧᏩ [kạnvtsuhwa] pg 85)
Panic grass: ᎧᏁᏍᎦ [kạnesga] pg 85)
Panicum spp: ᎧᏁᏍᎦ [kạnesga] pg 85)
Panther: ᏨᏓᏥ [tsvdạtsi] pg 109)
Pantherophis obsoletus: ᎦᎴᎩ [gạʔlegi] pg 69)
Paper: ᎪᏪᎵ [gohweli] pg 89)
Parent-in-law: ᎤᎾᏥ [unatsi] pg 57)
Parrot: ᏥᏍᏆᎦᏬᏂᏍᎩ [tsisgwagạwọʔnịsgi] pg 107)
Passenger pigeon: ᏬᏱ [woyi] pg 110)
Passer domesticus: ᏥᏍᏆᏯ [tsisgwaya] pg 107)
Passerina cyanea: ᎠᎵᏣᏃᏍᎦ [ạlitsạnosga] pg 23)

Passiflora incarnata: ᎤᏩᎦ [uwaga] pg 64)

Passing a bill (legislation): ᏍᎦᎶᎥᏗᏆ [galo³hisdiha] pg 71)

Passing a grade: ᎠᏍᎧᎣᏇ [akty³ɂleha] pg 14)

Passing by: ᏍᎦᎤᏇ [galo³hiseha] pg 72)

Passion flower: ᎤᏩᎦ [uwaga] pg 64)

Patchwork (for quilt): ᏗᎬᎯᏪᎥᏗ [digvleyosdi] pg 105)

Path: ᏒᎰᏗ [edasdi] pg 51)

Patriarch: ᎤᏫᎼᏲ [utvsonv] pg 63)

Paying: ᎠᏫᎥᏇ [akwiyiha] pg 27)

Paying him: ᎠᏫᏴᏴᏇ [akwiyvɂeha] pg 27)

Peach: ᏆᎾ [kwana] pg 95)

Peacock: ᏧᏗᎦᏫᏍᏗ [tsudigwasdi] pg 109)

Peanuts: ᏑᏯ ᎠᏂᎳᏗᏍᎩ [tuya aniladisgi] pg 107)

Pear: ᏎᏗᏳᏍᏗ [sediyusdi] pg 96)

Peas: ᎤᏂᏨᎾᏓᎵ [untsvndali] pg 58)

Pedicularis canadensis: ᎤᎫᎫᏍᏙ [ugukusdo] pg 54)

Pee wee (bird): ᏍᎪᏱᏴᏙᏍᏗ [dsgoyiɂdosdi] pg 107)

Peeking: ᎠᎧᏘᏇ [aka³tiha] pg 15)

Peeling: ᎠᎭᎨᏨᎯ [ahaketsyhi] pg 19), ᎤᏁᎦᎸᏅ [unegalyɂnv] (pg 57), ᎳᏴᎧᏍᎦᏍ [dayakeksga] (pg 102)

Pen: ᏗᎪᎭᏪᎶᏗ [digohweloɂdi] pg 105)

Pencil: ᏗᎪᎭᏪᎶᏗ [digohweloɂdi] pg 105)

Penetrating it: ᎠᏔᎳᎧᏍᎦ [atalaksga] pg 38)

Penis (his): ᎤᏩᏙᎵ [uwatoli] pg 64)

People with no clan affiliation: ᎠᏂᎩᏍᎩ [aniksgi] pg 26)

Pepper (black): ᏗᎪᏓᎵᏗ [dikodaldi] pg 104)

Pepper on a vine: ᎤᏂᏟᏏᎸᏴ [unitsilvɂi] pg 58)

Performing the scratching ritual: ᏔᏓᎱᎪᏍᎦ [dadahnugoh³sga] pg 101)

Persimmon: ᏏᎵ [sali] pg 95)

Person: ᏴᏫ [yvwi] pg 111)

Perspiring: ᎦᎵᏆᎦᎲ [gaɂliɂagaiha] pg 70)

PERSUADING HIM

Persuading him: ᎠᏍᏗᏰᏗᏇ [asdiyediha] pg 32)

Pestle: ᏍᏙᏍᏗ [sdosdi] pg 96)

Phaseolus lunatus: ᏑᏯᏁᏆ [tuyanegwa] pg 107)

Pheasant: ᏔᏗᏍᏗ [tvdisdi] pg 107)

Pheucticus ludovicianus: ᎦᏪᏍᎦᏩᎴᏅ [gaysgwalenv] pg 83)

Photograph: ᏗᏘᏣᎶᏍᏓᏅᎯ [ditsilosdanvhi] pg 105)

Photographer: ᏗᏗᏣᏣᎶᏍᏗᏍᎩ [didatsilosdisgi] pg 105)

Physalis spp: ᎤᏅᏚᎯᏍᏓ [unvduhisda] pg 59)

Phytolacca americana: ᏣᏰᎦ [tsahyiga] pg 107)

Picea rubra: ᏃᏥ ᏔᎨᏳᏍᏗ [notsi iyusdi] pg 94)

Picking it (a solid) up: ᎠᎩᏆ [agi³ɂa] pg 16)

Picking it (something flexible) up: ᎦᏁᏆ [ganeɂa] pg 75)

Picking it (something long) up: ᎠᏯᏆ [ayɂa] pg 47)

Picking it (something long) up from the ground: ᎠᏱᏆ [ayi³ɂa] pg 48), ᎫᏔᎩᏆ [guɂtagiɂa] (pg 90)

Picking on him: ᎠᎵᏌᎵᏇ [alsaliha] pg 22)

Picking up it (a liquid): ᎦᏁᎩᏆ [ganegi³ɂa] pg 75)

Picking up it (something flexible) or it (something alive) from the ground: ᎦᎾᎩᏆ [ganagiɂa] pg 73)

Picking up things that are alive: ᏓᏓᎾᎩᏆ [dada³nagi³ɂa] pg 100)

Pickling: ᏕᎦᏂᏦᏍᏗᏆ [degantsosdiha] pg 103)

Picture: ᏗᏘᏣᎶᏍᏓᏅᎯ [ditsilosdanvhi] pg 105)

Pie: ᎨᎵᏍᎩ [gelidsgi] pg 86)

Pig: ᏏᏆ [sikwa] pg 96)

Pigeon grapes: ᏆᎷᏥ [kwalu³si] pg 95)

Pigeon hawk: ᏌᎾᏩ [sanawa] pg 95)

Pileated woodpecker: ᎨᏲᎪᎬ [geɂgwogv] pg 86)

Pillow (his): ᎤᏍᏙᎯ [uksdohi] pg 53)

Pillow case: ᎠᎩᏍᏙᎯ ᎦᎸᏙᎯᏗ [aksdohi galvdohdi] pg 27)

Pin: ᏴᎩ [yvgi] pg 110)

Pinching: ᎠᎬᏁᎫᎩᏆ [agwenugiɂa] pg 27)

Pine lizard: ᏔᏳᎭᎵ [tayuhali] pg 102)

Pine tree (all varieties): ᏃᏥ [notsi] pg 94)

Pink: ᎩᎦᎨ ᎤᏍᎪᎸᏴ [gigage usgolvɂi] pg 87)

Pinus spp: ᏃᏥ [notsi] pg 94)

Pinus Strobus L: ᏙᏥ [doɂtsi] pg 106)

Pipe use for smoking: ᎦᏅᏬᎠ [ganvnowa] pg 79)

Pipilo erythrophthalmus: ᏧᏬᏍᎦ [tsuwosga] pg 109)

Piranga olivacea: ᏦᎳ [tsohla] pg 108)

Pistol (gun): ᏍᎧᎳ ᏍᎦᎶᎬᏪᎯ [skala galogwehi] pg 95)

Pitcher (baseball): ᏧᏕᎩ [tsudegi] pg 109)

Pitchfork: ᏴᎩ [yvgi] pg 110)

Pituophis catenifer sayi: ᎢᎾᏓ ᏐᎸᎨᏆ [inada solvgeɂi] pg 52)

Place for receiving: ᎤᏄᎯᏍᏗ [uɂluhisdi] pg 56)

Place of work: ᏗᎦᎸᎥᏫᏍᏓᏂ [digalvhwisdandi] pg 104)

Place to look: ᎤᏍᏗᏳ [usdiyu] pg 60)

Placing flexible things into a row: ᏓᏄᏁᎦ [danynega] pg 99)

Placing it (a solid) in a fire: ᎬᏔᏍᎦ [gvtah³sga] pg 92)

Placing it (a solid) on the ground: ᎠᏆᏍᎦ [aɂvsga] pg 13)

Placing it (something alive) on a raised surface: ᎦᎾᏆᏍᎦ [ganaɂvsga] pg 73)

Placing it (something alive) on the ground: ᎦᏅᏆᏍᎦ [ganv³ɂvsga] pg 79)

Placing it (something flexible) on the ground: ᎦᏅᏆᏍᎦ [ganv³ɂvsga] pg 79)

PLACING IT

Placing it (something long) on the ground: ᎠᏗᎠ [adiʔa] pg 40)

Placing living things in a row: ᏓᎧᎾᎦ [dakaṇega] pg 97)

Placing long things into a row: ᏓᏕᎦ [dadega] pg 101)

Placing solid things in a row: ᏓᏁᎦ [danega] pg 99)

Plaid: ᎤᏐᏃᏟ [uṇaloʔida] pg 57)

Planning to: ᎠᏕᎣᏖᎭ [adahnteha] pg 37)

Plantago lanceolata: ᎠᏍᏝᏃᏍᏗ [gosda³ṇisdi] pg 88)

Plantago major: ᎾᎾ ᎤᏕᎯᏘ [nan ụdehyti] pg 93)

Plantain, broadleaf: ᎾᎾ ᎤᏕᎯᏘ [nan ụdehyti] pg 93)

Planting: ᎠᏫᏍ [ahwih³sga] pg 47)

Planting seeds: ᏓᏫᏍ [dawisga] pg 102)

Platanthera ciliaris: ᎠᏣᏗ ᎠᏂᎦᏔ [atsadi aṇigwata] pg 44)

Platanus occidentalis: ᎫᎯᏳᎬᏍᏗ [kuhwiyụgsdi] pg 90)

Plate: ᎠᏖᎵᏚ [ahtelidu] pg 40), ᏍᏄᎲᎵᏗ [gaṇuhihldi] (pg 78)

Playing a game: ᏓᏁᎶᎲᏍ [daʔnelohvsga] pg 99)

Playing ball: ᎠᏁᏦᏍ [ahnetsoʔvsga] pg 26)

Playing cards: ᎠᏆᎾᏲᎯᎭ [akwaṇayo³hịha] pg 27)

Playing marbles: ᎦᏓᏲᎯᎭ [gada³yohịha] pg 82)

Playing music: ᎧᏃᎩᏍᏗᎭ [kaṇogisdịha] pg 85)

Playing with: ᏓᏁᎲᏗᎭ [daʔne³hldịha] pg 99)

Plowing: ᎦᏓᎷᎩᎠ [gadalu³gịʔa] pg 82)

Plucking a chicken: ᎫᏯᎩᎠ [guyagịʔa] pg 90)

Plugging it in: ᎫᏓᎸᏍ [gudalvʔvsga] pg 90)

Plum: ᎬᎾᏄᏂᏗ [gwaṇunsdịʔi] pg 95)

Pneumonia: ᎤᏍᎦᏎᏛ ᎤᏗᎴᎩ [ụsgased ụdịlegi] pg 60)

Pocket: ᎭᏦᏩᏛ [hatsowạdv] pg 92)

Pocket knife: ᎤᏍᏗ ᎭᏰᎳᏍᏗ [ụsdi hạyelạsdi] pg 60)

Podophyllum peltatum: ᎤᏂᏍᏇᏚᎦ [uṇisgweduga] pg 58)

Poecile carolinensis: ᏥᎩᎵᎵ [tsigịlili] pg 107)

Pointing at him: ᎠᏎᎯᎭ [ạse³hịha] pg 33)

Pointing for him: ᎠᏎᎮᎭ [ạse³heha] pg 33)

Poison ivy: ᎤᎸᏗ [ulvdi] pg 56)

Poison oak: ᎤᎸᏗ [ulvdi] pg 56)

Poke: ᏣᏱᎦ [tsahyịga] pg 107)

Poke salad: ᏣᏱᎦ [tsahyịga] pg 107)

Pokeweed: ᏣᏱᎦ [tsahyịga] pg 107)

Policeman: ᏗᏓᎯᏥᏍᎩ [dịdahnịtsịsgi] pg 105)

Pollywog: ᏗᎩᏥ [dịgitsi] pg 104)

Polygonatum biflorum: ᎢᎦᎾᏍᏗ [iganạsdi] pg 52)

Pond: ᎠᎻ ᎠᏍᏛᎯᏍᏛ [ạm asdỵhisdv] pg 25)

Poor: ᎤᏠᏕᎭ [ulẹsoda] pg 55)

Popcorn: ᎠᏂᏔᏍᎩᏍᎩ [aṇtasgisgi] pg 25)

Popping: ᎠᏔᏍᎩᎠ [atasgịʔa] pg 38)

Popping it: ᎠᏔᏍᎩᏍᏗᎭ [atasgisdịha] pg 38)

POST

Populus sect. Tacamahaca: ᎾᎦᎢᏘ [nạgeʔi] pg 93)

Populus spp: ᎠᏓ ᎬᏂᎯᏛ [adạ gỵnịhidv] pg 36), ᏥᏳ [tsiyu] (pg 108)

Porch: ᏙᏱᏨᎯ ᎠᏲᏓᏍᏱ [doyitsvhi ạyọdạsvʔi] pg 106)

Portion: ᎠᏯᏙᎸᏱ [ạyadohlỵʔi] pg 48)

Possession: ᎤᏤᎵ [utseli] pg 63)

Possum grapes: ᎨᎳᏗ [kelạdi] pg 86)

POST

Post: ᏗᎨᏛᏍᏗ [dịgedvsdi] pg 104)

Post oak: ᏧᏍᎪ [tsusgo] pg 109)

Postage stamp: ᎦᏯᎸᏗ [gayạlvdi] pg 83)

Pot scrapings: ᎤᏣᎳ [utsạla] pg 63)

Potato(es): ᏄᎾ [nuna] pg 95)

Pottery: ᎢᎾᏘ [vnti] pg 68)

Pounding: ᎠᏍᏙᎠ [asdoʔa] pg 32)

Pounding block: ᎧᏃᏅ [kạnonv] pg 85)

Pouring it: ᎠᏣᏴᏍ [atsỵʔvsga] pg 45)

Pouring it out: ᎠᏣᏴᏍ [atsv³ʔvsga] pg 45)

Pouting: ᎠᎵᏲᏬᏗᎭ [ahlịyowẹ³hdịha] pg 24)

Praying: ᎠᏓᏙᎵᏍᏗᎭ [adạdolisdiha] pg 37)

Preacher: ᎠᎵᏥᏙᎲᏍᎩ [altsịdọhvsgi] pg 24)

Preaching: ᎠᎵᏥᏙᎲᏍ [altsịdo³hvsga] pg 24)

Pregnant: ᎦᏁᎳᏗ [gaṇeladi] pg 76)

Preserving it: ᎠᎧᎵᏲᏗᎭ [ạkahyoh³dịha] pg 16), ᎦᎳᏛᏴᏍ [galhtaṇy³ʔvsga] (pg 72)

Prettier: ᏫᏥᏄᏬᏕᎭ [wịtsinuwodụha] pg 110)

Prettiest: ᏫᏥᏄᏬᏕᎭ [wịtsinuwodụha] pg 110)

Pretty: ᎤᏬᏕᎭ [uwodụha] pg 66), ᎤᏬᏕᎯ [uwodụhi] (pg 66)

Pricking it: ᎠᏣᏲᎵᎭ [atsạyo³hlịha] pg 44)

Prize: ᎠᏓᎪᎾᏙᏗ [adạgoṇạdodi] pg 36)

Probably: ᎠᏎᎿ [ạsehno] pg 34)

Process of lying down (in the): ᎦᎯᏅᎦ [gahny³ga] pg 79)

Procyon lotor: ᎬᎭᎵ [gvhỵli] pg 91)

Progne subis: ᏧᏧ [tsutsu] pg 109)

Pronunciation: ᏔᎪᏬᏗ [igọwesdi] pg 52)

Proper: ᏚᏳᎦᏔ [dụyukta] pg 107)

Pruning a tree: ᏕᎬᎾᎦᎳᏬᎣᎠᏗ [degvnạgạlạwọoʔa] pg 104)

Prunus domestica: ᎬᎾᏄᏂᏗ [gwaṇunsdịʔi] pg 95)

Prunus pensylvanica: ᏩᏯ ᏔᎾᎦᎢᏘ [tayạ ịnageʔi] pg 102)

Prunus persica: ᏆᎾ [kwana] pg 95)

Prunus spp: ᏩᏯ [taya] pg 102)

Pseudognaphalium obtusifolium: ᎪᏍᏗᏳᏍᏗ [kọsdiyụsdi] pg 88)

Puddle: ᎦᏁᎲᏱ [gaṇehvʔi] pg 75)

Puffball (fungus): ᏃᏆᏏ ᎤᏍᏗ [nokwịsi usdi] pg 94)

Pull (corn fodder or blades): ᎯᎵᏍᏛᏬᏨ [hilsdvwotsv] pg 93)

Pulling corn slades off: ᎠᎳᏍᏚᏬᎠ [ahlsdụ^{3}woʔa] pg 21)

Pulling leaves off of a tree: ᎠᎵᏍᏚᎩᎠ [ahlsdụgiʔa] pg 22)

Pulling rocks from the ground: ᏓᎬᏓᎳᎩᎠ [dakvdạlạgi^{3}ʔa] pg 98)

Pulling up weeds: ᎨᏄᎩᎠ [gẹnugiʔa] pg 86), ᎬᏄᏯᎩᎠ [gvnuyạgiʔa] (pg 91)

Puma concolor: ᏨᏓᏥ [tsvdạtsi] pg 109)

Pumpkin: ᎢᏯ [iya] pg 52)

Purple: ᏕᎷᎨ [dehlụge] pg 104)

Purple finch: ᎤᏦᏁᏗ [ụtsonedi] pg 64)

Purple martin: ᏧᏧ [tsutsu] pg 109)

Purple passionflower: ᎤᏩᎦ [uwạga] pg 64)

Pus: ᎠᏔᏍᎩᏍᎬᎢ [ạtạsgisgvʔi] pg 38)

Pushing aside: ᎧᏅᎠ [kạnvʔa] pg 85)

Pushing it: ᎠᏌᏙᏯᏍᎦ [ạsạdọ^{3}yhsga] pg 29)

Pushing it (a solid) aside: ᎠᏌᎲᎠ [asạhvʔa] pg 28)

Pushing it

Pushing it (something alive) aside: ᎠᎧᎲᎠ [ạkạhvʔa] pg 15)

Pushing it (something long) aside: ᎠᏏᏴᎠ [asi^{3}yvʔa] pg 34)

Pussywillow: ᏗᎵᎦᎵᏍᎩ [diligalịsgi] pg 105)

Putting a ribbon in his hair: ᎠᏇᎷᏍᎦ [agwelusga] pg 27)

Putting it (a liquid) into a container: ᎠᏥᎠ [ạtsị^{3}ʔa] pg 44)

Putting it (a solid) into a container: ᎦᎳᏍᎦ [gahlasga] pg 69)

Putting it (a solid) up: ᎠᏌᎲᏍᎦ [asạhvh^{3}sga] pg 28)

Putting it (something flexible) into a fire: ᎬᏛᎥᏍᎦ [gvhdv^{3}ʔvsga] pg 92)

Putting it (something flexible) into a liquid: ᏕᎬᏍᎦ [degvhsga] pg 104)

Putting it (something flexible) or it (something alive) into a container: ᎦᎸᎥᏍᎦ [gạlvʔvsga] pg 72)

Putting it (something flexible) up: ᎠᏒᎥᏍᎦ [asv^{3}vsga] pg 35)

Putting it (something long) into a container: ᎦᎳᏗᎠ [gạldịʔa] pg 69)

Putting it (something long) into a fire: ᎠᎲᏔᏍᎦ [ahv-tah^{3}sga] pg 20)

Putting it (something long) into a liquid: ᎠᎱᏗᎠ [ahudịʔa] pg 20)

Putting it (something long) up: ᎠᏌᏗᎠ [asa^{3}dịʔa] pg 29)

Putting liquid into a liquid: ᎠᏥᎠ [ạtsịʔa] pg 44)

Putting on a pair of pants: ᎠᏑᎵᎠ [ạsulịʔa] pg 35)

Putting on a sock: ᏓᎵᏲᎭ [dalihyoha] pg 99)

Putting on his shoulder: ᎦᏃᏒᎥᏍᎦ [gạnosvʔvsga] pg 78)

Putting on shoes: ᏓᏑᎳᏍᎦ [dalạ^{3}suhlasga] pg 98)

Putting something into a group: ᎨᎳᏗᎠ [gẹ^{3}hlạdịʔa] pg 86)

Putting up a wire: ᎠᏏᎳᏛᎥᏍᎦ [ạsịlạdvʔvsga] pg 34)

Pyrus communis: ᏎᏗᏳᏍᏗ [sedịyụsdi] pg 96)

Q

Quail: ᎤᎫᏇᎯ [ụgkwehi] pg 55)

Quakers: ᎠᏂᏇᎩ [ạnikwegi] pg 26)

Quartz crystal: ᎤᎸᏌᏘ [ulvsạti] pg 56)

Queen of the meadow: ᎠᎹ ᎠᏗᏙᏗ [ạm ạdịtodi] pg 25)

Quercus falcata: ᎫᎴᏧᎾᏍᏗ [gulẹtsunsdi] pg 89)

Quercus L: ᏔᎳ [tạla] pg 102)

Quercus nigra: ᏙᎳᏥ [dolạtsi] pg 106)

Quercus spp: ᎠᏓᏯᎯ [ạdạyạhi] pg 38)

Quercus stellata: ᏧᏍᎪ [tsusgo] pg 109)

Quercus velutina: ᏗᎬᏂᎨᎢ [digvnigẹʔi] pg 105)

Quick: ᎤᎵᏍᏓ [uhlịsda] pg 55), ᎦᏨᏄᎳ [gatsvnula] (pg 83)

Quiet: ᎡᎶᏪᎯ [elọwehi] pg 51)

Quilt: ᎠᏰᎧᎵ [ayẹkahli] pg 48)

Quilt top: ᎠᎬᎭᎴᏫᏓ [agvhạlewịda] pg 19)

Quitting: ᎠᏲᎯᏍᏗᎭ [ạyohisdịha] pg 49)

R

Rabbit: ᏥᏍᏚ [tsịsdu] pg 107)

Rabbit tobacco: ᎪᏍᏗᏳᏍᏗ [kọsdiyụsdi] pg 88)

Rabbit's tail: ᏥᏍᏚ ᏍᎩᏓᏘ [tsisdụ sgidạti] pg 107)

Raccoon: ᎬᎲᎵ [gvhvli] pg 91)

Racing: ᎠᎵᏙᎩᏱᎠ [altọgiyịʔa] pg 23)

Radio: ᎧᏃᎩᏍᏗ [kạnogisdi] pg 85)

Ragweed: ᎤᏆᏍᏓᎷᏱᏓ [ụgwạsdaluhyda] pg 60)

Railroad train: ᎠᏥᎳ ᏓᏆᎴᎷ [ạtsilạ dạgwạlelu] pg 44)

Rain: ᎠᎦᏍᎩ [agạsgi] pg 13)

Rain crow: ᏓᎶᎬ [dạlogv] pg 99)

Rain raven: ᏓᎶᎬ [dạlogv] pg 99)

Rainbow: ᎤᏅᎪᎳᏛ [uhnvgọladv] pg 59)

Rainbow trout: ᏧᏂᎶᎸᏗ [tsunilohldi] pg 108)

Raising: ᎠᏛᎯᏍᏗᎭ [atvhị^{3}sdịha] pg 42)

Raising an arm: ᎠᏐᎸᏔᏍᎦ [ạsolvtah^{3}sga] pg 34)

Raising children: ᏓᏛᎯᏍᏗᎭ [datvhịsdịha] pg 101)

Raising it: ᎠᏌᎳᏓ [asạladʔa] pg 28)

Ramps (plant): ᎤᏩᏍᏗ [ụwạsdi] pg 64)

Rana catesbeiana: ᎧᏄᏄ [kạnunu] pg 85)

Raspberries: ᏒᏗᏩᎵ [svdịwạʔli] pg 97)

Rat: ᏥᏍᏕᏥ [tsisdetsi] pg 107)

Rattle: ᎦᎾᏤᏗ [gạntsehdi] pg 74)

Rattle wrapped around the leg: ᎤᏅᏌᏗ [unṿsadi] pg 59)

Rattlesnake fern: ᎤᏎᎳᏘ [usẹlati] pg 60)

Rattus spp: ᏥᏍᏕᏥ [tsisdetsi] pg 107)

Raven: ᎪᎸᏅ [kolṿnv] pg 88)

Raven mocker: ᎪᎸᏅ ᎠᏰᎵᏍᎩ [kolṿnṿ ahyelisgi] pg 88)

Raven's Place (Big Cove): ᎪᎸᏅᏱ [kolṿnvyi] pg 88)

Raw: ᎠᎪᏍᏗ [ạgosdi] pg 18)

Razor: ᎠᎵᏍᏙᏯᏙᏗ [alsdohydohdi] pg 22)

Reading it: ᎠᎪᎵᏰᎠ [ạgoli^{3}yẹʔa] pg 17)

Rearing them: ᏓᏛᎯᏍᏗᎭ [datvhịsdịha] pg 101)

Rearing up: ᎠᏛᎯᏍᏗᎭ [atvhị^{3}sdịha] pg 42)

Receding: ᎦᏅᏬᏍᎦ [gạnvwosga] pg 81)

Receiving: ᏓᏓᏂᎸᎦ [dadạni^{3}lvga] pg 101)

Receiving a vaccine: ᏓᏓᏄᎪᏍᎦ [dadahnugoh^{3}sga] pg 101)

Receiving place: ᎤᎷᎯᏍᏗ [uʔluhisdi] pg 56)

Recognizing it: ᎪᎵᎧ [golka] pg 88)

Red (color): ᎩᎦᎨᎢ [gigạgeʔi] pg 87)

Red bird: ᏙᏧᏩ [totsuwa] pg 106)

Red buckeye: ᎤᏍᏆᏙ [ụsgwạdo] pg 60), ᏧᏆᏆ [tsugwagwa] (pg 109)

Red earthworms: ᎤᏂᏥᏯ [ụnịtsịya] pg 58)

Red fox: ᏧᎳ ᎩᎦᎨ [tsulạ gigạge] pg 108)

Red Horse: ᎣᎵᎦ [olịga] pg 53)

Red horsemint: ᏩᎴᎷ ᎤᏂᏣᎩᏍᏗ [wạlelụ ụnịtsạgisdi] pg 109)

Red maple: ᎩᎦᎨᏨᏩᎩ [gigạgetsvhwạgi] pg 87)

Red mulberry: ᎫᏩ [kuwa] pg 90)

Red oak: ᎫᎴᏧᎾᏍᏗ [gulẹtsunsdi] pg 89)

Red-eyed vireo: ᏧᏕᏒᎾᎵ [tsụdesṿnali] pg 109)

Red-headed woodpecker: ᏓᎳᎳ [dạlala] pg 98)

Red-tailed hawk

Red-tailed hawk: ᏔᏬᏗ ᎡᏆ [tạwodʔ egwa] pg 102)

Reflecting: ᎤᏔᎷᎩᎠ [uhtạlu^{3}gịʔa] pg 61)

Refrigerator: ᎠᏴᏣᏗᏍᏗᏍᎩ [ahyvtsạdịsdịsgi] pg 50)

Refusing to give him: ᎠᎨᏯᏗᎭ [ạgehydịha] pg 16)

Remembering it: ᎤᏅᏓᎭ [uhndaha] pg 59)

Removing an animal from pasture: ᎠᎩᎵᎩᎠ [ạkịligiʔa] pg 16)

Removing it (a solid) from a shelf: ᎠᏌᎩᎠ [asạgiʔa] pg 28)

Removing it (something long) from a container: ᎦᎵᏏᎭ [gạlisịha] pg 71)

Removing it (something long) or it (a liquid) or it (a solid) from a container: ᎦᎳᎩᎠ [gạlạgiʔa] pg 69)

Removing it from a shelf: ᎠᏏᎭ [asịha] pg 34)

Removing liquid from a container: ᎠᎫᎩᎠ [ạkugịʔa] pg 18)

Requesting: ᎠᏔᏲᎯᎭ [ahtạyohịha] pg 39)

Residing: ᎦᎾᎩᎳ [gạnạgịla] pg 74), ᎦᏁᎳ [gạnẹla] (pg 76)

Responsible for or to: ᎤᏚᏓᎳ [udu^{3}dạʔla] pg 63)

Resting: ᎤᏯᏪᏐᎵᎭ [uyạwe^{3}sohlịha] pg 66)

Returning: ᎢᎦᎷᎧ [igaʔlka] pg 52)

Returning an animal: ᎠᎧᏂ [ạkạni] pg 15)

Rheum rhaponticum: ᏧᏂᏦᏴᏍᏗ [tsuhnịtsohysdi] pg 108)

Rheumatism: ᏗᏙᎴᏍᎩ [dịdolesgi] pg 105)

Rheumatism root: ᎠᏨᎩ ᎢᎾᎨᎡᎯ [ahtsvgi ịnageẹhi] pg 45)

Rhinoceros: ᏣᏃᏏ [tsanosi] pg 107)

Rhododendron: ᏚᏐᎦ ᏨᏁᏆ [dụsog tsṿnegwa] pg 106)

***Rhododendron ferrugineum* L**: ᏚᏐᎦ ᏨᏁᏆ [dụsog tsṿnegwa] pg 106)

Rhus spp: ᏆᎶᎦ [gwaloga] pg 95)

Ribbon: ᎠᏇᎷᏍᏗ [ạgwehlusdi] pg 27)

Ribs: ᎠᏄᎳᏥᏴᎢ [ạnụlatsịyvʔi] pg 27)

Rice: ᎦᏃᎮᎾ [gạnọhena] pg 77)

Rich (becoming): ᎤᏪᏅᎦ [uwẹ^{3}hnvga] pg 65)

Ridiculing: ᏛᏐᏨᏤᎭ [dvsọtsvcheha] pg 107)

Ridiculing him: ᎠᏙᏥᏗᎭ [ado^{3}tsdịha] pg 42)

Right: ᎠᏘᏍᎩ [ạtisgi] pg 41)

Right-handedness (his): ᎠᏘᏍᎩ [ạtisgi] pg 41)

Ring (his): ᎤᎵᏰᏑᏍᏓᏬ [ulịyẹsụsdạwo] pg 56)

Ringing it (bell): ᎦᏃᏴᎮᏍᏗᎭ [gahnọyṿ^{3}hẹsdịha] pg 78)

Riparia riparia: ᏦᏯᎦ [tsoyạga] pg 108)

Ripping it: ᎠᎵᎬᎩᎠ [ạlịgvgiʔa] pg 21)

Rising from sitting: ᏓᎴᎲᏍᎦ [dalehvsga] pg 98)

River: ᎠᎹᏱ [ạmayi] pg 25), ᎡᏉᏂ [egwoni] (pg 51)

River (small): ᏂᎳᏛᏱ [nịldvyi] pg 94)

River birch: ᎦᏁᏗᏍᎩ [gạnedị^{3}sgi] pg 76)

River cane: ᎢᏯ [ihya] pg 52)

Road: ᎦᏅᏅ [gạnvhnv] pg 80), ᏅᏃᎯ [nvnọhi] (pg 95)

Roasting it: ᎠᏒᎾᏔᏍᎦ [asvnạtasga] pg 35)

Robbing him: ᎦᏅᏌᎲᏍᎦ [gạnhsạhvh^{3}sga] pg 80)

Robbinsville: ᏥᏲᎯ [tsiyọhi] pg 108)

Robin: ᏥᏍᏉᏉ [tsisgwogwo] pg 107)

Robinia pseudoacacia: ᎧᎶᏇᏗ [kạlọgwedi] pg 84)

Rock: ᏅᏯ [nvya] pg 95)

Rock armor: ᏅᏯ ᎤᏄᏬ [nṿʔyạ uhnụwo] pg 95)

Rock maple: ᏧᏩᎩ [tsuwagi] pg 109)

ROCK SHELTER

Rock shelter: ᏆᎣᏟᏍᎮᎢ [usdagalvɂi] pg 60)

Rocking a chair: ᏞᎻᎷᏫᎾᏚ [dahlilukesga] pg 98)

Rocky: ᏅᎲᎠ [nvɂyohi] pg 95)

Rolling (they are): ᎠᎾᏜᏋᏣᏟᏛ [anadasagwale³hiha] pg 25)

Rolling along: ᎠᏋᏣᏍᎵ [asagwalehli] pg 28), ᏛᏋᏣᏍᎵ [adasagwale³hli] (pg 37)

Rolling it: ᎠᏋᏣᏜ [asagwa³hleha] pg 28)

Rolling it around: ᎠᏋᏣᏛᏚ [asagwalesga] pg 29)

Rolling or skidding logs downhill: ᎠᏔᎮᎵᏛᏚ [ayuy-ohosga] pg 50), ᏎᏎᏔᎮᎰᎠᏛ [degayuyohohndiha] (pg 103)

Roof: ᏎᎡᎾᎵ [gasvnali] pg 81)

Roofing a house: ᎾᎵᎩᏇᏛᏚ [kaltsotah³sga] pg 84)

Rooster: ᎠᏣᏘᎤᎢ [atsvyaɂi] pg 46)

Root: ᏆᎾᏛᏍᏔ [unasdetsi] pg 57)

Rope: ᏅᏕᎤᏔ [sdeyadi] pg 96)

Rose twisted stalk: ᏒᏛᏘᏓ [tsuhitsgwa] pg 108)

Rose-breasted grosbeak: ᏎᏫᏜᏟᎤᎲ [gaysgwalenv] pg 83)

Rough: ᏆᏝᏣᏛᏔ [udatsakdi] pg 61)

Rubber, pitch, gum: ᎠᏣᎠ [atsahi] pg 43)

Rubus spp: ᎾᏍᎵ [nugahli] pg 94), ᏋᏟᎵ ᎠᏎᏯ [saloli akta] (pg 95), ᎡᏟᎶᎵ [svdiwaɂli] (pg 97)

Rudbeckia hirta: ᏌᏫᎾ [sotsena] pg 97)

Ruffed grouse: ᏅᏗᏛᏔ [tvdisdi] pg 107)

Ruined: ᎠᎦᏚ [ayo³ga] pg 48)

Ruining it: ᎠᎦᏜᏛ [ayo³sdiha] pg 49)

Ruler: ᎠᏘᏎᏛᏔ [atsilosdi] pg 44), ᏆᎬᏬᎦᎠ [ugvwiyuhi] (pg 55)

Rumex crispus: ᏞᏍᏴ [dagki] pg 97)

Running: ᏞᏫᏘᎵᏛ [dasgwahldiha] pg 100)

Running over him: ᎠᎪᏛᏔᏛ [atsoɂvsdiha] pg 45)

Running short of: ᏆᎲᎡᏚ [uhnigvga] pg 58)

Rusting: ᎠᏎᏔᏅᎠᏚ [agatsinvgoga] pg 14)

Rusty: ᏆᏎᏔᏅᎠᎲᏅ [ugatsinvgotsidv] pg 54)

S

Saddle: ᏎᏰᎦᎬ [gayyhulo] pg 84)

Safety pin: ᏆᏅᏣᏔ [usgwahdi] pg 60)

Salamander: ᏞᎦᏇᏅᏴ [daleyvsgi] pg 98), ᏚᏫᏯ [duweka] (pg 106)

Salix alba: ᏗᏪᏎᎵᏅᏴ ᎡᏣ [dilagalisgi egwa] pg 105)

Salix babylonica: ᏗᏎᏎᎰᎤᎭᏞ [digaɂgalvnyhida] pg 104)

Salix discolor: ᏗᎵᏎᎵᏅᏴ [diligalisgi] pg 105)

Salix eastwoodiae: ᏗᏪᏎᎵᏅᏴ ᏆᏅᏔ [dilagalisgi usdi] pg 105)

Salmo salar: ᏕᏛh [semoni] pg 96)

Salmon: ᏕᏛh [semoni] pg 96)

Salt: ᎠᎹ [ama] pg 25)

Sambucus canadensis: ᎠᎡᏚ [gosvɂga] pg 88)

Same: ᏆᏛᏬ [usoyi] pg 61)

Sand: ᏃᏯ [noya] pg 94)

Sand piper: ᏓᎪᎥ [agowv] pg 18)

Sandy: ᏃᏯᎭ [noyaha] pg 94)

Sap: ᏛᏪᏯᎾᎡᎢ [atasgisgvɂi] pg 38)

Sassafras: ᎾᎾᏫᏞᏘ [kansdatsi] pg 84)

Sassafras albidum: ᎾᎾᏫᏞᏘ [kansdatsi] pg 84)

Satin: ᏆᏓᎹᏯᏫᏯ [utalugisgi] pg 62)

Saturday: ᏞᏞᏫᏍh [dodagwideni] pg 106)

Saucer: ᏛᏙᎠᎠᏫᏗ [ahdoɂolvsdohdi] pg 41)

Sausage: ᏓᎾᏫ ᏛᏫᏛᎵ [hawiya asdoda] pg 93)

Saw: ᏎᎤᏙᏴ [gahndogi] pg 80)

Sawbrier: ᎾᎾ [nugahlv] pg 95)

Saxifraga micranthidifolia: ᏓᎠᏫᏍᏴᏫᏔ [agosdugisdi] pg 18)

Saying it: ᏓᏔᏛ [adiɂa] pg 40), hᏎᏫᏛ [nigawęɂa] (pg 94)

Scab: ᏆᎵᏫᏞᏛᎢ [ulsdalvɂi] pg 55)

Scald place: ᏆᏟᏔᏫᎾᏟ [udanelawoda] pg 61)

Scalded: ᏆᏟᏔᏫᎾᏟ [udanelawoda] pg 61)

Scalding and scraping it: ᏎᏔᏫᎾᏛ [ganelawo³ɂa] pg 76)

Scalping him: ᏛᏫᏆᏚᏎᎵᏛ [asdvnegaliha] pg 33)

Scar: ᏆᏙᎾᎡ [unelvsv] pg 58)

Scarf: ᏞᎵᏫᏎᎠ [alsdulohi] pg 23)

Scarlet tanager: ᎧᏪ [tsohla] pg 108)

Scattering: ᏎᏪᎶᏏᏫᎥᏛᏚ [galage³hydvɂvsga] pg 69)

Scattering from a pile: ᏓᏛᏎᎾᏛ [adigaleyaɂa] pg 40)

Sceloporus undulatus: ᏪᏎᎤᎵ [tayuhali] pg 102)

Schoenoplectus tabernaemontani: ᏎᎾᏛᏔ ᏆᏪᎾ [ganagatsi utana] pg 73)

School: ᏗᏎᏟᏫᏔ [didelkwasdi] pg 105)

Scissors: ᏗᎵᏫᏗ [dihlsdohdi] pg 105)

Sciurus carolinensis: ᏋᏟᎵ [saloli] pg 95)

Sciurus niger: ᏋᏟᎵ ᏪᏔ [saloli wohdi] pg 95)

Sciurus spp: ᏋᏟᎵ [saloli] pg 95)

Scotch thistle: ᏘᏘ [tsitsi] pg 108)

Scotchmen: ᏓᏅᏍᏔ [anisgatsi] pg 26)

Scraping (grit corn): ᏛᏫᎾᎠᏫᏚ [asdvgoh³sga] pg 33)

Scratching: ᏞᎬᎠᏫᏚ [datsagosga] pg 101)

Screech owl: ᎶᏘᎢ [wahuhu] pg 109)

Seed: ᏆᏎᏪ [ukta] pg 54)

Seeing it: ᏓᎪᏔᏛ [ago³whtiha] pg 18)

137

Seine

Seine: ᎠᎦᏳᎳᏗ [ągahyųladi] pg 14)

Seiurus aurocapilla: ᏧᏦᎵᏛ [tsųtsoldv] pg 109)

Selecting: ᏓᏑᏯᎩᎠ [dasuyągį³ʔa] pg 100)

Seller: ᎦᎾᏚᏍᎩ [gąndųsgi] pg 74)

Selling it: ᎤᎾᏕᎦ [unde³ga] pg 57)

Seminole: ᎠᏂᏎᎻᏃᎵ [ąnisemįnoli] pg 26)

Seneca: ᎠᏂᏎᏂᎧ [ąnisenįka] pg 26)

Separating: ᏓᎦᎴᏂᎠ [dagąlenįʔa] pg 97)

September: ᏚᎵᎢᏍᏗ [dųlįʔisdi] pg 106)

Serviceberry: ᎤᏙᎳᏂ [ųdoląni] pg 62)

Sessile bellwort. Wild oats: ᏧᏍᎦ ᏓᎶᏗ [tsusgą dąlo³hdi] pg 109)

Setophaga fusca: ᎦᏅᎩ [gąnvgi] pg 79)

Setophaga pensylvanica: ᏚᏯ [duya] pg 106)

Setting a trap: ᎠᏌᏛᎥᏍᎦ [asądvʔvsga] pg 29)

Setting it (a solid) down: ᎠᎲᏍᎦ [ahvsga] pg 20)

Setting out: ᎦᎧᎲᏍᎦ [gąkąhvh³sga] pg 68)

Setting up: ᎦᎧᎲᏍᎦ [gąkąhvh³sga] pg 68)

Seven: ᎦᎵᏉᎩ [gahlgwogi] pg 70)

Seven doctorings: ᎦᎵᏉᎩ ᎢᏳᏬᎵᏰᏓ [gahlkwogį įyuwohlįyeda] pg 70)

Seven year locust: ᎥᎴ [vle] pg 68)

Sevenbark: ᎦᎵᏉᎩ ᏧᏯᏍᏚ [gahlkwogį tsuyasdu] pg 71)

Seventeen: ᎦᎵᏆᏚ [gahlgwądu] pg 70)

Seventy: ᎦᎵᏆᏍᎪᎯ [gahlkwasgohi] pg 70)

Several: ᎢᏳᏓᎴᎦ [iyudąle³ga] pg 53)

Several months ago: ᎢᏯᏅᏓ [iyąnvda] pg 52)

Sevierville, TN: ᏏᏈᏲ [sigwiyo] pg 96)

Sewing: ᎦᏰᏫᏍᎦ [gąye³wisga] pg 83)

Sewing machine: ᎦᏰᏫᏒᎥᏍᎩ [gayewhsvʔvsgi] pg 83)

Shade (in the): ᎤᏙᏗᏍᎬ [ųdodisgv] pg 63)

Shaking his head no: ᎠᎵᏍᏛᏂᎯ [alsdv³hnįha] pg 23)

Shaking his head yes: ᎠᎵᏍᎫᏩᏍᎦ [ąhlsgu³whsga] pg 22)

Shaking it: ᎠᏖᎸᎲᏍᎦ [ahte³lvhvsga] pg 40)

Shaking it off of a tree: ᎦᎳᏐᏰᎯ [gahlso³ʔyeha] pg 69)

Shampooing: ᎠᎵᏍᏚᎵᎯ [alsduliha] pg 23)

Share: ᎠᏯᏙᎸᎢ [ąyadohlvʔi] pg 48)

Sharp-shinned hawk: ᏗᎦᎦᏛᎾᎯᏛ [digagdvnąhidv] pg 104)

Shaving him: ᎠᏍᏙᏰᎯ [asdo³yeha] pg 32)

Shawnee: ᎠᏂᏌᏩᏄᎩ [ąnisawąnugi] pg 26)

Sheep: ᎤᏃᏕᎾ [ųnodena] pg 59)

Sheet: ᎠᎬᎯᏓ [ąkvhįda] pg 19)

Sheet sling used to carry a baby on one's back: ᎤᏛᏃ [udvno] pg 63)

Sheets: ᏧᏛᏃᎯᏛ [tsudvnohįdv] pg 109)

Shell: ᎤᏯᏍᎦ [uhyasga] pg 66)

Shelling (peas): ᎬᏙᎩᎠ [gvtokį³ʔa] pg 92)

Shelling corn: ᏓᎦᏔᎵᎯ [daktąlįha] pg 97)

Shepherd: ᏗᎦᏗ [dikti] pg 104)

Shin bone (his): ᎠᏍᎬᏓᎨᏂ [ąsgvdągeni] pg 30)

Shingle: ᏒᏓᎷᎩ [svdąlugi] pg 97)

Shining: ᎤᏔᎷᎩᎠ [uhtąlu³giʔa] pg 61)

Shining (the sun): ᎠᎦᎵᎯ [ągalį³ha] pg 13)

Shirt

Shirt: ᎠᏅᏬ [ahnvwo] pg 27)

Shoals: ᎤᏍᏓᎾᎵ [ųsdąnali] pg 60)

Shoe: ᎤᎳᏑᎶ [uhląsulo] pg 55)

Shooting: ᎠᏲᎯᎯ [ąyohįha] pg 49)

Shopping: ᎠᏓᎾᎾᎩᎠ [adanąnągį³ʔa] pg 36)

Short: ᏍᏆᎳᎯ [sgwaląhi] pg 96)

Short height: ᎡᎳᏗ ᎢᎦᏗ [eląd igądi] pg 51)

Shouting: ᎠᏙᎯᎠ [ątohį³ʔa] pg 41)

Shovel: ᎪᏕᏍᎩ [kodęsgi] pg 88), ᎪᏕᏍᎩ [kodesgi] (pg 88)

Show: ᏗᎾᏛᏁᎵᏍᎬᎢ [dinądvnelįsgvʔi] pg 105)

Showing him: ᎠᏎᎮᎯ [ąsę³heha] pg 33)

Shrew: ᏓᎳᏍᎨᏫ [dahlsgewi] pg 98)

Shucking corn: ᏕᎦᏄᎳᎦᏓ [degąnulągdʔa] pg 103)

Shutting it: ᎠᏍᏚᎲᏍᎦ [asduhvh³sga] pg 33)

Sialia sialis: ᏣᏉᎳᏕ [tsagwolde] pg 107)

Sibling-in-law: ᎤᏪᎳᎦᏏ [uwęlaksi] pg 65)

Sick: ᎤᏨᎦ [uhtsvga] pg 64), ᏍᏗᏯᎯ [sdiyąhi] (pg 96)

Sickness: ᎤᏨᎬ [utsvgv] pg 64)

Side of a mountain (on the): ᎣᏛᏬᎣᏗ [odv-hlọohdi] pg 53)

Side of his body: ᎠᏍᏆᎨᏂ [ąsgwągeni] pg 30)

Sifter: ᎬᎪᏍᏗ [gvgosdi] pg 91)

Sifting: ᎦᎪᏍᏗᎯ [gagosdiha] pg 68)

Sifting flour: ᎠᎪᏛᎥᏍᎦ [ąkodvʔvsga] pg 18)

Signing it: ᎠᏍᏓᏱᏗᎠ [asdąʔyi³dįʔa] pg 32)

Silly: ᎤᏬᏥᏗ [uwotsdi] pg 66)

Simulium meridionale: ᏙᏌ [dosa] pg 106)

Singing: ᏕᎧᏃᎩᎠ [dekąnogįʔa] pg 103)

Sink: ᎠᎹ ᎠᏥᏍᏗ [ąm ątsįsdi] pg 25)

Sinking: ᎦᏃᏴᎦ [gąnoyv³ga] pg 78)

Sister's brother (female ego): ᎤᏙ [udo] pg 62)

Sister's daughter: ᎤᏙ [uto] pg 62)

Sister's sister: ᎤᎸᎢ [ulvʔi] pg 56)

Sitta carolinensis: ᏗᏪᏓᎶᎯ [dįwedąlohi] pg 105)

Sitting: ᎤᏬᎳ [uwohla] pg 66)

Sitting on it: ᎠᏍᎩᎸᎥᏍᎦ [asgįlvʔvsga] pg 29)

Six: � [sudạli] (pg 97)

Sixteen: ᏛᏯᏎᏬ [dạladụhi] (pg 98)

Sixty: � [sudahlsgohi] (pg 97)

Skating: ᏛᎾᏒᏬᏖ [dahlịnạsvsdịha] (pg 98)

Skilled: ᎠᏍᎾᏖ [asi³nạha] (pg 34)

Skilled (becoming): ᎠᏍᎾᎤᏍ [asi³nạsanvga] (pg 34)

Skillet: ᏍᏛᎮᏗ [gạtesạdi] (pg 82)

Skin (his): ᎤᏁᎦᏟᏴᏔ [unegạʔlvʔi] (pg 57)

Skink: ᏣᏁᎥ [tsạnenv] (pg 107)

Skinned place: ᎤᏛᏁᎦᎸᏛ [ụdạnegạlvda] (pg 61)

Skinning it: ᏍᏆᎦᏟᏖ [gahe³gạlịha] (pg 69)

Skinny: ᎤᎴᏍᏛ [ụlẹsoda] (pg 55)

Skirt: ᎠᎭᏃ [ạsạno] (pg 28)

Skunk: ᏗᎵ [dili] (pg 105)

Sky: ᏎᎷᎣᏘ [gạlvloʔi] (pg 72)

SLAPPING IT

Slapping it: ᎠᎩᎸᎯᏖ [akwạlvʔnịha] (pg 27)

Sled: ᏗᏛᏇᏅᎩ [dịdansịnegi] (pg 105)

Sleepy: ᏎᎸᏍ [gahlvsga] (pg 73)

Sleeve: ᎠᏬᏍᏔ [gohyạdvʔi] (pg 89)

Slender rush: ᎦᏁᏍᏍ [kạnesga] (pg 85)

Slicky mushroom: ᎤᏏᏣᏫ [ụnịlogwe] (pg 58), ᏣᏂᏣᎩ [tsụnihlọgi] (pg 108), ᏣᏂᏣᏫ [tsunihlogwe] (pg 108)

Sliding: ᎠᎤᏟᎮᏍ [ạsu³yọhohsga] (pg 35)

Sliding it: ᏎᏎᏇᎮᎣᏬᏖ [degạsu³yọhọnhdịha] (pg 103)

Slipper orchids: ᎤᏗᏫ ᎤᏫᏇᏩ [ụgkwẹ ụlạsula] (pg 55)

Slipping up on: ᏍᏃᎵ [gạno³li] (pg 78)

Slow: ᎠᏍᏎᎾᏆ [asgạnola] (pg 29)

Small amount: ᏎᎯᎵ [gạyohli] (pg 84)

Small pox: ᎤᎤᏫᎠᎵ [ụnvtagwạli] (pg 59)

Small river: ᎲᎯᎥ [hụnihịv] (pg 93)

Smelling it: ᎤᏣᏣᎡᏍ [uwạwsv³ga] (pg 65)

Smelly: ᏎᎦᎥᏍ [gagwsvga] (pg 81)

Smilax glauca: ᎤᏎᎧ [nugahlv] (pg 95)

Smilax herbacea: ᏏᏎᏛᎩ [sigạdasgi] (pg 96)

Smilax rotundifolia: ᎠᏂᏣᏴᎿ ᎤᎤᎾᏁᎭᏛ [ạnisgịnạ ụnạnẹsada] (pg 26)

Smiling: ᎤᏯᎮᏍ [uye³tsga] (pg 67)

Smoking: ᎠᏯᏍ [gogh³sga] (pg 87)

Smooth alder: ᎠᏤᏛ [ahtsehd] (pg 44)

Smooth carrionflower: ᏏᏎᏛᎩ [sigạdasgi] (pg 96)

Smooth herbaceous greenbrier: ᏏᏎᏛᎩ [sigạdasgi] (pg 96)

Smooth shadbush: ᎤᏙᏩᎲ [ụdolạni] (pg 62)

Snake: ᎢᎾᏛ [inạda] (pg 52)

Snake, with deer horns (mythical): ᎤᏠᎦᎾ [ụktena] (pg 54)

Snakeroot: ᎠᏫᏐᏯᏅᏗ [kolạkạgisdi] (pg 88)

Snapping turtle: ᎤᏫᏗᎩ [sạli³gu³gi] (pg 95)

Sneaking up on: ᏍᏃᎵ [gạno³li] (pg 78)

Sneezing: ᏍᏇᏅᎥᏫᏐᏍ [du¹ysdo³yhsga] (pg 107)

Sniffling: ᎤᏃᏯᎷᎥᏍ [u¹yỵ³sgiludoga] (pg 68)

Snoring: ᏛᎢ� [dakwạlagi³ʔa] (pg 100)

Snow on the ground: ᎤᎤᎦ [untsi] (pg 59)

Snowbird: ᏑᏗ [tuti] (pg 106)

Snowbird Community: ᏑᏗᏯᏏ [tutiyi] (pg 106)

Snowing: ᏚᏗᏖ [gutịha] (pg 90)

Snuff: ᎧᏫ ᎤᎤᏐᏯᎵ [tsolạ ụwosgili] (pg 108)

So long for now (idiom): ᎭᏩᏬ [hạwagwo] (pg 92)

Soaking it: ᎬᎦᏫᏐᏍ [gvʔhwạlah³sga] (pg 92)

Soap: ᎣᏩ [ohla] (pg 53)

Sochana: ᏐᏤᎾ [sotsena] (pg 97)

Sock (his): ᎤᎵᏲᎯᏆ [uliyọhi] (pg 56)

Soft: ᏩᎾ [wana] (pg 109)

Soft corn (roasting stage): ᏣᏩᏂᎨᎢᏔ [tsụwạnigeʔi] (pg 109)

Softstem bulrush: ᏎᎾᎦᏥ ᎤᏔᎾ [gạnagạtsị ụtana] (pg 73)

Solanum lycopersicum: ᎤᏂᏁᎫᎮᏍᏗ [ụnineguhịsdi] (pg 58)

Solanum tuberosum: ᏄᎾ [nuna] (pg 95)

Soldier: ᎠᏯᏐᎩ [ạʔyọsgi] (pg 49)

Sole of his foot: ᎤᏍᏛᏁᎦᏟᏴᏔ [usdạnegạʔlvʔi] (pg 60)

SOLID

Solid (object): ᎠᏍᏛᏯᏏ [ạsdayi] (pg 31)

Solomon's seal: ᏔᏎᏅᏗ [ịgạnạsdi] (pg 52)

Some other time: ᎢᏳᏝ [iyugwo] (pg 53)

Somebody: ᎩᎶᎢ [kịloʔi] (pg 87)

Someone: ᎩᎶᎢ [kịloʔi] (pg 87)

Something: ᏎᎦᎤᏍᏗ [gạhụsdi] (pg 69)

Something or things way off in the distance: ᎲᎢᎢᏔᏛ [nigeʔiyvda] (pg 94)

Son-in-law: ᎤᎤᎦ [unutsi] (pg 59)

Song: ᎧᏃᎩᏍᏗ [kạnogisdi] (pg 85)

Song sparrow: ᎢᏏᏎ [tsigtsa] (pg 107)

Songbook: ᎠᏬᎵ ᏗᎧᏃᎩᏍᏗ [gohweli dịkạnogisdi] (pg 89)

Soot: ᎤᎧᎣᏅᏗ [ụtsonvhida] (pg 64)

Sore: ᎤᎵᏐᏛᏴᏔ [ulsdạlvʔi] (pg 55), ᎤᏛᏁᎦᎸᏛ [ụdạnegalvda] (pg 61)

Sorrel tree: ᎤᎥᏙᏫᏯ [nvdọkwehya] (pg 95)

Soul: ᎠᏍᎩᎾ [ạsgina] (pg 30)

Soup: ᎤᏎᎻ [ugama] (pg 53)

Sour: ᏣᏂᎧᏐᏗ [tsuhnịtsosdi] (pg 108)

Sourwood: ᎤᎥᏙᏫᏯ [nvdọkwehya] (pg 95)

South: ᏧᏌᏃᏬᎢ [tsuganowv?i] pg 108)

Spade: ᎠᏍᎪᏯ [kodesgi] pg 88), ᎠᏍᎪᏯ [kodesgi] (pg 88)

Spaniards: ᎠᏂᏍᏆᏂ [anisgwani] pg 26)

Spanking him: ᎠᏨᎵᎥᏂᏆ [agwalvni³ha] pg 27)

Sparrow: ᏥᏍᏆᏯ [tsisgwaya] pg 107)

Sparrow hawk: ᎩᎩ [gigi] pg 87)

Speaking: ᎦᏬᏂᎭ [gawoniha] pg 83), ᎧᏁᎦ [kane³ga] (pg 84)

Speaking to him: ᎠᎵᏃᎮᏗᎭ [ahlinohe³hdiha] pg 22)

Spear: ᏴᎩ [yvgi] pg 110)

SpearFinger (Mythological): ᏴᎩ ᎤᏩᏑᎧᎵ [yvgi uwasukahli] pg 110)

Speckled: ᎤᎿᏟᏌᏗ [uhnvtsadi] pg 59)

Speckled trout: ᎤᎿᏟᏌᏗ [uhnvtsati] pg 59)

Speech: ᎢᎩᏁᎢᏍᏗ [igvne?isdi] pg 52)

Speeding it up: ᎠᏣᏄᎵᏗᎠ [atsanu³ldi?a] pg 44)

Spelling: ᎠᏍᏇᎵᏰᎠᎠ [asgweli³ye?a] pg 31)

Sphyrapicus varius: ᏧᎵᎢᎾ [tsuli?ena] pg 108)

Spicebush: ᏃᎮᏥ [nohdatsi] pg 94)

Spicewood: ᏃᎮᏥ [nohdatsi] pg 94)

Spicket: ᎠᎻ ᎤᏩᏙᏉᎯᏍᏗ [am uwado?ohisdi] pg 25)

Spider: ᎦᎾᏁᏍᎩ [gananesgi] pg 74), ᎧᎾᏁᏍᎩ [kanahnesgi] (pg 84)

Spiderwort: ᏔᎦᏩᎵ [tagwali] pg 102)

Spilling a non-liquid: ᎤᏤᏫᎠᎠ [utsewi?a] pg 63)

Spilling it (a liquid): ᎠᏨᏍᎥᏍᎦ [atsv³?vsga] pg 45)

Spinus tristis: ᏩᏓᎬ [wadagv] pg 109)

Spiny amaranth: ᏙᎵᏗᏳᏍᏗ [tohldiyusdi] pg 106)

Spirit: ᎠᏍᎩᎾ [asgina] pg 30)

Spitting: ᎠᎵᏥᏍᏈᏍᎦ [altsiskwsga] pg 23)

Split lip: ᏧᏚᎶᏗ [tsudulodi] pg 109)

Sponge morel: ᎤᏂᏍᎥᏙᏂ [unisvdoni] pg 58)

Spoon: ᎠᏗᏙᎭᏗ [aditohdi] pg 41)

Spotted touch-me-not: ᏩᎴᎷ ᎤᏂᎦᎴᎩᏍᏗ [walelu unigalegisdi] pg 109)

Spotted wintergreen: ᎠᏨᏍᎨᎢ ᎢᎾᎨᎮᎯ [ahtsvgi inageehi] pg 45)

SPOUT

Spout: ᎠᎻ ᎤᏩᏙᏉᎯᏍᏗ [am uwado?ohisdi] pg 25)

Spraining his ankle: ᎠᏛᎳᎦᎠ [advlag?a] pg 43)

Spring (of water): ᎠᎻ ᎦᏄᎪᎥᎢ [am ganugogv?i] pg 25)

Spring onion: ᎤᏩᏍᏗ [uwasdi] pg 64)

Sprinkling: ᎠᎪᏛᎥᏍᎦ [akodv?vsga] pg 18), ᎠᏍᏚᏥᏙᎭ [asdutsidoha] (pg 33)

Sprouting (a plant): ᎠᎵᏰᎲᏍᎦ [aliyehvsga] pg 24)

Spruce: ᏃᏥ ᎢᏳᏍᏗ [notsi iyusdi] pg 94)

Squash: ᏩᎩᎦ [wagiga] pg 109)

Squirrel: ᏌᎶᎵ [saloli] pg 95)

Stabbing him: ᎦᏣᏲ?ᎯᎭ [gatsayo³hiha] pg 83)

Stacking: ᏓᏰᎭᎳᏍᎦ [daykahlasga] pg 102)

Stacking it: ᎦᏑᏘᏍᎦ [gasvtasga] pg 81)

Stag: ᎦᎳᎩᎾ [galagina] pg 69)

Standing: ᎦᏙᎦ [gadoga] pg 82)

Star: ᏃᏈᏏ [nokwisi] pg 94)

Starting it: ᎠᎴᏂᎠ [aleni?a] pg 21)

Startling him: ᎠᏖᏍᏗᎭ [atesdiha] pg 40)

Starvation: ᎠᎪᎾ [agona] pg 18)

Staying: ᎡᏙᎮᏍᏗᎪᎠ [edo?hesdigwoa] pg 52)

Stealing: ᎦᏃᏍᎩᎠ [ganosgi³?a] pg 78)

Stealing from him: ᎦᏅᏌᎲᏍᎦ [ganhsahvh³sga] pg 80)

Stem: ᎤᏪᏅᏍᏛᎢ [uwenvsdv?i] pg 65), ᎤᎯᏴᏘᏅᏔ [uhyvtinvta] (pg 68)

Stepping: ᎠᎳᏍᎬᎡᎠ [alasgv?a] pg 20)

Stepping on it: ᎠᎳᏍᏛᎢᏍᎦ [alasdy?vsga] pg 21)

Stick: ᎠᎭᏓ [ahda] pg 35)

Stick pin: ᎤᏍᏆᏗ [usgwahdi] pg 60)

Sticking it: ᎠᏣᏲᎵᎭ [atsayo³hliha] pg 44)

Sticking it to something: ᎠᏯᎸᎢᏍᎦ [ayalv?vsga] pg 47)

Sticking to it: ᎦᏯᎸᎾᎦ [gayalvnga] pg 83)

Sticky: ᏧᏤᏲᏍᏗ [tsutseyosdi] pg 109)

Stinging him: ᎦᏨᎲᏍᎦ [gatsvhyhsga] pg 83)

Stirring it: ᎠᏑᎨᎭ [asu³geha] pg 35)

Stitch: ᎦᏰᏈᏍᎬᎢᎢ [gayekwsgv?i] pg 83)

Stomach: ᏍᎦᏬᎵ [sgwohli] pg 96)

Stone Mountain, GA: ᏙᏓᎷ ᏅᏯ [tsodaly ny?ya] pg 108)

Stopper: ᏚᏬᎵ [duwohli] pg 106)

Store: ᎠᏓᎾᏅᎥᎢ [ada?nanv?i] pg 36)

Store at a distance: ᏗᏓᏅᎥᎢ [didanv?i] pg 105)

Storm crow: ᏓᎶᎬ [dalogv] pg 99)

Stove: ᎠᏓᏍᏓᎯᏗ [adasdahydi] pg 37)

Strainer: ᎦᏁᏐᎵᏍᏙᎢᏗ [ganesolysdo?di] pg 76)

Strawberry: ᎠᏂ [ani] pg 26)

Stream: ᎭᏂᎯᎥ [hunihiv] pg 93)

Strengthening it: ᎠᏍᏓᏴᏱᏗᎠ [asda?yi³di?a] pg 32)

Streptopus lanceolatus: ᏧᎯᏥᏩ [tsuhitsgwa] pg 108)

Stretch mouth snake: ᎡᎧᏂᏯ [gwandiya] pg 95)

Stretching: ᏓᏓᎾᎩᎠᎠ [dadanagi³?a] pg 101), ᎦᏕᎫᏌᏂᎠᎠ [degutsangi³?a] (pg 104)

Stringing beans: ᎦᏕᎦᏓᏃᎳᎩᎠ [dega³danolagi?a] pg 103)

Striped horse: ᏧᏂᎶᎯᏗ ᏐᎩᎵ [tsunilohdi sogwili] pg 108)

Striped skunk: ᏟᎵ [dili] pg 105)

Striped wintergreen.   Wintergreen: Dℂꭹꮍ TꙆꝆRꭰ [ahtsvgi iᶇageehi] pg 45)

Strix varia: ᎣJJ [uguku] pg 54)

Strong: ᎤᏢhᎩꝈ [uhliᶇigida] pg 55)

Student: ᏥᏍᎢꭰꮍᎩ [dideᶅogwasgi] pg 105)

Studying: DAꭆᏰD [agoli³yeꭉa] pg 17)

Stumbling: SVꝆꭰVꙚ [dudogehidoha] pg 106)

Sturnella magna: ZᏝᏏ [ᶇokwisi] pg 94)

Subtracting: DᎱᎩᏏVD [asagisidoa] pg 28)

Sucking something.   (Continously, like his thumb.): ꮭꭰꚌᏖꝆ�Ꚅ [dasgwanuꭉtsga] pg 100)

Suffering: DᎩꭆᏙᏚ [agihli³yoga] pg 17)

Sugar: ꭷꭆᏎꝊ [kahlsetsi] pg 84)

Sugar maple: ᏣꮿᎩ [tsuwagi] pg 109)

Sumac: ᎢᏀᏕ [gwaloga] pg 95)

Summer (1st new moon in April to the 1st new moon in October): AᎩ [gogi] pg 87)

Summer grapes: ᎢᎷᏏ [kwalu³si] pg 95)

Sun: TᏍ RVᎣꝈ [iga edonvda] pg 52)

Sun drop: DꙩꝈꝊ [andatsi] pg 25)

Sun perch: ᎣᎪᏋ [ugolv] pg 54)

Sunday: VꝈᎢꮍꭱT [dodagwasgvꭉi] pg 106)

Sunflower: ᎤꝈᏗꙩh [nvdadikani] pg 95)

Surrendering: DꝈꭿꮪᏚ [adahyosga] pg 38)

Surrounding it: DꮼᏚᏴꙩᏗꙚ [ayadehysdiha] pg 47)

Sus: Ꮟꭲ [sikwa] pg 96)

Swallowing it: DᎩꮪᏚ [akisga] pg 17)

Swamp lily: ꭴꭰᏤᏣᏗ [kahngutsati] pg 84)

Sweater: ᏍᎤꙣꭱ [gasaᶅena] pg 81)

Sweeping: EZᎱꮪᏚ [gynosasga] pg 91)

Sweet: ᎤᏏꭱꮼꝈ [uganasda] pg 53)

Sweet birch: Dℂꭹꮍ ᎤᏏꭱꮼꝈ [atsvgi uganasd] pg 45)

Sweet bugleweed: DhꭱhꮼᎩ [aniwoꭉnisgi] pg 26)

Sweet potato(es): ꭶꭱ ᎤhᏏꭱꮼꝈ [nuᶇa uniganasda] pg 95)

Sweet white violet: ᏧꭱꮰꭰꮼᎩ ᎤhᏗᏁ [dihndas-dasgi uniᶇega] pg 105)

Sweetflag: ᎤꭿꝈꭅ [uyodahli] pg 67)

Swelling: AᏣꮼᏚ [ktisga] pg 88)

Swift water: AꭆꙣꝈᏴT [goᶅisdayyꭉi] pg 88)

Swimming: DꝈꭱD [adawo³ꭉa] pg 38)

Swimming along: DᏀᏛTh [ahyuꭉini] pg 49)

Swinging it: DꭆᎢᏥhꙚ [altelv³hniha] pg 23)

Sycamore: ᏤᏃᏍꮼᏗ [kuhwiyugsdi] pg 90)

Sylva, NC: ᏏWᏇᏉ [silagwo] pg 96)

Sylvilagus floridanus: ꝆꮂᏚ [tsisdu] pg 107)

Table: ᏎꮼᎩᎱT [gasgilvꭉi] pg 81)

Taboo: ᏚᏚᏒᏢ [gaktvda] pg 68)

Tadpole: ᏒᎩꝍ [digitsi] pg 104)

Taking it (a liquid) from him: ᏚᏞᎩRꙚ [ganegi³ꭉeha] pg 75)

Taking it (a solid) from a liquid: JᎩD [gugiꭉa] pg 89)

Taking it (a solid) from him: DᎩRꙚ [agiꭉeha] pg 16)

Taking it (a solid) off of a fire: EꝈᎩD [gvdagiꭉa] pg 92)

Taking it (something alive) or it (a solid) or it (something flexible) down: ᏚꝈᎩD [gadagiꭉa] pg 81)

Taking it (something alive) to him: DꭰᏞꭆ [akaneli] pg 15)

Taking it (something flexible) from a fire: EᏢᎩD [kd-vgiꭉa] pg 92)

Taking it (something flexible) or it (a solid) to him: DᎣRꙚ [anvꭉeha] pg 27)

Taking it (something flexible) or it (something alive) from him: ᏚᎣᎩRꙚ [ganagiꭉeha] pg 74)

Taking it (something long) down: DVᏏᏏꙚ [atosisiha] pg 42)

Taking it (something long) from a liquid: DꝆꮥᏏꙚ [ahuyi³siha] pg 20)

Taking it (something long) from him: DᏴRꙚ [ayv³eha] pg 50)

Taking it (something long) off a fire: DꞝꝈᎩD [ahvdagi³ꭉa] pg 20)

Taking it (something long) or it (a liquid) to him: DᏴRꙚ [ayvꭉeha] pg 50)

Taking liquid from liquid: DJᎩD [akugiꭉa] pg 18)

Taking off a pair of pants: DᏉWᎩD [asulagiꭉa] pg 35)

Taking off a ring: DꭆᏰᏉꮼꝈᎩD [aliyesusdagi³ꭉa] pg 24)

Taking off a shirt: DꙩꭱᎩD [ahnawogiꭉa] pg 25)

Taking off a sock: ꝈꭆꮍᎩD [daliyagi³ꭉa] pg 99)

Taking off running: DꭆᏗᎩD [ahlidgiꭉa] pg 23)

Taking off shoes: ꝈWᏉWᎩD [dalasulagi³ꭉa] pg 98)

Taking revenge: ᎣᏉᏒ [utse³ga] pg 63)

Taking revenge on him: DᏉᏙꙚ [atse³cheha] pg 44)

Taking someone along: DᏣh [ahtihni] pg 41)

Talking: ᏎꮼhꙚ [gawoniha] pg 83)

Talking to him: ꝆᎷh [geluᶾhni] pg 86)

Tall: TᏍᏗ [igadi] pg 52), ThᏍᏗ [inigadi] (pg 52)

Tall and skinny: ᏎᏉVꭆ [galvdohli] pg 73)

Tall height: Th TᏍᏗ [in igadi] pg 52)

Tame: ᏎᎤ [gaꭉᶇasa] pg 74)

Tamias striatus: ᎩᏀᏍ [kiyuga] pg 87)

Tape recorder: ᏎꮼhR DᎩꮼᎩ [gawonisv agisgi] pg 83)

Teacher: ᏥᏏꭿꙠꮼᎩ [didehyohysgi] pg 105)

Teaching: ᏓᏕᏲᎲᏍᎦ [dadehyohvsga] pg 101)

Teaching (ehyohv): ᏕᎨᏲᎲᏍᎦ [dekẹyọhvsga] pg 104)

Teasing him: ᎠᎵᏌᎵᎭ [alsạliha] pg 22)

Telephone: ᏗᎵᏃᎮᏗ [dihlịnọhehdi] pg 105)

Telephoning: ᎧᎸᏛᏂᎠ [kạlvdvnịʔa] pg 84), ᏓᎵᏃᎮᎭ [dahlịnọheha] (pg 99)

Telephoning (idiom): ᎦᎸᏛᏂᎭ [gạlvdv³ʔniha] pg 73)

Television: ᎠᎾᏓᏴᏔᏍᎩ [ạndạyvtạsgi] pg 25)

Telling it: ᎧᏃᎮᎭ [kạnọheha] pg 85)

Ten: ᏍᎪᎯ [sgohi] pg 96)

Tennessee: ᏔᎾᏏ [tansi] pg 102)

Terrapene carolina: ᏓᎦᏏ [dagsi] pg 97)

Terrapin: ᏓᎦᏏ [dagsi] pg 97)

Testicle (his): ᎤᎪᏅ [ukohnv] pg 54)

Thamnophis spp: ᎣᏛᎳᏘᎢ [ọdvhlaʔtịʔi] pg 53)

Thanking him

Thanking him: ᎠᎵᎮᎵᏤᎭ [alihelicheha] pg 22)

Thanks: ᏍᎩ [sgi] pg 96), ᏩᏓ [wạda] (pg 109)

That: ᏍᎩ [sgi] pg 96)

That much: ᏍᎩᎦ [sgiga] pg 96)

That so?: ᏍᎩᏕᎦ [sgidẹga] pg 96)

That's the one: ᏍᎩᎾᏂ [sgịnahni] pg 96)

That?: ᏍᎩᏄᏍᏗ(Ꭲ) [sgịʔnụsd(ị)] pg 96)

Thawing it out: ᎦᏁᏍᏓᎳᎩᎠ [gạnesdạlgị³ʔa] pg 76)

There: ᎭᎾ [hạna] pg 92), ᎾᏊ [nagwo] (pg 93)

Thick: ᎤᎭᎨᏓ [ụhạgeda] pg 55)

Thicket: ᏌᎷᏱ [sạluyi] pg 95)

Thigh (his): ᎦᎦᎷᎢ [gạgaluʔi] pg 68)

Thinking: ᎠᏓᏅᏖᎭ [adahnteha] pg 37)

Thinking that: ᎡᎵᎠ [eliʔa] pg 51)

Thirsty: ᎤᏔᏕᎩᎠ [uhtạdegịʔa] pg 62)

Thirteen: ᏦᎦᏚᎯ [tsogạdụhi] pg 108)

Thirteen months (a traditional year): ᏦᎦᏚ ᎢᏯᏅᏓ [tsọgạdụ ịyạnvda] pg 108)

Thirty: ᏦᎣᏍᎪᎯ [tsoʔọsgohi] pg 108)

This: ᎯᎠ [hiʔa] pg 93)

This is: ᎯᎠᏃᏄᏍᏗ [hiʔahnoʔnụsdi] pg 93)

This much: ᎯᎦ [hiʔga] pg 93)

This one: ᎯᎠ [hiʔa] pg 93)

This way: ᎯᎢᏨ [hiʔitsv] pg 93)

Thorny locust: ᎧᎵᏎᏥ [kahlsetsi] pg 84)

Threading a needle: ᎦᏌᏁᏅᏴᎥᏍᎦ [gạsạne³ndyʔvsga] pg 81)

Three: ᏦᎢ [tsoʔi] pg 108)

Throat (his): ᎤᎩᎯᏍᏗᏳ [ukịhịsdiyu] pg 54)

Throwing it: ᎤᏕᎦ [udega] pg 62)

Thryothorus ludovicianus: ᎠᎵᏔᎹ [ạlịtạma] pg 23)

Thunder: ᎠᏴᏓᏆᎶᏍᎩ [ahyvdạgwạlọsgi] pg 50)

Thundering: ᎠᏴᏓᏆᎶᎠ [a¹yvdạgwạlo³ʔa] pg 50)

Thursday: ᏅᎩᏁ ᎢᎦ [nvgịnẹ iga] pg 95)

Tick: ᎫᎫ [gugu] pg 89)

Tickling him: ᏓᏴᎩᎠ [da¹yv³gịʔa] pg 102)

Tightening it: ᎦᏅᏐᎯᎭ [gạnvsọ³hịha] pg 80)

Timber rattlesnake: ᎤᏦᎾᏗ [utsonạdi] pg 64)

Timber rattlesnake, male: ᎠᏨᏯ ᎤᏦᏅᏗ [ạtsvyạ ụt-sonvdi] pg 46)

Time: ᎢᏳᏩᏂᎸᎯ [iyụwahnịlvhi] pg 53)

Tin: ᏔᎷᎩᏍᎩ [tạlugisgi] pg 102)

Tin can: ᏔᎷᎩᏍᎩ [tạlugisgi] pg 102)

Tired: ᎤᏯᏪᎦ [uyạwe³ga] pg 66)

To be able to: ᏰᎵᏉ [yeligwo] pg 110)

Toad: ᏩᎶᏏ [wạlosi] pg 109)

Tobacco: ᏦᎳ [tsola] pg 108)

Tobacco, plug of: ᏦᎳ ᎠᏍᏓᏯᏔᏅᎯ [tsolạ ạsdạyhtạnvhi] pg 108)

Tobacco, twist of: ᏦᎳ ᎦᏄᏕᏲᎸᎯ [tsolạ gạnudeyohlvhi] pg 108)

Toe: ᎦᎾᏌᏛᎢ [gạnạsạdvʔi] pg 74)

Toe nail (his): ᎤᏑᎧᎸᎢ [usụkahlvʔi] pg 61)

Toilet paper: ᎠᏑᎴᏙᏗ [ạsuhldohdi] pg 35)

Tomato(es): ᎤᏂᏁᎫᎯᏍᏗ [ụninegụhịsdi] pg 58)

Tomorrow

Tomorrow: ᏑᎾᎴᎢ [sunalẹʔi] pg 97)

Tomorrow night: ᏑᎾᎴ ᎤᏒᎯ [sunalẹ ụsvhi] pg 97)

Tongue (his): ᎦᏂᎪᎢ [gangoʔi] pg 77)

Tonight: ᎤᏒᎯ [usv³hi] pg 61), ᎯᎪ ᎤᏒᎯ [higọ ụsvhi] (pg 93)

Too hard: ᏍᏓᏱ [sdahyi] pg 96)

Tooth: ᎦᏅᏙᎧ [gạndọka] pg 80)

Toothache (his): ᎤᏳᏍᏆᏗᏍᎬᎢ [uyụsgwạdịsgvʔi] pg 67)

Touching it: ᎠᏒᏂᎭ [ạsv³hnịha] pg 35)

Towards: ᎢᏣ [itsa] pg 52)

Towhee: ᏧᏬᏍᎦ [tsụwosga] pg 109)

Town at a distance: ᏗᎦᏚᎲᏱ [dịgadụhvʔy] pg 104)

Toxicodendron radicans: ᎤᎸᏗ [ulvdi] pg 56)

Toxostoma rufum: ᏩᏚᏰᎳ [wạdụyela] pg 109)

Tracking him: ᎨᎷᏂ [gelụ³hni] pg 86)

Tradescantia virginiana: ᏔᏆᎵ [tagwali] pg 102)

Trading: ᎠᏓᏍᏕᏓᎵᏴᎡᎭ [adạsdedạlịyvʔeha] pg 37)

Translating it: ᎠᏁᏍᏗᎭ [ahnesdịha] pg 26)

Transparent: ᎤᎸᏌᏘ [ulvsạti] pg 56)

Trapping: DᎻᏬᎥᏬᎦ [asadvᴖvsga] pg 29)

Traveling: DᏍᏇᏭD [ahneladiᴖa] pg 26)

Treacleberry: ᏫᎷᏢᏬᏭ [udihlisdi] pg 62)

Treating him (specify: bad or good): ᎴᏫᏔᏒᏍ [nuhwanadega] pg 95)

Treatment (medical): ᏫᏞᎠᏫᏬᎫ [didahnywohdohdi] pg 105)

Trembling: ᏫᎾᎾD [unawiᴖa] pg 57)

Try: ᏍᏁᎮᏭᏤ [ganehldiha] pg 76)

Tsuga caroliniana: ᏃᏓ [nonu] pg 94)

Tuberculosis: ᏫᎬᏫᏬᎮᎫ [ukyhyohldi] pg 55)

Tuesday: ᏔᎮᏁ [taline] pg 102)

Tufted titmouse: ᏫᏧᎩ [utsugi] pg 64)

Tulip tree: ᏥᏳ [tsiyu] pg 108)

Tumbling it end over end: ᏍᏍᏁᏬᏔᏭᏭᏤ [deganeh³sgwatdiha] pg 103)

Turdus migratorius: ᏥᏍᏇᎾᎾ [tsisgwogwo] pg 107)

Turk's cap lily: ᏭᎾᎵᏯᎫ [kahngutsati] pg 84)

Turkey: ᎬᎾ [kvna] pg 91)

Turkey vulture: ᏤᎵ [suli] pg 97)

Turning: DᏍᏯᏬᏛD [aktahyᴖa] pg 14)

Turning it around: DAᏓD [ago³hlyᴖa] pg 18)

Turning loose: ᏫᏂᏬᏍ [uyosga] pg 67)

Turning off a light: ᎬᎮᏭD [gvda³ᴖldiᴖa] pg 92)

Turning on a light: DᏓᎤᏇᏬᏍ [atsvstasga] pg 46), ᏝᏔᎤᏇᏬᏍ [datsvstah³sga] (pg 102)

Turnip: ᏫᎻᎾ [dosana] pg 106)

Turtle dove: ᎫᎷᏬᎯᎾᎿ [gulehdisgohnihi] pg 89)

Tuscarora: DᏂᏬᏍᎶᎴ [anisgaloli] pg 26)

Twelve: ᏔᎾᏍᏗ [tahlduhi] pg 102)

Twenty: ᏔᎶᏬᎯᏗ [tahlsgohi] pg 102)

Twenty-one: ᏔᎶᏬᎯ ᏤᏬ [tahlsgo sogwu] pg 102)

Twins: ᏗᏂᎭᎾ [dinihlowi] pg 105)

Twirling it: ᏍᎫᏗᎦᏍᏭᏤ [gadigwalydehdiha] pg 82)

Twisting it: ᏍᏓᎦᎯᏤ [ganuteᴖyoha] pg 79)

Two: ᏔᎵ [tali] pg 102)

Two hundred

Two hundred: ᏔᎮᏥᎢ [talitsgwa] pg 102)

Tying: ᏞᎭᎯᏤ [dakanhiha] pg 98)

Tying up: DᏓᎢᏤ [ahlv³iha] pg 25)

Tyrannus tyrannus: ᏭᎧᎢ [dilegwa] pg 105)

U

Ugly: ᏫᎮ ᏭᎾᎫ [uyo dikahndi] pg 67)

Ulcer: ᏍᏬᏬᎬ [gawosgv] pg 83)

Ulmus spp: ᏧᏳᏫ [tsuᴖginv] pg 108)

Unable to do it: ᏫᏓᏓᏬᏬᏍ [unu³lvhvsga] pg 59)

Unable to find: ᏫᎩᏍ [utsoga] pg 64)

Uncle: ᏫᏍᏥ [udutsi] pg 63)

Uncovering it: ᏧᎻᏴD [gusagi³ᴖa] pg 90)

Under: ᎰᎯᏣ [howinitsa] pg 93)

Under the house: ᏍᎯᏣᏬ [gani³svyi] pg 77)

Understanding it: ᎪᎵᎾ [golka] pg 88)

Undressing: DᎾᏇᏴD [ahnawogiᴖa] pg 25)

Unplugging it: ᏧᏝᏴD [gudalagiᴖa] pg 90)

Unravelling it: ᎬᏴD [gygi³ᴖa] pg 90)

Unripe: DAᏬᎫ [agosdi] pg 18)

Until: ᎢAᏬᏅ [igohidv] pg 52)

Unwinding it: ᏍᎦᏬᏬᏴD [galvweyagi³ᴖa] pg 73)

Up the mountain: ᏍᏍᏗ [gadusi] pg 82)

Upper back (his): ᏍᏩᏛᎢ [gasohiᴖi] pg 81)

Upstairs: ᏍᎦᏉᎫ [galv³ladi] pg 72)

Upstream: ᎦᏴ [tsogi] pg 108)

Upward: ᏍᎦᏉᎫᎬ [galvladitsa] pg 72)

Urging him: ᏍᎯᎮᏍᏤ [gani³lᴖdeha] pg 77), ᏍᎤᎾᏬᏤ [gahnywsdiha] (pg 80)

Urinating: DᏭᎬD [adi³kyᴖa] pg 40)

Urocyon cinereoargenteus: ᏧᏩ ᎻᎠᎯᏣ [tsula sakonige] pg 108)

Ursus americanus: ᎥᎾ [yona] pg 110)

Using: ᎬᏬ [gvhdi] pg 92)

Using it: ᎬᏬᏤ [gvhdiha] pg 92)

Uttering it: ᎯᏍᏬD [nigaweᴖa] pg 94)

Uvularia sessilifolia: ᏧᏬᏍ ᏝᎶᎫ [tsusga dalo³hdi] pg 109)

V

Vagina (her): ᏫᎤᏬᏝᎢᎢ [ulesdahlvᴖi] pg 55)

Value: ᏧᎬᏬᏩᎫ [tsugvwahldi] pg 108)

Veins: ᏧᎬᏍᎯ [tsuwaduni] pg 109)

Velvet: ᎮᏁᎮᎦᏬᎫ DᎾᏇ [tvnegwiyusdi ahnawo] pg 107)

Vendor: ᏍᏫᏬᏴᎩ [gandusgi] pg 74)

Venison: DᏔᎾᏬ [ahawiya] pg 19)

Veratrum viride: DᏬᎬᎿᏞ [asgwyneda] pg 31)

Very: ᏫᎮᎬ [udohyu] pg 63)

Very good: ᏬᏔᎬ [osiyu] pg 53)

Vespula maculifrons: ᎬᏍᏬ [tsgayᴖi] pg 107)

Vial: ᏧᏧ [gugu] pg 89)

Vine, to be on: ᎦᏙ [huda] pg 93)

Viola blanda: ᏗᎲᏓᏍᏓᏍᎩ ᎤᏂᏁᎦ [dihndasdasgi ụnịnega] pg 105)

Viola sororia: ᏗᎲᏓᏍᏓᏍᎩ [dihndasdasgi] pg 105)

Violets: ᎠᏂᏓᏍᏓᏍᎩ [anạdasdasgi] pg 25)

Vireo: ᏧᏕᏏᏅᎵ [tsụdesynali] pg 109)

Vireo olivaceus: ᏧᏕᏏᏅᎵ [tsụdesynali] pg 109)

Virginia: ᏩᏥᏂ [watsini] pg 110)

Virginia spiderwort: ᏖᎦᏩᎵ [tagwali] pg 102)

Virginia Strawberry: ᎠᏂ [ani] pg 26)

Virginia water horehound: ᎠᏂᏬᏂᏍᎩ [ạniwọʔnịsgi] pg 26)

Virginians: ᎠᏂᏩᏥᏂ [ạniwatsini] pg 26)

Viscum album: ᎤᏔᎵ [ụdahli] pg 61)

Visiting: ᎠᎲᏩᏗᎰᎭ [ahwạtvhidọha] pg 46)

Vitis aestivalis: ᎩᏩᎷᏏ [kwạlụ³si] pg 95)

Vitis baileyana: ᎨᎳᏗ [kelạdi] pg 86)

Vitis labrusca: ᎤᏂᏖᎷᏩᎵᏗ [ụnịtẹlvlahdi] pg 58), ᏖᏩᎵᏗ [tẹlv³ladi] (pg 104)

Vitis rotundifolia: ᎩᏩᎷᏏ [kwạlụ³si] pg 95)

Vote: ᎠᏆᎵ ᏧᏍᏗ [gohweli tsusdi] pg 89)

Vulpes spp: ᏧᏩ [tsula] pg 108)

Vulpes vulpes: ᏧᏩ ᎩᎦᎨ [tsula gigage] pg 108)

W

Wading: ᎠᏍᎬᎯᏙᎭ [aduhinịdọha] pg 42)

Wait: Ꮟ [sịh] pg 96)

Wait a minute: ᏏᎸᎢ [sịlvʔi] pg 96)

Wait a while: ᏏᏎᎦ [sịsega] pg 96)

Waiting for him, it: ᎠᏍᏣᏫ [ạktiya] pg 14)

Waking up: ᎠᏲᎦ [aye³ga] pg 48)

Walking: ᎠᏱ [aʔi] pg 13)

Walking about: ᎡᏙᎭ [edoha] pg 52)

Walking cane: ᎠᏙᎳᏅᏍᏗ [ạdolạnysdi] pg 42)

Walking stick: ᎠᏙᎳᏅᏍᏗ [ạdolạnysdi] pg 42)

Walkway: ᎡᏓᏍᏗ [edạsdi] pg 51)

Wall: ᎦᏅᏢᎦᏟᎢ [gansugahlyʔi] pg 74)

Wall paper: ᎭᎩᎦᎸᏛᎢ [hạyagalvdvʔi] pg 93)

Walnut: ᏎᏗ [sedi] pg 96)

Wanting it: ᎤᏚᎵᎭ [udu³liha] pg 63)

War: ᎠᏓᎾᏬᎢ [ạdahnọwi] pg 36)

War dance: ᎠᏓᏅᏩ ᎤᎾᎶᏍᎩᏍᏗ [ạdanhywạ ụnahlsgisdi] pg 36)

Warts: ᏩᎶᏏ [wạlosi] pg 109)

Washing dishes: ᏕᎬᏗᏤᎠ [degvdi³yẹʔa] pg 104)

Washing hair: ᎠᎵᏍᏚᎵᎭ [alsdulịha] pg 23)

Washing hands: ᏓᏑᎴᎭ [dasu³leha] pg 100)

Washing his face: ᎠᎬᏍᎬᏬᎠ [agvsgwoʔa] pg 19)

Washing it (a solid): ᎫᎯᎶᎠ [gụ³hilọʔa] pg 89)

Washing it (something alive): ᎩᎩᎶᎠ [gygilọʔa] pg 90)

Washing it (something flexible): ᎩᎩᎶᎠ [kgilọʔa] pg 90)

Washing it (something long): ᎫᏗᎶᎠ [gụʔilọʔa] pg 89)

Washing machine: ᏗᎩᎪᏍᎩ [dịgkịʔosgi] pg 105)

Washington, DC: ᎦᎾᏍᏚᎩ [gansdugi] pg 74)

Wasp: ᎧᎾᏟᏍᏕᏥ [kantsịsdetsi] pg 84)

Watching for him, it: ᎠᏍᏣᏫ [ạktiya] pg 14)

Watching it: ᎠᎧᏎᏍᏗᎭ [akạ³sẹsdịha] pg 15)

Watching over him, it: ᎠᏍᏣᏫ [ạktiya] pg 14)

Water: ᎠᎹ [ạma] pg 25)

Water beetle: ᎪᏳᏂᏏ [doyụnisi] pg 106)

Water birch: ᎦᏁᏗᏍᎩ [ganedị³sgi] pg 76)

Water cress: ᎠᎼ ᎤᎵᏏ [ạmọ ụlisi] pg 25)

Water fall: ᎠᎹ ᎦᏙᎤᏍᎬᎢ [ạm gạdoọsgvʔi] pg 25)

Water faucet: ᎠᎹ ᎠᏍᏚᎩᏍᏗ [ạm ạsdụgisdi] pg 25)

Water moccasin: ᎧᏁᎩᏬᏓ [kạnegwoda] pg 84)

Water oak: ᎪᎳᏥ [dolạtsi] pg 106)

Water pipe: ᎠᎹ ᎤᏪᏓᏍᏗ [ạm ụwẹdạsdi] pg 25)

Water that is moving swiftly: ᎪᎵᏍᏓᏴᎢ [gọlịsdayvʔi] pg 88)

Waterdog: ᏧᏩ [chuwa] pg 109)

Watermelon: ᎩᎩᏍᏗ [gygisdi] pg 90)

Way (in the): ᎠᎬᏴᏗᏣ [ạgvyịditsa] pg 19)

Way off: ᏂᎨᎢ [nịgei] pg 94)

Waynesville, NC: ᏐᎩ [soʔgi] pg 96)

We: ᎠᏴ [ạyv] pg 50)

Weak: ᎠᏩᏂᎦᎳ [ạwanigạla] pg 46), ᎤᎵᏍᏗ [ulisdi] (pg 55)

Weasel: ᏓᎶᏂᎨ ᏨᏍᏕᏥ [dạlonịgẹ tsịsdetsi] pg 99)

WEAVING

Weaving: ᎬᏍᎦ [gvsga] pg 91)

Wedge: ᎦᎭᏗ [gạhadi] pg 68)

Wednesday: ᏦᎢᏁ ᎢᎦ [tsoʔịnẹ iga] pg 108)

Weeds: ᎦᏄᎸᎯ [gạnulyhi] pg 79)

Week: ᏏᎾᏙᏓᎬᏩᏍᏗ [sundodạgwạsdi] pg 97)

Weeping: ᎠᏣᏱᎭ [adsyọ³hyịha] pg 45), ᎠᏦᎲᎭ [atsohyịha] (pg 45)

Weeping willow: ᏗᎦᎠᎦᎸᏅᎯᏓ [dịgaʔạgalvnyhida] pg 104)

Welcoming: ᏓᏓᏂᎸᎦ [dadạnị³lvga] pg 101)

West: ᏭᏕᎵᎬᎢ [wudeligvʔi] pg 110)

Western Indians: ᏭᏕᎵᎬ ᎠᏁᎯ ᎠᏂᏴᏫᎠ [wudeligv ạnẹhi ạniyvwiya] pg 110)

What: ᎦᏙ [gạdo] pg 82), ᏙᎢᏳᎲᏍᏗ [doʔiyụhsdi] (pg 105)

What can it be: ᎪᏗ ᎢᏳᎲᏍᏗ [dodi iyụsdi] pg 106)

144

Wheat bread: OGd&J [utsąlesdi] pg 63)

When: ᏫᏍTB [hvgaʔiyv] pg 93)

Where: ᏚᏨ [gatsv] pg 83)

Where?: ᏅP [hạdlv] pg 92)

While ago: A.ᎠᏱ [gohi] pg 87)

Whirlpool: DᏨ DᏚᎢᏫT [ạm ạdehyọhvʔi] pg 25)

Whiskey: ᎾᎣY [hwisgi] pg 110)

Whistling: DᏳᎡᏆᏪᏍᏚ [ạwhsᏴhasga] pg 46)

White: OᎢᏁᏚ [unega] pg 57)

White pine: VᏢ [doʔtsi] pg 106)

White violet: ᏗᎾᏓᏆᏓᎣY OᎢᏂᏁᏚ [dihndasdasgi ụnịnega] pg 105)

White walnut: A.ᎠᏱ [kohi] pg 87)

White willow: ᏗWᏚᏢᎣY RᎢ [dịlagalisgi egwa] pg 105)

White-breasted nuthatch: ᏗᎣᏓᏳᎠᏱ [dịwedạlohi] pg 105)

White-tailed deer: DᎾ [ahwi] pg 46)

Who is it?: ᎣYGᎣᏚ [kagịyụsdi] pg 84)

Who?: ᎾA [kago] pg 84)

Whooping cough: OᏅᎣY [ụsȩsgi] pg 61)

Whooping crane: ᎾᎾᎣᏚᎾ [kạnsgawi] pg 84)

Why: Vh [doni] pg 106)

Wide: DᏪᏛᎾ [ạyate³na] pg 48)

Wife: ᎣᏝBᏫᎣY [sdayᏴhᏴsgi] pg 96)

Wife (his): OᎢᏝᏢT [udạliʔi] pg 61)

Wild: TᎾᎢT [inạgeʔi] pg 52)

Wild (not tame): ᏫᏪWᏆᏱ [geᏴạtạhi] pg 87)

Wild allspice: ZᏝᏢ [nohdạtsi] pg 94)

Wild cherry: TᎾᏢ RᏆᏱ WᏫ [inạge ȩhi taya] pg 52), WᏫ TᎾᎢT [tayạ inạgeʔi] (pg 102)

Wild comfrey: OᎢhᎣᏚᏅᏚᏆ [ụnịsdȩlesdi] pg 58)

Wild grapes: OᎢhᏛᏆWᏆ [ụnịtȩlvlahdi] pg 58), ᏛᏆWᏆ [teḻy³ladi] (pg 104)

Wild hydrangea: ᏚᏢᏴᏓY ᏗᏫᎣᏚ [gahlkwogi tsuyasdu] pg 71)

Wild mandrake: OᎢhᏪᏚᏚᏚ [ụnịsgweduga] pg 58)

Wild passion vine: OᎢᏳᏚ [uwạga] pg 64)

Wild potato clan: DhAᏝᏅᎾ [ạnigodạgewi] pg 26)

Wild turkey: EᎾ TᎾᏢRᏆᏱ [kvnạ inạgeȩhi] pg 91)

Wild turnip: VRᎾ TᎾᏢ RᏆᏱ [dosᏴnạ inạge ȩhi] pg 106), SᏫᎣᏚ [dụyạsdi] (pg 107)

Wind: OᎢZᏗᏱ [ụnolȩhi] pg 59)

Wind blowing: ᏚZᏆᎥᏓᏍᏚ [gạnolv³ʔvsga] pg 78)

Winding a clock: ᏚOᏅᏢᏅ [gạnᏴsoheha] pg 80)

WINDING IT UP

Winding it up: ᏚᏆᏫᏫᎣᏚᏅ [gạlvhwẹysdịha] pg 73)

Winding thread or yarn: ᏚᏆᏫD [gạlvweʔa] pg 73)

Window lock: AᎡᎾWᏗᏫᏗᏳ [gọsvhnạldịsdiyu] pg 88)

Window pane: DᏝᏫᏗ [ạdakehdi] pg 36), KWh [tsolạni] (pg 108)

Wing (his): DEZᏫh [ạkᏴnogeni] pg 19)

Winning: DᏳᎣᏚ [aʔhlosga] pg 24)

Winter: AW [gola] pg 88)

Wiping himself: DᏴᏗᏅ [ạsuleha] pg 35)

Wiregrass: ᎣᏗᏁᏚ [kạnesga] pg 85)

Wiring: DᏏWᏁᎥᏚᏚ [ạsịlạdvʔvsga] pg 34)

Wishi mushroom: ᎾᏏ [wisi] pg 110)

Wishing to accompany: DᏢAᏗᏅ [alikọneha] pg 21)

Wishing to say: OᏴᏛᏅ [uyeh³lvha] pg 66)

Witch: ᏢYᏢ [tsgili] pg 107)

Witch-hazel: ᏚᎣᏴᏬG [gạnsudᏴlo] pg 74)

Witching: DᏝᏁᎩYD [adahnẹsạgiʔa] pg 36), ᏝVhᏅ [dadoniha] (pg 101)

With: EᏆ [gvhdi] pg 92)

Wolf: ᏳᏫ [wahya] pg 110)

Wolf clan: DhᏳᏫ [ạnihwạya] pg 26)

Wolftown: ᏳᎢᏱ [wahyohi] pg 110)

Woman: DᏫᏫ [ạgehya] pg 16)

Woman, elderly: DᏚBᏢᏫT [ạgạyvligeʔi] pg 14)

Wood: DᏝ [ahda] pg 35)

Wood betony: OᎢᏣᏫᏬV [ụgukusdo] pg 54)

Wood thrush: ᎾᏫE [kạwogv] pg 86)

Wood-fern: ᏏᎾ OᎢVᏫᏝ [yonạ ụtsesda] pg 110)

Woodchuck: ᎣᏚOᎢ [oganv] pg 53)

Wool: OᎢᏳh [uwạni] pg 64)

Word: TEᏗTᏫᏆ [igᏴneʔịsdi] pg 52)

Working: ᏚᏆᏫᏝᏗᏅ [duhlᏴwisdạʔneha] pg 106)

World: RGᏱ [elọhi] pg 51)

Worm: ᏢAᎥ [dsgoyi] pg 107)

Worm-eating warbler: YGᏁ [kịyugv] pg 87)

Worrying: OᎢᏝOᎢᏛᏗᏅ [udanhte³hdịha] pg 61)

Worth: DEᏳᏳᏆ [ạgvhwạldi] pg 19), ᏗEᏳᏳᏆ [tsug-vwahldi] (pg 108)

Wrapping it: DᏝWᎡᏫᏍᏚ [adạ³hlsᏴhvsga] pg 36)

Wringing it: DᏨᎦᏫᏚᏗᏅ [ạtsᏴwasdịha] pg 46)

Wrinkling: ᏚᏗAGᏚ [gạnegọyuga] pg 75)

Wrist (his): OᏴᏛᏨᎭh [uyesụtsvni] pg 67)

Wristwatch: ᏳᏢ [watsi] pg 109)

Writer: ᏗAᏫᏢᎣY [digohwelisgi] pg 105)

Writing: AᏫᏢD [gohweliʔa] pg 89)

X

Xyris caroliniana: ᏝGhᏢ OᎢᎾᏚᏢᏢ [dạlonige ụnạsdetsi] pg 99)

145

Y

Yard: TGⱵGᏝ [iyutsiloda] pg 53)

Yard (measurement): ᏉⱵGᏝ [sutsiloda] pg 97)

Yardstick: DⱵGᏯᎫ [atsilosdi] pg 44)

Year: OˀᏕᎫᏰᏌᏒT [udehdiyvsadisvɂi] pg 62), ᏉᏕᎫᏰᏝ [sudetiyvda] (pg 97)

Year, traditional: KᏕS TᏯOˁᏝ [tsogadu iyanvda] pg 108)

Yelling: DVᎠD [atohi³ɂa] pg 41)

Yellow breasted mockingbird: ᏓᏓ [huhu] pg 93)

Yellow dock: ᏝᏕᎩ [dagki] pg 97)

Yellow fringed orchid: DGᎫ DhᏔW [atsadi anigwata] pg 44), OˀJJ OᏯAᏂ [uguku uskoli] (pg 54)

Yellow Hill Community: RWᏋᎫ [elawohdi] pg 51)

Yellow jacket: GᏕᏵᎥ [tsgayɂi] pg 107)

Yellow poplar: ⱵG [tsiyu] pg 108)

Yellow root: ᏝGhᏔ OˀᏋᏯᏕⱵ [dalonige unasdetsi] pg 99)

Yellow shafted flicker: OˀᎫᏕᏝ [unegada] pg 57)

Yellow widelip orchid: OˀᏟᏝᏂGᏯᎫ [uyodahliyusdi] pg 67)

Z

Zea Mays: ᏇM [selu] pg 96)

Zebra: ᏧhGᎫ ᏱᏉᏟ [tsunilohdi sogwili] pg 108)

Zenaida macroura: JᎬᎫᏯAhᎠ [gulehdisgohnihi] pg 89)

Yellow-bellied sapsucker: ᏚᏂRᏛ [tsuliɂena] pg 108)

Yellow-billed cuckoo: ᏝGE [dalogv] pg 99)

Yellow-breasted chat: ᏓᏓ [huhu] pg 93)

Yellowhammer: OˀᎫᏕᏝ [unegada] pg 57)

Yes: ii [vv] pg 68)

Yesterday: OˀRᎠ [usv³hi] pg 61)

You too: TᎠᏯᏉ [ihisgwo] pg 52)

Young animal from a litter: DᏝᎠ [adahi] pg 36)

Your family: ᏕGᏟᎫᏛT [detsahldihnaɂi] pg 104)

Yucca flaccida: ᏇMᏉᏗ [selugwoya] pg 96)

Yuchi: DhGⱵ [aniyutsi] pg 27)

Grammar

Please take note:

- The following is from the "*Brief Specimens of Cherokee Grammatical Forms*" as printed in the "*The Cherokee Messenger (ᏣᏩᎩ ᎠᏂᎲᎣᎲᎢ?)*" in the years 1844 to 1846.

- The original text used 'ds' for the soft 'ts' sound. These have been replaced with 'ts' to be consistent with the entirety of the dictionary. Additionally "qu" has been replaced with "kw" to be consistent with the usage of "gw" in the rest of the text.

- The following description of Cherokee grammar is for 1840's Cherokee and not today's Cherokee. While most differences between the two are minor, *there are differences*. The material is very useful when working with the Cherokee New Testament, the Cherokee translation of Genesis, the Cherokee translation of Pilgrim's Progress, and so forth.

- The English text is also from the 1840's and has not been "modernized". It is important to understand that "thee" and "thou" are used to indicate "you one" and that "ye" and "you" are used to indicate "you two or more".

- Some re-arrangement of text, tables, and minor changes of wording have happened to facilitate e-book creation.

Syllabary

Characters as arranged by the inventor.

Ꭱ Ꭰ Ꮃ Ꮵ Ꮐ Ꮽ Ꮺ Ꮅ Ꮑ Ꮌ Ꭹ Ᏹ Ꮟ Ꮲ Ꭳ Ꮇ Ꮄ Ꭽ Ꮼ
Ꮰ Ꮤ Ᏼ Ꮈ Ꭿ Ꮝ Ᏺ Ꮁ Ꭺ Ꮷ Ꮍ Ꮞ Ꮠ Ꮯ Ꮘ Ꮗ Ꮜ Ꮖ Ꮓ Ꮿ
Ꮸ Ꮢ Ꮒ Ꭶ Ꮩ Ꭸ Ꮣ Ꭼ Ꮻ Ꭲ Ꭴ Ᏸ Ꮂ Ꮫ Ꭻ Ꮶ Ꮙ Ꮔ Ꮎ Ꮆ
Ᏻ Ꮴ Ꮧ Ꮾ Ꮪ Ꮥ Ꮳ Ꭵ Ꮕ Ꮦ Ꮉ Ꮡ Ꮱ Ꭾ Ꮀ Ꮋ Ꮭ Ꮚ Ꮹ Ꮨ
Ꮮ Ꮏ Ꭷ Ꮬ Ꮊ Ꮛ.

Chacters systematicaly arranged with the sounds.

Ꭰ a	Ꭱ e	Ꭲ i	Ꭳ o	Ꭴ u	Ꭵ v
Ꭶ ga Ꭷ ka	Ꭸ ge	Ꭹ gi	Ꭺ go	Ꭻ gu	Ꭼ gv
Ꭽ ha	Ꭾ he	Ꭿ hi	Ꮀ ho	Ꮁ hu	Ꮂ hv
Ꮃ la	Ꮄ le	Ꮅ li	Ꮆ lo	Ꮇ lu	Ꮈ lv
Ꮉ ma	Ꮊ me	Ꮋ mi	Ꮌ mo	Ꮍ mu	
Ꮎ na Ꮏ hna Ꮐ nah	Ꮑ ne	Ꮒ ni	Ꮓ no	Ꮔ nu	Ꮕ nv
Ꮖ gwa	Ꮗ gwe	Ꮘ gwi	Ꮙ gwo	Ꮚ gwu	Ꮛ gwv
Ꮜ sa Ꮝ s	Ꮞ se	Ꮟ si	Ꮠ so	Ꮡ su	Ꮢ sv
Ꮣ da Ꮤ ta	Ꮥ de Ꮦ te	Ꮧ di Ꮨ ti	Ꮩ do	Ꮪ du	Ꮫ dv
Ꮬ dla Ꮭ tla	Ꮮ tle	Ꮯ tli	Ꮰ tlo	Ꮱ tlu	Ꮲ tlv
Ꮳ ja	Ꮴ je	Ꮵ ji	Ꮶ jo	Ꮷ ju	Ꮸ jv
Ꮹ wa	Ꮺ we	Ꮻ wi	Ꮼ wo	Ꮽ wu	Ꮾ wv
Ꮿ ya	Ᏸ ye	Ᏹ yi	Ᏺ yo	Ᏻ yu	Ᏼ yv

Sounds represented by vowels.

a as *a* in *father*, or short as *a* in *rival*,
e as *a* in *hate*, or short as *e* in *met*,
i as *i* in *pique*, or short as *i* in *pin*,
o as *o* in *note*, but approaching to *aw*, in *law*,
u as *oo* in *moon*, or short as *u* in *pull*,
v as *u* in *but*, nasalized.

Consonant Sounds.

g is sounded hard, approaching to k; sometimes before e, i, o, u and v its sound is k. d has a sound between the English d and t; sometimes before o, u, and v, its sound is t, when written before l and s the same analogy prevails.

All other letters as in English.

Syllables beginning with g, except ga, have sometimes the power of k; syllables written with hl, except tla, sometimes vary to dl; la, le, li, lo, lu, lv, are sometimes sounded hla, hle, hli, hlo, hlu, hlv.

Pronouns

The Cherokee language has but two separable personal pronouns, viz.: First person singular and plural, *A-yv* (ᎠᏴ), “I and we.” Second person singular and plural, *ni-hi* (ᏂᎯ), “thou and you.” The third person is indicated by *na* (Ꮎ) or *na-ski* (ᎾᏍᎩ), “that,” or *hi-ya* (ᎯᏯ) or *hi-a* (ᎯᎠ) “this,” or by a verb expressing some attribute or condition of the person spoken of, as:—

ᏥᎦᏙᎦ,	tsi-ga-do-ga,	*the one who is standing,*
ᏤᏙᎠ,	tse-do-a,	*the one who is moving about,*
ᏧᏬᏝ,	tsu-wo-hla,	*the one who is sitting down,*
ᏥᎦᏅᎦ,	tsi-ga-nv-ga,	*the one who is lying down,*
ᏨᏓᏯᎢ,	tsv-da-ya-i,	*the one who is coming,*
ᏥᏩᎢ,	tsi-wa-i,	*the one who is going,*
ᏥᏲᎱᏒ,	tsi-yo-hu-sv,	*the one who is dead,*
ᏤᎭ,	tse-ha,	*the one who is living,*
ᏧᏢᎦ,	tsu-tlv-ga,	*the one who is sick,*

The Cherokee language has a form of personal pronouns, which may be termed *reflexive*; in which all the distinctions of person are indicated. This form has the sense of myself, thyself, &c., as the following will exhibit.

Singular.

1st person	ᎠᏋᏒ	a-gwv-sv	*myself,*
2nd person	ᏨᏒ	tsv-sv	*thyself,*
3rd person	ᎤᏩᏒ	u-wa-sv	*himself,*

Dual.

1st and 2nd person	ᎩᏅᏒ	gi-nv-sv	*ourselves, (thyself and myself)*
1st and 3rd person	ᎣᎩᏅᏒ	o-gi-nv-sv	*ourselves, (himself and myself)*
2nd person	ᏍᏛᏒ	sdv-sv	*yourselves, (two)*

Plural.

1st and 2nd person	ᎢᎬᏒ	i-gv-sv	*ourselves, (yourselves and myself)*
1st and 3rd person	ᎣᎬᏒ	o-gv-sv	*ourselves, (themselves and myself)*
2nd person	ᎢᏨᏒ	i-tsv-sv	*yourselves, (three or more)*
3rd person	ᎤᏅᏒ	u-nv-sv	*themselves*

The following table exhibits the possessive pronouns; the object possessed being singular.

Singular.

1st person	ᎠᏆᏤᎵ	a-kwa-tse-li	*mine,*
2nd person	ᏣᏤᎵ	tsa-tse-li	*thine,*
3rd person	ᎤᏤᎵ	u-tse-li	*his,*

Dual.

1st and 2nd person	ᎩᎾᏤᎵ	gi-na-tse-li	*ours, (mine and thine)*
1st and 3rd person	ᎣᎩᎾᏤᎵ	o-gi-na-tse-li	*ours, (his and mine)*
2nd person	ᏍᏓᏤᎵ	sda-tse-li	*yours, (two)*

Plural.

1st and 2nd person	ᎢᎦᏤᎵ	i-ga-tse-li	*ours, (yours and mine)*
1st and 3rd person	ᎣᎦᏤᎵ	o-ga-tse-li	*ours, (theirs and mine)*
2nd person	ᎢᏣᏤᎵ	i-tsa-tse-li	*yours, (three or more)*
3rd person	ᎤᎾᏤᎵ	u-na-tse-li	*theirs.*

Two degrees of intensity are denoted by adding *ga* (Ꭶ) and *gaya* (ᎦᏯ), as *akwatseliga* (ᎠᏆᏤᎵᎦ), “mine” (positively); *akwatseligaya* (ᎠᏆᏤᎵᎦᏯ), “mine” (really): i.e. “I alone am the real owner.”

When the posession of more than one object is to be denoted, the prefixes are varied thus:—

Singular.

1st person	ᴫᴝ	di-gwa	ᴫᴝᏤᏞ	di-gwa-tse-li	*mine,*
2nd person	ᴫᏛ	di-tsa	ᴫᏛᏤᏞ	di-tsa-tse-li	*thine,*
3rd person	ᴣ	tsu	ᴣᏤᏞ	tsu-tse-li	*his,*

Dual.

1st and 2nd	ᴫᎩᎾ	di-gi-na	ᴫᎩᎾᏤᏞ	di-gi-na-tse-li	*ours, (mine and thine)*
1st and 3rd	ᏦᎩᎾ	tso-gi-na	ᏦᎩᎾᏤᏞ	tso-gi-na-tse-li	*ours, (his and mine)*
2nd person	ᴫᏍᏓ	di-sda	ᴫᏍᏓᏤᏞ	di-sda-tse-li	*yours, (two)*

Plural.

1st and 2nd	ᴫᏍ	di-ga	ᴫᏍᏤᏞ	di-ga-tse-li	*ours, (yours and mine)*
1st and 3rd	ᏦᏍ	tso-ga	ᏦᏍᏤᏞ	tso-ga-tse-li	*ours, (theirs and mine)*
2nd person	ᴫᏛ	di-tsa	ᴫᏛᏤᏞ	di-tsa-tse-li	*yours, (three or more)*
3rd person	ᴣᎾ	tsu-na	ᴣᎾᏤᏞ	tsu-na-tse-li	*theirs.*

In the congugation of verbs the person is indicated by inseparable prefixes, as:—

Singular.

1st person	Ᏽ	tsi	ᏽᏁᏍ	tsi-ne-ga	*I speak,*
2nd person	Ᏺ	hi	ᏺᏁᏍ	hi-ne-ga	*thou speakest,*
3rd person	Ꮖ	ka	ᏩᏁᏍ	ka-ne-ga	*he speaks,*

Dual.

1st and 2nd	ᎿᏂ	i-ni	ᏍᏂᏁᏍ	i-ni-ne-ga	*we (thou and I) speak,*
1st and 3rd	ᎣᏍᏛ	o-sdi	ᎣᏍᏛᏁᏍ	o-sdi-ne-ga	*we (he and I) speak,*
2nd person	ᏍᏛ	sdi	ᏍᏛᏁᏍ	sdi-ne-ga	*you (two) speak,*

Plural.

1st and 2nd	ᎢᏛ	i-di	ᎢᏛᏁᏍ	i-di-ne-ga	*we (you and I) speak,*
1st and 3rd	ᎣᏥ	o-tsi	ᎣᏥᏁᏍ	o-tsi-ne-ga	*we (they and I) speak,*
2nd person	ᎢᏥ	i-tsi	ᎢᏥᏁᏍ	i-tsi-ne-ga	*you (three or more) speak,*
3rd person	ᎠᏂ	a-ni	ᎠᏂᏁᏍ	a-ni-ne-ga	*they speak.*

In some tenses the personal prefixes take the following form, as:—

Singular.

1st person	Ᏽ	tsi	ᏽᏁᏍ	tsi-ne-ga	*I speak,*
2nd person	Ᏺ	hi	ᏺᏁᏍ	hi-ne-ga	*thou speakest,*
3rd person	Ꮖ	ka	ᏩᏁᏍ	ka-ne-ga	*he speaks,*

Dual.

1st and 2nd	ᎿᏂ	i-ni	ᏍᏂᏁᏍ	i-ni-ne-ga	*we (thou and I) speak,*
1st and 3rd	ᎣᏍᏛ	o-sdi	ᎣᏍᏛᏁᏍ	o-sdi-ne-ga	*we (he and I) speak,*
2nd person	ᏍᏛ	sdi	ᏍᏛᏁᏍ	sdi-ne-ga	*you (two) speak,*

Plural.

1st and 2nd	ᎢᏛ	i-di	ᎢᏛᏁᏍ	i-di-ne-ga	*we (you and I) speak,*
1st and 3rd	ᎣᏥ	o-tsi	ᎣᏥᏁᏍ	o-tsi-ne-ga	*we (they and I) speak,*
2nd person	ᎢᏥ	i-tsi	ᎢᏥᏁᏍ	i-tsi-ne-ga	*you (three or more) speak,*
3rd person	ᎠᏂ	a-ni	ᎠᏂᏁᏍ	a-ni-ne-ga	*they speak.*

In some tenses the personal prefixes take the following, as:—

Singular.

1st person	DY	a-gi	DYЛᏟ	a-gi-ne-tsv	*I have spoken,*
2nd person	G	tsa	GЛᏟ	tsa-ne-tsv	*thou hast spoken,*
3rd person	Oᴵ	u	OᴵЛᏟ	u-ne-tsv	*he hast spoken,*

Dual.

1st and 2nd	Уh	gi-ni	УhЛᏟ	gi-ni-ne-tsv	*we (thou and I) have spoken,*
1st and 3rd	ᎣУh	o-gi-ni	ᎣУhЛᏟ	o-gi-ni-ne-tsv	*we (he and I) have spoken,*
2nd person	ᎣᎫ	sdi	ᎣᎫЛᏟ	sdi-ne-tsv	*you (two) have spoken,*

Plural.

1st and 2nd	ТУ	i-gi	ТУЛᏟ	i-gi-ne-tsv	*we (you and I) have spoken,*
1st and 3rd	ᎣУ	o-gi	ᎣУЛᏟ	o-gi-ne-tsv	*we (they and I) have spoken,*
2nd person	Тⱶ	i-tsi	ТⱶЛᏟ	i-tsi-ne-tsv	*you (three or more) have spoken,*
3rd person	Oᴵh	u-ni	OᴵhЛᏟ	u-ni-ne-tsv	*they have spoken.*

OVERVIEW OF VERBS

The simplest form in which we find being and tense, indicated in Cherokee, is in the Impersonal Substantive Verb *ge-sv-i* (ⱶRT), "being," and *i-gi* (ТУ), "is."

INDICATIVE MOOD

Verbal noun,	ⱶRT	ge-sv-i	*being*
Conditional or habitual,	ⱶᚺT	ge-so-i	*is, (usually, habitually, or on certain occasions,)*
Imperfect - conscious,	ⱶRУ	ge-sv-gi	*was, (with personal knowlege, or consciousness,)*
Imperfect - unconscious,	Ⱶ4T	ge-se-i	*was, (without personal knowlege, or consciousness,)*
Future tense,	Ⱶ4ᎣᎫ	ge-se-sdi	*will be.*

The distinctions indicated by the inflections of this verb, are combined with several of the simple tenses of regular verbs, forming compounds by which many very minute divisions of time, are marked with great precision.

The *ge-so-i* (ⱶᚺT) inflection modifies the principal tense, so, as to indicate the usual, customary or habitual prevalence of what is affirmed, in quantity, quality or frequency: or under certain circumstances or conditions.

> NOTE: The terms which, in this material, are given to the conjugations, moods, tenses, and other distinctions, indicated by the inflections of the Cherokee verb, are only used provisionally; such terms vary widely in other materials.

CONJUGATIONS

The regular Cherokee verb has nine conjugations, viz:

Radical	ⱶЛᏚ	tsi-ne-ga	*I speak, or I am speaking.*
Instrumental	ⱶЛТᎣᎫⱱ	tsi-ne-i-sdi-ha	*I speak with it, &c.*
Dative	ⱶЛVⱱ	tsi-ne-tse-ha	*I speak to or for him, &c.*
Departing	ⱶЛVᏚ	tsi-ne-tse-ga	*I go (to some place) to speak,*
Approaching	ⱶЛⱶᎠⱱ	tsi-ne-tsi-hi-ha	*I come (to some place) to speak,*
Ambulant	ⱶЛⱶVⱱ	tsi-ne-tsi-do-ha	*I speak about in various places,*
Frequentative	ⱶЛⱶGⱱ	tsi-ne-tsi-lo-ha	*I speak repeatedly,*
Perfective or Intensive	ⱶЛⱶbⱱ	tsi-ne-tsi-si-ha	*I speak confirming, or adding force to what has been spoken,*
Completive or Finishing	ⱶЛKᎣᎥᏚ	tsi-ne-tso-hv-sga	*I speak all, or finish speaking.*

152

THE RADICAL CONJUGATION

INDICATIVE MOOD

Present Tense and its Modifications.

ᎧᏁᎦ	ka-ne-ga	*he is speaking,*
ᎧᏁᎪᎢ	ka-ne-go-i	*he is peaking habitually, or on certain occasions,*
ᎧᏁᎬᏗ	ka-ne-gv-gi	*he was speaking with my personal knowledge,*
ᎧᏁᎨᎢ	ka-ne-ge-i	*he was speaking without my personal knowledge,*
ᎧᏁᎨᏍᏗ	ka-ne-ge-sdi	*he will be speaking,*
ᎧᏁᎬᎢ	ka-ne-gv-i	*his speaking, or his word.*

Of these forms, *ka-ne-gv-gi* (ᎧᏁᎬᏗ), indicates the presence or personal knowledge of the person who relates the fact: *ka-ne-ge-i* (ᎧᏁᎨᎢ), the absence of personal knowledge.

The Present Tense, showing the distinctions of person, and the modifications of tense.

Distinctions of Person:

Singular.

1st person	ᏥᏁ-	tsi-ne-
2nd person	ᎯᏁ-	hi-ne-
3rd person	ᎧᏁ-	ka-ne-

Dual.

1st and 2nd	ᎢᏂᏁ-	i-ni-ne-
1st and 3rd	ᎣᏍᏗᏁ-	o-sdi-ne-
2nd person	ᏍᏗᏁ-	sdi-ne-

Plural.

1st and 2nd	ᎢᏗᏁ-	i-di-ne-
1st and 3rd	ᎣᏥᏁ-	o-tsi-ne-
2nd person	ᎢᏥᏁ-	i-tsi-ne-
3rd person	ᎠᏂᏁ-	a-ni-ne-

Modifications of Tense:

-Ꮝ	-ga	*I am, thou art, &c. speaking.*
-ᎪᎢ	-go-i	*I am, &c. speaking habitually or on certain occasions.*
-ᎬᏗ	-gv-gi	*I &c. was speaking, with my personal knowledge.*
-ᎨᎢ	-ge-i	*I &c. was speaking, without my personal knowledge.*
-ᎨᏍᏗ	-ge-sdi	*I &c. will be speaking.*
-ᎬᎢ	-gv-i	*My, thy, his, &c. speaking, or word.*

By connecting each of these terminations with each of the persons of the verb, all the modications of this tense will be expressed in each person, thus, *tsi-ne-ga* (ᏥᏁᎦ), "I am speaking," *hi-ne-ga* (ᎯᏁᎦ), "thou art speaking," &c.

If the English affixed to each modification of this tense, varied to suit the person, be affixed to the verb, with the corresponding termination as in the tables, all the variations of person and tense will be expressed. This remark is applicable to the other tenses which admit of similar variations.

The Immediate Past Tense.

Singular.

1st person	ᎥᏥᏁᎩ	v-tsi-ne-gi	*I have just spoken,*
2nd person	ᎥᎯᏁᎩ	v-hi-ne-gi	*thou hast just spoken,*
3rd person	ᎥᎧᏁᎩ	v-ka-ne-gi	*he hast just spoken,*

Dual.

1st and 2nd	iᏂᏁᎩ	v-ni-ne-gi	*we (thou and I) have just spoken,*
1st and 3rd	ᎣᏍᏗᏁᎩ	o-sdi-ne-gi	*we (he and I) have just spoken,*
2nd person	iᏍᏗᏁᎩ	v-sdi-ne-gi	*you (two) have just spoken,*

Plural.

1st and 2nd	iᏗᏁᎩ	v-di-ne-gi	*we (you and I) have just spoken,*
1st and 3rd	ᎣᏥᏁᎩ	o-tsi-ne-gi	*we (they and I) have just spoken,*
2nd person	iᏥᏁᎩ	v-tsi-ne-gi	*you (three or more) have just spoken,*
3rd person	iᎠᏂᏁᎩ	v-an-ni-ne-gi	*they have just spoken.*

The Immediate Past Tense does not admit of being modified like the present, perfect and future tenses.

Modifications of the Perfect Tense.

Simple Perfect	ᎤᏁᏨ	u-ne-tsv	*he has spoken.*
Conditional Perfect	ᎤᏁᏦᎢ	u-ne-tso-i	*he has spoken, (whenever certain circumstances have taken place.)*
Imperfect of the Perfect	ᎤᏁᏨᎩ	u-ne-tsv-gi	*he spoke, with my personal knowledge.*
Imperfect of the Perfect	ᎤᏁᏤᎢ	u-ne-tse-i	*he spoke, without my personal knowledge.*
Future of the Perfect	ᎤᏁᏤᏍᏗ	u-ne-tse-sdi	*he will have spoken.*
Verbal Noun	ᎤᏁᏨᎢ	u-ne-tsv-i	*his having spoken, or his word (already spoken.)*

The Perfect Tense, exhibiting the distinctions of person and modifications of tense.

Distinctions of Person:

Singular.

1st person	ᎠᎩᏁ-	a-gi-ne-
2nd person	ᏣᏁ-	tsa-ne-
3rd person	ᎤᏁ-	u-ne-

Dual.

1st and 2nd	ᎩᏂᏁ-	gi-ni-ne-
1st and 3rd	ᎣᎩᏂᏁ-	o-gi-ni-ne-
2nd person	ᏍᏗᏁ-	sdi-ne-

Plural.

1st and 2nd	ᎢᎩᏁ-	i-gi-ne-
1st and 3rd	ᎣᎩᏁ-	o-gi-ne-
2nd person	ᎢᏥᏁ-	i-tsi-ne-
3rd person	ᎤᏂᏁ-	u-ni-ne-

Modifications of Tense:

-Ꮸ	-tsv	The Perfect Tense.
-ᏦᎢ	-tso-i	The Conditional Perfect.
-ᏨᎩ	-tsv-gi	Imperfect of the Perfect. *(With my personal knowledge.)*
-ᏤᎢ	-tse-i	Imperfect of the Perfect. *(Without my personal knowledge.)*
-ᏤᏍᏗ	-tse-sdi	Future Perfect.
-ᏨᎢ	-tsv-i	Verbal Noun.

If each of these terminations be connected with each person of the verb, as in the present tense, all the modifications of the tense will be expressed, in each person.

Future Tense, shewing the distinctions of person.

Singular.

1st person	ᏓᏥᏁᏥ	da-tsi-ne-tsi	*I will speak,*
2nd person	ᏘᏁᏥ	ti-ne-tsi	*thou wilt speak,*
3rd person	ᏓᎧᏁᏥ	da-ka-ne-tsi	*he will speak,*

Dual.

1st and 2nd	ᏓᏂᏁᏥ	da-ni-ne-tsi	*we (thou and I) will speak,*
1st and 3rd	ᏓᏲᏍᏗᏁᏥ	da-yo-sdi-ne-tsi	*we (he and I) will speak,*
2nd person	ᏓᏍᏗᏁᏥ	da-sdi-ne-tsi	*you (two) will speak,*

Plural.

1st and 2nd	ᏓᏗᏁᏥ	da-di-ne-tsi	*we (you and I) will speak,*
1st and 3rd	ᏓᏲᏥᏁ	da-yo-tsi-ne	*we (they and I) will speak,*
2nd person	ᏓᏥᏁᏥ	da-tsi-ne-tsi	*you (three or more) will speak,*
3rd person	ᎣᏂᏁᏥ	da-ni-ne-tsi	*they will speak.*

Imperfect of the Future Tense

(with my personal knowledge)

Singular.

1st person	ᏓᏥᏁᏥᏒᎩ	da-tsi-ne-tsi-sv-gi	*I did will or intend to speak.*
2nd person	ᏘᏁᏥᏒᎩ	ti-ne-tsi-sv-gi	*thou didst will or intend to speak.*
3rd person	ᏓᎧᏁᏥᏒᎩ	da-ka-ne-tsi-sv-gi	*he did will or intend to speak.*

Dual.

1st and 2nd	ᏓᏂᏁᏥᏒᎩ	da-ni-ne-tsi-sv-gi	*we (thou and I) did will or intend to speak.*
1st and 3rd	ᏓᏲᏍᏗᏁᏥᏒᎩ	da-yo-sdi-ne-tsi-sv-gi	*we (he and I) did will or intend to speak.*
2nd person	ᏓᏍᏗᏁᏥᏒᎩ	da-sdi-ne-tsi-sv-gi	*you (two) did will or intend to speak.*

Plural.

1st and 2nd	ᏓᏗᏁᏥᏒᎩ	da-di-ne-tsi-sv-gi	*we (you and I) did will or intend to speak.*
1st and 3rd	ᏓᏲᏥᏁᏥᏒᎩ	da-yo-tsi-ne-tsi-sv-gi	*we (they and I) did will or intend to speak.*
2nd person	ᏓᏥᏁᏥᏒᎩ	da-tsi-ne-tsi-sv-gi	*you (three or more) did will or intend to speak.*
3rd person	ᏓᏂᏁᏥᏒᎩ	da-ni-ne-tsi-sv-gi	*they did will or intend to speak.*

Distinctions of Person:

Singular.

1st person	ᏗᏥᏁᏥ-	di-tsi-ne-tsi
2nd person	ᏗᏁᏥ-	ti-ne-tsi
3rd person	ᏗᎧᏁᏥ-	di-ka-ne-tsi

Dual.

1st and 2nd	ᏗᏂᏁᏥ-	di-ni-ne-tsi
1st and 3rd	ᏗᏲᏍᏗᏁᏥ-	di-yo-sdi-ne-tsi
2nd person	ᏗᏍᏗᏁᏥ-	di-sdi-ne-tsi

Plural.

1st and 2nd	ᏗᏗᏁᏥ-	di-di-ne-tsi
1st and 3rd	ᏗᏲᏥᏁᏥ-	di-yo-tsi-ne-tsi
2nd person	ᏗᏥᏁᏥ-	di-tsi-ne-tsi
3rd person	ᏗᏂᏁᏥ-	di-ni-ne-tsi

Modifications of Tense:

-ᏐᎢ	-so-i	Conditional Future. *(shall will, or intend to, whenever certain things occur.)*
-ᏎᎢ	-se-i	Imperfect of the Future. *(did will, or intend to)*
-ᏎᏍᏗ	-se-sdi	Double Future *(shall at some future time be willing or intend to)*
-ᏒᎢ	-sv-i	Verbal Noun *(willing to speak)*

The terminations *gv-gi* (ᎬᎩ), *tsv-gi* (ᏨᎩ), *sv-gi* (ᏒᎩ), in addition to marking the tense, indicate personal knowledge of the speaker. And the terminations *ge-i* (ᎨᎢ), *tse-i* (ᏤᎢ), *se-i* (ᏎᎢ), denote the absence of personal knowledge.

Immediate Future Tense.

Singular.

1st person	ᎠᎩᏁᏥᏗ	a-ki-ne-tsi-di	*I am just about to speak,*
2nd person	ᏣᏁᏥᏗ	tsa-ne-tsi-di	*thou art just about to speak,*
3rd person	ᎤᏁᏥᏗ	u-ne-tsi-di	*he is just about to speak,*

Dual.

1st and 2nd	ᎩᏂᏁᏥᏗ	gi-ni-ne-tsi-di	*we (thou and I) are just about to speak,*
1st and 3rd	ᎣᎩᏂᏁᏥᏗ	o-gi-ni-ne-dsi-di	*we (he and I) are just about to speak,*
2nd person	ᏍᏗᏁᏥᏗ	o-gi-ni-ne-tsi-di	*you (two) are just about to speak,*

Plural.

1st and 2nd	ᎢᎩᏁᏥᏗ	i-gi-ne-tsi-di	*we (you and I) are just about to speak,*
1st and 3rd	ᎣᎩᏁᏥᏗ	o-gi-ne-tsi-di	*we (they and I) are just about to speak,*
2nd person	ᎢᏥᏁᏥᏗ	i-tsi-ne-tsi-di	*you (three or more) are just about to speak,*
3rd person	ᎤᏂᏁᏥᏗ	u-ni-ne-tsi-di	*they are just about to speak,*

This tense admits of modifications similar to those of the present, perfect and future tenses, as will be seen from the following. The personal prefixes the same as the foregoing.

ᎤᏁᏥᏗ	u-ne-tsi-di	*he is just about to speak,*
ᎤᏁᏥᏗᏒᎩ	u-ne-tsi-di-sv-gi	*he was (to my knowledge) just about to speak,*
ᎤᏁᏥᏗᏎᎢ	u-ne-tsi-di-se-i	*he was (without my knowledge) just about to speak,*
ᎤᏁᏥᏗᏐᎢ	u-ne-tsi-di-so-i	*he is about to speak whenever some vent occurs,*
ᎤᏁᏥᏗᏎᏍᏗ	u-ne-tsi-di-se-sdi	*he will be about to speak,*
ᎤᏁᏥᏗᏒᎢ	u-ne-tsi-di-sv-i	*his being about to speak.*

The following form marks the time just before the action of the verb, or the event referred to:

ᎤᏁᏥᏕᎾ	u-ne-tsi-de-na	*just before he spoke,*
ᎤᎷᏥᏕᎾ	u-lu-tsi-de-na	*just before he came,*
ᎤᏃᎱᎦᏂᏕᎾ	u-no-hu-ga-ni-de-na	*just before the flood,*
ᎤᎾᏙᏓᏈᏕᎾ	u-na-to-da-kwi-de-na	*just before the Sabbath;* i.e. Saturday.
ᎤᎩᏨᏂᏕᎾ	u-gi-tsv-ni-de-na	*just before day light.*

The personal prefixes are the same as in *a-ki-ne-tsi-di* (ᎠᎩᏁᏥᏗ) and its modifications.

Conditional Future Tense

The following form may be used as a conditional future tense of the Indicative Mood, or as a mild expression of the Imperative Mood.

Singular.

1st person	ᏥᏁᏨᎭ	tsi-ne-tsv-ha	*I will or shall speak,*
2nd person	ᎯᏁᏨᎭ	hi-ne-tsv-ha	*thou wilt or shalt speak,*
3rd person	ᎧᏁᏨᎭ	ka-ne-tsv-ha	*he will or shall speak,*

Dual.

1st and 2nd	ᎢᏂᏁᏨᎭ	i-ni-ne-tsv-ha	*we (thou and I) will or shall speak,*
1st and 3rd	ᎣᏍᏗᏁᏨᎭ	o-sdi-ne-tsv-ha	*we (he and I) will or shall speak,*
2nd person	ᏍᏗᏁᏨᎭ	sdi-ne-tsv-ha	*you (two) will or shall speak,*

Plural.

1st and 2nd	ᎢᏗᏁᏨᎭ	i-di-ne-tsv-ha	*we (you and I) will or shall speak,*
1st and 3rd	ᎣᏣᏁᏨᎭ	o-tsi-ne-tsv-ha	*we (they and I) will or shall speak,*
2nd person	ᎢᏣᏁᏨᎭ	i-tsi-ne-tsv-ha	*you (three or more) will or shall speak,*
3rd person	ᎠᏂᏁᏨᎭ	a-ni-ne-tsv-ha	*they will or shall speak,*

Aptness

Adjective indicating an aptness to the action of the Verbs.

Singular.

1st person	ᎠᎩᏁᏣᏔ	a-ki-ne-tsa-ta	*I am apt to speak,*
2nd person	ᏣᏁᏣᏔ	tsa-ne-tsa-ta	*thou art apt to speak,*
3rd person	ᎤᏁᏣᏔ	u-ne-tsa-ta	*he is apt to speak,*

Dual.

1st and 2nd	ᎩᏂᏁᏣᏔ	gi-ni-ne-tsa-ta	*we (thou and I) are apt to speak,*
1st and 3rd	ᎣᎩᏂᏁᏣᏔ	o-gi-ni-ne-tsa-ta	*we (he and I) are apt to speak,*
2nd person	ᏍᏗᏁᏣᏔ	sdi-ne-tsa-ta	*you (two) are apt to speak,*

Plural.

1st and 2nd	ᎢᎩᏁᏣᏔ	i-gi-ne-tsa-ta	*we (you and I) are apt to speak,*
1st and 3rd	ᎣᎩᏁᏣᏔ	o-gi-ne-tsa-ta	*we (they and I) are apt to speak,*
2nd person	ᎢᏣᏁᏣᏔ	i-tsi-ne-tsa-ta	*you (three or more) are apt to speak,*
3rd person	ᎤᏂᏁᏣᏔ	u-ni-ne-tsa-ta	*they are apt to speak,*

This form admits of modifications of tense similar to those of the present. The personal prefixes are the same throughout.

ᎠᎩᏁᏣᏔ	a-ki-ne-tsa-ta	*I am apt to speak,*
ᎠᎩᏁᏣᏛᎩ	a-ki-ne-tsa-tv-gi	*I was (knowingly) apt to speak,*
ᎠᎩᏁᏣᏖᎢ	a-ki-ne-tsa-te-i	*I was (unconsciously) apt to speak,*
ᎠᎩᏁᏣᏙᎢ	a-ki-ne-tsa-to-i	*I am apt to speak whenever certain events occur,*
ᎠᎩᏁᏣᏖᏍᏗ	a-ki-ne-tsa-tes-di	*I shall be apt to speak,*
ᎠᎩᏁᏣᏛᎢ	a-ki-ne-tsa-tv-i	*my being apt apt to speak, my aptness to speak.*

POTENTIAL MOOD.

Singular.

1st person	ᎬᎩᏁᎢᏍᏗ	gv-ki-ne-is-di	*I can speak,*
2nd person	ᎨᏣᏁᎢᏍᏗ	ge-tsa-ne-is-di	*thou canst speak,*
3rd person	ᎬᏩᏁᎢᏍᏗ	gv-wa-ne-is-di	*he can speak,*

Dual.

1st and 2nd	ᎨᎩᏂᏁᎢᏍᏗ	ge-gi-ni-ne-is-di	*we (thou and I) can speak,*
1st and 3rd	ᎦᏲᎩᏂᏁᎢᏍᏗ	ga-yo-gi-ni-ne-is-di	*we (he and I) can speak,*
2nd person	ᎨᏍᏗᏁᎢᏍᏗ	ge-sdi-ne-is-di	*you (two) can speak,*

Plural.

1st and 2nd	ᎨᎩᏁᎢᏍᏗ	ge-gi-ne-is-di	*we (you and I) can speak,*
1st and 3rd	ᎦᏲᎩᏁᎢᏍᏗ	ga-yo-gi-ne-is-di	*we (they and I) can speak,*
2nd person	ᎨᏣᏁᎢᏍᏗ	ge-tsi-ne-is-di	*you (three or more) can speak,*
3rd person	ᎬᏩᏂᏁᎢᏍᏗ	gv-wa-ni-ne-is-di	*they can speak,*

Conditional Potential Mood.

Singular.

1st person	BℏⲅꞰꝨ	yv-tsi-ne-gi	*I can speak if …,*
2nd person	BⱭꞰꝨ	yv-hi-ne-gi	*thou canst speak if …,*
3rd person	BⴱꞰꝨ	yv-ka-ne-gi	*he can speak if …,*

Dual.

1st and 2nd	BℏꞰꝨ	yv-ni-ne-gi	*we (thou and I) can speak if …,*
1st and 3rd	ꞪⱰꝆꞰꝨ	yo-sdi-ne-gi	*we (he and I) can speak if …,*
2nd person	BⱰꝆꞰꝨ	yv-sdi-ne-gi	*you (two) can speak if …,*

Plural.

1st and 2nd	BꝆꞰꝨ	yv-di-ne-gi	*we (you and I) can speak if …,*
1st and 3rd	ꞪℏⲅꞰꝨ	yo-tsi-ne-gi	*we (they and I) can speak if …,*
2nd person	BℏⲅꞰꝨ	yv-tsi-ne-gi	*you (three or more) can speak if …,*
3rd person	BDℏꞰꝨ	yv-a-ni-ne-gi	*they can speak if …,*

The Negative of the Conditional Potential Mood.

Singular.

1st person	BŞℏⲅꞰꝨ	yv-ga-tsi-ne-gi	*I cannot speak,*
2nd person	BŞⱭꞰꝨ	yv-ga-hi-ne-gi	*thou canst not speak,*
3rd person	BŞⴱꞰꝨ	yv-ga-ka-ne-gi	*he cannot speak,*

Dual.

1st and 2nd	BŞℏꞰꝨ	yv-ga-ni-ne-gi	*we (thou and I) cannot speak,*
1st and 3rd	BŞꞪⱰꝆꞰꝨ	yv-ga-yo-sdi-ne-gi	*we (he and I) cannot speak,*
2nd person	BŞⱰꝆꞰꝨ	yv-ga-yo-sdi-ne-gi	*you (two) cannot speak,*

Plural.

1st and 2nd	BŞꝆꞰꝨ	yv-ga-di-ne-gi	*we (you and I) cannot speak,*
1st and 3rd	BŞꞪℏⲅꞰꝨ	yv-ga-yo-tsi-ne-gi	*we (they and I) cannot speak,*
2nd person	BℏⲅꞰꝨ	yv-ge-tsi-ne-gi	*you (three or more) cannot speak,*
3rd person	BEℏꞰꝨ	yv-gv-ni-ne-gi	*they cannot speak,*

To this form is often prefixed the negative particle *tla* (Ꮭ), as *tla yv-ga-tsi-ne-gi* (Ꮭ BŞℏⲅꞰꝨ), (I cannot speak.)

THE SUBJUNCTIVE MOOD.

The same modifications are made in the tenses of the Subjunctive Mood as in those of the Indicative: except that the forms which end in *gv-gi* (EꝨ) and *gv-i* (EꚨꝨ), and which imply certainty and personal knowledge in the speaker, are wanting in this mood.

Singular.

1st person	ꝗℏⲅꞰꙄ	yi-dsi-ne-ga	*if I speak,*
2nd person	ꝗꞰꙄ	hyi-ne-ga	*if thou speak,*
3rd person	ꝗⴱꞰꙄ	yi-ka-ne-ga	*if he speaks,*

Dual.

1st and 2nd	ꝗℏꞰꙄ	yi-ni-ne-ga	*if we (thou and I) speak,*
1st and 3rd	ꞪⱰꝆꞰꙄ	yo-sdi-ne-ga	*if we (he and I) speak,*
2nd person	ꝗⱰꝆꞰꙄ	yi-sdi-ne-ga	*if you (two) speak,*

158

Plural.

1st and 2nd	ᎥᏗᏁᎦ	yi-di-ne-ga	*if we (you and I) speak,*
1st and 3rd	ᏲᏥᏁᎦ	yo-tsi-ne-ga	*if we (they and I) speak,*
2nd person	ᎥᏥᏁᎦ	yi-tsi-ne-ga	*if you (three or more) speak,*
3rd person	ᏯᏂᏁᎦ	ya-ni-ne-ga	*if they speak,*

tla (Ꮭ) prefixed to any tense in this mood makes it a negative; as *tla yi-tsi-ne-ga* (Ꮭ ᎥᏥᏁᎦ), (I do not speak.)

Modifications of the Present Tense of the Subjunctive Mood

The following are modifications of the Present Tense of the Subjunctive Mood. The personal prefixes the same as the Simple Present.

ᎥᏥᏁᎪᎢ	yi-tsi-ne-go-i	*If I speak habitually or contingently,*
ᎥᏥᏁᎨᎢ	yi-tsi-ne-ge-i	*If I was speaking unconsciously,*
ᎥᏥᏁᎨᏍᏗ	yi-tsi-ne-ges-di	*If I shall be speaking,*

Future Tense, Simple Form

Singular.

1st person	ᎥᏓᏥᏁᏥ	yv-da-tsi-ne-tsi	*if, at some future time, I should speak,*
2nd person	ᎥᏘᏁᏥ	yv-ti-ne-tsi	*if, at some future time, thou shouldest speak,*
3rd person	ᎥᏓᎧᏁᏥ	yv-da-ka-ne-tsi	*if, at some future time, he should speak,*

Dual.

1st and 2nd	ᎥᏓᏂᏁᏥ	yv-da-ni-ne-tsi	*if, at some future time, we (thou and I) should speak,*
1st and 3rd	ᎥᏓᏲᏍᏗᏁᏥ	yv-da-yo-sdi-ne-tsi	*if, at some future time, we (he and I) should speak,*
2nd person	ᎥᏓᏍᏗᏁᏥ	yv-da-sdi-ne-tsi	*if, at some future time, you (two) should speak,*

Plural.

1st and 2nd	ᎥᏓᏗᏁᏥ	yv-da-di-ne-tsi	*if, at some future time, we (you and I) should speak,*
1st and 3rd	ᎥᏓᏲᏥᏁᏥ	yv-da-yo-tsi-ne-tsi	*if, at some future time, we (they and I) should speak,*
2nd person	ᎥᏓᏥᏁᏥ	yv-da-tsi-ne-tsi	*if, at some future time, you (three or more) should speak,*
3rd person	ᎥᏓᏂᏁᏥ	yv-da-ni-ne-tsi	*if, at some future time, they should speak,*

Conditional or Contingent Future.

Modifications of the Future Tense.

Singular.

1st person	ᎥᏓᏥᏁᏥ	yv-da-tsi-ne-tsi	*if, on certain contingencies, I should intend to speak,*
2nd person	ᎥᏘᏁᏥ	yv-ti-ne-tsi	*if, on certain contingencies, thou shouldest intend to speak,*
3rd person	ᎥᏓᎧᏁᏥ	yv-da-ka-ne-tsi	*if, on certain contingencies, he should intend to speak,*

Dual.

1st and 2nd	ᎥᏓᏂᏁᏥ	yv-da-ni-ne-tsi	*if, on certain contingencies, we (thou and I) should intend to speak,*
1st and 3rd	ᎥᏓᏲᏍᏗᏁᏥ	yv-da-yo-sdi-ne-tsi	*if, on certain contingencies, we (he and I) should intend to speak,*
2nd person	ᎥᏓᏍᏗᏁᏥ	yv-da-sdi-ne-tsi	*if, on certain contingencies, you (two) should intend to speak,*

Plural.

1st and 2nd	ᎥᏓᏗᏁᏥ	yv-da-di-ne-tsi	*if, on certain contingencies, we (you and I) should intend to speak,*
1st and 3rd	ᎥᏓᏲᏥᏁᏥ	yv-da-yo-tsi-ne-tsi	*if, on certain contingencies, we (they and I) should intend to speak,*
2nd person	ᎥᏓᏥᏁᏥ	yv-da-tsi-ne-tsi	*if, on certain contingencies, you (three or more) should intend to speak,*
3rd person	ᎥᏓᏂᏁᏥ	yv-da-ni-ne-tsi	*if, on certain contingencies, they should intend speak,*

In the following modifications of the Future Tense the personal prefixes are the same as in the foregoing conditional or contingent form.

The Imperfect of the Future.

| ᏧᏗᏥᏁᏥᏎᎢ | yi-di-tsi-ne-tsi-se-i | *if I willed or intended to speak.* |

The Double Future, or Future of the Future.

| ᏧᏗᏥᏁᏥᏎᏍᏗ | yi-di-tsi-ne-tsi-ses-di | *if I shall, will, or intend to speak.* |

The Immediate Future Tense

Singular.

1st person	ᎥᎩᏂᏥᏗ	yv-ki-ne-tsi-di	*if I am about to speak,*
2nd person	ᏥᏣᏂᏥᏗ	yi-tsa-ne-tsi-di	*if thou are about to speak,*
3rd person	ᏳᏂᏥᏗ	yu-ne-tsi-di	*if he is about to speak,*

Dual.

1st and 2nd	ᏥᎩᏂᏂᏥᏗ	yi-gi-ni-ne-tsi-di	*if we (thou and I) are about to speak,*
1st and 3rd	ᏊᎩᏂᏂᏥᏗ	yo-gi-ni-ne-tsi-di	*if we (he and I) are about to speak,*
2nd person	ᏥᏍᏗᏂᏥᏗ	yi-sdi-ne-tsi-di	*if you (two) are about to speak,*

Plural.

1st and 2nd	ᏥᎩᏂᏥᏗ	yi-gi-ne-tsi-di	*if we (you and I) are about to speak,*
1st and 3rd	ᏊᎩᏂᏥᏗ	yo-gi-ne-tsi-di	*if we (they and I) are about to speak,*
2nd person	ᏥᏥᏂᏥᏗ	yi-tsi-ne-tsi-di	*if you (three or more) are about to speak,*
3rd person	ᏳᏂᏂᏥᏗ	yu-ni-ne-tsi-di	*if they are about to speak,*

Perfect Tense

Singular.

1st person	ᎥᎩᏂᏨ	ya-ki-ne-tsv	*if I have spoken,*
2nd person	ᏥᏣᏂᏨ	yi-tsa-ne-tsv	*if thou hast spoken,*
3rd person	ᏳᏂᏨ	yu-ne-tsv	*if he has spoken,*

Dual.

1st and 2nd	ᏥᎩᏂᏂᏨ	yi-gi-ni-ne-tsv	*if we (thou and I) have spoken,*
1st and 3rd	ᏊᎩᏂᏂᏨ	yo-gi-ni-ne-tsv	*if we (he and I) have spoken,*
2nd person	ᏥᏍᏗᏂᏨ	yi-sdi-ne-tsv	*if you (two) have spoken,*

Plural.

1st and 2nd	ᏥᎩᏂᏨ	yi-gi-ne-tsv	*if we (you and I) have spoken,*
1st and 3rd	ᏊᎩᏂᏨ	yo-gi-ne-tsv	*if we (they and I) have spoken,*
2nd person	ᏥᏥᏂᏨ	yi-tsi-ne-tsv	*if you (three or more) have spoken,*
3rd person	ᏳᏂᏂᏨ	yu-ni-ne-tsv	*if they have spoken,*

Modifications of the Perfect Tense.

Ꮣ ᏳᏂᏨ	tla yu-ne-tsv	*he has not spoken,*
Ꮣ ᏳᏂᏦᎢ	tla yu-ne-tso-i	*he has not been in the habit of speaking,*
Ꮣ ᏳᏂᏤᎢ	tla yu-ne-tse-i	*he did not speak.*
Ꮣ ᏳᏂᏤᏍᏗ	tla yu-ne-tses-di	*he will not have spoken.*

These modifications of the perfect tense are not often used without the negative *tla* (Ꮣ): with which prefixed, the word becomes negative instead of hypothetical. The particle *tla* (Ꮣ) has a similar effect before all other tenses in this mood.

160

IMPERATIVE MOOD.

Singular.

1st person	ƟⱲⲨⲨ	wi-tsi-ne-gi	*let me speak,*
2nd person	ⰀⲨⲨ	hi-ne-gi	*speak thou,*
3rd person	ƟⰀⲨⲨ	wi-ka-ne-gi	*let him speak,*

Dual.

1st and 2nd	ƬⱧⲨⲨ	i-ni-ne-gi	*let us, (thou and I) speak,*
1st and 3rd	ƟⱭⲨⲨⲨ	wo-sdi-ne-gi	*let us (he and I) speak,*
2nd person	ⱭⲨⲨⲨ	sdi-ne-gi	*speak ye (two),*

Plural.

1st and 2nd	ƬⲨⲨⲨ	i-di-ne-gi	*let us (you and I) speak,*
1st and 3rd	ƟⱲⲨⲨ	wo-tsi-ne-gi	*let us (they and I) speak,*
2nd person	ƬⱲⲨⲨ	i-tsi-ne-gi	*speak ye (three or more),*
3rd person	ꭹⱧⲨⲨ	wa-ni-ne-gi	*let them speak,*

INFINITIVE MOOD.

Singular.

1st person	ꭰⲨⲨꚍⱭⲨ	a-ki-ne-is-di	*I to speak,*
2nd person	ꮯⲨꚍⱭⲨ	tsa-ne-is-di	*thou to speak,*
3rd person	ꭳꞋⲨꚍⱭⲨ	u-ne-is-di	*he to speak,*

Dual.

1st and 2nd	ⲨⱧⲨꚍⱭⲨ	gi-ni-ne-is-di	*we, (thou and I) to speak,*
1st and 3rd	ꭳⲨⱧⲨꚍⱭⲨ	o-gi-ni-ne-is-di	*we, (he and I) to speak,*
2nd person	ⱭⲨⲨꚍⱭⲨ	sdi-ne-is-di	*you, (two) to speak,*

Plural.

1st and 2nd	ƬⲨⲨꚍⱭⲨ	i-gi-ne-is-di	*we, (you and I) to speak,*
1st and 3rd	ꭳⲨⲨꚍⱭⲨ	o-gi-ne-is-di	*we, (they and I) to speak,*
2nd person	ƬⱲⲨꚍⱭⲨ	i-tsi-ne-is-di	*we, (three or more) to speak,*
3rd person	ꭳꞋⱧⲨꚍⱭⲨ	u-ni-ne-is-di	*they to speak,*

THE DATIVE CONJUGATION

INDICATIVE MOOD.

Present Tense. Active Voice. [To him.]

Singular.

1st person	ⱲⲨꝞꙆ	tsi-ne-tse-ha	*I speak to him,*
2nd person	ⰀⲨꝞꙆ	hi-ne-tse-ha	*thou speakest to him,*
3rd person	ⱭⲨꝞꙆ	ka-ne-tse-ha	*he speaks to him,*

Dual.

1st and 2nd	ꭱⰀⲨꝞꙆ	e-ni-ne-tse-ha	*we, (thou and I) speak to him,*
1st and 3rd	ꭳⱭⲨⲨꝞꙆ	o-sdi-ne-tse-ha	*we, (he and I) speak to him,*
2nd person	ꭱⱭⲨⲨꝞꙆ	e-sdi-ne-tse-ha	*you, (two) speak to him,*

Plural.

1st and 2nd	ꭱⲨⲨꝞꙆ	e-di-ne-tse-ha	*we, (you and I) speak to him,*
1st and 3rd	ꭳⱲⲨꝞꙆ	o-tsi-ne-tse-ha	*we, (they and I) speak to him,*
2nd person	ꭱⱲⲨꝞꙆ	e-tsi-ne-tse-ha	*we, (three or more) speak to him,*
3rd person	ꭰⱧⲨꝞꙆ	a-ni-ne-tse-ha	*they speak to him,*

Present Tense. Active Voice. [To them.]

Singular.

1st person	ᏍᎯᏁᎥᏆ	ga-tsi-ne-tse-ha	*I speak to them,*
2nd person	ᎡᎠᏁᎥᏆ	ge-hi-ne-tse-ha	*thou speakest to them,*
3rd person	ᏎᎤᏁᎥᏆ	de-ka-ne-tse-ha	*he speaks to them,*

Dual.

1st and 2nd	ᎡᎯᏁᎥᏆ	ge-ni-ne-tse-ha	*we, (thou and I) speak to them,*
1st and 3rd	ᏙᏍᏗᏁᎥᏆ	do-sdi-ne-tse-ha	*we, (he and I) speak to them,*
2nd person	ᏎᏍᏗᏁᎥᏆ	ge-sdi-ne-tse-ha	*you, (two) speak to them,*

Plural.

1st and 2nd	ᎡᏗᏁᎥᏆ	ge-di-ne-tse-ha	*we, (you and I) speak to them,*
1st and 3rd	ᏙᏏᏁᎥᏆ	do-tsi-ne-tse-ha	*we, (they and I) speak to them,*
2nd person	ᏕᏏᏁᎥᏆ	de-tsi-ne-tse-ha	*we, (three or more) speak to them,*
3rd person	ᏓᏂᏁᎥᏆ	da-ni-ne-tse-ha	*they speak to them,*

Present Tense. Active Voice. [To thee.]

Singular. 1st	ᎬᏁᎥᏆ	gv-ne-tse-ha	*I speak to thee,*
Dual. 1st and 3rd	ᏒᏗᏁᎥᏆ	sdv-ne-tse-ha	*we, (he and I) speak to thee,*
Plural. 3rd	ᏨᏁᎥᏆ	i-tsv-ne-tse-ha	*we, (they and I) speak to thee,*

Present Tense. Active Voice. [To you (two).]

Singular. 1st	ᏒᏗᏁᎥᏆ	sdv-ne-tse-ha	*I speak to you (two),*
Dual. 1st and 3rd	ᏒᏗᏁᎥᏆ	sdv-ne-tse-ha	*we, (he and I) speak to you (two),*
Plural. 3rd	ᏨᏁᎥᏆ	i-tsv-ne-tse-ha	*we, (they and I) speak to you (two),*

Present Tense. Active Voice. [To you (three or more).]

Singular. 1st	ᏨᏁᎥᏆ	i-tsv-ne-tse-ha	*I speak to you (three or more),*
Dual. 1st and 3rd	ᏨᏁᎥᏆ	i-tsv-ne-tse-ha	*we, (he and I) speak to you (three or more),*
Plural. 3rd	ᏨᏁᎥᏆ	i-tsv-ne-tse-ha	*we, (they and I) speak to you (three or more),*

Present Tense. Passive Voice. [Spoken to by him.]

Singular.

1st person	ᎠᏱᏁᎥᏆ	a-ki-ne-tse-ha	*I spoken to by him,*
2nd person	ᏣᏱᏁᎥᏆ	tsa-ne-tse-ha	*thou art spoken to by him,*
3rd person	ᎤᏁᎥᏆ	u-ne-tse-ha	*he is spoken to by him,*

Dual.

1st and 2nd	ᎩᎯᏁᎥᏆ	gi-ni-ne-tse-ha	*we, (thou and I) are spoken to by him,*
1st and 3rd	ᎣᎩᎯᏁᎥᏆ	o-gi-ni-ne-tse-ha	*we, (he and I) are spoken to by him,*
2nd person	ᏍᏗᏁᎥᏆ	sdi-ne-tse-ha	*you, (two) are spoken to by him,*

Plural.

1st and 2nd	ᏘᏱᏁᎥᏆ	i-gi-ne-tse-ha	*we, (you and I) are spoken to by him,*
1st and 3rd	ᎣᏍᎯᏁᎥᏆ	o-tsi-ne-tse-ha	*we, (they and I) are spoken to by him,*
2nd person	ᏘᎯᏁᎥᏆ	i-tsi-ne-tse-ha	*we, (three or more) are spoken to by him,*
3rd person	ᎤᎯᏁᎥᏆ	u-ni-ne-tse-ha	*they are spoken to by him,*

Present Tense. Passive Voice. [Spoken to by them.]

Singular.

1st person	EYᎪVᏱ	gv-ki-ne-tse-ha	*I spoken to by them,*
2nd person	ᏩGᎩᎫᎠᎥ	ge-tsa-ne-tse-ha	*thou art spoken to by them,*
3rd person	EᏩᎠVᏱ	gv-wa-ne-tse-ha	*he is spoken to by them,*

Dual.

1st and 2nd	ᏩᎩhᎠVᏱ	ge-gi-ni-ne-tse-ha	*we, (thou and I) are spoken to by them,*
1st and 3rd	AᎩhᎠVᏱ	go-gi-ni-ne-tse-ha	*we, (he and I) are spoken to by them,*
2nd person	ᏩᏍᎯᎠVᏱ	ge-sdi-ne-tse-ha	*you, (two) are spoken to by them,*

Plural.

1st and 2nd	ᏩᎩᎠVᏱ	ge-gi-ne-tse-ha	*we, (you and I) are spoken to by them,*
1st and 3rd	AᏥᎠVᏱ	go-tsi-ne-tse-ha	*we, (they and I) are spoken to by them,*
2nd person	ᏩᏥᎠVᏱ	ge-tsi-ne-tse-ha	*we, (three or more) are spoken to by them,*
3rd person	EᏩhᎠVᏱ	gv-wa-ni-ne-tse-ha	*they are spoken to by them,*

Present Tense. Passive Voice. [Spoken to by thee.]

Singular. 1st	ᏍᎩᎠVᏱ	ski-ne-tse-ha	*I am spoken to by thee,*
Dual. 1st and 3rd	ᏍᎩhᎠVᏱ	ski-ni-ne-tse-ha	*we, (he and I) are spoken to by thee,*
Plural. 3rd	ᏍᎩᎠVᏱ	ski-ne-tse-ha	*we, (they and I) are spoken to by thee,*

Present Tense. Passive Voice. [Spoken to by you, (two).]

Singular. 1st	ᏍᎩhᎠVᏱ	ski-ni-ne-tse-ha	*I am spoken to by you (two),*
Dual. 1st and 3rd	ᏍᎩhᎠVᏱ	ski-ni-ne-tse-ha	*we, (he and I) are spoken to by you (two),*
Plural. 3rd	ᏍᎩᎠVᏱ	ski-ne-tse-ha	*we, (they and I) are spoken to by you (two),*

Present Tense. Passive Voice. [Spoken to by you, (three or more).]

Singular. 1st	ᏍᎩᎠVᏱ	ski-ne-tse-ha	*I am spoken to by you (three or more),*
Dual. 1st and 3rd	ᏍᎩᎠVᏱ	ski-ne-tse-ha	*we, (he and I) are spoken to by you (three or more),*
Plural. 3rd	ᏍᎩᎠVᏱ	ski-ne-tse-ha	*we, (they and I) are spoken to by you (three or more),*

Bibliography

Cherokee New Testament. 1860. Tulsa, Ok: American Bible Society - publisher.

Bunyan, John [author], ᏫᎵ [translator]. 1844. *Pilgrim's Progress - ᏛᏃᏎᏛ ᏚᏴᏒᏒᎢ* (Cherokee). Cherokee Baptist Mission, Ok: H. Upham - publisher. .

Feeling, Durbin. 1975. *Cherokee-English Dictionary.* Tahlequah, OK: Cherokee Nation of Oklahoma.

Holcomb, Sherry, Kristen Smith, Jeff Edwards, et. al. 2005-2010. *Cherokee Nation Immersion School Curriculae – Grades 0 - 4.* Tahlequah, OK: Cherokee Nation of Oklahoma.

Jones, Evan – editor. 1844 – 1846. *Cherokee Messenger, The* (Journal, Cherokee and English). Cherokee Baptist Mission, Ok: H. Upham - publisher.

King, Duane. 1975. *A grammar and dictionary of the Cherokee Language.* Athens, Ga: University of Georgia PhD dissertation.

Montgomery-Anderson, Brad. 2008. *A Reference Grammar Of Oklahoma Cherokee.* University of Kansas PhD dissertation.

Worcester, Rev. S. A. [translator]. 1856. *Genesis or the First Book of Moses* (Cherokee). Park Hill, Ok: Mission Press

CPSIA information can be obtained at www.ICGtesting.com
Printed in the USA
LVOW09s0230190516

488982LV00004B/117/P